# READING for SUCCESS
# in ELEMENTARY SCHOOLS

**Earl H. Cheek, Jr.**
Louisiana State University

**Rona F. Flippo**
Fitchburg State College

**Jimmy D. Lindsey**
Southern University–Baton Rouge

Brown & Benchmark
PUBLISHERS

Madison, WI  Dubuque  Guilford, CT  Chicago  Toronto  London
Mexico City  Caracas  Buenos Aires  Madrid  Bogotá  Sydney

**Book Team**

Executive Publisher *Edgar J. Laube*
Managing Editor *Sue Pulvermacher-Alt*
Developmental Editor *Suzanne M. Guinn*
Production Editor *Karen A. Pluemer*
Proofreading Coordinator *Carrie Barker*
Designer *Jamie O'Neal*
Art Editor *Rita Hingtgen*
Photo Editor *Leslie Dague*
Permissions Coordinator *Gail I. Wheatley*
Production Manager *Beth Kundert*
Production/Costing Manager *Sherry Padden*
Production/Imaging and Media Development Manager *Linda Meehan Avenarius*
Visuals/Design Freelance Specialist *Mary L. Christianson*
Marketing Manager *Amy Halloran*
Copywriter *Jennifer Smith*
Proofreader *Ann Morgan*

Basal Text *10/12 Garamond Book*
Display Type *Garamond Bold Italic*
Typesetting System *FrameMaker*
Paper Stock *45# Restorecote*

Executive Vice President and General Manager *Bob McLaughlin*
Vice President, Business Manager *Russ Domeyer*
Vice President of Production and New Media Development *Victoria Putman*
National Sales Manager *Phil Rudder*
National Telesales Director *John Finn*

 **A Times Mirror Company**

Cover design by Lesiak/Crampton Design, Inc.

Cover photograph © Bill Bachmann/Stock Imagery

Copyedited by Laurie McGee; proofread by Wendy M. Christofel

Library of Congress Catalog Card Number: 95-83801

ISBN 0-697-27926-X

Printed in the United States of America by Times Mirror Higher Education Group, Inc.
2460 Kerper Boulevard, Dubuque, IA 52001

10  9  8  7  6  5  4  3  2  1

# Contents

Chapter

**6**  Strategies for Studying and Learning from Text

Chapter

**7**  Developing Proficiency in Content Reading

*C h a p t e r*  **10**  *Literacy Learning in an Inclusive Setting*

**Section**    **IV**   *Assessment and Organizing for Instruction*

**Chapter**    **11**   *Assessment in the Elementary Classroom*

**Chapter**    **12**   *Approaches for Instruction*

# Preface

*T*he primary goal of all teaching is to help students learn. Teachers provide the opportunities and instruction to facilitate students' development in oral and written language and in cognitive endeavors. These include reading, writing, researching, studying, reflecting, and thinking. In other words, teachers must know how to develop these areas and to balance their students' learning opportunities and instruction for teaching to be most effective. Therefore, this text primarily focuses on the understandings and knowledge that teachers need to ensure that they can facilitate this balance for each student's maximum success in school.

It is clear from the authors' research and experiences that reading instruction has been undergoing changes and shifts in thinking and emphasis. This is substantiated by the current research and publications in reading education, writing, cognitive psychology, sociocultural influences, and teacher beliefs and effectiveness. Although the majority of school districts continue to require the use of basal reading programs, many teachers supplement their basal instruction with trade books and other authentic materials and assignments in an effort to provide the most effective and balanced instruction possible for each child in their classroom. There is new evidence and recognition from reading and other educational researchers that a "balanced," language-based, interactive view of learning that includes direct instruction, as well as time for children to read on their own, provides optimum opportunities to facilitate reading success. Instead of emphasizing bits and pieces of isolated reading and other language skills, facilitative reading instruction focuses more on reading, writing, and thinking as an interrelated communication process—a process that is fundamental to all academic learning activities. The emphasis on reading as a learning and communication skill necessitates providing students with a real purpose for utilizing reading. Function is stressed over terminology and labels. Comprehension and communication become the focus for reading instruction. Moreover, students learn that language and thinking systems operate together as inseparable parts of the entire language and learning process.

Using instructional approaches that encourage students to pursue their individual interests, study content materials, research relevant topics, share information, and read purposefully as well as for pleasure, rather than stressing isolated skill practice, will facilitate students' opportunities and desires to read. The result will be students who can and do read. Our goal then, in writing this text, is to provide basic, practical suggestions for teachers to reflect on and use to develop a facilitative reading and learning program in their elementary classrooms.

The thirteen chapters that comprise this text are presented in a progressive stage from theory to practical application.

Section I, "Foundations for Reading Literacy," consists of three chapters that present the basic theme of the text and discusses the foundations for emerging and developing literacy. In Chapters 1 and 2, current perspectives and definitions of reading are explored, and an emphasis on teachers developing their own balanced reading perspective and definition is encouraged. This perspective and definition is viewed as "developing," and text readers are encouraged to continue to reflect on and further develop their views as they move through the chapters of this text. The idea that the teacher's perspective and definition will have tremendous influence on his or her classroom is explained, and the role of the teacher as a facilitator of reading instruction is presented. Chapter 3 discusses the formative development of language, emergent literacy, social and cognitive development, the teacher's and parents'/families'/communities' roles in the child's development, and teaching strategies to enable young children to further develop their emerging literacy.

Section II, "Developing Literacy Skills and Strategies," focuses on the essential topics of word identification and vocabulary development, comprehension, strategies for studying and learning from text, content reading, and reading and writing. Chapter 4 describes the importance of word identification in the development of the student's vocabulary, presents strategies for learning vocabulary, and addresses the relationship between word identification and comprehension. The focus in Chapter 5 is on the vital component of comprehension, including current perspectives, its importance in a literate learning environment, and strategies designed to enhance understanding. Chapter 6 discusses the roles of the teacher and student in studying and learning from text, teaching techniques that enhance learning, and specific strategies for studying and learning from text. Chapter 7 examines the importance of developing proficiency in reading content materials with an emphasis on using reading as a tool for learning concepts presented in content materials. In Chapter 8, the relationship between reading and writing is presented with particular emphasis on creating a positive environment for integrating reading and writing in the elementary classroom.

Section III, "Meeting the Diverse Interests and Needs of All Learners," consists of two in-depth chapters devoted to helping teachers recognize and meet the many needs, motivations, and interests of all students in their classroom, to provide all students with opportunities for successful and rewarding school reading experiences. Chapter 9 develops the importance of encouraging personal reading opportunities for all students, and specific suggestions and literature for cultivating individual interests and motivating students to read are presented. The focus of Chapter 10 is to help teachers provide an environment conducive to the development of literacy in an inclusive setting that includes a wide range of students, such as at-risk/"at-promise" readers, linguistically and culturally diverse students, gifted and talented students, and other learners with special needs/challenges.

Section IV, "Assessment and Organizing for Instruction," explores the topics of assessment, approaches to teaching, and organizing and managing the classroom. Chapter 11 discusses the importance of gathering information through the use of portfolios and other informal and formal assessment procedures. Also, the idea that continuous and current assessment is necessary and an important part of providing effective instruction for each student is presented. In Chapter 12, the facilitative teacher perspective, one that balances the use of approaches with students' needs, skills, strategies, motivations, and cultures is reviewed; and five approaches for teaching and developing reading are presented. These approaches include: language experience, individualized reading, literature-based, basal reader, and eclectic.

Chapter 13 concentrates on managing the elementary classroom, organizing and grouping for instruction, arranging facilities, organizing for parent/family participation and involvement, using and managing technology, and continuing reflection and professional development.

Each chapter of the text opens with an overview and a list of its main ideas; includes reflection activities to promote reader interaction with ideas presented throughout the chapter; and closes with a summary, closing activities for applying the information presented, and a reference section. Text readers are asked to keep a "reflection journal" to record their responses to the reflection activities found at appropriate points throughout the text. These activities are numbered to correspond to particular chapters and locations (e.g., Reflection Activity 1.1 is the first reflection activity found in Chapter 1; Reflection Activity 1.2 is the second reflection activity found in Chapter 1; Reflection Activity 2.1 is the first reflection activity found in Chapter 2; and so on). Following the last text chapter, two appendices provide an interest inventory, and information on professional organizations and refereed journals that focus on literacy and related educational research and application. Accompanying the text will be an instructor's guide, which includes questions and other pedagogical aids to assist instructors, as well as transparency masters. Also, *Reading for Success in Elementary Schools* is part of the **Brown & Benchmark Methods Series.** The **Methods Series** allows instructors to create black and white methods texts by combining chapters from this text with two other texts: *Language Arts: Process, Product, and Assessment,* 2nd edition, by Farris, and *Elementary and Middle School Social Studies: A Whole Language Approach,* 2nd edition, by Farris/Cooper. Additionally, an instructor can add his/her own material to customize the combined text for a particular course.

## *Acknowledgments*

We want to thank those at Brown & Benchmark who assisted us throughout this project. We are deeply grateful to Sue Pulvermacher-Alt, who believed in the viability of this project, to Suzanne Guinn, who served as our developmental editor and team leader, to Karen Pluemer, our excellent and dedicated production editor, and to Laurie McGee, our wonderful copyeditor. We also sincerely appreciate the efforts put forth by the Brown & Benchmark staff during the production of our book.

Very special thanks is extended to Karla Lemoine, Julie Lester, and Johan van der Jagt; to Florida State University, the University of Florida, and the University of Georgia for the learning opportunities they provided us; and to our parents, colleagues and students, and our families.

Rona wishes to acknowledge the following very special contributions. First, thank you to classroom teachers Marcia Haimila, McKay Campus School, Fitchburg, Massachusetts, and Peggy Marrano, Wildwood School, Wilmington, Massachusetts, who provided many wonderful samples of their young students' writings and invented spellings. Also thank you to their students, Kenneth Adams, Sabrina Fanelli, Kimberly Silvia, Mark Walsh, Jaclyn White, and

Sarah Winchell, whose wonderful and imaginative writings were selected for sharing in this edition. Thank you, too, to classroom teacher Robin Coughlan, Spaulding Memorial School, Townsend, Massachusetts, for her insight in using word processors to generate computer stories and for use with special learners; thank you to Kelly Coughlan for providing her wonderful computer-generated writing samples for inclusion in this edition. Recognition and thanks are extended to all of Rona's teacher education students at Fitchburg State College who contributed their memories of former teachers and their scenarios depicting the importance of prior knowledge and experiences—especially to Jim Klock, Dawn LaRocco, Lynda Magner, Patty McGregor, Janet Reid, Marcia Robinson, and Sharon Rosenfelder, whose contributions were selected for inclusion in Chapter 2.

Terry Dorsey, school librarian at South Street Elementary Complex in Fitchburg, Massachusetts, and Janice Ouellette, librarian at Fitchburg State College, are acknowledged for their expertise and help with the children's literature references. Appreciation goes to JoAnn Pellecchia for generously typing some of the examples used in Chapter 6 and to Margaret Daoust for verifying reference citations, in between their very demanding other tasks.

Thank you to the classroom teachers and other educators taking graduate classes at Fitchburg State College for trying out the ideas, reacting to ideas, and critiquing ideas and figures developed for Chapter 1 ("An Introduction to Reading"), Chapter 2 ("The Facilitative Classroom Teacher"), Chapter 3 ("Reading and the Young Child"), Chapter 6 ("Strategies for Studying and Learning from Text"), Chapter 8 ("Reading and Writing"), Chapter 9 ("Developing Personal Reading: Meeting Diverse Interests and Motivations"), the sections on "Cultural Diversity," "The Cultural Difference Model," and "Bilingual and ESL Programs" in Chapter 10; and Figures 12.1, 12.2, and 13.9. Special thanks also to: Robin J. Athanas, Country Day School, Groton, MA; Charlene C. Cormier; Julie DeCiero, Templeton Center School, Templeton, MA; Susan Jane Dudley, Major Victor E. Edwards Elementary School, West Boylston, MA; Christine Fanos, Elm Street School, Gardner, MA; Elizabeth M. Foster; Deborah Kemp, Crocker Elementary School, Fitchburg, MA; Gina Marie Longo, Memorial School, Winchendon, MA; Tracy J. Mainville, Murkland School, Lowell, MA; Christine Page; Richard Maynard, South Street Elementary Complex, Fitchburg, MA; and Jacqueline M. Rouisse, who each suggested many insightful questions and ideas for the text ancillary materials. Also, Rona would like to recognize her Chairperson, Dr. Ronald Colbert, for his support. Additionally, we want to thank Kerry Lester and Charles Lowder of Louisiana State University for their contributions to several of the figures in Chapter 1.

Thank you to the wonderful staff of the International Reading Association (IRA) for their usual assistance and cooperation. And thank you especially to Tyler Fox for his creative ideas, editorial insights, moral support, and frequent consultations; and to Tara Flippo for her ideas, wisdom, and continuous support. I am also grateful to my children, Todd Graham and Tara Flippo, for the inspiration for many of my ideas—watching them each grow up into being avid readers and successful students of each school, college, and university they've attended.

Finally, thank you to the reviewers who contributed their ideas and expertise to this text:

Susan Clark Thayer
Suffolk University
Boston, Massachusetts

June G. Hornsby
William Carey College
Hattiesburg, Mississippi

Swannee Dickson
Pembroke State University
Pembroke, North Carolina

Sharon Lee
University of South Dakota–Vermillion
Vermillion, South Dakota

John D. Beach
SUNY–Cortland
Cortland, New York

Mary Ann Wham
University of Wisconsin–Whitewater
Whitewater, Wisconsin

Sondra Lettrich
Seton Hill College
Greensburg, Pennsylvania

Deborah Ann Jensen
Wagner College
Staten Island, New York

Scott Beesley
Grand Canyon University
Phoenix, Arizona

E.H.C.
R.F.F.
J.D.L.

*Dedication*

To the students at Louisiana State University in Reading Education

E. H. C.

To Tyler, Tara, and Todd, and to my mother, Molly, with all my love

R. F. F.

To my maternal grandparents, Wilsie J. Chauvin and

Cecilia A. Chauvin, and to my great aunt, Miss Agnus Ayo

J. D. L

# Section I

## Foundations for Reading Literacy

S ection I, "Foundations for Reading Literacy," consists of
three chapters that present the basic theme of the text and
discuss the foundations for emerging and developing literacy.
Current perspectives and definitions of reading are explored,
and an emphasis on teachers developing their own balanced
reading perspective and definition is encouraged. This perspective and definition is viewed as "developing," and text readers
are encouraged to continue to reflect on and further develop
their views as they move through the chapters of this text. Reflection activities are first introduced in these foundation chapters and occur as well in all the other chapters of this text.
Readers are asked to keep a "reflection journal" to record their
responses to these reflection activities.

The idea that the teacher's perspective and definition of
reading will have tremendous influence on his or her classroom
and students is explained in the section, and the role of the
teacher as a facilitator of reading instruction is presented, with
many examples given of what is involved. Additionally, the formative development of language, emergent literacy, social and
cognitive development, the teachers' and parents'/families'/
communities' roles in the child's development, and teaching

strategies to enable young children to further develop their emerging literacy are introduced and discussed. To provide illustrations from the lives of real children, three youngsters—Rosario, Josh, and Tiffany—and their early learnings are presented and woven into the last chapter of this section.

Each chapter in this section, and throughout the rest of the text, opens with an overview and a list of the main ideas to indicate its primary focus; includes reflection activities to promote reader interaction with ideas presented throughout the chapter; and closes with a summary, closing activities for applying the information presented, and a reference section.

# *A*n Introduction to Reading

© Margaret Miller/Photo Researchers, Inc.

# *Overview*

*I*n this introductory chapter, you are asked to consider your current beliefs about reading and the reading process. Your own beliefs establish a starting point from which to study the reading process and the development of your students as successful readers. Perceptions of reading and reading as a complex process are discussed. Interrelated components of this complex process are described as (a) sensory; (b) perceptual; (c) sequential; (d) experiential; (e) linguistic; (f) cognitive; (g) learning; (h) association; (i) affective; (j) constructive; and (k) cultural.

Three major perspectives, or theories, of reading also are identified and described: skills-based, whole language, and interactive. Just as there are different perspectives of the reading process, there are also many definitions of reading; thus, several definitions relating to each of the three perspectives of reading are presented. The reading process has implications for all school-related learning. Reading is discussed as crucial to learning and is an integral part of all content to be studied in school situations.

Finally, your current perspective and definition of reading is viewed as a developing one. Your reading perspective and definition will have the most influence on your classroom and on your students. Thus, the primary focus of this chapter is to introduce you to the major current professional perspectives relating to the teaching of reading. As you read each chapter of this book and further consider the reading process, your own perspective and definition of reading is likely to change or broaden.

## *Main Ideas*

- Reading is a complex multidimensional process composed of sensory, perceptual, sequential, experiential, linguistic, cognitive, learning, association, and affective, constructive, and cultural components.
- Skills-based, whole language, and interactive are three current major perspectives of reading.
- Definitions of reading are based on one's reading perspective.
- Personal and learning experiences significantly influence teachers' formulations of reading perspectives and definitions.
- A logical reading perspective and definition, developed through experience, study, and reflection, are important to have because they influence how you will teach reading.
- Reading is crucial to learning and is applied across the school curriculum and content areas.

What is reading? What does it involve? Is it the ability to analyze and pronounce individual letters or combinations of letters? Is it picking out words? Is it understanding written communication? As you begin to study the reading process, considering these and many other questions is important. As a classroom teacher, your perception of the answers to these questions will greatly influence how you approach the teaching of reading. You probably already have some ideas about what reading is. After all, you have had a great deal of experience with reading in that you are a reader and probably have been for years.

## Reflection Activity 1.1

*T*ake a few minutes to think about reading and what it involves. Then, in your reflection journal, using the heading Reflection Activity 1.1 (as mentioned in the preface, 1.1 means Chapter 1, Reflection Activity 1; 2.2 would mean Chapter 2, Reflection Activity 2; and so on), answer the question What Is Reading? using the designation Part A (there will be Parts B and C later, so leave space after Part A for them). Write or diagram what you know about reading at this point in time. After you have finished, date what you have written so that you can later reexamine it. As you read this book and engage in other activities that increase your knowledge about the reading process, you may want to change your diagram or notations. But, for now, your diagram is just right. It is where you are beginning and represents your current perception of reading and the reading process. Another name for your "diagram of the reading process" is your "schema of the reading process." A schema is an individual's conceptual description, plan, or structure for something. It can also be the way one visualizes and organizes ideas and information about something. (Note, the plural for "schema" is "schemata.")

In this chapter, the reading process as well as different perspectives of reading will be discussed. You will discover that there is not just one reading perspective, but probably as many different perspectives as there are individuals involved in thinking about and studying the reading process. However, for the sake of brevity and clarity, we are only going to introduce and discuss the three most common and widely accepted professional perspectives. Then we will provide and discuss several definitions of reading. Just as there is a proliferation of different perspectives of reading, there is also an equal or larger number of definitions of reading. However, only a few representative definitions from each of the perspectives will be delineated. The chapter ends with a brief discussion of your own developing reading perspective and definition and its importance to your role as a facilitative classroom teacher.

Did you write in your reflection journal under Reflection Activity 1.1 ("What Is Reading? Part A") what you currently believe reading involves? If not, please do so before reading the next section, and again, remember to leave space for Parts B and C, which you will work on later.

# The Reading Process

There is no single simple explanation we can give to introduce you to or to adequately describe the entire reading process. However, we feel it is important at this stage in the text to provide you with some explanation and to make this explanation as succinct as possible so that it helps you understand what appears to be, and is, a complex process. We believe that the reading process is complex because it requires and interweaves all the language and learning skills. Further, it involves and is significantly affected by experiences with language, books and other print media, verbal and nonverbal ideas, and exposure to infinite content and concepts.

The reading process also involves print awareness, perceptual development, and comprehension. When we look at printed communication, relate it to some context or task, and can understand what we have "read," then we would say that the reading process has been demonstrated. Please note at this time that the reading process involves much more than just decoding, verbalizing, or recognizing printed words. We believe that in addition to identifying words, readers must make sense of words and relate words in some way to a known context or assignment in order for us to say that someone has really "read." Comprehension must be part of the act, or reading has not taken place. It is, in essence, interacting with the text and becoming involved at a level that enables you to activate your experience and prior knowledge to gain a greater understanding of the writer's message and your interpretation of that message.

The reading process involves the use and integration of many complex components that are essential to the successful understanding of text (see Figure 1.1). According to Burns, Roe, and Ross (1996), the reading process includes the sensory, perceptual, sequential, experiential, thinking (cognitive), learning, association, affective, and constructive elements. We would also add two others: linguistic and cultural. We believe that an understanding of these interrelated aspects of reading will enable you to better identify your students' needs and to provide students with more effective reading instruction. Each aspect or component of reading is described in the sections that follow.

## Sensory Component

The sensory component of the reading process involves visual and auditory acuity to see and hear written symbols and their sounds. Visual acuity refers to the actual sharpness of seeing. Auditory acuity refers to the keenness of hearing. The presentation of symbols is typically visual, although learning to read also involves the activation of certain auditory acuity capabilities. To accommodate students who are visually impaired or hearing impaired, tactile and kinesthetic methods can be used instead. Tactile methods involve using the sense of touch. Kinesthetic methods utilize the sense of movement, for instance body movement or positioning.

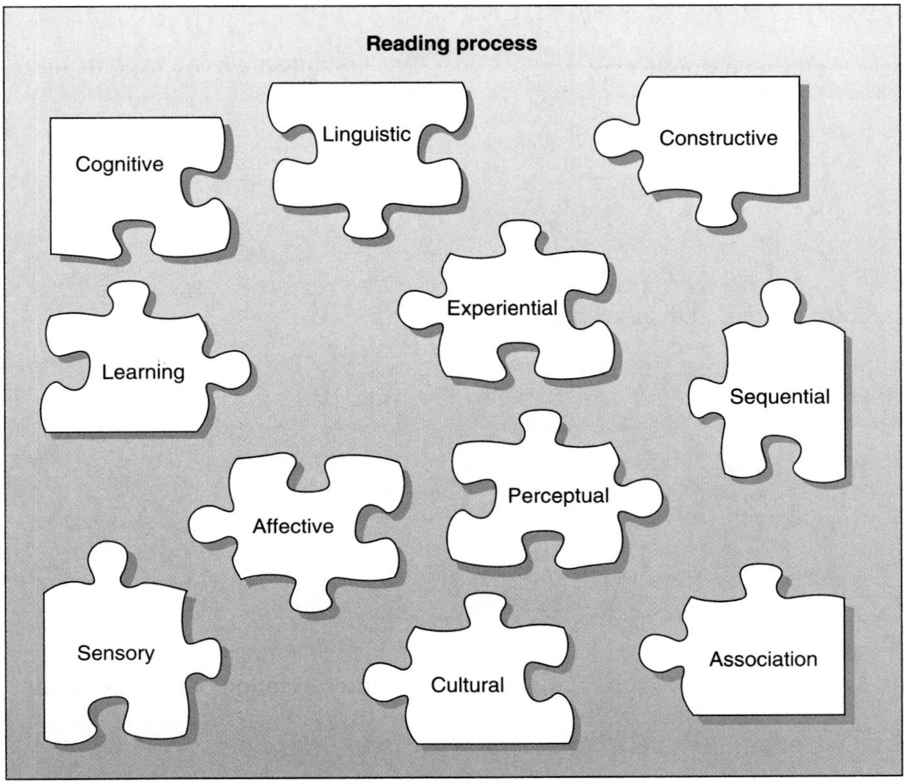

**Reading process**

Cognitive

Linguistic

Constructive

Learning

Experiential

Sequential

Affective

Perceptual

Sensory

Cultural

Association

*Figure 1.1*
Components of the
reading process.

## Perceptual Component

The perceptual component of the reading process involves students' use of their perceptual abilities to interpret what they see or hear. The information that they read is processed according to each student's experiential background. The meaning that your students are able to gain from the information they read is also associated with and dependent on their experiential backgrounds. This gleaned information is transmitted both visually and auditorially. Visual perception involves the identification and interpretation of various aspects of letters and words such as size, shape, and position. Auditory perception is primarily concerned with sound blending, memory, and discriminating likenesses and differences.

## Sequential Component

Sequential processing of text involves developing the awareness that English print is read from left to right and involves a top-to-bottom orientation. Following this sequence enables your students to gain meaning from the printed page. Another important aspect of this component is the awareness that language follows a sequential pattern of grammar and logic. This awareness involves an understanding that the printed page represents someone's thoughts or a recording of spoken language.

## Experiential Component

Both direct and indirect experiences are necessary for the development of the experiential component of the reading process. These experiences enable students to develop a richer vocabulary, which in turn enhances their understanding of concepts essential for their development into successful readers. Many students will come to your classroom with varied experiences that enhance their effectiveness as readers, but others may not. Those students lacking direct relevant experiences can be provided with indirect experiences that will enable them to become more successful readers.

## Linguistic Component

Linguistic aspects of the reading process involve and overlap with many of the other aspects already cited, particularly aspects involving sight and sound of words in language; grammar and structure of words in sentences; meaning of language and vocabulary associated with particular meanings; and all experiences with language, both oral and written. Because children with normal hearing, speech, and sight are hearing, speaking, and seeing language from infancy, they have developed an extensive linguistic background by the time they enter school. Continued and rich opportunities to practice with oral and written language, once in school, will help children further develop this important aspect of the reading process.

## Cognitive Component

Reading requires the utilization of cognitive abilities to facilitate the recognition and understanding of words through the interpretation of printed or written text. These cognitive abilities involve intellectual activities such as knowing, comprehending, thinking, applying, analyzing, synthesizing, and evaluating information and ideas. Understanding text also depends on reading critically and creatively. Critical reading involves evaluating the relevancy and adequacy of what one reads. Creative reading involves making use of what one reads by relating ideas or information read to one's experience or problems. Your students will use specific cognitive abilities or functions to promote critical and creative reading by relating information to their past experiences, interpreting figurative language, determining authors' purposes, evaluating the ideas presented, and applying the ideas presented to actual situations they have experienced. To develop or activate necessary cognitive abilities, teachers can design and use appropriate questioning strategies that cause students to engage in critical reading rather than just reading and learning isolated facts. These questions will also enable your students to deal more readily with real-life situations through the use of higher-level thinking skills.

## Learning Component

Reading is the key to learning in all aspects of life. For most school-related learning to occur, students must be effective readers. You will enhance the development of effective readers if your students are motivated, given meaningful practice, and provided with relevant and interesting reinforcement opportunities. Being effective readers increases success in school, helps students cope with real-life situations away from school, enhances their image in others' eyes, and provides them with a form of recreation. Reading is essential if your students are to be active learners in the various content areas such as social studies, science, and mathematics. Thus, seeing and understanding the relationship between reading and learning is very important to successful learning in school.

## Association Component

The process of association is essential in learning to read. Students learn to associate objects and ideas with spoken language and then perceive the association between spoken language and print. It is important that students be given opportunities for appropriate activities and immediate reinforcement to assist them in establishing these desired associations. Although repetition may be helpful in the development of associations, the associations that have some meaning to your students, either from prior knowledge or through experiences, tend to be learned more quickly.

## Affective Component

Although the development and activation of cognitive functions are essential to successful reading, affective factors may be more influential in motivating students to read. "Affective" refers to emotional activities or feelings. Four of the more important affective aspects of the reading process are interest, motivation, attitude, and self-esteem. For example, your students who are interested in the materials that they read will typically exert a greater effort in the reading process than students who have little or no interest in the same materials. This intensified effort may also be related to the motivations and attitudes your students exhibit toward a particular reading. Students who are motivated to read something, and with positive attitudes about the reading will usually put forth more of an effort than students who are unmotivated. Attitudes and motivations about reading are significantly influenced by your students' homes, communities, and entire sociocultural environments. "Socio-" refers to factors that can include social standing, education, income, and position. "Cultural" refers to the behaviors of a social group, including language, customs, and values. Students from environments where reading is frequently used often tend to see the purposes and uses of reading.

Your students' self-esteem also plays an important role in the reading process. Students with poor self-esteem may fear failure in reading and consequently may try to avoid reading activities. On the other hand, students with positive self-esteem often tend to be more confident in their ability to read and enjoy reading opportunities. In developing your students' reading abilities, you can help them feel accepted and successful by providing activities that enhance reading accomplishments.

### Constructive Component

As readers interact with print, they are continuously activating their visual and auditory senses in conjunction with their experiences and prior knowledge to construct a personal meaning in relationship to the text. Their experiences and prior knowledge are developed from the cultural and societal goals of all their learnings. Thus, the personal meaning constructed will be very different for each reader. In classrooms today there will be much diversity among students. Because of this diversity represented by children of many cultural and experiential backgrounds, each of the students will construct a meaning from the text representative of his or her own beliefs, experiences, and prior knowledge. This is to be expected in our culturally diverse society and simply indicates the necessity of providing students with appropriately diverse reading materials and activities.

### Cultural Component

Cultural aspects of the reading process involve and overlap with all of the other aspects cited. Culture shapes children's linguistic, cognitive, and affective learnings and development from infancy and continues throughout their lives. Children are developing their motivations, learnings, and other knowledge through the lenses of their own experiences. These experiences will be different for all children, and, therefore, no two children or individuals will see or understand something in the exact same way. Teachers and children need to be accepted and respected for these individual differences. The different experiences, understandings, and perceptions of individuals can help make a classroom a vital sharing and learning community.

## Perspectives of Reading

As we noted at the beginning of this chapter, there are many perspectives of reading. These different perspectives have developed because of different family, school, community, cultural, and other personal experiences as well as because of different learnings and exposures to reading research and practice; they influence the way one feels about reading and learning and how reading should be taught in the schools. The perspective that you embrace will influence your goals concerning reading instruction and enhancement, and the climate for reading that will be present in your classroom. The perspective that you develop about reading and reading instruction is crucial because it will affect your teaching and the students you teach.

Professional reading educators and researchers also have different perspectives, and we believe that these perspectives have evolved and been developed through different family, school, community, cultural and personal experiences. We also know that these professional perspectives have been additionally developed through a careful study and examination of the research, literature, and practices related to reading instruction. Although many different perspectives of teaching reading exist, we will examine only three of those that currently dominate the reading education research and literature:

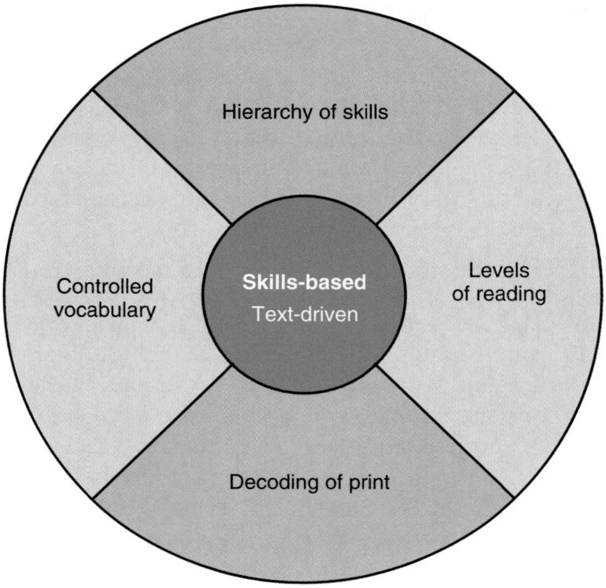

*Figure 1.2*
Skills-based reading perspective.

the skills perspective, the whole language perspective, and the interactive perspective. These perspectives tend to segment, if only superficially at times, much of the thinking about reading and have been responsible for the advancement of an infinite number of variations and differing theories about reading. However, for the sake of simplicity and clarity, we have chosen to present these three perspectives of reading in their broadest sense. We believe that they encompass most of the current varying theories and perspectives of reading. When we later examine definitions of reading, several definitions that can be categorized under each of these broad perspectives will also be presented.

## The Skills Perspective

During the first half of the twentieth century, until at least the late sixties, most of the research and literature in the field of reading (e.g., Austin and Morrison 1963, Guthrie 1973, and Samuels 1980) espoused a skills-based perspective (see Figure 1.2). Harris and Hodges (1995) indicated that these views had their roots in an associational, behavioristic concept of learning (p. 206). Reading was viewed as a collection of skills and subskills, and some reading researchers tried to differentiate these skills into a scope-and-sequence (hierarchy) type of relationship (i.e., what skills would be taught at what grade level and in what order), and attempts were made to dissect skills into smaller component parts and subparts. Other reading authorities felt that skills were much more global in nature and could not be divided like the slicing of a cake or pie. However, a common element among reading educators was that many considered the act of reading to be a skill, and they saw reading instruction as beginning with the development of smaller lower-level skills or units of communication and building up to larger or higher-level communication skills. For example, students might first be taught to recognize letters, then to recognize words, next to read simple sentences, then to read paragraphs, next to read stories, and, finally, to read books. Another skills-based example is the idea that students would be taught a decoding skill (an analysis of symbols), like phonics; and word parts, like syllables, before the comprehension skills. When the comprehension skills were taught, they would start with literal skills and work up to more complex application and analysis abilities (going beyond what is stated in the text).

Some reading authorities refer to this perspective as the "bottom-up theory." This hierarchical type of model lends itself to the idea that you start with the simple skills (at the bottom) and work up to the more difficult skills (at the top). Gough, Ehri, and Treiman (1992) believe that the connections between phonology and orthography (sounds and letters) should be the primary focus of beginning reading instruction. Even at the language acquisition stage of a child's development, some researchers are convinced that meaningful words are formed by combining a small inventory of meaningless units in a structured way, a bottom-up process (Lieberman and Lieberman 1990).

Another fairly common idea among reading educators who support a skills-based reading perspective is that reading success can be measured by how closely the readers can approximate or decode an author's stated words, or what the author intended to convey. In other words, the information in the text is "fixed" information exactly as presented by the author. The perspective was, and is today, a text-based perspective: Reading starts at the bottom (with the text and the less complex skills) and moves toward the top (toward meaning by utilizing the more complex skills).

Once again, we have purposely simplified the skills-based perspective. As we later examine several definitions of reading, you will see that the definitions grouped under this skills-based  umbrella elaborate more aspects of this perspective. Furthermore, reading educators and researchers who might be regarded as skills-based adherents do not necessarily have identical beliefs. However, the majority of them would not disagree with the notion that (1) reading is the utilization of many skills, and (2) the successful reader can approximate an author's words and message as they are stated in the text.

## The Whole Language Perspective

In the late 1960s and early 1970s, reading research and literature that presented more of a holistic view of the reading process (now known as the whole language perspective) began to emerge (e.g., Goodman 1976, Levin and Kaplan 1970, Smith 1971) (see Figure 1.3). Reading was described as a natural process and as a part of the other language processes, and within these contexts there was considerable interest in students' psycholinguistic experiences. Rather than treating reading as a set of text-based skills and levels, reading began to be viewed as a holistic process that begins with the reader's experience and predictions about meaning. In this process, the student's comprehension becomes the prime focus. Instead of focusing on skill development and the understanding of the author's very exact textual meaning, comprehension and relating textual information to

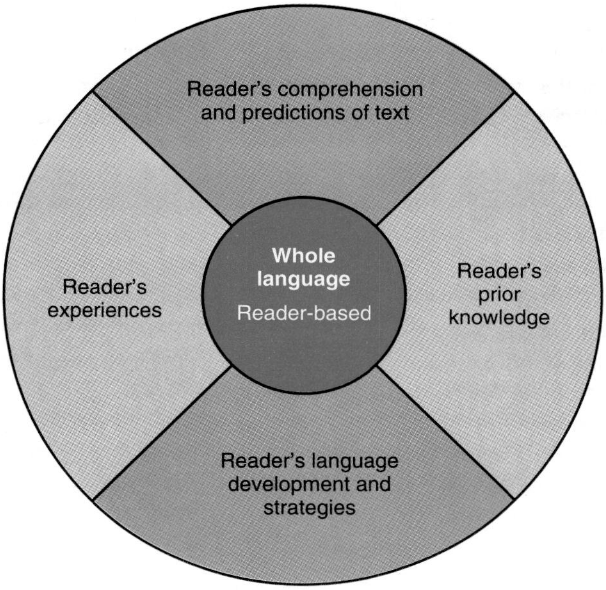

Figure 1.3
Whole language
reading perspective.

the reader's own experience and knowledge are the primary objectives. In the emerging whole language perspective, reading for understanding became the main focus, with skills knowledge only considered as particularly relevant when it caused a loss or breakdown in comprehension. This holistic view became increasingly strong in reaction to the skill and drill emphasis many educators saw in the schools. Reading strategies for dealing with a variety of materials and purposes were to replace the skills and levels of the skills-based models.

Some reading professionals refer to this holistic perspective of reading as the "top-down theory." Here you are more concerned with a higher order of communication and comprehension (at the top) and will work on the lower skills and units of communication as necessary (at the bottom). Meaning begins with the reader and moves down to a lower level of processing, using the text as needed.

Although many classroom teachers and others both inside and outside the educational community believe that whole language is of relatively recent origin, its roots can be traced back to the 1920s and 1930s progressive education movement, particularly to the work of John Dewey (Moorman, Blanton, and McLaughlin 1994). Furthermore, this progressive movement flourished in other English-speaking countries such as New Zealand, Australia, and England well before it became popular in this country. The term *whole language* was actually popularized in Canada and is similar in philosophy to the "real books" educational movement in England (K. S. Goodman 1992). During the 1970s, the whole language movement in the United States began to gain its earliest momentum. Although he is somewhat modest about his contribution, there can be no doubt that one of the most influential proponents of this movement in this country is Kenneth Goodman. In his 1992 article "I Didn't Found Whole

Language," he discussed the origins of this movement and his role as a contributor. Goodman believes that whole language is an inclusive philosophy of education that involves five important views (Goodman refers to them as "pillars"): a specific view of language; learning; teaching; curriculum; and a learning community. Specifically, he believes that whole language is a holistic integrated reading and writing philosophy that advocates the use of real, authentic literature and other real books for students' reading materials. In whole language classrooms, students and teachers are empowered to learn together in a democratic learning community. His 1992 article also includes Goodman's view that whole language is compatible with such educational concepts and movements as process writing, developmentally appropriate experiences, multigrade and family grouping, cooperative and collaborative education, language across the curriculum, language-experience reading, thematic units, literature-based reading instruction, questioning strategies for students and teachers, child-centered instruction, critical thinking, nongraded schools, emergent literacy, authentic assessment, and conflict resolution. Goodman further stated that whole language is incompatible with outcome-based education, phonics-only reading programs, and direct instruction.

The whole language movement has become enormously influential in the instruction of reading. We believe that the influence of this movement cannot be overstated. The basic tenets of this perspective are important concepts of which all teachers should be aware. Many positive changes in reading instruction in recent years can be directly attributed to the whole language movement. It has forced all of us to reexamine our beliefs about reading instruction and to become more flexible in our attitudes toward helping children learn to read.

## *The Interactive Perspective*

In the latter part of the 1970s and in the 1980s, an increasing number of research studies that advocated that reading is an interactive process were published (e.g., Rumelhart 1984, 1994). In this particular perspective of reading (see Figure 1.4), the reading process was conceptualized as neither bottom-up nor top-down but rather as a combination of these two theories of reading. In this context, and as Mason (1984) has reported, fluent readers process characteristics of texts as well as activate their language abilities, prior knowledge, and experiential backgrounds to learn, understand, and remember printed language. Reading can be text- or student-centered, or both.

The primary difference between the interactive perspective and the skills-based and whole language theories is that the interactive perspective is based on the theory that both the reader's hypotheses of the text and the written text itself are used by the reader in an attempt to gain meaning (Heilman, Blair, and Rupley 1994). This more interactive involvement and view continues to develop as researchers build on the current research and apply new learnings from cognitive psychology as well as from some constructivist, sociocultural, and other influences.

Thus, the interactive perspective supports the differential use of these informational sources at different times and under different conditions. The

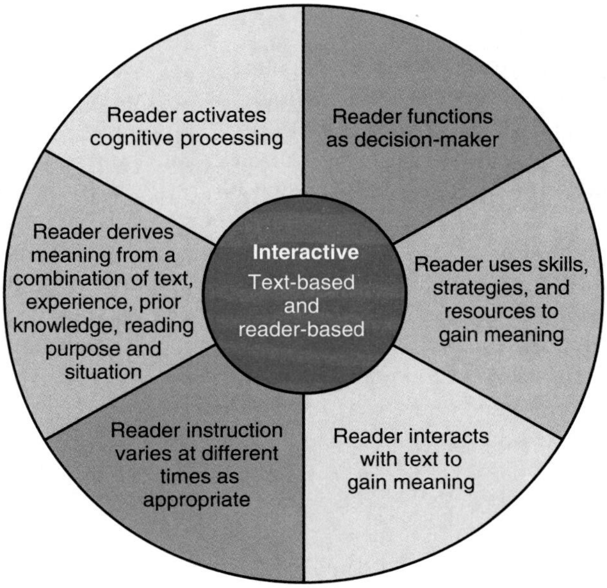

**Figure 1.4**
Interactive reading perspective.

Figure 1.4 Interactive reading perspective.

*Circular diagram with center labeled "Interactive / Text-based and reader-based" surrounded by segments reading: "Reader activates cognitive processing", "Reader functions as decision-maker", "Reader uses skills, strategies, and resources to gain meaning", "Reader interacts with text to gain meaning", "Reader instruction varies at different times as appropriate", "Reader derives meaning from a combination of text, experience, prior knowledge, reading purpose and situation".*

reader activates features of both the bottom-up (skills-based) and top-down (whole language) perspectives one at a time, or simultaneously, and meaning results from the interaction between the reader and the text. This active behavior allows the reader to use whatever sources are necessary and eliminates the need to rely on only one or the other. Here the reader is encouraged to make the decision to move to the bottom to decode as necessary, using lower-level skills, and to the top to comprehend using higher-level strategies when possible. The key elements or beliefs of the interactive perspective include the following:

1. Reading is a cognitive process.
2. Meaning results from the interaction between the reader and the text.
3. Understanding of reading information develops from the whole (stories and paragraphs) to the parts (words and sentences) as well as from the parts to the whole.
4. Different emphases in instruction are appropriate at different times.
5. Meaning is not in the text to be extracted by the reader, as the bottom-up theorists proposed.
6. Meaning is not in the reader to be triggered by the text, as the top-down theorists suggested.
7. Meaning is an endeavor where the reader makes the decision to use necessary skills, strategies, and resources (from the bottom and/or the top) to gain meaning.
8. Meaning is developed in the mind of the reader from the combination of information gleaned (1) from the text, (2) from the reader's cognitive experience, and (3) from the reading purpose and situation.

# Definitions of Reading

Your perspective of reading sets the stage for your definition of reading. Harris and Hodges (1995) have stated that "definitions need to be seen in the context of the theoretical and pragmatic orientations of the definer" (p. 207). For example, if you have a skills-based perspective, you might define reading as "the utilization of many skills and subskills." However, if you have a whole language perspective, you could define reading as "a natural process that is part of all the other language processes." Yet, if you view reading from an interactive perspective, you might define reading as "a cognitive process with meaning resulting from the interaction between the reader and the printed page."

In this section, we will explore several definitions of reading by looking at some of those stated by reading educators and researchers. We think that if you read and analyze others' definitions of reading you will profit in three ways. First, you will have additional information to assist you in answering the question "What is reading?" Second, as you continue to develop your own definition of reading, you will consider the varying definitions that have been given and will not be as likely to adhere to a narrow or stagnant definition of reading. Third, and perhaps the most important reason for considering a number of definitions, you will discern how your definition of reading is going to influence your view about reading and the way in which you teach reading. Even though trying to define reading might seem to be somewhat limiting or abstract, it is very important for you to continue to consider your beliefs about reading and instruction and continue to conceptualize your specific definition.

The final section of this chapter will discuss in detail the importance of your having your own definition of reading and your involvement in the reading process. At this point, however, we want you to take a few minutes to review and think more about the diagram or notations you made concerning the reading process in Reflection Activity 1.1 under "What Is Reading? Part A." Now under the subheading Part B, write your own personal definition of reading. You might want to refer again to your notes or diagram to formulate this definition. Keep in mind that your definition cannot be wrong. It is *your* definition, and it represents your current understanding of what reading is. As you did with Part A, date the definition you write in Part B.

## Skills-Based Definitions

According to Harris and Sipay (1990), skills-based definitions of reading are rooted in the philosophy that reading is the translation of graphemes (e.g., our letters of the alphabet) into inner speech or language during silent reading or into oral speech or language during oral reading. During silent or oral reading, readers utilize their "listening comprehension" abilities for comprehension purposes. Thus, "written language is subservient to, or dependent on, oral language; the only activity unique to reading is 'breaking the written code'" (p. 12). Some skills-based reading definitions given by well-known educators are cited in the paragraphs that follow:

Flesch (1955), in his nationally acclaimed book *Why Johnny Can't Read,* defined reading from a very limited skills-based mode. He stated:

> Reading is getting meaning from certain combinations of letters. Teach the child what each letter stands for and he can read. (pp. 2–3)

As you may have discerned, Flesch's definition is specifically based on a phonics-skills emphasis. Reading, according to Flesch, is teaching your student how to use phonic rules and generalizations.

Fries (1963) has also published a widely quoted skills-based definition of reading. Fries maintained:

> The process of learning to read in one's native language is the process of transfer from the auditory signs for language skills, which the child has already learned, to the new visual signs for the same signals. (p. 120)

Fries's reading definition is based on the concept of linguistics, where reading is teaching your students to associate their spoken language with acceptable written language and by having them recognize contrasting spelling patterns (e.g., "bat," "cat," "fat," and so on) that represent their oral language.

In 1967 Chall published the first edition of her book *Learning to Read: The Great Debate* and asserted that her review of the research indicated that the code-emphasis view of beginning reading—that is, a view that advocates emphasizing learning of the printed code before emphasizing the meaning of words—produces better readers. Chall's definition would include the importance of the learning of many reading skills, including the use of phonics, as a foundation for learning to read. At the time, Chall was concerned that many schools had been emphasizing a "whole word learning" approach to teaching reading, where children simply memorized words. Sometimes this was called the "look-say" approach. The debate then was whether children should be taught by a "look-say" or by a phonics emphasis.

More recently, Adams's (1990) *Beginning to Read: Thinking and Learning about Print* was published. Adams's extensive research led her to report that approaches that include systematic code instruction (including phonics) along with a meaning emphasis, language instruction, and connected readings are superior (p. 49). Adams did emphasize that readers should learn this code instruction systematically, first beginning with letters and letter sounds, and later blended together (p. 48). Then through repeated attention to sequences of individual letters, readers would gain the ability to perceive words and syllables as wholes (p. 130). Both Chall's (1967) and Adams's (1990) views are quite different and far broader and more comprehensive than Flesch's (1955); even within each of the major perspectives we describe, views keep evolving and developing based on additional research, practice, and the knowledge gleaned from other views, perspectives, and influences.

## *Meaning-Based Definitions*

It has been stated (cf. Harris and Sipay 1990) that a top-down definition must stress or imply that meaning is predicted before print is processed, that visual cues (e.g., letters alone or in combination) are inspected as needed, and that meaning predictors are continually rejected, confirmed, and refined. Whole language–based definitions imply that readers play an active role in the reading process and supply the additional information needed to understand what is on the printed page.

An International Reading Association publication, Harris and Hodges's (1995) *The Literacy Dictionary: The Vocabulary of Reading and Writing,* presents a number of top-down or holistic definitions of reading. K. Goodman's composite definition, taken from two of his early publications, is representative of these meaning-emphases definitions and states: "Reading is a sampling, selecting, predicting, comparing, and confirming activity in which the reader selects a sample of useful graphic cues based on what he sees and what he expects to see . . . [and] . . . the reader attempts to reconstruct a message from the writer" (p. 207). Goodman (1970) has also defined reading as "a complex process by which a reader reconstructs to some degree a message encoded by a writer in graphic language" (p. 5). Goodman's definitions are predicated on his belief that reading is a meaning-getting task and that readers' prior knowledge and psycholinguistic competence are important. Smith (1971) proposed that reading "is an act of communication in which information is transferred from a transmitter to a receiver" (p. 12). Additionally, some reading educators see reading and comprehension as the same process, and their definitions of reading reflect this oneness. For example, Jerry Harste (another whole language authority), stated in an interview with Monson and Monson (1994), "While we have looked at literacy as involving print, I see literacy as the using of any kind of sign system to make sense and share meaning . . . [b]y my definition, I can see all the disciplines and the humanities as forms of literacy" (p. 519).

Cambourne (1994) has stated that linguistic rules are learned under conditions that are significantly different from those typically found in schools. When these natural conditions are interfered with, the acquisition of language is seriously compromised.

Again, reading educators who subscribe to the whole language or meaning-emphasis perspective have proposed reading definitions that emphasize comprehension. These definitions also stress that reading is a form of meaningful communication, and these definitions continue to develop and be refined based on continued research, reflection, and practice within the whole language movement, as well as from some constructivist, sociocultural, and other influences.

### *Interactive Definitions*

Rumelhart (1994) has published one of the most widely cited descriptions of the interactive reading process. His work has been used by other educators and researchers to formulate their own interactive definitions of reading. These definitions propose that skills-based and whole language processes are at work one at a time or simultaneously to affect comprehension. The proficient reader validates comprehension by decoding important text (analyzing symbols) and/or by using prior knowledge (existing information and familiarity).

Lapp and Flood (1986) have advanced a widely accepted interactive definition of reading within Rumelhart's perspective. They stated:

Reading is an interaction between the author and the reader. To understand the printed message, the readers must perceive, interpret, hypothesize, and evaluate. These processes occur in varying degrees depending on the readers' familiarity with the content of the text and with their purposes for readings. (p. 6)

Durkin (1993) has indicated that reading involves intentional thinking during which meaning is constructed through interactions between text and the reader. Pearson (1985) proposed that readers play a much more active role in their own reading than we once thought. He stated:

A teacher can no longer regard the text as the ultimate criterion for defining what good comprehension is; instead she must view the text, along with students' prior knowledge, students' strategies, the task, and the classroom situation as one facet in the complex array . . . [called reading] . . . Now a teacher must know as much about the influence of these other facets (prior knowledge, strategies, tasks, situation) as she knows about the text itself. (p. 726)

Furthermore, Pearson suggested that students build mental models or diagrams as they read. The models may be different than the fixed text of the author, but these actively constructed reader-built models will be the result of the students' previous knowledge about the topic or concept.

Another interactive definition has been proposed by Wixson and Peters (1984). They defined reading as "the process of constructing meaning through the dynamic interaction among the reader's existing knowledge, the information suggested by the written language, and the context of the reading situation." The reader is engaged in an interactive process involving prior cognitive experiences, the text material, and the reader's construction of meaning based on these inputs. Or, as Harris and Sipay (1990) stated, "a hypothesis generated by top-down processing is guided by the result of bottom-up processing, and the bottom-up processing is guided by the expectations imposed by top-down processing" (p. 13).

## *Perspectives and Definitions: Our Reaction*

As you read the preceding perspectives and definitions, you probably thought, "It doesn't seem clear-cut at all. How can these reading authorities be categorized by perspectives or by definitions? Some of those definitions do not seem to fit any of the perspectives, and some seem to fit in a different one, or in all three, or overlap somehow." If this was what you were thinking, you are quite correct. It is difficult to make these judgments, but it is important that you examine various reading perspectives to better understand the reading process.

Why is it important? Why does it make a difference? Most of us actually formulate our own reading perspectives and definitions from our personal experiences and from what we have learned about the reading process. This is what we hope you will also do. Just as the reading professionals we have cited have their own thoughts, definitions, and complex ideas concerning the reading process based on their particular research, study, and personal introspection, and influenced as well by the research and thinking of others, we want you to develop your own thoughts and ideas about reading based on what you know now and what you will study, read, observe, and learn throughout your educational career. Keep in mind that your perspective and definition will continue to develop as you study and learn more about the reading process.

We do not advocate that you adopt any particular one of the three reading perspectives discussed in this chapter. The thesis of this chapter, and in fact of our entire text, is that there is much to be valued and applied within each of the major perspectives of reading. No value judgments have been made or will be made regarding preferences for any of these particular perspectives or their related definitions. Instead, as we have already pointed out, these perspectives may overlap in some instances, as suggested by several of the definitions we grouped for you. Additionally, we believe that *only you* will be able to advocate an appropriate perspective suited to your needs. We hope that you will study the reading process carefully and then integrate the best of what you learn into your present beliefs and knowledge about reading, developing your own balanced ideas.

Based on our collective research and experiences, we find that as a research team we use and believe in ideas from each of the three presented evolving perspectives. We believe that reading development is based on students' emerging experiences with language and that the reader's comprehension is of paramount importance. We also believe that the reader's prior knowledge and experiences do affect his or her understanding of what he or she reads. (These are some of the ideas we have taken from the whole language perspective.) But we also believe that reading is an interactive process and for us, it involves the cognitive processing of information in the text and use of many skills, strategies, and resources to gain meaning. We see the reader as someone who must interact with the text to develop meaning, meaning that will be shaped by a combination of text, experience, prior knowledge, purpose, and situation. (These are some of the ideas we have taken from the interactive perspective.) We have "balanced" our views with a belief that it is necessary at times for teachers to provide direct instruction in skills (including phonics) to students needing this instruction, and we also believe that the decoding of print is part of reading. (These ideas have been taken from the skills-based perspective; however, we do not believe in any particular sequence or hierarchy of skills, or in the need to control students' exposure to vocabulary.) In addition, we believe that students should receive direct instruction, as needed, in various strategies to help them develop their proficiency as readers. (This idea of direct instruction to enhance reading strategies comes from interactive research.)

Finally, even though we do not want you to "just simply" accept our beliefs and views, we do present for you throughout this text our concept of "the facilitative teacher" perspective. We have come to believe that this is the teacher who we would each try to be if we were to be classroom teachers again. In other words, "the facilitative teacher" in our text values the learnings that have evolved from all the major reading perspectives and adopts strong beliefs in using students' language experiences as well as their cognitive and cultural learnings to help them develop into successful readers. The facilitative teacher understands that the major reading perspectives have evolved over time through research efforts and reflection, as well as through trial-and-error learning. Each of the reading views and beliefs were a reaction to or building on the ones that came before it. Because of this understanding, our facilitative teacher does not worry about labeling herself or himself as a member of any particular camp or group. Instead, our idea of a facilitative teacher suggests that this teacher is capable of reflecting and making decisions based on what is best for each individual child in her or his classroom, *balancing* the use of methods, material, and instruction.

You will see, as you continue to read this text, that our facilitative teacher uses many of the newest ideas, including use of authentic assessments, collaborative learning, and the integrated teaching of various subject areas; the facilitative teacher also balances these using many of the ideas from the more traditional beliefs, like direct instruction of skills and strategies. In summary, our facilitative teacher is reflective, knowledgeable, and makes professional decisions that are in the best interest of all students' reading development.

Harris and Hodges (1981) in an earlier reading dictionary publication have noted the importance and the impact that different points of view have on actual reading instruction by citing the work of the late, noted reading educator Ruth Strang:

> If we think of reading primarily as a visual task, we will be concerned with the correction of visual defects and the provision of legible reading material. If we think of reading as word recognition, we will drill on the basic sight vocabulary and word recognition skills. If we think of reading as merely reproducing, we will direct the student's attention to the literal meaning of it. If we think of reading as a thinking process, we shall be concerned with the reader's skill in making interpretations and generalizations, in drawing inferences and conclusions. If we think of reading as contributing to personality development and effecting desirable personality changes, we will provide our students with reading materials that meet their needs or have some application to their lives. (p. 264)

 **Reflection Activity 1.2**

*W*hy is it important for a teacher to be able to articulate a definition of reading? What are some instructional implications of that definition? Take a few moments and reflect on these questions. Then, in your journal under the heading Reflection Activity 1.2, write your answers based on what you have read thus far in this text.

# Your Reading Perspective and Definition

So how does all this affect you? How will you be involved with reading as a classroom teacher? Our answer to this is quite simple: You will be involved in every possible way because reading is part of everything you will teach. Reading is crucial in every aspect of the school curriculum as well as in daily aspects of life. Your perspective of the reading process and reading definition will guide your teaching practices.

Reading should not be perceived as a subject that must be attended to for only one class period per day. Instead, we hope you will accept the position that reading is a process that must be attended to and integrated in every class that you teach. Reading is without content itself but plays an integral role in instruction and in the study of science, social studies, English, and all the other content subjects. Reading is a process to be applied to all school- as well as nonschool-related forms of written communication. You should be teaching and encouraging the use of reading strategies throughout the day in all curricula and content areas.

We believe that if you accept and implement this concept of reading, you will become a more effective teacher. You will also become a teacher who can provide a successful and realistic reading and learning environment. The reading perspective and definition you develop should enhance your classroom instruction and assist you to view your students as individuals with intelligence, feelings, interests, and needs. It should also lead you to accept responsibility for encouraging learning, facilitating positive outcomes, and nurturing the love and usage of reading in and out of the classroom. The role of this text is to provide information and ideas that will lead you toward adopting such a facilitative reading philosophy.

## Reflection Activity 1.3

*H*ow might the teacher's definition and way of teaching reading affect the students' definitions of their "ideas" about reading? Once again, take a few moments to reflect on this question. Then under the heading Reflection Activity 1.3, write your answer based on what you know thus far about reading.

## Summary

It has been the purpose of this chapter to advance your understanding of the reading process. We have also attempted to help you develop your own existing perspective and definition by presenting descriptions of three major professional perspectives of reading instruction and by examining definitions proposed by several reading educators. We concluded this chapter with a discussion of our perceptions and your role in the reading process. Additionally, we emphasized the importance of reading in all school subjects and areas. Before leaving this chapter, we ask you to return to your reflection journal and reread what you initially wrote or diagrammed about the reading process under the heading Reflection Activity 1.1 "What Is Reading? Part A." Below your notations or diagram use the space left for Part C to rewrite or make any changes to your notes or diagram. If your beliefs have not been altered, it is not necessary to make any changes or additions. Likewise, take a second look at your definition of reading under Part B. Do you wish to alter or add to your definition of reading? If so, go ahead and make the changes. What do you now think reading is? It will be interesting for you to see how much or little your perception of reading has been altered after reading this initial chapter. As you continue to read this text and to study and discuss the reading process, you will be asked to reconsider your position and make any desired alterations to your current view of reading instruction.

## *Closing Activities*

1. This chapter has emphasized the importance of one's experiences in determining a personal view of reading. Make a list of some of the things that you feel have influenced your own personal definition and schema (diagram) of reading.
2. In a small group, share your diagram, definitions, and list of influences with others in your reading methods class. Discuss your reactions with your group. Did this discussion influence your perceptions to any extent?
3. Analyze your diagram and definition. Does it lean toward the skills-based perspective, whole language perspective, or interactive perspective? In what ways does it seem similar to or different from each of these perspectives?
4. Using your college library, find articles about reading in professional journals like *The Reading Teacher, Reading Horizons,* and *Language Arts.* Read three articles and try to write what you feel each author's personal definition of reading might be.
5. Using your college library, examine three recently published elementary reading methods textbooks and try to determine the basic theory or perspective of each text. Write a brief statement for each. Then indicate which of these texts most closely reflects your current beliefs about the teaching of reading and the reading process. Why?
6. Interview reading and language arts and other teacher-education faculty at your college and ask for their personal definitions of reading. Meet in a small or large group and share these definitions. Groups should discuss the implications of each shared definition. What is each person's probable philosophy? What in their background or professional training could have influenced their philosophies?
7. Observe a teacher teaching a reading lesson in an elementary classroom. By your own observations, try to determine what definition and perspective of reading is suggested. Describe and explain it.
8. Interview the elementary school teacher whom you observed. Ask the following questions and record the teacher's answers: (a) "What is your definition of reading?" and (b) "What strategies, ideas, or practices about teaching reading do you endorse?" Next, analyze how the teacher's definition, ideas, and practices are related. Document and explain your analysis.

*References*

Adams, M.J. (1990). *Beginning to Read: Thinking and Learning about Print.* Cambridge: MIT Press.
Austin, M.C., and C. Morrison. (1963). *The First R: The Heward Report on Reading in the Elementary Schools.* New York: Macmillan.
Burns, P.C., B.D. Roe, and E.P. Ross. (1996). *Teaching Reading in Today's Elementary Schools,* 6th ed. Boston: Houghton Mifflin.

Cambourne, B. (1994). "The Rhetoric of 'The Rhetoric of Whole Language.'" *Reading Research Quarterly* 29:330-332.

Chall, J.S. (1967). *Learning to Read: The Great Debate.* New York: McGraw-Hill.

Durkin, D. (1993). *Teaching Them to Read,* 6th ed. Boston, MA: Allyn & Bacon.

Flesch, R. (1955). *Why Johnny Can't Read and What You Can Do About It.* New York: Harper & Row.

Fries, C.C. (1963). *Linquistics and Reading.* New York: Holt, Rinehart & Winston.

Goodman, K.S. (1970). "Behind the Eye: What Happens in Reading." In K.S. Goodman and O. Niles, eds., *Reading Process and Programs.* Urbana, IL: National Council of Teachers of English.

Goodman, K.S. (1976). "Reading: A Psycholinguistic Guessing Game." In H. Singer and R. Ruddell, eds., *Theoretical Models and Processes of Reading.* Newark, DE: International Reading Association.

————. (1992). "I Didn't Found Whole Language." *The Reading Teacher* 46:188-199.

Gough, P.B., L.C. Ehri, and R. Treiman. (1992). *Reading Acquisition.* Hillsdale, NJ: Erlbaum.

Guthrie, J.T. (1973). "Models of Reading and Reading Disability," *Journal of Educational Psychology* 65:9-18.

Harris, A.J., and E.R. Sipay. (1990). *How to Increase Reading Ability,* 9th ed. New York: Longman.

Harris, T.L., and R.E. Hodges, eds. (1981). *A Dictionary of Reading and Related Terms.* Newark, DE: International Reading Association.

————, eds. (1995). *The Literacy Dictionary: The Vocabulary of Reading and Writing.* Newark, DE: International Reading Association.

Heilman, A.W., T.R. Blair, and W.H. Rupley. (1994). *Principles and Practices of Teaching Reading,* 8th ed. New York: Macmillan.

Lapp, D., and J. Flood. (1986). *Teaching Students to Read.* New York: Macmillan.

Lieberman, I.Y., and A.M. Lieberman. (1990). "Whole Language versus Code Emphasis: Underlying Assumptions and Their Implications for Reading Instruction." *Annals of Dyslexia* 40:51-76.

Levin, H., and E.L. Kaplan. (1970). "Grammatical Structure and Reading." In H. Levin and J. Williams, eds., *Basic Studies in Reading.* New York: Basic Books.

Mason, J.M. (1984). "A Schema-Theoretic View of the Reading Process as a Basis for Comprehension Instruction." In G. Duffy, L. Roehler, and J. Mason, eds., *Comprehension Instruction: Perspective and Suggestions* (pp. 26-38). New York: Longman.

Monson, R.J., and M.P. Monson. (1994). "Literacy as Inquiry: An Interview with Jerome C. Harste." *The Reading Teacher* 47(7):518-521.

Moorman, G.B., W.E. Blanton, and T. McLaughlin. (1994). "The Rhetoric of Whole Language." *Reading Research Quarterly* 29:308-329.

Pearson, P.D. (1985). "Changing the Face of Reading Comprehension Instruction." *The Reading Teacher* 38:724-738.

Rumelhart, D.E. (1984). "Understanding Understanding." In J. Flood, ed., *Understanding Reading Comprehension* (pp. 1-20). Newark, DE: International Reading Association.

————. (1994). "Toward an Interactive Model of Reading." In R.B. Ruddell, M.R. Ruddell, and H. Singer, eds., *Theoretical Models and Processes of Reading,* 4th ed. (pp. 864-899). Newark, DE: International Reading Association.

Samuels, S.J. (1980). "The Age-Old Controversy between Wholistic and Subskill Approaches to Beginning Reading Instruction Revisited." In C. McCullough, ed., *Inchworm, Inchworm: Persistent Problems in Reading Education* (pp. 202-221). Newark, DE: International Reading Association.

Smith, F. (1971). *Understanding Reading: A Linguistic Analysis of Readings and Learning to Read.* New York: Holt, Rinehart & Winston.

Wixson, K.K., and C.W. Peters. (1984). "Reading Redefined: A Michigan Reading Association Position Paper." *Michigan Reading Journal* 17(1): 4-7.

# *T*he *Facilitative Classroom Teacher*

© Elizabeth Crews/The Image Works

## *Overview*

*I*n this chapter the importance of the elementary classroom teacher's philosophy concerning reading and learning is emphasized. Examples of facilitative and nonfacilitative teachers are used to illustrate how their philosophies affect the classroom environments, learning goals, and their students' learning attitudes and interests. Because teachers exert such a strong and lasting influence on their students, it is especially important that teacher education majors experience opportunities to assimilate and integrate information from their coursework and professional readings into their philosophies of teaching.

The importance of students' varied backgrounds, cultures, experiences, and prior knowledge are also discussed. Case-study examples are provided to illustrate the effects of prior knowledge, students' concepts, and their vocabulary backgrounds on their learning.

The facilitative teacher is further introduced as a teacher who values students' individualities and facilitates their learning by being aware of and by providing for their differences, experiences, needs, strategies, motivations, cultures and interests, and he or she balances instruction to meet these diversities. Examples are given to illustrate the importance of those differences, and to provide ideas as to how teachers can adapt instruction to the student and the learning environment. Additionally, suggestions are made to help teachers assess students prior to any instructional attempts.

Facilitative reading and learning instruction involves certain attitudes and ideas. Guidelines are presented to further expand the facilitative reading concept.

## *Main Ideas*

- Teachers' philosophies can be the basis for how teachers perceive their roles and actually teach.
- Teachers' philosophies about reading and learning influence every aspect of their classrooms and also influence their students' perceptions about reading and learning.
- Facilitative teachers encourage learning, facilitate positive environments and outcomes, and nurture the love and usage of reading in and out of the classroom.
- Students' prior knowledge and culture and their concept development and vocabulary are taken into consideration by facilitative teachers when they plan instruction.
- Facilitative teachers adapt instruction to the students and learning environment by assessing the students and the learning situation, by deciding instructional goals and content using assessment information, and by developing an integrated-facilitative instructional program.

- There are numerous guidelines teachers could consider to contemplate and implement facilitative reading and learning programs.
- The teacher-effectiveness research has included attempts to identify and measure teacher characteristics and competencies as well as attempts to examine teachers' judgments, decision making, and beliefs.

In Chapter 1 we introduced major reading perspectives, a variety of definitions of reading, and our thoughts about the reading process. We also established a need for your personal definition and thoughts about reading. Additionally, we asked you to use your existing knowledge concerning reading, as well as information presented in this text and in your other professional encounters and readings, to develop and state your own perspective and definition. As you are now probably aware, a definition and a perspective of reading are another way of indicating your philosophy or theory about reading and learning. However, we consider a philosophy and a theory of reading and learning to be much broader and much more encompassing than a definition.

Teachers' philosophies will often be the basis for the way they perceive their roles as teachers, set up their classrooms, determine their learning goals, manage their learning environments, assess their students, make instructional decisions, work with parents and families, cooperate with other professional educators, and work with their students. Sometimes, of course, what people say they believe may not be reflected in what they actually do. The facilitative teacher not only talks about positive teacher behaviors but also embodies or manifests them, particularly in reading-related instruction.

In this chapter, the facilitative teacher concept is introduced and examples of facilitative and nonfacilitative teacher behaviors are given. Additionally, the importance of individual student characteristics, backgrounds, experiences, and prior knowledge and concepts is emphasized with discussion and examples to help you see how instruction can be adapted to the student and the learning environment and situation. Learnings from effective-teaching research, which includes examination of teachers' thinking and beliefs, has made an impact on the schools. This research will be discussed near the end of the chapter. Finally, you are asked to consider your own facilitative characteristics and attributes.

## *The Facilitative Teacher*

Because teachers' beliefs concerning reading and learning often affect every aspect of their classrooms, it is imperative that your developing philosophy have the potential for positively affecting students' growth and development. Furthermore, because teachers have a tremendous impact on students and these effects can be long-lasting, it is desirable for you to develop a philosophy that will nurture the learning environment. We believe that the facilitative teacher has a nurturing philosophy, exhibits the behaviors needed to effectively meet the reading needs of students, and creates a positive classroom learning environment.

## A Definition

Facilitative teachers are professional teachers who believe that their role is to encourage learning, facilitate positive environments and outcomes, and nurture the love and usage of reading in and out of the classroom. These teachers are learner-oriented and understand the importance of reading in the learning process. They understand that reading is a crucial part of the language and communication process and encourage the development of all aspects of this process. The primary goal of facilitative teachers is to help develop independent learners who use reading and other related strategies for research, content area study, and personal interests, growth, and satisfaction.

## Facilitative and Nonfacilitative Teachers

Most of us can think back to our elementary days and remember with clarity several of our teachers. We tend, however, to remember most those teachers who had a significantly positive or negative impact on our learning experiences. What was it about these teachers that made them unforgettable to us? We would like to suggest to you that it was their philosophies and beliefs concerning teaching and learning that made them so memorable. We will never forget those teachers who seemed to so strongly exhibit facilitative and nonfacilitative behaviors.

Consider the following descriptions of facilitative teachers from the memories of two of our students:

> My fourth-grade teacher was the best! She encouraged us to work in groups and to talk if we wanted to. Although we had considerable freedom, not one of us was a behavior problem. We put on three school plays during the course of the year as well as learned a lot. She helped us when we were in trouble and gave of her time freely whenever we needed her. This teacher believed in a student-centered classroom environment, and she emphasized each part of life as a learning experience. Although the school's curricula were important to her, she also believed that the classroom was a social environment and that we needed to develop socially as well as academically.

> Miss D _____ welcomed us into her classroom with a warm smile. Our second-grade classroom was a friendly environment with desks clustered in groups, and we were allowed to chat quietly among ourselves. Miss D _____ had a very caring personality and showed this to us often. She stressed sharing and cooperation. Miss D _____'s philosophy of teaching and learning had positive outcomes. She stressed working together and guided this type of learning environment. We were always given time for input and she followed up on our ideas. She gave us time to work on things we thought were important and valued our finished products. She showed us she cared about us and our learning, and, as a result, we wanted to show her our respect by doing a good job on what she asked of us. Her role was as a guide and a facilitator of learning.

Did the teachers whom you fondly remember exhibit some of the behaviors of the above fourth- and second-grade teachers? Would you like to be remembered by your students as positively as the teachers depicted? These teachers, as you have already gathered, were student-oriented and were facilitators of learning.

$\mathcal{T}$ake a few moments to scan your memory for the elementary school teacher you most positively remember. We suspect this was a facilitative teacher. Then try to recall a classroom experience with that teacher. In your reflection journal under the heading Reflection Activity 2.1, respond to the following: (a) Describe the scenario from your memories; (b) briefly tell what you feel this teacher's philosophy of teaching was; (c) how did this teacher view himself/herself and his/her role in the classroom? (d) what effect has this teacher had on you? and (e) what effect will this teacher have on your teaching philosophy and behavior?

The following are descriptions of nonfacilitative teachers or teachers who negatively affected two of our students' learning experiences:

Miss B _____ was a very uncaring teacher. When we entered her classroom, we were to keep our mouths closed at all times unless called on, to sit in our seats, and to do our work without disturbing anyone. We would have a pile of work sheets waiting for us every day. Our desks were all lined up neatly in rows and no one dared move. Miss B _____ always used verbal punishment that was harsh and demeaning. It was torture to enter this sixth-grade classroom, and we all feared walking through the door. Miss B _____'s philosophy of teaching was definitely to be in control. She placed heavy emphasis on work sheets, and we were to learn the necessary things by drill and more drill. Miss B _____'s role was that of a strict disciplinarian, and an overseer of drill work.

I remember my second-grade teacher vividly, mainly because she had such a negative impact on my desire to read. She didn't seem to value the importance of reading for pleasure. For example, one day I was reading a book and was totally absorbed by the story. The next thing that I noticed was the entire class standing in line, giggling and laughing at me, as I remained in my seat, reading. The teacher made some derogatory statement about my reading. I was thoroughly embarrassed. From that school year on, I stayed away from reading as much as possible. I would only read if absolutely necessary. It wasn't until I met my husband, who enjoys reading, that I started buying and reading books of interest to me. This, by the way, did not take place until I was 30 years old!

I feel this teacher wasn't really interested in reading, nor in the emotional well-being of children. Had she been concerned, she would have praised my reading interests. Instead, she chose to allow the students to ridicule me, and showed that she was more concerned with the fact that I had not paid attention to her. In retrospect, I probably did overreact to the situation; however, I know that my negative attitudes toward reading for pleasure instilled by this particular teacher were very real.

Did you have a Miss B _____, or was one of your teachers like the second-grade teacher described? Do you want to be remembered or depicted by one of your students like these teachers? These teachers were perceived by these students as nonfacilitative individuals who seemed to put more value on control than on learning.

$W$e ask you to again take a few moments to scan your memory but this time to remember the elementary school teacher who most negatively affected you as a student. We suspect this individual was a nonfacilitative teacher. Then in your reflection journal under the heading Reflection Activity 2.2, try to recall a specific classroom experience with that teacher and record the following: (a) Describe this scenario from your memories; (b) briefly tell what you feel this teacher's philosophy of teaching was; (c) how did this teacher view himself/herself and his/her role in the classroom? (d) what effect has this teacher had on you? and (e) what effect will this teacher have on your teaching philosophy and behavior?

As we have tried to point out through case studies and your own memories, when teachers act out their philosophies of teaching and learning, there is certainly an effect on the classroom environment and students' attitudes and learning outcomes. Furthermore, these effects can be very long-lasting because teachers' behaviors can make a difference, as opposed to the many other variables that come into play in the school setting. For that reason, your philosophy and beliefs are very important to us. Your developing philosophy about learning and reading, or what you believe is really important, and what you believe is really not so important, will set the tone for your total classroom environment.

## *Understanding and Using Students' Backgrounds, Experiences, and Prior Knowledge*

Your students will come to your classroom with an extreme diversity of backgrounds and abilities. Likewise, their cognitive and linguistic (language-related) experiences, their prior knowledge, and their concept development and vocabulary in all aspects of content and other school-related learning will be different. Such tremendous variation is one of the greatest challenges a teacher can have. Therefore, as a teacher, it is important that you understand how unique each of your students really is. Their uniqueness and experiences will have to be a consideration in your instructional procedures and in everything you hope that your students will learn. No one can really individualize for all the differences and experiences in an average-sized classroom population; however, the teacher who is aware of these differences and experiences will be more likely to provide some opportunities for all learners. We believe this teacher will be a facilitative teacher who values each individual and who facilitates learning for those individuals by being in touch with "where they are" and "where they are coming from."

In the sections that follow, specific case-study examples are presented to illustrate the importance of knowing your individual students and their backgrounds and experiences as those relate to their prior knowledge, and to their concept development and vocabulary.

## Prior Knowledge

The understandings your students bring to their readings—their prior knowledge of concrete (e.g., toys) and abstract (e.g., love) concepts—will have a significant impact on their ability to comprehend text. For example, your students reared on a farm, as compared with their peers who were reared in an urban area or a suburb, will have developed more rural background schemata, and this knowledge will promote their understanding whenever you are reading or discussing ideas that require prior knowledge in that area. Consider the following case study and the prior-knowledge dilemma:

> The classroom teacher of inner-city fourth-graders from a disadvantaged neighborhood introduced a lesson on various recreational and leisure-time activities. The teacher mentioned a variety of activities (camping, white-water rafting, racquetball, sailing, golf, down-hill skiing, and so on) and then asked the students what they knew about these activities. Very few of the students participated in this discussion.

What do you think was responsible for the students' lack of participation in this discussion? That's right! Many of the students probably had little experience with the activities named, and thus had little or no prior knowledge of them. Instead, growing up in an inner-city neighborhood, these students are probably more familiar with other recreational activities like rollerblading, stickball, and basketball. Most of the students had never been out of the city, so they would have limited firsthand knowledge of many of the leisure activities the teacher suggested. The leisure activities mentioned may be appropriate examples for students from some rural communities or from an affluent suburb, but not necessarily for students in this inner-city neighborhood school. The teacher must gear the lesson and discussion  to the background, experiences, and prior knowledge of the students, if it is to be a successful learning experience. Facilitative teachers would be aware of their students' prior knowledge and would also design their lesson based on this prior knowledge or implement activities that would develop the necessary concepts.

In this second case study, another teacher faces a situation where several students' prior knowledge and experiences are very different. Following the case study are some suggestions of what a facilitative teacher might have done.

> In a first-grade classroom in rural Pennsylvania Dutch country, students bustled with excitement because Halloween was coming. Pictures of jack-o-lanterns and ghosts floated across the bulletin boards. During story time, the teacher read a story about Boo, a friendly little ghost, and then put the children to work developing a huge class mural about Halloween.  A few students of Amish background were lost because their families do not participate in secular

celebrations such as Halloween. To them, this was all very new and strange, as would be later holiday-related activities that included Santa Claus, valentines, and the Easter Bunny. Later in the day the Amish students did not participate in a class discussion about television shows, like "It's the Great Pumpkin, Charlie Brown." Television shows have little meaning to these students because they live in homes without electricity and they do not have television sets.

The students' lack of prior knowledge could negatively affect the outcome of these activities. However, a facilitative teacher could do a number of things prior to such a lesson, to determine as well as to develop the Amish students' prior knowledge. The Amish students could have been asked beforehand what Halloween means to them in order to assess their prior knowledge. If they lacked Halloween concepts, students in the classroom could share with their Amish classmates their impressions through classroom or small-group discussions, or by engaging in role playing. The Amish students could then have been encouraged to share with the class something about one of their interesting customs.

## *Concepts and Vocabulary*

The extent to which children are familiar with concepts (abstract ideas) and related vocabulary also has a direct impact on their abilities to read with success. Roberts (1992) found that children both develop and refine their concepts of words as they reflect upon and consider relational aspects of their vocabulary. She stated that the teacher's awareness of the children's cognitive development is crucial to the development of vocabulary concepts. We agree with Roberts that teachers must provide appropriate experiences with written language to assist children in making the connection between speech and print. McKeown (1993) suggested that developing a "learner's dictionary" for young children might be an effective way for teachers to help their students learn new vocabulary. While Goodman, Smith, Meredith, and Goodman (1987) reported that if students have a limited understanding of words as they attempt to read, then when they are not reading, they further indicated that vocabulary cannot be built in isolation from language and experience.

Although attention to vocabulary builds knowledge of specific words and has a positive impact on comprehension, it is important for teachers to provide instruction that uses words in a meaningful way, such as discussion and dramatization that will result in the students gaining a deeper understanding from print (Blachowicz and Lee 1991). We believe that facilitative teachers not only assess their students' conceptual understanding but also use thoughtfully planned and relevant activities to develop their understanding. Consider this case study:

Mrs. Anderson, a second-grade teacher, begins her lesson on natural habitats: "Today, class, we're going to explore natural habitats. Does anyone know the meaning of the term, 'natural habitat'?" (No response) "Let's look at this picture of beavers building their dam. The beavers are in their natural habitat. Can anyone tell me what I might mean when I say 'natural habitat'?" Mrs. Anderson smiles.

Most of the class are eagerly waving their hands to respond. "Yes, Jackie?" "Natural habitat means home," Jackie replies. "Yes, Jackie, an animal's natural habitat is its natural home," Mrs. Anderson says, reinforcing the idea. "Now, I'd like all of you to choose your favorite animal and draw it in its natural habitat."

Mrs. Anderson circulates as her class draws a variety of animals in appropriate habitats. She comments positively to each of the children. One student, Tommy, is drawing a lion in a cage—not exactly what she had in mind. "Tommy, look at how Jackie put her deer in a forest. That's its natural home. What is the natural home of your lion?" "Oh, I get it," responds Tommy, and he proceeds to draw another lion in a jungle setting.

Once Mrs. Anderson analyzes what has transpired, she will not be surprised. Tommy's first drawing did reflect his concept of natural habitat. For Tommy, animals' homes are cages because that is what he has always seen. Tommy's concept is the result of his experience. Mrs. Anderson may decide to design some additional activities for Tommy to further develop his concept of animals' natural habitats. The use of the students' drawings was a good way to diagnose how well they understood the meaning of natural habitat. Comparing peer drawings was also a way to further develop concepts and related vocabulary.

Concepts and vocabulary also come into play during reading-writing activities. Consider the following case study:

A group of five second graders are working with the teacher on a lesson dealing with the language rule of "doubling the final consonant before adding 'ing.' " The students are taking turns reaching into a brown paper bag and pulling out a plastic Easter egg. Inside each egg is a word that the students can identify. After getting and reading the word, these students must write this word on the chalkboard and apply the doubling rule.

Matthew takes his turn and writes the word "put" on the chalkboard. The teacher asks Matthew to change the word "put" to "putting." Matthew adds the "ing" but does not double the final consonant. The teacher then tells Matthew to double the "t" before adding the "ing." Matthew takes the chalk and makes the letter "t" twice as big. It takes the teacher a minute before she realizes what Matthew has done. Matthew has misunderstood the meaning of the word "doubling" as the teacher intended it to be used.

Do you think Matthew was alone in not understanding the concept of "doubling"? How many times do students make errors because they do not know the concept that a teacher is emphasizing or they do not know the meaning of the words used in the directions? Can you remember an incident where you did not have the needed or related vocabulary to correctly follow a teacher's instruction? Knowing the concepts and related vocabulary promotes comprehension and the following of directions. Facilitative teachers not only ascertain their students' concepts and related vocabulary but also develop background in areas where they find incomplete or inadequate information.

## Reflection Activity 2.3

*O*nce more, think back to your own elementary school days. Do you recall a situation when you were confused because of your background and prior knowledge, or because you misunderstood a concept?

In your reflection journal under Reflection Activity 2.3, develop a scenario to show the importance of students' backgrounds, experiences, and prior knowledge. Use an elementary classroom setting and indicate the grade level. Use any content-subject area you would like for your illustration, but choose one that is appropriate to the grade level of the students. If you like, you can use an actual situation from your own experience as a learner or from your observation or experience with students in a classroom. You can also choose to make up a fictitious scenario to illustrate your ideas. In any case, try to include misconceptions or misunderstandings of content or concepts because of different backgrounds, a lack of cognitive experience with specific content, or inaccurate prior knowledge.

# Adapting Instruction to the Student and the Learning Environment

Facilitative teachers do everything that they can to adapt instruction and adjust learning activities to their students. Yet, this is easier said than done. Probably no teacher can completely adapt instructional procedures to all the backgrounds, needs, experiences, and interests of all students at all times, but the facilitative teacher tries to accommodate instruction for the students. How do facilitative teachers arrive at this awareness, and how do they accommodate for the students? They do this by assessing the students, assessing the learning situation, deciding on instructional goals and content based on those assessments, and developing an integrated-facilitative instructional program.

## Assessing the Students

To be a facilitative teacher and to adapt instruction to your students' individual needs (e.g., prior knowledge, experience, motivations, and interests), you must first assess your students.

The general purpose of assessment is to find out "where your students are" and "where they are coming from." Specifically, you will administer informal and formal instruments to answer these questions:

1. What do my students already know about the content or concept under consideration?
2. Do my students have some misconceptions about the content or process, and if so, what are these misconceptions?
3. Do my students have the vocabulary, reading, study, and writing background to handle this content or concept?

4. If not, what specific vocabulary, reading, study, and writing abilities or strategies might be a limitation to my students?
5. To what degree are my students interested in this content or concept? If interest is lacking, is there something that the students are interested in that can be related or used in some way with this particular content or concept?

Although you will be reading a chapter on assessment later in this text, we want to suggest, at this point, an informal approach such as having students write, diagram, or draw what they know about a given content, topic, or concept is an excellent initial assessment procedure. This is much the same approach that we pursued with you earlier, when we asked you to write or diagram what you thought reading was. Students' writings, diagrams, or drawings and related discussion can provide you with an idea of the depth of their knowledge, possible misinformation or misconceptions, completeness of information, knowledge of related vocabulary, and interest. A follow-up activity such as a preview or introductory library assignment can also provide additional information regarding your students' reading, study, and writing abilities as related to the content. You can use these writings, diagrams, drawings, discussions, and preview assignments both to assess your students and to introduce new contents or concepts to them. Also, you will have gathered valuable information to use as a basis for making decisions about instructional goals, organizing for instruction, and adapting the learning environment. Later, you could present material and ideas that the students can accommodate into their present writings, diagrams, or drawings, thus building on their prior knowledge. Once again, in much the same way as we hope to build on your knowledge of the reading process, you will be using your assessment data to facilitate learning.

## *Assessing the Learning Situation*

What is the best way to provide instruction and facilitate the learning of a content or concepts? What are the constraints of the learning environment? How much flexibility do you have? Do you have the variety of resources you need? How can you adapt for the missing resources and for the constraints of the learning environment? Instituting assessment procedures to evaluate your learning situation will help you to not only answer these questions but also to establish a classroom environment conducive to learning.

Facilitative teachers realize that the classroom environment is often not the perfect setting or only place to facilitate all that is to be learned. Each situation, content, or concept presents a new challenge. We are not suggesting that you completely reorganize your classroom for every new concept you teach or present. However, we are suggesting that you should be aware of the environment and do your best to develop instructional situations that are conducive to the needs of the students and to the needed resources and learning situations for the contents or concepts you hope to teach.

| 1. What types of transportation are most of my students somewhat familiar with (that is, students can identify or can draw a visual image of)? | | | | |
|---|---|---|---|---|
| | Yes | No | ? | Comments |
| Cars & minivans | ✓ | | | |
| Trucks | ✓ | | | |
| Taxis | ✓ | | | |
| Limousines | | | ✓ | Most students seem to have "heard" of a limousine, but only a few really seem to know what it is. |
| Buses | ✓ | | | |
| Trolley cars | | ✓ | | Nicholas, Kristen, & Jenny were the only students who indicated recognition and knew the name when they saw the picture of the trolley car. |
| Passenger trains | ✓ | | | |
| Subways/mass transit trains | | | ✓ | Students called it a "train," but most seemed to know that it was a different type of passenger train than that used on a cross-country trip. |
| Airplanes | ✓ | | | |
| Jets | ✓ | | | |
| Helicopters | ✓ | | | |
| Balloons | | | ✓ | Students recognized the hot air balloon, but they didn't seem to associate it with any means of transportation. |
| Hovercraft | | ✓ | | |
| Ocean liners | ✓ | | | |
| Freight ships | ✓ | | | |
| Sailboats | ✓ | | | |
| Fishing boats | ✓ | | | |
| Motor boats | ✓ | | | |
| Air boats | | ✓ | | |
| Canoes | ✓ | | | |
| Row boats | ✓ | | | |
| Walking | ✓ | | | |
| Rollerblades | ✓ | | | |
| Bicycles | ✓ | | | |

**Figure 2.1**
Prior knowledge, experience, and interests checklist for transportation.

## Deciding Instructional Goals and Content

When you have assessed your students and the learning situation, you are in a better position to make decisions about your instructional goals and content (what will be taught or presented). Figure 2.1 presents an example of a completed checklist that a second-grade teacher developed as she assessed her students' prior knowledge, experiences, and interests related to the study of transportation. Looking over Figure 2.1, you will see that this facilitative teacher first assessed her students' familiarity with a full spectrum of various modes of transportation (see Question 1 and the responses). The teacher's purpose was to see whether most of the students had "heard" of or had a recognition-level type of knowledge of these different means of transportation. After a brief class discussion using pictures, the teacher determined that most of the students were familiar with most of the transportation suggested, with the exception of trolley cars, hovercraft, and air boats. Additionally, although students had heard of limousines, only a few really knew what they were.

2. What types of transportation do most of my students seem to have some knowledge of (that is, students can discuss or otherwise indicate more than recognition level knowledge)?

| | Yes | No | ? | Comments |
|---|---|---|---|---|
| Cars & minivans | ✓ | | | |
| Trucks | ✓ | | | |
| Taxis | ✓ | | | |
| Limousines | | ✓ | | Brittany & Daniel thought we were talking about flooring. Chris & Matthew thought we were talking about some type of fuel. Only Nicholas & Jenny associated limousine with a chauffeur. |
| Buses | ✓ | | | |
| Trolley cars | | ✓ | | Kristen, Jenny, and Nicholas knew what a trolley car was. The other students either didn't know at all or weren't offering ideas. Daniel indicated that it was "a thing you pull behind your car." |
| Passenger trains | ✓ | | | |
| Subways/mass transit trains | | | ✓ | |
| Airplanes | ✓ | | | |
| Jets | ✓ | | | |
| Helicopters | ✓ | | | |
| Balloons | | ✓ | | |
| Hovercraft | | ✓ | | |
| Ocean liners | ✓ | | | |
| Freight ships | ✓ | | | |
| Sailboats | ✓ | | | |
| Fishing boats | ✓ | | | |
| Motor boats | ✓ | | | |
| Air boats | | ✓ | | Jessica thought an air boat was like the pirate ship in Peter Pan. |
| Canoes | ✓ | | | |
| Row boats | ✓ | | | |
| Walking | ✓ | | | |
| Rollerblades | ✓ | | | |
| Bicycles | ✓ | | | |

**Figure 2.1**
Prior knowledge, experience, and interests checklist for transportation (*continued*).

Although students recognized a hot-air balloon, they did not really associate it with any means of transportation.

Next this teacher assessed the students' knowledge of the various modes of transportation (see Question 2 and the responses). The purpose was to see whether the students could discuss or could indicate more than a recognition level of knowledge with each of these modes of transportation. Again, through large- and small-group discussion, this facilitative teacher learned that her second graders had some knowledge of most of the transportation suggested. However, there were some misconceptions or misinformation concerning several modes of transportation. Specifically, "limousines" was not an understood concept. Brittany and Daniel thought the teacher was talking about flooring, whereas Chris and Matthew thought it was a type of fuel. Only two students, Nicholas and Jenny, seemed to make some appropriate associations between limousines and chauffeurs. Again, trolley cars were not really known to most of the students, along with balloons, hovercraft, and airboats. Also, during this

| 3. What types of transportation have most of my students had some experience with (that is, students have actually seen or used this type of transportation)? | | | | |
|---|---|---|---|---|
| | Yes | No | ? | Comments |
| Cars & minivans | ✓ | | | |
| Trucks | ✓ | | | |
| Taxis | | | ✓ | Kristen, Jenny, & Nicholas are the only students who indicated riding in a taxi. |
| Limousines | | | ✓ | Nicholas & Jenny had ridden in a limousine on their way to the airport. |
| Buses | ✓ | | | |
| Trolley cars | | ✓ | | |
| Passenger trains | | | ✓ | Nicholas, Pedro, Amy, & Sophie have all traveled on a passenger train. Amy & Nicholas have traveled on trains overnight. |
| Subways/mass transit trains | | ✓ | | |
| Airplanes | | | ✓ | Kristen, Jenny, Nicholas, Pedro & Amy have all traveled by air. They were unsure whether it was on a regular airplane or a jet. |
| Jets | | | ✓ | |
| Helicopters | | ✓ | | |
| Balloons | | ✓ | | |
| Hovercraft | | ✓ | | |
| Ocean liners | | ✓ | | |
| Freight ships | | ✓ | | |
| Sailboats | | | ✓ | Nicholas, Jenny, Kristen, & Chantele all indicated that they have been out on a sailboat on the lake. |
| Fishing boats | ✓ | | | |
| Motor boats | ✓ | | | |
| Air boats | | ✓ | | |
| Canoes | ✓ | | | |
| Row boats | ✓ | | | |
| Walking | ✓ | | | |
| Rollerblades | ✓ | | | |
| Bicycles | ✓ | | | |

**Figure 2.1**

Prior knowledge, experience, and interests checklist for transportation (*continued*).

more in-depth level of assessment, the teacher learned that the concept of "mass transit" was not very clear among the students. Although they had a recognition-level knowledge of a subway, on further probing the teacher found a lack of depth and understanding.

The next area that this teacher explored was the students' actual experiences with these different types of transportation (see Question 3 and the responses). This facilitative teacher wanted to know whether any of her second graders had actually seen or used any of these types of transportation. Here is what the teacher learned: Most of the students did have actual prior experiences with cars & minivans, trucks, buses, fishing boats, motor boats, canoes, row boats, walking, rollerblades, and bicycles. They had absolutely no concrete prior experiences with trolley cars, subways/mass transit trains, helicopters, balloons, hovercraft, ocean liners, freight ships, and air boats. There were some means of transportation with which a few students had prior experiences but most of the students had no experience. These means

4. What types of transportation do most of my students seem most interested in (that is, students appear animated when discussing these or otherwise indicate interest)?

| | Yes | No | ? | Comments |
|---|---|---|---|---|
| Cars & minivans | ✓ | | | Many of the students were very excited discussing different types of cars & minivans. |
| Trucks | | ✓ | | |
| Taxis | | ✓ | | |
| Limousines | | | ✓ | Several children, particularly Nicholas, Jenny, Katie, Sonia & Carlos, were interested in limousines. |
| Buses | | ✓ | | |
| Trolley cars | ✓ | | | |
| Passenger trains | ✓ | | | |
| Subways/mass transit trains | ✓ | | | |
| Airplanes | ✓ | | | |
| Jets | ✓ | | | |
| Helicopters | ✓ | | | |
| Balloons | ✓ | | | |
| Hovercraft | ✓ | | | |
| Ocean liners | ✓ | | | |
| Freight ships | | ✓ | | |
| Sailboats | | | ✓ | Nicholas, Jenny, Kristen, Chantele & Carlos were interested in sailboats. |
| Fishing boats | | ✓ | | |
| Motor boats | | ✓ | | |
| Air boats | ✓ | | | |
| Canoes | | ✓ | | |
| Row boats | | ✓ | | |
| Walking | | ✓ | | |
| Rollerblades | ✓ | | | |
| Bicycles | ✓ | | | |

**Figure 2.1**

Prior knowledge, experience, and interests checklist for transportation (*continued*).

included taxis, limousines, passenger trains, airplanes, jets (note there was a little confusion over airplanes and jets), and sailboats.

Next the teacher was interested in finding out which modes of transportation most interested her students and judged their interest by their animation during large-group discussion and other indications of interest like continued discussions, questions, and sharing of experiences (see Question 4 and the recorded responses). The teacher discovered that the group as a whole was more interested in cars & minivans, trolley cars, passenger trains, subways/mass transit trains, airplanes, jets, helicopters, balloons, hovercraft, ocean liners, air boats, rollerblades, and bicycles than any of the other modes of transportation. However, the teacher also learned that a few students were particularly interested in limousines, and a few others in sailboats.

The teacher next looked at her available materials and other resources (for example, books, magazines, videos, catalogs, brochures, and guest speakers) to ascertain what resources were available to provide information on the various transportation modes and their related concepts and issues. As the teacher inventoried these resources, consideration was given to any special reading, writing,

5. What materials or resources do I have or can I get on transportation (that is, books, magazines, videos, catalogs, brochures & guest speakers)? And, are there any special reading, writing, and study skill considerations for use of these materials?

| | Yes | No | ? | Comments |
|---|---|---|---|---|
| Cars & minivans | ✓ | | | books, catalogs |
| Trucks | ✓ | | | books, catalogs |
| Taxis | ✓ | | | books, guest speaker |
| Limousines | ✓ | | | catalogs, books |
| Buses | ✓ | | | books, schedules (may be difficult for students to read) |
| Trolley cars | ✓ | | | encyclopedias, San Francisco brochures (the reading material may be difficult), video |
| Passenger trains | ✓ | | | books, brochures, video, schedule (difficult) |
| Subways/mass transit trains | | | ✓ | only a subway schedule |
| Airplanes | ✓ | | | video, books |
| Jets | | | ✓ | video, books |
| Helicopters | ✓ | | | books |
| Balloons | ✓ | | | books, video |
| Hovercraft | | | ✓ | only travel brochure (difficult reading) |
| Ocean liners | ✓ | | | books, brochures |
| Freight ships | ✓ | | | books |
| Sailboats | ✓ | | | books, video |
| Fishing boats | ✓ | | | books |
| Motor boats | ✓ | | | books |
| Air boats | | ✓ | | |
| Canoes | ✓ | | | books, brochures |
| Row boats | ✓ | | | books, brochures |
| Walking | ✓ | | | magazines |
| Rollerblades | ✓ | | | book, guest speaker, brochure |
| Bicycles | ✓ | | | books, brochures, guest speaker |

**Figure 2.1**

Prior knowledge, experience, and interests checklist for transportation (*continued*).

and study-skill needs or problems that might arise (see Question 5). Please note that this facilitative teacher was not driven by the availability of materials but was first interested in students' prior knowledge, experiences, and interests concerning transportation and other special considerations before selecting materials. A less facilitative teacher might have made instructional decisions based on the availability of materials, rather than first considering the students' knowledge, experiences, and interests, and ability to use the materials.

Finally, this facilitative teacher considered the possibilities for providing the students with needed experiences (see Question 6). Note, once again, the facilitative teacher is most concerned about her students' needs and desires; rather than just making decisions based on what is available or easiest, this teacher bases decisions on her students' prior knowledge, experiences, and interests.

Look over the data in each part of Figure 2.1. Can you predict which transportation modes the teacher will facilitate study of in the classroom? Can you predict which types of transportation or field trips the teacher will select to facilitate student experiences? How did you predict this? We think you already know. The facilitative teacher will not elect to teach things that the students already know (or do not need) or to teach things in which they demonstrated

| 6. What types of transportation could we try out and/or have some sort of access to for possible field trips? | | | | |
|---|---|---|---|---|
| | Yes | No | ? | Comments |
| Cars & minivans | ✓ | | | |
| Trucks | | | ✓ | |
| Taxis | ✓ | | | |
| Limousines | | | ✓ | |
| Buses | ✓ | | | |
| Trolley cars | | ✓ | | |
| Passenger trains | ✓ | | | |
| Subways/mass transit trains | | | ✓ | |
| Airplanes | ✓ | | | |
| Jets | ✓ | | | |
| Helicopters | | | ✓ | |
| Balloons | | ✓ | | |
| Hovercraft | | ✓ | | |
| Ocean liners | | ✓ | | |
| Freight ships | | ✓ | | |
| Sailboats | ✓ | | | |
| Fishing boats | ✓ | | | |
| Motor boats | ✓ | | | |
| Air boats | | | ✓ | |
| Canoes | ✓ | | | |
| Row boats | ✓ | | | |
| Walking | ✓ | | | |
| Rollerblades | ✓ | | | |
| Bicycles | ✓ | | | |

**Figure 2.1**
Prior knowledge, experience, and interests checklist for transportation (*continued*).

limited interest. This teacher will try to facilitate learning in areas and concepts in which the students exhibit the greatest interest. Also, this teacher will try to find materials and guest speakers to use for each of the areas selected, and, if at all possible, she will provide meaningful field trips to enrich or develop students' experiences.

We even think you might be able to figure out what individual or small-group research and study areas the teacher might suggest within the transportation study unit. Perhaps a few interested students could study one means of transportation and report their research to the rest of the class.

## Developing an Integrated-Facilitative Program

Using students' prior knowledge, experiences, and interests as illustrated in Figure 2.1, to develop instructional decisions regarding goals and content, is representative of an integrated-facilitative type of program. In this type of program, reading, content area study, writing, and strategies development are integrated as opposed to being taught in isolation. For example, students researching a particular mode of transportation are developing their study skills and strategies to locate specific material, their reading skills and strategies to read and summarize the information, their reporting skills and strategies to deliver the information to the other students and the teacher, and their content skills and strategies to relate the information to the study of transportation. In an integrated program, you need not announce, "It is time for writing. Write your sentences on transportation." In an integrated program, your students simultaneously and continuously use their reading, writing, studying, researching, reporting, and content skills and strategies. They are using them in a natural and meaningful way. This happens because they are interested, and because you have planned appropriate and meaningful activities to meet your individual students' needs and interests within the framework of the material you must teach during the school year.

## *Considering Facilitative Reading Instruction*

As you prepare yourself for your role as a teacher, we encourage you to organize your classroom program from a facilitative as well as integrated perspective. The teacher case-study examples you have read were selected because they allowed us to focus your attention on facilitative and integrated teacher behaviors. The facilitative teacher with an integrated program emphasis is not an either/or type of teaching perspective. Instead, this perspective permits you to be structured, logical, and humanistic and to design and balance reading, writing, and learning activities based on the needs and attributes of your students and the characteristics of the learning situation and environment. Facilitative teachers who integrate learning do so without isolating instruction. These teachers tend to view reading and other language and communication areas and content area learning as a whole, and as their overall instructional responsibility; they plan and balance instruction to meet students' needs and the curriculum goals.

Reading is a process that is not a subject in itself. It is a tool to be used to learn, to enjoy, and to pursue a variety of topics, concepts, ideas, and interests. This, in essence, means that in the integrated-facilitative classroom, students will use reading in a natural way (e.g., learning to read, as they read, and learning to apply reading strategies in situations where they must apply them). It also means that students will share their reading interests and ideas developed from reading with others through discussions and writings. Students will not see reading as a separate subject, or writing and speaking as isolated and separate activities. Instead they will be allowed to read to pursue their assignments and interests, write to record their ideas, and research and speak to share and respond. But the facilitative teacher with an integrated program will intervene and teach specific skills and strategies where and when individual students need them, using a balance of relevant methods and materials that fit the situation and students' needs. This teacher will not have to wait for "reading group" time or for the language-arts block to intervene or to provide needed instruction. The facilitative teacher is an integrator of learning and a professional-education decision maker. Learning is the real goal, not student control; and student independence, not dependence, is the desired outcome.

# Guidelines for Facilitative Reading Instruction

We present the following guidelines to further express our ideas concerning aspects of an integrated-facilitative program. They do not represent absolute instructional practices because there are no absolutes in teaching. Instead, these guidelines provide parameters within which you could contemplate, conduct, and evaluate your own reading program. They are indicative of student-centered learning and can be used by teachers throughout the various grade levels. These guidelines further represent a synthesis of our interpretation of the most effective and facilitative attitudes and values teachers can hold for teaching reading in today's elementary schools and embodies our concept of facilitative instruction.

1. *Reading is a language-based process.* Perhaps the most essential concept that we hope students will come to understand in their early years of development is that there is a relationship between spoken language, thoughts, and print. This language and print awareness is important to the development of successful readers. The more opportunities children have to develop this awareness through various experiences in their formative years, the better. Additionally, the larger and more diverse a student's language experience, vocabulary, and language skills, the more likely it is that the student will become a successful reader. Children come to school with a fairly large speaking and listening vocabulary. This vocabulary and the concepts it represents are a product of the children's cultures, experiences, and other early learnings. The importance of students' language experiences and language processes for their future reading success are discussed throughout this text.

2. *Reading is a complex process with many variables that can affect it.* The reading process as described earlier involves the integration of a number of complex components that are important to the successful understanding of text. Each component interacts with others for successful reading to occur. Facilitative teachers are aware of these components and their relationship to effective classroom instruction. These components include sensory, perceptual, sequential, experiential, linguistic, cognitive, learning, association, affective, constructive, and cultural elements.

3. *Reading instruction should meet the needs of each student.* The elementary classroom is a microcosm of society. Within all classrooms, students manifest varying abilities, skills, strategies, interests, and motivations. Facilitative teachers identify the needs and interests of their individual students and provide the appropriate instructional and learning opportunities for them. These various needs will require knowledgeable instruction based on a sound philosophy of reading. Also, the students within such a diverse classroom will require the use of differentiated approaches to learning, individualized assignments and activities, and time for their own personal reading pursuits.

It is important to note that there is not one correct way to teach reading. Each student has strengths and needs that will determine the type of instruction you should provide. You will find one reading approach effective with one student but ineffective with another. Instruction should be matched to the needs and interests of your students, rather than forcing students into an inappropriate match with certain materials, or a particular reading approach.

4. *Teachers should continually assess their students' reading skills and strategies and use this information as a basis for instruction, and students and their families should be given opportunities to assess students' growth and development as part of this process.* The assessment of your students' reading skills and strategies is essential to daily as well as long-range planning. Although formal assessment may not take place every day, there are many types of informal assessment you can use (e.g., observation, evaluation of students' work, listening to students read, students' self-assessments, or just interacting with your students in instructional and noninstructional settings), within the context of actual classroom work, to collect student reading data. Assessment is crucial because it provides opportunities for determining students' individual strengths and needs. This information then provides the foundation for designing, implementing, and monitoring an effective instructional program in your classroom. Also, if assessment is to be used successfully in your program, it must be continuous and must allow students opportunities to participate through their own reflections and self-evaluations. This entails using various assessment techniques throughout the school year as an integral part of your instructional program, because continuous assessment enables you to maintain a current evaluation of each student's development and continued needs.

Assessment can be done as part of and during classroom instruction. Varied assessment techniques should be used to gain the maximum information possible concerning your students' skills, strategies, and their ideas concerning their own development. Additionally, parents and family members can and should be involved in various aspects of this assessment.

5. *Reading is part of written language and is also closely related to all the other language processes—both oral and written.* There is a close relationship between reading, listening, oral language, and writing. It is clear that reading is a language-based process, but how important are listening and writing to becoming a successful reader?

Listening is a receptive language function and essential to the reading process because of the importance of the association of sounds, comprehension, and word forms with print. Children develop an early awareness of the relationship between sounds and print. They also develop an awareness that the word forms they interact with in print have sounds, and that these word forms have meanings. Many children first learn to associate language with print through listening to stories read to them at home.

Writing, like oral language, is an expressive language process. It is a process that enables students to associate what they hear, speak, and see with print. Writing is crucial to the reading process because it enables students to make the connection between what the writer does and what the reader does. When students write down what they read, they reinforce the concept of print and language. Thus, writing becomes reading, and reading becomes writing.

6. *Integrating reading into content area learning is important for effective and facilitative instruction.* One area facilitative teachers do not neglect when designing an effective classroom program is that of integrating reading into the content areas. Reading instruction is not an end in itself. Students learn to read as a tool for reading content-area materials as well as for research, personal enrichment, and recreation. Reading is the tool that gives students access to vast amounts of information about such content areas as mathematics, science, social studies, and literature. For students to acquire information and concepts found in content materials, they need to use and read these materials. One way of enhancing content reading is to encourage students to practice and use their reading and study strategies with a variety of content materials in meaningful ways. In doing this, the application value of reading is reinforced.

   In some elementary classrooms, students are not given opportunities to learn to use reading strategies in subject areas. When this content-reading encouragement and instruction are missing, students do not see the relationship between reading and learning, and often miss the important content information in their various subject-matter texts.

7. *Personal reading is a crucial element of the total classroom program.* One of the primary reasons for learning to read is for pursuing and researching areas of personal interests and needs and for personal enjoyment. However, instead in many elementary schools, because of outside pressures and demands, a great deal of time and energy is spent on the repetitious teaching of skills without regard to their application or to their use for these very real pursuits. Because school districts want to be able to measure the progress of their students, they have put considerable emphasis on implementing instruction that is measurable. Since skills progress can be assessed to some extent, many school districts have placed much emphasis on reading instruction that emphasizes skill development. Certainly, some skill instruction is needed in our schools, but it is important to remember that the eventual goal of reading instruction is the production of successful readers. This means that your students should be able to apply reading skills and strategies to real-life situations, needs, and materials. In other words, they should be able to pick up and successfully read informational and recreational materials such as newspapers, magazines, library books, or any other types of material of importance or interest to them. Time should be set aside every day for your students to read books and other materials for personal purposes and enjoyment. Personal reading provides

opportunities to apply many of the reading and study strategies that are important to developing successful readers.

8. *Reading should be a positive experience for students.* Reading is enjoyable because it opens up new horizons. For students to develop a positive attitude about reading, they must experience some success with the printed page. You can help develop this positive feeling about reading by implementing a program that encourages students to read. Emphasis should be placed on reading for a purpose and using reading to enhance all other learning. Skills should be taught from an application perspective that encourages their use in research and personal reading pursuits. The classroom atmosphere and teachers' attitudes about reading will affect the students' perceptions. Facilitative teachers can enhance learning to read and their students' desire to read. Learning to read is more successful in classrooms where the teachers provide all students with positive experiences and feelings of success.

9. *Learning to read is a continuous and developmental process and starts with a child's earliest experiences.* Students develop their reading skills and strategies throughout their early childhood and their school-age years. As students begin their educational experiences, facilitative teachers build on their existing strengths and strategies that they have already developed at home through their exposure to language and cognitive learnings. Layers of learning occur with additional information building on the children's earlier foundations. Although students will learn different skills and strategies at different times of their development, all your students will continue to develop their reading strategies throughout elementary school and high school, and on through life, further refining and developing their existing strategies.

10. *Students with special needs must be provided for within the regular classroom program.* As a result of Public Law 94-142, the Education for All Handicapped Children Act, and the Individuals with Disabilities Education Act (IDEA) many exceptional students are being taught in the regular classroom. These students may have specific learning, behavioral, and physical situations that require their teachers' patience and attention. One of the primary difficulties that classroom teachers encounter when working with these students is the wide range of reading needs and abilities they exhibit, which requires considerable organizational-management ability on the teachers' part, as well as knowledge of these students' particular challenges or strengths. Providing instruction for these students in the regular classroom requires careful planning and the development of an individualized program for each student.

   Additionally, classroom teachers will also work with learners who are gifted, talented, and diverse (e.g., those who speak English as their second language). These students also need individualized instructional planning that emphasizes reading strategies appropriate to their needs, strategies, interests, motivations, and cultures. However, in general, we believe that if you recognize that all students have some special needs, you will be more prepared to handle the variety of skills, strategies, talents, needs, motivations, cultures, and interests of all the students you teach.

11. *The ultimate goal of reading is comprehension, and students should be encouraged to reflect on their understandings of text.* Sometimes teachers and students become entangled with the practice of sounding out letters and words in isolation. This practice overemphasizes the sounds of words and neglects the primary reason for reading—comprehension. It is important not to become so involved with the mechanics of reading that understanding and reflecting on the printed page becomes secondary. This is critical even in the earliest grades, because reading is a continuous developmental process and children should be encouraged, right from the beginning, to read for meaning and to discuss and reflect on their readings. As they become more proficient readers, the idea of reading for meaning will continue to be the goal.

12. *Facilitative teachers understand effective reading instruction.* The classroom environment is student-centered, emphasizing principles of student growth and development. In this type of environment, the teacher is well organized and uses effective management strategies. Students receive instruction appropriate to their particular reading needs, strategies, motivations, interests, and culture; this instruction is designed to maximize their learning potential. Facilitative teachers are knowledgeable of the different approaches to teaching reading and know how best to implement these approaches for their students to receive the greatest benefit from the learning opportunities provided. These teachers design and implement programs that feature an integrated perspective of reading. The emphasis is on gaining meaning from print with support from the various skill areas resulting in the students' ability to apply their knowledge of reading to the content areas, as well as to their personal reading pursuits. The ultimate goal of facilitative teachers is to produce successful independent readers.

13. *Facilitative teachers are professional.* Facilitative teachers recognize the importance of continued learning and growth not only for their students but also for themselves. Because of this, facilitative teachers read the professional literature, engage in professional in-services and take college classes, attend professional meetings and conferences, and take part in professional research opportunities in their classrooms. This desire for professional growth separates facilitative teachers from their counterparts who often see their diplomas and teaching certificates as an end, rather than as the beginning, of a rewarding professional career.

Many opportunities are available to the professionally oriented teacher within school districts, college communities, and professional associations. One such professional opportunity for classroom teachers is membership and participation in the International Reading Association (IRA) as well as other national, state, and local professional associations. The IRA is the largest professional association in the world for classroom teachers involved with reading instruction and publishes several professional journals and a newsletter. *The Reading Teacher* is the journal that is particularly useful for elementary teachers and *Reading Today,* the IRA's bimonthly newsletter, has information that would greatly help you work with parents, families, communities, administrators, other professionals, and your students. The IRA also conducts international, state, and local conferences and disseminates a wide variety of other publications that are particularly helpful to both teachers and parents/families. We encourage you to join IRA and also to consider membership in other professional organizations.

# Effective-Teaching Research

A great deal of the teacher-education research has been focusing on issues related to "effective teaching" or "effective schooling." Effective-teaching research refers to attempts to characterize or evaluate those attributes that make a teacher effective in the classroom. This research movement developed because it became more apparent to educational researchers that the teacher is by far the most important variable of the schooling and learning experience. In the past, it was thought that the other aspects of the educational process such as students' materials, the physical plant, the curriculum, school facilities, and school discipline played an equal if not greater importance in teaching and learning. However, the more recent research and practice have continued to indicate that although most aspects can be shown to make a difference, the most important of all, by far, and the one that contributes the most to the students' achievement, is "the teacher" (Rupley, Wise, and Logan 1986). Therefore, new interest has once again been focused on the teacher, on what the teacher is doing in the classroom, on attributes of effective teachers, and, more currently, on interaction in the classroom, teachers' judgments, teachers' decision making, and teachers' beliefs.

What follows is a brief review of different research efforts related to the quest for effective teaching and teachers. These efforts have included the use of rating scales and process-product studies, and teachers' judgments, beliefs, and decision-making studies.

## Rating Scales and Process-Product Studies

Initial inquiries into teacher effectiveness began about 1900, peaked in the late 1920s and early 1930s, and then remained an area of interest until the 1950s (Ellena, Stevenson, and Webb 1961). This first era of teacher-effectiveness research was described by Cruickshank (1986) as a search for teacher traits that described and permitted identification of someone as a "good" teacher. Most of these studies involved the use of rating scales and raters and the use of student-achievement gains as criteria. Rupley, Wise, and Logan (1986) have noted that these ratings were usually done by supervisors who attempted to evaluate such areas as discipline, promptness, personality, and techniques of instruction. Additionally, they indicated that these ratings tended to be subjective judgments with low reliability and validity. The result of these early or first-era studies was that little was learned about teacher effectiveness or how to select, train, encourage, or evaluate that effectiveness (Biddle and Ellena 1964).

Cruickshank (1986) identified the second era of teacher-effectiveness research as beginning about the 1960s and continuing today. Cruickshank (1986) and Rupley, Wise, and Logan (1986) characterized this period as one that utilized more objective classroom-observation instruments, like the ones developed by Flanders (1960) and Medley and Mitzel (1958), and that later used "process-product" studies, which attempted to identify relationships between teacher behaviors and student gains or changes in learning outcomes (see Duncan and Biddle 1974, Hoffman 1986, and Rosenshine and Furst 1967). However, Rupley, Wise, and Logan saw this use of process-product studies as the beginning of a new period of teacher-effectiveness research, one that signaled a major advance in the study of teaching.

Although this second period of teacher-effectiveness research is still in progress, Silcock (1993) has stated that all of this research may do no more than indicate that effective teachers provide maximum opportunities to learn. We believe that the most basic goal of every teacher should be to provide a classroom environment that is conducive to learning for each student. Heilman, Blair, and Rupley (1994) suggested that effective teachers of literacy help students focus on learning to read by (1) providing more time for reading instruction; (2) keeping students actively engaged during instruction; (3) providing appropriate feedback related to instruction; (4) setting specific purposes for reading; (5) presenting an overview of what is to be learned before the lesson is taught; (6) using illustrations and examples to relate new learning to previous learning to activate their schemata and to help them learn how to apply this information; and (7) monitoring students' participation to increase the probability of success.

It is essential that teachers project an attitude of high expectations for each child. Good and Brophy (1987) found that students for whom teachers expect little will frequently receive less instruction, be given less work to do, receive little or no praise, receive less attention, be given more literal-level questions and less time to respond, be seated farther away from the teacher with less eye contact, be smiled at less often, and receive less assistance and more negative reinforcement during class discussion.

Clark (1995) reviewed and summarized the characteristics of effective instruction that he found most pertinent to literacy and reading fluency. These are as follows: (1) effective instruction involves high but achievable expectations, (2) effective instruction is direct and explicit, and (3) the tasks that the students engage in to learn and to practice should be meaningful and functional for them (pp. 250–251). Clark's review is consistent with the summary of findings for effective teaching provided by Rosenshine and Stevens (1986) and also more recently discussed by Parkay and Stanford (1995).

We believe that the facilitative teacher is in the best position to become an effective teacher. As effective-facilitative teachers, we must provide a classroom environment that encourages the participation of each student, using a variety of activities, materials, and strategies, and that ensures each student receives positive and supportive praise.

## Teachers' Judgments, Beliefs, and Decision-Making Studies

Most recently, the research in teaching has focused on teachers' judgments, beliefs, and their decision making. As Rupley, Wise, and Logan (1986) stated:

> With the increased interest in cognitive psychology and cognitive information processing, many teacher effectiveness researchers are looking beyond direct instruction, management, and psychological conditions to determine goals, intentions, judgments, decision, and information processing. Teacher effectiveness researchers have begun to examine the nature of teacher rationales. (pp. 32–33)

Unfortunately, and as Duffy and Ball (1986) pointed out, the process-product studies that had dominated the teacher-effectiveness research suffered from a serious limitation because they had investigated only observable behaviors and had ignored the less visible cognitive processes that teachers engaged in when teaching. In other words, teachers' thinking, and the possibility that teacher thinking could be an important part of teacher effectiveness, had not been considered. Duffy (1982a) stated that teachers' behaviors are guided by what they think. Additionally, other researchers (Duffy and Ball 1986, Harste and Burke 1977, Kamil and Pearson 1979) have stated that teachers' decision making is influenced by their theoretical or philosophical orientations.

Research exploring teachers' judgments and decision making as influenced by their theoretical orientations and beliefs is the newest area of teacher-effectiveness research. Research and observation have indicated that most teachers are strongly influenced by the way they were taught (Clark and Newby 1984; Shulman 1986). Additionally, the research published to date has suggested that teachers do hold beliefs about reading and these beliefs do seem to have some influence on their decisions and choices of instruction (Borko and Niles 1982, Deford 1985, Harste and Burke 1977, Kinzer and Carrick 1986). Preservice teachers often have idealistic attitudes, stating they would not teach the way they were taught (Moore 1986). However, beliefs and attitudes can be overridden by the influences of the school situation in which teachers find themselves (Borko and Cadwell 1982, Duffy 1982b). Other research (Bean 1980) has indicated that teachers' beliefs and views about reading can be changed by the study of the more-updated teaching and learning theories. Finally, Lehman, Freeman, and Allen (1994) have indicated that their research suggests that teachers' perceptions do influence teachers' practices and that more self-awareness about beliefs will benefit those teachers' practices. They have further suggested that teachers need time to sort out their beliefs and to reflect on the practices they use (p. 20). We hope that this text and the reflection activities we ask you to engage in, as well as your other professional readings, reflections, encounters, and observations, will make a positive impact on your beliefs, philosophy, and practices.

As we have seen, teachers need opportunities to reflect on their experiences, beliefs, and teaching practices. They also need time to read and discuss various theories, philosophies, and their own evolving perspectives. Effective teachers need to have the time to think and plan about what they wish to accomplish, why they wish to accomplish it, and how they should proceed to facilitate students' understanding, independence, and interests.

## A Recapitulation

As previously indicated, your developing perspective, theory, and definition of reading are most important because of their influence on your classroom practices and on all the students you will eventually teach during your educational career. You are responsible for setting the goals and the climate for reading, and those goals and climate affect everything that transpires in your classroom. A description of the facilitative teacher as a model for your use has been presented. We hope that you will assimilate and accommodate some of these facilitative qualities into your own developing reading perspective.

### Reflection Activity 2.4

*T*ake a few minutes to review your Chapter 1 reflection journal notes, diagram, and thoughts. After doing so, in your reflection journal under the heading Reflection Activity 2.4, "Facilitative Teacher Attributes," note any other attributes, characteristics, or ideas that you see in your diagram and definition that are indicative of the facilitative teacher concept presented. How facilitative are you right now?

Finally, it is most important that as a developing facilitative teacher you have

1. knowledge of your own beliefs about reading,
2. knowledge of the nature of reading,
3. knowledge of the foundations of teaching and enhancing reading, and
4. knowledge of classroom management and a plan for implementing it.

The remaining chapters of this text will help you to continue to develop knowledge and competence in each of these four very important areas.

## Summary

This chapter has defined what a facilitative teacher is and provided some examples of facilitative and nonfacilitative teachers. It illustrated and discussed the importance of individualizing instruction based on students' needs, strategies, interests, motivations, cultures, and backgrounds. Some guidelines for the elementary classroom teacher were described to provide more structure to the facilitative concept and to promote continued professional development. Additionally, effective-teaching research was presented and discussed.

As we have learned from the extensive studies and reviews of teacher effectiveness, the easiest characteristics to measure are not necessarily the most important ones. The more intangible beliefs, values, and philosophies you are developing will greatly influence your effectiveness. The facilitative teacher is much more than a technician who only follows a teachers' guide and other dictated procedures. Facilitative teachers know how to select, analyze, and evaluate instruction and materials that fit their students and classroom situation.

Facilitative teachers understand the importance of expediting their students' learning and the importance of integrating learning whenever possible. Facilitative teachers assess their students' strengths and needs in all learning situations and give attention to their students' varied, unique, and diverse strategies, motivations, cultures, and interests as they make judgments and decisions regarding their teaching and as they organize and manage learning in their classrooms. The facilitative teacher selects and uses the most appropriate ideas that fit his or her own beliefs and philosophy from each of the three perspectives described earlier: (a) the bottom-up or skills-based perspective, with attention given to assessing students' strengths and needs in every aspect of a learning situation; (b) the whole language meaning-based perspective, with attention given to students' linguistic and other prior experiences, and their effect on overall understanding; and (c) the interactive perspective, with attention given to students' cognitive experiences and the use of strategies and all available sources to gain understanding. The teacher then utilizes methods, materials, and procedures to develop her or his own balanced, facilitative perspective from what she or he considers to be most appropriate for individual students' learning.

There are no absolutes we can offer you. There are no absolutes when you are dealing with human beings. Your goal should be to develop into a professional with confidence in your own abilities, and with an attitude that directs you to be critical of your own work and therefore allows you to make changes when appropriate. Finally, we have embodied our facilitative teacher as a professional, effective, multidimensional person who has the knowledge and sensitivity to encourage, teach, and nurture students into independent readers, learners, and thinkers. In the chapters that follow, you will be provided the necessary guidelines for becoming the type of facilitative teacher we have portrayed in this chapter.

## Closing Activities

1.  In a small group in class, share and discuss your Reflection Activity 2.1, the facilitative teacher you described.
2.  In a small group in class, share and discuss your Reflection Activity 2.2, the nonfacilitative teacher you described.
3.  In a small group in class, share and discuss your Reflection Activity 2.3, the importance of prior knowledge, concepts, and so on.
4.  In a small group, share, discuss, and justify the facilitative attributes you listed in your reflection journal under Reflection Activity 2.4, "Facilitative Teacher Attributes." Also, share with the group your perceptions of the facilitative teacher attributes you presently have and those that you hope to develop.
5.  Using your own notes and diagram for your definition of reading, consider your present feelings about teaching and learning and respond to the following questions or recommendations: (a) What is your emerging philosophy or thinking? (b) What evidence is available in the professional literature (for example, *The Reading Teacher, Reading Horizons, Reading Psychology, Reading Research and Instruction,* and *The Elementary Teacher*) to support your emerging philosophy or theory? (c) In a small group in class, share your emerging philosophies and the evidence you found in the professional literature to support your current position.
6.  Observe an elementary classroom when the teacher is presenting a content-related lesson, topic, or concept (for example, a science or history lesson). Then (a) describe the content, topic, or concepts that were taught; (b) develop a list of the vocabulary, ideas, and/or concepts the students were expected to know; (c) list the learning tools (for example, reading, writing, study skills, and so on) the students

needed to handle the lesson; (d) describe how, if you were the teacher, you would have assessed whether your individual students could handle the necessary learning tools you listed in (c); and (e) describe what activities you would have used with those students you identified in (c) as not having the necessary learning tools.

7. In a small group, share and discuss teaching situations that you have observed in your field or classroom experiences that represent both facilitative and nonfacilitative teaching environments. What would you change about either environment and how would you implement that change?

8. Using this chapter and your own personal knowledge, develop a checklist that can be used during observations to evaluate the extent to which facilitative teaching is occurring in a classroom.

## References

Bean, T. W. (1980). "Can We Update Experienced Teachers' Beliefs and Practices in Reading?" *Reading Horizons* 20:183–187.

Biddle, B., and W. Ellena. (1964). *Contemporary Research on Teacher Effectiveness.* New York: Holt, Rinehart & Winston.

Blachowicz, C. L. Z., and J. J. Lee. (1991). "Vocabulary Development in the Whole Literacy Classroom." *The Reading Teacher* 45(3):188–195.

Borich, G. D. (1993). *Clearly Outstanding: Making Each Day Count in Your Classroom.* Needham Heights, MA: Allyn & Bacon.

Borko, H., and J. Cadwell. (1982). "Individual Differences in Teachers' Decision Strategies: An Investigation of Classroom Organization and Management Decisions." *Journal of Educational Psychology* 7:598–610.

Borko, H., and J. Niles. (1982). "Factors Contributing to Teachers' Judgments about Students and Decisions about Grouping Students for Reading Instruction." *Journal of Reading Behavior* 14:127–136.

Clark, C. H. (1995). "Teaching Students about Reading: A Fluency Example." *Reading Horizons* 35(3):250–266.

Clark, D. C., and T. J. Newby. (1984, April 23–27). *Origins of Teaching Behaviors of First Year and Student Teachers.* Paper presented at the annual meeting of the American Educational Research Association, New Orleans, Louisiana.

Cruickshank, D. R. (1986, Winter). "Profile of an Effective Teacher." *Educational Horizons,* 80–86.

Deford, D. (1985). "Validating the Construct of Theoretical Orientation in Reading Instruction." *Reading Research Quarterly* 20(3):351–367.

Duffy, G. (1982a). "Fighting Off the Alligators: What Research in Real Classrooms Has to Say about Reading Instruction." *Journal of Reading Behavior* 14:357–372.

————. (1982b). "Response to Borko, Shavelson, & Stern: There's More to Instructional Decision-Making in Reading Than the 'Empty Classroom.' " *Reading Research Quarterly* 17:295–300.

Duffy, G. G., and D. L. Ball. (1986). "Instructional Decision Making and Reading Teacher Effectiveness." In J. V. Hoffman, ed., *Effective Teaching of Reading: Research and Practice* (pp. 163–180). Newark, DE: International Reading Association.

Duncan, M., and B. Biddle. (1974). *The Study of Teaching.* New York: Holt, Rinehart & Winston.

Ellena, W., M. Stevenson, and H. Webb. (1961). *Who's a Good Teacher.* Washington, DC: American Association of School Administrators, Department of Classroom Teachers of the National Education Association, and National School Boards Association.

Flanders, N. (1960). *Interaction Analysis in the Classroom: A Manual for Observers.* Ann Arbor, MI: University of Michigan.

Fullan, M. G. (1993). "Why Teachers Must Become Change Agents." *Educational Leadership* 50(6):12–17.

Good, T. L., and J. E. Brophy. (1987). *Looking in Classrooms,* 4th ed. New York: Harper & Row.

Goodman, K. S., E. B. Smith, R. Meredith, and Y. M. Goodman. (1987). *Language and Thinking in School: A Whole-Language Curriculum,* 3rd ed. New York: Richard C. Owen Publishers.

Harste, J. C., and C. Burke. (1977). "A New Hypothesis for Reading Teacher Research: Both the Teaching and Learning of Reading Are Theoretically Based." In P. D. Pearson, ed., *Reading: Theory and Practice: Twenty-Sixth Yearbook of the National Reading Conference.* Clemson, SC: National Reading Conference.

Heilman, A. W., T. R. Blair, and W. H. Rupley. (1994). *Principles and Practices of Teaching Reading,* 8th ed. New York: Macmillan.

Hoffman, J. V. (1986). "Process-Product Research on Effective Teaching: A Primer for a Paradigm." In J. V. Hoffman, ed., *Effective Teaching of Reading: Research and Practice* (pp. 39–51). Newark, DE: International Reading Association.

Kamil, M., and P. D. Pearson. (1979, Winter). "Theory and Practice in Teaching Reading." *New York University Education Quarterly:* 10–16.

Kinzer, C. K., and D. A. Carrick. (1986). "Teachers Beliefs as Instructional Influences." In J. A. Niles and R. V. Lalik, eds., *Solving Problems in Literacy: Learners, Teachers, and Researchers* (pp. 127–134). Rochester, NY: National Reading Conference.

Lehman, B. A., E. B. Freeman, and V. G. Allen. (1994). "Children's Literature and Literacy Instruction: 'Literature-based' Elementary Teachers' Beliefs and Practices." *Reading Horizons* 35(1):3–29.

McKeown, M. G. (1993). "Creating Effective Definitions for Young Word Learners." *Reading Research Quarterly* 28(1):18–31.

Medley, D. M., and H. E. Mitzel. (1958). "A Technique for Measuring Classroom Behavior." *Journal of Educational Psychology* 49:86–93.

Moore, S. A. (1986). "A Comparison of Reading Education Students' Instructional Beliefs and Instructional Practices." In J. A. Niles and R. V. Lalik, eds., *Solving Problems in Literacy: Learners, Teachers, and Researchers* (pp. 143–146). Rochester, NY: National Reading Conference.

Parkay, F. W., and B. H. Stanford. (1995). *Becoming a Teacher,* 3rd ed. Boston: Allyn & Bacon.

Roberts, B. (1992). "The Evolution of the Young Child's Concept of Word as a Unit of Spoken and Written Language." *Reading Research Quarterly* 27(2):124–138.

Rosenshine, B., and N. Furst. (1967). "Research on Teacher Performance Criteria." In B. O. Smith, ed., *Research in Teacher Education.* Englewood Cliffs, NJ: Prentice-Hall.

Rosenshine, B., and R. Stevens. (1986). "Teaching Functions." In M. C. Wittrock, ed., *Handbook of Research on Teaching* (pp. 376–391). New York: Macmillan.

Rupley, W. H., B. S. Wise, and J. W. Logan. (1986). "Research in Effective Teaching: An Overview of Its Development." In J. V. Hoffman, ed., *Effective Teaching of Reading: Research and Practice* (pp. 3–36). Newark, DE: International Reading Association.

Shulman, L. S. (1986). "Paradigms and Research Programs in the Study of Teaching: A Contemporary Perspective." In M. C. Wittrock, ed., *Handbook of Research on Teaching* (pp. 3–36), 3rd ed. New York: Macmillan.

Silcock, P. (1993). "Can We Teach Effective Teaching?" *Educational Review* 45(1):13–19.

Zehm, S. J., and J. A. Kottler. (1993). *On Being a Teacher: The Human Dimension.* Newburg Park, CA: Corwin Press.

# *R*eading and the *Y*oung Child

© Robert Finken/Photo Researchers, Inc.

# Overview

*T*his chapter explores the development or emergence of the literacy of young children. This discussion of emergent literacy development shows the importance of children's very earliest experiences with language and print, both oral and written. Included in this discussion are such topics as print awareness; stories and story structure; affective development; linguistic development; cognitive development; and the importance of social, parental/family, community, and teacher interactions and involvement. From these discussions and examples we will see how three youngsters, Rosario (age 2½ years), Josh (age 4 years), and Tiffany (age 5 years), have developed some of their literacy learnings. These learnings shape their understandings about themselves and their cultures as related to the use of literacy skills. These learnings also provide a foundation for emerging reasoning, thinking and problem-solving abilities; concepts and vocabulary; and schemata.

This chapter also provides and summarizes many implications for teachers based on the reviewed emergent literacy research. Practical teaching and classroom strategy ideas are delineated, and additional resources for teachers of young children are given. These teaching ideas and literature resources should help teachers of young children provide the environment and instructional support that are developmentally appropriate for the children in their classrooms. We believe that this foundation will facilitate the kind of teaching and learning that emergent literacy research has shown to be "natural" for children from most sociocultural backgrounds.

## Main Ideas

- Young children's earliest experiences with language play an important part in the development of their reading and writing strategies and skills.
- Print awareness, oral and written language development, story structure awareness, and learning to appreciate and see the usefulness of writing and reading are all part of children's emerging literacy.
- Emergent literacy research and the earlier constructivist research have shown how important children's sociocultural environments are to their literacy development and motivation to read and write.
- Social and cognitive development and learnings provide the insights children have to their cultures and values and facilitate the development of reasoning abilities, concepts and vocabulary, and schemata.
- Early reading, other literacy development, and continuing reading/literacy development can be facilitated in school through the continued

involvement of parents/families, and the opportunities teachers develop for children and older students to nurture their own natural learning.

- Many teaching and classroom strategies "fit" the emergent literacy view of learning and are recommended for the continued development of young children.

An understanding of children's language development, both oral and written, is extremely important for all teachers, no matter what grade levels they teach. This is because literacy development, which includes the foundations for reading and writing, begins at birth, as soon as babies can see, hear, and cry out. As they communicate they begin to develop awareness of, appreciation for, and skill with oral and, later, written language. Obviously, teachers of young children need this understanding of literacy development, but it is just as important that teachers of older students understand the foundations of literacy. If they do, they will choose teaching strategies, environments, and materials that will continue to foster learning, and will provide supportive classroom atmospheres that facilitate development of readers, writers, thinkers, and independent learners.

## *Importance of Early Experiences*

Young children's early experiences with language and their development of various literacy-related concepts and skills have been widely studied and acknowledged in the reading research and literature from various prospectives, cultures, and parts of the world (e.g., Adams 1990; Chall 1967; Clay 1991; Durkin 1966; Ferreiro 1986; Flesch 1981; Goodman 1990; Harste, Woodward, and Burke 1984; Heath 1983; Holdaway 1979; Piaget 1955; Teale and Sulzby 1986, 1989; and Vygotsky 1978). This research has led to theories about how young children develop as readers and writers. Those theories can be broadly grouped into two models of learning: the transmission model and the transactional model.

The transmission model, which views children as empty vessels into which knowledge must be poured, comes from behavioral psychology ideas. On the other hand, the transactional model views children as already having a rich prior knowledge and background and comes from the cognitive psychology and psycholinguist learnings about acquisition of language (Weaver 1994). Today, some call this transactional model a constructivist view of learning (translations and republications of Vygotsky's early work, e.g., 1978, are usually credited for this view). This view leads to schooling that values what the individual child already knows about language and attempts to create learning environments that allow the child to continue to develop (Weaver 1994, p. 87).

Prior to the mid-1980s, many educators talked about children's "readiness to read" or "reading readiness." This was thought of as the degree to which children were ready to learn a particular reading skill or strategy when they come to school. Many educators also talked about other various skills and prereading factors that were believed to affect reading success, such as psychomotor skills, intelligence quotients, visual perception, and auditory discrimination, to name a few. This view of reading readiness and prereading factors was more of an example of the transmission model of learning. Children were viewed as young persons who must be made ready and must be taught certain skills, often in isolation, before they could learn to read. However, since the mid to late 1980s, earlier ideas about readiness skills and other factors have evolved to a more inclusive view of the young child's early experiences. This more current view is known as "emergent literacy" (Strickland and Morrow 1989; Teale and Sulzby 1986) and fits the transactional model of thinking about the young child.

The emergent literacy view gives credence to everything that happens in a child's development, from birth on, that shapes the child's concepts about oral and written language and the use of language in all its forms. The sections that follow discuss this early development and experience from an emergent literacy perspective.

### *Emergent Literacy: An Introduction*

Emergent literacy can be defined as "one's emerging or developing literacy." It begins at birth and continues to develop as the young baby and child is exposed to all aspects of language in the home, extended family, community, and sociocultural groups. In the beginning it may not look like or seem like the conventional literacy of the educated world; however, it is emerging and it will continue to develop as the child continues to have more experiences and encounters with language in his or her world. Emergent literacy development occurs in all children from all socioeconomic groups and all ethnic and cultural backgrounds (Sulzby and Barnhart 1992), and it includes awareness and development of both reading and writing literacy (Teale 1987). Therefore, when children begin their formal schooling in kindergarten or first grade, they have often developed some sense of awareness of print; oral and written language; stories and story structure; and the uses of speaking, writing, and reading. The following examples of emergent literacy illustrate this development.

The first example is Rosario, a young 2½-year-old toddler, who goes shopping with her grandmother every day. Grandma writes a shopping list before they go and reads it, checking off items, as she goes through the market searching for the groceries on the list. Rosario helps Grandma with the shopping and unpacking. Rosario is developing an awareness of print, written language, and the use of writing and reading. At bedtime, when Mommy is there, she reads Rosario a bedtime story. Rosario has some favorites. She sometimes helps Mommy pick out the bedtime book. Rosario loves it when Mommy reads to her. She knows some of the stories so well that she can tell what will happen next. Rosario is developing an awareness and appreciation of print, stories, and reading. She is also developing a sense of story structure and sees the usefulness and enjoyment of reading.

*W*hat are your earliest recollections of your own emergent literacy development? Do you remember shopping list experiences, bedtime stories, receiving birthday cards, or recognizing your name on a present? In your journal, under the heading Reflection Activity 3.1, make note of your earliest literacy memories. What aspects of literacy awareness do you think these fostered?

## *Print Awareness*

As you noted in the previous Rosario example, children begin to acquire concepts about print at very early ages. These concepts about print develop based on children's experiences with written language. Clay's Concepts about Print test, reprinted in her 1993 publication and also available in a Spanish reconstruction (Escamilla, Andrade, Basurto, and Ruiz, with Clay 1996), assesses various aspects of print awareness that are generic to many languages and cultures. Some of these print concepts include an awareness that

1. Books have a specific orientation with identifiable fronts and backs, and pages have identifiable tops and bottoms.
2. Print is important because the print, not the picture, is to be read.
3. Certain rules govern directionality; for example, print on the left page is read before print on the right page; and print on a page progresses from left to right and from top to bottom.
4. Letters in a word and words in sentences are ordered from left to right, and by changing the order the meaning is altered.
5. Punctuation has meaning.
6. Lowercase letters have corresponding capital letters.
7. Letters are letters, and words are words.

When children attend to these and other concepts about print, they are showing print awareness. This print awareness is part of emergent literacy and is developmental and based on children's previous experience with print (Sulzby and Barnhart 1992).

Adams (1990) has summarized what children who grow up in a print-rich environment seem to learn about print (pp. 334–335):

1. Print is very different from other kinds of visual patterns in their environment.
2. Print is print across any of a variety of media—on paper, television screens, signs, or even written with their fingers or with sticks in the dirt.
3. Print seems to be all over the place—even on labels inside your clothes.

4. Different samples of print are used by adults in different ways; they read picture books to you, but newspapers to themselves; they sometimes read signs and labels aloud, but sometimes there is print that they seem to ignore.
5. Adults mysteriously extract meaning from print.
6. There appears to be different categories of printed materials, each with their own characteristic appearances and uses—like books, magazines, signs, labels, instructions, telephone books, lists, price tags, cards, party invitations, and menus.
7. Print holds information.
8. Print can be produced by anyone.

Adams (1990) has argued that although many privileged children do grow up in a print-rich environment, many other children do not; therefore, these other children do not necessarily develop the insights about print necessary for beginning reading. Adams believes that these children will require more instruction in phonological awareness, print awareness, word awareness, and letter recognition if they are to succeed in the primary grades (pp. 336–337). Later in this chapter some suggestions for teaching are outlined that will enhance children's future development of print awareness and other aspects of emergent literacy.

## Oral and Written Language

As noted in the previous sections, children are exposed to oral and written language from their earliest experiences. However, this is not to say that oral language and written language are the same. Although they are inextricably related, oral language and written language involve different mediums and conventions for using language. Oral language involves use of speech (to create oral language) and hearing (to hear the oral language created). Written language involves use of writing (to record written messages) and reading (to decipher or decode the written messages). Emergent literacy research indicates that even though these literacy processes are not the same, they do develop together. In other words, children often develop an awareness and understanding of these processes concurrently. Note in the next example how Josh's (age 4) developing awareness and understanding of oral language and written language are enhanced by a literacy event in his family.

Josh's parents are talking and arguing with each other. Both of them are clearly upset and this worries Josh. He hears his mother say words like "out of work," "pay the bills," "money for groceries," and "what about the rent." His father keeps responding with words like "don't worry," "we'll work it out," and "I'll talk to the foreman again," but Josh's father seems worried, too. Josh's mother holds up a paper with lots of print typed on it and says, "It's no use, didn't you read this? What are we going to do?" Josh's father says, "I know. I know. But they sent that letter to almost everyone. I'll talk to the foreman and see." Josh can't help but worry. He is aware that the powerful speech his parents spoke, and what he heard, means that the family has trouble. He is also aware that the print on that letter explains what happened. The letter came from where Josh's father works and both of his parents read the message on the paper. The message is obviously something bad. Josh can't read yet, but when his parents go to bed, he is going to ask his big brother, Jason, to read the letter to him.

Smith (1994) has pointed out that children must have two special insights regarding oral and written language to learn to read. First, children must be aware that print is meaningful and, second, that written language is not just the same as speech (p. 204). Smith explained that print is all around children. This environmental print can be loaded with meaning if children have opportunities to make hypotheses about the print and test out their hypotheses. For example, a sign that indicates "Toys" is indeed the place in the department store that has lots of toys displayed for sale. Or in our example of Josh and the crisis in his family, when Josh's brother reads the letter to him, Josh's hypothesis that the letter says something bad is confirmed when his brother reads: "We are sorry to tell you that you, and most of the people in your work area, are being let go."

As we can see by the Josh example, literacy events are learnings about literacy that happen in the child's environmental experience, and not all of these environmental experiences are necessarily positive. But, even so, whether good or bad or even neutral, literacy learning does take place from children's sociocultural and family experiences. Although common sense tells us that positive oral language and print experiences are best, the environment of children is full of various literacy learning experiences. Teale's (1986) research indicates that parents from low socioeconomic status can and do provide rich literacy learning environments for their children.

## Reflection Activity 3.2

*W*hat do you believe? Do you agree with the emergent literacy view that children are immersed in oral and written language within their own cultures and families, and that this environmental print and language exposure provides literacy learnings? Or do you believe in Adams's (1990) argument that many children without print-rich environments will fail in school reading unless they receive instruction in sound, letter, print, and word recognition? Or do you see elements of truth in both views? In your reflection journal, jot your response down and explain why you believe as you do.

The conventions of written language are different from the medium and conventions of speech. As Smith (1994, pp. 206–208) has pointed out, children who expect written language to be exactly the same as speech can have difficulty predicting and comprehending its conventions and thus in learning to read. Children need familiarity with how written language works, and one of the best ways for children to develop this familiarity is by being read stories. All full cohesive stories, whether from a storybook or from a newspaper or magazine, as well as more informal written language, like letters or other written personal communications, can provide children with some awareness of the conventions of written language.

# Stories, Story Structure, and Storybook Reading

When parents and other family members read and share stories with young children, the readings and talk surrounding the words and pictures in the books lead to questions about print (Taylor and Strickland 1986); provide models of written language, its structure, and its conventions (Smith 1994); and foster literacy development and nurture an appreciation for and interest in reading (Spiegel 1994).

Some of the language (linguistic) and other literacy development learnings from story reading and sharing include awareness and observations of

1. the processes and conventions of written language—the increased conscious awareness of, and the development of insights about, language as both an object and a process is known as "metalinguistic awareness" (Rowe and Harste 1986; Templeton 1986);
2. the structure and usage of written language, including the words, ideas, and sentences in the story or writing—
   - *graphophonics*—what words look like and sound like when we see them in the story
   - *syntax*—putting words together when reading or writing in a grammatically acceptable way
   - *semantics*—what words mean when they are embedded in the specific situation of the story
   - *pragmatics*—what words are appropriate to use in the particular social setting or purposes of the communication;
3. the language and structure of stories—how they begin, evolve, and end, and their predictability; and
4. what readers do when they read books.

Martinez and Roser (1985) examined the concept of the familiarity of stories and its relationship to children's understanding. They found that when parents/family members repeated readings of the same story to children, there were four positive benefits. The first benefit was that children tended to talk more when the story was familiar. Second, the children's story talk changed in form as the story became more familiar (e.g., children asked fewer questions but made more comments). A third benefit of repeated readings of familiar stories was that children's story talk changed in focus, and they were able to attend to other dimensions such as character identification. A fourth benefit of repeated readings of familiar stories was that children experienced a more in-depth understanding of the story. Clearly, these repeated readings improved the ability of children to interact with the printed page.

When children model reading activities based on their emergent literacy experiences of being read to, they engage in what Holdaway (1979) has described as "successive approximations." Successive approximations are really steps toward literacy, even though they may not always be accurate or fit the conventional idea of reading. In other words, children will use what they know thus far about story structure and storybook reading to read a storybook.

Observing children read a storybook can tell teachers a lot about children's emergent or emerging literacy.

Sulzby's (1985, 1991) storybook reading and classification work has described the different categories of emergent reading. She designed her observational assessments to be used with children's favorite storybooks and has indicated that they have been successfully used with both Anglo and Hispanic children from low-income as well as middle-income families. The following list is a summary of Sulzby's simplified version of the categories and descriptions of what teachers can look for to observe the child's approximations of each category:

1. The child refers to pictures in the story and labels or talks about the picture but doesn't really tell the story with the pictures. (Here the child doesn't sound like a "storyteller" or a "reader.")
2. The child refers to pictures in the story and tells the story by referring to the pictures. (Here the child sounds like a "storyteller," not a "reader.")
3. The child refers to pictures in the story and combines telling the story with pictures and reading the pictures to tell the story. (Here the child sounds sometimes like a "storyteller," but also sometimes sounds like a "reader.")
4. The child refers to the pictures in the story but is telling the story in the language of its author. (Here the child sounds like a "reader.")
5. The child refers to the print in the story and attempts to read the story using the printed text. (Here the child sometimes may refuse to read if he or she cannot identify the words, may read using only some aspects of the print, or may actually read the story.)

It is important for teachers to understand that during any one reading, children may shift from one category to another, and that these categories are meant only to describe children's approximate development. The categories themselves overlap and there are no clear boundaries between each. Sulzby's work instead provides teachers with a means of observing children's attention to print and their modeling of the reading process.

## Appreciation and Seeing Usefulness of Writing and Reading

As young children's literacy develops, it is hoped that they learn that writing and reading are both useful and pleasurable activities. Children experiencing this sense of usefulness, and deriving enjoyment and pleasure from reading and writing activities, are likely to continue to pursue these activities. Writers get better and better at writing by writing. Readers get better and better at reading by reading.

A resurgence of interest in the affective aspects of reading has occurred in recent years (Cramer and Castle 1994). This is because more and more research has pointed to the strong relationships between motivation, interest, and cognitive learning, including reading comprehension and metacognition (e.g., Guthrie 1994). Young emergent learners who are given opportunities to enjoy storybook reading and other positive and pleasurable literacy events are learning that reading can be truly something to be savored. Remember Rosario's happiness and enjoyment concerning Mommy's bedtime story reading?

We have also seen how young children learn that writing and reading can be useful and purposeful. Remember Rosario's shopping list experiences with Grandma, and Josh's experience of learning from "the letter" about what happened to worry his parents so very much? Writing and reading become meaningful and purposeful to children through literacy experiences like these.

Now let's look at one other example. This young child, Tiffany, is learning about writing and reading and its usefulness and pleasures.

Tiffany is almost 5 years old. She lives with her Daddy and her younger brother, Tyrone. Tiffany's Daddy plans a big birthday party for Tiffany. Together they write a list of who they will invite, pick out funny party invitations, write the important information inside each, and finally address and mail each invitation. Daddy and Tiffany also make a list of what they have to buy for the party. Some of the things on the list include: candles, balloons, party hats, and paper plates. They go shopping together and buy everything on the list. Daddy decides that he and Tiffany will make the cake themselves. They have to read and use Auntie's recipe book to do it. Tyrone can't help because he can't read yet. It is fun! After the party, Daddy reads one of Tiffany's new storybooks to Tiffany and Tyrone. They love the book and make Daddy read it over and over again. It is about a funny monkey named George. Tiffany loves stories about monkeys! She has others about the monkey called George. The next day, Tiffany reads the new book to Tyrone. The pictures help Tiffany remember how to read it. Tyrone loves it when Tiffany reads him storybooks. Lots of times she begins with "Once upon a time."

Tiffany is modeling reading behavior and practicing her emerging literacy. She knows that writing and reading are useful and pleasurable. She knows about story structure because Daddy has read her many different storybooks. She knows how to hold a book, read the pictures, and retell the story that the author tells. Tiffany also knows a lot about the main characters in the Curious George books. She knows that George always gets into trouble, but the kind "man" always forgives him. Tiffany knows that these stories are predictable. She also knows that they are literature that she really likes. In fact, when Auntie asked her what she wanted for her birthday, Tiffany told her more Curious George books.

## Reflection Activity 3.3

$W$e have read that through storybook reading young children learn about the conventions of written language, the structure of written language, the language and structure of stories, what readers do when they read, and the pleasures of reading. We have also read that the research indicates that purposes, motivations, and interests affect children's understanding of what they read. Obviously, storybook reading is important to emergent literacy development. In your journal, under the heading Reflection Activity 3.3, please note your own ideas regarding the importance of storybook reading. What evidence have you seen in your own childhood, or in your children's development, to illustrate its importance?

# Social and Cognitive Development

Thus far most of our discussion regarding the young child and emerging literacy has focused on the child's language development, particularly the child's learnings, awareness, and appreciation of written language. Another label for this language development is "linguistic development" or "linguistic experience." However, it is clear that while young children develop experience and learnings about language they also are developing socially and cognitively. This section of the chapter will explore some of these social and cognitive learnings and development.

## Young Children's Sociocognitive Learnings

Let's revisit some of the young children and scenarios we have previously described and identify some of the social and cognitive learnings to which each has been exposed.

### Rosario's Learnings

When Rosario (age 2½) and Grandma make a shopping list and go grocery shopping, Rosario learns that reading from a list in the grocery store is a social event. In other words, she learns that one context and use of writing and reading is in the grocery store with Grandma. If Rosario continues, throughout her early childhood years, to shop this way with Grandma, Rosario will feel that one appropriate and comfortable use of writing and reading is for shopping.

Rosario also learns cognitively from the grocery shopping trips. She probably learns the names ("vocabulary") for many foods that she and Grandma look at or buy. She learns what kind of things one finds in a grocery store, and she develops a "schema" for grocery stores. She also probably has other cognitive learnings. For example, she may have learned how to get from her house, and back again, from the grocery store; that bags filled with groceries are generally heavy, but some items that are big, like paper towels, aren't heavy and they can fill grocery bags, too; and that to take the groceries home, Grandma must exchange them for pennies and dollars before they leave the store.

When Rosario's Mommy reads her a bedtime story each night, this is a social occasion for Rosario. Rosario learns that bedtime reading is an appropriate and comfortable time and location for reading. Rosario has cognitive learnings from the bedtime readings, too. She learns new vocabulary for the things she and Mommy read about. She also develops schemata for the things she and Mommy read about.

### Josh's Learnings

When Josh (age 4) hears his parents talking and arguing about their problems caused by what they read in "the letter," Josh learns that receiving letters is a social event; an event that can bring good or bad news into your home. He also sees that reading and talking about letters is a grown-up endeavor, one that involves very serious discussion. Even though the news in this letter wasn't pleasant, Josh has learned that receiving and reading letters is an appropriate event in his family and culture.

Cognitively, Josh has learned the importance adults put on having a job. He has further developed his schema for "having a job," and "for not having a job." He has also possibly further developed his schema for the vocabulary word *foreman* and for other words his parents discussed.

## Tiffany's Learnings

Now, we would like you to try it. Review the scenario describing the preparations for Tiffany's fifth birthday party, and also the storybook reading following the party. What social and cognitive learnings do you think Tiffany might have had from these experiences?

**R e f l e c t i o n   A c t i v i t y   3 . 4**

*R*eflect on Tiffany's experiences and learnings, and then, in your journal, under the heading Reflection Activity 3.4, list the learnings you are able to glean from those events and experiences. Later in this chapter, we will revisit these reflections about Tiffany's learnings.

The sections that follow review and discuss some of the areas and research associated with social and cognitive development.

## The Social Context of Reading and Writing

The idea that reading and writing are social processes and that children learn about written language through social interactions can be traced back to the research and writings of Russian-born social psychologist Lev Vygotsky (two of his books were republished in 1978 and 1986). Although Vygotsky died long before he was rediscovered and credited for his constructivist views of the development of knowledge and learning, educational researchers today are referring to Vygotsky's ideas about child development and literacy learning. This section summarizes what we have learned from some of these ideas.

1. Children develop their thinking abilities by communicating with "others" in their social world. These others include their parents, families, siblings, peers, and other community members.
2. Children's intelligence should not be evaluated as something that does not change, or as something in isolation from others. For example, measures of intelligence quotients (IQ tests) do not tell what a child is capable of learning. Vygotsky indicated that what he calls the "zone of proximal development" (1978) instead is the distance between a child's mental age and what the child could learn with the help and interaction of another person.

3. Using language, children develop their abilities for higher-order thinking and reasoning. Children learn to "talk themselves through" their learning, building on the language interactions they have already had with others.

4. Learning experiences, which begin early on, in the home and in the community, influence children's literacy development; conversely, children are not waiting until they start school to learn. Ideas about "readiness," or "being developmentally ready" to learn, are inappropriate to what we know about children's emergent literacy.

5. Children's learning can happen anytime, as long as they have adults or peers available to help them extend their current knowledge and skills.

6. Children's play with writing and reading is one way that they learn to be writers and readers. Children emulate or try to model the behavior of adults or older siblings whom they admire. (We saw this role playing of "a reader" when Tiffany read a storybook to her younger brother, Tyrone.)

In summary, from the work of Vygotsky, and the work of the many others cited who have further developed the emergent literacy perspective of literacy development, we know that learning to read and write takes place within a social context. This social context usually begins with the child and a parent or family caregiver. Together they interact, and the child continually learns about language and learns about the world around him or her (concepts, vocabulary, and reasoning skills). When children are interested in expanding their knowledge, they interact with adults and peers in the family and community, asking questions, observing, and modeling what they glean. A child is a product of all he or she has experienced and learned, and will continue to experience and learn, in the world—the world of the child's family, community, and culture.

## Cognitive Learnings: Culture, Vocabulary, and Schemata

When young children learn about their written language in specific social contexts, they become comfortable using what they know about writing and reading in those same contexts. For instance, because Rosario has learned that writing and reading lists are part of the shopping experience in her family, culture, and community, she is likely to continue to write and read lists when she goes shopping. Again, because Rosario has learned that bedtime reading is appropriate and very enjoyable in her family, culture, and community, she is likely to continue to read at bedtime. These cognitive learnings about writing and reading will be productive to Rosario's future as a person who writes and reads, and they match the values and purposes of writing and reading in most American schools. But what about the child who grows up in a family, culture, and community that uses or values writing and reading in different ways? For instance, consider a child whose culture uses writing and reading only for bible study. Would that child value reading at bedtime and writing and reading lists for secular purposes? Of course, this is an extreme example, but the point is that as emergent readers and writers, children have been developing in their own unique families, communities, and cultures. How those families, communities, and cultures use written language will greatly affect how their children use written language. Much of the research on literacy and learners from diverse cultures has indicated that we have to value and respect each child's emergent literacy and be prepared to enhance their continued development as readers and learners by providing appropriate learning opportunities and instruction (e.g., Au 1993; Banks 1994; and many others). The sections at the end of this chapter will provide some ideas that are conducive to what we have learned from Vygotsky's work (1978, 1986) and the work of others (e.g., Cambourne 1988; Holdaway 1979; Strickland and Morrow 1989; and Teale and Sulzby 1986) with emergent literacy views.

Some of the other cognitive learnings children develop relate directly to their abilities to understand what they read. In order to understand what they read, they need reasoning and problem-solving skills, an understanding of the concepts and vocabulary in the reading, and some schemata for what they will read about. These cognitive learnings are discussed next.

### *Reasoning, Thinking, and Problem Solving*

As previously indicated, young children develop their reasoning, thinking, and problem-solving skills by communicating and interacting with others. This was one of our greatest learnings from Vygotsky's work (republished in 1978). A basic premise of his theory about learning is that higher forms of mental activity are jointly constructed and transferred to children through the dialogues that they have with other people. These ideas have been stimulating researchers and educators toward designing educational opportunities that encourage discussion and joint problem-solving activities (Berk 1994). When children engage in cooperative dialogues with more mature children or adults, they can intellectualize the language of those dialogues and use it to organize their independent efforts in the same way (Berk 1992).

Berk (1994) also reviewed the research of Vygotsky (republished in 1978 and 1987) and described children's social pretend play and its importance to the development of their thinking. She has indicated that make-believe has a "critical role . . . in developing reflective thoughts as well as self-regulatory and socially cooperative behavior" (p. 38). Additionally she has emphasized that teachers should view social pretend play as the ultimate activity for nurturing early childhood capacities that are crucial for academic success.

It is very clear from our discussions that language and thought are so interrelated that we cannot discuss one of them without discussing the other. When children have intellectualized the dialogues they have with others, they are able to use these dialogues, engaging in "talking to themselves," as a means of seeking and planning solutions to problems. In other words, through repeated interactions with others, children learn to regulate their own problem-solving activities by mediating their own internal speech (Galda, Cullinan, and Strickland 1993). The term *scaffolding,* coined by Bruner (1983), describes the learning process by which learners learn to gradually support themselves, by first receiving support from more capable others. As learners become more capable themselves, the support is gradually withdrawn.

Teachers can use scaffolding in their classrooms as a way of providing instruction that supports the kind of learning children naturally engage in as emergent learners.

We believe that the reasoning, thinking, and problem-solving development of young children is directly linked to the reflective thinking older children must engage in if we are to call them "metacognitively aware." Metacognitive strategies involve self-monitoring our understanding of what we hear or read. Baker and Brown (1984) indicated that metacognitive abilities help learners keep track of how well they are comprehending. Although metacognitive awareness will be more fully discussed in this text, we think it is important to note here that the young child's emergent literacy, especially reasoning, thinking, and problem-solving development, serves as a foundation to the higher-order thinking and reflection required for reading comprehension and metacognitive monitoring.

## *Concepts and Vocabulary*

Young children are learning new concepts and vocabulary every day. Remember Rosario's grocery store experience? She's probably learning concepts like "heavy," "light," "big," "small," "money," and "buying" every time she goes to the store with Grandma. She's also learning the vocabulary that matches those concepts. Moe's (1989) review of the research indicated that by the time children have reached the age of 5, they have speaking vocabularies of approximately two thousand words. When they begin first grade, their speaking vocabularies exceed four thousand words and may be as high as fifteen thousand words. Moe noted that even the most disadvantaged of inner-city children have extensive speaking vocabularies, and the listening vocabularies of young children are even larger. He also indicated that although the research findings vary, first graders can listen to and understand between ten thousand and twenty thousand different words (p. 24).

Finally, Smith (1994) has suggested that all of the aspects of thought that language distinguishes can be seen as the manipulation of cognitive relationships. Learners are not doing different things when they reason, draw inferences, or solve problems; they only appear to be different because of the context in which they are done or the consequences of doing them. He illustrated this by defining

- "reasoning" as the relationships within a series of statements or states of affairs—the way one thing follows another;
- "inference" as involving relationships between particular statements or states of affairs and more general circumstances;
- "problem solving" as relating existing states of affairs to desired states; and
- "classification," "categorization," "concept formation," and other manifestations of "higher order" or "abstract" thinking as imposing and examining relationships among statements or states of affairs (p. 21).

According to Stanovich (1986), knowing word meanings is the most important background knowledge required for comprehension. Beck, McKeown, and Omanson (1987) have indicated that knowing a word is not an all-or-nothing situation. Instead, children's word knowledge should be viewed in terms of the degree or the extent to which they know the word. For example, Carey's (1978) study indicated that 6-year-old children "know," to some degree, approximately fourteen thousand words. Carey pointed out that learning a word involves a gradual process of refining one's understanding and adding "partial knowledge" on successive encounters. She estimated four to ten encounters are necessary for word learning to be "complete."

## Schemata

A *schema* (singular of *schemata*) is a collection of related information and experience that our brain organizes to give us a mental picture of whatever the schema is for. Anderson and Pearson (1984) defined it as "knowledge already stored in memory" (p. 255).

As we go through life experiencing our world, we develop schemata to abstract what we are learning, modifying, or using. These schemata band together, where they are related. Our experiences assist us to develop specific schemata for people, places, events, functions, roles, and feelings, among other concrete and abstract concepts. For instance, your "genetic family schemata" would be a cognitive abstraction of your immediate family (for example, father, mother, siblings, grandparents, and so on) and distant relatives. The schemata that we or your students develop are our "knowledge" of our existence, and they become part of the "prior knowledge" we bring to listening, writing, or reading activities to help us interpret or comprehend oral or written language.

Referring back to Rosario's grocery shopping experiences, Figure 3.1 depicts what young 2½-year-old Rosario's developing schema for a grocery store might look like.

As you can see, Rosario has a schema for the grocery store based on the information she has learned about it through her experiences there with Grandma. Likewise, Rosario is probably developing other schemata for other things and concepts she is learning about through her emergent literacy. When Rosario begins school and is required to read certain stories and texts, she will have an easier time understanding what she reads when she has existing schemata for the concepts and topics. Of course, schemata aren't stagnant. Children continue to learn more about things within their family, community, and cultural experiences, and more about the things their parents/families read to them. Therefore, their schemata are continually developing and changing. Furthermore, because children construct their own knowledge, by forming and reforming concepts in their minds, their knowledge does not come fully developed and is often quite different from that of an adult (McGee and Richgels 1996, p. 7).

Piaget (1969) indicated that two processes make these changes and development possible. *Assimilation* is the cognitive development process that allows new information from a child's environment to be integrated into or added to the child's existing schema. The other process, *accommodation,*

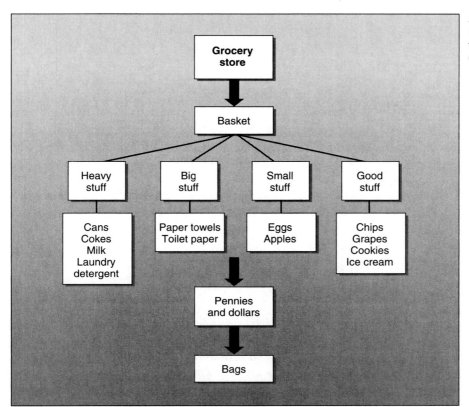

**Figure 3.1**
Rosario's "schema"
for "grocery store"
(age 2½).

involves modifying the existing schema, by sometimes rearranging or discarding some information, to accommodate new information that has been experienced and learned.

Look at Figure 3.2, which shows Rosario's hypothetical and further developed schema for the grocery store at age 4. As you can see, by a process of assimilation and accommodation, Rosario has added more information and categories to her schema. She has also classified several pieces of information into more than one category, showing that her schema for a grocery store is more sophisticated, and she has further refined her ideas and labels for the grocery store. For example, she actually now calls the store "Manny's Grocery Store" and has refined her label "big" to "large."

What happens when youngsters must read a text about a topic or concept they have no schemata for? Usually, they have trouble comprehending it. Here is an example of what this might be like. Read the piece of text below and see what you understand:

> Standing on the outside, watching, waiting, searching, and often scurrying out of the way of cars and people. Watching and searching and watching and searching some more, and then finally sleeping. Much of his life is spent this way. Sometimes

**Figure 3.2**
Rosario's "schema"
for "grocery store"
(age 4).

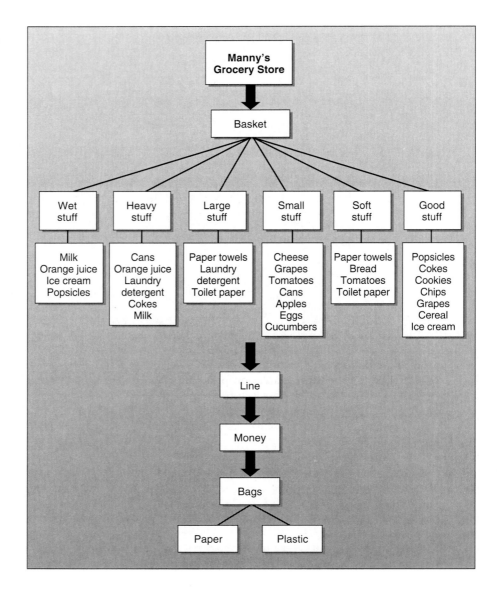

he goes hungry for long periods of time. Sometimes he stuffs himself when he can. Sometimes he experiences kindness, sometimes cruelty. However, this is what his life is like and he has adjusted.

What did you understand this to be about? Is it about a person, perhaps a "street person"? Is it about an animal, "a squirrel," or "a rat," or some other scavenger? Or is it about something else? Your understanding of this piece will depend on your schema for the actual topic. The piece was actually written to describe "a homeless cat in the city." Your reading task, as an adult, was much easier than it might be for a child, because you probably have a schemata for all of the possibilities mentioned, and with additional and fuller text, you could have narrowed down the possibilities and been able to accurately match a schema for the reading. Rumelhart (1976) indicated that reading is an interaction between the schema of the author and the schema of the reader. It involves predicting, then checking, and finally "schema matching."

## A Revisit to Tiffany's Learnings

Now that we have had an opportunity to present more background information about sociocognitive learning to you, we would like you to revisit the list you generated in your journal under the heading Reflection Activity 3.4, and compare it with the list we have developed. It will be interesting for you to see whether you noted some learnings of 5-year-old Tiffany that we did not think of. Likewise, perhaps we noted some that you did not notice or think to be significant. Let's see.

### Tiffany's Learnings: Our List

1. Reading, to select party invitations, and writing party invitations are appropriate contexts for reading and writing.
2. Writing and reading lists, for people to invite to a party and for things you need to buy, are appropriate contexts for writing and reading.
3. Reading directions (like Tiffany and Daddy did to make a cake) is an appropriate context for reading.
4. Reading books at bedtime is an appropriate time and context for reading.
5. Tiffany possibly learned some new vocabulary words and is able to associate these words to what they look like (graphophonic awareness) when they are written down—for example, candles, balloons, party hats, paper plates.
6. Tiffany possibly learned more about pragmatics and the appropriate language to use for party invitations.
7. Tiffany probably developed or further developed her schemata for "birthday party planning," "baking a cake," and "writing, addressing, and mailing invitations."
8. Tiffany probably learned some new vocabulary from the book that Daddy read her.
9. Tiffany's schema for "the mischief that Curious George gets into" has been enlarged. (Assimilation has further developed her schema. But that is not fair, you probably would not have known that until you read beyond Reflection Activity 3.4.)
10. Tiffany has also probably further developed her reasoning, thinking, and problem-solving skills by engaging in conversations with Daddy, working out solutions to problems, during party planning and preparation. (Again, this isn't fair, because the idea that reasoning and thinking are developed and enhanced through active conversations and interactions with an interested older person wasn't introduced until after you wrote Reflection Activity 3.4.)

Well, how did you do, and how did we do? We would like to have you reflect a little more now. Please try the next reflection activity.

## Reflection Activity 3.5

*R*eview all of the early experiences and the linguistic, social, and cognitive development and learnings discussed to this point in this chapter. Then reflect on these questions: What experiences and learnings do you think are most important to children's emerging literacy? Why? In your journal, under the heading Reflection Activity 3.5, write your responses. Feel free to indicate experiences from your own emerging literacy development or your own experiences with children that may have led you to answer the way you have.

## *Enhancing Literacy Development*

The theme of this chapter has clearly been that literacy development begins at birth and that children are moving closer and closer to attaining literacy in the conventional sense as their emerging literacy continues to develop. To make our points about this theme, we have reviewed and discussed the relevant research and literature, and we have provided examples of three young children's emergent literacy learnings.

We agree with the emergent literacy view of language and literacy development. Our review of the literature has indicated that children from various socioeconomic groups and many sociocultural communities develop an awareness of print. Likewise, when children are read storybooks and are given ample opportunities to interact with caring adults, they develop affectively, linguistically, and cognitively. Nevertheless, we still believe that children's existing literacy, when they begin school, must be nurtured and opportunities must be given for continued literacy development.

In this section we discuss and list ways that parents/families, communities, teachers, and the children themselves can enhance literacy development opportunities after children begin school to ensure children's success. We feel that these ideas and opportunities are applicable to working with all young children, including those who have not had as "print-rich" and "language-rich" of a background as others, and culturally diverse and other diverse learners who may have additional developmental and learning needs.

### *The Parents'/Families' and Communities' Roles*

The importance of "family literacy" and the involvement of parents, families, and communities in children's literacy and schooling have been a strong presence in the literature, education profession, and American politics (see, for example, Morrow 1994, 1995; Morrow, Paratore, Gaber, Harrison, and Tracey 1993; and U.S. Department of Education 1994). The International Reading Association (IRA) established a commission on family literacy in 1991 to study issues and initiatives in family literacy from a global perspective. In 1994, the U.S. Department of Education set aside funding for a parent/family/community initiative as part of the Goals 2000 legislation. The main thrust of all of this is to respect the role that parents, families, and communities play in children's education; involve them more; and continue to study the broadened concept of family literacy.

The IRA Family Literacy Commission's (1994) broadened concept of family literacy involves much more than just parent involvement in their children's schooling. The Commission has indicated that family literacy also involves the following: how families provide literacy to their children; how they use literacy at home; and special cultural considerations. The family interactions and literacy scenarios that have been provided in this chapter have already given you several examples of this broadened concept of family literacy.

It is important that the classroom teacher allow parents/families to actively continue the emergent literacy development that they started. Parents/families can be encouraged to take part, after children begin school, when teachers encourage them to continue the following activities as delineated by Chapman (1986):

1. *Relating events in books to their children's lives.* It is important for parents/family members to relate characters and events in books to people and situations in their children's own lives. By doing this, parents provide an important link that increases their children's understanding of the story at a deeper level.
2. *Expanding their children's world.* Parents can focus on events in stories to enlarge the world of their children. This may include helping their children develop a clearer perspective about the story being read, clarifying a picture, or expanding a concept.
3. *Providing information about books and reading.* When parents/family members share books with children, they provide them with input opportunities to develop technical as well as functional concepts about reading. These concepts may include learning that books have a beginning, middle, and end; that books are read from front to back; that books are written by people; and that books are paginated.
4. *Helping their children get meaning from pictures.* Children should be encouraged by their families to "read" pictures for meaning. Parents/family members can accomplish this by asking questions and making comments about specific pictures. This establishes a recurring and highly structured routine that supports language acquisition.
5. *Helping their children get meaning from the text.* Parents/family members can help children view text as a source of meaning by repeating phrases and sentences and by focusing on specific words in the text.

6. *Encouraging their children to behave like readers.* Parents/family members should encourage their children to assume the role of the reader, thus advancing their children's approximation of readerlike behaviors. It is important for parents to treat their children as readers, and to encourage their children to assume this role. (However, this should not be forced if the child is not interested or not willing.)

Additionally, we would add the following suggestions for parents/family members:

7. *Continue to "talk with" and "interact" with your youngster.* When parents continue to use language and communication, modeling how they "work things out," young school-age children can continue to use these interactions to further develop their reasoning, thinking, and problem-solving skills.

8. *Ask questions about what went on in school, what was learned, what was fun, what was hard, and what was easy, and ask why.* When parents/family members give their children an opportunity to reflect on their learning, children will learn (a) that what they think is important; and (b) to think of themselves as knowledgeable, thoughtful, and capable learners who know when something is difficult or easy and why. (Again, we believe this will add to children's abilities to think and problem-solve, and we see it as an opportunity for developing metacognitive awareness early on.)

There is no doubt that the parents'/family's contribution to the reading process is critical. The experiences they provide in the home environment set patterns that affect and will continue to affect children's literacy for the remainder of their lives. Greaney (1986) summarized six areas in which parents/families exert influence over their childrens reading:

1. *Verbal interaction.* It is now clear that the verbal interactions between children and parents at home have a significant impact on the development of children's language abilities and their relationship to reading. The development of a story language foundation at home allows children to develop a vocabulary that increases the likelihood of success in early reading.

2. *Interest in reading.* It is important that parents act as a role model for children so that an interest in reading is developed. Parents who are interested in reading can contribute both to their children's confidence and interest in reading. Those children who have not indicated an interest in reading before entering school may experience some difficulty in developing this interest after entering school. Unfortunately, a lack of interest in reading can impede the probability of achieving success as a reader.

3. *Parental reading.* The importance of reading to children at an early age has already been mentioned; however, home reading activity cannot be overemphasized. Early parent-child interactions with print exert a major influence on future reading success. Parents should read to their children as often as they can. Parents' own reading habits also affect children's

values. Parents who read often for their own pleasure show their children that reading is a pleasurable and important aspect of their lives.

4. *Access to reading materials.* One of the essential ingredients in early reading is the accessibility of reading materials in the home. Unfortunately, in many homes there is a lack of reading materials. However, parents must be made aware of the need to provide materials for their children. These materials can include children's own books as well as library books.

5. *Opportunity for reading.* It is important to provide both an appropriate atmosphere and an opportunity for children to read. This is more likely to encourage children to develop effective personal reading habits that will help them develop into successful independent readers.

6. *Parent-child reading.* Parents who read to their children help their children understand the meanings of written words long before they can read them and also stimulate their children's imaginations. This activity also encourages an appreciation of reading and of books.

Finally, keep in mind that many child-family or parent relationships will not fit a traditional model. The "parent" may be an older sibling, grandparent, aunt, or neighbor. Whoever accepts responsibility and provides the nurturing for the child should be treated with respect and treated as "a parent." This is the older person who has and will be the one the child interacts with, reads with, shops with, and learns with.

## *The Teacher's Role*

Your primary role in enhancing reading development is to provide a classroom atmosphere that is conducive to learning and literacy. Many opportunities should exist for children to interact, play, read, write, draw, and work collaboratively with others. All of these opportunities should enhance interest in written language, both reading and writing; story sharing; problem solving; and learning and discovering new concepts, ideas, and things.

Holdaway (1986) has indicated that to continue children's "natural" learning, you might follow these suggestions:

1. Display in an imitative way what it is like to be a reader.
2. Give beginning readers an environment in which the conditions for learning are readily available. You are responsible for providing an environment in the classroom that invites participation.
3. Although developing readers frequently attempt various tasks and may exhibit many errors, try to show tolerance and patience in using these errors as learning experiences. Encourage approximating behaviors and provide time for unmonitored and self-regulated practice. In the early stages of schooling, promote children's role playing as readers and their enjoyment of these approximations of reading a book. These activities should be regarded as the first stage of reading.
4. When children seek and accept help, supply it without an overwhelming amount of explaining and moralizing. Thus, your role is to provide the

exact amount of assistance requested, to observe with sensitivity and appreciation the needs of the learners, and to intervene in helpful ways when necessary.

5. Create a rich environment of language in use, drawing attention to a few challenging concepts but keeping the environment free from anxiety about the curriculum.
6. Try to maximize the meaning in reading.
7. Avoid negative interactions but encourage student self-correction and self-regulation.
8. It is important to select a rich literature that your children will enjoy and from which they will create a hierarchy of favorites by insistently requesting that certain books be read over and over again.

Cambourne's "conditions for learning" (1988) have indicated how he believes children learn to read and write in a natural way, proceeding in much the same way as when they acquired language. These "conditions for learning" can serve as a guide to teachers of young children as they plan learning opportunities for their class. These conditions or steps are summarized, listed, and explained as follows:

- Immersion and Demonstration—"immerse" children in all kinds of texts, "engaging" them through demonstration that this is something they can do; this is something useful; and this is something that they will not be punished for if they are not fully correct. (For example, Brown and Cambourne [1987], suggest immersion in fables, fairy tales, and myths; narrative literature that develops atmosphere, characters, and setting; and various types of expository materials that describe, instruct, persuade, and inform.)
- Expectation—"expect" that the children will be successful; show confidence.
- Responsibility—"empower" the children to decide what, how, and when they learn the "bits" necessary to the learning task.
- Use—give children time and many opportunities to use their reading and writing attempts in "real ways."
- Approximation—let children be free to "approximate" the desired model; mistakes are okay and are in fact essential for learning to develop.
- Response—give children your feedback in a timely relevant manner without any sense of threats or force.

The environment and conditions for children's learning that you create in your classroom are certainly important. However, of equal importance is the environment and conditions for parents/family involvement that you create. This involvement is important all through the school-age years. Upper elementary, middle, and high school teachers, as well as teachers of younger children, should design opportunities to facilitate the parent/family involvement of all students. Giving parents a chance to play a role in the assessment and the learning of their children in school facilitates opportunities to succeed as a teacher. Parents/family members have a tremendous amount of information and insight about their children. By involving them in assessment and instructional planning you have an opportunity to "tap" and use that information and insight in ways that will help you work with their children. Parents can tell you about their child's emergent literacy and interests, make observations about their child as a reader and writer, tell you about literacy activities in their home, and participate in ongoing assessment and conferencing situations that will be meaningful to the child's learning. For some examples of specific ways of gathering and using information from parents/families for assessment, and ideas for child-family-teacher "three-way conferencing and planning sessions," see Flippo (1997).

Parent/family education and involvement efforts are part of the classroom teacher's role and responsibility. Many teachers have successfully developed programs to educate and work with parents. Fredericks and Taylor (1985) provided step-by-step procedures to help teachers initiate such programs in their classrooms and schools. Flippo and Branch (1985) developed a parent-information program for the parents of very young children and young school-aged children. The program consisted of summarizing research literature for parents to show them the extreme importance of their role in the reading process and also provided suggestions for simple parent-child activities and interactions that would foster reading development. Fredericks and Rasinski (1990) have suggested many ideas for parent involvement:

1. Continuously provide parents with written and visual materials and information; do this over the entire school year, not just at the beginning.
2. Make parental involvement a schoolwide endeavor.
3. Recognize the parents/families who make a commitment to reading.
4. Let children recruit their parents'/families' involvement by writing invitations and preparing awards.
5. Develop activities that include all of the family so that reading is a family project.
6. Consider including other members of the community in your plans, such as senior citizens and people from business and government, and try to get their endorsement of your efforts.
7. Make your classroom a comfortable place for parents to visit.
8. Communicate "good news" over the telephone to parents/families—not just bad news.
9. If parents/families don't get involved, try to find out why.
10. Make your activities schedule flexible enough so more parents can be involved; consider using occasional late afternoon, evening, and weekend times.
11. Consider establishing a parent/family hot line to keep parents informed.
12. Consider preparing videotapes of special literacy events and programs and have them available for parents.

Many other researchers and educators have suggested ideas for communicating with parents of young school-age children (e.g., Bruneau, Rasinski, Shehan 1995; Flippo and Smith 1990; Shockley, Michalove, and Allen 1995; Vukelich 1984). Others have suggested ways of explaining your emergent literacy teaching rationale to parents (e.g., Fields 1995). Finally, Cramer (1994) has made some additional suggestions for "reading on family trips," which teachers could send home to families before the summer begins. We have summarized and listed some of Cramer's suggestions to help you with your parent/family education efforts:

1. Family members can take turns being the "designated reader" of a favorite book that can be read as the family travels.
2. Play the "alphabet game" in which family members watch for letters of the alphabet, in sequence, from signs along the road. When a letter is spotted, read the word and/or phrase in which the letter was found.
3. On long trips, give children a map and have them find the road being traveled on, the next town, and the number of miles to the next stop.
4. Whenever possible, stop and read historical markers, and discuss the significance of the events described. Use math to calculate the years since the events occurred (p. 140).

We have a few other ideas to add to Cramer's suggestions:

5. Whenever possible, collect free brochures about places you are going or would like to visit on your trip. Encourage children to read them by reading the pictures. Older family members can read the brochures to younger children.
6. Make a point of "reading menus" aloud together, discussing the possible selections.
7. If the family is interested in history, old graveyards can be fascinating places to read gravestones, note historical significance, and calculate the years a person lived and how long ago that has been.

As pointed out earlier, parent/family involvement and literacy go beyond the home. Family literacy includes the sociocultural environment and the community in which the child lives. Flippo, Hetzel, Gribouski, and Armstrong (in press) describe their efforts to nurture and develop literacy opportunities in the community while also fostering and developing an appreciation for the rich cultural diversity of the population with which they worked.

Finally, as you work with parents, families, and communities, you can make use of many helpful resources. The International Reading Association (IRA) publishes many materials, brochures, and booklets for parents. Many of these are free for the asking or are available at very nominal charges. Also, the IRA publishes a column called "Parents and Reading" in their bimonthly newspaper, *Reading Today.* This column contains many creative ways of working with and involving parents/families in school. It also contains useful information about current and new publications that might be helpful to parents. The IRA and the Children's Book Council make a list of favorite children's books available each year and publish it in *The Reading Teacher* journal. Others have published booklets to educate and inform parents/families about a wide variety of literacy-related issues (see, e.g., Anderson 1990; Colbert 1991; Flippo, 1982; Gerecke 1990; Hetzel 1991; and Zide and Shaw 1990). Additionally, Morrow, Burks, and Rand's (1992) annotated bibliography is recommended as a source of books, chapters, pamphlets, journals, journal articles, and videos that can be used for parent/family outreach and education efforts.

As we have tried to show you, the teacher's role is a critical one, but it is one that must interweave with the roles of parents/families and community, and with the children themselves. Dwyer and Dwyer (1994), after reviewing the research and literature regarding the affective domain, literacy, and teachers' attitudes, stated: "Teachers must create within each classroom a positive atmosphere, a way of life conducive to promoting reading through positive affect. Positive teachers are competent teachers, constantly striving to better their skills. They realize that positive effect coupled with a high level of teaching ability promotes maximum achievement from their students" (p. 72). Your attitude toward children's emergent literacy and their continued development will affect everything that happens in your classroom.

## The Child's Role

Just as parents/families, communities, and teachers play vital roles in the emerging reading process, so do children. Contrary to what some believe, children are not just containers waiting for information to be poured into them. They also have a role to play in learning to read, and their early interaction with print prepares them to a large extent for this role.

Forester (1986) viewed children as apprentices learning to use language. In this role, they are language creators who do so by adjusting vocabulary, syntax, tone, volume, or imagery to meet the needs of each new encounter. Since there are not enough explicit rules to teach children how to respond to and then create each new combination of words or intonation patterns in daily conversation, it appears that children innately activate implicit learning. This activation enables children to interact physically and emotionally with rich and varied environments and to synthesize large amounts of sensory information into patterns or rules that allow recognition of the many subtle variants in the environment. By activating implicit learning strategies, children replicate and generalize various behaviors that they have observed.

Forester (1986) also suggested that learning through active participation in the language process requires more than just simple practice. Children need to be immersed in an environment where written language is as natural and viable a part of communication as spoken language. The opportunity to interact and practice freely within this type of learning environment enables children to shift roles from passive receiver to active participant in the reading process.

May (1994) called children "constructivists," constantly reinventing or "constructing" their own versions of what they encounter (p. 58). He also said they are "producers of knowledge," creating their own language rules and testing them out through writing and reading (p. 59). Michel (1994) looked at reading and literacy acquisition through the eyes of children. In this study of emergent readers, she showed the rich understandings and insights that can be gleaned when teachers and parents listen to young children's thinking about reading. Michel has suggested that when teachers really listen to children and their views about reading, they can use children's perceptions as a way of gauging instruction and its effectiveness. Children's perceptions should be monitored on a regular basis. Michel also indicated that certain categories of perceptions have been created through children's articulation of what reading means to them. These categories can serve as a framework for helping teachers understand each child's development, and include the following:

1. What children do when they read—their tasks, as they see them.
2. How children learn to read—the process they use, as they see it.
3. What purposes children have for reading.
4. How well children feel they are doing in reading.
5. How children feel about reading.
6. What children think about reading at home and reading at school.
7. What children think about their siblings as teachers (p. 143).

According to McInees (1986), literacy learning is an active, creative process, and all children invest much time, ingenuity, and energy inventing language-learning strategies for themselves. This process begins early in children's lives and is refined through practice with language. Part of this process involves children's use of imagination as readers and writers, and, as language players. Children playing with these language functions frequently pretend that they can do what adults and older children can do. This use of models is directly dependent on their ability to imagine being a reader or a writer. The ability to try on learning roles helps children shape images of themselves as learners.

Again, children appear to have an innate sense of language from birth. They are able to emulate and adapt their language as environmental or emotional factors require. This ability enables them to relate their spoken-language patterns to print, which in turn facilitates the development of the reading process. As children assume their role in the reading process, so must you. Children bring various degrees of language development and print awareness to the school setting, and it is crucial to the learning process that you let them utilize these language and awareness capabilities to the fullest extent. For children to achieve success, try to emphasize reading and writing for meaning, usefulness, and enjoyment, so that all their learning strategies can be activated and tried out.

## Reflection Activity 3.6

*I*t has been established in the previous sections that the involvement and interactions of parents/families, communities, teachers, and children are interwoven and crucial to continuing and enhancing literacy development. Think about this involvement and the kinds of interactions and environments you will want to promote in your own classroom as a facilitative teacher. Then, in your journal under the heading Reflection Activity 3.6, indicate the specific kinds of interactions and environments you will want to promote, and jot down ideas about how you could promote them.

# A Summary of the Emergent Literacy Research

Based on our review of the emergent literacy research, and the reviewed research of many others (e.g., see Teale and Sulzby 1986, 1989 and others cited throughout the chapter), we have summarized the following for you:

1. The development of reading and writing begins very early in life.
2. Reading and writing concepts and abilities develop concurrently and are interwoven.
3. Reading and writing concepts, functions, and abilities are developed through real-life experiences with reading, writing, and literacy materials.
4. Parents, family members, and other significant older persons demonstrate literacy to children as they read, write, use literacy materials, and interact with children.
5. Children are immersed in language from birth on; use of language with older/significant persons promotes thinking and cognitive development; children's language attempts and usage (oral and written) are products of their sociocultural environment; literacy development is fostered when children's attempts are treated positively and they are seen as capable persons; and social play with other children does promote further language development (linguistic) and cognitive development including problem-solving and reasoning abilities.

## Implications for Teachers

The emergent literacy research provides many important implications for teachers of young children regarding how they can further enhance children's literacy. It also provides important implications for teaching strategies that teachers can use for young children who have been neglected or deprived of literacy-building environments and other diverse learners in need of many literacy immersion opportunities. First we will provide you with a listing of the implications for teachers. Following that, we will suggest and briefly summarize many teaching strategies and ideas, which fit the emergent literacy and constructivist views of learning as well as our own view of what facilitative teachers do in their classrooms.

1. Realize that social imaginative play and other verbal peer interactions enhance language and cognitive development, and allow many opportunities for them to happen in your classroom.
2. Develop learning activities that integrate listening, speaking, reading, and writing (oral and written language).
3. Use art, music, and drama activities to further develop language opportunities.
4. Read many books and stories to children every day.
5. Choose books and stories that you believe will be of high interest to children and will further stimulate their interests in reading books.
6. Give children opportunities to respond to the books and stories you read.

7. Reread favorite stories as often as children request them.
8. Give children opportunities to retell and/or act out stories in their own words after listening to you read them.
9. Give children many opportunities to make their own books. (Sometimes children can dictate stories as the teacher writes the stories down in the children's own words. Other times, let the children write their own books using scribble writing, pictures, and invented spellings or other symbols of their own choosing to tell their stories in their own words.)
10. Give children many opportunities to share the stories they write with others.
11. Accept "less than perfect" readings, retellings, writings, and other literacy attempts for all children.
12. Provide classroom activities and an environment that enhances the idea that literacy is part of communication and that meaning is essential for communication to take place.
13. Give all children many opportunities to be and "feel" successful with their literacy activities and attempts.
14. Don't try to teach isolated skills and terminology about reading , like "words," "letters," and "sentences," but instead allow children to naturally learn these terms and concepts by using reading and writing in your classroom in meaningful reading and writing activities.
15. Use your observations of each child's literacy development to plan opportunities for each child's continued development, by continually assessing children as you work with them on a day-to-day basis.

## Teaching Strategies

What follows is a listing and brief overview of several teaching strategies and ideas that should enhance the emerging literacy development of most children. As pointed out earlier, we believe that these strategies are consistent with the learning from emergent literacy research and constructivist views about the development of learning.

## Use of Big Books

Using "Big Books" or enlarged versions of a children's book that children can easily see, the teacher can model the reading process to children as he or she reads and shares the book with them and they follow along. Holdaway (1979) has described use of this shared book experience and indicated that shared reading resembles the developmental learning that many children have experienced at home during parents' storybook reading. The teacher demonstrates reading the text and then children are given opportunities to experiment independently, approximating the story. Teachers can now purchase Big Books and accompanying smaller ones for children's individual reading and rereading; however, some teachers prefer making their own Big Books to be used with favorite children's stories. Slaughter's (1993) book fully describes many uses of the shared book experience and is an invaluable resource for teachers of young children.

## Use of Predictable Books

Similar to use of Big Books, using predictable books is a continuation of the emerging literacy storybook experience, and it is particularly helpful for youngsters who have not had many opportunities for storybook reading with their parents. Predictable books are books with repetitious text and simple, predictable language and events. For instance, in the book *The Very Hungry Caterpillar* by Eric Carle (1981), the caterpillar eats his way through the days of the week and the pages of the book. Predictable texts allow young children to use prediction, sampling, confirming, and disconfirming strategies right away, practicing the same process that more mature readers use (Bridge 1979). Slaughter (1993) is suggested as a good source of information on using predictable books with children and a listing of many such books to help get you started. Also, Tompkins and Hoskisson (1995) give suggestions for the step-by-step reading of predictable books, with examples of four different types of predictable books.

## Modeling and Scaffolding

Modeling and scaffolding are ways teachers can support the learning and development of young children. As teachers we can "model" the skills, strategies, behaviors, and values we hold concerning reading. When we model and demonstrate reading by reading for pleasure and information, we reinforce its importance to children. When we talk about the skills and strategies we use to read and find information, we demonstrate to children how readers read. This is very similar to how parents and family members model and demonstrate literacy in their homes.

Scaffolding goes hand-in-hand with modeling. Similar to the way parents do activities and support the literacy development of their young children, teachers can do the same. For instance, parents often coach their children, showing them how to do something and then gradually allowing them to do it themselves. Teachers can "scaffold instruction" to first model literacy activities and various literacy strategies and skills and then, little by little, to allow children to model back the activity and necessary skills/strategies. Researchers have indicated (Applebee and Langer 1983; Cazden 1980, 1983) that through these demonstrations and interactions teachers provide a framework to support the learning of complex tasks. As children learn and develop, the need for the scaffolding is less, and children assume more and more responsibilities for doing the tasks on their own. In other words, teachers provide as much or as little support as children need, gradually withdrawing support as children are able to do the tasks or activities independently.

## Make-Believe, Pretend Play, and Role Playing

As we already learned, pretend play is an opportunity for children to role-play and talk and act out various interactions and situations that enhance the development of their thinking and problem-solving abilities (Berk 1994). Therefore, opportunities for this social play and interaction are to be encouraged in the early childhood classroom. Teachers can facilitate these opportunities by creating various "centers" for various kinds of pretend play and interactions. For example, a housekeeping center, with various props (pots, pans, grocery boxes) and costumes (aprons, hats, and so on) can promote dialogue and problem-solving play. A block center, with other props like small cars, trucks, buildings, and little people can promote other dialogue and problem-solving play. A storytime center, with a rocking chair, many books, stuffed animals and dolls, can provide another setting for role playing and dialogue. Additionally, teachers could provide opportunities for children to dramatize stories they have heard, read, or written. Teachers need to understand the importance of these make-believe and role-playing opportunities for their young children's literacy development.

## Cooperative Learning

Cooperative learning and other group discussion and work enhances children's language development, problem-solving abilities, and literacy development. For example, writing groups and story-sharing groups are excellent opportunities for children to share their ideas and get help from each other. Group planning, group problem solving, and group sharing are all part of cooperative and peer-group learning.

## Cross-Age Tutoring

Cross-age tutoring, or grouping, involves older youngsters helping younger children. As we know from the reviewed emergent literacy and constructivist research, children become literate by being involved with literate older, more knowledgeable "others," like their parents, grandparents, or older siblings. Therefore, arranging for your early childhood youngsters to work on various literacy-related projects with older students makes excellent sense. Many very successful cross-age tutoring and learning programs have been described in the literature. For instance, Marden, Richard, and Flippo (1991) reported positive learning results when fifth-grade youngsters mentored kindergarten children; Samway, Whang, and Pippitt (1995) described their successful multiethnic, multilingual program involving fifth- and sixth-grade youngsters and first- and second-grade learners; and Morrice and Simmons (1991) described the advantages of a whole language cross-age program. Both tutors and tutees benefit. Teachers of young children are encouraged to develop these positive shared learning literacy opportunities with teachers of older children.

## Literary Immersion

Literary immersion involves immersing children in literature and print in your classroom. Remember Cambourne's (1988) "conditions for learning," described earlier in this chapter? Cambourne indicated that these conditions would provide a foundation for the learning of literacy skills in the classroom. Children learn about reading and writing by reading and writing. Children learn about what readers and writers do by being readers and writers. By immersing children in certain literature, children become familiar with reading and writing that particular literature.

Brown and Cambourne (1987) have fully described how they use reading, retelling, and writing activities to immerse children in various types of literature. For several weeks at a time children read, discuss, share, and write, discuss, and share selected genre. Through this immersion in literature children learn about the specific genre, as well as learn what readers and writers must do. Also see Flippo (1997) for a detailed step-by-step outline of how teachers can implement literary immersion in their classrooms.

## Children's Literature and Resources for the Teacher of Young Children

Although many citations have been given throughout this chapter, we want to emphasize that excellent children's literature and other resources for classroom teachers are constantly being published. Teachers of young children will want to watch for and review the many delightful children's books that come available each year. We have also listed some resources that we think will help you locate good children's literature and other valuable resources for your school and classroom literacy development program. Additionally, the International Reading Association (IRA) and the Children's Book Council (CBC) should be consulted for their yearly updated list of children's favorite books.

*Beyond Storybooks: Young Children and the Shared Book Experience* (1993) by Judith Pollard Slaughter.
*Book Talk and Beyond: Children and Teachers Respond to Literature* (1995) edited by Nancy L. Roser and Miriam G. Martinez.
*Fostering the Love of Reading* (1994) edited by Eugene H. Cramer and Marrietta Castle.
*Invitation to Read: More Children's Literature in the Reading Program* (1992) edited by Bernice E. Cullinan.
*More Kids' Favorite Books* (1995) compiled by the IRA and CBC.
*Research and Professional Resources in Children's Literature* (1995) edited by Kathy G. Short.
*Resources in Early Literacy Development: An Annotated Bibliography* (1992) compiled and edited by Lesley Mandel Morrow, Susan P. Burks, and Muriel K. Rand.
*Teachers' Favorite Books for Kids* (1994) compiled by the IRA.
*Teaching Multicultural Literature in Grades K–8* (1993) edited by Violet J. Harris.

 **Reflection Activity 3.7**

*T*hese last sections of the chapter have summarized the emergent literacy research, offered implications for teachers based on this research, and suggested teaching strategies and ideas to enhance the continuation of emerging literacy development in your classroom. How do these "fit in" with the ideas you noted in your journal entry in Reflection Activity 3.6? Now, in your journal, under the heading Reflection Activity 3.7, add any additional ideas and organization and teaching strategies you will want to use in your classroom to implement a reading and writing development program consistent with the emergent literacy research.

# Summary

In this chapter we explored the development of literacy and the importance of young children's early experiences with literacy. This development of literacy has come to be known as emergent literacy, which includes the development of print awareness; oral and written language; familiarity with stories, story structure, and storybook reading; and appreciation for writing and reading. We have also seen how children's social and cognitive development and learning are part of their emerging literacy. The social context of reading and writing were explored, as well as various cognitive learnings related to culture, and development of reasoning, vocabulary, and schemata.

We discussed the importance of the parents' and families' roles in literacy development. We have also seen how the teacher's role and the child's involvement are both important to continued literacy development in school. Additionally, we summarized the emergent literacy and constructivist research, pointed out the implications for teachers, and suggested certain teaching strategies and ideas that seem consistent with the research. These teaching strategies and ideas include use of Big Books; use of predictable books; modeling and scaffolding; make-believe, pretend play, and role playing; cooperative learning; cross-age tutoring; and literary immersion. Finally, we suggested some sources for children's literature and other resources for teachers of young children.

# Closing Activities

1. How would you describe "emergent literacy"? How is it different from the more traditional idea of "reading readiness"? Be prepared to share your answers in a small-group discussion.
2. How does home and community environment contribute to children's interest in reading? What implications does this have for parenting and families?
3. How can the school environment contribute to children's interest in reading? What implications does this have for teachers and schools?
4. What are some strategies that teachers can use to involve parents and family members in their student's literacy development? Be prepared to share these in a small-group discussion.
5. What is print awareness? How does it relate to literacy development?
6. Find an article written in one of the more recent issues of a professional journal (e.g., *The Reading Teacher, Reading Horizons, The Elementary Teacher*) that provides suggestions for working with parents and families. Read the article and then summarize the suggestions.
7. Find an article written in one of the more recent issues of a professional journal that provides ideas for enhancing the affective, cognitive, or linguistic strategies of young children. Read the article and then summarize the suggestions.
8. As part of your field activities for this course, observe for one hour in a kindergarten or first-grade classroom. (You may observe during any type or subject area of instruction.) Then do the following: (a) Describe the teaching/learning situation you observed; (b) describe any teaching strategies you observed the teacher implement; (c) describe the effect of those strategies on the children; (d) ask the teacher why she/he felt that those strategies were particularly relevant to those particular children; and (e) describe, in your opinion, how effective these strategies were for the continued development of the children's emerging literacy.

### References

Adams, M. J. (1990). *Beginning to Read: Thinking and Learning about Print.* Cambridge, MA: The Massachusetts Institute of Technology Press.

Anderson, R. C., and P. D. Pearson. (1984). "A Schema-Theoretic View of Basic Processes in Reading Comprehension." In P. D. Pearson, ed., *Handbook of Reading Research* (pp. 255–292). New York: Longman.

Anderson, F. (1990). *A Guide to Your Child's Language Development.* Fitchburg, MA: Fitchburg State College, Parent Education Outreach Publications.

Applebee, A. N., and J. A. Langer. (1983). "Instructional Scaffolding: Reading and Writing and Natural Language Activities." *Language Arts* 60: 168-175.

Au, K. H. (1993). *Literacy Instruction in Multicultural Settings.* Ft. Worth, TX: Harcourt Brace College Publishers.

Baker, L., and A. L. Brown (1984). "Cognitive Monitoring in Reading." In J. Flood, ed., *Understanding Reading Comprehension* (pp. 21-44). Newark, DE: International Reading Association.

Banks, J. A. (1994). *An Introduction to Multicultural Education.* Boston: Allyn & Bacon.

Beck, I. L., M. McKeown, and R. Omanson. (1987). "The Effects and Uses of Diverse Vocabulary Instructional Techniques." In M. McKeown and M. Curtis, eds., *The Nature of Vocabulary Acquisition* (pp. 147-163). Hillsdale, NJ: Erlbaum.

Berk, L. E. (1992). "Children's Private Speech: An Overview of Theory and the Status of Research." In R. M. Diaz and L. E. Berk, eds., *Private Speech: From Social Interaction to Self-Regulation* (pp. 17-53). Hillsdale, NJ: Erlbaum

———. (1994). "Vygotsky's Theory: The Importance of Make-Believe Play." *Young Children* 50(1): 30-39.

Bridge, C. A. (1979). "Predictable Materials for Beginning Readers." *Language Arts* 56(5): 503-507.

Brown H., and B. Cambourne. (1987). *Read and Retell.* Portsmouth, NH: Heinemann.

Bruneau, B., T. Rasinski, and J. Shehan. (1995). "Parent Communication in a Whole Language Kindergarten: What We Learned from a Busy First Year." In J. E. DeCarlo, ed., *Perspectives in Whole Language* (pp. 351-357). Boston: Allyn & Bacon.

Bruner, J. (1983). *Child Talk: Learning to Use Language.* New York: Holt, Rinehart, & Winston.

Cambourne, B. (1988). *The Whole Story: Natural Learning and the Acquisition of Literacy in the Classroom.* Auckland, NZ: Ashton Scholastic.

Carey, S. (1978). "The Child as Word Learner." In M. Halle, J. Bresnan, and G. A. Miller, eds., *Linguistic Theory and Psychological Reality* (pp. 264-293). Cambridge, MA: MIT Press.

Carle, E. (1981). *The Very Hungry Caterpillar.* New York: Putnam.

Cazden, C. B. (1980). "Peekaboo as an Instructional Model: Discourse Development at Home and at School." *Papers and Reports of Child Language Development* 17:1-29.

———. (1983). "Adult Assistance to Language Development: Scaffolds, Models, and Direct Instruction." In R. P. Parker and F. A. Davis, eds., *Developing Literacy: Young Children's Use of Language* (pp. 3-18). Newark, DE: International Reading Association.

Chall, J. S. (1967). *Learning to Read: The Great Debate.* New York: McGraw-Hill.

Chapman, D. L. (1986). "Let's Read Another One." In D. R. Tovey and J. E. Kerber, eds., *Roles in Literacy Learning: A New Perspective* (pp. 10-25). Newark, DE: International Reading Association.

Clay, M. M. (1991). *Becoming Literate: The Construction of Inner Control.* Portsmouth, NH: Heinemann.

———. (1993). *An Observation Survey of Early Literacy Achievement.* Portsmouth, NH: Heinemann.

Colbert, R. P. (1991). *How to Pick a Special Day Care Center.* Fitchburg, MA: Fitchburg State College, Parent Education Outreach Publications.

Cramer, E. H. (1994). "Connecting in the Classroom: Ideas from Teachers." In E. H. Cramer and M. Castle, eds., *Fostering the Love of Reading: The Affective Domain in Reading Education* (pp. 125-141). Newark, DE: International Reading Association.

Cramer, E. H., and M. Castle, eds. (1994). *Fostering the Love of Reading: The Affective Domain in Reading Education.* Newark, DE: International Reading Association.

Cullinan, B. C., ed. (1992). *Invitation to Read: More Children's Literature in the Reading Program.* Newark, DE: International Reading Association.

Durkin, D. (1966). *Children Who Read Early: Two Longitudinal Studies.* New York: Teachers College Press.

Dwyer, E. J., and E. E. Dwyer. (1994). "How Teacher Attitudes Influence Reading Achievement." In E. H. Cramer and M. Castle, eds., *Fostering the Love of Reading: The Affective Domain in Reading Education* (pp. 66–73). Newark, DE: International Reading Association.

Escamilla, K., A. M. Andrade, A. G. M. Basurto, and O. A. Ruiz, with M. M. Clay. (1996). *Instrumento de Observación: De los Logros de la Lecto-Escritura Inicial.* Portsmouth, NH: Heinemann.

Ferreiro, E. (1986). "The Interplay between Information and Assimilation in Beginning Literacy." In W. Teale and E. Sulzby, eds., *Emergent Literacy: Writing and Reading* (pp. 15–49). Norwood, NJ: Ablex.

Fields, M. V. (1995). "Talking and Writing: Explaining the Whole Language Approach to Parents." In J. E. DeCarlo, ed., *Perspectives in Whole Language* (pp. 351–357). Boston: Allyn & Bacon.

Flesch, R. (1981). *Why Johnny Still Can't Read.* New York: Harper & Row.

Flippo, R. F. (1982). *How to Help Grow a Reader.* Atlanta: Metro Atlanta/Georgia State University Chapter of Phi Delta Kappa. (Reprinted by Fitchburg State College, Parent Education Outreach Publications, Fitchburg, MA.)

———. (1997). *Reading Assessment and Instruction: A Qualitative Approach to Diagnosis.* Ft. Worth, TX: Harcourt Brace College Publishers.

Flippo, R. F., and H. Branch. (1985). "A Program to Help Prepare Pre-Schoolers for Reading." *Reading Horizons* 25(2): 120–122.

Flippo, R. F., C. Hetzel, D. Gribouski, and L. A. Armstrong. (in press). "Literacy, Multicultural, and Socio-Cultural Considerations: Student Literacy Corps and the Community." *Phi Delta Kappan.*

Flippo, R. F., and J. A. Smith. (1990). "Encouraging Parent Involvement through Home Letters." *The Reading Teacher* 44(4): 359.

Forester, A. D. (1986). "Apprenticeship in the Art of Literacy." In D. R. Tovey and J. E. Kerber, eds., *Roles in Literary Learning: A New Perspective* (pp. 66–72). Newark, DE: International Reading Association.

Fredericks, A. D., and T. V. Rasinski. (1990). "Whole Language and Parents: National Partners." *The Reading Teacher* 43(9): 692–694.

Fredericks, A. D., and D. Taylor. (1985). *Parent Programs in Reading: Guidelines for Success.* Newark, DE: International Reading Association.

Galda, L., B. E. Cullinan, and D. Strickland. (1993). *Language, Literacy, and the Child.* Ft. Worth, TX: Harcourt Brace College Publishers.

Gerecke, L. (1990). *How to Use Wordless Picture Books with Your Child.* Fitchburg, MA; Fitchburg State College, Parent Education Outreach Publications.

Goodman, Y. M., ed. (1990). *How Children Construct Literacy: Piagetian Perspectives.* Newark, DE: International Reading Association.

Greaney, V. (1986). "Parental Influences on Reading." *The Reading Teacher* 39(8): 813–818.

Guthrie, J. T. (1994). "Creating Interest in Reading." *Reading Today* 12(1): 24.

Harris, V. J., ed. (1993). *Teaching Multicultural Literature in Grades K–8.* Norwood, MA: Christopher-Gordon Publishers.

Harste, J. C., V. A. Woodward, and C. Burke. (1984). *Language Stories and Literacy Lessons.* Portsmouth, NH: Heinemann.

Heath, S. B. (1983). *Ways with Words.* Cambridge, MA: Cambridge University Press.

Hetzel, C. W. (1991). *How to Be an Active Part of Your Child's School Reading Program.* Fitchburg, MA: Fitchburg State College, Parent Education Outreach Publications.

Holdaway, D. (1979). *The Foundations of Literacy.* Sydney, Australia: Ashton Scholastic.

———. (1986). "Guiding a Natural Process." In D. R. Tovey and J. E. Kerber, eds., *Roles in Literacy Learning: A New Perspective* (pp. 42–51). Newark, DE: International Reading Association.

International Reading Association. (1994). *Teachers' Favorite Books for Kids.* Newark, DE: International Reading Association.

International Reading Association and the Children's Book Council. (1995). *More Kids' Favorite Books.* Newark, DE: International Reading Association.

International Reading Association Family Literacy Commission. (1994). *Family Literacy: New Perspectives, New Opportunities.* Newark, DE: International Reading Association.

Marden, M. R., M. Richard, and R. F. Flippo. (1991). "Fifth Grade/Kindergarten Mentor Program: Beginnings." *New England Reading Association Journal* 27(2): 2-4.

Martinez, M., and N. Roser. (1985). "Read It Again: The Value of Repeated Readings during Storytime." *The Reading Teacher* 38(8): 782-786.

May, F. B. (1994). *Reading and Communication,* 4th ed. New York: Macmillan.

McGee, L. M., and D. J. Richgels. (1996). *Literacy's Beginnings: Supporting Young Readers and Writers,* 2nd ed. Boston: Allyn & Bacon.

McInees, J. (1986). "Children's Quest for Literacy." In D. R. Tovey and J. E. Kerber, eds., *Roles in Literacy Learning: A New Perspective* (pp. 73-76). Newark, DE: International Reading Association.

Michel, P. A. (1994). *The Child's View of Reading: Understandings for Teachers and Parents.* Boston: Allyn & Bacon.

Moe, A. J. (1989). "Using Picture Books for Reading Vocabulary Development." In J. W. Stewig and S. L. Sebesta, eds., *Using Literature in the Elementary Classroom* (pp. 23-34). Urbana, IL: National Council of Teachers of English.

Morrice, C., and M. Simmons. (1991). "Beyond Reading Buddies: A Whole Language Crossage Program." *The Reading Teacher* 44(8): 572-577.

Morrow, L. M. (1994). "Family Literacy: An Overview for the Year of the Family." *Reading Today* 12(2): 12.

———. ed. (1995). *Family Literacy Connections in Schools and Communities.* Newark, DE: International Reading Association.

Morrow, L. M., S. P. Burks, and M. K. Rand, eds. (1992). *Resources in Early Literacy Development: An Annotated Bibliography.* Newark, DE: International Reading Association.

Morrow, L. M., J. R. Paratore, D. Gaber, C. Harrison, and D. Tracey. (1993). "Family Literacy: Perspective and Practices." *The Reading Teacher* 47(3): 194-200.

Piaget, J. (1955). *The Language and Thought of the Child.* New York: Meridian.

———. (1969). *The Psychology of Intelligence.* Paterson, NJ: Littlefield, Adams.

Roser, N. L., and M. G. Martinez, eds. (1995). *Book Talk and Beyond: Children and Teachers Respond to Literature.* Newark, DE: International Reading Association.

Rowe, D. W., and J. C. Harste. (1986). "Metalinguistic Awareness in Writing and Reading: The Young Child as Curricular Informant." In D. Yaden Jr. and S. Templeton, eds., *Metalinguistic Awareness and Beginning Literacy* (pp. 235-236). Portsmouth, NH: Heinemann.

Rumelhart, D. E. (1976). *Toward an Interactive Model of Reading* (Technical Report No. 56). San Diego, CA: Center for Human Information Processing.

Samway, K. D., G. Whang, and M. Pippitt. (1995). *Buddy Reading: Cross-Age Tutoring in a Multicultural School.* Portsmouth, NH: Heinemann.

Shockley, B., B. Michalove, and J. Allen. (1995). *Engaging Families: Connecting Home and School Literacy Communities.* Portsmouth, NH: Heinemann.

Short, K. G., ed. (1995). *Research and Professional Resources in Children's Literature: Piecing a Patchwork Quilt.* Newark, DE: International Reading Association.

Slaughter, J. P. (1993). *Beyond Storybooks: Young Children and the Shared Book Experience.* Newark, DE: International Reading Association.

Smith, F. (1994). *Understanding Reading: A Psycholinguistic Analysis of Reading and Learning to Read,* 5th ed. Hillsdale, NJ: Erlbaum.

Spiegel, D. L. (1994). "A Portrait of Parents of Successful Readers." In E. H. Cramer and M. Castle, eds., *Fostering the Love of Reading: The Affective Domain in Reading Education* (pp. 74–87). Newark, DE: International Reading Association.

Stanovich, K. (1986). "Matthew Effects in Reading: Some Consequences of Individual Differences in the Acquisition of Literacy." *Reading Research Quarterly* 21:360–406.

Strickland, D., and L. Morrow, eds. (1989). *Emerging Literacy: Young Children Learn to Read and Write*. Newark, DE: International Reading Association.

Sulzby, E. (1985). "Children's Emergent Reading of Favorite Storybooks: A Developmental Study." *Reading Research Quarterly* 20(4): 458–481.

———. (1991). "Assessment of Emergent Literacy: Storybook Reading." *The Reading Teacher,* 44(7): 498–500.

Sulzby, E., and J. Barnhart. (1992). "The Development of Academic Competence: All Our Children Emerge as Writers and Readers." In J. W. Irwin and M. A. Doyle, eds., *Reading/Writing Connections: Learning from Research* (pp. 120–144). Newark, DE: International Reading Association.

Taylor, D., and D. S. Strickland. (1986). *Family Storybook Reading*. Portsmouth, NH: Heinemann.

Teale, W. H. (1986). "Home Background and Young Children's Literacy Development." In W. H. Teale and E. Sulzby, eds., *Emergent Literacy: Writing and Reading* (pp. 173–206). Norwood, NJ: Ablex.

———. (1987). "Emergent Literacy: Reading and Writing Development in Early Childhood." In J. Readence and S. Baldwin, eds., *Research in Literacy: Merging Perspectives* (pp. 45–74). Rochester, NY: National Reading Conference.

Teale, W. H., and E. Sulzby (1986). *Emergent Literacy: Writing and Reading*. Norwood, NJ: Ablex.

———. (1989). "Emerging Literacy: New Perspectives." In D. S. Strickland and L. M. Morrow, eds., *Emerging Literacy: Young Children Learn to Read and Write* (pp. 1–15). Newark, DE: International Reading Association.

Templeton, S. (1986). "Literacy, Readiness, and Basals." *The Reading Teacher* 39(5): 403–409.

Tompkins, G. E., and K. Hoskisson. (1995). *Language Arts: Content and Teaching Strategies,* 3rd ed. Englewood Cliffs, NJ: Prentice-Hall.

U.S. Department of Education. (1994). *Strong Families, Strong Schools.* Washington, DC: U.S. Department of Education.

Vukelich, C. (1984). "Parents Role in the Reading Process: A Review of Practical Suggestions and Ways to Communicate with Parents." *The Reading Teacher* 37(6): 472–477.

Vygotsky, L. S. (1978). *Mind in Society: The Development of Higher Psychological Processes.* M. Cole, V. John-Steiner, S. Scribner, and E. Souberman, eds. Cambridge, MA: Harvard University Press.

———. (1986). *Thought and Language.* Cambridge, MA: MIT Press.

———. (1987). "Thinking and Speech." In R. Rieber and A. S. Carton, eds. *The Collected Works of L. S. Vygotsky: Vol. I. Problems of General Psychology* (pp. 37–285). New York: Plenum.

Weaver, C. (1994). *Reading Process and Practice: From Socio-Psycholinguistics to Whole Language,* 2nd ed. Portsmouth, NH: Heinemann.

Zide, M. M., and B. E. Shaw. (1990). *Growing More Social, Day by Day: A Parents' Handbook.* Fitchburg, MA: Fitchburg State College, Parent Education Outreach Publications.

# Section II

## *Developing Literacy Skills and Strategies*

$S$ ection II, "Developing Literacy Skills and Strategies," consists of five chapters that review and present various areas of literacy that teachers are responsible for developing and teaching. These areas include the word-identification skills and strategies that students must rely on and be able to use when they encounter unknown words in text, and vocabulary development strategies that teachers can use to help their students to continue to develop their reading vocabularies throughout their schools years.

Comprehension skills and strategies are given special attention. First the comprehension process is discussed, along with different factors that influence comprehension. Then readers are asked to consider the many aspects of comprehension, focusing on comprehension skills, schema theory, and prior knowledge research, metacognitive strategies, language-processing factors, text factors, story structure, and different textual demands.

Strategies for studying and learning from text, developed especially to meet the classroom teachers' needs, are highlighted. The focus is on helping elementary students "know how to learn." Mrs. Argueta, a fourth grade teacher is introduced, and her study-learning assignment for students is used to show classroom teachers how to apply the latest ideas on study-learning to their elementary curricula. Many examples, activities, and figures are provided to illustrate the instructional ideas and techniques for elementary teachers from the early elementary through the intermediate and upper elementary grades. Content-reading skills, strategies, and other considerations are explored and a content-reading approach is suggested.

Finally, the relationship between reading and writing is explained as interrelated and recursive. Teachers are presented with information on invented spelling and other approximations of written literacy, process writing stages, using children's literature to model and stimulate writing, and use of journal writing in the classroom. Additionally, we present teaching strategies and processes to enhance students' reading and writing development, as well as samples of children's invented spellings.

A new feature introduced in this part is a section in each chapter entitled "Computer Hardware and Software Considerations." Because of the advances in technology, we feel it is particularly important for classroom teachers to be made aware of the newest available teaching and learning programs.

# Word Identification and Vocabulary Development

© Jim Whitmer

*Overview*

$T$ his chapter overviews general and specific concepts relative to developing and expanding elementary students' vocabulary and word-identification abilities. Vocabulary and word identification are described and their importance to students' reading comprehension is discussed. Factors that affect vocabulary development and word-identification strategy learning and guidelines that can be used to plan and conduct vocabulary lessons are delineated and described. Five vocabulary strategies elementary teachers can adopt or adapt to introduce or teach vocabulary are identified and their instructional steps delineated and discussed. Defined also are four word-identification skills/ strategies—using sight-words, contextual analysis, structural analysis, and graphophonic analysis—that students can apply to identify unknown words. Examples of using these skills/strategies are provided, theories and principles underlying their use are discussed, and instructional considerations are presented. It should be noted that information regarding these word-analysis skills/ strategies is presented based on the belief that efforts in word-analysis instruction are only beneficial if they promote comprehension. The chapter ends with a discussion of computer hardware and software concepts related to literacy learning and vocabulary and word-identification development and expansion.

## Main Ideas

- Students enter school with an oral and listening vocabulary that is fairly large and can be used to develop and expand their reading vocabularies and word-identification abilities.
- Vocabulary instruction and various word-identification skills and strategies assist students in developing general, specialized, and technical reading vocabularies.
- Students' experiential, cognitive, linguistic, and sociocultural backgrounds affect their vocabulary development and learning of word-identification skills/strategies.
- Elementary teachers should use research-based guidelines to design and conduct vocabulary-literacy events or instructional strategies.
- Elementary teachers can adopt or adapt numerous strategies to introduce or teach target vocabulary.
- Sight words are words students recognize "on sight" without needing to carefully inspect the words. Sight words can be taught or developed in several ways.
- Contextual analysis is the word-identification strategy in which students use the sentence(s) and surrounding words to figure-out and

comprehend unknown words. A variety of instructional activities can be used to develop this strategy.

- Structural analysis is the word-identification strategy involving students recognition of word elements such as root words, affixes, compound words, syllables, and accents to identify unknown words. These skills can be taught using a variety of instructional procedures.
- Graphophonic analyses are word-identification strategies that involve students learning and applying relationships between graphemes (letters), phonemes (sounds), and words. These word-identification strategies can be taught in many different ways.
- Students should be encouraged to use all their available strategies to identify unknown words.
- Elementary teachers can use computer hardware and software to develop students' vocabulary and various word-identification strategies.

When students enter school, they begin with an oral and listening vocabulary that has been influenced by numerous factors, including their linguistic, cognitive, experiential, and sociocultural backgrounds. Although some children already recognize many words "on sight," their oral and listening vocabularies far exceed their reading vocabulary, and the richness of their language depends on the factors previously mentioned. Thus, you can use students' existing language as a foundation for helping them develop their reading vocabularies and word-identification skills/strategies to recognize printed words. One of your ultimate objectives as a teacher should be to promote students' development of reading vocabularies that parallel as closely as possible their oral and listening vocabularies. Additionally you will want to use authentic and functional events to assist your students in extending their existing oral and listening vocabularies to serve as a foundation for the continued development of vocabulary, word identification, and other literacy abilities.

## *The Vocabulary and Word-Identification Process*

The act of reading is a complex process affected by many factors and the interaction of these factors (e.g., the reader's prior knowledge and language facility or the qualities of the printed text). With respect to the focus of this chapter, Heilman, Blair, and Rupley (1994) reported that two significant variables that contribute to reading success are the students' reading vocabulary and their abilities to apply word-identification strategies. Although reading educators have always been concerned with how students learn words and develop their vocabulary (Manzo and Manzo 1991), Collins and Cheek (1993) have noted that the concept of "reading vocabulary" has now become a major concern for reading researchers and writers. However, reading educators also have been and will continue to be concerned with the word-identification strategies that students can be taught to identify unknown words. This section introduces you to important concepts and ideas related to word knowledge, reading vocabulary, and word-identification strategies.

## *Word Knowledge*

Numerous researchers have provided us with basic and unique insight into the concepts of "words" and "word knowledge." Savage (1994) reported that students' word knowledge is paramount in the literacy process and is related to experiences, represents conceptual developmental levels, and is essential for their reading competency—particularly comprehension. According to Savage (1994):

> Words are the currency of communication, the main medium in the exchange of ideas through language. Words are essential to any spoken or written language experience. For this reason, vocabulary development is an essential part of language arts in the elementary schools. . . . As part of literacy development in the classroom, three aspects of vocabulary study/development are typically addressed . . . [e.g., word knowledge (students' receptive and expressive vocabularies), word recognition (students' abilities to know a word and its meaning), and word analysis (students' abilities to figure out the pronunciation and/or meaning of unknown words encountered in context)]. (p. 137)

One of your primary teaching-learning objectives will be the development of your students' receptive and expressive word knowledge. To ensure that this word knowledge is not learned in isolation you will want to have your students engage in authentic and functional language experiences. Then, and as noted by Alvermann and Phelps (1994), you could design and conduct literacy events that assist your students in labeling and applying learned words ". . . to existing schemata, build on existing schemata, and develop entirely new schemata" (p. 239).

## *Reading Vocabulary*

The concept of "reading vocabulary" is quite simple in theory but involves multidimensional aspects. May (1994) stated:

> Reading vocabulary . . . incorporates one's sight vocabulary. All of one's reading vocabulary, by its very nature, requires the ability to quickly pronounce a word out loud or decode it silently. All of one's reading vocabulary requires the ability to quickly determine a word's meaning in the context of the author's message. (p. 154)

In essence, students' reading vocabulary is the printed words they are able to identify and give meaning to upon sight. This vocabulary can be developed by using research-based guidelines to plan and conduct lessons that introduce or teach vocabulary, by adopting or adapting effective vocabulary strategies, and by applying appropriate word-identification skills and strategies—all of which will be presented in upcoming sections.

Finally, Brozo and Simpson (1995) reported that "[r]esearch studies suggest that vocabulary is best taught from a unifying context" (p. 157). As with word knowledge, it is important that vocabulary activities help students to apply new labels to their existing schemata, to build on existing schemata, and to develop new schemata (Alvermann and Phelps 1994).

# Word Identification

Oral language is of particular importance in developing a foundation for word-identification strategies and reading vocabularies. As we have already noted, students enter school with many language skills and strategies already developed. You should be aware of these strategies and use them to their best advantage to assist your students in learning to read. One of your concerns is to help your students make the connection between their existing spoken language and printed language. According to Harris and Smith (1986), numerous factors will affect your students as they make this connection. Three specific language processes or "cue systems" form the basis of word identification.

1. Graphophonic cues involve the relationship between symbols and sounds. The recognition of letters and words (grapho) and the sounds they represent (phonic) enables the reader to interpret the letters, when seen, as sounds, and to recognize words.
2. Syntactic cues involve the patterns or structure into which words are arranged to form phrases, clauses, and sentences. The ability to use syntax (i.e., the order of words or structure of words in sentences) and grammar (i.e., word functions and relationships) enables the reader to make use of the location of nouns, verbs, adjectives, and so on. The ability to use these cues effectively allows a reader to predict what an unknown word might be by its location in the sentence.
3. Semantic cues involve gaining the meaning of individual words and combinations of words from the sentences or the paragraph these words are in. Understanding the meaning expressed by adjacent words and sentences enables the reader to often predict the meaning of words that are unknown.

Although many beginning readers can "naturally" recognize syntactic and semantic cues and can use them to some extent, they cannot rely entirely on context to understand the written passage. They must be taught how to use other ways of identifying the printed word within its context. To achieve this objective, students will have to learn how to decode unknown words through the development of a cadre of word-identification skills and strategies. The effective teaching of word-identification strategies is essential to the development of good readers. These strategies can be developed in a variety of ways, but there are two notes of caution before we proceed.

First, instruction in the word-identification strategies of using sight words, contextual and structural analysis, and graphophonic analysis is just one step in the instructional-reading process. Although some skills in these areas are essential for your students to read, we do not want you to feel that by teaching these skills and strategies you have taught everything necessary for reading. Rupley and Blair (1983) used the term "facilitative" skills and instruction to describe abilities and teaching techniques in areas that have an impact on the actual reading process but are not, in and of themselves, reading. Many of the word-identification skills discussed in this chapter are facilitative (i.e., they facilitate the reading process, but they are not actually "reading"). Skills that are "actually reading," like overall comprehension, the ability to see cause-and-effect relationships, the ability to synthesize information, and other actual reading skills, have been labeled "functional skills" (cf. Rupley and Blair 1983). These functional skills are what reading is all about, and so we must caution you to not lose sight of differences between facilitative and functional skill instruction. You will teach word-identification skills and strategies as necessary, to help your students develop their functional reading abilities. However, you must also remember that teachers who spend too much time on facilitative skills, like those who spend too much time on word-identification skills, often deemphasize the teaching of essential functional reading.

Second, because instruction in word-identification skills is intended to facilitate the functional reading process, you should select and focus on those word-identification skills and strategies that your students need to read with comprehension. For example, if students can read and understand text, yet are weak in some of their phonics skills, we do not believe that you should focus their instruction on phonics. Phonics is a tool that your students use in word identification to help pronounce an unknown word in print. If your students can encounter and comprehend words in print with their present abilities, then additional phonics instruction is not necessary. The same would hold true of the other word-identification skills.

Conversely, if your students cannot comprehend what they read and have limited phonics skills or lack other word-identification skills and strategies, then instruction in appropriate word-identification skills and strategies is necessary. You will have to use your professional judgment and understanding of what is really important in reading to teach your students word-identification skills that will have a significant impact on their reading comprehension. Your role as a classroom teacher should be to facilitate reading in your classroom and use appropriate instruction to do so. We define "appropriate instruction" as instruction that "fits" the needs of a student and is relevant to your objectives or goals in the classroom.

## Reflection Activity 4.1

*C*an you think of skills that you would classify as "facilitative" for reading instruction but that are not really reading in and of themselves? We have already suggested the word-identification skill of phonics as one facilitative skill. What others can you come up with? In your reflection journal under the heading Reflection Activity 4.1, Part A, list as many skills as you can that you would call facilitative. Next, in Part B, list as many "functional" skills as you can. We already suggested that overall comprehension, cause-and-effect relationships, and synthesizing information are functional, or real reading skills. Can you think of others?

The development of an effective sight vocabulary is an important part of word-identification development. When developing your students' sight vocabulary, pay particular attention to those words that they will most frequently encounter in their reading. Young readers usually start with a relatively limited sight vocabulary, but many often do bring to the reading setting the ability to read quite a few words at sight. It is not necessary for them to have to apply other identification techniques to recognize these words, because these words are part of their memory. Sight words, then, are words that students know "on sight," or by memory. They are words that students instantly recognize without any need for assistance. Many schema-related words can be added to this existing sight vocabulary as new concepts are taught in school. Additionally, you will find that some words can be taught best as sight words because they cannot be easily identified by other word-identification strategies. It is important for readers of all ages to continuously expand their sight-word vocabulary. The recognition of sight words is a part of the graphophonic cue system we introduced earlier. "Grapho-" referred to the recognition of letters and words.

The second word-identification strategy that students can be taught to use is contextual analysis. Contextual analysis involves using the meaning of a known surrounding word, phrase, sentence, or passage, or the grammar or structure of the sentence, to identify and get meaning from an unfamiliar word. Contextual analysis is often heavily used by readers to compensate for the lack of an established sight vocabulary. Contextual analysis is a part of the semantic and syntactic cue systems. When students use the meaning of other words as clues, they are utilizing their semantic system. When they use the sentence structure or grammar of surrounding words in context, they are utilizing their syntactic system.

Another word-identification strategy that students can be taught to use is structural analysis. This strategy enables the reader to examine word parts or structural parts, such as affixes (prefixes and suffixes), root words, contractions, and compound words, to determine a word's appropriate pronunciation and meaning. Structural analysis involves both the grapho (sight) and phonic (sound) aspects of the graphophonic cue system. The ability to use syllabication principles is also a structural-analysis procedure.

The fourth word-identification strategy that students learn to use to pronounce and recognize words involves graphophonic skills: learning to associate phonemes (sounds) with graphemes (symbols). Phonics instruction is part of this strategy development. Unfortunately, some teach students to rely too heavily on phonics as a word-identification technique. One of the problems of relying only on phonics is that even if you are successful at pronouncing a word, you may still not know the meaning of the word. Therefore, it is best to teach your students that phonics is not the only way to decode unknown words. Instead, you teach them to use phonics as only one of several word-identification tools.

Finally, Alvermann and Phelps (1994) stated that you " . . . should . . . emphasize strategies that readers can use to tackle unfamiliar words in other contexts" (p. 253). We have introduced here four word-identification strategies

Word identification development should fit the needs of students.

© James L. Shaffer

that students can apply to pronounce and/or determine the meaning of unknown words encountered in context. Additional information about these strategies—using sight words, contextual analysis, structural analysis, and graphophonic analysis—is also presented later in this chapter. Again, we must state that most word-analysis skills are "facilitative" and should be focused on and are beneficial if they promote your students' reading comprehension.

## Factors Affecting Vocabulary and Word-Identification Development

To more fully understand the importance of the role that vocabulary and word identification occupy in the reading process, you should be aware of and consider numerous factors as you develop these literacy areas. The primary factors that significantly affect your students' ability to develop effective vocabulary and word-identification strategies include your students' experiential, cognitive, linguistic, and sociocultural backgrounds. Other important factors you should be cognizant of include the particular characteristics of the English language, and your students' maturation and learning styles (Collins and Cheek 1993).

The development of the English language was influenced by many languages and dialects. As would be expected when varied language principles are integrated, our language has irregularities in elements such as grammar, spelling, and pronunciation. This language-integration problem becomes evident, and even more pronounced in the schools, when we try to teach students to read primarily with a code-emphasis approach such as synthetic phonics. (Synthetic phonics refers to a part-to-whole approach in which the student is taught the sounds represented by letters in isolation from real words.) Many words that have been added to our language do not follow acceptable phonic patterns and spelling principles.

Maturation is another factor that plays an important role in the reading vocabulary and word-identification process. Some students may not have well-developed auditory- and visual-discrimination skills when entering school. As a result, these students at first experience difficulty in learning and using reading vocabulary and word-identification strategies. Their lack of maturation can also adversely affect their speech and language development, which is essential in the reading process. For instance, poorly developed speech and language abilities, particularly the inability to understand or pronounce certain sounds and the inability to aurally (by hearing) distinguish differences between particular sounds, make learning phonics difficult.

The learning styles of your students are also important considerations in the reading vocabulary and word-identification process. Some students learn effectively in large group settings while others function better in small groups. Some students need a structured, teacher-directed classroom environment, whereas others learn more effectively in a student-centered setting. There are students who are able to use all of their sensory and perceptual abilities during word-identification procedures, whereas others may experience perceptual problems due to sensory or other disabilities or special needs that adversely affect their reading development. Such varied learning styles and sensory and perceptual factors may require you to select alternative word-identification instruction methods for some of your students. For example, a student with a hearing impairment and poorly developed auditory skills may experience more success if you use visual and kinesthetic teaching procedures. Also, those students who appear to profit from more self-directed experiences should be allowed many choices and opportunities for independent reading as part of their reading instruction.

In sum, the development of students' reading vocabulary and word-identification skills/strategies is a complex process that is affected by many factors. These include their experiential, cognitive, linguistic, and sociocultural backgrounds; the unique characteristics of the English language; the students' degree of maturation; and students' individual learning styles. These factors and their impact should be taken into consideration as you further develop your students' word-identification and vocabulary acquisition strategies.

*Y*our college-educational experiences have resulted in the continued development of your vocabulary and word-identification abilities. Take a few minutes at this time and reflect on the development of these abilities because of your enrollment in a liberal arts and/or sciences course (e.g., mathematics, foreign language, history, or science) and in one of your education courses. Then, based on the information in the section you have just read and your reflection, list under Reflection Activity 4.2 in your reflection journal the factors that you believe affected your vocabulary and word-identification development in both courses. After creating your list, compare and contrast these factors with respect to which ones had the most and least impact on your vocabulary and word-identification abilities in the liberal arts/sciences and education courses.

## *Guidelines for Effective Vocabulary Instruction*

As Brozo and Simpson (1995) reported, and we concur, there is no single superior method you can select to develop and expand your students' reading vocabulary. These researchers have recommended using a variety of approaches to achieve this literacy objective and adopting research-based guidelines to structure vocabulary instruction. In the sections that follow, we will describe five language-based and functional strategies and four word-identification strategies (e.g., structural analysis) that you can use to develop and expand your students' reading vocabulary abilities. With respect to research-based guidelines to structure vocabulary instruction, numerous reading educators (see Alvermann and Phelps 1994; Heilman et al. 1994) in addition to Brozo and Simpson (1995) have presented guidelines to consider when planning and conducting vocabulary literacy events. Ten research-based guidelines we believe you could use to structure vocabulary instruction are as follows:

1. *Select words for vocabulary instruction that your students will encounter and are expected to "own" when reading classroom materials (reading and content texts).* The reading vocabulary development process begins with the selection of words students will encounter that are important to their understanding printed materials and related concepts—vocabulary that appears to be important to the text or you believe may be unknown to the students. Four criteria that you and your students could utilize to select vocabulary include: (a) the vocabulary's relationship to the key concepts to be read; (b) the relative importance of the vocabulary to the key concepts to be explored; (c) the students' prior knowledge and language abilities; and (d) the vocabulary's

potential for enhancing independent learning strategies (Alvermann and Phelps 1994).

2. *Determine your students' prior knowledge and build vocabulary concepts upon that prior knowledge.* We have discussed throughout this text the role of prior knowledge in literacy learning and assessment procedures to secure this information (e.g., observations and checklists). Students' prior knowledge is essential in the vocabulary development process, and this importance has been stated by Savage (1994):

> The meaning of new words are connected to familiar concepts and experiences. New words are taught not as separate labels or isolated items, but they are introduced and developed as their meaning relates to familiar concepts and experiences. As new words are taught, they are integrated with words that pupils already know. (pp. 140–141)

After determining your students' prior knowledge, varied instructional techniques can be used to link your students' prior knowledge and known vocabulary with new words and their meanings.

3. *Build a conceptual base for word learning with varied activities and contexts.* As noted earlier, vocabulary is not learned in isolation. In addition to using students' prior knowledge for vocabulary instruction, you should also assist your students in building a conceptual base to learn new vocabulary. Heilman et al. (1994) recommended developing this conceptual base by using

> analogies, language features, characteristics (sets, e.g., a horse is an animal), and relationships to know words (such as relating newspapers, magazines, and catalogs as information sources that can be read or looked at selectively) to achieve students' background knowledge of concepts and to relate new words. (p. 139)

Furthermore, the use of varied activities and contexts to build conceptual bases also promotes vocabulary learning because different literacy events will reduce student boredom (Alvermann and Phelps 1994).

4. *Create a language-rich classroom environment.* We also have discussed throughout this text the importance of a language-rich classroom and the creation of this environment by promoting authentic receptive and expressive language events. To this end we hope you will promote and develop vocabulary learning activities that provide students with specific listening, reading, speaking, and writing experiences. As your students explore vocabulary through receptive and expressive language functions, these experiences also promote the thinking and problem-solving abilities they will need to use and understand vocabulary (May 1994).

5. *Emphasize your students' active role in the vocabulary learning process.* There is a direct relationship between students' vocabulary efforts and their vocabulary learning outcomes (Brozo and Simpson 1995). Whenever possible, encourage your students to become actively involved in the vocabulary learning process. To facilitate this involvement you may need to teach your students how to use various vocabulary

learning strategies (e.g., context clues or word parts) and monitor and reinforce their application of these strategies.

6. *Be an enthusiastic model of vocabulary use.* The manner in which you convey your feelings about vocabulary learning to your students is important. Because modeling influences learning, you should show your enthusiasm about words and the application of strategies that build vocabulary. Feel free to use the dictionary in front of your students to determine the meaning of words you do not know or to clarify definitions.

7. *Use direct vocabulary instruction to take advantage of the many forms (such as mental pictures, kinesthetic associations, smells, and tastes) used to store word knowledge.* Direct and systematic instruction based on varied sensory and imagery experiences will promote students' vocabulary abilities (Heilman et al. 1994). The adoption or adaption of the vocabulary strategies described in the next section will focus and structure your vocabulary lessons as well as permit the integration of multisensory and imagery activities.

8. *Reinforce word learning with repeated exposures over time.* Savage (1994) reported that repetition is a primary quality of effective vocabulary instruction and that students must repeatedly use words if they are to "own" them. Therefore, use teacher- and student-directed activities to ensure vocabulary repetition not only in written contexts but also in speaking, listening, and writing situations.

9. *Promote vocabulary transfer through vocabulary learning and strategy development.* It is important to promote your students' vocabulary transference abilities. To this end Alvermann and Phelps (1994) recommended that teachers "[c]oncentrate on words and strategies that have the widest possible application to other subjects and other reading situations" (p. 246). For example, you should ensure that your students have learned the vocabulary that they will again encounter in future literacy events. Also, teach your students to use various vocabulary learning strategies (e.g., context clues or familiar word parts) to identify known and unknown words during future literacy events.

10. *Have your students read widely in and out of the classroom.* Savage (1994) has described the effect that wide reading has on students' vocabulary learning. According to this reading educator:

> Reading itself is a major means of acquiring word knowledge. The relationship between reading success and word meaning is a reciprocal one. Knowledge of word meaning contributes greatly to reading ability. At the same time, wide reading contributes significantly to vocabulary acquisition. (p. 147)

Encourage your students to read varied printed materials and to read these materials at school, in the home, and in the community.

Although there is no single superior approach to develop or expand your students' reading vocabulary, numerous guidelines have been proposed for vocabulary instruction. We have delineated and discussed the preceding research-based guidelines that we hope you will consider when planning and conducting vocabulary instruction and other literacy events. Use of these guidelines will not only structure your vocabulary development efforts but also increase your students' vocabulary learning outcomes.

## Reflection Activity 4.3

*O*ne of your primary teaching objectives will be the development and expansion of all of your students' reading vocabularies. Because of the variability of their vocabulary and literacy learning experiences, you will find yourself selectively using the preceding ten guidelines to structure and individualize instructional lessons for the development of all students' vocabulary acquisition. In your reflection journal under Reflection Activity 4.3, rank-order the ten guidelines as you perceive their importance—from the most important to the least—for developing vocabulary instruction for students with more limited vocabulary experience. Then, rank-order the guidelines as you perceive their importance—from most to least—for developing vocabulary instruction for students with more extensive reading vocabularies. Finally, compare and contrast your rankings of the guidelines for students with more limited vocabulary experience and those with more extensive reading vocabularies with the rankings of one of your classmates. End this reflection activity by discussing any similarities or differences in ranking found that might have surprised you. Why did they surprise you?

## *Strategies for Developing and Expanding Vocabulary*

You can use a myriad of language-based and functional strategies, alone or in combination, to develop or expand your students' reading vocabularies. For the most part, these strategies can be implemented within the guidelines discussed in the last section, are easily carried out in elementary classrooms, and can be used to introduce or teach targeted vocabulary. Because these strategies have proven to be equally effective in promoting vocabulary development, you should select the strategy that is most appropriate for you based on your philosophy, students' characteristics, and vocabulary teaching-learning objectives. Alvermann and Phelps (1994) have also suggested that you consider the cost-benefit ratio, or the relationship of the complexity of the vocabulary to be learned and time needed for instruction, when selecting a vocabulary development strategy. Five strategies that you can adopt or adapt to achieve your vocabulary teaching-learning outcomes are presented next.

## *Vocabulary Self-Collection Strategy*

Haggard's (1986) vocabulary self-collection strategy is an excellent method to introduce new words or to enhance vocabulary development. It is student centered, permits students to select and explore pertinent vocabulary, and capitalizes on students' prior knowledge and interest. The four steps you can adopt or adapt to implement the vocabulary self-collection strategy follow:

1. *Determine the vocabulary.* The students, individually or in cooperative groups, begin the vocabulary self-collection process by surveying the printed material(s) to read. As they survey the material(s), they are to write in their vocabulary journals known and unknown words they encounter that they believe are meaningful to the content and that should be explored and learned. While the students are identifying and recording pertinent vocabulary you also should survey the printed material(s) and determine words important to understanding the content to be read.

2. *Define the vocabulary.* The second step of the vocabulary self-collection strategy is a whole-class activity that has you and your students recommending words to be explored and learned. The recommended words are recorded (e.g., on the chalkboard or overhead), rationales for selecting the words are provided by individuals making the recommendations, and the words are defined based on their context in the printed material(s). In addition to using the context to define the words, you and your students could also use prior knowledge or reference materials (e.g., a dictionary) to clarify or enhance the definitions generated.

3. *Develop the final vocabulary list.* You and your students now evaluate the words delineated and defined in step two to eliminate unnecessary words. The words could include duplications, words already in the students' reading vocabulary, or words unimportant to understanding the printed material(s) to be read. After developing the final vocabulary list, you and your students review the words and definitions, and if necessary, enhance the definitions provided. The students then write the final vocabulary list and definitions in their vocabulary journals.

4. *Augment students' vocabulary knowledge.* The final step in this strategy involves your utilization of teacher- and student-directed activities to augment the students' knowledge of the targeted vocabulary by clarifying or enhancing the definitions on the final word list. These activities should not only make use of the printed material(s) to be read but also use the students' prior knowledge, reference documents, and other sources.

Again, Haggard's (1986) vocabulary self-collection strategy is student centered and is an excellent teaching strategy for introducing or teaching new words. Can you modify the preceding four steps to adapt this strategy for postreading purposes or to teach targeted vocabulary?

# List-Group-Label Strategy

Taba's (1967) list-group-label strategy is another language-based and functional teaching procedure that you may want to use for your students' continued vocabulary development. The general purpose of this strategy is to use students' prior knowledge to promote their acquisition of new vocabulary and classification abilities and to structure their understanding of verbal concepts and relationships. You will also find that this strategy reinforces previously learned as well as newly acquired reading vocabulary words. You can adopt or adapt the following three steps to implement the list-group-label strategy:

1. *List or delineate vocabulary.* This strategy begins with your preview of the printed material(s) to be read and the selection of a single word or phrase that corresponds to the central focus of the content. For example, your students are to read a passage about transportation, so you select "Forms of Transportation" as the topic phrase. This topic phrase is written (e.g., on the chalkboard or overhead), and you ask your students to engage in brainstorming and provide you with words or phrases that are related to "Forms of Transportation." Acceptable students' responses are recorded while responses not related to the topic are rejected and reasons for their rejection given. The listing of related words or phrases continues until a reasonable number has been generated or the activity time expires. Possible student responses for the topic phrase identified above could include the following:

### Forms of Transportation

| | | | |
|---|---|---|---|
| Cars | Canoes | Trains | Taxis |
| Jet airplanes | Hot air balloons | Subways | Elephants |
| Horses | Camels | Ferries | Walking |
| Trucks | Buses | Blimps | Running |
| Bicycles | Motorcycles | Motorboats | Ocean liners |

2. *Group and label delineated vocabulary.* After listing acceptable responses, you point to and orally read the words or phrases listed. Your students are then asked to group the listed words or phrases that are similar and to give a label or title indicating the relationship(s) common to the groups created. Students are told that listed words or phrases can be used in more than one group and that they should have at least two words or phrases in each group.

3. *Follow-up activity.* The list-group-label strategy ends with you asking students to present their word or phrase groupings and the labels created. You record the students' groupings and labels (on the chalkboard or overhead), and after doing so, ask the students to state their reason(s) for the particular groupings. This follow-up activity is important because it provides students with the opportunity to see groupings and labels that they may not have considered. Possible labels

and groupings for the "Forms of Transportation" example could include the following:

*Human movement*—walking and running

*Animals used for transportation*—horses, camels, and elephants

*Highway vehicles*—cars, trucks, buses, taxis, and motorcycles

*Air transportation*—jet airplanes, hot air balloons, and blimps

*Water transportation*—ocean liners, canoes, motorboats, and ferries

*Two-wheel transportation*—bicycles and motorcycles

*Public transportation*—taxis, buses, trains, ferries, and subways

This teacher- and student-directed strategy activity can also be used to teach new words. Can you modify the preceding list-group-label steps to design a postreading vocabulary learning lesson?

## Feature Analysis Strategy

You can implement Johnson and Pearson's (1984) feature analysis strategy to facilitate your students' vocabulary, semantic, and categorization abilities. It can also be used to help your students determine differences and similarities among related words. The six steps for using feature analysis to introduce and explore vocabulary include the following:

1. *Select the category.* The first step is to select a category for listing words based on your students' prior knowledge or related vocabulary in the printed material(s) to be read. For example, your students will read a passage about different fast foods, their classification within the basic food groups, and their nutritional value. You or your students select "Fast Food" as an appropriate category for this feature analysis activity.

2. *Delineate the category words.* After determining the category, you or your students delineate the vocabulary to be analyzed that is related to the category selected and that may be found in the printed material(s). For example, the "Fast Food" passage the students will read focuses on fried chicken, hamburgers, french fries, pizza, tacos, and salad. You apply your knowledge of the vocabulary in the printed material(s), or your students use their prior knowledge, to delineate these and other fast-food items for feature analysis.

3. *Delineate the vocabulary features for analyses.* You and your students have selected the category ("Fast Food") and the vocabulary (fried chicken, hamburgers, etc.). The third step is to delineate the features (e.g., characteristics or attributes) to be used for examining the vocabulary selected. For example, the features that could be listed for analyzing the fast-food vocabulary could include the four basic food groups—dairy, vegetable, meat, and bread products. You or your students would then create a matrix using the vocabulary and features delineated.

| Fast food categories | Four basic food groups | | | |
|---|---|---|---|---|
| | Dairy | Vegetable | Meat | Bread products |
| Fried chicken | N | N | Y | S |
| Hamburgers | S | S | S | Y |
| French fries | N | Y | N | N |
| Pizza | S | S | S | Y |
| Tacos | S | S | S | Y |
| Salad | S | Y | S | S |

Key: Yes (Y)  No (N)  Sometimes (S)

**Figure 4.1**
Matrix for fast-food vocabulary, features, and relationships.

| Fast food categories | Four basic food groups | | | | Other considerations | |
|---|---|---|---|---|---|---|
| | Dairy | Vegetable | Meat | Bread products | Saturated fat | Caloric content |
| Fried chicken | | | | | | |
| Hamburgers | | | | | | |
| French fries | | | | | | |
| Pizza | | | | | | |
| Tacos | | | | | | |
| Salad | | | | | | |
| Egg rolls | | | | | | |
| Donuts | | | | | | |

**Figure 4.2**
Matrix for fast-food vocabulary and features (expanded).

4. *Identify vocabulary and features and/or relationships.* In the fourth step of feature analysis, you and your students adopt a procedure to indicate the vocabulary and features or relationships. Simple procedures could involve the use of paradigms (e.g., Yes or No), whereas more-complex procedures could be based on a Likert scale (e.g., 1 = Strongly Agree, 2 = Agree, 3 = No Opinion, 4 = Disagree, 5 = Strongly Disagree). After devising the relationship procedure, you and your students move through the category matrix and indicate the vocabulary features and/or relationships (see Figure 4.1).

5. *Delineate additional vocabulary and features.* Depending on your students' prior knowledge or the literacy events, the fifth step involves adding vocabulary and features to the matrix. For example, if the fast-food passage the students read also described egg rolls and donuts, these words could be added. If the passage addressed the saturated fat and caloric content of the fast foods, these features could be added (see Figure 4.2).

6. *Identify added vocabulary and features and/or relationships, and review the matrix.* The final step in feature analysis has two components. First, you and your students again move through the category matrix and

explore the relationships of the added vocabulary and features. Second, you and your student review the feature analysis process and the developed category matrix—vocabulary, features, and vocabulary and features or relationships.

Johnson and Pearson's (1984) feature analysis strategy can also be adapted to teach students new words and their similarities and differences. Can you modify the preceding steps to use this strategy for postreading vocabulary instructional purposes?

## *Vocabulary and Sentence Scaffolding Strategy*

Cudd and Roberts (1993/1994) have proposed a vocabulary and sentence scaffolding procedure that can be used to introduce or teach new words to students with a limited reading background. In addition to developing and expanding your students' vocabulary, using this direct strategy will also promote their understanding of sentence structure and organization. The five steps you can adopt or adapt to use vocabulary and sentence scaffolding are as follows:

1. *Select the vocabulary.* You begin this strategy by previewing the printed material(s) to be read and selecting vocabulary your students should know to understand the content. Important words should be selected from throughout the printed material(s) and from low, moderate, and high reading contexts. For example, if students are to read a passage about the life cycle of butterflies, you select the following new words to introduce—*Lepidoptera, caterpillar, cocoon,* and *chrysalis.*
2. *Determine a specific sentence structure.* Based on your students' prior knowledge and the sentence structure in the printed material(s), you determine a specific sentence structure to embed the targeted vocabulary and to guide the scaffolding activity. These sentence structures can be simple, compound, or complex or a combination of the three.
3. *Create personalized sentence stems with the targeted vocabulary embedded.* During this step, you create two to five sentence stems with the targeted vocabulary embedded in the stems. Cudd and Roberts (1993/1994) suggested personalizing the stems

   . . . by adding your children's names and familiar events, people, or places, drawing upon as much common experience as possible. Having each child as the subject of a sentence several times during the year is effective in building self-esteem. (p. 347)

   Sentence stems that could be created with the vocabulary listed in step one are:

   Although biologists refer to them as Lepidoptera, we _____ .
   A caterpillar is _____ .
   Michael Wang found a cocoon _____ .
   The chrysalis is a stage in the life of a butterfly, and _____ .

4. *Write, discuss, and complete the sentence stems.* The sentence stems are recorded (e.g., on the chalkboard or overhead). You read the first stem, discuss the concepts involved, and ask a student to complete the stem. You and the other students evaluate the response, modify it if necessary, and record an appropriate ending. The remaining stems are read, concepts discussed, and suitable endings recorded.

5. *Review targeted vocabulary and sentences.* This strategy ends with reviewing the targeted vocabulary and sentences created. Students could be asked to write the sentences in their reading journals or to use the stems and develop different appropriate endings. They could also work alone or in cooperative groups to write a brief composition using the targeted vocabulary, stems, and endings (or modified stems and endings).

In addition to introducing new words and providing practice with sentence structure, this scaffolding strategy will promote your students' self-esteem and written-language abilities. Can you modify the preceding steps to use this strategy for postreading vocabulary learning purposes?

## *Semantic Mapping*

The final vocabulary strategy we would like to present is Johnson and Pearson's (1984) semantic mapping. Semantic mapping is somewhat similar to Taba's (1967) list-group-label activity and is becoming one of the most widely used vocabulary development strategies in the elementary classroom (Alvermann and Phelps 1994). According to Heilman et al. (1994):

> Semantic mapping incorporates many of the guidelines for vocabulary teaching and enables students to expand their vocabularies, understand relationships between existing and new concepts, understand multiple meanings of words, and learn actively. Semantic mapping structures information categorically so that students can more readily see relationships between new words and concepts and their existing knowledge base. (p. 140)

This teacher-directed strategy is typically used for prereading purposes, but you could also create semantic maps after reading events to reinforce and relate new vocabulary concepts to the students' prior knowledge. The six steps you can adopt or adapt to develop the semantic map in Figure 4.3 are as follows:

1. *Select the central word or phrase.* You initiate this activity by reviewing the printed material(s) to be read and selecting a word or phrase that corresponds to the central focus of the context. For example, your students will read a passage about automobiles, so you select "Car" as the topic word or phrase.

2. *Write the central word or phrase and discuss the concept.* You record the word or phrase in what will be the center of the semantic map and briefly discuss the concept represented. For example, "Car" is written on the chalkboard or overhead, and you use pictures and other vicarious experiences to promote a common understanding of the concept "Car" (see May 1994).

**Figure 4.3**

Example of a semantic map activity.

Source: Developed by Lane Gauthier, University of Houston.

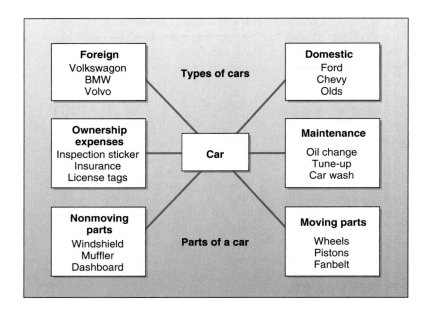

3. *Delineate related vocabulary.* You ask your students to work alone or in cooperative groups to delineate as many words as possible that relate to the central word or phrase. To generate the vocabulary for the "Car" semantic map, your students would write "Car" in their reading journals and list words associated with this concept (e.g., Volkswagen, Ford, inspection sticker, oil change, windshield, wheels).

4. *Group related vocabulary.* You ask students one at a time to give you words they delineated for the topic word or phrase. As the words are presented, you discuss the categorization or mapping of the words and record them by categories on the chalkboard or overhead in specific locations around the central word or phrase. For example, different students provide the words *Ford, Chevy,* and *Olds,* and you record these words in a group on the semantic map and discuss that these automobiles are domestic, or American-made, cars (see Figure 4.3).

5. *Determine the labels for vocabulary groupings.* After the words have been recorded by categories, you and your students determine a label, or title, for the vocabulary groupings. Each label presented should be evaluated to ensure its appropriateness and then recorded above or below the word categories. Vocabulary categories could also be clustered and given an accurate label. At this step you or your students can also add new vocabulary to the word categories. Appropriate labels for the word categories in Figure 4.3 could include Foreign and Domestic (Types of Cars), Ownership Expenses, Maintenance, and Nonmoving Parts and Moving Parts (Parts of a Car).

6. *Create and review the semantic map.* The final step in semantic mapping involves two components. First, you and your students select a

geometric shape (e.g., square or rectangle) to outline the categories and then connect the outlined groupings with lines. Second, you and your students review the central word or phrase, the category labels, and the related vocabulary.

Again, semantic mapping is one of the most widely used strategies in the elementary classroom to introduce new words. You and your students not only will enjoy creating semantic maps but also will find this strategy effective for developing and expanding vocabulary and schemata.

We believe you can employ the preceding five language-based and functional strategies alone or in combination to develop or expand your students' vocabulary knowledge. Since research has not indicated that one strategy is superior (Brozo and Simpson 1995), you should select the strategy that is most appropriate for your vocabulary lessons based on your philosophy, students' characteristics, vocabulary teaching-learning objectives, and what Alvermann and Phelps (1994) called the cost-benefit ratio (i.e., the relationship of the complexity of the vocabulary to be learned and time needed for instruction). As you experiment with these strategies, you will determine which strategies are more effective for introducing new words and which ones should be adopted or adapted for postreading vocabulary learning purposes.

## *Various Word-Identification Strategies*

For students to become independent and effective readers, they will need to develop a variety of word-identification strategies. In this section, we describe four word-identification strategies—sight recognition, contextual analysis, structural analysis, and graphophonic analysis—that you can teach your students to apply as needed when they encounter unknown words in context.

These word-identification skills and strategies will play an important role in your students' learning to read, but just how significant a role each of these play is somewhat open to debate (Gunning 1995). Some researchers (Anderson and Freebody 1979; May 1994) have suggested that word-identification competence (e.g., identifying sight words) may not be related to reading comprehension, whereas others (Barrett and Graves 1981; Shad 1993; Yap 1979) have reported that the evidence has suggested that students with good word-identification abilities also evidence superior comprehension. Regardless of the contrasting views on students' word-identification abilities and their comprehension performance, we believe that the development of more effective word-identification strategies for students who need them could benefit those students and should be an integral part of your instructional program. (Think back to the previous discussion regarding facilitative and functional skills and instruction.)

In beginning word-identification instruction, one problem that may arise is that of your students' ability to conceptualize the term *word* (Durkin 1980). As Savage (1994) noted, the knowledge of words is important because "[w]ords represent concepts, and concepts are tied to experiences" (p. 140). Downing

(1976) stated that this problem for beginning readers may be a result of cognitive confusion due to a phase that all people pass through when they begin to learn a new skill. Hare's (1984) review of the literature also found that young readers experience difficulty in the areas of word consciousness, word boundaries, and word referent relationships; therefore, you may need to introduce and model what is meant when one refers to a "word" with your early childhood learners. As they have more and more opportunities to use, write, read, and discuss language and words, children develop more consciousness of words, word boundaries, and, eventually, word referent relationships. (This is discussed in depth in a later chapter of this text.)

As students mature and further develop their vocabularies, they usually actually build three reading vocabularies:

1. *General vocabulary:* Words that comprise the major portion of our vocabulary usage in everyday communication, such as *table, house, chair,* and *school.*
2. *Specialized vocabulary:* Words with multiple meanings that change from one content area to another, such as *mass, root, rims,* and *raise.*
3. *Technical vocabulary:* Words that are essential to the understanding of a specific content area. These words relate to only one content area and are crucial to the understanding of its concepts. These words include *genes* (science), *embargo* (social studies), and *exponents* (mathematics).

Providing effective word-identification instruction within your literacy program is contingent upon a number of variables. First, create an atmosphere conducive to learning by using the various word-identification strategies to demonstrate their use and then providing your students opportunities to apply them in context in their printed materials (HuffBenkoski and Greenwood 1995).

Another important variable is the matching of instructional procedures with specific student abilities. In other words, your instruction in word-identification strategies must capitalize on your students' interests, prior knowledge, and linguistic and other cognitive experiences. Failure to match instructional elements with student characteristics could result in ineffective teaching, frustrated students, and an unpleasant reading experience that may affect your students' long-term reading progress (Collins and Cheek 1993).

The final variable to consider as you plan and implement effective word-identification procedures involves the use of context. When teaching students to identify words, avoid teaching words in isolation, and, at all times, relate them to context. In fact, we believe that you should do your best to introduce and emphasize all words within a meaningful context because such teaching procedures enable students to better understand the relationship between word identification and comprehension (McKeown, Beck, and Worthy 1993).

In summary, your responsibility is to develop a literacy program that enhances vocabulary development through meaningful word-identification instruction. From a philosophical perspective, Heilman et al. (1994) stated that the following should be kept in mind when designing and conducting word-identification literacy events:

1. Word-identification instruction is not reading; it is providing tools to help understand the meaning of written language. Instruction must provide opportunity for students to apply their word-identification skills in meaningful reading situations.

2. Students must develop flexibility in identifying words so that they can use all available cue systems to determine meaning. They need to develop independent and fluent mastery in areas of whole-word recognition, phonics, structural analysis, and contextual analysis . . . to focus on the meaning of what they read rather than just word pronunciation. The ability to decode a word with minimal effort is called automaticity of word identification. (pp. 83–84)

And, from an instructional perspective, Blachowicz (1985) has recommended that you use logical guidelines or principles to structure your word-identification instructional program. These guidelines and principles would include but not be limited to the following:

1. *Build a conceptual base for word learning.* Develop a schema for teaching new words that will assist your students in developing more effective word-identification strategies. Stress the deepest levels of semantic relationships possible.

2. *Stress learner involvement.* Always use student-centered discussions when presenting new words, and whenever possible, have the students define new words themselves rather than using a reference tool or having you give the definitions.

3. *Focus on usable vocabulary.* Be selective in choosing words to teach word-identification competence. Ask yourself three questions in the selection process: Is it important for your students to know this word? Will knowing a particular word help them identify and comprehend other words? Is the word essential to understanding the selection? If the answer is yes to all or to the first two questions, teach your students the words for long-term retention. If only the third criterion is met, you should teach for the short term.

4. *Create opportunities to use new word-identification skills and vocabulary.* Encourage your students to use new word-identification and vocabulary skills not only during reading instruction but also in school-related and personal reading.

5. *Make word-identification instruction a long-term goal.* Adopt instructional programs that will have a long-term effect and use consistent follow-up procedures to reinforce word-identification skills and strategies.

6. *Introduce your students to resources for word-identification learning.* For motivation and to encourage practice and use, introduce many types of books and literature, as well as appropriate computer programs, among other word-study materials, into the curriculum.

7. *Develop transferable skills.* Give your students practice in using new word-identification strategies within context and teach them how to use word learning tools such as the dictionary and the thesaurus.

Again, there are four word-identification skills and strategies you could help your students develop to identify unknown words in text. As you read the following general and specific descriptions of these skills/strategies, please keep the previously described word-identification guidelines in mind, as well as our previous discussion involving facilitative and functional skill instruction.

## Sight Words

May (1994) reported that there are approximately two hundred basic sight words and defined sight words as "*high frequency words* whose meaning we should already know, so that when we recognize them in print we have both pronunciation and meaning available within one second" (p. 155). In general, sight words are recognized immediately on visual contact "as whole words," and identification and meaning occur with limited examination. To illustrate this independent word-identification ability, we ask you to look at the following words:

| | |
|---|---|
| a | lateralization |
| the | dolabriform |
| was | septuagenarian |
| from | polynomial |
| there | notwithstanding |

Now, were the words in the left column sight words for you? Did you identify those words in the right column with another independent word-identification strategy? Any words in the right column that you may have identified without careful examination would also be sight words for you.

Savage (1994) has stated the importance of developing students' sight-word vocabulary:

> It stands to reason that the more words pupils can recognize instantly as they read, the more smooth and efficient their reading will be. The goal of instruction in word recognition is to help pupils recognize printed words as quickly and as easily as possible. If the process of identifying words is unreasonably difficult and time consuming, the impact on enjoyment and understanding is negative. (pp. 147–148)

Also, Heilman et al. (1994) have delineated the following three reasons that you should plan and conduct sight-word instruction within your classroom reading program:

1. A child who knows a number of words as whole words can better understand, see, and hear similarities between these known words and new words. Having a large sight vocabulary is invaluable in helping identify other words.
2. When words are recognized instantly, analysis is minimal. The reader can focus on reading for meaning.

*Figure 4.4*
Possible word identifiers.

| Configuration (Word shapes) | was       hat       elephant |
| Top vs. bottom half words | It is fun to play in the snow.<br>The little boy ran to the store. |
| Consonant vs. vowel clues | Pl_y_ng f_ _tb_ll c_n b_ f_n.<br>__e _a_ u_e__o _ui__ _i_ _ou_e. |

3. Numerous high-frequency words (e.g., was, the, those, etc.) should be learned as units simply because students see them over and over in any reading situation and they contribute significantly to using syntax as a means of getting meaning from reading. (p. 86)

## Theories and Principles

Reading educators are not entirely sure why readers are able to distinguish one word from another, but some would have you consider such factors as determining word configuration, inspecting the top half of words, or analyzing consonant clues (see Figure 4.4). But, and as Karlin and Karlin (1987) noted, studies indicate that students (a) utilize the beginning and final elements of words rather than the middle structure; (b) use the initial position of the word and the context to determine the remainder of the word; and (c) see small words as wholes but see only familiar words of two or more syllables in their entirety. Regardless, your students may enter school with the ability to recognize many high-frequency words (e.g., Dolch words) or words they have encountered repeatedly at home or in the community (e.g., *McDonald's, Ford,* and so on), and you can use these words as a starting point for reading instruction.

The process of identifying words by sight is also referred to by some reading educators as the whole-word method. This method is based on the theory that students should be taught to identify certain high-frequency words by sight rather than through the application of other word-identification strategies. When they learn words by sight, students are able to participate more quickly in the reading process. Additionally, many words can become part of their individual sight vocabulary because these words have a special meaning for them—schemata for the word have been developed at home, in school, or in the community. We must also note at this time that your students' ability to use sight words effectively is frequently associated with their word-identification performance on various word lists such as the *Dolch Basic Sight Word List,* the *Fry New Instant Word List,* the *Slosson Oral Reading Test* (SORT), or word lists provided with the various reading programs that many school systems use for reading instruction.

Sight-word instruction, or presenting words as wholes, is essential for students to learn those high-frequency words that you want them to recognize on sight or without using phonics, structural analysis, or other word-identification skills. Those sight words that are more concrete with a higher level of visual imagery (e.g., *apple*) are easier for students to learn and remember than those words that are abstract with a lower level of visual imagery (e.g., *was*) (Hargis and Gickling 1978). In their research, Kolker and Terwilliger (1981) found that word imagery enhanced the memory of sight words for both good and poor readers. You may have to spend time teaching low-imagery words that are similar in configuration such as *was, were, where, when, the,* and *then* among others. You should approach this instruction by providing these words in a variety of materials, within context, and with as much concreteness as possible in your reading instruction.

## *Instructional Considerations*

When teaching your students to identify sight words, you will probably have to employ more than one strategy. One strategy that has proved successful in helping students remember sight words, particularly those that are similar in configuration, is using picture cues. Another successful strategy involves teaching abstract sight words within the context of a sentence. The use of the language-experience approach is also effective in teaching sight words to students. Whichever strategy you select, some students will require practice and repetition using a variety of games and activities.

Lapp and Flood (1986) have described a very specific procedure to develop sight-word competence. They suggested that you use the following guidelines to conduct your sight-word development:

1. When appropriate, use pictures to illustrate the word. Ask you students to study the picture and predict what is being said in the selection.
2. Ask your students to read along with you as you read the various words. This will assist them in determining whether their predictions are correct.
3. Have your students follow along as you reread the passage and point to the picture.
4. Encourage your students to read the passage with you.
5. While the students follow the story visually ask individual students to read the sentence.
6. When you have finished reading a sentence, reinforce the individual words by pointing them out to the students.
7. Discuss the meaning of each word, and explain that some words (e.g., *the, is,* and *am*) serve as helpers to complete sentences.
8. Emphasize those words with irregular spelling patterns, such as *sight, of, who, laugh,* and *the.*
9. Frame each word for your students so that they can familiarize themselves with its length, configuration, initial letter(s), and other letter features.
10. Have students reread the sentence with you.

Also, May (1994) has presented a very effective meaning-based, interactive, and functional procedure that you can adopt or adapt to develop and expand your students' sight-word abilities. The ten steps in this procedure are as follows:

1. The teacher selects enjoyable patterned books that emphasize the . . . [target sight words (e.g., Bill Martin's *Brown Bear, Brown Bear, What Do You See?* or Bruno Munari's *The Elephant's Wish*)].
2. The teacher reads the book out loud.
3. The teacher reads the book again, with the children joining in whenever they can predict what comes next.
4. The children take turns with echo and choral reading.
5. The teacher reads the text from teacher-made charts with no picture clues. Then the children echo-read and/or choral-read.
6. The children place matching sentence strips on charts. (The teacher has made charts so that a sentence strip can be taped under a sentence on the chart.)
7. The children later place matching word strips on charts, saying the word order the first time this is done and in random order later.
8. The children and teacher chorally read the entire story.
9. The teacher places word strips in random order at the bottom of the chart. The children come up and match the strips to words in the story saying each word as they match it to one in the story.
10. [The teacher has the children] . . . write the target words as well as read them. This will help the children commit them to their sight vocabulary. (pp. 161–162)

Finally, there are a number of educational games, teaching aids, and specialized techniques that you may want to use with students who are having difficulty developing sight words. Duffy and Roehler (1986) have described the following three "fix-it" educational games that you and your students will enjoy playing and that will promote sight-word learning:

Make up racing games in which students race by pronouncing . . . sight words to be learned. For example, construct an auto racing course, dividing the track into equal squares. Give each student a toy racing car and provide yourself with a pack of cards upon which are printed the words you want the class to learn. . . .

Play a fishing game in which students are given a pole constructed of a stick and a string having a magnet tied to the end. Place paper fish with target words printed on them in a box. . . . Attach a paper clip to each fish. Students drop their line into the pond . . . [and] pull the fish out and get to keep it if they can correctly pronounce the word printed on its side. . . .

Play a variation of the television game Concentration. Place the words to be learned on cards and put them face down on the table. The student must remember where there are two cards exactly alike and try to pick up matching pairs. As the players turn over each card, they must pronounce the word on the card. (pp. 288–290)

Two teaching aids Choate (1987) suggested that you construct and have your students use to develop and expand their sight-word vocabulary are tachistoscopes and word wheels (see Figure 4.5). Choate (1987) also observed

**Figure 4.5**
A tachistoscopic device and word wheel.

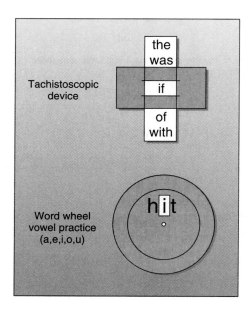

Tachistoscopic device

the
was
if
of
with

Word wheel
vowel practice
(a,e,i,o,u)

h i t

that "[r]epeated exposure and practice in and out of context are the most efficient strategies for helping students remember sight words" (p. 82). And for students with special needs who continue to exhibit significant problems learning sight words, we would recommend that you use multisensory procedures with them. Some of these procedures (e.g., Fernald's VAKT Approach) are discussed in a later chapter.

Finally, one of the major sight-word obstacles some of your students will face is distinguishing between easily confused words. For example, some students may have difficulty identifying such similar-looking words as *was* and *saw, them* and *then,* and *where* and *there* among others. Figure 4.6 presents an instructional activity that you can use to promote your students' visual attention to and accurate identification of easily confused sight words within context. This sight-word strategy is particularly beneficial to help students focus on sight words in text and to help students who reverse or transpose letters.

## Contextual Analysis

Contextual analysis is another word-identification strategy that you can help your students develop to enable them to determine an unknown word by analyzing its position or function in a sentence or passage and by knowing the meaning of surrounding words (Brozo and Simpson 1995). Look at the following sentences and try to identify the missing words:

The farmer rode a _____(1)_____ in the field.
Mary ate ice _____(2)_____ at the _____(3)_____party.
_____(4)_____ can be used to look at the moon.

1. Read a passage like the one above to your students.  As you read, model appropriate reading behavior such as pace, intonation, and pronunciation.

2. Reread the same passage with your students, again modeling the use of appropriate behavior.

3. Now frame for your students the "easily confused" words:
   As I was walking to my friend's house, I suddenly saw them.  There were two frisky puppies playing in my friend's yard, but then, they quickly disappeared. Where did they go?

4. Then, encourage the students to read the passage together.

5. After Step 4 is completed, use a collaborative grouping format where the students can further explore the use of "easily confused" sight words in trade books or other teacher- or student-selected materials.

**Figure 4.6**
Literacy activity to promote students' attention to and identification of "easily confused" sight words.

Did you use your contextual-analysis strategies and identify (1) *tractor,* (2) *cream,* (3) *birthday,* and (4) *Telescopes* as the unknown words? In general, contextual analysis involves the use of syntactic clues (or the grammatical position of unknown words within the sentence) and semantic clues (or insight into the meaning of unknown words based on previous or later printed context) (Savage 1994). The more complex the materials to be read, the more opportunities that are available to employ contextual analysis (Karlin and Karlin 1987). This word-identification strategy has received positive reviews concerning its value in assisting students to increase their vocabulary, and you will find that even your youngest readers can use this strategy to deal with unknown words.

## *Theories and Principles*

Spache and Spache (1986) stated the theories and principles that underlie contextual analysis. According to these reading educators:

> Apparently, most contextual clues demand some degree of inferential thinking. As a result, some teachers assume that contextual analysis is not much more than guesswork and therefore should not be promoted. The truth is that such inferential thinking is an essential part of the reading process at all maturity levels and should be strongly encouraged. Pupils should not be burdened with learning the technical terms . . . [but] emphasis should be placed upon helping readers use the sense of the sentence or the surrounding sentences as an aid in identifying the probable meaning of a difficult word. The goal of contextual analysis is not always an exact recognition of a word or its pronunciation. These may be

approached by other means, such as phonics or structural analysis. But when these techniques are successful, they do not necessarily result in the derivation of the meaning of a word, for it may not be encompassed in the reader's auditory vocabulary. Thus contextual analysis takes the reader beyond pronunciation to meaning, which in many situations is more significant for ultimate comprehension. (p. 503)

In essence, contextual analysis is a thinking process that facilitates the identification of unknown words by use of students' syntactic and semantic cue systems.

A rather unique aspect of contextual clues is that, unlike other word-identification strategies, they seem to become more usable as readers mature. There is research (cf. Spache 1981) that has indicated that adult readers rely less on phonics or structural analysis and more on contextual analysis as their primary word-analysis tool. Also, research with younger students has found that although first graders definitely use contextual analysis, as students matured and moved to higher grade levels (third grade), they greatly increased their use of this strategy (Goodman 1965).

Much of the research concerning contextual clues is related to the classification of these clues. In general, the contextual clues used by children to identify words include pictorial and graphic aids, typographical clues, and especially syntactic and semantic clues. Heilman et al. (1994) reported that syntactic clues include structure words (e.g., nouns or verbs), phrases (e.g., a phrase may describe or refine a word), language grammar (e.g., a subject, verb, or object), and appositives (e.g., a word or words that explain the previous word), whereas context clues include definitions or explanations, synonyms or antonyms, figurative language, and summary statements. Perhaps the most widely accepted classification of contextual clues that are used by readers was proposed by Ames (1966). Ames proposed that there were fourteen types of clues students could use to identify a word: (a) language experience or familiar expression, (b) modifying phrases or clauses, (c) definition or description, (d) words connected in a series, (e) comparison or contrast clues, (f) synonym clues, (g) tone, setting, and mood clues, (h) referral clues, (i) association clues, (j) the main-idea and supporting-detail pattern, (k) the question-answer pattern in a paragraph, (l) preposition clues, (m) nonrestrictive clauses or appositive phrases, and (n) the cause-effect pattern of a sentence or paragraph. Collins and Cheek (1993) also noted that in addition to syntactic and contextual clues, students can use the printed material's title and theme, or a combination of these clues with graphophonic and structural clues, to identify unknown words.

### *Instructional Considerations*

The contextual-analysis teaching-learning process involves use of syntax, semantic, and other contextual clues. Using these are natural and involve real reading and language. Numerous reading educators (see Collins and Cheek 1993; Heilman et al. 1994) have recommended that you employ modeling, discussion, and cloze procedures to develop your students' contextual-analysis strategies.

For example, you would write a sentence or sentences on the chalkboard or overhead and replace a word or words with a line denoting a space (modified cloze procedure):

Mary's _____ ice cream is chocolate.

Tom and Juan went to the park to swing. Instead of swinging they played on the _____. They enjoyed sitting across from each other, talking and laughing, and going up and down.

or

Mary's f_____ ice cream is chocolate.

Tom and Juan went to the park to swing. Instead of swinging they played on the t_____. They enjoyed sitting across from each other, talking and laughing, and going up and down.

Modeling would involve your thinking out loud and providing students with the syntactic, semantic, structural, graphophonic, and other clues you are using to identify the pronunciation and/or meaning of the unknown word(s). Your thinking out loud could result in the following:

"Mary's /f/_____ ice cream is chocolate. What word beginning with an f is logical or would fit? Could it be first? No. Final? No. Favorite? Oh, yes, it could be favorite."

"Let me see. Tom and Juan were in the park, and they played on something that goes up and down. What can a friend and I sit on in the park that goes up and down? I cannot pronounce 'teeter-totter' but I believe it must be a seesaw."

A discussion session would involve you and your students discussing syntactic, semantic, structural, graphophonic, and other clues that can be used to identify the pronunciation and/or meaning of the unknown word. You and your students would discuss the theme(s) of the sentence(s), the context(s) of the missing word(s), and possible words based on different clues. The discussion(s), if necessary, would end by you providing the appropriate word(s) and identifying which clues support the appropriate word(s).

Harris and Smith (1986) have also recommended that you teach your students to go through a series of questioning strategies to serve as a guide to using contextual clues to analyze unknown words. These questioning strategies are as follows:

1. After reading the whole sentence or paragraph, can you think of a word that would make sense in that spot?
2. Using context and the sound of the first part of the word, can you figure out what the word should be?
3. Using context, the first part of the word, and the sound of the last part of the word, can you figure out what the word should be?

4. Using context and applicable sound-spelling patterns across the whole word, can you figure out what the word should be?
5. If you still do not know the word, go to a dictionary to look it up, or ask someone.

Finally, Duffy and Roehler (1986, pp. 290–291) have recommended the following two activities to use with students who are having difficulty developing contextual-analysis strategies:

> Once students develop a sight-vocabulary, you can use these words to create sentences where you ask them to read a sentence and to provide the missing word. If the students cannot yet read independently, you can do the same thing as a listening activity. . . .
>
> Give students riddles in which the context supplies only a minimum outline of the missing word. For instance, you could provide the sentence, "The swimmer dived into the _____." Elicit student response encouraging a variety of answers, such as "water," "pool," "lake," "river." Then place a letter card (such as the letter *w*) at the left of the blank space and say, "What word must go in the blank space?"

Again, it is important that you teach students to combine contextual analysis and other strategies when they encounter large or complex contents. For example, in addition to using the sentence or surrounding known words, students should also employ structural and phonic analysis to identify difficult words. The combination of contextual structural, and letter-sound clues will increase successful word-identification and comprehension performance. The three sentences that follow illustrate this combination concept:

_____ fell on the _____ ice and _____ her _____.
M_____ fell on the m_____ ice and br_____ her a_____.
M_____y fell on the m_____ing ice and br_____ her a_____m.
Mary fell on the melting ice and broke her arm.

## Structural Analysis

Structural analysis is a word-identification strategy your students can use to help determine the meaning and pronunciation of a new word by examining word elements or parts (Collins and Cheek 1993). This identification is achieved through an examination and analysis of words and their parts by separating these words into meaningful units, identifying and giving meaning to the individual units, and then recombining these parts into meaningful wholes. Structural analysis includes such skills as dealing with syllabication, prefixes, suffixes, contractions, compound words, and inflectional endings. Look at the following sentence with two unknown words and follow our suggested use of structural analysis to identify these words:

_____, the _____ boy was _____.
Never_____, the dis_____ boy was mis_____.

Never.the_____, the dis_____ful boy was
mis.chie_____.
Never. the . less, the dis. grace. ful boy was mis.chie.vous.

The primary difference between phonic analysis and structural analysis is that with structural analysis larger units are dealt with in analyzing the structure of words, and the study of word parts (such as affixes) includes the meaning of those parts. In other words, phonic analysis is devoid of meaning, whereas structural analysis includes an emphasis on meaning.

## *Theories and Principles*

Savage (1994) stated that structural analysis

> involves trying to determine the meaning of words by their morphemic (meaning) units. The major classes of morphemes in English are roots and affixes. The root (base or stem) carries the essence of word meaning. Prefixes—morphemes attached to the beginning of root words—and suffixes—morphemes attached to the end of words—modify meaning by creating new words. Recognizing these morphemic elements enables readers to reach for the meaning of the words they read. . . . Structural analysis also includes learning about [compound words and] contractions. (p. 164)

In essence, students use their structural-analysis strategies to attend to the various word structures that have meaning, and based on the meaning provided by these structures, they identify the words.

Various terms are used in discussions of structural analysis. Some of these terms and examples include:

*Root or Base Word.* A word that is a free morpheme that does not have an affix or inflectional ending and is not compounded (e.g., *school, wind, etc.*)

*Affix.* A prefix or suffix added to a word to change its meaning (e.g., *cat + s = cats*) or its grammatical function (e.g., *quick + ly = quickly*)

*Prefix.* A word component (for example, *pre, un,* and so on) attached to the beginning of a root or base word to change its meaning (e.g., *preview, unhappy*).

*Suffix.* A word component (e.g., *er, ing*) attached to the end of a root or base word to change its meaning (e.g., *faster, going*).

*Inflectional Ending.* A word ending that, when added to a root or base word, denotes tense, number, degree, gender, or possession, such as *cars, parted,* and *closing.*

*Syllabication.* The process of decoding words by dividing them into parts such as *run-a-way, nec-es-sar-y,* and *bro-ken.*

*Compound Words.* The combination of two or more root or base words to form a single word such as *Sun + day = Sunday, air + plane = airplane,* and *birth + day = birthday.*

## *Instructional Considerations*

As Spache and Spache (1986) reported, "[T]he purpose of training in structural analysis is, then, the development of the habit of recognition by larger, more meaningful units within words" (p. 492). You could begin the process by teaching students to identify root words and affixes, to recognize compound words, and to identify syllables and inflectional endings.

Karlin and Karlin (1987) have described instructional procedures you could adapt to develop your students' abilities to identify root words, affixes, and compound words. After your students are aware of root words and sentence-completion tasks (e.g., "I have a cat. Sue has two _____"), you would use a five-step procedure to help students recognize these word parts: (1) recognizing root words and affixes in print; (2) noting modified forms of root words; (3) identifying more difficult root words; (4) reading root words with varied affixes; and (5) finding the meaning of affixes by using the context.

The instructional procedure recommended by the Karlins for teaching identifying of compound words is easily adaptable to your students' needs. You begin instruction by having students aurally and visually discriminate these words. For example, you and your students would read compound words composed of known sight words (e.g., *dogfish* or *grandfather*), and your students would mark the individual words in each compound word. Second, you would read a list of compound and noncompound words aloud (e.g., *watercolor* vs. *holder*) and have students aurally discriminate the compound words. Third, you would have your students use known root words to build compound words. For example, they could combine the flashcards (e.g., *horse* and *play* to form *horseplay*) to build a file of compound words. And fourth, you would have your students apply their contextual-analysis abilities by putting the compound words they have learned into incomplete sentences. For example, they would have used the compound-word examples we utilized in this paragraph to complete the following sentences:

My _____ is 63 years old.
You should not engage in _____ in class.
My father caught a _____ at the lake.
I like to paint with red _____.

We must begin our discussion of the teaching of syllabication and inflectional endings with a note of caution. Most reading authorities (e.g., Spache and Spache 1986) are not in favor of classroom teachers having their students memorize complicated syllabication and inflectional endings and rules/generalizations. However, there are rules and generalizations for you and your students to refer to and to use as necessary. For example, Harris and Smith (1986) have suggested the following syllabication generalizations:

1. When two consonants are between two vowels, the word is usually divided between the two consonants (*rab-bit, sis-ter*).
2. When a vowel is followed by a single consonant, the consonant usually begins the second syllable (*be-fore, to-ken*).

3. When a word ending in *le* is preceded by a consonant, that consonant goes with the *le* syllable (*ta-ble, fum-ble*).
4. If a word contains a prefix, it is divided between the prefix and the root or base word (*re-view, con-form*).
5. If a word contains a suffix, it is divided between the suffix and the root or base word (*like-ly, fool-ish, long-er, long-est*).
6. Consonant digraphs and blends are never divided (*part-ner, eth-ics*).

Furthermore, there are numerous generalizations concerning spelling when inflectional endings are present that you might want to have available. These generalizations as outlined by Harris and Smith (1986) include the following:

1. The spelling of the root or base word does not usually change when inflectional endings are added (*walking, matches, called, girls*).
2. If the base word ends in *e*, the *e* is usually dropped when adding an inflectional ending that begins with a vowel (*hope–hoping; take–taking*).
3. When a root or base word ends in a single consonant following a single vowel, the final consonant is usually doubled when an ending is added (*run–running; drop–dropped*).
4. When a word ends in *y* preceded by a consonant, the *y* is usually changed to *i* before adding the ending (*cry–cried; pony–ponies*).
5. If the final *y* is preceded by a vowel, the ending is added with no change in the root or base word (*buy–buys; monkey–monkeys*).
6. If the word ends in *f*, the *f* is usually changed to *v* before the addition of an ending (*wolf–wolves; scarf–scarves*).

Finally, we do not recommend that you teach your students, or have your students memorize, long lists of rules and generalizations. The material is presented here for your reference. When a particular rule or generalization is appropriate to one or many of your students' needs, you can present it in the context of a familiar story or familiar material and explain it as needed.

### *Graphophonic Analysis*

Graphophonic analysis is the fourth word-identification strategy that students can develop to identify unfamiliar words through pronunciation and symbol relationships. In general, graphophonic analysis involves students learning and applying the relationship between the written symbols (graphemes, or our twenty-six letters of the alphabet) and the sounds (phonemes, or the forty-four to forty-six sounds in the English language) associated with those symbols.

The teaching of phonics (which is a major part of graphophonic analysis) was the central focus of the great reading debates of the 1950s and 1960s, and these arguments resulted in significant research efforts and the development of phonic-oriented basal reading programs that were used throughout the 1970s and some far into the 1980s. Although the holistic movement, which flourished in the 1990s moved many away from basal readers and research in code-emphasis approaches, the teaching of phonics and other code-emphasis instruction continues to be a subject of debate for reading educators (e.g., see

Graphophonic analysis involves strategies students use to identify unfamiliar words through letter and sound relationships.
© Jim Whitmer

Adams 1990; and Smith 1994), and the general public is bombarded daily with media coverage polarizing the benefits of learning phonics or being taught by a whole language perspective. However, this polarization is more political than representative of the real issues. Those who advocate for whole language do not believe that phonics is not important. Instead they argue about how it should be presented to students.

If you wish to balance your instruction and want to include attention to phonics, it is prudent that you provide a systematic presentation of the sound-symbol relationships your students need to successfully use graphophonic analysis to help them figure out unfamiliar words in text. The following sections present information to help you understand various phonic concepts and implement appropriate graphophonic-analysis development in your classroom.

## Theories and Principles

Terminology used in graphophonic-analysis instruction is often confusing to teachers and other school-related professionals. To assist you with these terms, we have defined those that you may encounter in your future teaching and in the professional literature.

### Graphophonic Analysis Terminology

***Phonics Instruction.*** Phonics instruction is a teaching procedure that focuses on students' understanding as well as learning that printed language represents the spoken sounds that are heard when words are pronounced. It is teaching students the association that each sound is represented by a particular letter or combination of letters.

***Phonetics.*** Phonetics is the study of speech sounds, and how they are made physiologically and acoustically. In other words, it involves how sound is made, how it changes, and what a sound's relationship is to the overall language process. Although educators have taken the term *phonics instruction* from phonetics, the word-identification skill known as *phonics* represents only a small part of the area of phonetics.

***Phoneme.*** A phoneme is the smallest unit of sound in a language that can be used to differentiate one word from another. For example, in the words *car* and *jar*, the letters *c* and *j* represent two distinct sounds. The phonemes /c/ and /j/, as identified by the letters enclosed with slanted lines, reflect the only difference in their pronunciation. This single difference in sounds also significantly changes the meaning of these words.

***Grapheme.*** A printed symbol representing a speech sound or phoneme is a grapheme (or letter of the alphabet). Some phonemes are represented by a single grapheme or letter, while others require a combination of two or more of these printed symbols. These clusters of two letters that represent one phoneme are referred to as *digraphs*, and clusters of three letters representing one phoneme are referred to as *trigraphs*.

***Phoneme-Grapheme Correspondence.*** Phoneme-grapheme correspondence is the relationship between sounds (phonemes) and the symbols (graphemes) that represent them. Because the English language has approximately forty-four phonemes and only twenty-six graphemes, there is not always a one-to-one relationship between the correspondence of phonemes and graphemes. This lack of a one-to-one phoneme-grapheme relationship creates problems that are most evident in the spelling patterns of words that have become established in English writing.

***Morphemes.*** The smallest unit in the English language that contains meaning is the morpheme. There are two types of morphemes, free and bound. A free morpheme is one that functions independently, such as *cat, fog,* and *rain*. A bound morpheme such as *s* must combine with a free morpheme, such as *dog* in *dogs*.

## Phonics Instruction

The history of phonics instruction in the United States schools has been both interesting and controversial. As already pointed out, the primary focus of the early debates regarding phonics instruction was whether to teach unknown words as sight words (the whole-word approach), or to stress the sound of individual letters within these words (the phonics approach). The current debates tend to instead focus on how to teach phonics, rather than whether to teach it or not. Two methods of teaching phonics, the analytic and the synthetic, are briefly described for your review. Each presents a different view of how instruction should proceed. Analytic phonics instruction is based on a comparison of words already known to the student and then teaching sounds within those words. For example, students are taught to read

/cat/ and then are taught the grapheme-phoneme relationships /c/ /a/ /t/ that compose /cat/. Synthetic phonics instruction, however, uses generalizations of rules and stresses the isolated sounds in words and then the blending of these sounds to form words. Within synthetic phonics instruction, you teach students the phoneme-grapheme relationships /c/, /a/, and /t/, and then you teach them to blend these relationships to form the word /cat/.

Research regarding these two methods of phonics instruction is somewhat mixed (cf. Burns, Roe, and Ross 1996). Chall (1967) found that the use of intensive synthetic phonics instruction yielded better results than did analytic phonics instruction. This was substantiated by the classic First Grade Studies conducted by Bond and Dykstra (1967), although Dykstra (1968) later found that students receiving synthetic phonics instruction did not outperform their peers who received another type of reading instruction. Later research (cf. Norton and Hubert 1977) found that those students receiving both analytic and synthetic phonics instruction were superior in word-identification ability, whereas those students receiving meaning-emphasis instruction excelled in comprehension. More recently, Adams's (1990) research has indicated that even though trying to isolate phonemes can result in some distortion, there are more advantages than disadvantages to asking children to produce phonemes in isolation.

Although Collins and Cheek (1993) indicate that the published research regarding analytic and synthetic phonics instruction is not too useful to teachers, it is important to note that your students will respond differently to the different phonics methods. Thus, perhaps the most expeditious approach for you is to determine which, if either, of these two phonics methods is appropriate for your students on an individual or small-group basis. Then use your professional decision-making abilities to teach these and other facilitative skills when needed, teaching the ones that are necessary for your particular students in contexts that will facilitate their acquisition of these skills.

## Instructional Considerations

In teaching graphophonic analysis, you may present certain rules or generalizations in various activities and in varied instructional materials. The basic premise of phonics instruction is that a certain degree of regularity occurs in the English language and its spelling patterns. Instruction in graphophonic analysis expands your students' awareness of this regularity and allows them to use the phonic aspect of the graphophonic cuing system to apply those phonic cues during the reading process. The ultimate objective of phonics instruction is to get your students to appropriately apply various phonics generalizations.

As in other aspects of reading instruction, there is some debate regarding the usefulness of teaching a large number of phonics generalizations to your students. One definitive study of this topic was conducted by Spache (1981), who identified 121 different phonics generalizations that were reported in the literature. However, Spache discovered that only 10 of these 121 generalizations meet the criterion of at least 75 percent utility in application. The generalizations that were found to be useful 75 percent of the time, and therefore the generalizations that Spache (1981) found most appropriate for students to eventually learn, were as follows:

> *Vowels.* When *y* is the final letter in a word, it usually has a vowel sound. When there is one *e* in a word that ends in a consonant, the *e* usually has a short sound.

> *Vowel Digraphs.* When the letter *r* follows a vowel, the sound is neither long nor short. This is also true for vowels followed by *l* or *w.*

> *Consonants.* Only one sound is formed when *c* and *h* are next to each other. In this letter-sound relationship, *ch* is pronounced as in *kitchen, catch,* and *chair,* not as *sh.* The sound /k/ is usually heard when the letter *c* is followed by *o* or *a.* The sound /s/ is usually heard when *c* is followed by *e* or *i.* Only one sound is heard when two of the same consonants are side by side.

Since some teaching materials for beginning readers contain reference to or instruction in some of the phonics generalizations, Harris and Smith (1986) suggested that teachers should have a minimum knowledge of these generalizations to help students develop specific decoding skills. Teachers may also want to consider modeling some of these generalizations to students, when appropriate, to meet their needs.

1. *Short Vowel Rule.* When there is only one vowel in a word or syllable, that vowel usually has a short sound if the vowel is at the beginning or in the middle of the word (e.g., *at, met, it, hot, but*).
2. *Long Vowel Rule 1.* When a two-vowel word or syllable has a silent *e* at the end, the first vowel in the word usually is long (e.g., *made, ride, hope, tune*).
3. *Long Vowel Rule 2.* When there is a double vowel in a word or syllable, the first vowel is usually long, and the second vowel is silent (e.g., *maid, beat, toast*).
4. *Murmur Rule.* When a vowel is followed by the letter *r,* it has a modified sound that is neither characteristically long nor short (e.g., *car, hurt*).
5. *Diphthong Rule.* Certain double vowels have linked sounds that make use of both vowels, such as the *ou* in *house,* the *ow* in *now,* the *oi* in *oil,* and the *oy* in *boy.*

Lapp and Flood (1986) reviewed several suggestions that are helpful to teachers in implementing effective strategies for teaching phonics. These suggestions include the following:

1. Implement vowel instruction early in the beginning reading program. Some teachers and publishers prefer teaching consonants first because of the regularity of the phoneme-grapheme correspondences of the consonants. However, this view fails to consider the high correlation between the phoneme-grapheme correspondences of many vowels and the ability of students to decode vowels in order to read independently. Because most children can clearly articulate vowels by the ages of 4 or 5

and have had some experiences in decoding vowels, the early introduction of vowels enhances their prospects of becoming independent readers at an earlier stage of the reading process.

2. Letter pairs that contrast visually such as *b* and *d* should be introduced early in your reading program. Although previous opinions discouraged this practice because of the possibility of confusing the letters with one another, the current thought is that the introduction of these visually contrasting letters teaches students to focus on the distinctive features of each letter within a specific context.

3. When teaching the first consonants, you should use the /f/, /s/, /v/, and /m/ sounds in words.

4. Your students should be introduced to variations in phoneme-grapheme correspondences from the beginning of reading instruction to prepare them for later reading.

5. Use four natural-order strategies to help your students learn to decode words and to develop independent phonics strategies: (a) look at the beginning letter; (b) next, look at the final letter; (c) then look at the medial letter; and (d) study the configuration of the word.

6. Use phonograms to introduce word families. For example, ask your students to write as many words as they can with *b, s, r,* and *t* as the beginning letter. Then, use these lists to develop games and other instructional activities.

7. Use language-development activities to practice new words learned through phonics. This aids your students' retention and application.

Finally, Stahl (1992) has recommended the following nine guidelines that you may want to consider to ensure the best graphophonic-analysis instruction you can provide:

1. *Develop students' concepts about print functions.* The development of print concepts (e.g., left-to-right orientation, phoneme-grapheme relationships, etc.) begins at home and is reinforced in kindergarten and in the first grade. These concepts can be developed through the use of language-experience activities, shared-book experiences, and authentic literacy learning tasks.

2. *Promote students' phonemic awareness.* Phonemic awareness is the awareness of sounds, or phonemes, in spoken words, which correlates highly with reading success. It is important that you promote your students' phonemic awareness by engaging in speaking and listening vocabulary activities that require students to attend to, reflect on, and orally produce individual sounds.

3. *Use clear and direct language.* Your oral language should be clear, precise, and direct when you engage in graphophonic-analysis instruction. If you use appropriate diction and enunciation, you will not only model proper speech patterns but also reduce your students aural errors (i.e., their hearing the incorrect pronunciation of words or sounds).

4. *Integrate graphophonic analysis into the total literacy program.*
   Phoneme-grapheme relationships and generalizations should not be
   presented in isolation. You should use the text students are to read to
   develop specific graphophonic-analysis skills. This instruction should be
   across the curriculum and could occur prior to literacy learning activities
   or in a minilesson following the literacy events.
5. *Focus on reading words and not learning rules.* Graphophonic rules
   should not be specifically taught or memorized by students. You should
   point out these rules to your students to highlight our English spelling
   patterns and to promote students' use of these patterns when analyzing
   unfamiliar words.
6. *Make extensive use of onsets and rimes.* Instead of teaching your students
   graphophonic rules, you can show them how to use onsets and rimes to
   analyze unfamiliar words. Onsets are the parts of words before the vowel,
   whereas rimes are the parts of words from the vowel onward. For
   example, when students encounter the unfamiliar word *wheat,* they
   should determine that *wh* is the onset and *-eat* is the rime. The students
   then associate the rime *-eat* with known words (e.g., *meat* or *heat*) to try
   to pronounce *wheat.* Teaching students to use onsets and rimes increases
   their accuracy in pronouncing syllables and promotes their comprehension
   of sentences and stories. The following thirty-seven rimes can be used by
   students to derive approximately five hundred words:

| -ack | -ain | -ake | -ale | -all | -ame |
|------|------|------|------|------|------|
| -an | -ank | -ap | -ash | -at | -ate |
| -aw | -ay | -eat | -ell | -est | -ice |
| -ick | -ide | -ight | -ill | -in | -ine |
| -ing | -ink | -ip | -ir | -ock | -oke |
| -op | -or | -ore | -uck | -ug | -ump |
| -unk | | | | | |

7. *Permit students to engage in invented spelling.* You should permit your
   students to use invented spelling during written-language activities (e.g.,
   "I am hape" for "I am happy"). The use of invented spelling in authentic
   contexts promotes students' phonemic awareness and
   graphophonic-analysis competencies.
8. *Have students focus their attention on the internal structure of words.*
   Teach your students to strategically examine the internal orthographic
   patterns in words and to use these patterns to identify unfamiliar words.
   These strategies could include "sounding out" a word with a
   letter-by-letter analysis or using the onset and rime of the unfamiliar word
   to pronounce it.
9. *Develop automatic word-identification abilities.* The purpose of
   graphophonic-analysis instruction is to teach students to identify
   unfamiliar words in text so that they can comprehend the intended
   "message." After students have identified unfamiliar words using
   graphophonic analysis, you should use a variety of instructional strategies
   to ensure quick and automatic word identification.

*M*any word-identification strategies and techniques for teaching them were described in this section. Also, the major cuing systems that encompass these strategies have been listed and discussed. Furthermore, conflicting information concerning what strategies to teach and how they should be taught has been presented. How are you to know what to do? How can even the best of teachers approach the task of teaching word-identification strategies without making reading boring or turning kids off? These are not easy questions to answer.

Reflect again on your diagram and your definition of reading that you developed in Chapter 1. Do your own beliefs about reading give you a clue as to how you would handle the word-identification strategies? Now, consider what you have read in the preceding sections, and under the heading Reflection Activity 4.4 in your journal, list the strategies you would work on and indicate how you might do it. Then indicate how this fits in with your own current beliefs about reading instruction.

## *Computer Hardware and Software Considerations*

This section describes general hardware concepts and explores technology for developing and expanding your students' reading vocabulary and word-identification skills and strategies.

If you decide to use technology in your literacy program, you should consider the following computer hardware.

*Multimedia Computer.* Probably the most exciting change in educational computing in recent years has been the advent of multimedia technology. Multimedia technology permits the integration of varied hardware (computers, televisions, video cameras and videocassette recorders, interactive videodisc players, etc.) and the use or creation of software that incorporates two or more types of media (e.g., text, graphics, still or motion video, animation, audio, and voice). If you are afforded the opportunity to select a computer, we recommend that you purchase a multimedia computer system that is compatible with the software available in your school district (e.g., Macintosh for Apple-Macintosh software or IBM/Compatible for OS2, Windows 3.11 or 95, PC-DOS and MS-DOS software). The Macintosh PowerPC (e.g., 9500/132) and the IBM Series 850 or Dell XPS P133c are three of the many multimedia computers you could consider. These systems have powerful microprocessors, expandable random-access memory (RAM)—we would recommend a minimum of four megabytes—and massive hard-disk storage devices—we would recommend a gigabyte hard drive—single or dual disk drives, SVGA monitors, and mice. They can also be fitted with a modem or fax/modem for telecommunication capabilities.

**CD-ROM Drive.** Multimedia computers are equipped with a CD-ROM drive that can access but not store information on CD-ROM disks. A CD-ROM disk can store 550 megabytes of media, and educational software producers are increasingly using this format to offer their memory-intensive programs (e.g., Reader Rabbit's Interactive Reading Journey). If your classroom computer does not have a CD-ROM drive, consult with your school district's technology specialist to determine the possibility of interfacing with a fast internal or external CD-ROM drive (e.g., NEC's 6X or six speed).

**Two Floppy Disk Drives.** If the situation permits, we would recommend that you buy a computer with two floppy disk drives—3.5 inch and 5.25 inch. First, having two different floppy drives will permit you to access programs on both 3.5-inch and 5.25-inch diskettes. Second, having two different disk drives will permit you to copy or back up programs to either 3.5-inch or 5.25-inch diskettes (e.g., copying from Drive A to Drive B or vice versa). Finally, two disk drives would reduce the program and data disk swapping activities that must be done when you use one disk drive to access a program (e.g., Drive A and a word processing program) and the other disk drive to save data created (e.g., Drive B and an appropriately formatted diskette to save the word processing files created). Finally, we would also recommend that you secure floppy disk drives that can access or save on high-density diskettes (e.g., 3.5-inch 1.44 megabytes and 5.25-inch 1.2 megabytes).

**SVGA Color Monitor.** Software developers are using graphics and color elements in their programs to increase instructional value and motivational attributes. If you have a high-resolution VGA or Super-VGA color monitor, you and your students will be able to take advantage of software with graphics and color elements.

**Interactive Videodisc Player.** A number of excellent literacy programs (e.g., Churchill's Curious George: The Making of Curious George) are available on interactive videodisc—a shiny, white, metallic long-playing record that holds 54,000 high-resolution frames on each side of the disc. You would need an interactive videodisc player to access these discs (e.g., Sony's Lasermax), and we would recommend that you secure a Level III player to interface with your computer. Interfacing a Level III videodisc player with your computer would permit you and your students to create and display computer- and videodisc-generated literacy materials.

**Laser or Near Letter Quality (NLQ) Printer.** You should obtain a laser (e.g., Hewlett Packard Laserjet 4L) or a NLQ printer (e.g., Apple Imagewriter II or Panasonic KX-P1624). These printers can be used with most software programs and print (produce hard copy) text as well as graphics. As you probably already know, laser or NLQ capabilities will give your text, particularly letters and reports, a businesslike look or quality.

**Modem or Fax/Modem.** A very useful input/output device is a modem (Modulate/Demodulate). With a modem and appropriate software, you and your students can engage in telecommunication activities such as accessing databases (e.g., the Internet), using electronic mail and bulletin boards (e.g., local computer club bulletin boards), establish home–school communications and literacy events, and retrieve instructional software or lessons through telecommunications. You should select a modem with 14.4 or higher baud capabilities and user-friendly software (e.g., Telix 3.2.2 or higher). Having telecommunications capabilities will enable you and your students to communicate with computer libraries, database resources, and individuals throughout the United States. Having a fax/modem, you and your students could also send and receive facsimiles.

***Alternative Input/Output Devices.*** We have just described standard input/output devices your computer should have (e.g., SVGA monitor, disk drive, and printer). Although we have not mentioned this, the keyboard is the standard input device you and your students will most likely use. However, there are alternative input/output devices that will increase the instructional capabilities of your computer. For example, if your computer has a mouse, joystick, touch screen, graphics tablet, or voice recognition unit, your students with limited keyboard skills could input data or respond to software program commands by moving the mouse or joystick to the correct area, by touching the computer screen to select an answer, by marking or writing on the graphics tablet, or just talking to the computer. If you have an optical character reading and inputting system such as a document scanner, you can also have your computer read and input (store) entire pages of text, graphics, and pictures. Also, a speech synthesizer output device will enable your computer to use human and robotic speech functions. Speech synthesis can assist young students or older students with limited reading strategies because the computer will "orally produce" what is on the screen or give verbal directions or commands.

***LCD Panel.*** One of the major disadvantages of computer-learning activities is the limited number of students who can access the computer at one time (e.g., one student, student dyads, or a small cooperative group). You can remedy this situation and use the computer with a large group or the whole class by securing a liquid crystal display (LCD) panel. An LCD panel is a projection device that is typically connected to a computer and used with an overhead projector to display computer-generated text, graphics, and other visual media on a screen or on the wall. Certain LCD panels have interactive pointing systems (e.g., Proxima's Desktop Project 2750 Cyclops) that permit you or a student to control the computer and software program by simply pointing at projected images. Also, there are LCD panels (e.g., Sharp Electronics's QA 1500) you can purchase that do not have to be connected with your computer. Again, an LCD panel would permit you to maximize your computer resources by allowing large groups or the whole class to view and discuss computer programs.

***Local Area Networks (LAN).*** Your school district or school may have a computer LAN, or computers connected by sharing a common line of communication. This is a very interesting and cost-effective system because it would permit you to communicate with other professionals in your district and share programs or files. You should consult with your school district's technology specialist to determine the existence of LANS and the possibility of interfacing with these networks.

As you go about the business of selecting reading vocabulary and word-identification software programs, you should keep in mind a number of software considerations. These considerations are as follows.

***Software Evaluation.*** Use external evaluation (e.g., program reviews in professional journals or books) and internal evaluation (e.g., program reviews in the school district) to determine what software may be appropriate and effective for developing and expanding your students' reading vocabulary and word-identification strategies. You may also want to collaborate with other elementary teachers in your district to establish an internal evaluation software review database.

***Varied Software Programs.*** Use various types of software programs. For example, you and your students could use applications programs (e.g., word processing, database, spreadsheet) to develop lessons, to use to teach particular skills, or to do classroom and homework assignments. Reading vocabulary and word-identification programs that are tutorial, demonstration, simulation, games, and utility in format are also useful. These program formats will give your students varied educational experiences and allow them to use different skills and strategies to interact with the software.

***Software Attributes.*** Select programs that have graphics and color elements, an edit mode to add to or revise the program, and a built-in management system. The edit mode and management system are particularly useful because they allow you to incorporate your specific reading data into the program and to keep track of the correct and incorrect responses of those students who use the program. Software with speech-synthesis capabilities would also be beneficial to your less-abled readers.

***Authoring Systems.*** If you have access to few software programs or there are limited programs that meet your needs, you could secure and learn how to use an authoring system to create your own programs. Unfortunately, the more powerful the system, the more time you will have to give to master these programs. However, some programs are user-friendly and have the features you would want in an authoring system. For example, if you have a multimedia computer and are unable to find appropriate multimedia software for your reading vocabulary or word-identification strategies, you could use an authoring system such as Apple's HyperCard, Macromedia's Authorware Professional, Asymetrix's Multimedia Toolbook, or IBM LinkWay Live and develop your own multimedia programs. Your students could also use Sunburst's My Media Text Workshop to create multimedia reading vocabulary or word-identification programs. And, you and your students could use word processing programs (Random House's Snoopy Writer or Spinnaker's Kidwriter) and publishing programs (The Learning Company's The Children's Writing & Publishing Center) to develop reading vocabulary and word-identification instructional materials and work products.

Literally hundreds of reading vocabulary and word-identification software programs are available to you. Some of these are listed for you here by area (Reading Vocabulary in Context, Contextual Analysis, etc.) and provide the title, suggested grade level (GL), and the company to contact.

## Reading Vocabulary in Context

| *Name* | *Company* |
|---|---|
| Learning to Read (GL 1–12) | Guarantee Software |
| Troll Reading Games (GL 4–6) | Troll Associates |
| Laser Learning Series (GL 4–10) | Laser Learning |
| Reader Rabbit 3 (GL 2–4) | The Learning Company |
| Joseph's Reader (GL 1–6) | JFL Enterprises |
| Language Experience Recorder Plus (GL K–12) | Teacher Support Software |
| My Favorite Monster (GL 1–3) | Quene |

## Sight Words

| | |
|---|---|
| The Montana Reading Program (GL K–3) | PDI |
| Word Recognition & Picture Sentences (GL 1–2) | CEEDE/Profiles |
| Word Works (GL 1–6) | Teacher Support Software |
| Word Memory Program (GL 1–3) | I/CT |
| Word-A-Tach (GL 1–3) | Hartley |
| Tunbunch Elementary (GL 1 and above) | Unicorn |

## Contextual Analysis

| | |
|---|---|
| Cloze Plus (GL 1–8) | Milliken/I/CT |
| Reading & Thinking I–IV (GL 2–12) | Intellectual Software |
| Word Blaster (GL 3–6) | American School Publishers |
| Cloze Power: Reading in Context (GL 3–8) | Orange Cherry New Media |
| Cloze Reading Comprehension (GL 3–8) | Intellectual Software |
| Gapper Reading Lab and Anthology (GL 2–8) | HRM Software |
| Fay's Word Rally (GL 1–7) | Didatech |
| Success with Reading (GL 3–4) | Scholastic |
| M-ss-ng L-nks (GL 3 and above) | Sunburst Communications |
| Using the Context (GL 3 and above) | Barnell Loft, LTD |
| Mission Control Word (GL 1 and above) | Hart, Inc. |

## Structural Analysis

| | |
|---|---|
| IBM Vocabulary Series (GL 3–8) | IBM |
| Roots and Affixes (GL 2–6) | Hartley |
| Prefix Power (GL 3–6) | MECC |
| Suffix Sense (GL 3–5) | MECC |
| Contraction Action (GL 2–4) | MECC |
| Compound it (GL 3–6) | MECC |
| Prefixes/Suffixes/Base Words (GL 3 and above) | Microlearning |
| Microcourse Reading (GL 3 and above) | Houghton Mifflin |

## Graphophonic Analysis

| | |
|---|---|
| Lexia Learning Series (GL 1–3) | Lexia Learning Systems |
| Starting & Winning Phonics Plus (GL 2–4) | K–12 Micromedia |
| Winning with Vowels (GL 2–3) | Hartley |
| Reader Rabbit 1 and 2 (GL K–3) | The Learning Company |
| Reading Machine (GL K–3) | Southwest EdPsych |
| Word Magic (GL 1–4) | Mindscape Education Software |

## Alphabet

| | |
|---|---|
| Talking Stickybear Alphabet (GL PreK–1) | Stickybear Software |
| Reader Rabbit's Ready for Letters (GL PreK–1) | The Learning Company |
| First Letter Fun (GL PreK–K) | MECC |
| Letter Recognition Skill Builders (GL PreK–2) | Edmark |
| Kinder Koncepts: Reading (GL PreK–1) | Midwest Software |
| Mickey's ABC's (GL PreK–K) | Walt Disney/Buena Vista |

## Phonemic Awareness

| | |
|---|---|
| Reader Rabbit's Interactive Reading Journey (GL K–1) | The Learning Company |
| First-Start Micro Reading Labs (GL K–2) | Troll Associates |

Finally, there are also a number of software programs that have voice-recognition capabilities (i.e., students can interact with the program by using verbal responses and commands) and speech-synthesis functions (i.e., the computer uses human or robotic speech to give verbal responses or commands) that are excellent for students with limited keyboard skills and reading strategies. One word-identification and reading vocabulary program that students can "talk to" and the program "talks back to them" is Chatterbox: the Voice Reading Ability Drill (Voice Learning Systems, Boulder, CO). This program uses eight hundred words to develop graphophonic strategies, sight vocabulary, and reading vocabularies, and students go through a number of steps as they interact with The Voice Reading Ability Drill software. Although The Voice Reading Ability Drill is just one of the many available programs that uses voice recognition and speech synthesis to develop reading vocabulary and word-identification skills, we would recommend that you develop your own specific multimedia software programs to match students' characteristics, literacy objectives, and technology attributes.

# *Summary*

This chapter presented general and specific concepts relative to developing and expanding elementary students' vocabularies and word-identification skills and strategies. The vocabulary and word-identification process was described and its importance in students' reading comprehension was discussed. Factors that affect vocabulary development and word-identification strategy learning and guidelines that can be used to plan and conduct vocabulary lessons were delineated and described. Five vocabulary strategies elementary teachers can adopt or adapt to introduce or teach vocabulary were identified and their instructional steps delineated and discussed. Also defined were four word-identification skills/strategies—using sight words, contextual analysis, structural analysis, and graphophonic analysis—that students can apply to identify unknown words. Examples were provided, underlying theories and principles were discussed, and instructional considerations were presented. We ended this chapter with a discussion of hardware and software to help you use technology to further develop and expand your students' vocabulary and word-identification skills and strategies.

## *Closing Activities*

1.  Go back to Reflection Activity 4.1 and the list of facilitative and functional skills you developed. Share and discuss these in a small group.
2.  Reading materials that contain specialized vocabulary and technical vocabulary may require many other facilitative skills to be understood. In a small group, choose a content area and then list all the skills your group feels would be "facilitative" in dealing with the content area. For instance, if history were the content area selected, your group might feel that a sense of sequence would be one important facilitative skill. Once you agree on the facilitative skills necessary to read that content area, separately list any functional or "real reading" skills you anticipated.
3.  In the same group, develop a list of concrete words that have a high level of visual imagery (suitable for sight learning) and would be relevant and probably highly frequent in the selected content-area reading materials. For instance, if history were the content area, then words like *war, flag,* and *government* might be appropriate sight words. Next, separately list harder-to-remember words—more abstract and less visual words that might be more difficult to learn by sight, but necessary to learn anyway because of their frequency in the content-area materials. (Include words that would be difficult to identify by word-identification techniques other than sight.)
4.  Find a difficult paragraph to read in an elementary-level textbook or other elementary-level book. Explain how you could use contextual analysis to figure out some of the words. Particularly note when you would use syntactic cues, when you would use semantic cues, and when you would use both cue systems. Could you explain this to a student? Your ability to explain your use of these cues to a student is modeling the analysis strategies. This modeling is an important instructional procedure.
5.  In a small group, share and discuss beliefs concerning the teaching of reading vocabulary and word-identification skills and strategies (as you listed and explained in Reflection Activity 4.3). How do your beliefs fit with the controversies regarding how to teach phonics and some of the other word-identification skills? Discuss this in, and with, your group.
6.  Using the library resources at your college, find a recent journal article discussing or reporting research on reading vocabulary development or on one of the word-identification skills or strategies described in this chapter. Read, summarize, and reflect on the article. Be prepared to share your summary and reflection in class.

### *References*

Adams, M. J. (1990). *Beginning to Read: Thinking and Learning about Print.* Cambridge, MA: The MIT Press.

Alvermann, D. E., and S. F. Phelps. (1994). *Content Reading and Literacy: Succeeding in Today's Diverse Classrooms.* Boston: Allyn & Bacon.

Ames, W. S. (1966). "The Development of a Classification Schema of Contextual Aids." *Reading Research Quarterly* 1:57–82.

Anderson, R. C., and P. Freebody. (1979). *Vocabulary Knowledge and Reading.* Urbana, IL: Center for the Study of Reading: University of Illinois. (Reading Educational Project No. 11).

Barrett, M. T., and M. F. Graves. (1981). "A Vocabulary Program for Junior High School Remedial Readers." *Journal of Reading* 25:146–151.

Blachowicz, C. L. Z. (1985). "Vocabulary Development and Reading: From Research to Instruction." *The Reading Teacher* 38:876-881.

Bond, G. L., and R. Dykstra. (1967). "The Cooperative Research Program in First Grade Reading Instruction." *Reading Research Quarterly* 2:5-141.

Brozo, W. G., and M. L. Simpson. (1995). *Readers, Teachers, Learners: Expanding Literacy in Secondary Schools,* 2nd ed. Englewood Cliffs, NJ: Merrill/Prentice-Hall.

Burns, P. C., B. D. Roe, and E. P. Ross. (1996). *Teaching Reading in Today's Elementary Schools,* 6th ed. Boston: Houghton Mifflin.

Chall, J. S. (1967). *Learning to Read: The Great Debate.* New York: McGraw-Hill.

Choate, J. S. (1987). "Reading Word Recognition." In J. S. Choate, T. Z. Bennett, B. E. Enright, L. J. Miller, J. A. Poteet, and T. A. Rakes, eds., *Assessing and Programming Basic Curriculum Skills* (pp. 67-92). Boston: Allyn & Bacon.

Collins, M. D., and E. H. Cheek. (1993). *Diagnostic-Prescriptive Reading Instruction: A Guide for Classroom Teachers,* 4th ed. Madison, WI: Brown & Benchmark Publishers.

Cudd, E. T., and L. L. Roberts. (1993/1994). "A Scaffolding Technique to Develop Sentence Sense and Vocabulary." *The Reading Teacher* 47:346-349.

Downing, J. (1976). "The Reading Instruction Register." *Language Arts* 53:762-780.

Duffy, G. G., and L. R. Roehler. (1986). *Improving Classroom Reading Instruction: A Decision-Making Process.* New York: Random House.

Durkin, D. (1980). *Teaching Young Children to Read,* 3rd ed. Boston: Allyn & Bacon.

Dykstra, R. (1968). "Summary of the Second Phase of the Cooperative Research Program in Primary Reading Instruction." *Reading Research Quarterly* 4:49-70.

Goodman, K. S. (1965). "A Linguistic Study of Cues and Miscues in Reading." *Elementary English* 42:639-643.

Gunning, T. G. (1995). "Word Building: A Strategic Approach to the Teaching of Phonics." *The Reading Teacher* 48:484-488.

Haggard, M. R. (1986). "The Vocabulary Self-Correction Strategy: Using Student Interest and World Knowledge to Enhance Vocabulary Growth." *Journal of Reading* 29:634-642.

Hare, V. C. (1984). "What's in a Word? A Review of Young Children's Difficulties with the Construct 'Word.'" *The Reading Teacher* 37:360-364.

Hargis, C. H., and E. F. Gickling. (1978). "The Function of Imagery in Word Recognition Development." *The Reading Teacher* 31:870-873.

Harris, L. A., and C. B. Smith. (1986). *Reading Instruction: Diagnostic Teaching in the Classroom.* New York: Macmillan.

Heilman, A. W., T. R. Blair, and W. H. Rupley. (1994). *Principles and Practices of Teaching Reading,* 8th ed. New York: Macmillan

HuffBenkoski, K. A., and S. C. Greenwood. (1995). "The Use of Word Analogy Instruction with Developing Readers." *The Reading Teacher* 48:446-447.

Johnson, D. D., and P. D. Pearson. (1984). *Teaching Reading Vocabulary.* New York: Holt, Rinehart & Winston.

Karlin, R., and A. R. Karlin. (1987). *Teaching Elementary Reading: Principles and Strategies,* 4th ed. San Diego: Harcourt Brace Jovanovich.

Kolker, B., and P. N. Terwilliger. (1981). "Sight Vocabulary Learning of First and Second Graders." *Reading World* 20:251-258.

Lapp, D., and J. Flood. (1986). *Teaching Students to Read.* New York: Macmillan.

Manzo, A. V., and U. C. Manzo. (1991). *Content Area Reading: A Heuristic Approach.* Columbus, OH: Merrill.

May, F. B. (1994). *Reading as Communication,* 4th ed. New York: Merrill/Macmillan.

McKeown, M. G., I. L. Beck, and M. J. Worthy. (1993). "Grappling with Text Ideas: Questioning the Author." *The Reading Teacher* 46:560-566.

Norton, D. E., and P. Hubert. (1977). *A Comparison of the Oral Reading Strategies and Comprehension Patterns Developed by High, Average, and Low Ability First Grade Students Taught by Two Approaches—Phonic Emphasis and Eclectic*

*Basal.* College Station, TX: Texas A & M University (ERIC Document Reproduction Service No. ED 145393).

Rupley, W. H., and T. R. Blair. (1983). *Reading Diagnosis and Remediation: Classroom and Clinic,* 2nd ed. Boston: Houghton Mifflin.

Savage, J. F. (1994). *Teaching Reading Using Literature.* Madison, WI: Brown & Benchmark Publishers.

Shad, M. (1993, May). *The Role of Vocabulary in Developmental Reading Disabilities. Technical Report No. 576.* Urbana, IL: Center for the Study of Reading (ERIC Document Reproduction Service No. ED 356458).

Smith, C. B., moderator. (1994). *Whole Language: The Debate.* Bloomington, IN: EDINFO Press and ERIC Clearinghouse on Reading, English, and Communication.

Spache, G. D. (1981). *Diagnosing and Correcting Reading Disabilities,* 2nd ed. Boston: Allyn & Bacon.

Spache, G. D., and E. B. Spache. (1986). *Reading in the Elementary Schools,* 5th ed. Boston: Allyn & Bacon.

Stahl, S. A. (1992). "Saying the 'P' Word: Nine Guidelines for Exemplary Phonics Instruction." *The Reading Teacher* 45:618–625.

Taba, H. (1967). *Teacher's Handbook for Elementary Social Studies.* Reading, MA: Addison-Wesley.

Yap, K. O. (1979). "Vocabulary: Building Blocks of Comprehension?" *Journal of Reading Behavior* 11:49–59.

# *C*omprehension

© Elizabeth Crews/The Image Works

# *Overview*

*T*his chapter explores the comprehension process. Various factors that influence comprehension are discussed. These include cognitive experiences, sociocultural factors, experiential background, prior knowledge, interest in materials, purpose for reading, linguistic experience, and reading rate.

A section on perspectives of comprehension presents the current models of comprehension that influence the reading process. Those discussed are the skills-based, holistic, and interactive models. Within this section, the comprehension process is classified into the two primary perspectives of traditional and contemporary. Both of these theoretical perspectives are examined in detail.

Within the traditional perspective of comprehension, a skills-centered philosophy is presented. The discussion of the contemporary perspective focuses on the importance of schema theory and prior knowledge, language-processing factors, and text factors incorporating the theoretical aspects of both the holistic and interactive models.

Final sections of the chapter discuss implications for the classroom teacher, and several comprehension strategies are presented.

## *Main Ideas*

- Comprehension should be the primary objective of the reading process.
- The current models of reading comprehension can be categorized into traditional and contemporary philosophies.
- Classroom teachers should be aware of past and present comprehension research to provide effective instruction.
- Important aspects of comprehension include higher-level comprehension skills, schema theory and prior knowledge, language-processing factors, and text factors.
- Classroom teachers can use many comprehension strategies and resources for basal reading, other story-type reading materials, and content area materials.

Comprehension is the complex process of understanding the meaning of one word or a series of words presented in oral or printed form. It includes not only the ability to decode words but also the awareness of their meaning. Thus, the ultimate objective of a reading program is to help students understand what they are reading.

# The Comprehension Process

Comprehension, the final goal of all reading activities, requires thinking and interaction with the text. It is not only difficult to observe, but it is also difficult to measure. It is the process of understanding the author's meaning. Savage (1994) has suggested that even more is involved in comprehension than understanding the intended meaning of the author. We must also consider the distinction between comprehension and interpretation. Comprehension is concerned with understanding what is contained in story text, whereas interpretation involves an individual reaction or response to that material. These are both closely related, and both are crucial to fully understanding the text.

One of the primary reasons that the concept of comprehension is difficult to grasp is that we are unable to fully observe the various ongoing perceptual, cognitive, and linguistic processes. Although the concept of comprehension may be elusive, it is essential to your students' success as readers for you to have a clear understanding of the importance of comprehension. You may ask why some students comprehend information more readily than others, and what enhances successful reading. You should also be concerned with your students' reading-comprehension on a daily basis by helping them to better understand those materials that they are required to read.

The concern about reading comprehension has intensified over the years. Public officials, parents, and teachers have expressed dismay at the apparent inability of many students to understand what they are asked to read. This concern has manifested itself in various ways, but perhaps the most important manifestation has been to encourage reading educators to focus on comprehension as a complex process that is essential to better understanding. Pearson (1985) has advanced three reasons for this intense interest in comprehension: (a) We no longer expend as much energy on issues that once dominated the reading field such as the best way to teach reading, the question of teaching the alphabet as a prerequisite to reading instruction, and how schools can build sound individualized programs; (b) practitioners are more concerned about comprehension; and (c) psychologists have an interest in reading comprehension as an area of research.

Pearson (1985) suggested the following six changes that would improve comprehension instruction:

1. Accept comprehension for what it is.
2. Change the types of questions we ask about selections students read.
3. Change our attitude toward and practices of teaching vocabulary.
4. Change the way we teach comprehension skills.
5. Develop curricular materials that recognize the fact that comprehension and composition are remarkably similar in process.
6. Change our conception of the teacher's role in the reading program.

In a more recent discussion, Fielding and Pearson (1994) recommended a number of suggestions to improve children's comprehension. These included providing enough time for actual text reading, emphasizing more teacher-directed

**Figure 5.1**
Factors that may
affect students'
comprehension.

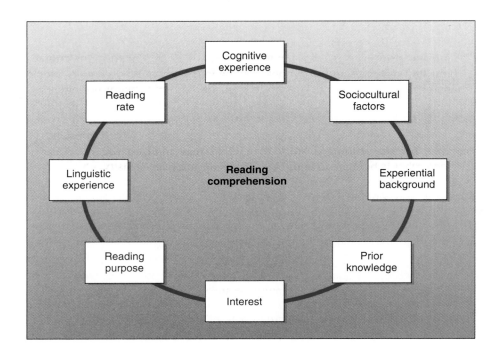

comprehension strategy instruction, providing more opportunities for peer
and collaborative learning, taking more time for discussing what has been read,
and devoting more of the children's instructional time to self-selected materials
within a student's reach.

# *Factors That Affect Comprehension*

A number of factors (see Figure 5.1) may directly affect students' comprehension of the various materials that they are assigned or choose to read. Eight of
these factors that have been identified are cognitive experience, sociocultural
factors, experiential background, prior knowledge, interest, purpose for reading, linguistic experience, and reading rate (Collins and Cheek 1993). Following is a brief discussion of each of these factors.

## *Cognitive Experience*

Cognitive experience is a critical factor in all aspects of learning; however, it is
especially crucial to reading comprehension. The ability of your students to
employ deductive/inductive reasoning as they read helps them to better analyze and interpret higher-order texts and questions as well as to develop the
strategies to recall and relate information and concepts from various selections
that require the activation of higher-order thinking. Reading is a complex process, and cognitive experience is an important part of this process.

*What can you learn*

## Sociocultural Factors

Another factor that influences comprehension is sociocultural experience. Students from "print rich" backgrounds have usually experienced more contact with written materials and storybook reading in their homes and communities, whereas those students from less "print rich" backgrounds might not have had as much access to printed material and story reading. Some families have a tendency to rely more on verbal than written communication, whereas others make more of a concerted effort to relate oral language to printed symbols. For example, parents reading a story to a child may indicate the relationship between what is being read and the symbols on the page. This type of reading experience develops an early awareness in many children that printed symbols on pages represent ideas and spoken words.

Another aspect of sociocultural background relates to the lack of experience with the complexities of standard English. For example, some children develop a different cultural and language perspective than others. Language differences and dialectical differences may create problems in comprehending materials written in standard English. However, Gemake (1981) found that although the oral reading of some students speaking a nonstandard English was adversely affected by dialectical patterns, the reading comprehension process was not. Comprehension of complex sentence patterns, however, was found to be more difficult for these students.

## Experiential Background

A factor that may exert a significant influence on your students' comprehension is their experiential background. For those students with varied experiences, the chances for success in reading are greatly increased; students with fewer experiences may have less of an opportunity to be successful. Many of those students will encounter selections in the basal reader or other materials with which they have difficulty relating. For example, students from the bayou country in Louisiana may be asked to read a selection about winter camping in the mountains of New England. If they have not had experience winter camping in the mountains (and have few ideas about what may be involved with topics such as ice-climbing, snow-shoeing, and frostbite, for instance), this could increase the likelihood that they may have difficulty understanding the selection.

## Prior Knowledge

A fourth factor that is closely related to experiential background, and crucial for your students to understand what is being read, is prior knowledge. Studies (e.g., Langer 1984; McKeown, Beck, Sinatra, and Loxterman 1992; Schumm, Vaughn, and Leavell 1994) have indicated that prior knowledge plays a major role in students' ability to comprehend, and a lack of prior knowledge can prevent students from activating the schemata that enable them to successfully comprehend whatever materials they are reading. If your students lack prior knowledge about topics that you ask them to read, there are numerous steps that you can take to improve their probability of reading-comprehension success. Tierney and Cunningham (1984) stated that you could (a) teach vocabulary as a prereading step; (b) provide different types of experiences in the classroom that fill in and expand on your students' existing knowledge; and (c) use a framework of concepts similar to the text or materials being read that will enable your students to build an appropriate background of knowledge.

### Interest

Interest in a topic or area is another factor that you will find affects your students' comprehension. Although many variables interact with the text to influence comprehension, students are more likely to read more effectively if the materials and content match their interests. Some of the variables that can affect comprehension by indirectly affecting the interest in the materials used are vocabulary, readability, concept load (the number of concepts in a selection), the compact presentation of information, and different organizational text patterns. Thus, the way in which the materials are written and presented to students affects not only their interest but also their comprehension. Additionally, the syntactic and semantic structure of materials can positively or negatively affect interest and comprehension.

### Reading Purpose

Another important factor that can affect your students' comprehension is their purpose for reading, or the purpose you give them for reading. Anytime that students are given an assignment, they need a purpose to direct and focus their reading. Setting a purpose for reading enables them to activate their background of experiences and to bring their prior knowledge to the reading task. Purpose setting helps your students to activate the schemata necessary for better understanding the material to be read.

Although you should set a purpose for reading when assigning materials, your students also play an active role in the purpose for reading. Once aware of the purpose, students can adjust their reading rate, reading strategies, and other cognitive strategies toward the stated purpose. For example, if the purpose is to review a chapter and develop an outline, students skim and scan for topics and details, seeking appropriate organization based on the concepts covered in the chapter. This involves the implementation of strategies that differ from those used to read a story for the main idea, to read a novel to analyze characters and plot, or to read and follow the steps necessary for a science experiment.

### Linguistic Experience

A seventh factor that affects comprehension is linguistic experience: syntactic, semantic, phoneme-grapheme, and other language experience. Students who enter school with well-developed language experience have a greater likelihood of becoming successful readers. Students who lack extensive language experience need to be given numerous opportunities to experiment with and increase their language skills. These opportunities will permit students to experiment with known as well as new vocabulary to further develop their semantic cuing system, to develop their syntax or structural language awareness, and to facilitate their phoneme- (sound) and grapheme- (sight) relationship knowledge. A rich linguistic base will also improve the likelihood that students will be able to read with comprehension. Many school districts are implementing language-development programs for those students entering school with fewer language experiences. Successful reading programs for such students typically emphasize a language-based curriculum using the language-experience approach or a variation of this procedure. Many of these students are from diverse cultural backgrounds that speak languages other than standard English. Because of the correlation between language learning and learning to read, the development of your students' language experience must be a primary objective.

### Reading Rate

The final factor we discuss that affects reading comprehension is reading rate. Many of your students will be unaware that their rate of reading can enhance or deter their comprehension. Thus, it is important that students are taught to adjust their reading rate to the type of material read. For example, students may read a book for recreation with a high interest level at a fairly rapid rate and still maintain adequate comprehension. However, students may read an assigned selection from the basal or a content text at the same fairly rapid rate but find that their comprehension decreases. For many students, this is a rather common occurrence, and it is important that you are able to assist them in determining an appropriate rate for various materials. Students should be taught to decrease their speed for certain types of content materials, such as science and math, and to select a comfortable rate for basal stories and recreational materials. Just helping your students become aware of how rate can affect comprehension may prevent many of the difficulties that they may encounter.

## Different Perspectives of Comprehension

For many years, comprehension was viewed as a process involving the systematic development and application of various skills, which were arranged in hierarchies that progressed from the lowest levels of thinking to the highest. As a result of the instructional procedures developed based on this theoretical perspective of teaching reading comprehension, some doubt has arisen concerning the opportunities for students to effectively develop their cognitive abilities to the fullest. The primary reason for this skepticism about teaching lower-level comprehension skills first, and then progressing to higher levels, is the apparent infrequent use of higher-level reading-questioning strategies by classroom teachers. In fact, a lot of instruction often focuses on basic-recall types of questions that may require only a one- or two-word answer. Thus, many students read primarily to locate the main idea, supporting details, and other such lower-level information. Because students are less frequently asked to evaluate and synthesize information, it is more difficult for them to develop the higher-level cognitive strategies they must have to become more critical readers. In other words, students should be able not only to identify the facts from a selection but also to understand the writer's intent.

A number of research studies investigating the issue of questioning strategies revealed some interesting information. For example, Taba (1965) found that teachers give out large amounts of information to students and then encourage them to give it back almost word for word. Guszak's (1967) study of second, fourth, and sixth graders further substantiated the belief that the questioning strategies used by elementary teachers were primarily of a literal nature. This study indicated that literal-level questions emphasizing recall and recognition composed 78.8 percent of all questions asked in the second grade, 64.7 percent in the fourth grade, and 57.8 percent in the sixth grade. Questions requiring evaluation and translation were used only 20 percent of the time, and in some instances, these required only a yes or no response. In a later study, Durkin (1981b) found not only a lack of the use of higher-level questioning strategies by teachers but also very limited instruction by teachers in higher-order comprehension. As a result of these and other studies examining the appropriate use of questioning strategies, teacher educators as well as teachers have become more aware concerning this important aspect of comprehension.

Comprehension instruction has traditionally focused on the widely accepted idea of the use of three levels of comprehension: literal, inferential, and critical. This focus has further centered on the theory of using taxonomies (classification systems) to indicate how students progress from the lowest levels of thinking to the highest and to assist teachers in developing appropriate questioning strategies for students at each level. These taxonomies have provided guidance to teachers in examining the learning process and in developing questioning strategies appropriate to the needs of individual students.

In examining the models of reading comprehension, you will see that some disparity clearly exists among the different perspectives. Each of the models is viewed as an integral component of various philosophies of how reading should be taught. For example, the skills-based model provides the basis for many materials you will use in teaching your students to read, especially many of the basal reading series, and is considered to be the foundation of the traditional philosophy of teaching reading. The holistic and interactive models provide the basis for a more contemporary philosophy. Although these latter two models of reading comprehension represent something of a break from traditional views and have similar goals, there are still differences between the two models that will have to be reconciled in order for the contemporary philosophy to make more of an impact on the schools. In the following sections on the traditional and contemporary philosophies of reading, a discussion of the essential elements of both views is presented for your information (see Figure 5.2).

Figure 5.2

Elements of traditional and contemporary comprehension philosophies.

> **Traditional philosophy**
>
> Implementation of a skills-based perspective
>
> Close parallel between certain taxonomies and the hierarchy found in the comprehension process
>
> Emphasizes the development of skills in a sequential progression from the literal level through the inferential level to the critical level

> **Contemporary philosophy**
>
> Implementation of the holistic and/or interactive perspective
>
> Certain language-processing factors including semantic and syntactical clues affect the comprehension process
>
> Certain text factors including story structure and expository structure affect the comprehension process
>
> Effective comprehension requires the reader to interact actively with the text

## *Traditional Reading-Comprehension Concepts*

The traditional philosophy of teaching reading comprehension typically encompasses the following views:

1. The implementation of the skills-based perspective of teaching comprehension includes the belief that the page brings more information to the reader than the reader brings to the page (Strange 1980). In other words, this is a text-based perspective.
2. Reading occurs primarily as the result of a two-stage process of decoding words and comprehension.
3. Reading involves letter identification, letter-sound correspondence, the putting together of sounds, and lexical (the denotative or dictionary-type meaning of words) search for word meaning, with the meaning of each word in a group used to understand the meaning of the group (Lapp and Flood 1986).
4. Comprehension skills are divided into a three-level hierarchy of literal, inferential, and critical skills. These skills are then arranged in ascending order of cognitive demand, meaning that the literal domain is less cognitively demanding than the inferential, and the inferential domain is less cognitively demanding than the critical domain.

5. The hierarchy operates in a linear manner, with the processing such that proficiency must occur at the literal level before the inferential domain can become operative, and inferential-domain proficiency must occur before the critical domain becomes operative (Gough, Ehri, and Treiman 1992).

Perhaps the most important element in the implementation of the traditional philosophy of reading-comprehension instruction, especially for teachers, is the effective application of reading skills at the appropriate level. This involves the important component of providing instruction for each student at the literal, inferential, and critical levels of comprehension. This essential step in the comprehension process is explored in the following section.

## Comprehension Skills

The comprehension skills are divided into three primary areas of literal, inferential, and critical, which are categorized according to their appropriate cognitive level of processing. In other words, each skill's placement in the comprehension hierarchy is determined as a result of being text-explicit (literal), text-implicit (inferential), or experience-based (critical) (Lapp and Flood 1986). A brief discussion of each of the three comprehension skill areas is presented here.

## Literal-Level Comprehension

Those comprehension skills that play a fundamental role in the total reading process and that are essential to the development of a sound foundation in comprehension are literal skills. For those advocates of a skills-based perspective of reading comprehension, students must learn the application of literal skills and develop proficiency in their use to progress to those skills of a higher cognitive order, that is, inferential and critical. Developing an adequate vocabulary is particularly important in the development of literal comprehension skills, since students with well-developed vocabularies typically find that literal-level cognitive processing is less difficult for them. On the other hand, students with less-well-developed vocabularies may experience greater difficulty in functioning at this level.

In the skills-based model of teaching reading comprehension, teachers establish some organizational structure of the various literal skills. This structure or hierarchy of skills is believed to enable your students to more effectively learn the skills at each of the cognitive levels. Those comprehension skills that are categorized as literal are to (a) understand concrete words, phrases, clauses, and sentence patterns; (b) identify stated main ideas; (c) recall details; (d) remember stated sequences of events; (e) select stated cause-effect relationships; (f) contrast and compare information; (g) identify character traits and actions; (h) interpret abbreviations, symbols, and acronyms; (i) follow written directions; and (j) classify information.

### Inferential-Level Comprehension

In moving from the lowest level of comprehension to the highest level, the second or middle level of cognitive processing involves those comprehension skills referred to as inferential. Such skills are believed to require a higher level of cognitive functioning than those on the literal level. In analyzing this cognitive domain, it is clear that more than just a superficial perusal of a selection is necessary. The reader must interact more with the text to understand the deeper meaning of the selection. Such essential skills as drawing conclusions, predicting outcomes, and synthesizing ideas must be employed in this process. The reader must also be aware of the language patterns used by the writer.

Other inferential skills of particular importance are context clues and signal words. The development of these skills is especially useful in understanding the material read. Some inferential skills that are most usually believed to be particularly valuable to the student are (a) predicting outcomes; (b) interpreting character traits; (c) drawing conclusions; (d) making generalizations; (e) perceiving relationships; (f) understanding implied cause and effect; (g) interpreting figurative language; (h) understanding mood and emotional reactions; (i) understanding the author's purpose; (j) using signal words to understand meaning; (k) examining language patterns including capitalization and punctuation; (l) summarizing information; (m) recognizing implied sequence; (n) using context clues to determine meaning; and (o) synthesizing information.

### Critical-Level Comprehension

The highest level of cognitive processing required of the reader encompasses those comprehension skills found at the critical level. Such skills are believed to require a higher level of cognition than those skills either at the literal or inferential levels. At this level of cognitive functioning, the reader is required to evaluate the material read and to make judgments about that material. To achieve success at this level, readers would employ their highest level of cognition.

Developing critical comprehension and critical reasoning will influence students throughout their school careers and in adulthood. Students do need to learn to perceive bias, differentiate between fact and opinion, and deal with various other situations that require a critical analysis of printed information.

Critical comprehension skills believed to be essential to effective cognitive development are (a) identifying relevant and irrelevant information; (b) interpreting propaganda techniques; (c) perceiving bias; (d) understanding the reliability of an author; (e) differentiating facts and opinions; (f) separating real and unreal information; and (g) understanding fallacies in reasoning.

## Contemporary Reading-Comprehension Concepts

We have elected to use the term *contemporary* to refer to the relatively more recent developments in reading-comprehension research that have strong implications for reading instruction and should continue to make an impact in the schools in the future. This body of research represents an emerging view of the comprehension process.

There are a number of views relative to the contemporary philosophy of reading comprehension, which includes both holistic and interactive models, that could affect the way you teach your students. These views include the following:

1. In the holistic model, the reader brings more information to the page than the page brings to the reader (Goodman 1967, Smith 1979). In other words, readers activate their prior knowledge to assist their understanding of the text, and they also develop a hypothesis that is verified by reading the material.

2. An integral part of the holistic model is that while an individual reads the brain carries on a search for meaning (at the top) and only descends into the lower (or bottom) levels to process the stimulus or gather the information to prove or disprove its original premise (Goodman 1976).

3. In the interactive model, reading is neither a bottom-up nor a top-down function, and information can be processed and synthesized at any point in the comprehension process (Frederiksen 1981, Rumelhart 1984, Stanovich 1980). In this model, each level functions independently, with input free to engage all levels of comprehension at any point. Thus, sound-symbol correspondences, letter-sequencing correspondences, and syntactical cues can be engaged at the literal, inferential, or critical levels.

4. Another characteristic of the interactive model is that simultaneous input is allowed to enter at any point in the reading process, and after a specific level is activated, information can be transferred to any other level without stopping to interact with its bordering level. For example, if the critical level of comprehension was activated by the reader, the literal level could be activated next if the reader's cognitive processing required this.

5. The primary premise of the interactive model is that cognitive processing need not occur in any specific place. The reader comprehending text at the critical level would not have to stop and interact at the inferential level before entering the literal domain. Thus, in the preceding example, the reader moves directly from the critical level to the literal domain, with the inferential domain used only as a directional link (Gauthier 1982).

In the following sections, some of the basic concepts that form the foundation for the contemporary perspective of reading comprehension are presented. The contemporary elements addressed are schema theory and prior knowledge, language-processing factors, and text factors.

### *Schema Theory and Prior Knowledge*

The educational implications of schema theory were recognized as early as the 1930s (Bartlett 1932), but it was not until the late 1970s that its impact on reading began to be felt. Since the influence of schema theory on the study of reading comprehension has increased dramatically, it is important that you are aware of this emphasis and also its applicability in designing and implementing reading-comprehension instruction.

What is schema theory? What is the relationship between schema theory and prior knowledge? Rumelhart (1984) stated that schema theory is concerned with knowledge—particularly how it is presented and how the representation enhances its use in certain ways. Since prior knowledge represents the information that readers have acquired from a lifetime of experiences and is essential to your students' comprehension abilities, an understanding of how it is stored and activated when needed is important.

Thus, schema theory is concerned with explaining just how the storage and activation of prior knowledge affects the comprehension process. Because comprehension is an active process, it relies on units or structures of knowledge referred to as schemata to organize and interpret what is heard or read (Lapp and Flood 1986). Therefore, a schema (remember, "schemata" is plural) is essential to the reader's understanding of the text.

There is evidence that students' schemata perform certain valuable functions for them as they interact with text. These essential functions include the following:

1. Summarizing the information that is known about a concept and how these pieces of information are related (Harris and Sipay 1990)
2. Relating other information to the generic concept and indicating how this knowledge should be used (Rumelhart 1984)
3. Providing a network of hierarchically arranged concepts (Durkin 1981a, 1984)
4. Allowing for the addition of new information into areas, or "empty slots," where pieces of information are missing in a schema as well as permitting for modification by new information (Harris and Sipay 1990)
5. Providing for concurrent utilization of more than one schema, since any one schema may not contain as much information as needed at any given time (Samuels and Eisenberg 1981)

Although schemata perform valuable operational functions that will assist students in successfully interacting with text, it will be the students' responsibility to determine when these schemata are needed to understand the text (Harris and Sipay 1990).

It is also important to keep in mind that schemata are acquired as a result of students' varied experiences. These experiences allow for the development of a knowledge base predicated on their encounters in life. The development of a knowledge base permits students to formulate hypotheses that are activated when they are involved with text. Since each reader's experiences vary to some extent from every other reader, you can expect text material to be interpreted differently by each of your students. This is one reason that reading the same text material may result in several different interpretations of its meaning. Each person's experiences facilitate the development of a knowledge base that influences that reader's interpretation of the written information. However, it is important to note that there is also published evidence suggesting that the hypotheses formulated by your students as a result of the interaction between their schemata and the text can be progressively refined, modified, or discarded (Mason et al. 1984).

As a facilitative teacher, you should ascertain just what your students know about given concepts, ideas, or terms. Remember, earlier in this text, we asked you to diagram the reading process (develop a written schema for reading) as you know it to be. We emphasized that your ideas were important because they were what you believed and were your starting point for reading education. In the same way, it is important to ascertain what your students already know about their world. When your students' points of origin are known, you can start there. If their schemata are incomplete, you can provide them with additional material and experiences to help them assimilate new information into their existing schemata. However, if they have misinformation in their schemata for a given topic, your job will be more difficult, since you will need to present additional material and experiences so that they will recognize their misinformation and accommodate the new information by either discarding information from their present schemata or by rearranging information to allow the newly learned information to fit. You can find out about your students' schemata by encouraging individual or class discussions, asking students to show pictures sharing what they know about a topic or concept, or getting students to diagram their knowledge (schemata).

Activities that could promote schemata development could include relevant educational television programs such as those on PBS and The Discovery Channel, using videotapes that allow students to better understand cultural differences in this and other countries, field trips, guest speakers, and films. It is also essential that you discuss new vocabulary with your students so that they can relate these to previously learned concepts and to new information. These are just a few examples of ways to help students construct meaning from text.

Closely related to the importance of prior knowledge in the comprehension process is the concept of making inferences. The ability to understand the writer's intent is critical if students are to be successful in their comprehension endeavors. Each student activates schemata that go beyond the stated information in text material to interpret the writer's meaning and also gain a deeper understanding of the writer's intent. Students who are able to draw on a wide range of knowledge have a better chance to spontaneously integrate the desired information and to make inferences, assumptions, and "best guesses" (Lapp and Flood 1986). Thus, the ability of your students to infer information concerning the writer's intent depends on the experiences and prior knowledge they have developed and their activation of the appropriate schemata essential to understanding text.

The following is an example of inferring information regarding the intent of the writer. What do you think is bothering these children?

> The sun was low in the sky, and the children were home from school.
> Mom was outside working in the flower bed. Dad had not yet arrived.
> Mom noticed that the children were irritable, somewhat less cooperative than usual, and she began rushing to finish.

Based on the information provided by the writer, you might guess that the children were tired, sleepy, hungry, or just wanted Mom in the house. If the facts are considered as presented—(a) the sun was low in the sky, (b) the children were home from school, (c) Mom was outside, (d) Dad was not home yet, and (e) the children were behaving erratically—you would probably guess that the writer's intent was to indicate to the reader that the children were hungry. In this example, you were asked to use your experiences and prior knowledge to activate the appropriate schema to understand the writer's intent.

## Metacognitive Strategies

We believe that students' activation of schemata when interacting with print is not enough. It is also important that students can monitor their own reading in a way that allows them to better understand what they are reading. This process of self-monitoring is *metacognition.* Most good readers do this without really thinking about it, but those readers who do not use effective self-monitoring strategies require the teacher's help in constructing meaning. Teachers can teach students how to self-monitor by modeling the appropriate strategies. It is becoming increasingly obvious that teaching students to use metacognitive strategies while they read is essential to constructing meaning from print. Assisting beginning readers and less-mature and/or less-abled readers who are not as adept at self-monitoring in developing these metacognitive strategies is particularly important. For example, students could be taught how (a) to query themselves "why" as they are reading; (b) to determine the main ideas and to use this information to self-generate questions to guide their reading; (c) to find the answers to the questions they have generated; and (d) to review their questions and answers to ascertain how the text information is being presented and how they are comprehending this text.

A variety of activities can be planned to develop your students' self-awareness and self-assessment abilities, as well as to help them develop strategies to self-regulate or make adjustments to comprehend what they read. Because comprehension is involved in every aspect of the school curriculum, your metacognitive and other comprehension activities can be developed as part of any aspect of your school-reading-related work and study.

One such activity was developed by Flippo and Lecheler (1987) to emphasize metacognitive awareness by the use of a simple rate-adjustment activity that encourages children to modify their reading rates and modify their concentration according to how difficult the material is. The steps in this activity are as follows:

1. Tell the students, by providing the reason, what you would like them to do. In other words, explain to them that because some sentences are more difficult than others, their reading rate should vary according to the difficulty of the content being read.
2. Use several sentences to illustrate what you mean and explain why you would read these slowly, moderately, or fast.

3. Ask "Why are some sentences read faster than others?" List the students' responses on the board.
4. Ask the students to suggest some sentences that they would read slowly, moderately, or fast. Write these on the board exactly as they dictate them.
5. Ask them to explain why they would read those sentences at those rates.
6. Ask students to comprehend the sentences before stating what their reading rates should be.
7. Have them find sentences in varieties of materials and textbooks, read them silently, and then give the rates they suggest for themselves.
8. Allow many opportunities for the students to share their sentences, suggested rates, and reasons.

Many activities similar to the preceding one can be developed for use in the elementary classroom. You will be limited only by your imagination.

## Reflection Activity 5.1

*D*o you see how easily metacognitive-awareness and self-regulation activities can be designed and implemented to fit your day-to-day instruction in the elementary classroom? Now, take a few minutes and brainstorm to see how many possibilities you can envision for developing metacognitive-awareness and self-regulating activities for your classroom. You do not need to detail the steps for these activities at this time, but just list in your reflection journal under the heading Reflection Activity 5.1 as many possibilities as you can imagine. Later, you might want to share these ideas and discuss them. You might even want to fully develop one or more of them for future use in your classroom.

## Language-Processing Factors

Language-processing factors and their effect on students' ability to successfully comprehend written text comprise a primary component of the contemporary philosophy regarding how an individual learns to read. These language-processing factors focus primarily on the influence of the semantic and syntactic structure of English and how this relates to the reading process. Note that semantics refers to the meanings of words, and that syntax is concerned with the structure of language, or how words interact to develop a working relationship.

The importance of semantics to successful reading has been well known to educators for many years. Students' use of semantic strategies is readily apparent early on, because these strategies involve using the meaning of surrounding words and other meaning clues to make appropriate inferences concerning new words in the text.

Clearly, your students will enter school with varied semantic strategies. These differences in strategies and vocabulary knowledge result primarily from their varied experiences and development of prior knowledge. As previously discussed, students activate their schemata to comprehend vocabulary and larger written text. If they have no prior experiences on which to draw, your students will be unable to relate to certain vocabulary and the concepts, ideas, or information it represents. Lack of relevant schemata for specific areas, and topics related to required readings, necessitates that you help develop pertinent schemata for students.

It is important for you to provide experiences to help your students develop their schemata. However, it is also important that students develop their own strategies for identifying unknown vocabulary. These strategies may have them asking someone for assistance or using the dictionary, but perhaps their most valuable strategy would involve their use of context. The use of context will allow your students to use surrounding words as clues to determine a specific word's appropriate use and meaning in that context.

Because of the importance of semantics in emerging literacy, some educators tend to overlook the importance of also using syntactic structure in learning to read or in comprehending text. Syntax plays a key role in the reading process because it is concerned with the order of language and how it works. For example, each sentence in standard English contains a subject and a predicate, and we use the order of these words in sentences to assist us in understanding written text. This order of words, in fact, is a crucial factor in signaling meaning.

The primary word classes in standard English sentences are nouns, verbs, adjectives, adverbs, and structure words. The first four classes of words are considered to be content words, which transmit the content of the message, and the fifth class of words is considered to be structure or function words (Hittleman 1983). These classes carry no meaning in and of themselves, but they act as markers of the content of words and establish relationships between classes of words. Furthermore, in a generative-transformational theory of grammar, each sentence has a deep structure and a surface structure. The deep structure is concerned with the basic syntactical relationships among the elements of a sentence, whereas the surface structure of the sentence is what we actually see on the printed page. Since meaning is derived from the interaction of words, the surface structure is retrieved from the deep structure of the sentence through a series of formal operations referred to as transformations. These transformations occur according to the basic principles of syntactical structure and represent the primary means through which the reader is able to gain meaning from the writer's message. In this series of transformations, the reader is taken from the surface structure of written text to the deep structure, thus enabling the reader to fully understand the meaning of the writer. Therefore, the ability of the reader to fully understand text is contingent on the reader's ability to retrieve deep structure.

## Text Factors

A third component of the contemporary comprehension perspective of gaining meaning from print involves text factors, with the primary focus on the interaction between the reader and the written text. Of major concern to reading educators interested in text factors is the extent to which text enhances or interferes with comprehension. It seems likely that there are various factors related to the written materials that your students will be expected to deal with as they read. It is these factors that we will examine more closely in the following sections.

## Story Structure

Narrative stories, such as stories children/students are exposed to before and after entering school, can be analyzed through their structure. This formal structural analysis would define the extent to which a story fits a particular structure or "grammar." Whaley (1981) defined story grammars as a set of rules that define the structure of text and one's mental perception of story structure.

Since these story structures appear to be an inherent part of our cultural background, exposure to stories at an early age increases the likelihood that we will internalize story grammars and use them to develop schemata for recognizing appropriate story patterns. These recognizable story patterns can help children anticipate what will happen next and make other predictions, providing more support for comprehending text.

## Expository Text

As students progress in school, they encounter textbooks that are expository rather than narrative in the manner in which information is presented to the reader. Such textbooks are concerned with teaching basic concepts and factual information in content areas like science or social studies. The emphasis on providing basic concepts and factual information to the reader represents a shift from story structures that are inherent in our culture to expository text that utilizes a variety of organizational patterns. Furthermore, because of the progressively increasing focus on content area material, some students moving into higher grades may experience difficulty in successfully comprehending this material. Thus, it is important that you become aware of this potential problem and be prepared to assist your students in comprehending expository text.

Meyer (1984) has summarized the research related to text structure and recommended the following:

1. Significant ideas found in the top levels of the content structure are more easily remembered than lower-level ideas.
2. The types of relationships found within expository-text structure affect recall more at the top levels of content structure than at the lower levels.
3. Different types of relationships at the top level of content structure affect recall in a variety of different ways.

4. Those students who can identify and use top-level structure develop more effective recall capabilities.

5. Students can be taught to identify top-level text structures.

Developing the ability to identify the various types of text organizational patterns and to become more aware of text structure is important if your students are to understand expository text. Meyer (1984) suggested several steps to follow in teaching your students to more effectively use text structure. These suggestions included the following:

1. Have your students use real-life situations to identify relationships (e.g., cause-effect, comparison-contrast, and so on), and explain how these relationships affect the structure of their texts.

2. Demonstrate to the students how to look for signal words that indicate relationships.

3. Use questioning techniques that emphasize inferring the relationships among ideas, and teach your students to ask themselves similar types of questions.

4. Provide guided practice designed to enhance instruction.

## *Implications for Classroom Teachers*

In examining comprehension, we have presented the basic concepts of two major perspectives of reading comprehension: what we have called "traditional" and "contemporary." Aspects of these perspectives have been researched and used in schools over a period of years and have been used to design reading-comprehension instruction. If the differences among the perspectives were strictly theoretical in nature and irrelevant to classroom instruction, you would not need to be concerned or involved. However, the differences and their implications go to the very core of reading-comprehension instruction. As a result, you and your instructional program may be left in something of a quandary. Is the skills-based model of comprehension more effective, or are the holistic and/or interactive models more effective in developing students' comprehension? These are crucial questions that have a direct impact on your classroom reading instruction. In our exploration of the issues involved in comprehension instruction, we elected to classify the skills-based model of comprehension as traditional, and the holistic and interactive models as contemporary.

We believe that it is important for you to be aware of these differences concerning theories of comprehension. It is also logical to assume that some basic ideas from both the traditional and contemporary perspectives are essential to gaining meaning from texts and facilitating learning. It is also important to be aware of such topics as the influence of prior knowledge and schemata on the ability of your students to gain meaning from print. Likewise, the facilitative teacher must know about language-processing elements and the various text factors that affect understanding. There is little doubt that each of these form an integral part of the comprehension process.

In further examining the question of which model of comprehension is more effective for your classroom, it is important to note that much of the research that we classified as contemporary is still evolving and much of the contemporary ideas and research have developed out of more traditional learnings. Also, although many schools are still implementing the more traditional model, many have included aspects of contemporary ideas and research. Thus, the primary question is whether the students' probability of success in gaining meaning from print can be improved by utilizing this contemporary knowledge and by integrating this knowledge with the ongoing experiences and knowledge learned from school implementation. We believe that the answer to this questions is yes. Yes, balancing and using ideas from traditional and contemporary learnings about comprehension best serve the needs of students. The facilitative teacher uses knowledge, research, and his or her own professional reflections to select and use the best from both to meet students' instructional needs.

## Comprehension Strategies

One of the challenging tasks that teachers have is developing their students' reading comprehension. Because reading is comprehension and because some students will have difficulty comprehending, it is important that you place the teaching of comprehension as your number-one program priority. As you have gathered from reading this far into this chapter, many books and articles have been written that state varied positions on what the comprehension process is and what should be done to develop comprehension abilities. We are keenly aware that it is impossible to describe adequately the numerous comprehension strategies that could be effectively used in your reading program. However, some principles and specific strategies that may be worth considering as you design and implement your reading program are reviewed in the following section.

### General Instructional Strategies

The following list provides some general strategies to use for enhancing comprehension in your reading program.

- Provide strategies that emphasize vocabulary development through interaction with authentic texts to help students construct meaning.
- Use questioning techniques that emphasize the use of appropriate questions and that encourage interaction among students and between students and yourself.
- Encourage students to become more involved by using positive feedback when using questioning strategies. Use modeling, scaffolding, and positive reinforcement as integral components of direct instruction.
- Modeling metacognitive strategies for students should occupy a primary role in comprehension instruction. Use strategies that clearly indicate to your students a direct or indirect connection to your instruction.

## Specific Instructional Strategies

A number of strategies also are available to implement your comprehension activities or to promote your students' reading-comprehension processes. These strategies can be used with your authentic materials as well as with commercial reading program materials (basals) and not only are easy to employ but also can be used with both younger and older elementary students. The effective use of these strategies could very easily be one of the determining factors in whether or not students learn to construct meaning from text. Because of their importance to the reader, this section is devoted to the discussion of selected comprehension strategies that you can demonstrate and model for your students. Remember, students must be given enough time to learn how to use these strategies effectively through practice, teacher feedback, and assessment.

## Directed Reading and Thinking Activity (DRTA)

The first instructional strategy that we suggest for your consideration is the DRTA. The objective of the DRTA, which was developed by Stauffer (1969), is to improve comprehension performance by having students focus their attention on particular text (e.g., story titles) and to make predictions about what they are to read based on those text features. Although the DRTA is a dynamic procedure and can be conducted in various ways, a number of steps can be used in implementing this comprehension procedure. These steps include the following:

1. Direct the students' attention to the story title and ask them to predict what the story is about based on the title. After students have volunteered their hypotheses and reasons for their predictions, you may want to ask selected students whether they agree or disagree with the stated hypotheses and to give their reasons for agreeing or disagreeing.

2. Have the students read specific subtitles and ask them to predict what the story is about based on the subtitles. Ask selected students whether they agree or disagree with the stated hypotheses and to give their reasons for agreeing or disagreeing.

3. Direct the students' attention to particular vocabulary, phrases, and sentences and ask them to use these text features to hypothesize what the story is about. Select other students to tell the class whether they agree or disagree with the stated hypotheses and why they have reached these decisions.

4. Have the students visually inspect specific pictures, tables, and figures and ask them to hypothesize what the story is about based on this graphic information. Ask selected students whether they agree or disagree with the stated predictions and to give their reasons for agreeing or disagreeing.

5. Ask the students to read the text to confirm or negate their predictions or hypotheses.

Rude and Oehlkers (1984, pp. 223–24) have also described how to adapt the DRTA to meet the needs of less-abled readers. According to these reading educators, you can improve these students' comprehension performance by doing the following:

1. Whenever possible, focus [these] students' attention on one question throughout the story. . . . Question[s] that focus [attention] can be identified by determining the central problem or conflict.
2. Limit the number of predictions. It is not necessary for every student to make a personal prediction.
3. Delay a request for prediction until students are well into the story. . . .
4. Rewrite portions of high-interest stories at the students' instructional level . . . [You could] read portions of the original version . . . [to your students] while the students read selected paragraphs in a simplified version.

One of the recurring problems inherent in using the DRTA with younger elementary students involves the difficulty in eliciting responses from these children. Johnston (1993) suggested several ideas that could improve the students' responses and increase the likelihood of their participation. These include modeling for students; providing choices; using predictable books; maintaining neutrality in commenting on whether predictions are good or bad, right or wrong; asking students to write down their ideas if they are reluctant to voice a prediction; inviting revision by offering students the opportunity to change their predictions when more information is available; allowing students to collaborate with other students; encouraging less-vocal students by calling on these students first; eliciting brief summaries of what has just been read to encourage those students who are unsure of what to say; and offering outrageous inaccurate predictions of your own that will require the students to think about and to refute your predictions.

Again, the DRTA is a dynamic comprehension teaching strategy that is easy to implement and can more actively involve your students in the comprehension process.

## Modeling Using Think-Alouds

We believe that modeling appropriate literacy learning behavior for your students is one of your most important responsibilities. Although many of your students will be able to effectively construct meaning from print without modeling, others will not. One of the more effective modeling strategies that encourages discussion and teacher-student interaction is think-alouds. Baumann, Jones, and Seifert-Kessell (1993) concluded from their research that think-alouds help students develop the ability to monitor their reading comprehension and to activate strategies to correct comprehension breakdowns. Fawcett's (1993) review of the literature suggested that using students as think-aloud models represents a more recent theory of knowledge as socially constructed and represents more authentic thinking.

Think-alouds represent an effort by the teacher to demonstrate to the students the thinking processes that are activated during reading. This is achieved primarily by the students following along as the teacher interacts with the text material by analyzing vocabulary, demonstrating how prior knowledge is activated, making predictions, and discussing how to critically construct meaning from print. After modeling reading experiences to the students, you may wish to use collaborative groups to allow the students to model the reading process to each other. To vary this strategy and to provide more extensive one-to-one instruction, you could tape-record individual students and take notes of their nonverbal behavior to better analyze their reading progress.

## Scaffolding

Scaffolding is a strategy that originated from developmental theories of learning suggested by Vygotsky (1978). He believed that adults could assist children in functioning at higher psychological levels. He theorized that the assistance of an adult allowed a child to operate in the "zone of proximal development," which is a level between completely independent learning and assisted learning. This concept of learning has led to the idea of *scaffolding* in the educational community in the belief that teachers could provide assistance within the child's learning comfort zone without impinging on the child's ability to internalize a specific task or concept.

Beed, Hawkins, and Roller (1991) indicated that scaffolding has three essential features. First, interaction takes place in a collaborative setting and closely follows the student's intention; second, the teacher and the student operate within the parameters of the student's zone of proximal development; and third, support is gradually withdrawn, with a final goal of independence by internalizing the knowledge taught. These authors conceptualized a strategy for implementing this theoretical construct in regard to reading instruction in the elementary classroom. This strategy involves the use of five scaffolding levels that can be applied to any number of comprehension or other learning tasks such as vocabulary development. The first level is the least independent and most concrete and involves teacher modeling, a concept we discussed in regard to think-alouds. Next, the teacher models with verbal explanations and invites student participation. Third, the teacher identifies appropriate strategies for students as they work through the task in a collaborative effort. The fourth level involves verbal cuing without reference to the specific elements of a strategy. The teacher refers to the name of a strategy, such as "looking back in the text," but then the student completes the task alone. At the fifth and final level, general verbal cuing occurs, which will extend to any context and provides the least teacher support. Teachers encourage students to think critically by asking such questions as, "What strategy can you activate to help you?"

We believe that scaffolded instruction has much potential in teaching reading to elementary students, especially for those children who require additional teacher support. Scaffolding enables the teacher to become more directly involved in the learning process without detracting from the students' natural progression to becoming independent learners.

**Figure 5.3**

An example of a basic story frame format.

Developed by Heather Gaspard, Audubon Elementary School, Baton Rouge, Louisiana.

**Title:** _____

**Author:** _____

| Beginning | Middle | End |
|-----------|--------|-----|
|           |        |     |

_____

_____

_____

_____

_____

_____

## Story Frames

Story frames are particularly useful in giving students, especially primary-grade elementary students, some structure to a story. Using story frames enables these students to add a concrete dimension to the content of the stories that they read, as if they were "framing out a house," if you will. First, they pour the foundation, then put up the sides and the roof before starting on the inside of the house. This technique has proven to be quite successful with teaching reading comprehension to younger to middle-grade elementary school children. It is particularly helpful to those children who lack appropriate experiences to have developed a sufficient knowledge base to effectively comprehend some children's stories. This strategy is especially effective in integrating reading and writing and can be adapted to meet the needs of a variety of stories.

In a typical story frame, students search for the problem, events that contribute to solving the problem, how the events are sequenced, what the author's message is, and why the students may or may not have liked the story. A story frame can also portray the feelings and beliefs of the characters in the story and can serve to analyze one or more of the characters (see Figures 5.3, 5.4, and 5.5).

Duncan (1993) suggested that comparing film and text helps elementary students to build critical comprehension. She believes that if children have adequate schemata, they should read the text before viewing the film; however, if

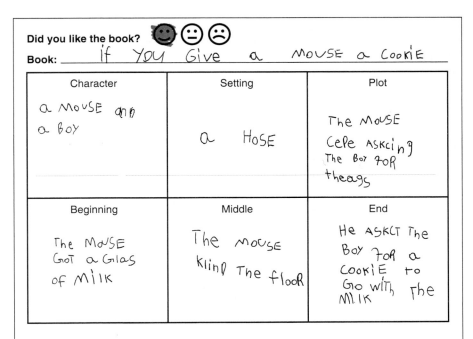

**Did you like the book?** 😄 😐 😞

**Book:** ____If  YOU  Give  a  MOUSE  a  CookiE____

| Character | Setting | Plot |
|---|---|---|
| a MOUSE and a BOY | a HOSE | The MOUSE CePe ASKCing The BOY 7OR theags |

| Beginning | Middle | End |
|---|---|---|
| The MOUSE GoT a GlaS oF Milk | The MOUSE KlinP The flooR | He ASKCT The BOY 7oR a CookiE to Go wiTh the MILK |

**Figure 5.4**
An example of an extended story frame format with a student's responses to a story.
Used with permission of Heather Gaspard, Audubon Elementary School, Baton Rouge, Louisiana.

*The Secret Garden*

they do not, she believes that they should view the film first to enhance their prior knowledge of the story to be read. One of the activities that she used was an adaptation of a story frame. In this adapted story frame she had the students view the film and then read the book of a popular children's story. Students were asked to complete a story frame that analyzed the main character in the story and compare this with the film version of the character. This activity required a critical evaluation of the character traits in both venues and a response to dramatic interpretation.

We believe that Duncan's suggestion of comparing films and books is an instructionally sound and highly motivating teaching procedure. Not only did she use a story frame activity in this lesson, but she used three other activities that we believe would facilitate children's comprehension of a story. These included a Venn diagram that compared and contrasted characters in the film and books of another popular children's book, writing a film review of a popular children's movie, and creating a storyboard for an animated film story that the children would create collaboratively and with the teacher (see Figure 5.6 for an example of a Venn diagram).

We believe that the use of story frames in giving structure to children's stories would be helpful to most students in developing their understanding of concepts and in constructing meaning from text.

**Figure 5.5**

An example of an extended story frame format with a student's responses to a story.

Used with permission of Heather Gaspard, Audubon Elementary School, Baton Rouge, Louisiana.

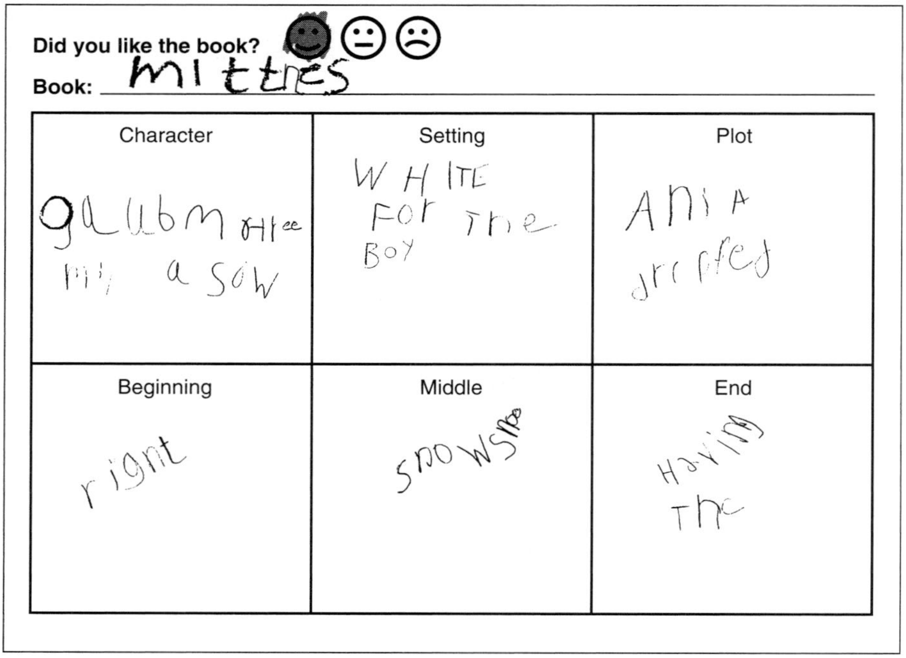

## Readers' Theater

Readers' Theater is a technique that empowers readers by actively projecting them into the text through their voices and gestures. Through this medium, students use "reading rate, intonation, and an emphasis on the meaning-bearing cadences of language to make the print come alive" (Hoyt 1992, p. 582). Readers' Theater is an excellent motivational strategy for children that integrates oral communication and comprehension in a way that captures the students' imagination and interest. It can be used in a variety of ways with one child or several; however, we believe that this strategy is more effective when used as a collaborative activity involving several children. Readers' Theater can be done with narrative stories from your basal, trade books, as well as with certain expository text (such as from a history selection).

The teacher's role in Readers' Theater is that of a facilitator who uses modeling to demonstrate the use of different reading rates, intonation, and expression. Sloyer (1982) suggested several steps that the teacher should follow in using this strategy. These include selecting material that fits the needs of students; discussing the theater or a movie as a natural springboard for Readers' Theater; introducing students to a short story for which a natural, built-in script exists and then allowing them time to explore the nuances of the script; using the existing script as a model in adapting another story and then adapting the story; preparing for theatrical production by introducing students to some aspect of stage craft, to different areas of the stage where action might occur

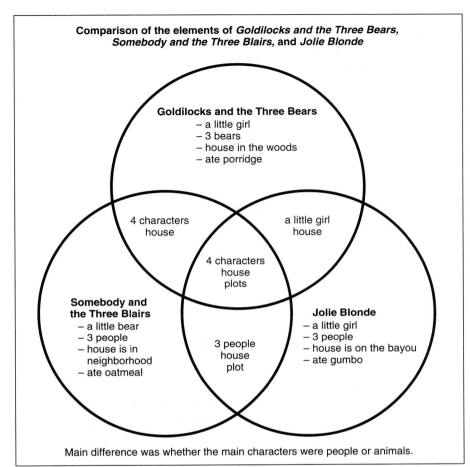

**Comparison of the elements of *Goldilocks and the Three Bears*, *Somebody and the Three Blairs*, and *Jolie Blonde***

**Goldilocks and the Three Bears**
– a little girl
– 3 bears
– house in the woods
– ate porridge

4 characters
house

a little girl
house

4 characters
house
plots

**Somebody and the Three Blairs**
– a little bear
– 3 people
– house is in neighborhood
– ate oatmeal

3 people
house
plot

**Jolie Blonde**
– a little girl
– 3 people
– house is on the bayou
– ate gumbo

Main difference was whether the main characters were people or animals.

**Figure 5.6**
An example of a Venn diagram.

Developed by Judy Burch, Audubon Elementary School, Baton Rouge, Louisiana.

and characters might be located, to the use of props and body movements, and to practice for the performance; performing the play (story) and then following up with discussions about different aspects of the play (story) such as characters and setting to provide feedback to the children; and finally, preparing a full-length program, if you decide that is appropriate.

## Computer Hardware and Software Considerations

Another chapter introduced you to state-of-the-art hardware that can be used in the elementary classroom.

A myriad of software issues should be considered before purchasing and using programs for comprehension instructional purposes. Generally, you will find that word-identification and vocabulary software programs are more plentiful and better designed than reading-comprehension programs. Regardless, the

Readers are empowered by actively interacting with text.
© Michael Siluk

software you select to support your comprehension instruction should permit personal and instructional productivity (e.g., simulation and opportunities to practice needed skills and strategies) and as much as possible should match the printed materials your students are using (e.g., Scholastic's WiggleWorks– seventy-two trade books and matching software) and your instructional goals and needs. Additionally, because so many comprehension software programs are available for group purposes (e.g., networking) or for individual activities, you will need to determine your purposes and needs before evaluating and using any of these materials. For example, series software that you could use within your literacy program to promote your students' reading comprehension include the following (GL = Recommended Grade Level):

| Name | Company |
| --- | --- |
| The Big Book Maker Series (GL Pre-8) | Toucan |
| Reading for Comprehension (GL 2-6) | Intellectual Software |
| Reading for Meaning (GL 2-8) | IBM |
| Comprehension Power (GL 1-12) | Milliken & I/CT |
| Comprehension Connections (GL 4-9) | Milliken |
| Multimedia Story Book Series | EBook |
| Troll Micro Mysteries (GL 2-4) | Troll Associates |
| Troll Reading Games (GL 4-6) | Troll Associates |
| Incredible Adventure of Quentin (GL 1-5) | Pelican/Toucan |

| | |
|---|---|
| Reading Well Series (GL 2-5) | Mindscape Educational Software |
| Living Books (GL K-3) | Broderbund |
| The Amazing Reading Machine (GL 3-6) | MECC |
| Express Delivery Reading Series (GL 2-6) | MECC |
| Relevant Reading Series (GL 1-8) | Aquarius |
| Twistaplot Reading Adventure (GL 4-8) | Scholastic |

Individual software programs that you could decide to use to further develop or reinforce your students' specific and varied comprehension skills and strategies include:

| Name | Company |
|---|---|
| Beginning Reading Comprehension (GL K-2) | EPC |
| Primary Steps to Comprehension (GL 1-3) | EPC |
| Steps to Reading Comprehension (GL 1-8) | EPC |
| Scholastic Reading Comprehension (GL 4-6) | Scholastic |
| Pickleface and Other Stories (GL 4-5) | Hartley |
| Stickybear Reading Comprehension (GL 2-6) | Stickybear |
| Reading Comprehension (GL 4-7) | Stickybear |
| Four Basic Reading Skills (GL 4-8) | Brain Bank |
| Cause and Effect (GL 3-6) | Hartley |
| Multiple Meanings (GL 4-6) | Hartley |
| Facts or Opinions (GL 3-6) | Harvard Associates |
| Reading for Meaning (GL 2-4) | Harvard Associates |
| Getting the Main Idea (GL 2-5) | Saddleback Educational, Inc. |
| Context Clues (GL 2-5) | Saddleback Educational, Inc. |
| Drawing Conclusions (GL 2-5) | Saddleback Educational, Inc. |
| Inference (GL 2-5) | Saddleback Educational, Inc. |
| Fantasyland/Reading between the Lines (GL 3-6) | Learning Well |
| Galaxy Search/Predicting Outcomes (GL 2-6) | Learning Well |
| Ace Detective (GL 3+) | Mindplay |
| Ace Reporter (GL 3+) | Mindplay |
| Ace Explorer (GL 3+) | Mindplay |
| Ace Inquirer (GL 3+) | Mindplay |
| Super Solvers Midnight Rescue (GL 3-6) | The Learning Company |
| Favorite Fairy Tales (GL 1-3) | Quene |
| Aesop's Fables (GL 1-5) | Unicorn |
| The Puzzler (GL 3-6) | Sunburst Communications |
| Charlotte's Web (GL 3-6) | Sunburst Communications |

If you cannot find appropriate multimedia software for your reading-comprehension classroom needs, you may want to consider designing comprehension programs using an authoring system such as Apple's HyperCard,

Macromedia's Authorware Professional, Asymetrix's Multimedia Toolbook, or IBM LinkWay Live. Your students could also use Sunburst's My Media Text Workshop to create multimedia comprehension programs. Finally, you and your students could use integrated programs (Claris Works or Microsoft Works), word processing programs (Microsoft Word, WordPerfect, Random House's Snoopy Writer, or Spinnaker's Kidwriter), and publishing programs (The Learning Company's The Children's Writing & Publishing Center) for reading-comprehension-writing purposes.

## Summary

This chapter explored comprehension and its role in the reading process. Several factors were discussed that influence reading comprehension. These included cognitive experiences, sociocultural factors, experiential background, prior knowledge, interest, purpose for reading, linguistic experience, and reading rate. Also, perspectives of comprehension currently advocated by reading educators were delineated and reviewed and classified as either traditional or contemporary perspectives. Within the traditional perspective of comprehension, a skills-centered perspective was presented. The discussion of the contemporary model of comprehension focused on the importance of schema theory and prior knowledge, language-processing factors, and text factors incorporating aspects of both the holistic and interactive models. Classroom teachers were encouraged to note that many of the contemporary ideas are outgrowths and refinements of the more traditional perspective and that it is important for facilitative teachers to use and balance ideas that fit the instructional needs of their students along with their own beliefs and professional study and reflections.

The final sections of this chapter discussed pedagogical implications for classroom teachers and presented several comprehension instructional strategies appropriate for group or individual settings.

## Closing Activities

1. In a small group, share and discuss any implications you see for teaching based on your current understanding of schema theory. Are you assimilating and accommodating the materials presented thus far in the text into your existing schemata? How do you see that evolving?

2. As we indicated, many school systems are still implementing the more traditional model of comprehension, although many have also included aspects of contemporary ideas and research. Do you see ways of incorporating even more aspects of the contemporary model into the existing school programs? Write a short position paper discussing this problem. Be prepared to share your paper in class.

3. As a part of your field activities for this course, have three students read several passages to you. When each has finished reading the passages, ask several questions on the literal, inferential, and critical levels. As each student answers these questions, note at which level or levels of questioning the student had more success. What other information about each student's comprehension do you think is important for you to know? Why?

4. As part of your field activities for this course, review a story from a children's book actually being used in a second-grade classroom. Then select, develop, and implement one of the following three strategies or activities with a small group of children. After implementing the strategy, summarize the results, and be prepared to share them in class with your peers.
   (a) DRTA
   (b) Think-alouds
   (c) Story Frame

5. Using the library resources at your institution, examine the information pertaining to the traditional and contemporary aspects of comprehension. Write a brief research paper discussing the implications for present and future classroom reading instruction.

## References

Bartlett, F. C. (1932). *Remembering: A Study in Experimental and Social Psychology.* Cambridge, England: Cambridge University Press.

Baumann, J. F., L. A. Jones, and N. Seifert-Kessell. (1993). "Using Think-Alouds to Enhance Children's Comprehension Monitoring Abilities." *The Reading Teacher* 47(3): 184–193.

Beed, P. L., E. M. Hawkins, and C. M. Roller. (1991). "Motivating Learners Toward Independence: The Power of Scaffolded Instruction." *The Reading Teacher* 44(9): 648–655.

Collins, M. D., and E. H. Cheek. (1993). *Diagnostic-Prescriptive Reading Instruction: A Guide for Classroom Teachers,* 4th ed. Madison, WI: Brown & Benchmark Publishers.

Duncan, P. H. (1993). "I Liked the Book Better: Comparing Film and Text to Build Critical Comprehension." *The Reading Teacher* 46(8): 720–725.

Durkin, D. (1981a). "What Is the Value of the New Interest in Reading Comprehension?" *Language Arts* 58:23–43.

———. (1981b). "Reading Comprehension Instruction in Five Basal Reader Series." *Reading Research Quarterly* 16(4): 515–544.

———. (1984). "Is There a Match between What Elementary Teachers Do and What Basal Readers Recommend?" *The Reading Teacher* 37:734–744.

Fawcett, G. (1993). "Using Students as Think Aloud Models." *Reading Research and Instruction* 33(2): 95–104.

Fielding, L. G., and P. D. Pearson. (1994). "Reading Comprehension: What Works." *Educational Leadership* 51(5): 62–68.

Flippo, R. F., and R. L. Lecheler. (1987). "Adjusting Reading Rate: Metacognitive Awareness." *The Reading Teacher* 40(7): 712–713.

Frederiksen, J. R. (1981). "Sources of Process Interaction in Reading." In A. Lesgold and C. Perfetti, eds., *Interactive Processes in Reading* (pp. 361–385). Hillsdale, NJ: Erlbaum.

Gauthier, L. R. (1982). *A Study of the Three-Level Hierarchy of Information Processing in Reading Comprehension with Respect to Cognitive Demand.* Unpublished doctoral dissertation, Louisiana State University, Baton Rouge, Louisiana.

Gemake, J. (1981). "Interference of Certain Dialect Elements with Reading Comprehension for Third Graders." *Reading Improvement* 18:183–189.

Goodman, K. S. (1967). "Reading: A Psycholinguistic Guessing Game." *Journal of the Reading Specialist* 6:126–135.

———. (1976). "Reading: A Psycholinguistic Guessing Game." In H. Singer and R. Ruddell, eds., *Theoretical Models and Processes of Reading.* Newark, DE: International Reading Association.

Gough, P. B., L. C. Ehri, and R. Treiman. (1992). *Reading Acquisition.* Hillsdale, NJ: Erlbaum.

Guszak, F. J. (1967). "Teaching Questioning and Reading." *The Reading Teacher* 21:227–234.

Harris, A. J., and E. R. Sipay. (1990). *How to Increase Reading Ability: A Guide to Developmental and Remedial Methods,* 9th ed. New York: Longman.

Hittleman, D. R. (1983). *Developmental Reading, K–8: Teaching from a Psycholinguistic Perspective,* 2nd ed. Boston: Houghton Mifflin.

Hoyt, L. (1992). "Many Ways of Knowing: Using Drama, Oral Interactions, and the Visual Arts to Enhance Reading Comprehension." *The Reading Teacher* 45(8): 580–584.

Johnston, F. R. (1993). "Improving Student Response in DR-TAs and DL-TAs." *The Reading Teacher* 46(5): 448–449.

Langer, J. A. (1984). "Examining Background Knowledge and Text Comprehension." *Reading Research Quarterly* 19(4): 468–481.

Lapp, D., and J. Flood. (1986). *Teaching Students to Read.* New York: Macmillan.

Mason, J., and the Staff of the Center for the Study of Reading. (1984). "A Schema-Theoretic View of the Reading Process as a Basis for Comprehension Instruction." In G. G. Duffy, L. R. Roehler, and J. M. Mason, eds., *Comprehension Instruction: Perspectives and Suggestions* (pp. 26–38). New York: Longman.

McKeown, M. G., I. L. Beck, G. M. Sinatra, and J. A. Loxterman. (1992). "The Contribution of Prior Knowledge and Coherent Text to Comprehension." *Reading Research Quarterly* 27(1): 78–93.

Meyer, B. J. F. (1984). "Organizational Aspects of Text: Effects on Reading Comprehension and Applications for the Classroom." In J. Flood, ed., *Understanding Reading Comprehension* (pp. 113–138). Newark, DE: International Reading Association.

Pearson, P. D. (1985). "Changing the Face of Reading Comprehension Instruction." *The Reading Teacher* 38(8): 724–738.

Rude, R. T., and W. J. Oehlkers. (1984). *Helping Students with Reading Problems.* Englewood Cliffs, NJ: Prentice-Hall.

Rumelhart, D. E. (1984). "Understanding Understanding." In J. Flood, ed., *Understanding Reading Comprehension* (pp. 1–20). Newark, DE: International Reading Association.

Samuels, S. J., and P. Eisenberg. (1981). "A Framework for Understanding the Reading Process." In F. Pirozzolo and M. Wittrock, eds., *Neuropsychological and Cognitive Processes in Reading* (pp. 31–67). New York: Academic Press.

Savage, J. F. (1994). *Teaching Reading Using Literature.* Madison, WI: Brown & Benchmark Publishers.

Schumm, J. S., S. Vaughn, and A. G. Leavell. (1994). "Planning Pyramid: A Framework for Planning for Diverse Student Needs During Content Area Instruction." *The Reading Teacher* 47(8): 608–615.

Sloyer, S. (1982). *Readers' Theater: Story Dramatization in the Classroom.* Urbana, IL: National Council of Teachers of English.

Smith, F. (1979). "Conflicting Approaches to Reading Research and Instruction." In L. Resnick and P. Weaver, eds., *Theory and Practice of Early Reading,* vol. 2 (pp. 31–42). Hillsdale, NJ: Erlbaum.

Stanovich, K. E. (1980). "Toward an Interactive-Compensatory Model of Individual Differences in Development of Reading Fluency." *Reading Research Quarterly* 16(1): 32–71.

Stauffer, R. G. (1969). *Teaching Reading as a Thinking Process.* New York: Harper & Row.

Strange, M. (1980). "Instructional Implications of a Conceptual Theory of Reading Comprehension." *The Reading Teacher* 33: 391–397.

Taba, H. (1965). "The Teaching of Thinking." *Elementary English* 42:534.

Tierney, R. J., and J. W. Cunningham. (1984). "Research on Teaching Reading Comprehension." In P. D. Pearson, ed., *Handbook of Reading Research* (pp. 609–656). New York: Longman.

Vygotsky, L. S. (1978). *Mind in Society: The Development of Higher Psychological Processes.* Cambridge, MA: Harvard University Press.

Whaley, J. F. (1981). "Reader's Expectations for Story Structures," *Reading Research Quarterly* 17(1): 90–114.

# Strategies for Studying and Learning from Text

© Robert Finken/Photo Researchers, Inc.

# *Overview*

*T*his chapter presents a rationale and many ideas and examples for teaching and developing elementary-grade students' study-learning skills and strategies. "Learning how to learn" is explained as the goal of all schooling. When teachers and students are aware of the study-learning tasks, the skills and strategies involved, and the methods and expectations regarding assessment and performance, "knowing how to learn" can become a reality. Even when the goal is clearly to develop students' independence, students often need teacher demonstration, guidance, and support.

Teachers can use many of the same good teaching techniques that they use to enhance and develop reading, writing, thinking, and learning across the curriculum. We especially endorse the use of demonstration, modeling, and scaffolding. Additionally, the teaching techniques of "scaffolded reading experiences," use of study guides, and "fading" are explained in this chapter as techniques that can be particularly developed to enhance study-learning. Mrs. Argueta, a fourth-grade teacher, is introduced in this chapter, and her study-reading assignment is used to illustrate "how to do" meaningful study-learning work with elementary-grade students. In addition, several study-learning examples of prereading, during-reading, and postreading activities, and an assortment of study guides for use with elementary-grade students are given.

Various study-learning skills as well as important student organizational skills are identified and described. Also, many specialized study-learning skills are identified and discussed.

Finally, we present several specific strategies for studying and learning from text. We also reiterate the need to embed the teaching of study-learning skills and strategies in authentic active content learning and assignments. Students must view study-learning activities as purposeful, helpful, and rewarding in order to benefit. Otherwise, they could be viewed as just exercises that take away from the time students really need to get their "real work" done.

## *Main Ideas*

- "Learning how to learn" should be the main goal of schooling.
- Study-learning skills and strategies can be introduced in the early elementary grades and continued throughout the elementary school years.
- It is important for students and teachers to be aware of study-learning tasks, skills, and strategies that will be needed, and how learning and performance will be evaluated.

- Many teaching techniques are especially suited for the study-learning development of elementary students: demonstration, modeling, scaffolding, fading, use of scaffolded reading experiences, and use of many different study guides.
- Study-learning skills and strategies instruction should be embedded in the regular content instruction of the elementary classroom.
- Study-learning assignments, tasks, and activities should be motivating and intrinsically rewarding for your elementary students.
- Reference and research skills include use of dictionaries, encyclopedias, and library resources to locate and learn information.
- Organizational skills include use of outlining, underlining and student glossing, and note taking and note making.
- Specialized study-learning skills include using parts of textbooks to find information, reading graphically displayed information, skimming and scanning, adjusting reading rate, and test-taking and test-preparation skills.
- Several specific strategies for reading, learning from, and studying texts can be used with your intermediate- and upper-grade elementary students. These include: PARS, K-W-L, SIP, RIPS, and Inference Awareness.

The traditional emphasis of reading instruction in the elementary schools tended to focus on word-identification and comprehension skills. However, as we have seen thus far in this text, literacy development and learning involves much more than just developing reading skills. McKenna and Robinson (1993) have indicated that the research on the psychology of learning suggests that students must be actively engaged with the content we expect them to learn in order to actually learn it. As students move from the early grades toward the upper grades, we can correctly assume that they will be confronted with more and more complex study and learning demands. Will they have the skills and strategies to deal with these increasing demands? What can elementary teachers do to help students meet these learning tasks and demands? This chapter will present information that will answer these and other questions related to studying and learning from texts and assignments.

## Learning How to Learn

We believe that helping students learn how to learn should be our main goal in school. School is an artificial environment, one that is supposed to prepare students to handle the future academic demands of life. Teachers can never begin to teach *everything. Everything* is too much! Instead, we must create an environment that enables students to teach themselves as needed. In that way, when students leave the artificial world of the classroom, they will be able to direct their own learning when necessary or at their discretion. But we have to allow our students the opportunity to practice while under our guidance. Study skills are tools that, combined with reading, writing, and thinking skills and strategies, will equip your students for learning how to learn. Just as you will devote time to literacy instruction in meaningful situations, you must also devote time to teach your students how to learn. The key is for learners to be interested; motivated; actively engaged; able to adapt to the task, text, their own learning style and needs; and able to apply the strategies that are needed for each occasion. Turner and Paris (1995) have indicated that "If students are to be motivated readers and writers, we must give them the tools and the reasons to read and write and allow them to discover the many paths to literacy—paths that fit the diverse goals, purposes, interests, and social needs of children" (p. 672).

Anderson and Armbruster (1984) noted that studying is a special form of reading. That it differs from other forms of reading is evident because students are expected "to study and learn" specific information that they will have to discuss or on which they will be tested. Students have to visualize the outcomes of studying as a function of the interaction between stated and processing variables. *Stated variables* relate to the status of the student and the material to be studied. Student elements include such variables as knowledge of the criterion task, knowledge of the content in the material to be studied, and interest and motivation. Text elements are features that affect the readability of the material, such as content and organization. *Processing variables* are concerned with getting information from the printed page through the students' thought processes. These processing variables include the initial focusing of attention, subsequent encoding of information, long- and short-term memory storing, and retrieval of the information.

As you can see, learning how to learn is just as complex a task for students as learning to read. It is your responsibility to help your students to learn how to learn, but it is their responsibility as well. "Knowing how to learn" can become the goal for both teachers and students when both are aware of the tasks and skill and strategy demands involved.

## Reflection Activity 6.1

*I*n your own words, what does learning how to learn involve? How does a curriculum that emphasizes learning how to learn fit in with your current beliefs and schema concerning the reading process? You might want to again refer to your diagram and notations concerning those beliefs in Chapter 1, before you address these questions in your journal, under Reflection Activity 6.1.

## *Studying and Learning Considerations*

Studying and learning involves task awareness, strategy awareness, and awareness of how to think about and monitor learning and performance (Anderson and Armbruster 1984; Baker and Brown 1984; Wade and Reynolds 1989). This involves being metacognitively aware. Just as students' awareness in these areas is important to studying and learning, teachers' awareness is also critical. In the sections that follow, each of these areas are discussed, and examples are given of both the teacher's and students' roles in teaching and learning how to learn.

## Awareness of the Study-Learning Task

Knowing and understanding what is expected, or what the actual task is, is critical to being able to perform or do the task (Anderson and Armbruster 1984). For example, if students are expected to know certain information for a test, they must be aware of what that information is and how they will be tested on it (Flippo 1988). Here is another example: If students are expected to write a report, they must be aware of what should be included in the report, the format and other requirements for the report, and how it will be evaluated. Clearly, if a person is to perform satisfactorily on a task assigned by someone else, the assigner must provide the criteria for the task and the guidelines he or she will use to evaluate the success of the task. Both the assigner and assignee have certain roles and responsibilities if the task or assignment are considered to be satisfactorily completed.

## Teacher's Role

As teachers, we can basically make any educationally sound learning or study assignments we elect to make. But important considerations must be *(1) have we analyzed what is required of students to complete the assignment? and (2) do the students have a clear idea of the purpose(s) and guidelines for the assignment, and the criteria that will be used to evaluate it?*

The assignment analysis sheet, as depicted in Figure 6.1, will provide you with guidance and a procedure to analyze the study and learning strategies students will need to have or to use for assignments you give them. Additionally, the reflection questions in Figure 6.1 should help you delineate guidelines or criteria to go with your assignments.

To illustrate how the assignment analysis sheet can be used, see Figure 6.2. In this figure, Mrs. Argueta has analyzed the study skills and strategies her fourth-grade students will need to complete their first research paper. As you can see, a lot of independent work is involved. How can Mrs. Argueta guide students and help them successfully fulfill their roles as learners?

## Students' Role

When the teacher has explicitly made the study or learning assignment and purpose clear, students are in a better position to complete the task. Even so, students have their own roles and obligations concerning their learning and the completion of assignments. Some "learning to learn helpers" your students can use to clarify the task at hand and what is expected of them are as follows:

1. Students should be encouraged to ask the teacher for clarification of any aspect of the assignment they are unsure of, or do not understand.
2. Students should be encouraged to ask the teacher to show them a sample of what a successfully completed assignment might look like and/or to model some of the study skills and strategies involved.

**Figure 6.1**
Assignment analysis
sheet.

**Assignment Analysis Sheet**

1. Specific assignment or learning: _____
   _____
   _____
   _____

2. Authentic purpose(s) for assignment or learning: _____
   _____
   _____
   _____

3. Steps students will need to take in order to complete this assignment or learning: ____
   _____
   _____
   _____
   _____
   _____

4. Specific study skills and strategies needed to complete each step: _____
   _____
   _____
   _____
   _____
   _____

5. How this assignment or learning will be evaluated: _____
   _____
   _____
   _____
   _____
   _____

6. What is my exact criteria and requirements for this assignment or learning? _____
   _____
   _____
   _____
   _____
   _____

3. Students should be encouraged to discuss the assignment and criteria with other students when they feel this would be helpful.
4. Students should be encouraged to ask older peers, or adults in school, their family, or community for advice and suggestions if they feel this would be helpful. (e.g., the school or community librarian might have some research advice to offer.)

**Assignment Analysis Sheet**

1. Specific assignment or learning: _Students will research, develop, and write their "first" research papers on self-selected topics related to our integrated unit on rainforests._

2. Authentic purpose(s) for assignment or learning: _In order for all students to learn as much about rainforests as possible, individual students will select the aspects they find most interesting, research them, write reports, and share their reports with the class._

3. Steps students will need to take in order to complete this assignment or learning: _(a) Brainstorm possible topics of interest, consider them, select one, and plan what they want to research. (B) Go to library, research topic, write notes, and make a list of sources. (c) Write report and bibliography from notes. (d) Edit report and bib. with help of writing group, and publish report. (e) Gather any pictures or artifacts to go with report. (f) Orally share with class._

4. Specific study skills and strategies needed to complete each step: _(a) Narrowing down a topic. (b) Planning and organizational skills. (c) Library reference and research skills (using cataloguing system, finding materials, using references to research). (d) Skimming and scanning, adjusting rate as necessary, using graphic information (tables, graphs, maps). (e) Note-taking from text skills. (f) organizing notes and outlining information. (g) Summarizing. (h) Report writing. (i) Editing skills (including use of dictionary). (j) Oral reporting/sharing._

5. How this assignment or learning will be evaluated: • _Students library search activities will be evaluated by their participation and success at finding material on topic._ • _Students reports and bibliography will be evaluated by their successful coverage of their topics and listing of materials used._ • _Students sharing will be evaluated by their publication of their reports and participation in oral sharing of their reports._

6. What is my exact criteria and requirements for this assignment or learning? _(a) Select a topic related to rainforests. (b) Find and use at least 5 library sources to get information on the topic. (c) Take notes from at least 5 different library sources. (d) Write a report that is at least 3 pages long. (e) Include at least 5 library references (print references) in the bibliography, according to format provided for books, newspapers, magazines, and encyclopedias. (f) Publish and orally share report (artifacts and pictures are optional)._

*Figure 6.2*
Teacher's analysis of the study skills and strategies needed to complete the assignment.

5. Students should be encouraged to internalize the purpose for the assignment and make the assignment and the work involved "their own." If students view the purpose for the assignment as "authentic," this will more easily happen. (See the following example of how one fourth-grade student, Carmen, has internalized Mrs. Argueta's research paper assignment.)

Carmen understands that Mrs. Argueta wants each student to select the most interesting aspect of their integrated unit on rainforests, do library research on that aspect, and then write a report on it. At first Carmen was a little overwhelmed by the assignment, but after she asked lots of questions and talked and brainstormed with other students, she felt better and began to look forward to the assignment. Carmen is very interested in snakes and other reptiles, and she now knows that she can do her research and report on the more common snakes and reptiles found in the different rainforests of the world. Because Mrs. Argueta told the students they may use pictures and artifacts when they share their reports, Carmen is planning to bring photos and some samples she has of how snakes shed their skins, but first she must do research and find out whether the snakes in rainforests shed their skins. This will be fun for Carmen because she is highly motivated to pursue this area of study. Her understanding of the assignment, and her motivation and internalization of the assignment are a very good beginning toward her satisfactory completion of the assignment. However, the next considerations, awareness of the skills and the strategies to use to complete the assignment, are equally important.

## Awareness of the Skills and Strategies to Use

As we have seen in Figures 6.1 and 6.2, awareness of the study-learning task/assignment is different from awareness of the skills and strategies necessary to complete the assignment. Knowing the necessary skills and strategies and how to apply them to the study-learning task at hand involves both teacher and student responsibilities.

### Teacher's Role

For every assignment we give students, teachers must be aware of the skills and strategies that students will need to complete the task. This involves first a delineation of the steps students must take to complete the task (see #3 on Figures 6.1 and 6.2), and then an analysis of the specific study skills and strategies needed to complete each step (see #4 on Figures 6.1 and 6.2). *Next teachers must decide whether students in their classroom have or know how to use the necessary study skills and strategies.* One of the best ways to determine this is by observing students do their usual classroom work. If teachers want to be systematic about these observations, they can do so by recording their findings on a simple class list or grid over a period of time, noting individual students' skill and strategy abilities and use. For an idea of what this might look like, see Figure 6.3.

It seems opportune here to differentiate between skills and strategies. Dole, Duffy, Roehler, and Pearson (1991) indicated that "strategies" imply an

| Study Skills and Strategies | | | | | | | | | | | | | |
|---|---|---|---|---|---|---|---|---|---|---|---|---|---|
| Students' names: | Planning and organizing | Library research | Skimming and scanning | Adjusting rate | Using graphic information | Note taking | Outlining | Summarizing | Report writing | Editing | Using dictionary | Oral reporting | Notes: |
| | | | | | | | | | | | | | |
| | | | | | | | | | | | | | |
| | | | | | | | | | | | | | |
| | | | | | | | | | | | | | |
| | | | | | | | | | | | | | |
| | | | | | | | | | | | | | |
| | | | | | | | | | | | | | |
| | | | | | | | | | | | | | |
| | | | | | | | | | | | | | |
| | | | | | | | | | | | | | |
| | | | | | | | | | | | | | |
| | | | | | | | | | | | | | |
| | | | | | | | | | | | | | |
| | | | | | | | | | | | | | |
| | | | | | | | | | | | | | |
| | | | | | | | | | | | | | |
| | | | | | | | | | | | | | |
| | | | | | | | | | | | | | |
| | | | | | | | | | | | | | |
| | | | | | | | | | | | | | |
| | | | | | | | | | | | | | |
| | | | | | | | | | | | | | |
| | | | | | | | | | | | | | |
| | | | | | | | | | | | | | |

**Figure 6.3**
Study skills and strategies checklist.

awareness or reflection on what we do while we are learning; and "skills" instead imply a more automatic response to learning (p. 242). Paris, Wasik, and Turner (1991) proposed that a developing skill can become a strategy when it is intentionally used. Flippo (1997) has indicated that skills involve the ability to perform a task, and that sometimes many skills used together can form a strategy. Flippo (1997) has defined strategies as the way we go about working out problems.

If a teacher observes that some students lack the necessary study skills and strategies to do an assignment, the teacher's responsibility is to model and teach these skills. However, it is important to keep in mind that good study skill and strategy instruction is embedded rather than isolated instruction (Ruddell and Ruddell 1995, p. 468). In other words, study skill and strategy instruction, like reading and writing instruction, needs to be part of the larger instruction in your classroom. Children and older students will learn study skills when you develop opportunities to present them within the broader context of your curriculum (i.e., as part of reading the social studies chapter, as part of studying for the science quiz, etc.).

## Students' Role

Students often have a lot to do in order to satisfactorily complete a given assignment. For example, to complete Mrs. Argueta's research paper assignment, take another look at Figure 6.2, #3, to see what the fourth graders must do. This can sometimes be overwhelming for an elementary-age student. In fact, many high school (Alvermann and Phelps 1994; Zemelman and Daniels 1988) and even college students (Risko, Alvarez, and Fairbanks 1991) are often overwhelmed by this type of assignment. However, when elementary-age students are guided and instructed on doing such assignments, they can be successful. Various reading educators have pointed out the importance of starting study and learning skills development at an early age by engaging elementary students in real study and inquiry activities (e.g., Flippo and Borthwick 1982; Irvin and Rose 1995; Moore, Moore, Cunningham, and Cunningham, 1994).

To guide your elementary students, to keep them from feeling overwhelmed, and to help them satisfactorily complete their study-learning tasks, you might encourage their planning and organizing activities. See the "think-through" sheets we have developed for this purpose in Figures 6.4 and 6.5. These will give you some ideas to help guide your students. You may want to combine these sheets. You can also design your own "think-through" and other planning and organizing activities, and skill-awareness sheets to fit your own instructional purposes.

Students also need to feel that they have enough time to complete the study-learning task. Your encouragement, belief in your students' abilities to successfully do the assigned task, and your students' motivation for completing the task will all contribute to your students' potential for success (e.g., see Cramer and Castle 1994; Dwyer and Dwyer 1994; Good and Brophy 1978; and Guthrie 1994).

Sometimes students will need help from you to understand how to perform and use necessary study skills and strategies. As can be seen in Figure 6.5, they need to know that they can come to you for help and guidance. Various teaching techniques—modeling, scaffolding, and fading—can be used by you to provide this assistance and will be explained, along with study skill and strategy examples, later in this chapter. Additionally, specific information on a variety of study-learning skills and strategies are also provided.

**Figure 6.4**
Think-through "to do"
sheet.

# Think–Through "To Do" Sheet

| What I have to do: | Check when it is done: |
|---|---|
| | |
| | |
| | |
| | |
| | |
| The order I should do it in: | |
| | |
| | |
| | |
| | |
| When I should do it: | |
| | |
| | |
| | |
| | |

## *Awareness of How to Monitor Learning and Performance*

Ongoing evaluation and overall performance evaluation are an important part of studying and learning. Teachers must know how to monitor and assess students' work and success with the learning task. Students must also know how to self-monitor and evaluate their own learning and performance (Alvermann and Phelps 1994, p. 224). This monitoring and assessment on the part of both the teacher and the students involve reflection and thinking. This reflection and thinking are a part of students' metacognitive strategies and control. Students with metacognitive control can use their learning strategies and skills as tools (Paris and Winograd 1990). Their self-regulated assessment and learning will help them accomplish academic goals and tasks (Borkowski, Carr, Rellinger, and Pressley 1990). Moore et al. (1994) emphasized that self-monitoring and self-regulating learners plan to use strategies appropriate to specific learning tasks, check on their progress, and make adjustments as needed.

# Think-Through "How To Do" Sheet

| I have to...<br>(List study skills you<br>have to use below) | Do I know how to?<br>(Yes, No, Maybe) | Where I can<br>get help...<br>(From the teacher,<br>librarian, friend,<br>family, etc.) |
|---|---|---|
| | | |
| | | |
| | | |
| | | |
| | | |
| | | |
| | | |
| | | |
| | | |
| | | |
| | | |
| | | |
| | | |
| | | |
| | | |

*Figure 6.5*
Think-through "how to do" sheet.

## Teacher's Role

When teachers are clear about how they will evaluate assignments and learnings, and specify their criteria and requirements for assignments and learnings, students can use this information when they self-assess and reflect on their work. (Refer back to #5 and #6 on Figures 6.1 and 6.2.) *Teachers must be sure that students have or know the criteria for the assignment and how it will be evaluated.* Anderson and Armbruster (1984) indicated that the most effective approaches to study assignments are those that are the best match to the criteria that the teacher will use to assess students' learning and performance. For example, students in Mrs. Argueta's class would not do very well if their approach to writing the research report on rainforests focused on summarizing their textbook chapter on the rainforest and using National Geographic videos to supplement this information. Instead, because Mrs. Argueta made students aware of the criteria for the assignment, and how it will be evaluated, they would do much better to focus on using printed library materials to research one aspect of rainforests; and using at least five different sources, including books, newspapers, magazines, and encyclopedias.

However, all students may not have "performance awareness." Alvermann and Phelps (1994) have indicated that performance awareness enables students to monitor whether they have understood the task and used appropriate study skills and strategies. They have further suggested that a good way to develop students' performance awareness is to ask students to determine whether the strategies they used for study or for an assignment were effective. Teachers can use the following list, which we have created using some of Alvermann and Phelps's ideas and some of our own, to develop "performance awareness" with elementary students:

1. When students are finished with an assignment that involved study and learning strategies, ask them to make a list of all the strategies they used to complete the assignment. (For younger elementary children, the teacher can ask children to draw a picture of the strategies they used, or tell about the strategies they used.)
2. Ask students to tell how each strategy helped them.
3. Ask students to rate the strategies from most helpful to least helpful.
4. Ask students to share with the group which strategies were most helpful to them, telling "why" and "how."
5. The teacher can participate and share how she (or he) did the assignment, the strategies she used, and which were most helpful and why. (If children are younger elementary students, or if students do not fully understand what the teacher wants them to do, the teacher should provide a model by sharing her strategy use, and so on, before students are asked to list, rate, and discuss their study strategies.)

## Students' Role

Reflection and metacognition are components of students' performance awareness. As we have seen, teachers can help students develop their performance awareness by asking students to reflect and consider "how they learned." Students can help themselves too, by being reflective learners and thinkers. Figure 6.6 shows a student reflection guide that we developed for your elementary school students. When you first introduce this guide, we suggest that you model the questions and answers for your students with an assignment you and they have all recently completed. Then, when students see how you use it, they can try it out on their own in small groups. The reflection questions can be answered orally, in written responses, or in a check-sheet type of format. The most important idea is for students to realize that they have a good bit of the control of their learning and of how well they learn and do on their assignments. You will want them to remember to ask themselves these or similar reflection questions whenever they do a study-learning assignment.

## Student Reflection Guide

1. Did I complete the study or learning assignment as explained by the teacher? (To be sure, compare the teacher's criteria to your work and see if it is complete or finished.)

2. What kind of grade or evaluation do I think I will get on this assignment, activity, or test? Why?

3. Is there something else I could do to get a better grade or evaluation on it? What?

4. Do I have the time to do more to get the better grade? How much more time do I need? Will it be worth it?

5. What did I learn from this study or assignment? Is this what the teacher was expecting me to learn? Is there something else I can do to learn more or to meet the teacher's criteria? Am I willing to do it? Why or why not?

6. Overall, am I satisfied with my learning or work? Why or why not? If not, how can I improve it?

*Figure 6.6*
Student reflection guide.

$W$hat studying and learning considerations do you view as most important, and why? In your reflection journal, under the heading Reflection Activity 6.2, note your ideas and rationale.

## Teaching Techniques

Throughout this text, we have suggested a variety of teaching strategies and techniques for enhancing students' emergent literacy, vocabulary, comprehension, content reading, and other reading and writing development. Many of these teaching techniques are equally applicable to enhancing students' study skills and strategies. Teachers should use these techniques, especially modeling, scaffolding, metacognitive questioning, cooperative learning, and peer and cross-age tutoring, to enhance and develop their students study-learning skills and strategies. Because these teaching techniques are discussed elsewhere in this text, they will not be elaborated here. However, we do want to emphasize here that we believe these teaching techniques are fundamental to all teaching and student learning. These are not just reading or literacy education techniques. In fact, more and more we see these techniques being suggested, although sometimes under different names or labels, across all the elementary and all school curriculum areas (see Hyde and Bizar 1996; Maxim 1995; and Sivertsen 1993).

In this section we highlight two additional teaching techniques or tools that are especially appropriate for study-learning development and teaching: scaffolded reading experiences and the use of study guides.

### Scaffolded Reading Experiences

Graves and Graves (1994) have described a "scaffolded reading experience" as a set of prereading, during-reading, and postreading activities especially designed to assist a particular group of students in successfully understanding, learning from, and enjoying a particular reading (p. 5). Graves and Graves indicated that they have developed this scaffolded reading technique from research and ideas that include but are not limited to:

- the need for student success (that is, Brophy 1986);
- schema theory (Rumelhart 1980);
- constructivist ideas, including learners constructing their own meanings;
- the importance of working with others, as in cooperative learning (Slavin 1987);
- interactive model ideas, especially the idea that readers use both text and their background knowledge to understand their readings;

- "generative learning" (Wittrock 1986, 1990), which is meaningful learning that results in real understanding, remembering what is learned, and being able to apply what is learned to new situations, and which comes about when learners generate meaningful relationships involving ideas that are in the text; and
- scaffolding, which involves teacher support and a gradual release of that support as learners can take over more and more of the task demands on their own—scaffolding involves modeling, guided supported practice, and adjustment of supports, as needed.

We believe that the Graves and Graves (1994) scaffolded reading experience is an excellent teaching technique, which can be especially appropriate to study-learning assignments and development. We have outlined here the possible components of this technique, taken from the extensive work of Graves and Graves (1994); with each component we provide a brief example of how the component or step can be used with a study-learning assignment. For a full range of examples and development ideas for each component, we suggest you refer to the Graves and Graves (1994) book *Scaffolding Reading Experiences: Designs for Student Success.*

## *Prereading Activities*

These activities can include such things as motivating students, relating the material to students' lives, activating students' background knowledge, building their text-specific knowledge, preteaching vocabulary and other concepts, prequestioning techniques, predicting from the text, setting directions, and suggesting strategies that could work for the reading assignment.

Overall, prereading activities are intended to motivate and prepare students to read the text assignment. Any combination of prereading activities can be used. The teacher is in the best position to select and design activities appropriate to the particular students, particular assignment, and the particular reading involved. Here is an example of how Mrs. Argueta might have motivated and prepared her fourth graders for reading a text chapter selection on rainforests. Keep in mind, this is only one set of possibilities for prereading activities that Mrs. Argueta might have selected and designed:

1. Mrs. Argueta first read students a recent newspaper article she found that described how rainforests are disappearing off the face of the earth, and how their gradual disappearance is causing many kinds of animals, reptiles, insects, and plants to have no place to live.
2. Students were asked to predict what would happen to these animals, reptiles, insects, and plants.
3. Students were asked to predict what would happen to them (the students) and their families if our world, the environment in which we live, were to disappear.
4. Mrs. Argueta indicated that "the chapter that we are going to read will help us understand more about rainforests and the problems being caused by their gradual disappearance." She suggested that "as we read,

individual students may want to make a list of these problems, and, later, the group will discuss them and other information about rainforests that students are interested in talking about."

## *During-Reading Activities*

These activities can include such things as students reading silently, teacher reading to students, teacher-guided reading, students reading orally, and modifying the text. Overall, the purpose here is to have students read and interact with text so that they can construct meaning from the text. We have explained next one combination of activities that Mrs. Argueta could have used with her students as they read the rainforest chapter. Keep in mind that another teacher might, just as effectively, designed different during-reading activities for a different group of students. Graves and Graves (1994, p. 85) have pointed out some questions teachers can ask themselves to help plan this stage of activities: How might this reading task and assignment best be accomplished? What can I do to involve students actively with this text, or to make this material come alive for them? What can I ask students to do as they read the text to make it more understandable, enjoyable, or memorable?

Here is what Mrs. Argueta decided:

1. She began by reading the first half of the chapter to the students herself to more fully hold their attention.
2. She modified the text by skipping several sections in the beginning and middle of the chapter that might be boring to some of the students, and she explained to them that later, if some of them were particularly interested in learning about this information, as background for their research reports, they could come back to it. In this way, she focused the reading on the parts of the chapter she thought they would find most interesting.
3. She asked them to silently read the ending of the chapter to themselves. She thought that the ending of the chapter, which described the plight of the wildlife of the rainforest would be of particular interest to the students. She reminded students to keep taking notes about the problems they were reading about so that they could discuss them later.

## *Postreading Activities*

These can include questioning, discussion, writing, drama, graphic, application, and reteaching activities. Overall, these activities are intended to encourage students to do something with material they have just read. Graves and Graves (1994) noted that "until we do something with it (the material), it isn't really ours" (p. 115). Once again, the teacher must decide what activities, if any, are appropriate to any particular reading or assignment. Let's see how Mrs. Argueta planned some postreading activities for her students to fit their assignment:

1. Students discussed the problems, which they had individually noted, that are being caused by the disappearance of rainforests. Some of these problems were of particular interest to individuals and to groups of students.

2. Mrs. Argueta used the discussion as an opportunity to reteach or highlight the important problems and associated concepts from the chapter on the chalkboard.
3. Mrs. Argueta suggested that because different students seemed particularly interested in different topics, problems, or aspects of what they read, it might be interesting to individually do research and find out more. Then students could share their research with the whole group. Mrs. Argueta assigned the research report as an application, outreach, and reading-writing activity assignment. (Refer back to Figure 6.2 for the details of Mrs. Argueta's assignment.)
4. To keep their interest active and to further motivate the students, Mrs. Argueta suggested that the class do a whole wall mural depicting the different problems and aspects of the overall rainforest situation, based on the textbook reading, the newspaper article Mrs. Argueta read, and their discussion thus far. Students worked in small groups to illustrate whatever problems/aspects they were most concerned about. Students individually decided which problem-group in which to work on the mural.

## Use of Study Guides

Wood, Lapp, and Flood (1992) have provided an extensive and comprehensive review of study guides, including the many different types of study guides, and how to use them. They have explained that study guides are teacher-developed tools for helping students understand instructional reading materials. These guides often consist of a series of activities or questions related to the text or other materials students will use in class or for study. Students engage in the activities or respond to the questions as they read and pursue their assignments (p. 1).

Using study guides with reading assignments gives teachers some control over the concepts and ideas they hope students will learn, and it provides students with a clear understanding of what the teacher expects them to know. Furthermore, study guides provide support and assistance to students, without taking all control away from them. Students use the study guide, thereby retaining some control of their own learning (Wood et al. 1992).

Classroom teachers can use numerous types of study guides to direct students' reading and learning. Wood et al. (1992) have emphasized that these study guides should be used carefully and that the teacher should always remember that they are only to be used as a stepping-stone to independent learning. Once students have a successful strategy for learning from the text, then the study guide should be obsolete. Teachers' ultimate purpose is to lead students to the point where they can independently read and study on their own without the support of a study guide (p. 4). Although Wood et al. described many different types of study guides, we have selected only those that they indicated are appropriate for use with both primary grade and intermediate grade elementary-age students and seem most appropriate to us for use as a study-learning tool. See Figure 6.7 for our overview of these selected study guides, developed by summarizing descriptions provided by Wood et al. (1992); then see the sections that follow for more information and an example

**Overview of Study Guides**

| Type of study guide | For study-learning materials in: | Use/purpose of study guide: |
|---|---|---|
| Point-of-view guide | • History<br>• Science | • To help students elaborate as they read<br>• To help students develop mental recitation skills<br>• To help students learn content |
| Interactive reading guide | • Social Studies<br>• Science<br>• Other content area learning | • To promote cooperative reading and learning<br>• To promote use of predictions, associations, and recalling and reorganizing information |
| Extended anticipation guide | • Literature<br>• All content area learning | • To stimulate thinking and activate prior knowledge<br>• To stimulate hypothesizing and discussion |
| Concept guide | • All content area learning | • To help students organize and categorize sub-ordinate information under major concepts |
| Analogical study guide | • Science<br>• Other content area learning | • To help students make abstract concepts more understandable<br>• To encourage students to connect new information with their everyday experiences |
| Reading road map | • All content area learning | • To help guide students through reading materials by helping them adjust their reading rate to correspond with the importance of the information they encounter |
| Glossing | • Literature<br>• All content area learning | • To help direct students' attention as they read, improving their understanding of the text<br>• To use marginal notes in the text to help engage students as they read/study |

*Figure 6.7*

Overview of study guides appropriate for use with elementary students for study-learning.

Developed from information in Karen D. Wood, Diane Lapp, and James Flood (1992). *Guiding Readers Through Text: A Review of Study Guides.* Newark, DE: International Reading Association.

of each. We recommend that interested readers also refer to the Wood et al. book, and to the other authors cited in this section, for their complete descriptions and examples of these and other study guides.

## Point-of-View Guide

In the Point-of-View Guide (Wood 1988), students are asked questions in an interview-type format to help them gain different perspectives on the events or information described in the reading materials. Teachers should usually model the kinds of responses they hope to solicit from students when they begin. See the following questions that have been developed to go with encyclopedia articles on the "Pilgrims," "Mayflower," "Mayflower Compact," and "William

Bradford." Keep in mind that similar kinds of questions could be developed to use with content textbook materials, magazine articles, and other study-learning materials.

### "Pilgrims" (Volume 15, pp. 415–416)

1. As one of the pilgrims, tell why you came to America?
2. Explain what led up to your coming to America, and who were your leaders?

### "Mayflower" (Volume 13, p. 261)

3. What was the name of the ship that you came on and what was the trip like?

### "Mayflower Compact" (Volume 13, pp. 261–262)

4. You were one of the signers of the Mayflower Compact. Tell us what it was and what it was for.

### "William Bradford" (Volume 2, p. 454)

5. William Bradford was a friend of yours. Tell about him and what he did for the colonists.

## Interactive Reading Guide

The Interactive Reading Guide (Wood 1988) is a study guide that promotes cooperative learning. The teacher directs the use of it by asking for responses from individuals, small groups, pairs of students, or from the whole class by use of symbols. When students complete each part, activity, or question, the teacher instigates a class discussion of the material. This is a good technique to use when the teacher feels the entire class needs additional help or guidance with a particular reading and study assignment. See the questions and symbols detailed in Figure 6.8 for an abbreviated example of how a teacher might develop an Interactive Reading Guide for a social studies selection and study on the students' state. These third-grade students live in Massachusetts.

## Extended Anticipation Guide

Duffelmeyer, Baum, and Merkley (1987) developed the idea of the Extended Anticipation Guide, which stimulates discussion, provides opportunities for the teacher to find out what students know about a topic, and stimulates prior knowledge and hypothesizing. Duffelmeyer (1994) further recommended the anticipation guide, which evolved from Herber's (1978) ideas, as a prereading teaching strategy; Duffelmeyer also indicated that the guide can be used to promote reading to learn from expository text. See Figure 6.9 for an example of what an Extended Anticipation Guide for the study of "bats" might look like. This one was developed for use in a second-grade classroom.

# Massachusetts

Directions:  Use the interaction codes to tell you who to work with.  Then read the directions for each one and do what it says.  If you need help, ask someone in your group or the teacher.

Interaction codes:

    ◯ = Work alone

    ⊛ = Work with your group

    ◯◯ = Work with a partner

    ◯ = The whole class will work on this together

---

⊛ 1.  In your group, list everything you can think of that you know about Massachusetts.

◯◯ 2.  On your own, or with a partner, read pages 59–60 and see if you can write down anything else you found out about Massachusetts.

⊛ 3.  Share the new things you found out in your group, and add all the new things to the group list.

◯ 4.  The whole class will share their lists and one big class list will be made.  We will all look at the map of Massachusetts to see if anything we listed happens in any particular places.

*Figure 6.8*
Massachusetts: A study guide for group interaction.

Developed from the creative ideas and an example in Karen D. Wood (1988), "Guiding Students Through Informational Text," *The Reading Teacher, 41*(9), pp. 912–920.

**Bats**

Directions: Read the sentences in Part I. If you agree, put a ☺ in the column. If you disagree, put a ☹ in the column. Be ready to explain your choices.

---

**Part I**

Agree  Disagree

_____  _____  1. Bats are only in scary movies and Halloween stories.

_____  _____  2. Bats live in dark, wet places.

_____  _____  3. Bats are a kind of bird.

_____  _____  4. Bats have very bad eyesight.

Directions: Read about bats in your "Weekly Reader." If you read something that supports your choices, put a ☺ in the column. If what you read doesn't support your choices, put a ☹ in the column. Then write what the "Weekly Reader" says about bats, using your own words.

---

**Part II**

Support  No support                   In your own words

1. _____   _____   _____
                    _____

2. _____   _____   _____
                    _____

3. _____   _____   _____
                    _____

4. _____   _____   _____
                    _____

*Figure 6.9*
Extended anticipation guide for the study of bats.

Developed from the creative ideas and an example in F. A. Duffelmeyer, D. D. Baum, and D. J. Merkley (1987), "Maximizing Reader-Text Confrontation with an Extended Anticipation Guide," *Journal of Reading, 31,* pp. 146–150.

## Concept Guide

Baker (1977) originated Concept Guides to help students see the relationship of more- and less-significant concepts. These guides are designed to help students organize information from texts, categorizing them and listing subordinate information under major concepts. This is similar to the process students must use when they outline information and can serve as an important text-study technique. See Figure 6.10 for one sample of a Concept Guide. This one was developed for fifth graders for their readings on and study of jellyfish, part of their marine science unit.

## Analogical Study Guide

Bean, Singer, and Cowan (1985) developed the Analogical Study Guide to reinforce learning of content area materials. Use of these guides encourages students to connect new information with known information, and helps make abstract ideas more understandable. Bean et al. suggested three steps in developing these guides:

1. Analyze the reading-learning task to determine what concepts students should learn, focusing on the most essential information.
2. Construct appropriate analogies for the material to be learned.
3. Explain and demonstrate to the students how the guide works, showing how analogies are used as retrieval/memory cues (mnemonic devices) to help students recall and remember information from the text material to be learned.

Wood et al. (1992) suggested that by using small, cooperative groups, teachers can encourage students to brainstorm and come up with their own analogies for the material to be learned. Furthermore, teachers can creatively use known information to help students learn more difficult material. Here is an example of some analogies developed in a Wood et al. example of how a primary grade teacher used an Analogical Study Guide to help students see how a plant receives nutrients by drinking water in similar ways to a person drinking through a straw. After students read a selection with the teacher, the teacher provided a poster identifying plant parts and their functions, and then showed a second poster of a person drinking through a straw. The study guide contained some of these analogies:

1. root to cup (collects and holds nutrients/food/water),
2. stem to straw (carries food/water/nutrients upward), and
3. leaf to person drinking (receives food/water/nutrients).

## Reading Road Map

Wood et al. (1992) explained that the Reading Road Map (Wood 1988) helps guide students through the reading and study of text that otherwise might be particularly difficult for students who have not yet learned to adjust their reading rate. They have indicated that it is particularly important to explain the purpose of the Reading Road Map to the students and suggested that parallels can be drawn between the textbook journey and an actual trip to another location. Figure 6.11 illustrates an example of a Reading Road Map, stimulated from the creative ideas and an example provided in Wood (1988), to help you see how an elementary teacher can use this to guide students through the readings for a unit of study.

## Jellyfish

**Part I:**

Directions: Read each of the statements given below. If you believe them to be true, check the "true" column. If you believe them to be false, check the "false" column.

| True | False | **Information statements** |
|------|-------|----------------------------|
| ____ | ____ | 1. Jellyfish are sea animals. |
| ____ | ____ | 2. Jellyfish get their names from the jellylike material between two layers of cells that make up the animal's body. |
| ____ | ____ | 3. The jellyfish body looks like a bell or umbrella shape. |
| ____ | ____ | 4. A group of projections, called tentacles, hang down from the body. |
| ____ | ____ | 5. Corals, sea anemones, and hydras are also sea animals. |
| ____ | ____ | 6. Some jellyfish can inflict painful and sometimes poisonous stings into people and other animals. |
| ____ | ____ | 7. Sea wasps are a kind of jellyfish. |
| ____ | ____ | 8. Sea nettles are a kind of jellyfish. |

**Part II:**

Directions: Read the information given in your textbook, in the encyclopedia article, and in the *National Geographic* article on jellyfish. Then organize each of the informational statements given above, in Part I, under one of the following three headings. If you find other information that you think should go under a heading, go ahead and list it and we can discuss these in class.

**Headings**

"Kinds of Sea Animals"

_____

_____

_____

_____

    "Types of Jellyfish"

    _____

    _____

    _____

    _____

        "Characteristics of Jellyfish"

        _____

        _____

        _____

        _____

*Figure 6.10*
Concept guide on jellyfish.

Developed from the creative ideas and an example in Karen D. Wood, Diane Lapp, and James Flood (1992). *Guiding Readers Through Text: A Review of Study Guides*, p. 52. Newark, DE: International Reading Association.

# Reading Road Map: Spiders

Directions: Our science unit on spiders will uncover a lot of new and interesting information. Some of the information in our textbook, other books on spiders, and in our *National Geographic* articles will have to be found and read more carefully in order to not miss important information and details. To make this more of an adventure for you, we will go on a "trip" through two of the materials we will be reading using this Road Map for Spiders. The map will point out important places to slow down, and think and write about what you are learning. The map will also point out places you can read more quickly and other road map clues and signs for speed.

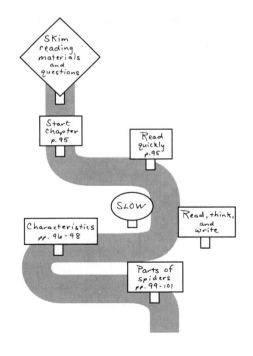

## Learning quest

1. List and know all the "major characteristics" of spiders.

2. What are the parts of a spider's body?

3. How does the spider eat his/her food?

4. What are some of the most interesting things you have read and learned about the spider's characteristics and body parts?

**Figure 6.11**
Reading road map for the study of spiders.

Developed from the creative ideas and an example in Karen D. Wood (1988), "Guiding Students Through Informational Text," *The Reading Teacher, 41*(9), pp. 912–920.

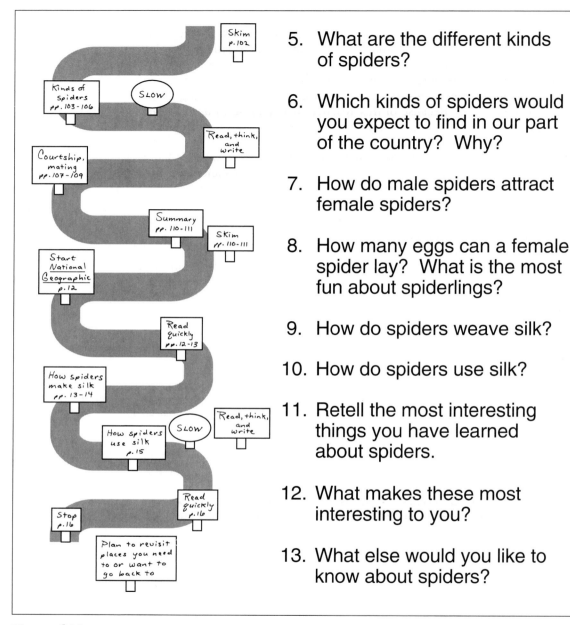

Skim
p.102

Kinds of
Spiders
pp. 103-106

SLOW

Read, think,
and
write

Courtship,
mating
pp.107-109

Summary
pp. 110-111

Skim
pp. 110-111

Start
National
Geographic
p.12

Read
quickly
pp. 12-13

How spiders
make silk
pp. 13-14

How spiders
use silk
p. 15

SLOW

Read, think,
and
write

Read
quickly
p. 16

Stop
p. 16

Plan to revisit
places you need
to or want to
go back to

5. What are the different kinds of spiders?

6. Which kinds of spiders would you expect to find in our part of the country? Why?

7. How do male spiders attract female spiders?

8. How many eggs can a female spider lay? What is the most fun about spiderlings?

9. How do spiders weave silk?

10. How do spiders use silk?

11. Retell the most interesting things you have learned about spiders.

12. What makes these most interesting to you?

13. What else would you like to know about spiders?

**Figure 6.11**
Reading road map for the study of spiders (*continued*).

## Glossing

Otto, White, Richgels, Hansen, and Morrison (1981) are credited with demonstrating how the use of marginal notes, or glossing, can help students understand textual reading materials. Glossing can be used to direct students' attention to specific content of the reading by pointing out facts, information, and important concepts in the piece. This technique involves the teacher writing in the margins of the material. Because of this, teachers may choose to use an overhead projector to point out and highlight the material. The kind of notations that teachers choose to make will depend on the age and needs of the students, and the content to be focused on and learned. Wood et al. (1992) suggested that teachers make sure that the gloss notations are brief and used only to meet lesson objectives. Teachers will not want the notations to make the reading more cumbersome and difficult for students. We have developed a short example of a teacher's glossing of material on spiders to illustrate what this may look like (see Figure 6.12). You also can let students gloss their own reading and study material to highlight and note information they believe is important or helpful for them to learn. See Figure 6.13 for an example of how a student glossed this same material.

**Reflection Activity 6.3**

*S*everal ways and many ideas for helping students read, study, and learn from text and other content-reading assignments have been suggested and explained. Each of these has involved teacher guidance and the teacher's retention of some control over students' reading and learning. Because the goal of all teaching should be enabling the learner to "learn how to learn" and to be in control over his/her own learning, we know that too much teacher control could be detrimental. In your reflection journal, under the heading Reflection Activity 6.3, write your opinion regarding teacher control—how much is too much? Then list what you feel are the strengths of some of the specific teaching techniques and ideas presented, and what you feel are the cautions teachers must take when using them.

## *Identifying Study-Learning Skills*

What are the study-learning skills that elementary students must develop and must learn how to use? After reviewing the literature and available materials for the development of study and learning skills for elementary-grade youngsters (e.g., Irvin and Rose 1995; and Mangrum 1989), we have grouped the study-learning skills into three categories: reference and research skills, organizational skills, and specialized study-learning skills. Each of these categories of study-learning skills are discussed in the sections that follow, with definitions and examples for your reference.

# Spiders

The spider is a small, [eight-legged] animal. Spiders are best known for the [spinning of silk] webs, which they use [to catch insects to eat.] The webs are so strong that even large insects have trouble escaping from the spider's web. Even though all spiders spin silk, they do not all make webs. Some spiders use the silk to trap other insects in different ways. For example, the bolas spider spins a single line of silk that is sticky at the end. The bolas spider swings the line at insects that fly near and catch them at the end of the line. [In this chapter, much more interesting information on spiders will be described and discussed.]

*Handwritten annotations:*

What are two characteristics of spiders?

How do spiders use silk to catch insects?

This is one way spiders use silk to catch insects.

This is another way.

What do you think this chapter will be about?

**Figure 6.12**
Sample of teacher's glossing of material on spiders.

Developed from the creative ideas and an example in Karen D. Wood, Diane Lapp, and James Flood (1992). *Guiding Readers Through Text: A Review of Study Guides,* p. 65. Newark, DE: International Reading Association.

## Spiders

[The spider is a small, eight-legged animal.] Spiders are[best known for the spinning of silk webs,]which they use to catch insects to eat. The webs are so strong that even large insects have trouble escaping from the spider's web. [Even though all spiders spin silk, they do not all make webs.] Some spiders use the silk to trap other insects in different ways.  For example,[the bolas spider spins a single line of silk that is sticky at the end.] The bolas spider swings the line at insects that fly near and catch them at the end of the line.  In this chapter, much more interesting information on spiders will be described and discussed.

*Spiders have 8 legs*

*Spiders spin silk*

*Not all spiders make webs! (This looks important to remember!)*

*The Bolas Spider is one kind of spider.*

*Figure 6.13*
Sample of a student's glossing of material on spiders.

### Reference and Research Skills

Reference and research skills are used to locate information from a variety of sources (e.g., library reference sources and encyclopedias), to use the dictionary, and to gather information on an infinite variety of topics (either teacher-directed, self-directed, or both). Elementary school students should be encouraged to develop these skills as early as possible because they will use them extensively in content-reading assignments as well as in personal-interest research areas. Armbruster and Armstrong (1993) indicated that students in elementary school are expected to engage in search tasks ranging from locating a single fact for answering a question to locating and synthesizing information for a report. For example, you may ask your primary students to use trade books and supplementary materials, in addition to their textbooks, to locate information about a particular topic. As students reach the middle and upper elementary grades and beyond, the need to use these research skills is further intensified. Thus, the development and refinement of these skills is important if your students are to succeed in doing content-related research assignments or to locate specific information of their own choosing.

A study with fifth graders searching for information in a textbook (Dreher and Sammons 1994) confirmed an earlier study (Cole and Gardner 1979) that students need guidance and real context to convert their verbal understandings to actual competence. Search tasks are common school and workplace demands (Dreher 1993). Search tasks involve a type of strategic reading that occurs when readers seek specific goal-related or assignment-related information. The task often involves looking for very specific information and ignoring irrelevant or non-task-specific information. Research has indicated (see Dreher and Sammons 1994) that search-strategy instruction using real social studies and other school subjects' research projects should improve the likelihood of the transfer of search-related skills to students. Salend (1994) in his text directed toward effective mainstreaming and inclusive classrooms emphasized a similar need for authenticity and using real classroom textbooks for the study and learning assignments for all students. Just telling students how to, and/or teaching reference and research skills in isolation from real research and text assignments, is not effective.

Miller (1979) has identified some of the more widely used library skills that should be developed in the primary grades. Other educators (cf. Nelson 1973) have also suggested that closer cooperation between the school librarian and teacher is essential if students are to effectively learn how to use reference and research skills, and that close cooperation between schools and public libraries would also be beneficial in helping reinforce student use of these study skills (McCabe 1984). Finally, in their comprehensive review of various library and research skills of college students, Risko et al. (1991) indicated that there is a difference between library skills (which involve searching for information) and research skills (which involve searching for knowledge) (p. 229); they also implied that all students need relevant assignments to use these skills, not workbook-type practice exercises that have little to do with what is required of students in their subject areas.

Reference and research skills that can be developed and cultivated with the teacher's guidance and modeling include the use of the dictionary, encyclopedias, and other reference materials, and use of the library card catalog or computerized catalog (Cheek and Cheek 1983). Using the dictionary involves knowing how to alphabetize and use guide words to locate specific words and knowing the meaning of words to further one's search purposes. Also, the ability to find and comprehend information about a particular topic in reference materials is helpful for a better understanding of many content texts and assignments. Thus, your students' abilities to use reference materials in the library, encyclopedias, and other printed materials should be encouraged and developed as early as possible in the elementary classroom. Likewise, the ability to use the different types of library card catalogs (and in many school districts and public libraries, a computerized version of this) is important if your students are to locate and use information in the library. Furthermore, the use of these resources requires that students really know the topic or subject being sought and are able to generate other descriptors for the topic in the event it is listed in other ways.

Elementary teachers, even of the primary and intermediate grades, can develop many relevant reference and research learning assignments for their students. These assignments can easily fit the curriculum for the various content area units and integrated units that they teach. Refer back to Mrs. Argueta's assignment, earlier in this chapter, for an idea of how this can be done. It is not hard to be authentic when we believe in and teach an authentic curriculum. Can you think of ideas for authentic reference and research assignments that you could develop for elementary students?

## Reflection Activity 6.4

*I*n your reflection journal, under the heading Reflection Activity 6.4, first brainstorm and then jot down ideas you have for developing a reference and research skills assignment for elementary youngsters that leads them to use library books and resources, encyclopedias, dictionaries, and other reference materials to locate and learn specific information. Tell how you will make the assignment real, motivating, and part of the authentic learning of the content you will teach.

## *Organizational Skills*

These skills require an ability to synthesize and evaluate material so that it can be organized into an efficient learning format. Because higher-level cognitive functions are used in organizational activities, it is important that your students become more aware of their responsibility in self-initiating and self-regulating their own reading and learning behaviors (Tierney 1982). Metacognitive behavior, which involves self-awareness, self-monitoring, and self-control while learning, should be cultivated and used as part of developing necessary organizational study-learning skills. The research and literature over the past two decades has indicated that teachers and learners need to do more than be aware; they must further develop their awareness and knowledge to make teaching and learning more effective. This is particularly true if your students are to cultivate their analysis, synthesis, and judgment among other higher-order thinking skills (see Baker and Brown 1984; Bereiter and Scardamalia 1987; Dansereau 1985; Dreher and Slater 1992; Mier 1984; Palincsar and Brown 1984; Paris et al. 1991; Pearson and Fielding 1991; and Roehler and Duffy 1991).

The organizational skills we include and detail in this section are the study-learning skills of outlining, which involves classifying, summarizing, and sequencing information; underlining and student glossing, which involves selecting or noting important information in texts; and note taking and note making, which again involves classifying, summarizing, and sequencing information.

## *Outlining*

The primary objective of outlining is to locate and list the main ideas and supporting details in a selection. By doing this, students are better able to identify and learn the information that is important for them to read and understand. This skill can be particularly effective for your students, but they may only learn if you provide appropriate educational experiences (Hansell 1978). Harris and Sipay (1990, p. 617) suggested the following procedure to teach students the effective use of outlining:

1. Discuss the importance of outlining with your students.
2. Demonstrate how to outline using previously read material.
3. Present a series of exercises in outlining in which a lot of assistance to the students is given at first, and then less and less assistance is provided.

In the first step of outlining instruction, the teacher discusses the importance of each idea, its relationship to other ideas in the selection, and its place in the selection. The demonstration step involves you outlining a selection that your students are familiar with, and then modeling for them how and why certain ideas are outlined as they are. The last step of this procedure, presenting a series of outlines, involves several substeps. These substeps would include (a) displaying a complete outline on which the complete skeleton is shown but only part of the outline itself is given; (b) giving the structure of the outline but not filling in any information; (c) giving students main headings and having them fill in supporting ideas; and (d) having your students prepare a complete outline without assistance.

Additionally, we suggest that the outlining exercises you do with students should be done with real and meaningful reading and study assignments from your various content texts, so that they are not just isolated exercises; rather, they are exercises that will help students develop outlining skills while learning otherwise necessary and relevant content. For those students who need more assistance, you could use small-group and one-to-one sessions to promote their development of outlining skills. As you can see, the teaching outlining procedure involves scaffolded instruction, with the teacher providing maximum support in the beginning and gradually withdrawing support as the students take on more and more responsibility. Moore et al. (1994) refer to this as *fading*.

When using fading, the teacher demonstrates what she or he expects students to do, fades out assistance as students practice the task with the teacher's help, and finally fades out more as the teacher provides opportunities for independent application. "Fading moves from demonstration to guided practice to independent application as teachers fade out and students fade in" (Moore et al. 1994, p. 20). The idea is to eventually develop student independence. This fading can be applied to all study-learning skills and strategies instruction. We will continue to recommend it to you as we highlight other study-learning skills and strategies in this chapter.

## *Underlining and Student Glossing*

Underlining and student glossing are related and useful study-learning skills. The primary objective of underlining is to select the most important concepts and information in text, underlining them, or highlighting them, for future reference. The primary objective of student glossing is to select the most important concepts and information in text, making margin notes about them, for future reference. (Refer back to Figure 6.13 for an example of student glossing.)

Unfortunately, some students have a tendency to underline or highlight more information than they should, thus negating the benefit of having only the most important information marked in the text for future study references. Without teacher modeling and demonstration (as in Figure 6.12) students will not know how much is too much when they try to gloss their own texts. Some research studies (e.g., Blanchard 1985) have shown underlining to be the most popular organizational study skill, even though other research has presented mixed results in determining its effectiveness when compared with other strategies (Harris and Sipay 1990; McAndrew 1983).

Poostay (1984) suggested that teachers use the following instructional sequence to assist students in developing their underlining skills:

1. Copy a selection of 100 to 150 words.
2. Preview the selection, then underline key concepts. Include five to seven key concepts per one hundred words.
3. Make copies of the underlined selection for your students.
4. As you read a portion of the selection, have the students point to each underlined concept.
5. Demonstrate and discuss how and why each concept was selected.
6. Read the selection again and ask students to predict the content of the selection using only the underlined concepts.
7. Collect the underlined selection, and give out the original source and ask the students to read it.
8. Use unaided and aided recall strategies to check the students' comprehension of the selection.
9. Allow students to practice on other selections, and then encourage them to use this technique on their own.

We have developed a similar instructional sequence for helping your students see how they can use their own glossings to study and learn from their content reading materials. The steps are detailed for your future use:

1. Copy a selection from a textbook, of at least four paragraphs in length, that all the students are currently using in class for content study, and display it using your overhead projector.
2. Read the entire selection aloud to your students as they follow along.
3. Use teacher marginal glossing (as in Figure 6.12); and model, mark, and gloss the first paragraph or part of the displayed selection, as you explain to students why you are noting certain concepts or information.

4. Next, solicit students' input, suggestions, and rationales to mark and gloss the second part (or second paragraph) of the displayed selection, reiterating what they told you to mark and their reasons.

5. Let individual students, who volunteer, come forward to mark and gloss and explain their rationales on the third part (or third paragraph) of the displayed selection.

6. Suggest that students work in cooperative groups to mark and gloss the fourth part (or paragraph) in the selection. Leave the overhead material on display, and give each student in the cooperative group a copy of the fourth part of the selection to finish.

7. When they are done, have volunteers from the cooperative groups come forward and mark the fourth part on the overhead selection, explaining their group rationale.

8. When the entire selection is marked, suggest that the class help you look back at the glossings, and on chart paper, solicit a list of important glossed concepts and information that might help students on a test, or is important for them to know.

9. Solicit students' ideas as to the benefits of students glossing their own important reading materials.

As noted in the previous section, again the teacher uses scaffolding or fading to teach these skills. Students are encouraged to use these skills on their own as study-learning tools whenever they feel ready, but the teacher is available to fade in support when students need or want it.

### Note Taking and Note Making

Note taking and "note making" (Flippo 1988) are important study-learning skills. Note taking is useful to students as they listen to information presented in teacher lectures and discussions (Anderson and Armbruster 1991), and as they read and study their textbooks (Caverly and Orlando 1991). Extensive review of the research on note taking has shown that "[t]he process of taking notes can help the note taker learn and remember information, and the notes themselves can preserve information for later use" (Anderson and Armbruster 1991, p. 190). However, students must be taught to take notes that are appropriate to the demands being placed on them (Caverly and Orlando 1991). Notes seem helpful to the extent that they contain information that will be tested, but what students do with their notes is equally important. Students must cognitively process the noted information, encoding it in the same way that they will need to use it on a test (Anderson and Armbruster 1991).

Flippo (1988) developed ideas and strategies for note taking and note making. Flippo emphasized the importance of students note-making activities to assist their internalization and encoding of the material to be learned. She suggested that students develop skill in condensing their study notes by rewriting them several times. Each time the notes are condensed further, students have to redetermine what is most important and synthesize the information further. Additionally, Flippo described note-taking and note-making strategies that include organizing notes into topic cards, lists, outlines, and diagrams, and organizing class-lecture notes.

Kiewra (1984) delineated a sequence of steps to facilitate note-taking success, which included the following: (1) using effective techniques during class lectures and discussion; (2) taking extensive notes at first; (3) employing paraphrasing or summarizing note-taking procedures; (4) revising notes as quickly as possible after they are taken; (5) reviewing notes before the next class (note-taking session); and (6) incorporating externally provided notes in all note-taking and reviewing procedures.

Although many schemes and formats are provided in the literature for taking notes, we like the one suggested by Lindsey (1985) and illustrated in Figure 6.14. Students use a 2″ × 3″ × 3.5″ × 2″ format to divide their notebook pages for note-taking purposes. The students can use the 2-inch column to jot down key words and phrases for notes, the 3-inch column can later be used to enhance notes with remembered and text information, and the 3.5-inch column can be reserved for later translations of the notes into test-taking cues. The 2-inch bottom area can be used for you or students to respond to or reflect on each page of notes.

## Reflection Activity 6.5

*I*n your reflection journal, under the heading Reflection Activity 6.5, first brainstorm and then jot down ideas you have for developing the outlining, underlining and student glossing, and note-taking and note-making skills of elementary-age students. Tell how you will make your instruction motivating and part of authentic student content learning needs. Also, tell how you can use fading to provide the necessary supports for student learning while fostering the development of independence.

## Specialized Study-Learning Skills

Students need various specialized study-learning skills to successfully carry out and complete different study-learning assignments, and to use and learn information obtained from the books and other materials they must use. The specialized study-learning skills are discussed next. As with other study-learning skills discussed in this chapter, we recommend that teachers make use of modeling, demonstrating, and fading instruction to provide the support students need as well as the opportunities for independent learning development.

## Using Parts of Textbooks

To use textbooks effectively, students need a good working knowledge of the resources found in a textbook and where and how to use them to find certain types of information. For example, your students should know that the table of

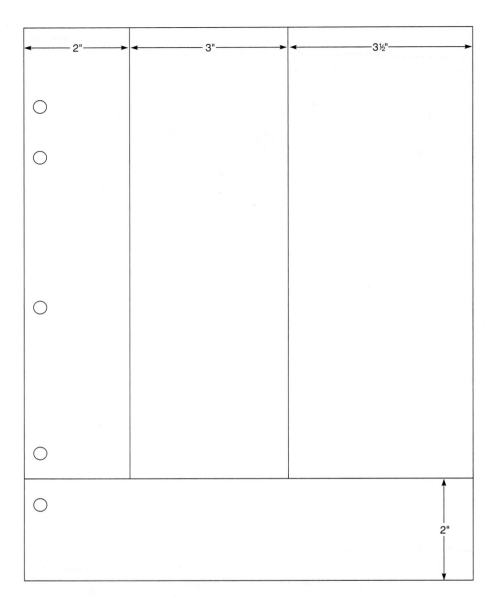

**Figure 6.14**

A notetaking format: 2″ × 3″ × 3.5″ × 2″.

contents is in the front of the text and that it is useful in getting an idea of what is in each chapter. They also need to know that the index is usually in the back of the textbook and can be helpful in locating more specific details and topical information. Understanding what the glossary, the title and copyright pages, and the bibliography or references are for can facilitate your students' research and other information-gathering needs.

Teachers can ask students to use these various text resources as part of their content-reading assignments, modeling where each can be found and how to use them. For example, when beginning the rainforest unit, Mrs. Argueta had students review the table of contents in their text and guess in what chapter the information on rainforests would be found. Students were asked to explain their rationales for guessing. Then, using the table of contents, students found the page numbers and turned to the indicated chapters to confirm or disprove their guesses. She also asked students to check the index at the back of the book to see whether "rainforests" were cited on any particular pages. Students then looked on those pages to see what was said about rainforests. Mrs. Argueta wanted students to know how to cite a reference, so she showed them how to cite their texts using the title and copyright pages. When students were introduced to new vocabulary in their text reading on rainforests, she suggested and modeled use of the glossary. Finally, when she wanted students to notice the bibliography at the end of the text chapter, she asked them to see whether they could find a list of other books and sources with information on rainforests. She showed students how to scan the bibliography for appropriate sources students might want to find to give them more information on rainforests.

## Reading Graphically Displayed Information

Graphically displayed information skills include reading graphs, tables, charts, and maps. The importance of these skills is reinforced by research that has suggested that both children and adults remember pictures of objects better than names of objects (Levin 1976), as well as by recognition that graphical literacy is an important communication tool and deserves a place in the school curriculum (Fry 1981).

Teachers can enhance students' skills at reading and using graphically displayed information by more often using and discussing the maps, tables, and other graphic displays found in students' textbooks. These displays, which are sometimes ignored by teachers, can be used to make the content materials more interesting and meaningful for students. Students can also be encouraged, with the teacher's support, to do their own meaningful research and develop their own graphic displays to share their research findings. This helps students understand the use of graphic materials better and helps them understand the relationships more clearly (Devine 1987; Moore et al. 1994; and Flippo 1997). Flippo (1997) presents several of these ideas for developing graph- and table-reading skills and strategies by using student-generated questions and research.

Flippo and Frounfelker (1988) developed a map-reading activity that emphasizes basic map-reading concepts, vocabulary, and symbol interpretation for middle-grade elementary students and encourages them to self-assess their understandings and knowledge (see Figure 6.15). First the teacher introduces the subject of map study and displays a variety of maps. Then the teacher gives each student the self-assessment sheet and asks one student to volunteer to read a question aloud from the sheet. After allowing time for all students to answer the question for themselves, the teacher has another volunteer answer and tell how she or he arrived at the answer. If the student gives a full and accurate answer, the teacher says "You knew the answer" and tells the other students, if they responded similarly, to check the "I knew the answer space"

## Self Assessment of Sample Map Reading Skills

| Questions | I knew the answer | I knew part of the answer | I did not know the answer | Unknown words |
|---|---|---|---|---|
| 1. What is a map? | ____ | ____ | ____ | _____ |
| 2. What is a compass rose? | ____ | ____ | ____ | _____ |
| 3. What are the four cardinal directions? | ____ | ____ | ____ | _____ |
| 4. What is a map scale? | ____ | ____ | ____ | _____ |
| 5. What is a map key or legend? | ____ | ____ | ____ | _____ |
| 6. What are symbols used in a map key? | ____ | ____ | ____ | _____ |
| 7. What is a map grid? | ____ | ____ | ____ | _____ |
| 8. What does parallel mean? | ____ | ____ | ____ | _____ |
| 9. What does perpendicular mean? | ____ | ____ | ____ | _____ |
| 10. What are coordinates? | ____ | ____ | ____ | _____ |
| 11. What is a political map? | ____ | ____ | ____ | _____ |
| 12. What is a boundary? | ____ | ____ | ____ | _____ |
| 13. What is a capital? | ____ | ____ | ____ | _____ |
| 14. Name one common kind of map that is a political map. | ____ | ____ | ____ | _____ |
| 15. What is a physical map? | ____ | ____ | ____ | _____ |
| 16. How are things or features shown on a physical map? | ____ | ____ | ____ | _____ |
| 17. What is an elevation map? | ____ | ____ | ____ | _____ |
| 18. What are contour lines? | ____ | ____ | ____ | _____ |
| 19. What is a demographic map? | ____ | ____ | ____ | _____ |
| 20. Name two things you can learn from a demographic map. | ____ | ____ | ____ | _____ |

**Figure 6.15**
Self-assessment of sample map reading skills.

From R. F. Flippo and C. R. Frounfelker, III, (1988), "Teach Map Reading Through Self Assessment." *The Reading Teacher, 42* (3):259. Reprinted by permission of Rona F. Flippo and the International Reading Association, Copyright by the International Reading Association, Newark, Delaware.

following the question on the self-assessment sheet. If an answer is only partially accurate, the teacher says, "You knew part of the answer. Keep thinking, maybe you will get the rest of it." Other students with similar answers would check the "I knew part of the answer" space. The teacher solicits a more complete answer from volunteers. If the answer is inaccurate, the teacher says "You don't know the answer, but it was a good try." Students with similar responses would check the "I did not know the answer" space. Again, the teacher solicits volunteers to come up with the correct answer. As other questions are read, students write any words they do not know in the right column of the sheet. These words can later serve as individual vocabulary research lists. When all the questions have been reviewed and checked, the teacher can use the information to make instructional decisions. Later, after instruction has been provided, students can reassess their understanding using the same procedure.

Flippo and Frounfelker have indicated that this sharing and clarifying of information, along with the self-assessment activity, enhances learning and motivates students. Teachers can develop their own similar activities for table- and graph-reading skills and to enhance skills for reading and using other graphic displays.

## Skimming and Scanning

The specialized study-reading skills of skimming and scanning enable readers to preview material, to search for specific details, and to develop a general impression of the material. Skimming material involves a brisk reading of that material to form an overall general impression. Scanning, however, involves very rapid reading with the task of searching for specific details or pieces of information. Both skills are used singularly or in combination to read and study content.

Fry (1989) has developed materials for teaching and helping upper-grade elementary students to develop skimming and scanning skills. But classroom teachers can use their own materials if they have some guidance as to how to proceed. Using the following procedures, you can demonstrate and provide practice to teach your students these important specialized skills:

1. Select full excerpts of text, that are at least a thousand to fifteen hundred words long. (It is best to use text that students will have to read anyway as part of your content reading plans.)
2. Demonstrate the skills of skimming and scanning by modeling how you do it with the selected text projected on an overhead projector. (Explain what you are doing when you skim: You are trying to quickly review the material to see whether it is what you were looking for, and to see whether you need to read it more carefully. Explain what you are doing when you scan: You are reading the material rapidly and looking for specific information.)
3. Pose some questions about the material and ask students to scan with you to search for the specific answers. (Work through the selection with the students helping you find the specific information.)
4. Using a second excerpt of the same length, give all students a copy with some specific questions, and let students practice skimming and scanning in small cooperative learning groups.
5. For variety and more practice opportunities, students can skim and scan a variety of materials (e.g., lists, indexes, newspaper articles, schedules, tables, TV guides).

As you can see, skimming and scanning needs to be modeled and taught, but once learned, the teacher can fade out and let students use their skimming and scanning techniques as another study-learning tool.

## *Adjusting Reading Rate*

Students need to be able to vary their reading rates according to specific purposes and materials. Often students will instead read all materials at the same
rate, which results in sporadic comprehension of important text information.
This seems to be more prevalent when they read different types of content
materials, such as mathematical, science, social studies, or literature texts. In
general, the more technical the information and vocabulary, the slower the rate
your students may need to use. However, the purpose for reading the material
should also help students moderate their rates.

Flippo and Lecheler (1987) developed a procedure to encourage
intermediate-grade elementary students to be more aware of their reading
rates, and to adjust their rates and concentration for different materials based
on the difficulty of the materials. This procedure causes students to become
aware of how fast they can read something and still understand it. It requires
them to decide whether they can read certain material *slowly, moderately,* or
*fast,* words that youngsters can easily understand. We recommend that you utilize this procedure and develop activities using curriculum materials from your
own classroom to develop rate awareness and adjustment proficiency. The procedure is outlined for your use:

1. Tell students what you would like them to do by providing the reason:
   "Because some materials are more difficult to read than others, your
   reading rate shouldn't always be the same. It should vary."
2. Use several examples to illustrate what you mean and explain why you
   would read these slowly, moderately, or fast.
3. Ask "Why are some materials read faster than others?" List students'
   responses on the board.
4. Ask students to suggest materials that they would read slowly,
   moderately, or fast, but emphasize that understanding the material is still
   important. Write these suggested materials and the rates students provide
   on the board.
5. Ask individual students to explain their rationales for the suggestions they
   made in #4. Accept individual reasons. What might be difficult for one
   student to read and understand might not be for another.
6. Ask students to find passages and excerpts from varieties of textbooks
   and materials you use in class, read them silently, and then give rates they
   suggest for themselves. Establish this as an ongoing assignment.
7. Allow many opportunities for students to share their passages and
   excerpts, suggested rates, and reasons. This can be done over an
   extended period of time in small or large groups. This helps students
   develop their individual metacognitive rate awareness.

## Test-Taking and Test-Preparation Skills

Test-preparation skills and strategies actually involve use of most of the other study-learning skills. Application of study-learning skills is really what good test preparation is all about (Flippo 1988). Flippo has recommended many strategies for helping students use the various study-learning skills to study for and otherwise prepare for upcoming essay and objective tests. Simpson (1984) indicated that when students have had little or no instruction in the use of study and learning strategies, their comprehension of content materials in middle and secondary schools can be seriously affected. Weinstein and Mayer (1986) have summarized some of the major categories of study-learning skills and strategies, which we have displayed for you and further developed with examples of elementary classroom learning tasks in Figure 6.16, to show the relationship between the study-learning skills and test study and preparation strategies. When students know how to learn, they can have control over their learning and studying.

Teachers tend to assume that students will develop efficient test-preparation and test-taking skills as they mature, and they often do not teach these skills to students. Unfortunately, many students never learn the skills. Flippo and Borthwick (1982) have noted that test-taking instruction is not part of most teacher education programs. They hypothesized that teachers were never taught test-taking and test-wiseness strategies, and therefore they do not know how to teach these strategies to their students. It is important for teachers to assist students in developing the ability to apply systematic procedures in studying for and taking tests. The research literature supports the idea that special instruction in preparing for and taking tests can lead to better test results (Wark and Flippo 1991).

Learning to be test-wise depends on learning how to apply different strategies to different types of tests, as well as other important aspects of study preparation. These aspects include the following (Flippo 1988):

1. organizing study materials for a test;
2. actually studying for the specific test;
3. knowing how to use various test-taking cues and understanding the different characteristics of different types of tests; and
4. actually taking the test using time-management organization, knowledge of topic information, and internal cues in the test.

A summary of test-preparation suggestions by Flippo (1988) and Pauk (1993) can provide you with a listing that could be given to your upper elementary grade students in the form of a checklist. The checklist could consist of the following points:

1. Review lecture and reading notes periodically.
2. Plan a definite exam study schedule and stick to it.
3. Prepare and study a master outline of the test subject (an informal, condensed version of all your notes). Making an outline or master set of important notes is an excellent review. Recite to yourself the facts and ideas related to each item in the outline or notes.

**Figure 6.16**
Categories of
study-learning
strategies.

Derived and developed
from C. E. Weinstein and
E. Mayer (1986), "The
Teaching of Learning
Strategies," in M. C.
Wittrock, ed., *Handbook
of Research on Teaching,*
3d ed., pp. 315–317. New
York: Macmillan.

## Categories of Study-Learning Strategies

(Each category includes strategies and practices that influence aspects of the encoding process which facilitate one or more types of learning outcome and performance.)

*Rehearsal/Strategies* for basic learning tasks—such as repeating the names of items in an ordered list. Common school tasks in this category include remembering the order of the planets from the sun and the order in which the major battles of the Civil War occured.

*Rehearsal/Strategies* for complex learning tasks—such as copying, underlining or highlighting the material presented in class. Common school tasks in this category include underlining the main events in a story or copying the most important ideas from the text about the causes of the Civil War.

*Elaboration strategies* for basic learning tasks—such as forming a mental image or sentence relating the items in each pair for a paired-associate list of words. Common school tasks in this category include forming a phrase or sentence relating the name of a state and its major agricultural product, or forming a mental image of a scene described by a poem.

*Elaboration strategies* for complex tasks—such as paraphrasing, summarizing, or describing how new information relates to existing knowledge. Common school tasks in this category include creating an analogy between the operation of a school and the operation of the government, or relating the information presented about the planets of the solar system to the information presented about the sun.

*Organizational strategies* for basic learning tasks—such as grouping or ordering to-be-learned items from a list or a section of text. Common school tasks in this category include organizing new vocabulary words into categories for various parts of speech, or creating a chronological listing of the events that led up to the Declaration of Independence.

*Organizational strategies* for complex tasks—such as outlining a section of a chapter or creating a hierarchy. Common school tasks in this category include outlining assigned chapters in the textbook, or creating a diagram to show the relationship among the various forms of life in the rainforest.

*Comprehension monitoring strategies*—such as checking for understanding. Common school tasks in this category include using self-questioning to check understanding of the material presented in class and using the questions in a study guide to guide one's reading focus while studying a textbook.

*Affective strategies*—such as being ready, sure of oneself, and relaxed, to help overcome test anxiety. Common school tasks in this category include reducing external distractions by studying in a quiet place or using relaxation techniques as necessary during a test.

4. Besides memorizing, synthesizing, and analyzing, try to see the interrelationships. (Examine material from your own point of view.)
5. Ask about the type of test that is to be administered. Make up test questions or an exam, take it, and grade it.
6. Remember that the best way to know a concept is to be able to state it correctly in your own words. Study with this objective in mind.

7. Pay special attention to important points and ideas. Make a list of hard-to-remember facts and information. Note cards are a good idea. Repeatedly summarize, write, further condense, rewrite, and recite important points noted on your cards.
8. Do not be afraid to cram (Flippo 1988). Have a final review the night before an exam, and continue to review and recite important information right up until exam time. (Although cramming sometimes carries a negative connotation, Flippo has noted that cramming is "just intense studying" and, in fact, good students do it all the time [pp. 54–55].)

Students need to be aware of the differences between objective and essay tests to effectively prepare for them and take them. Objective tests usually consist of true and false, multiple-choice, matching, and fill-in questions. True-false are absolute statements, in that you either answer a question "true" or "false." A strategy to remember is that when a true-false statement is only partly true, the answer is false. Also, absolute modifiers are words that tend to appear in false statements. Examples of such words are *always, all,* and *only.* However, qualifiers such as *frequently, some,* and *many* tend to more often appear in true statements.

Multiple-choice questions are incomplete statements followed by possible answers. The question is referred to as the stem and the choices are called options. There are usually four or five choices, with one answer being the correct option and the others the distractors. One strategy your students could use for answering multiple-choice questions is to eliminate as many of the distractors as possible, and to analyze the remaining stem and possible options as though they were true-false questions. Flippo (1988, pp. 115–118, and 122–123) has recommended the following techniques which should help students learn how to select the best multiple-choice option:

1. Read the stem and anticipate the answer before you look at the options.
2. Lightly mark in pencil a T or F by the options as you review each; only the Ts are usually possibilities.
3. Use cues in the options, for instance:
   (a) The most general alternative is often the most encompassing of the choices and may be the correct choice.
   (b) Two similar alternatives often have nearly the same meaning; both cannot be correct unless it is a key word that is different.
   (c) The use of two alternatives of opposite meaning often indicates that one of them is correct; when teachers make up alternatives for questions, an antonym for the correct answer is often the first thing that comes to mind.
   (d) "None" or "all-of-the-above" alternatives can be eliminated or selected by noting whether you put all Fs or all Ts by the options.
4. Using these and other cues and your knowledge of the material, eliminate as many of the options as possible, and if more than one option is still left, take your best guess from the remaining options.

Shepherd (1994) has suggested that teachers provide the following procedures to students for answering matching and fill-in questions.

## Matching Questions

1. Examine both lists to understand the types of items you are to match.
2. Use one list as the starting place to make all matches.
3. If one list has longer statements, use it as the starting place to make all matches.
4. Cross out items as you match them.
5. Match first only those items that you are certain are matches.
6. If possible, use logical clues to match items about which you are uncertain.

## Fill-In Questions

1. Decide what type of answer is wanted.
2. When a question contains two blanks with a space between them, give a two-word answer.
3. When a blank is preceded by the word "an," give an answer that begins with a vowel (*a, e, i, o,* or *u*).

When applying test-wiseness strategies to matching and fill-in type of questions, you should encourage your students to also use their own prior knowledge of the particular subject matter under consideration to monitor their choice of responses, along with the preceding suggestions.

Essay tests differ from objective tests in that the answers must be constructed rather than recognized, and these answers will be graded in a more subjective manner than those on objective tests. The advantage of essay tests is that they maximize the use of the knowledge and understandings students have. Students' success also depends on developing and using their understandings of the content materials, organizing that content, and writing clear, well-developed responses that rely on their understandings and organization. To prepare for an essay test, Flippo (1988, pp. 57–76) has recommended the following advice, which could be explained and demonstrated to upper elementary students:

1. Use your notes and knowledge of the content that will be tested to predict the types of questions you will be asked.
2. Predict the questions and practice writing answers to them, using your notes and other resources you gathered for study. (Even if the questions you predict are not exactly the same as those on the test, the process of predicting and answering questions will help you learn the material more thoroughly.)

Figure 6.17, derived from the Flippo (1988) book, displays the kinds of questions, and the key words and phrases that signal various types of essay questions and the responses that are required. Using your own class content materials and notes, your students can practice predicting and answering potential essay exam questions.

A strategy that students can use for studying for an essay or objective test is the use of mnemonic acronyms. The mnemonic acronym "COW" can be used to remember the three steps for taking essay tests. *Mnemonic* means "to help the memory" and *acronym* is a word made from the initial letters of other

| Kinds of questions | Key words | Phrases that signal questions |
| --- | --- | --- |
| Short-answer | List<br>Name<br>Define<br>Identify | |
| Long-answer | Trace | Describe the steps in ...<br>Trace the development of ...<br>Trace the events leading up to ...<br>Outline the history of ... |
| | Compare and contrast | Tell how _____ and _____ are alike or different.<br>Consider the advantages or disadvantages of ...<br>Compare and contrast _____ and _____ .<br>Show the similarities and differences between _____ and _____ . |
| | Discuss | Discuss the significance or the problems of ...<br>What is the relationship between _____ and _____?<br>Discuss the effect of ...<br>Discuss the role of ... |

**Figure 6.17**

Kinds of essay questions.

Derived from R. F. Flippo (1988), *TestWise: Strategies for Success in Taking Tests,* pp. 57–76. Parsippany, NJ: Fearon Teacher Aids/Simon & Schuster.

words. "COW" stands for: Construct; Organize; and Write. Mnemonic devices are also used in making up sentences, but this strategy should be used selectively.

Finally, the key to receiving a good grade on an essay test is being able to organize ideas. An exam taker needs to develop a line of thinking and use examples to illustrate a theme. Some students know all the facts, write everything they know, and yet receive little credit for their essay answers. Studying facts in isolation, failing to understand the facts, not following directions, and not dividing test time properly are common errors. For example, your students can write a mini-outline for each essay question. The mini-outline briefly lists the major points intended for their answers. Other strategies for responses to essay tests are to answer the question directly, reflect on the organization of the potential answer, use facts to support statements, use examples to help clarify points made, and in conclusion to be sure the essay answer is organized with thoughts clearly exemplified. In reflecting and self-monitoring their answers, students can determine whether their conclusion summarizes their response.

Flippo (1988) provides practice on various study skills and strategies as part of her test-preparation and test-taking strategies by applying the study skills to actual test-preparation situations. Many test-preparation strategies include skills and strategies that teachers may traditionally teach as part of their usual study-skills instruction (e.g., note taking, outlining, summarizing).

However, when teaching your students these skills and strategies as part of their test-taking preparation, you are providing a tangible purpose for students to become accomplished in important related study-learning skills. Furthermore, appropriate use of the various specialized study skills is important to your students' success in the various study-learning assignments they undertake.

## Reflection Activity 6.6

*W*hat do you think of the idea of teaching your students how to study for and take tests? Do you feel that somehow this is cheating or not ethical? Several researchers have indicated that they believe that students have a right to test-preparation and test-taking instruction, and that success in test taking is an important aspect of school, often affecting students entire lives (i.e., Flippo 1988; Flippo and Borthwick 1982; Pauk 1993; and Shepherd 1994). Take a stand. How do you feel? Under the heading Reflection Activity 6.6 in your reflection journal, indicate why you do or do not believe your students should be taught these skills and the other related study-learning skills.

### *Study-Learning Skills: A Summary*

In summary, study-learning skills are worth teaching. Students need these skills to pursue and do the many learning tasks and assignments that elementary teachers and upper-grade teachers assign. However, like all other teaching, study-learning skills should be embedded in the authentic content curriculum of your classroom and should be intrinsically motivating to students. They should be presented to be used for real purposes, real situations, and in the pursuit of real and interesting assignments. Guthrie and Pressley (1992, p. 257) reviewed and summarized the research relative to cognitive competence and indicated the following:

1. Students comprehend text more fully and remember the information longer if they view the texts as a means for learning an idea or gaining an experience, as opposed to objects to be understood and recalled.
2. Cognitive strategies are learned more rapidly when reading goals are immersed in substantive and intrinsic purposes.
3. Students learn to search for ideas and locate information across a variety of texts and references most efficiently when the texts are provided as tools and resources among other resources for learning.
4. Students will read more independently and voluntarily when reading is part of a substantive, intrinsically oriented goal, rather than just for teacher-directed purposes.

In the section that follows we present descriptions of several specific study-reading and learning strategies that elementary school students and their teachers can use to help students read, learn from, and study text. Johnston (1985) has emphasized the difference between "teaching strategies" and "learning strategies" and advocated that teachers transfer their efforts to assisting students in learning various learning strategies. When students become involved in a learning strategy, they are more likely to effectively use the strategy independently and in varied situations.

## *Specific Strategies for Studying and Learning from Text*

It is important that both you and your students are aware of a number of strategies that can be used to enhance students' abilities to read, study, and learn from textual materials. Even though another chapter in this text focuses on content reading, we present a number of selected study-reading and teaching strategies here that you can introduce to your students and use with your students as you and they develop skills and strategies for learning how to learn. As you introduce the study-reading strategies to your students, you will want to model the correct usage and application of each strategy so that your students will gain an understanding of its use and effectiveness with various text materials. It is also important to give students an appropriate amount of time to practice and to receive feedback from you in order to enable them to use these strategies effectively. However, always let students practice and apply the study-reading strategies to materials they really need to read or really want to read in order to do their school assignments and other personal research, rather than to just "practice materials." As emphasized previously, making schoolwork authentic and assignments real and meaningful is an important part of the classroom teacher's role.

Additionally, in this section, we provide two teaching strategies for you to try, which we believe are particularly helpful when introducing students to new learning areas and to readings that you know might be especially difficult to understand. Although these are teaching strategies rather than learning strategies, we feel that these selected teaching strategies will lead students toward becoming more independent learners, readers, and thinkers. In the content reading chapter of this text, you will be introduced to other reading and teaching strategies you can apply to your content teaching.

### *PARS*

This study-reading strategy developed by Smith and Elliot (1979) is particularly useful for elementary students with limited prior experience in using study-reading strategy techniques. The PARS steps to teach your students are as follows:

1. *Preview* the material to better understand its organization, that is, its important headings or concepts.
2. *Ask questions* before reading to help you understand the purpose or purposes inherent in your reading.
3. *Read* with those purpose-setting questions as a guide.
4. *Summarize* the reading by analyzing information gained against your questions.

## K-W-L

This teaching strategy developed by Ogle (1986) is designed to help you facilitate your students' abilities to activate prior knowledge when interacting with text, and to increase their level of interest in reading and studying about selected topics. The three steps in this strategy are as follows:

1. *K—What I Know.* The students collaboratively respond to a concept presented by you before they read a selection. You record their ideas on the chalkboard, poster board, or any convenient place in order to use them as a beginning point for discussion. After this, collaboratively generate categories from their responses to help students better understand the text.
2. *W—What Do I Want to Learn?* Students develop questions that highlight their area of interest as a result of the activities in the first step. Students then read the selection.
3. *L—What I Learned.* After completing the text selection, students list what they have learned, check this against their questions, and answer any remaining questions.

## SIP

Dana (1989) developed this study-reading strategy that is designed to help readers with special needs concentrate their attention on content while reading. It is effective with both narrative and expository text. The three steps for SIP are as follows:

1. *Summarize* the content of each page, or naturally divided section, of the text. This enables your students to reflect on and interact with the text more effectively.
2. *Imaging* reminds the students to try to form an internal visual display of content encountered while reading. It also provides a second imprint of the text's content but is economical because it adds no time to the reading task.
3. *Predict* while reading. Students should try to pause after each page, or naturally divided section in the text, reflect on the text, and predict what might happen next. During this step, your students can verify, revise, or modify predictions based on what they have learned.

## RIPS

Dana (1989) designed this study-reading strategy for readers with special needs to combat difficulties understanding text while reading. It is also effective in converting negative impressions toward the text material into more positive ones. The four steps of RIPS are as follows:

1. *Read on* and then *reread* when necessary. If comprehension deteriorates while reading, students should be encouraged to stop and reread until their understanding of the text improves.

2. *Imaging* is a crucial component of this strategy and students are asked to visualize the content to provide themselves with an imprint of the material. Visual images that make no sense are an indication to students that comprehension difficulties are continuing.
3. *Paraphrase* those sections that are problem areas, and then ask students to try to restate the information in their own words.
4. *Speed up, slow down, and/or seek help.* Explain to students that during the "reading on" and "rereading" of text, they may need to speed up or slow down their rate of reading. When all else fails, students should seek your assistance.

### Inference Awareness

This teaching strategy was described by Gordon (1985) as a procedure to assist readers in locating information that is implied rather than directly stated in content materials. The five steps of this strategy are as follows:

1. Discuss with your students that in order to understand some text materials, readers must activate their own prior knowledge and experiences to understand what the writer intended but did not directly state.
2. In the second step, you model "inferencing" by reading a selection from the text material, then ask an inference question, give your own answer, and discuss with your students the cognitive processing involved.
3. The third step of this strategy involves a collaborative effort between you and your students. You ask and then answer another inference question, but in this step the students are asked to provide documentation that supports or refutes your answer. Encourage dialogue among your students and between your students and yourself.
4. During this step, students write the answers to the inference questions while you provide the supporting documentation; then, students and teacher discuss the responses and supporting documentation.
5. In the last step, students are completely responsible for locating the answers to the questions, finding supporting documentation, and explaining the cognitive processes involved.

## Computer Hardware and Software Considerations

The hardware considerations relative to using your computer to develop your students' study skills and strategies are similar, with one exception, to those we have discussed in earlier chapters. As we previously stated, these considerations include the following: (a) selecting hardware that matches the software programs you want to use (e.g., Macintosh or IBM/IBM compatible); (b) securing hardware that has multimedia capabilities (e.g., Macintosh 5300/100 or IBM Aptiva M71) and a fast and powerful microprocessor (e.g., PowerPC, Pentium, or P6), a large hard disk (e.g., one gigabyte), extensive random-access memory (e.g., a minimum of four megabytes of RAM), a fast CD-ROM drive (e.g., NEC's 6X or 8X), and a state-of-the-art monitor (e.g., Sony or Panasonic 17" SVGA) and printer (e.g., Hewlett Packard or Cannon laser printer); and (c) using adaptive and/or alternative input and output devices (e.g., IntelliKeys, TouchWindow, voice recognition, and speech synthesis). The one exception at this time is that we strongly recommend that you also secure a high-speed fax/modem (e.g., Hayes or US Robotics 14.4 or 28.8) and appropriate software (e.g., MicroPhone Pro for Power Macintosh and IBM/Compatible WinFax Pro and WinComm Pro) to engage in telecommunication activities. You and your students could use the fax/modem (MOdulate–DEModulate) and software to send and receive "faxes" and to access other computers, local bulletin boards for elementary students' access, and national online services (e.g., America Online, Compuserve, and Prodigy), and the international bulletin boards (e.g., the Internet and the World-Wide-Web) through an Internet provider (e.g., an online service). By accessing, we mean that you would be able to use your computer and standard telephone lines to communicate directly or indirectly with other professionals and students who are "telecommunicating" (e.g., "chatting" and sending/receiving electric- or e-mail) and to communicate with online services to search for, find, upload (or send), and download (or retrieve) needed information or files (e.g., newspaper or magazine articles). Your students could also use your computer's telecommunication capabilities: (a) to establish pen or e-mail pals; (b) to interact with local or distant mentors; and (c) to fax documents or transfer files such as letters, reports, and papers to other individuals for informational, editorial, and other study skills and strategies purposes. There are costs, of course, associated with online services (e.g., yearly or monthly fees) and with long distance telephone activities. And your students should be carefully monitored as they use your computer to interact with strangers.

You should continue to keep in mind two software considerations as you use your computer system to develop your students' study skills and strategies. First, you should use internal and external procedures to carefully evaluate available programs to determine whether they match your students' characteristics, your study-skills/strategies goals and objectives, and your hardware attributes. Internal procedures could include consulting with other professionals in your district to obtain their evaluations of available programs. You could also collaborate with these professionals to establish a local software evaluation database. External procedures could include reading software reviews in your professional journals or in commercial magazines. Another excellent external procedure is to access software information from local and national bulletin boards or online services. Second, you should select software programs that promote personal and instructional productivity and offer varied formats. In addition to application and utility software, you should obtain simulation and demonstration programs for study and teaching-learning outcomes. Some programs you may want to secure and evaluate that develop, reinforce, or apply study skills and strategies include:

| Program | Company |
|---|---|
| **General Learning Abilities/Processes** | |
| Learning Improvement Series (GL 6–12) | Lawrence Productions/MCE |
| Mind Benders (GL 2–6) | Critical Thinking Software |
| | |
| **Organization and Planning** | |
| Kid Works 2 or Deluxe (GL PreK–4) | Davidson |
| Kid Pix Studio (PreK–8) | Broderbund |
| Kid Desk (PreK–6) | Edmark |
| Pacesetter (GL 6–12) | Mindplay |
| | |
| **Document Saving, Editing, and Publishing** | |
| Children's Writing & Publishing Center (GL 2–9) | The Learning Company |
| Also—Kid Works, Kid Pix, and Kid Desk | |
| | |
| **Studying and Test-Taking Skills** | |
| A Silly Noisy House Multimedia Study Bundle (GL K–3) | Humanities Software |
| How to be a Better Test Taker (GL 3–6) | Scholastic |
| Microcourse Reading/Study Skills Component (GL 2–6) | Houghton Mifflin Company |
| Test-Taking Tactic Software (GL 3–6) | EBSCO Curriculum Materials |
| | |
| **Dictionary/Thesaurus** | |
| Dictionary Skills (GL 3–6) | American School Publisher |
| Dictionary Skills (GL 4–5) | Intellectual Software |
| Macmillan Dictionary for Children (GL 1–6) | Macmillan New Media |
| Random House Webster's Electronic Dictionary & Thesaurus (GL 5–12) | WordPerfect Corporation |
| | |
| **Encyclopedia** | |
| Random House Encyclopedia (GL 4–12) | Microlytics/Software Holdings |
| Encarta Encyclopedia (GL 2–9) | Microsoft Corporation |
| Grolier's Multimedia Encyclopedia (GL 3–12) | Electric Publishing |
| Compton's Encyclopedia (GL 2–12) | Compton's New Media |
| | |
| **Maps** | |
| Map Skills (GL 4–12) | Optimum Resource |
| My First World Atlas (GL 1–4) | Impressions |
| Picture Atlas of Our World (GL 4–12) | National Geographic |
| World Atlas (GL 5–12) | The Software Toolworks |
| U.S. Atlas (GL 5–12) | The Software Toolworks |
| | |
| **Research** | |
| How to Do Research (GL 7–12) | Intellectual Software |
| Study Skills (GL 3–6) | C. C. Publications |

**Library**

| | |
|---|---|
| Foundations of Library Skills (GL 3–6) | EPC |
| Library Skills (GL 4–12) | Looking Glass Learning |
| Library Search and Solve (GL 4–8) | K-12 Micromedia Publishing |
| Let's Learn about the Library (GL 4–8) | Troll Associates |

Finally, if you are unable to find appropriate software for your students' study strategy needs, you could design these programs with multimedia formats using an authoring system such as Apple's HyperCard, Macromedia's Authorware Professional, Asymetrix's Multimedia Toolbook, or IBM LinkWay Live. Your students could also use Sunburst's My Media Text Workshop to create multimedia study programs. And, you and your students could use integrated programs (ClarisWorks or Microsoft Works—word processing, database, spreadsheets, etc.), stand-alone word processing programs (Random House's Snoopy Writer or Spinnaker's Kidwriter), and publishing programs (The Learning Company's The Children's Writing & Publishing Center) to develop documents for study skills and strategies purposes.

## Summary

Study-learning skills and strategies enable students to pursue and accomplish the many assignments and study tasks they are given in school. They also provide students with the tools that they need to acquire and learn information from texts and other resources. Developing these skills and strategies is important to your students "learning how to learn." Learning how to learn is the main goal of school instruction.

Studying and learning considerations explored in this chapter included: awareness of the study-learning task, awareness of the skills and strategies to use, and awareness of how to monitor learning and performance. Both students and teachers have a role in each of these.

Two major teaching techniques for enhancing students study-learning development were discussed and examples were provided. The scaffolded reading experience—which consists of prereading, during-reading, and postreading activities—and the use of various study guides were recommended. Additionally, teachers were reminded that many of the teaching techniques described elsewhere in this text are also applicable to the development of students' study-learning strategies. Use of demonstration, modeling, scaffolding, and fading are strongly recommended as teaching techniques that go across all reading and study-learning curricula.

A variety of study-learning skills were identified and discussed. They include the reference and research skills, like using the dictionary, encyclopedia, and library reference materials. Also included and discussed were the organizational skills of outlining, underlining and student glossing, and note taking and note making. Finally, many study-learning skills, which we grouped as specialized skills, were discussed. These included using parts of textbooks, reading graphically displayed information (maps, graphs, tables, etc.), skimming and scanning, adjusting reading rate, and test-taking and test-preparation skills. Study-learning skill instruction should be embedded in your content learning instruction so that it is seen as meaningful and purposeful to your students, rather than as instruction in isolation.

In the last major sections of the chapter we presented several specific strategies for studying and learning from text, as well as information concerning use of computer technology. When used, these strategies, and the suggested computer applications, should empower your students and encourage the active, self-directed, and independent learning we recommend and want to encourage.

# *Closing Activities*

1. In a small group in class, explain what you now believe that learning how to learn involves and how it fits with your existing schema. You may want to refer back to your response to Reflection Activity 6.1 that we asked you to write early in this chapter. Feel free to amend your earlier reflection if you wish.

2. Design your own scaffolded reading experience for any particular grade level you choose. Include at least one prereading, during-reading, and postreading experience to fit a particular content study-learning unit of your choice. If possible, try this out with a group of students. Take notes and share the scaffolded reading experience you designed, and the results (if you were able to try it out), with your peers in class.

3. Design a study guide for reading, study, and learning of science-related material for any particular grade level you choose. If possible, try it out with a group of students. Take notes and share the study guide you designed, and the results (if you were able to try it out), with your peers in class.

4. Design a different type of study guide for reading, study, and learning history or other social studies–related material for any particular grade level you choose. If possible, try it out with a group of students. Take notes and share the study guide you designed, and the results (if you were able to try it out), with your peers in class.

5. In Reflection Activity 6.4, you noted ideas for developing a reference and research skills assignment for elementary youngsters. Refer back to that, select one of your ideas, and detail a lesson or activity you could try out in an elementary grade classroom for any particular grade level you choose. Remember to use fading and application to authentic content learning. If possible, try it out with a group of students. Take notes and share the lesson/activity you designed, and the results (if you were able to try it out), with your peers in class.

6. In Reflection Activity 6.5, you noted ideas for developing the outlining, underlining and student glossing, and note-taking and note-making skills of elementary youngsters. Refer back to that, select one of your ideas, and detail a lesson or activity you could try out in an elementary grade classroom for any particular grade level you choose. Remember to use fading and application to authentic content learning. If possible, try it out with a group of students. Take notes and share the lesson/activity you designed and the results (if you were able to try it out), with your peers in class.

7. Develop an original lesson or activity for enhancing one of the specialized study-learning skills described in this chapter. You may develop it for any particular grade level you choose. Remember to use fading and application to authentic content learning. If possible, try it out with a group of students. Take notes and share the lesson/activity you designed, and the results (if you were able to try it out), with your peers in class.

8. Select one of the specific study-reading strategies for studying and learning from text, as described in the section near the end of this chapter. Show students, in whatever grade level you choose, how to use the selected study-reading strategy. Use the teaching techniques of demonstrating, modeling, scaffolding, and fading to help students read, learn, and apply the strategy to real content material. Take notes and share the results with your peers in class.

Alvermann, D. E., and S. F. Phelps. (1994). *Content Reading and Literacy: Succeeding in Today's Diverse Classrooms.* Boston: Allyn & Bacon.

Anderson, T. H., and B. B. Armbruster. (1984). "Studying." In P. D. Pearson, R. Barr, M. L. Kamil, and P. Mosenthal, eds., *Handbook of Reading Research* (pp. 657-679). New York: Longman.

———. (1991). "The Value of Taking Notes During Lectures." In R. F. Flippo and D. C. Caverly, eds., *Teaching Reading & Study Strategies at the College Level* (pp. 166-194). Newark, DE: International Reading Association.

Armbruster, B. B., and J. O. Armstrong. (1993). "Locating Information in Text: A Focus on Children." *Contemporary Educational Psychology* 18:139-161.

Baker, R. L. (1977). "The Effects of Inferential Organizers on Learning and Retention, Content Knowledge, and Term Relationships in Ninth Grade Social Studies." In H. L. Herber and R. T. Vacca, eds., *Research in Reading in the Content Areas: The Third Report.* Syracuse, NY: Syracuse University Reading and Language Arts Center.

Baker, L., and A. L. Brown. (1984). "Metacognitive Skills and Reading." In P. D. Pearson, R. Barr, M. Kamil, and P. Mosenthal, eds., *Handbook of Reading Research* (pp. 353-394). New York: Longman.

Bean, T. W., H. Singer, and S. Cowan. (1985). "Analogical Study Guides: Improving Comprehension in Science." *Journal of Reading* 29:246-250.

Bereiter, C., and M. Scardamalia. (1987). "An Attainable Version of High Literacy: Approaches to Teaching Higher-Order Skills in Reading and Writing." *Curriculum Inquiry* 17(1): 9-30.

Blanchard, J. S. (1985). "What to Tell Students about Underlining . . . and Why." *Journal of Reading* 29:199-203.

Borkowski, J. G., M. Carr, E. Rellinger, and M. Pressley. (1990). "Self-Regulated Cognition: Interdependence of Metacognition, Attribution, and Self-Esteem." In B. F. Jones and L. Idol, eds., *Dimensions of Thinking and Cognitive Instruction* (pp. 53-92). Hillsdale, NJ: Erlbaum.

Brophy, J. (1986). "Teacher Influences on Student Achievement." *American Psychologist* 41:1069-1077.

Caverly, D. C., and V. P. Orlando. (1991). "Textbook Study Strategies." In R. F. Flippo and D. C. Caverly, eds., *Teaching Reading & Study Strategies at the College Level* (pp. 86-165). Newark, DE: International Reading Association.

Cheek, E. H., and M. C. Cheek. (1983). *Reading Instruction through Content Teaching.* Columbus, OH: Merrill.

Cole, J., and K. Gardner. (1979). "Topic Work with First-Year Secondary Pupils." In E. Lunzer and K. Gardner, eds., *The Effective Use of Reading* (pp. 167-192). London: Heinemann.

Cramer, E. H., and M. Castle, eds. (1994). *Fostering the Love of Reading: The Affective Domain in Reading Education.* Newark, DE: International Reading Association.

Dana, C. (1989). "Strategy Families for Disabled Readers." *Journal of Reading* 33:31-32.

Dansereau, D. F. (1985). "Learning Strategy Theory." In J. W. Segal, S. W. Chipman, and R. Glaser, eds., *Thinking and Learning Skills: Vol. 1: Relating Instruction to Research* (pp. 209-239). Hillsdale, NJ: Erlbaum.

Devine, T. G. (1987). *Teaching Study Skills: A Guide for Teachers,* 2nd ed. Boston: Allyn & Bacon.

Dole, J. A., G. G. Duffy, L. R. Roehler, and P. D. Pearson. (1991). "Moving from the Old to the New: Research on Reading Comprehension Instruction." *Review of Educational Research* 61(2): 239-264.

Dreher, M. J. (1993). "Reading to Locate Information: Societal and Educational Perspectives." *Contemporary Education Psychology* 18:129-138.

Dreher, M. J., and R. B. Sammons. (1994). "Fifth Graders' Search for Information in a Textbook." *Journal of Reading Behavior* 26(2): 301-314.

Dreher, M. J., and W. H. Slater. (1992). "Elementary School Literacy: Critical Issues." In M. J. Dreher and W. H. Slater, eds., *Elementary School Literacy: Critical Issues* (pp. 3–25). Norwood, MA: Christopher-Gordon Publishers.

Duffelmeyer, F. A. (1994). "Effective Anticipation Guide Statements for Learning from Expository Prose." *Journal of Reading* 37(6): 452–457.

Duffelmeyer, F. A., D. D. Baum, and D. J. Merkley. (1987). "Maximizing Reader-Text Confrontation with an Extended Anticipation Guide." *Journal of Reading* 31:146–150.

Dwyer, E. J., and E. E. Dwyer. (1994). "How Teachers' Attitudes Influence Reading Achievement." In E. H. Cramer and M. Castle, eds., *Fostering the Love of Reading: The Affective Domain in Reading Education* (pp. 66–73). Newark, DE: International Reading Association.

Flippo, R. F. (1988). *TestWise: Strategies for Success in Taking Tests.* Parsippany, NJ: Fearon Teacher Aids/Simon & Schuster.

———. (1997). *Reading Assessment and Instruction: A Qualitative Approach to Diagnosis.* Ft. Worth, TX: Harcourt Brace College Publishers.

Flippo, R. F., and P. Borthwick. (1982). "Should Testwiseness Curriculum Be a Part of Undergraduate Teacher Education?" In G. H. McNinch, ed., *Reading in the Disciplines, Second Yearbook of the American Reading Forum* (pp. 117–120). Athens, GA: American Reading Forum.

Flippo, R. F., and C. R. Frounfelker III. (1988). "Teach Map Reading Through Self Assessment." *The Reading Teacher* 42(3): 259.

Flippo, R. F., and R. L. Lecheler. (1987). "Adjusting Reading Rate: Metacognitive Awareness." *The Reading Teacher* 40(7): 712–713.

Fry, E. B. (1981). "Graphical Literacy." *Journal of Reading* 24:383–389.

———. (1989). *Skimming & Scanning: Intermediate Level*, 2nd ed. Providence, RI: Jamestown Publishers.

Good, T. L., and J. Brophy. (1978). *Looking in Classrooms.* New York: HarperCollins.

Gordon, C. J. (1985). "Modeling Inference Awareness Across the Curriculum." *Journal of Reading* 28(5): 444–447.

Graves, M., and B. Graves. (1994). *Scaffolding Reading Experiences: Designs for Student Success.* Norwood, MA: Christopher-Gordon Publishers.

Guthrie, J. T. (1994). "Creating Interest in Reading." *Reading Today* 12(1): 24.

Guthrie, J. T., and M. Pressley. (1992). "Reading as Cognition and the Mediation of Experience." In M. J. Dreher and W. H. Slater, eds., *Elementary School Literacy: Critical Issues* (pp. 241–260). Norwood, MA: Christopher-Gordon Publishers.

Hansell, S. T. (1978). "Stepping up to Outlining." *Journal of Reading* 22:248–252.

Harris, A. J., and E. R. Sipay. (1990). *How to Increase Reading Ability: A Guide to Developmental and Remedial Methods,* 9th ed. New York: Longman.

Herber, H. L. (1978). *Teaching Reading in Content Areas.* Englewood Cliffs, NJ: Prentice-Hall.

Hyde, A. A., and M. Bizar. (1996). *Thinking in Context: Teaching Cognitive Processes Across the Elementary School Curriculum,* 2nd ed. New York: Longman.

Irvin, J. L., and E. O. Rose. (1995). *Starting Early with Study Skills: A Week-by-Week Guide for Elementary Students.* Boston: Allyn & Bacon.

Johnston, P. (1985). "Teaching Students to Apply Strategies That Improve Reading Comprehension." *The Elementary School Journal* 8(5): 635–644.

Kiewra, K. A. (1984). "Acquiring Effective Notetaking Skills: An Alternative to Professional Notetaking." *Journal of Reading* 27:299–302.

Levin, J. R. (1976). "What Have We Learned about Maximizing What Children Learn?" In J. R. Levin and V. L. Allen, eds., *Cognitive Learning in Children: Theories and Strategies.* New York: Academic Press.

Lindsey, J. D. (1985). "Strategies for Mainstreamed Students: Can We Do More?" Speech given at the annual conference of the National Council of Teachers of English, Houston, Texas, March 28.

Mangrum, C. T. (1989). *Learning to Study* series, 2nd ed. Providence, RI: Jamestown Publishers.

Maxim, G. W. (1995). *Social Studies and the Elementary School Child,* 5th ed. Englewood Cliffs, NJ: Merrill/Prentice-Hall.

McAndrew, D. A. (1983). "Underlining and Notetaking: Some Suggestions for Research." *Journal of Reading* 27:103–108.

McCabe, P. P. (1984). "Stretch Your Budgets: Have Schools and Public Libraries Cooperate." *Journal of Reading* 27:632–635.

McKenna, M. C., and R. D. Robinson. (1993). *Teaching through Text: A Content Literacy Approach to Content Area Reading.* New York: Longman.

Mier, M. (1984). "Comprehension Monitoring in One Elementary Classroom." *The Reading Teacher* 37(8): 770–774.

Miller, M. J. (1979). "The Primary Child in the Library." In L. Monson and D. McClenathan, eds., *Developing Active Readers: Ideas for Parents, Teachers, and Librarians.* Newark, DE: International Reading Association.

Moore, D. W., S. A. Moore, P. M. Cunningham, and J. W. Cunningham. (1994). *Developing Readers & Writers in the Content Areas K-12,* 2nd ed. New York: Longman.

Nelson, R. M. (1973). "Getting Children into Reference Books." *Elementary English* 50:884–886.

Ogle, D. M. (1986). "K-W-L: A Teaching Model That Develops Active Reading of Expository Text." *The Reading Teacher* 39:564–570.

Otto, W., S. White, D. Richgels, R. Hansen, and B. Morrison. (1981). *A Technique for Improving the Understanding of Expository Text: Gloss and Examples* (Theoretical Paper No. 96). Madison, WI: Wisconsin Center for Education Research.

Palincsar, A. S., and A. L. Brown. (1984). "Reciprocal Teaching of Comprehension-Fostering and Comprehension-Monitoring Activities." *Cognition and Instruction* 1:117–175.

Paris, S. G., B. A. Wasik, and J. C. Turner. (1991). "The Development of Strategic Readers." In R. Barr, M. Kamil, P. B. Mosenthal, and P. D. Pearson, eds., *Handbook of Reading Research: Volume II* (pp. 609–640). New York: Longman.

Paris, S. G., and P. Winograd. (1990). "How Metacognition Can Promote Academic Learning and Instruction." In B. F. Jones and L. Idol, eds., *Dimensions of Thinking and Cognitive Instruction* (pp. 16–51). Hillsdale, NJ: Erlbaum.

Pauk, W. (1993). *How to Study in College,* 5th ed. Boston: Houghton Mifflin.

Pearson, P. D., and L. Fielding. (1991). "Comprehension Instruction." In R. Barr, M. L. Kamil, P. Mosenthal, and P. D. Pearson, eds., *Handbook of Reading Research: Volume II* (pp. 815–860). New York: Longman.

Poostay, E. J. (1984). "Show Me Your Underlines: A Strategy to Teach Comprehension." *The Reading Teacher* 37:828–830.

Risko, V. J., M. C. Alvarez, and M. M. Fairbanks. (1991). "External Factors that Influence Study." In R. F. Flippo and D. C. Caverly, eds., *Teaching Reading & Study Strategies at the College Level* (pp. 195–236). Newark, DE: International Reading Association.

Roehler, L. R., and G. G. Duffy. (1991). "Teachers' Instructional Actions." In R. Barr, M. L. Kamil, P. Mosenthal, and P. D. Pearson, eds., *Handbook of Reading Research: Volume II* (pp. 861–883). New York: Longman.

Ruddell, R. B., and M. R. Ruddell. (1995). *Teaching Children to Read and Write: Becoming an Influential Teacher.* Boston: Allyn & Bacon.

Rumelhart, D. E. (1980). "Schemata: The Building Blocks of Cognition." In R. J. Spiro, B. C. Bruce, and W. F. Brewer, eds., *Theoretical Issues in Reading Comprehension* (pp. 33–58). Hillsdale, NJ: Erlbaum.

Salend, S. J. (1994). *Effective Mainstreaming: Creating Inclusive Classrooms,* 2nd ed. New York: Macmillan.

Shepherd, J. F. (1994). *College Study Skills,* 5th ed. Boston: Houghton Mifflin.

Simpson, M. L. (1984). "The Status of Study Strategy Instruction: Implications for Classroom Teachers." *Journal of Reading* 28:136–143.

Sivertsen, M. L. (1993). *State of the Art: Transforming Ideas for Teaching and Learning Science.* Washington, DC: Office of Research, U.S. Department of Education.

Slavin, R. E. (1987). *Cooperative Learning: Student Teams,* 2nd ed. Washington, DC: National Education Association.

Smith, C. B., and P. G. Elliot (1979). *Reading Activities for Middle and Secondary Schools.* New York: Holt, Rinehart & Winston.

Tierney, R. J. (1982). "Essential Considerations for Developing Basic Reading Comprehension Skills." *School Psychology Review* 11(3): 299–305.

Turner, J. C., and S. G. Paris. (1995). "How Literacy Tasks Influence Children's Motivation for Literacy." *The Reading Teacher,* 48(8): 662–673.

Wade, S. E., and R. E. Reynolds. (1989). "Developing Metacognitive Awareness." *Journal of Reading* 33:6–14.

Wark, D. M., and R. F. Flippo. (1991). "Preparing for and Taking Tests." In R. F. Flippo and D. C. Caverly, eds., *Teaching Reading & Study Strategies at the College Level* (pp. 294–338). Newark, DE: International Reading Association.

Weinstein, C. E., and E. Mayer. (1986). "The Teaching of Learning Strategies." In M. C. Wittrock, ed., *Handbook of Research on Teaching,* 3rd ed. (pp. 315–317). New York: Macmillan.

Wittrock, M. C. (1986). "Students' Thought Processes." In M. C. Wittrock, ed., *Handbook of Research on Teaching,* 3rd ed., (pp. 297–314). New York: Macmillan.

———. (1990). "Generative Processes of Comprehension," *Educational Psychologist* 11:87–95.

Wood, K. D. (1988). "Guiding Students through Informational Text," *The Reading Teacher* 41(9): 912–920.

Wood, K. D., D. Lapp, and J. Flood. (1992). *Guiding Readers through Text: A Review of Study Guides.* Newark, DE: International Reading Association.

Zemelman, S., and H. Daniels. (1988). *A Community of Writers: Teaching Writing in the Junior and Senior High School.* Portsmouth, NH: Heinemann.

# *D*eveloping Proficiency in Content Reading

© James L. Shaffer

*E* lementary teachers are responsible for teaching their students how to read mathematics, science, social studies, and other content area materials. They could do this by providing instruction in the reading of all textbooks that students use in their classrooms. This instruction should focus on pertinent content and the strategies students must use to read content. In a previous chapter, our focus was on "learning how to learn." In this chapter, we turn our focus on content reading, or "reading to learn." This chapter, then, is designed to help teachers understand the content-reading process and assume their role in developing students' content-reading abilities. Various perspectives on content reading are examined, and some considerations regarding content reading are delineated. A directed content-reading approach (DCRA) that can be used by elementary teachers to guide content lessons is described. We also discuss the importance of cognitive experience, concepts, and schemata in the content-reading process, and detail activities that can be used to develop study-reading strategies for reading lengthy textbook assignments. Additionally, the use of thematic units to integrate curricula and provide literacy experiences across the curricula is discussed. Finally, content-reading computer hardware and software considerations are presented.

## Main Ideas

- Content reading is reading to learn.
- Content instruction focuses both on the content to be learned and the reading factors and strategies that facilitate this instruction.
- Many factors may affect students' content-reading proficiency.
- Teachers should consider using a directed content-reading approach (DCRA) to organize their instruction and to develop students' content-reading abilities.
- Students' concepts and schemata promote content-reading success.
- Planning and implementing thematic units makes content learning more interesting as well as academically beneficial to students.
- Reading-to-learn strategies can be used to provide students with a system for reading lengthy content materials.
- Computer hardware and software can be used to develop content abilities.

An interesting adage that you may have heard is "In grades K through three you learn to read, but in grades four and above you read to learn." If you think about your own school experiences, you will probably come to the conclusion that there is some truth to this adage. Your kindergarten teacher probably worked diligently to get you ready to learn to read, and your first-, second-, and third-grade teachers were unrelenting in their efforts to develop your word-identification and comprehension abilities. But then what? Somewhere near the fourth grade, your teachers might have begun to spend less time trying to teach you how to read and more time having you and your classmates actually read various kinds of content materials (e.g., chapters in social studies and science books). You then probably spent your upper-elementary, middle, and secondary school years reading more textbooks and more content-reading materials.

Instruction in reading in the content areas should actually begin in the first grade (or earlier) and continue throughout students' formal education experiences. This was noted by William S. Gray, one of the pioneers of reading education in the United States, almost a hundred years ago (Dishner and Olson 1989). This chapter is intended to promote your understanding of reading in the content areas and to promote your instruction in these areas beginning in the earliest elementary grades. Reading in the content areas is closely related to the study and learning strategies that were covered in another chapter. However, study skills and strategies, and other strategies for learning from text, are only part of what is involved in content area reading. Students will use those study and learning strategies as well as all other comprehension and word-identification skills and strategies in their content area reading. You, as an elementary teacher, will play a very important role in your students' development of content-reading competence. Content reading is "reading to learn" and learning to be active and independent learners in the areas of social studies, science, health, and other school subjects (Alvermann and Phelps 1994). Additionally, content reading is "reading to learn to learn." By this we mean that content reading employs all the reading strategies in an educational setting where students are reading to learn from their textbooks and learning how to learn more about the content areas they study. Reading programs should have a K–12 content perspective (Cheek, Lindsey, Rutland, and Doyle, 1984).

## *Reading in the Content Areas*

What is reading in the content areas? You probably already know that it involves reading-content materials and the students' schemata for the content; content-related vocabulary, interest, motivation, and attitudes; needs and purposes; higher-level comprehension abilities; and study-reading skills abilities. You are also probably aware that when educators talk about reading in the content areas they are referring to reading printed materials that focus on social studies, science, and other school-related subjects. However, we would like to add more specificity to your perception of what reading in the content areas is by presenting selected excerpts on this topic published by reading educators over the past two decades. Their perspectives will provide you with insight into content reading's philosophical evolution, add to your existing knowledge about content reading, and enable you to define what reading in the content area involves.

Cheek and Cheek (1983) have presented the concept of reading in the content areas by contrasting it with general reading instruction:

> Content reading differs from general reading instruction in that content reading is provided in conjunction with content teaching, while reading instruction is usually thought of as instruction given in a special reading class or an elementary classroom. General reading instruction places emphasis on skill development and independent reading relates reading instruction to specific content materials. . . . [C]ontent instruction is most effective when the need for reading instruction via content reading is recognized. (p. 5)

In essence, reading in the content areas is that activity that takes place in content lessons—such as reading social studies materials. However, it is necessary that teachers realize the importance of content reading, and plan and conduct instructional activities that will show their students how to independently read content materials. Students need specific abilities (e.g., knowing specific technical vocabulary) to successfully read a social studies chapter, and teachers must do what is necessary to see that their students develop these abilities.

Vacca and Vacca (1986) have stated a reading-in-the-content position emphasizing the importance of the classroom teacher's role:

> Although content traditionally has been king to many teachers, process has achieved the stature of prime minister in today's classroom. Showing students how to learn comes with the territory. When textbooks [or other content materials] are the vehicle for learning, the teacher has a significant role to perform. In effect, the classroom teacher is a "process helper," bridging the gap that often exists between students and the [content materials] . . . (p. 11)

Simply stated, Vacca and Vacca noted that content reading has two components. First, there is the content or written materials. Second, there are the processes that students must have if they are to become competent content readers. Teachers can teach content, but they must also engage in activities that will develop the processes their students must employ to successfully read content.

Conley (1992) has defined one of the components of content reading to consider within the "process helper" position noted by Vacca and Vacca:

> *Content reading* is a field in education devoted to helping students acquire specific strategies for reading in various subject areas, termed reading-to-learn strategies. Reading-to-learn strategies provide . . . ways for thinking and communicating in different subjects. . . . These strategies help students continuously increase their knowledge, update their skills, and improve communication with the world around them. (pp. 4–5)

According to Conley, the purpose of the content-reading program is to develop students' reading-to-learn strategies. Students are then provided with appropriate experiences so that they can use these strategies to become literate in content-subject areas, more effective learners, and better world citizens.

Alvermann and Phelps (1994) have addressed the issue of the textbook, the changing demographics of content classrooms, specific behaviors good content readers exhibit, and the benchmark students will use to evaluate themselves:

> . . . content area reading instruction involves much more than covering the subject matter in a particular specialty area. It includes making decisions about the role of the textbook and developing active and independent readers in culturally diverse classrooms. Students who self-question, monitor their reading, organize information, and interact with peers, possess some of the strategies necessary for becoming independent learners. But their overall sense of themselves as learners will depend to a larger extent on how they see themselves as readers and what it means to be literate in a fast-changing world. (p. 43)

Finally, according to Brozo and Simpson (1995), content-reading programs promote literacy and empower students:

> Literacy teaching and learning in . . . [content areas] could provide the necessary experiences for . . . [students] to take on political, social, and economic challenges in the near and long term. Making literacy and learning meaningful on a sociopolitical level could help students look more critically at their own lives as well as the lives of their neighbors and society and imbue them with the courage to become involved in helping to improve our political, social, and economic condition. (p. 2)

What did you think about the content positions advanced by these authors? They are, in all likelihood, similar to what you may perceive that reading in the content areas is all about. They may also have refined your content-reading definition and given you other elements (e.g., basic vs. content-reading instruction, processes, etc.) to incorporate into your understanding of content reading.

You will need to teach your students how to read and how to read to learn, starting as early as kindergarten or first grade. You will also have responsibility for selecting many content materials, and you will be responsible for designing and implementing instructional activities to develop the abilities your students will need to read the content selected. Before describing a general content-reading instructional model (our recommended DCRA) and specific techniques you could consider to structure content instruction, we provide information relative to factors that will positively or negatively affect students' success as they read in the content areas. This discussion might also provide you with some insight into why you or other college/university students experience success or problems when tackling college/university reading assignments. College/university reading assignments usually involve reading in the content areas.

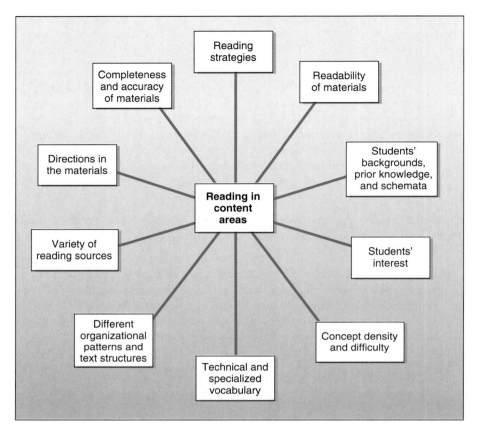

*Figure 7.1*

Factors that may affect students' reading in the content areas success.

# Content Area Reading Considerations

There are numerous factors that may affect your students as they read content materials. Conley (1992), Smith (1991), Anthony and Raphael (1989), Herber (1978), and H. Robinson (1978) among others have delineated and discussed these important content-literacy factors, which are displayed in Figure 7.1. Following this figure, we include a discussion of some of these considerations and some short passages for you to read, to simulate how your students can be affected.

## *Less-Abled Readers*

The chances are quite likely that during your teaching career you will have students who are nonreaders. These students' limited reading strategies will significantly affect their understanding and success when trying to read content materials. To simulate what nonreaders might experience as they attempt to read, try to read the following paragraph (it is about a groundhog resting at his home) and answer the comprehension questions. You should know that this passage has a fifth-grade readability level (as calculated quantitatively using the Fry [1977] readability formula).

## Die Wette[*]

An einem schönen Sonntagmorgen steht ein Igel vor der Tür seines Hauses. Es ist Sommer, die Sonne scheint hell am blauen Himmel, und ein frischer Wind bläst über die Fleder. Der Igel raucht zufrieden seine Pfeife und denkt: Wie schön das Wetter ist! Ein wunderbarer Morgen! Wenigstens für mich. Leider nicht für meine Frau. Sie hat die Hände voll. Zuerst muss sie die Kinder waschen, und dann macht sie das Frühstück. Nun, ich arbeite die ganze Woche, und wenn ich sechs Tage schwer arbeite, dann brauche ich meiner Frau am Sonntag nicht zu helfen. Ein Mann braucht seine Ruhe. Ich habe also Zeit, bis das Frühstück fertig ist. (pp. 5, 7)

### Fragen
1. Was für ein Tag ist es?
2. Welchen Beruf hat der Igel?

If you have taken courses in German or have a reading knowledge of German, you probably were able to read some if not all of this passage. If you have no proficiency in German, you have just experienced to some degree the nonreader's content-reading nightmare.

The reading-in-the-content experiences of your less-abled readers will be very different. Some of these children will have various word-identification difficulties, whereas others will exhibit comprehension difficulties. Many will have both. We would like you to try to read the following passage that has been modified so that you can experience the content-reading dilemma for less-abled students. Do your best to read this passage, written at the college level, and to answer the comprehension questions.

## Blake's Classification Process[†]

Our purpose for classifying _____ is to be sure _____ they get the special _____ and related services they _____. We classify pupils by _____ important in doing the _____ tasks because pupils who _____ extraordinarily on these characteristics _____ special needs to which _____ must fit education so _____ they can learn and _____ the cultural tasks. _____ practice, we usually classify _____ on one characteristic and _____ them by that characteristic, for example, speech- or language-impaired _____ physically handicapped. Sometimes we classify on more than one _____ and label pupils multihandicapped or with a compound name, _____ deaf/blind. (p. 49)

### Questions
1. Name the kinds of task we must do when classifying.
2. What happens when we don't classify students?

If you were able to read Blake's passage and answer the questions, we congratulate you. The chances are you were more "less abled" than "able" as

---

[*]G. F. Schmidt (1964). _Hör gut zu: A Beginning German Audiolingual Reader_ (New York: Macmillan).

[†]K. A. Blake (1981). _Educating Exceptional Pupils_ (Reading, MA: Addison-Wesley).

you read and struggled through the passage; your students with limited reading abilities will also struggle with the content you have them read in much the same way you have just struggled.

You can use a variety of strategies to help your nonreaders and less-abled readers read content materials. We recommend the following three general procedures:

1. Use prereading and postreading activities to assist your students in recognizing the vocabulary. Some of these activities are discussed in the "Technical and Specialized Vocabulary" and "The Directed Content-Reading Approach" sections that follow. These activities could include such traditional procedures as the use of flashcards and multisensory activities.

2. Develop prior knowledge and schemata to facilitate comprehension. Prereading strategies you could utilize are presentations, discussions, and audiovisual sessions. The sections that follow provide suggestions for developing concepts, schemata, and cognitive strategies.

3. Schedule direct-teaching lessons and use internal and external adjunctive aids to promote comprehension skill and strategy development. Direct teaching would focus on pertinent text and comprehension processes that students could use. Also, adjunctive aids could be used to focus attention as well as help develop schemata and metacognition.

It is an extremely difficult and arduous process to develop nonreaders and less-abled readers' content-reading abilities. Structure, flexibility, creativity, and hard work within your classroom program are your keys to success with these students.

## *Readability of Materials*

Klare (1989) defined readability as "the quality that makes . . . [printed matter] relatively easy or hard to understand" (p. 35). The readability level of a passage is affected by many factors, including vocabulary, sentence structure, and content (Durkin 1978). For example, based on a quantitative analysis using one of the many readability formulas, second-grade materials, as compared with materials written at a sixth-grade level, would have fewer polysyllabic words (or more shorter words) and simpler sentences (subject-verb-object) rather than compound and complex sentences. Additionally, a qualitative analysis should reflect content and concepts appropriate to the readers' backgrounds, prior knowledge, schemata, purposes, interests, strategies, and motivations.

A number of mathematical formulas (e.g., Spache 1953) and graphs (e.g., Fry 1977, Raygor 1977) have been developed to estimate the quantitative readability levels of written materials. A copy of the Fry Readability Graph and the directions for using this procedure are found in another chapter. It is desirable, however, to rely more on the strategies, interests, motivations, backgrounds, purposes, prior knowledge, and schemata of your students, and the text structure and other textual considerations of the materials to be read, to make appropriate decisions regarding the difficulty of the content materials you select or suggest, rather than just to use estimated quantifiable data. Remember that readability may be affected by many factors—quantitative factors (e.g., length of words and sentences) and qualitative factors (e.g., difficulty of concepts, schemata, prior knowledge, interests and purpose, and text structure).

We have selected the following passage for you to read so that you can experience what your students might encounter when they read materials that may be very difficult for them. This passage has a 16+ readability level (as assessed by quantitative readability formulas only, approximately college senior year) but addresses learning and retention concepts important to elementary teachers. See if you can read this passage and answer the comprehension questions.

## *Memorial Reduction*[*]

The attractiveness of the assimilation process inheres not only in its ability to account for the superior retention of meaningfully learned ideas, but also in the fact that it implies a plausible mechanism for the subsequent forgetting of these ideas, namely, the gradual "reduction" of their meanings to the meanings of the corresponding anchoring ideas to which they are linked. Thus, although the retention of newly learned meanings is enhanced by anchorage to relevant established ideas in the learner's cognitive structure, such knowledge is still subject to the erosive influence of the general reductionist trend in cognitive organization. Because it is more economical and less burdensome merely to retain the more stable and established anchoring concepts and propositions than to remember the new ideas that are assimilated in relation to them, the meaning of the new ideas tends to be assimilated or reduced, over the course of time, to the more stable meanings of the established anchoring ideas. (p. 93)

### *Questions*

1. What is the attractiveness of the assimilation-process concept?
2. Why are the new ideas harder to remember than already-anchored concepts?

Were you able to comfortably read the preceding passage and answer the questions? Your students might have the same types of experiences with content materials that you give them if those materials are too difficult (as assessed quantitatively); or are based on concepts and ideas that are not within their schemata, interest, or purposes, or have unusual or unfamiliar textual structure and other text variables (as assessed qualitatively). Because the readability will vary within your instructional materials (e.g., one page is quantitatively graphed at the third-grade level while the next page graphs at the fifth-grade level, or the materials deal with familiar concepts in one section but unfamiliar concepts in another), you can expect your students to have various degrees of success as they read their content assignments. Also, because readability formulas and graphs only give you an estimated quantitative readability level, you

---

[*]D. A. Ausubel (1968). *Educational Psychology: A Cognitive View* (New York: Holt, Rinehart and Winston).

should use your knowledge of your students' strategies, schemata, concept knowledge, cognitive and linguistic experiences, and interests/motivations to select appropriate materials.

We would like to recommend the following two activities that you could undertake to possibly counteract some readability problems.

1. Help students use internal and external adjunctive aids to focus their attention on pertinent concepts and to promote their comprehension. These aids could include learning goals, questions, and outlines.
2. Develop your students' word-identification and comprehension strategies by using schemata-development activities, metacognitive questioning, and cognitive and linguistic cues. New vocabulary could be taught using direct teaching procedures, language-experience activities, and crossword puzzles or games, among other more traditional methods.

## Students' Backgrounds, Prior Knowledge, and Schemata

May (1994) refers to background knowledge or semantic cues as minitheories that the reader brings to content materials based on past schemata. For example, if you have science materials describing concepts and principles of space shuttles and space travel that you want your students to read, you can expect those students who have some understanding of space shuttles and space flight to be more proficient readers. Unfortunately, and as you well know, your students will come to school with varying knowledge about their world (e.g., people, places, events), and this knowledge has been developed by their exposure to books, television and videos; travel opportunities; participation in community activities; verbal interactions with parents, siblings, and other family members; and other linguistic, cognitive, and sociocultural variables. It is thus logical to assume that the more familiar your students are with the topics they are to read, prior to actually reading, the more likely they will be able to read and to achieve your content objectives. Let us demonstrate this to you. Read the following passage published by May (1994), which simulates the effect of a lack of concept or prior knowledge on your reading comprehension.

## No Title[*]

This operation is really not that difficult. First you remove them from the room you've just used and take them into the other room. Next you remove the material you no longer want and place each one in the appropriate place. Don't worry if this sometimes seems difficult. In time you'll get used to all the possibilities that are available to you. After you're satisfied with the arrangements, just follow the directions on the front and you'll be finished for a while. Later, when you have a need for them again, you can use them some other time. It's true that you have to repeat the operation many times in the course of living, but I'm sure you'll agree that it's worth it. (p. 16)

_____

[*]F. B. May (1994). See reference section.

## Questions

1. What is a good title for this passage?
2. What shouldn't you worry about when you do the above operation?

Well, could you answer the questions? Now, let us give you some information about the preceding passage that would help you to apply previously developed cognitive experiences to comprehend what you have just read. Are you ready? *This passage describes the operation of washing dishes in the dishwasher.* If you were to go back and read the above passage, you would use the schema for "washing dishes in a dishwasher" and easily read this passage.

It is important that you develop your students' cognitive experience and schemata before you give them content materials to read. These activities could involve helping them to understand the concrete and abstract concepts they are to read or getting them to verbally use the vocabulary they will encounter. General procedures that you could employ to develop cognitive experience and, in turn, schemata are as follows:

1. Prepare a presentation, question-and-answer, or discussion session to introduce pertinent background knowledge. Do everything you can to get your students actively involved in these sessions.
2. Assign large-group, small-group, or one-to-one, audiovisual, technology, paper-and-pencil, art, or drama projects that require your students to see, hear, and touch elements of the concepts before they are to read. In addition to these multisensory activities, your students could read and answer questions, construct dioramas, or put on plays related to the concepts they are to read.

Additionally, two other important variables that relate to the understanding of concepts are student interest and concept density. First, as we have indicated elsewhere in this textbook, student interest is very important. If students are not interested in what you want them to read, then they may not attentively and strategically read the material you assigned. Although we know that a facilitative teacher tries to plan instruction and materials around students' interest, we also know that there are some materials, interesting or not, that you must assign. Therefore, it is imperative that before assigning those materials you do your best to "create or develop student interest" by using some of the suggestions listed for developing cognitive experience and schemata. Also, you could try to relate materials that you believe do not meet students' interest to other areas in which they are interested.

Concept density, or the number of concepts presented in a passage, is another important variable related to cognitive background. When too many concepts are presented in a paragraph or reading selection, the result may be concept overload for your students. In other words, if many concepts (and therefore the need for many schemata) are embedded in a paragraph, the paragraph is likely to be very difficult to read, affecting your students' comprehension and recall. Once again, you can only counter this by your instructional approaches. You would need to point out concepts and familiarize students with them prior to reading. Then, during reading, students could be alerted to syntactic and other structural cues that will help them separate concepts as they read.

A question before we leave this subsection: What would happen if you gave the "No Title" passage to someone who knew absolutely nothing about dishwashing or dishwashers (someone who had no previous concept or schemata for it) but told them, "You are going to read a paragraph about the operation of a dishwasher"? That's right! This statement would not help them because they have no cognitive experience, or dishwasher schemata, to use as they read the passage. (Of course, we will note here that your statement might help them linguistically through syntax, if they observed the position of "dishwasher" as you used it in your question.)

## *Technical and Specialized Vocabulary*

The very nature and purpose of content materials dictate that technical and specialized vocabularies must be used to develop these passages. As you read and recognize such vocabularies, they give you insight into the types of content you are reading and bring into play schemata you have already developed for content. For example, in what content areas would you expect to find the words *malignant, ligament, communicable diseases, cardiac, orthopedic?* Now, try the next group: *schema, linguistic, syntax,* and *phonics.* We hope these words look familiar! Finally, what comes to your mind as you think about the meaning of the words *watering, fertilizing, weeding,* and *pruning?* Having technical and specialized vocabulary competencies will significantly increase your students' ability to read and understand the content materials you assign them to read. These vocabularies trigger existing concepts and schemata, and as you have already seen in the dishwasher example, and in other places throughout this text, without prior knowledge of the concepts, some materials are not possible to understand. This is particularly true of very technical and specialized content reading. We want you to read the following excerpt, and answer the comprehension questions, to experience the effect of unfamiliar vocabulary on your content-reading proficiency.

## *The Benefit-Cost Concept*[*]

One school of thought argues that the best approximation to an ideal social discount rate is the net yield or return on private investment projects, that is, the marginal productivity of capital in private investment. Technically, this would be a weighted average of the opportunity-cost rate in private investment for all sectors of the economy from which the government investment would withdraw resources. However, imperfections in capital markets do not allow a clear discernment of the marginal productivity of private capital investment. In practice, the discount rates utilized in the benefit-cost efforts of the federal government frequently have not approximated this version of the social discount rates. (p. 321)

---

[*]B. P. Herber (1979). *Modern Public Finance* (Homewood, IL: Richard D. Irwin).

## Questions

1. How do you determine the ideal social discount rate?
2. What are the imperfections in capital discernment of marginal productivity of private capital investment?

The preceding passage is written at the college level (as assessed quantitatively) but what might have prevented you from satisfactorily answering the comprehension questions is unfamiliarity with the technical and specialized vocabulary within the passage (e.g., "social discount rate"). You can assist your students in recognizing and comprehending content-specific vocabulary in a number of ways. We suggest you consider using the following procedures:

1. As you develop your students' prior knowledge, delineate and define pertinent technical and specialized vocabularies. Also, encourage students' discussions and questions so that they are using these vocabularies.
2. Use vocabulary-development activities before and after the students read the content materials. These activities could involve implementing traditional tasks such as discussions, paper-and-pencil assignments, and small-group projects. Other procedures you could use include taking field trips and developing computer-software vocabulary programs using authoring systems.

There is no doubt that you will employ other creative and structured activities to develop the technical and special vocabularies for your students with special needs. In another chapter, we present multisensory activities (e.g., Fernald's VAKT procedure) and an analytical peer-tutoring method that you can adopt or adapt.

## Additional Factors

Brozo and Simpson (1995), Collins and Cheek (1993), and Rothkopf (1976) have identified additional factors related to students' success with content area reading. These factors include the following.

## Different Organizational Patterns and Text Structures

Content materials can be organized into enumeration, persuasive relationship, and problem-solving patterns. Elementary students may have difficulty reading certain patterns and text structures because important information (e.g., cause-effect relationships) may not be explicitly stated and must be inferred. You can help your students read content materials with different patterns and text structures by teaching them how to recognize and use the passage structure to comprehend pertinent information.

## Variety of Reading Sources

The content-reading activities you use will require your students to read in a variety of sources. In addition to reading the content textbook, they will also have to read related materials in magazines, encyclopedias, newspapers, and other books to collect needed information. Primary-grade students in particular will have problems going from one reading source to another, because their "reading and learning experiences" may have been limited to using one book at a time. You can help your students develop competencies with a variety of reading sources by planning and supervising lessons where they use one, then two, then three, then four reading sources. Elements you want to help your students deal with when they use different sources are the varying structure, organization, formats, and vocabularies found in multiple sources.

## Directions in the Materials

The directions embedded within content materials or provided by external means significantly affect students' ability to read important content information. Where specific reading purposes are not stated or general directions are provided (e.g., "Read and remember as much as you can"), your students' attention may not focus on specific information that they should recall later. However, where specific directions such as learning goals, external and embedded questions, internal graphic material, structural cues, outlines, and other cognitive organizers and cues are given, your students' attention can be directed to the particular facts and concepts you expect them to read and remember. You should select content materials that have internal directions and other aids (e.g., embedded questions, graphics) that give your students specific directions and assistance to comprehend materials. If your content materials lack these types of directions, you can use study guides, questions, and outlines among other adjunctive aids to focus your students' attention on important content concepts.

## Completeness and Accuracy of the Materials

The completeness and accuracy of the content materials you use in your classroom will affect your students' ability to achieve your content objectives. As you already know, printed materials that are incomplete do not provide all the information that readers need to completely understand the concepts presented. For example, how could your students read and completely understand the dangers of pollution if toxic wastes are not mentioned? Also, printed materials that present inaccurate facts can negatively affect students' ability to read and comprehend important content information. How can your students read that the elimination of pollutants is the only solution to cleaning up the environment and at the same time completely understand the logical necessity for an accelerated increase of toxic wastes? You should do everything you can to select content materials that are complete and accurate, or use supplementary materials to make your materials complete and accurate.

The preceding factors alone or in combination will influence reading in content instructional practices and literacy development. If your students are to become active and independent learners, you must design content-reading plans in which you function as a facilitative "process helper" and students develop pertinent "reading-to-learn" strategies. Using the Directed Content-Reading Approach described in the next section will support both outcomes. This approach also directs your attention to the critical aspects of teacher-learner task-setting interactions (Smith 1991).

## Reflection Activity 7.1

$W$e have presented a variety of factors and considerations that may affect content area reading. Under the heading Reflection Activity 7.1 in your reflection journal, rank-order these factors and considerations as to which ones you believe could have the greatest to least impact on your students' reading in content areas. As you rank-order each, briefly justify why you have selected it for that particular ranking.

## *A Content-Reading Approach*

Conley (1992), Roehler and Duffy (1989), and other reading educators have stated that content-reading activities must be highly structured and skillfully directed if they are to achieve their objectives. These authors have also noted that (a) there is no single content-reading approach for you to adopt; (b) activities must be flexible so that you can respond spontaneously and creatively to emerging situations; and (c) procedures and materials you use should be varied to meet the needs of all your students. In addition to the preceding three general guidelines, you should keep in mind another important idea as you design and implement content-reading activities. As suggested by Cheek and Cheek (1983), (d) content reading is a developmental process, introduced in the primary grades and refined as students move through school.

Your content-reading program must be more than "lesson planning and student reading." It must be conceptualized and conducted so that your students acquire the skills and strategies that they will utilize in future educational and societal settings. Just think how important your content abilities are to you at this stage of your academic career!

We are in agreement with content-reading authors that teachers and students should be actively involved in a well-conceived, flexible, and developmental content-reading program. To accomplish this, we recommend that you consider our Directed Content-Reading Approach (DCRA). The DCRA will allow you to organize content area learning activities and at the same time allow for the necessary flexibility and variety that has been called for. Figure 7.2 portrays the components of our DCRA. We believe that it (a) provides some structure for your content lessons so that you can meet your content objectives and (b) permits you to address the unique content strategies of all of your students.

The next section describes our DCRA. Please be advised that what you will read is only a brief explanation of what is a complex teaching-learning process (i.e., entire books have been written on content reading), and we can only introduce a framework you can use for a directed but flexible content approach with all your students. Because you have just read and personally experienced

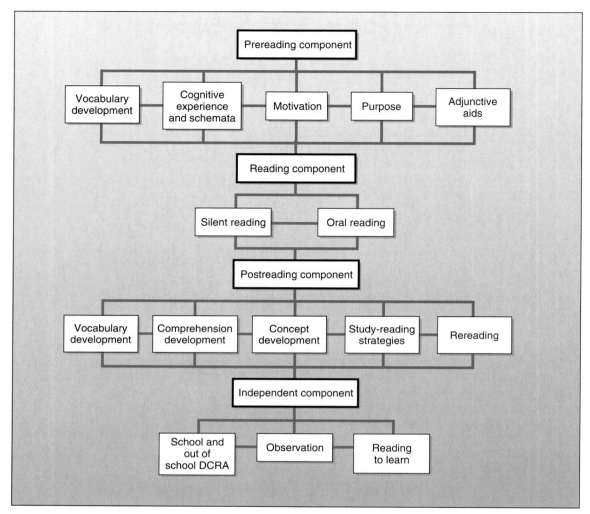

*Figure 7.2*
Directed content-reading approach (DCRA) components.

factors that affect content-reading proficiency and have been given general teaching strategies available to you to deal with the effects of these factors, we are comfortable at this point that you appreciate the complexities of content reading demands. Additionally, the fact that your success in college may be directly related to your content-reading abilities has probably already convinced you of the importance of this instruction. Regardless, to supplement our brief description of the DCRA, we have also included specific recommendations you could utilize to develop your students' content-reading strategies.

## *The Directed Content-Reading Approach (DCRA)*

The Directed Content-Reading Approach (DCRA) should provide you with the framework you need to become an organized facilitative teacher and an effective "process helper." It is implemented by applying specific prereading, reading, postreading, and independent reading activities that have been designed to fit pertinent content materials. However, the DCRA can be individualized and adapted to the needs and characteristics of students. If you are organized, but are also responsive to your individual students, you greatly increase the chances of having a successful program.

### *Prereading Component*

The prereading component is the first step in the DCRA. This component has numerous purposes, but in general you conduct these activities to prepare your students to read the selected content materials. Prereading activities are extremely important for students with limited language and reading abilities and may have to be extended for the nonreaders and less-abled readers. The DCRA prereading component includes the following five elements:

1. *Vocabulary Development.* Content materials tend to have their own particular vocabularies (e.g., science content has science-related words). These technical or specialized vocabularies tend to be listed at the beginning of the materials or in the teacher's guides. You could use varied means (overhead projectors, teaching strategies, etc.) to encourage

your students to recognize and comprehend these words. Multisensory procedures could also be used to develop their vocabulary competence.

2. *Cognitive Experience and Schemata.* Cognitive experience, as discussed earlier, affects content-reading proficiency. Students' background knowledge and schemata could be developed or enhanced using discussions, audiovisuals, and other activities. Extensive cognitive experiences provide students with basic concepts and schemata they need to activate comprehension.

3. *Motivation.* A motivated reader is more apt to be an active reader. Your enthusiasm about the materials you give students to read is likely to affect their motivation. Develop activities (e.g., field trips, guest speakers, question-and-answer sessions) to get your students enthused about the content to be read. If a lengthy content passage is to be segmented to produce two or more reading assignments, each reading would be preceded by a motivational activity.

4. *Purpose.* Providing a reading purpose can be the single most important step you can take to prepare your students to read and comprehend specific content concepts. This activity can also help students develop and activate the schemata and metacognitive strategies they need to search for and to understand pertinent content concepts.

5. *Adjunctive Aids.* Learning goals, questions, outlines, and study guides are adjunctive aids that can serve multiple purposes. They can direct your students' attention to specific content, build prior knowledge, and activate schemata. Your students could use these aids during the prereading, reading, and postreading components. A previous chapter presented many ideas for using study guides and learning goals as adjunctive aids.

Because we advocate a facilitative approach to instruction, the prereading component elements you begin or end with should be selected based on the students and content involved. Content attributes and student characteristics would dictate what you should do first, second, third, and so on, or what you could completely omit. Again, prereading activities for nonreaders and less-abled readers should be more extensive to develop pertinent backgrounds.

## Reading Component

The second step in the DCRA is the reading component. This component has two elements that involve reading the content material for meaning, and using the materials for diagnostic purposes:

1. *Silent Reading.* Silent reading of the content materials is usually the primary procedure of this step. Your students should be encouraged to use internal and external aids while reading, or to use a specific study-reading strategy (like SQ3R discussed in a later section) to structure their reading behaviors.

2. *Oral Reading.* We do not advocate extensive use of oral-reading activities for whole-class functions. However, we do think you should employ oral-reading tasks in one-to-one settings for diagnostic purposes. Listening to

individual students read orally can help you gain insight into their particular strategies (e.g., use of syntax, semantic, and graphophonic cues; and many comprehension strategies). You can then use this information to plan your students' postreading activities or to provide more activities listed under the prereading component.

The reading assignments you give in this component should be structured so that students are guided to read selectively, noting important details and concepts, and the students should also have opportunities to respond and react to what they have read. Many of the study guides suggested in a previous chapter can be successfully used during this stage.

## Postreading Component

The DCRA's third step is the postreading component. The five elements of this component have as their purpose the reinforcement of previously learned skills and strategies and the further development of content knowledge. This component is extremely important for students who need extra assistance and involves most of the major reading areas discussed in this text. Postreading activities include the following:

1. *Vocabulary Development.* The postreading vocabulary development activities can be similar to the prereading activities you develop. You could use any additional information you gathered during the silent- and oral-reading assignments and assessments to plan these activities. Traditional paper-and-pencil tasks, art and drama projects, and a variety of other activities could be employed. Multisensory procedures could also be used with students who have limited vocabularies.

2. *Comprehension Development.* The reinforcement of previously learned comprehension skills and refinement of new content information are the purposes of this postreading element. You should plan and conduct activities that focus not only on literal text-explicit information but also on higher-level inferential, critical, and evaluative content questioning and understanding.

3. *Concept Development.* Your students may have difficulty understanding some concepts due to the many factors discussed in this and other chapters. Misunderstood or underdeveloped concepts that were encountered in content materials should be developed or clarified so that they are meaningful to your students. Follow-up discussions and other postreading activities should help to identify those underdeveloped concepts, and also to assist in clarifying them for the students.

4. *Study-Reading Strategies.* For those students who have difficulty reading and achieving your content objectives, we suggest that you reinforce the application of one of the specific study-reading strategies (e.g., SQ3R). Again, these strategies are discussed later in this chapter.

5. *Rereading.* The final postreading element we recommend is having your students reread selected parts of the content materials. This reading could be oral or silent, could involve using adjunctive aids and organizers,

and could be teacher- or student-centered. Requesting that students read specific sentences and asking them to answer questions or discuss ideas is an effective procedure for further developing pertinent content vocabulary, comprehension, and concepts.

Which postreading element you implement first or last, or omit altogether, depends on the content material you are using and your students' characteristics. The postreading component is important, so be deliberate and thorough as you implement postreading activities. This is an excellent component for one-to-one and small-group work.

### *Independent Component*

The last step in the DCRA is the independent-reading component. This is a student-centered component, in that your students select content materials that they want to read. You facilitate the process by providing guidance and scheduling reporting and other activities to complement their research, selection, and reading of these materials. This step has three purposes: First, it provides the students with the opportunity to use the content-reading skills and strategies they have developed within your DCRA or in other school settings (e.g., library, science lab, etc.) and in outside school settings (e.g., home, community, etc.). They can select appropriate content materials they want to read and read these materials using their own procedures. Second, it provides you with a vehicle to observe your students to determine whether they are internalizing and applying the content skills you are trying to develop. Third, it provides the students with the opportunity to really "read to learn" and empowers them to learn more about the content under study than just what is in their textbooks.

This component should provide your students with exciting as well as successful reading experiences. Your students should also be aware of their responsibilities and use their independent content-reading activities to further develop their content area knowledge and interest. The flexible and facilitative nature of the DCRA permits you to move more knowledgeable and proficient or mature learners in a given content area from the prereading component directly to the independent component. No lockstep procedure is implied. However, for many students in your class, some prereading activity, followed by silent reading, then followed by some postreading activity, and finally by opportunities for independent reading, will be most beneficial.

## *Activities to Promote Active and Independent Learners*

The extent to which your students progress through your DCRA and acquire the content area concepts you want them to learn can be directly proportional to the efforts you put forth to assist them to develop their concepts and schemata. Examples of activities that you could use during the reading, postreading, and independent components include use of adjunctive aids, structured overviews, and other reading-to-learn and concept-facilitating activities. (Also see the chapter on strategies for studying and learning for more prereading, during reading, and postreading ideas.)

## Adjunctive Aids

Adjunctive aids such as the learning to learn study-guide ideas (illustrated in a previous chapter), external and embedded questions, outlines, and related prose materials can be used to develop cognitive background, concepts, and schemata. They can be discussed and given to the students during the prereading component and used by them during the reading and postreading components. Learning goals can be particularly effective with less-abled readers. (Read and find (1) _____, (2) _____, and so on). You could develop learning goals and other study-guide ideas for use with all of your content area materials.

## Structured Overviews

Structured overviews, or graphic organizers, are used to give students information relative to the content materials to be encountered and to support the knowledge-building process (Brozo and Simpson 1995). These structured overviews develop concepts and schemata and also provide cognitive structure to assist students to read content materials. Structured overviews present superordinate, ordinate, and subordinate displays of the content materials.

## Other Concept-Facilitating Activities

You can use a myriad of other activities, limited only by your imagination, to develop your students' concepts and schemata. These activities can be developed to fit your specific content area materials and your students' needs and interests. Audiovisual activities (e.g., videos, cassettes) are excellent because they tend to hold student attention as well as be informative and, of course, can be used over and over. Discussion, question-and-answer, and role-playing sessions can also be planned for large- or small-group settings or can be utilized in one-to-one situations. Specific reading assignments could be planned to serve as a brief overview of what is to be read or to provide important information needed as background knowledge. Paper-and-pencil tasks could be conducted to overview the materials or order important ideas and information. Field trips, art and drama projects, computer software programs, resource persons and mentors, and peer buddy systems could also be used to develop needed cognitive experience and content area concepts.

Using one or more of the suggested activities could give your students the experience and background important to developing schemata. These schemata and cognitive structures will help your students to activate lower- and higher-order comprehension skills and strategies to understand and remember concepts that they read. Activities such as these and others in this text can be used to enhance students' concepts and understanding during the use of the DCRA.

## Specific Reading-to-Learn Strategies

How many times during your school career has a teacher or professor given you and your peers the following assignment: "Read Chapter _____ for tomorrow and be prepared to discuss the major issues presented." And after looking at the chapter and the number of pages to read, you thought or said, "How am I going to read this entire chapter and remember what is in it?" Believe it or not, as an elementary teacher you will probably give your students similar-type assignments and have them read entire chapters or lengthy content passages. Also, you will expect them to be able to recall for future discussion important issues and concepts that are presented. There are many reading-to-learn strategies you could teach your students to use that will assist them with these lengthy content-reading activities and direct their reading-studying behaviors to promote comprehension and recall. The four strategies we suggest that you consider are QSCP, SQ3R, PQ4R, and KWLA.

## QSCP

Palincsar and Brown (1988) have described listening and reading comprehension as problem solving and recommended that teachers and students use a four-step process to maximize thinking during text-based listening or reading activities. The four steps are *q*uestioning, *s*ummarizing, *c*larifying, and *p*redicting (QSCP). You would use, or teach students to use, this QSCP process to structure thinking, reading, and learning behaviors as follows:

***Questioning.*** During group, minilesson, and student conference content-related activities, you would determine what is to be read (e.g., a chapter section), generate questions that would be answered when reading, and have students provide possible answers to the questions posed. Brainstorming techniques could also be used to generate additional questions and possible answers. When students are independently reading content materials, they would frame questions they want answered.

***Summarizing.*** During teacher-student formats, you or a student would summarize what was read (e.g., a chapter section) and cooperatively comment or elaborate on the summary. Students engaged in independent content reading would summarize what was read at an appropriate juncture. Questions generated could be used to structure the summary, and content needing clarification is identified.

***Clarifying.*** You and your students would return to the text to secure information to clarify points of concern (e.g., rereading and discussing what was read). Consulting other resources (e.g., a dictionary) could also be used for clarification purposes. Students reading independently could reread and reflect on appropriate text or use other resources to clarify concerns.

***Predicting.*** When questions have been generated, text read and summarized, and ambiguities clarified, you or a student would signal to move to the next part of the printed materials and make predictions regarding this content. Independent readers would also predict what they will encounter.

## SQ3R or PQ4R

F. Robinson (1970) has defined and discussed one of the most widely used reading-to-learn strategies for content purposes, the SQ3R approach (also see Paporollo 1991; Schumm 1992). The SQ3R steps that you could teach your students to use to read lengthy content materials include the following:

***Survey.*** Students would survey (or quickly read) the introduction, the major headings and subheadings, and the conclusion or summary. This survey procedure will help them to get the main idea(s) of the content as well as the length of the assignment.

***Question.*** Because setting a purpose for reading facilitates comprehension and recall, students should be taught how to formulate questions to guide their reading. These questions could come from questions identified during the survey step or changing important headings to questions. For example, the heading "Major Shipping Centers in the United States" would become "What are the major shipping centers in the United States?"

***Read.*** At this step students should carefully read the content materials. They should use the questions they have formulated to structure their reading (i.e., to find the answers).

***Recite.*** This step involves students reciting the answers to the questions they have formulated. They should try to recite the answers from memory, rather than using notes or referring back to the text.

***Review.*** The final step in the SQ3R strategy involves students reviewing specific sections of the content materials to determine whether they have correctly answered their questions. They could also review their notes at this juncture to evaluate their reading-comprehension.

A variation of Robinson's (1970) SQ3R strategy is Thomas and Robinson's (1972) PQ4R. Their PQ4R method shown next, if applied systematically and used often, can promote content-reading proficiency and recall:

***Preview.*** Your students would preview the materials from first page to last. They should consider developing general questions prior to and during the previewing to structure their attention during this important step.

***Question.*** Similar to SQ3R "Question" step.

***Read.*** Similar to SQ3R "Read" step.

***Reflect.*** After reading the passage, your students should take a few moments to reflect on what they have read. They may also want to skim over or reread content that was very important or difficult to understand.

***Recite.*** Similar to SQ3R "Recite" step.

***Review.*** Similar to SQ3R "Review" step.

## KWLA

Ogle's (1986) K-W-L strategy, also discussed in a previous chapter, is an excellent technique to develop students' content informational learning and can be used to assess the quality and quantity of their responses (McAlister 1994). To do this you would first provide students with printed materials they are to read and a K-W-L worksheet that has three columns—Know, Want to Know, Learned. Prior to reading the printed materials the students would reflect or brainstorm on the topic and in column one, Know, write what they know about the topic. Alvermann and Phelps (1994) recommended that students categorize known information and predict other categories that may be encountered when reading. Then students would list in column two, Want to Know, questions they want answered when reading the printed materials. Next students would read the printed materials and list in column three, Learned, the answers to questions in column two or new information acquired. Finally, you would conference with the students and collaboratively discuss the quality and quantity of their K-W-L responses.

We believe you can use the K-W-L strategy in content-subject areas to promote an individual student's or groups of students' activation of prior knowledge, problem-solving abilities, and comprehension outcomes. However, we would suggest that you also consider using Mandeville's (1994) KWLA model, which further links your students' cognitive and affective domains during the content reading process. Students would be given content printed materials and a KWLA worksheet with four columns—Know, Want to Know, Learned, and Affect. Students alone, in groups, or in a whole-class format would complete columns one, two, and three as described in the last paragraph. After reflecting on or discussing the information in the three columns, students would use column four to provide affective responses to what they knew and learned. These responses could answer such questions as: Was this interesting? Why or why not? Did I like or dislike what I learned? Why? Is what I learned important to me? Why or why not? According to Mandeville (1994), the use of an Affect column gives students an avenue to address personal perspectives about the content as well as strengthens their construction of new learning by linking the cognitive and affective domains.

If you have never been taught or used the QSCP, SQ3R, PQ4R, or KWLA learning-to-read strategies, you are probably thinking you could not use them because they would take too much time! We want you to know that your thinking is quite true (i.e., SQ3R requires extra time) and that your students will come to the same conclusion when you introduce these strategies to them. Nevertheless, we believe that you and your students will read, comprehend, and recall more pertinent information when using a specific reading-to-learn strategy than reading without using a systematic procedure. Using such strategies will indeed require additional time, but if they are used often and internalized as a habit, they promote content-reading success. This is especially true for students who have limited reading-study abilities (Hadaway and Young 1994). You and your students can experiment with different combinations of learning-to-read strategies (e.g., combining QSCP and SQ3R and other steps you may want to add) to come up with your own approach for systematically reading content materials. This would be fun and would make the collaborative strategy more meaningful to the students in your class.

### *Thematic Units and Integrated Curricula*

We believe that at this point in this chapter you realize that one of the more challenging tasks you will face in the elementary classroom is developing your students' content-reading abilities while achieving your content-subject area objectives. You will meet this challenge by (a) using a structured but flexible content-reading approach such as the Directed Content-Reading Approach (DCRA) we described earlier; (b) teaching your students how to use reading-to-learn strategies such as the QSCP, SQ3R, PQ4R, and KWLA just described; and (c) incorporating appropriate technology concepts into your content-reading program as described at the end of this chapter. However, there is another instructional practice that we would like you to consider within your DCRA or as a stand-alone approach to promote content-subject area success. This instructional practice is planning and implementing thematic units to integrate curricula (e.g., mathematics, social studies, and science) and to engage students in reading and writing across the curricula. Skillfully using thematic units will promote your students' literacy and content learning.

Lapp and Flood (1994) have delineated and described the following basic steps to plan and guide a thematic unit.

### Select a Theme

You would collaborate with your students to select a theme for the unit that is relevant to your grade-level curricular objectives and your students' interests and needs. The theme could focus on a school event (e.g., a future field trip to the zoo), on a community activity (e.g., a local festival), or on an upcoming holiday (e.g., Presidents' or Martin Luther King, Jr. Day). Themes could also focus on somewhat nontraditional topics. For example, Evans (1994) described a unique thematic unit on "Monstrous, Pesadillas, and Other Frights" that everyone enjoyed and that proved to be academically rewarding. When considering themes, however, you and your students should take two things into account. First, the theme should be broad enough to incorporate your grade-level curricula (e.g., literacy and content-subject areas) and should be of interest to both you and your students. Second, the theme selected should provide a logical venue for content area instructional activities and skill development.

### Collect Texts and Other Materials

You and your students next would collaborate to collect the needed thematic materials (e.g., mathematics, social studies, and science). The types of materials collected are only limited by your creativity but would probably include textbooks, trade books, videos, magazines, computer software programs, resource persons, and games. With respect to printed materials, Hartman and Hartman (1993) stated that "the object is to arrange a set of texts that are potentially rich with connections and that complement your goals and objectives as well as students' responses and interests" (p. 204). To this end they recommended that you use companion books (i.e., by the same author), complementary books (i.e., by different authors and not series based), synoptic texts (i.e., "a single story, idea, or event and read across the versions, variations, and accounts of it" [p. 206]), and texts with different points of view. Other materials secured should match curricular objectives and student differences.

### Engage Students

After selecting the theme and collecting the necessary materials, you would establish your goals and objectives. The two specific purposes of your thematic unit will be developing your students' literacy-learning abilities and increasing their content area knowledge bases. You would then determine which activities you will use to achieve your goals and objectives. It has been reported (see Grant, Guthrie, Bennett, Rice, and McGough, 1993/1994) that you can promote motivation and cognitive and affective development by engaging students in concept-oriented instruction (e.g., real-world activities and problems). We also recommend that you use the planning-learning pyramid described in a later chapter to establish goals and objectives.

### Group Students

Your goals, objectives, and activities will determine your student grouping patterns. These formats will include individual students, dyads, small and large groups, and whole-class formats. Where possible, follow up whole-class instruction with small-group activities, and maximize your use of student conferences, integrated reading and writing minilessons, and cooperative groups to achieve literacy and content outcomes (Wiggins 1994). Also, for students who need additional assistance, design and guide group practices that use time appropriately, provide immediate needed interventions, stress quality over quantity, move students from whole-class to group activities, and offer ongoing evaluation procedures (Kameenui 1993).

### Expand the Theme

As your thematic unit progresses, you and your students will find yourselves identifying additional activities to expand the unit (e.g., a class art project or a parallel home project). You should collaborate with the students to determine unit expansions, but only select those activities that promote the achievement of the unit's goals and objectives. Expansion parallel home activities, particularly for students who need additional assistance should also be considered.

### Assess Student Growth

Your thematic unit should have ongoing evaluation procedures that provide qualitative and quantitative assessment data. According to Lapp and Flood (1994), these procedures should " . . . complement your designed goals and instructional activities" (p. 418). We also recommend that your evaluation methods match the needs of your students (e.g., a student with limited reading and/or writing skills could be given an oral test).

Planning and implementing thematic units will be exciting as well as academically beneficial. You can use them within your DCRA or stand-alone to integrate curricula and to provide reading and writing experiences across the curricula. Thematic units promote meaningful learning and assist students in making literacy connections across the curricula. (For example, remember Mrs. Argueta's rainforest unit in the chapter on strategies for studying and learning from text.)

$A$t the beginning of this text and again at the beginning of this chapter, we emphasized that content area reading instruction should start when students begin other reading instruction, usually in the first grade. We have further emphasized that reading is a tool to be applied to all the content areas and is not a "subject" in and of itself. However, some educators in the elementary schools do not agree with this position. They maintain that content area reading is traditionally a secondary-education concern and that elementary teachers should not deal with reading in the content areas, or, as they call it, "secondary reading." What do you think? In your reflection journal under Reflection Activity 7.2, state your position regarding content area reading instruction.

## Computer Hardware and Software Considerations

The hardware and software issues you consider for your content-reading program parallel the considerations we have discussed in earlier chapters. Additionally, from a hardware perspective, it would be very helpful if you were a part of a local area network (LAN) with other teachers or instructional information centers (e.g., school libraries). Your school district could concentrate its funds by purchasing state-of-the-art hardware and software to establish LANs in schools or across the school system. All teachers would then have access to the latest content-subject area software because instructional resource and library personnel and teachers would collaborate to purchase and use software in established computer networks. The ability to use your computer for telecommunication purposes to access local and national databases and bulletin boards (e.g., Internet's FrEdMail—Free Educational Electronic Mail) would also promote your content teaching-learning objectives (Norden and Moss 1993).

We also suggest that you have at least one stand-alone computer with related peripherals for your specific use and for your students' individual use. An ideal work station would have a microcomputer with multimedia capabilities, a touch screen, graphic tablet, or voice recognition unit for easy input, a speech-synthesis unit to assist your less-abled and nonreaders (and visually impaired students), a modem for telecommunication activities, and a dot-matrix or laser printer for near-letter-quality and graphics functions. As stated earlier, you should first select the software you think is compatible with your reading program and then purchase the hardware, be it Apple's Macintosh or an IBM or compatible system to run those programs.

The software considerations for your content-reading instruction are similar to other aspects of reading instruction. You should do everything you can to work with district personnel to evaluate and to purchase quality application, utility, and instructional programs. We recommend that you use Claris Works (Claris Corporation, Mountain View, CA) or the Bank Street series (Broderbun, San Raphael, CA) or Microsoft Works (Microsoft Corporation, Redmond, WA) for word processing, database, and spreadsheet activities. You could use these application software for personal and instructional productivity purposes (e.g., organizational functions, grading, and writing letters), while your students would use these programs for content reading-writing projects (e.g., conceptualizing reports), for generating databases (e.g., organizing names, dates, and accomplishments of historical figures), and for mathematical-content situations (e.g., developing spreadsheets to understand and complete a science project focusing on the names of planets, their distance from the sun, their size, their atmospheric compositions, and the number and names of their moons). You should also have an easy-to-use authoring system to develop multimedia lessons (e.g., Apple's HyperCard, Macromedia's Authorware Professional, Asymetrix's Multimedia Toolbook, or IBM LinkWay Live), a program to produce instructional materials or published reports with pictures and text (e.g., The Learning Company's The Children's Writing & Publishing Center), an electronic dictionary, thesaurus, and encyclopedia (e.g., Microsoft's Encarta, Random House's Encyclopedia, and Webster's Electronic Dictionary & Thesaurus), and a program to create content-subject area tests and manage students' assessment data (e.g., Slosson Publications' Quest Make). You should also have a variety of demonstration, simulation, tutorial, game, and utility programs in diskette, CD-ROM, or videodisc media that correspond to your subject area content and objectives. Selected social studies programs (with suggested grade levels) that you may want to secure and evaluate are as follows:

| Name | Company |
| --- | --- |
| **Geography** | |
| SchoolWorks: Social Studies (GL K–12) | K–12 Micromedia |
| Social Studies Tool Kits GL (5–12) | Great Lakes/Tom Snyder |
| Geography Skills Series (GL 5–Adult) | Focus Media |
| World Geography (GL 6–Adult) | MECC |
| Great Cities of the World (GL 5–Adult) | InterOptica |
| States and Capital (GL 4–Adult) | Gameco |
| My First Atlas (GL 1–4) | Impressions |
| PC Globe Maps 'n' Facts (GL 6–Adult) | Broderbund |
| Geography Skills (GL 5–Adult) | Focus Media |
| Map Skills (GL 3–6) | Coronet/MTI |
| Decisions, Decisions Series (GL 4–12) | Tom Snyder Productions |
| Carmen Sandiego Series (GL 4–12) | Broderbund |
| **History** | |
| TimeLiner Series (K–Adult) | Tom Snyder Productions |
| Time Treks (GL 4–Adult) | Magic Quest/Earthquest |
| World History (GL 4–8) | January Publications |
| Those Were the Days (GL 5–6) | Right on Programs |
| Time Tunnel: The America Series (GL 4–Adult) | Focus Media |
| Point of View 2.0 and Community History Kit (GL 4–12) | Scholastic |
| Operation U.S. Presidents (GL 4–Adult) | Tanager |

**Women and Cultural**

| | |
|---|---|
| Women of Courage Series (GL 4–6) | EPC |
| World Cultures and Youth (GL 5–Adult) | Coronet/MTI |
| The Multicultural Chronicle (GL 5–9) | K-12 Micromedia |
| Struggles for Justice (GL 5–12) | Scholastic |
| Celebrate (GL K–8) | Coronet/MTI |

If you want to experience the emerging capabilities of social studies software, we recommend that you try EPC's Interviews in History and Historical Perspectives. Both programs are interactive and controlled by the students. The students interview prominent figures in history (e.g., Abraham Lincoln) by selecting questions from a menu or typing questions they want answered.

The following are selected science and health programs with suggested grade levels that you may want to secure and evaluate:

| Name | Company |
|---|---|
| **Science** | |
| Science Helper (GL K–8) | Learning Team |
| Learning About Science (GL 1–5) | AIMS |
| Science Toolkit Plus Series (GL 4–Adult) | Broderbund |
| Science Adventure 2.0 (GL 5–Adult) | Knowledge Adventure |
| Science in Your World Series (GL 1–6) | Macmillan/McGraw-Hill |
| Scientific Method (GL 5–12) | Micro Power & Light |
| Your Universe (GL 4–8) | Focus Media |
| Our Planet (GL 5–7) | EPC |
| Ecology for Beginners (GL K–3) | Coronet/MTI |
| Water: Air in Action Series (GL 5–8) | AIMS |
| Classification (GL 2–4) | EME |
| The Multimedia Animal Encyclopedia (GL 2–4) | Applied Optical |
| Planets: Nature's Food Factory (GL 6–Adult) | Ventura Education |
| BodyWorks 3.0 (GL 6–Adult) | Software Marketing |
| Physical Science Series (GL 4–7) | Churchill |
| Rocks: Properties and Uses of Minerals (GL 3–Adult) | Spectrum Software |
| **Health** | |
| Drugs: Friend or Foe? (GL 2–4) | Marshware |
| It's Wise to Say NO to Alcohol (GL 2–6) | Right on Programs |
| Nutrition Nabber (GL 2–5) | MECC |
| House-A-Fire: Science 1 (GL 2–8) | Decision Development |
| AIDS: A Different Germ (GL K–3) | Coronet/MTI |
| Less Stress (GL 4–7) | Churchill |

Finally, you maximize content area teaching-learning outcomes by integrating traditional instructional practices with technology based on the needs of your students. However, finding the right commercial software programs tailored to content curricular and students' needs will be almost impossible. You can use one of the multimedia authoring programs identified previously and your content-subject area objectives and materials to develop software programs specific to the needs of your students. You can also involve your students in the content curriculum-technology development process by teaching them how to use a multimedia authoring program (e.g., Sunburst's My Media Text Workshop).

## Summary

A very important reading-instructional responsibility you will have is designing and implementing effective content reading in your classroom. The information presented in this chapter has provided you with general as well as specific knowledge relative to understanding what content reading involves in the elementary grades and your role. Reading in the content areas is "reading to learn" in such subject areas as social studies and science and should be developed so that you not only stress content but also teach your students how to read and learn from content materials. It is important that you are aware of the factors that positively or negatively affect your students' content-reading successes. To enhance content-reading instruction, you may wish to use the directed content-reading approach (DCRA) we described. In the final sections of this chapter, activities to promote the development of students' concepts and schemata were presented, reading-to-learn strategies were outlined, and computer hardware and software considerations were discussed.

## Closing Activities

1. In a small group, share and discuss your position regarding content area reading instruction in the elementary school. Refer to what you wrote in Reflection Activity 7.2 in this chapter.
2. In a small group, share and discuss your reactions to the factors and considerations we identified that may affect reading performance in content areas. Which do you believe might affect elementary students the most? Which factors would affect elementary students the least? Also, come up with additional activities other than the ones we described that you could use to deal with some of these factors and content-reading considerations.
3. Develop an appropriate activity to promote concept development utilizing a selection from a content area textbook from your field-experience classroom or from the curriculum library in your school, college, or university. You may develop the activity utilizing adjunctive aids, structured overviews, or other concept-facilitating activities described in this chapter. Be prepared to share the activity with peers in your class.
4. As part of your field experience for this course, examine three recent but different content area textbooks for elementary students. List the name, publisher, and publication date of each, noting the following aspects of each text and recording your findings: (a) internal adjunctive aids (graphs, tables, glossaries, questions, outlines, and so on); (b) length of chapters; (c) number of concepts usually dealt with on each page, or in each chapter; (d) vocabulary considerations (number of technical or specialized words introduced on each page or chapter); (e) format considerations (organization of material, table of contents, usability of text); and (f) appeal level (stimulating, interesting, colorful, attractive).

### References

Alvermann, D. E., and S. F. Phelps. (1994). *Content Reading and Literacy: Succeeding in Today's Diverse Classrooms.* Boston: Allyn & Bacon.

Anthony, H. M., and T. F. Raphael. (1989). "Using Questioning Strategies to Promote Students' Active Comprehension of Content Area Materials." In D. Lapp, J. Flood, and N. Farnan, eds., *Content Area Reading and Learning: Instructional Strategies* (pp. 244–257). Englewood Cliffs, NJ: Prentice-Hall.

Brozo, W. G., and M. L. Simpson. (1995). *Readers, Teachers, Learners: Expanding Literacy in Secondary Schools,* 2nd ed. Englewood Cliffs, NJ: Merrill/Prentice-Hall.

Cheek, E. H., and M. C. Cheek. (1983). *Reading Instruction through Content Reading.* Columbus, OH: Merrill.

Cheek, E. H., J. D. Lindsey, A. D. Rutland, and T. S. Doyle. (1984). "In Defense of a K–12 Reading Perspective." *Reading Horizons* 25(1): 43–49.

Collins, M. D., and E. H. Cheek. (1993). *Diagnostic-Prescriptive Reading Instruction: A Guide for Classroom Teachers,* 4th ed. Madison, WI: Brown & Benchmark Publishers.

Conley, M. W. (1992). *Content Reading Instruction: A Communication Approach.* New York: McGraw-Hill.

Dishner, E. K., and M. W. Olson. (1989). "Content Area Reading: A Historical Perspective." In D. Lapp, J. Flood, and N. Farnan, eds., *Content Area Reading and Learning: Instructional Strategies* (pp. 2–13). Englewood Cliffs, NJ: Prentice-Hall.

Durkin, D. (1978). *Teaching Them to Read,* 3rd ed. Boston: Allyn & Bacon.

Evans, C. (1994). "Monstrous, Pesadillas, and other Frights: A Thematic Unit." *The Reading Teacher* 47:428–430.

Fry, E. B. (1977). "Fry's Readability Graph: Clarification, Validity, and Extension to Level 17." *Journal of Reading* 21:242–252.

Grant, R., J. Guthrie, L. Bennett, M. E. Rice, and K. McGough. (1993/1994). "Developing Engaged Readers through Concept-Oriented Instruction." *The Reading Teacher* 47:338–340.

Hadaway, N. L., and T. A. Young. (1994). "Content Literacy and Language Learning: Instructional Decisions." *The Reading Teacher* 47:522–527.

Hartman, D. K., and J. M. Hartman. (1993). "Reading Across Texts: Expanding the Role of the Reader." *The Reading Teacher* 47:202–211.

Herber, H. L. (1978). *Teaching Reading in the Content Areas,* 2nd ed. Englewood Cliffs, NJ: Prentice-Hall.

Kameenui, E. J. (1993). "Diverse Learners and the Tyranny of Time: Don't Fix Blame; Fix the Leaky Roof." *The Reading Teacher* 46:376–383.

Klare, G. R. (1989). "Understanding the Readability of Content Area Tests." In D. Lapp, J. Flood, and N. Farnan, eds., *Content Area Reading and Learning: Instructional Strategies* (pp. 34–42). Englewood Cliffs, NJ: Prentice-Hall.

Lapp, D., and J. Flood. (1994). "Integrating the Curriculum: First Steps." *The Reading Teacher* 47:416–419.

Mandeville, T. L. (1994). "KWLA: Linking the Affective and Cognitive Domains." *The Reading Teacher* 17(8): 679–680.

May, F. B. (1994). *Reading as Communication,* 4th ed. New York: Merrill/Macmillan.

McAlister, P. J. (1994). "Using K-W-L for Informal Assessment." *The Reading Teacher* 47:510–511.

Norden, H., and B. Moss. (1993). "Virtual Schools: Reading and Writing." *The Reading Teacher* 47:166–168.

Ogle, D. M. (1986). "K-W-L: A Teaching Model That Develops Active Reading of Expository Text." *The Reading Teacher* 39 (6):564–570.

Palincsar, A. S., and A. L. Brown. (1988). "Teaching and Practicing Thinking Skills to Promote Comprehension in the Context of Group Problem Solving." *Remedial and Special Education* 9:53–59.

Paporollo, A. G. (1991). *SQ3R: A Must of Teaching Science Concepts in the Sixth Grade.* Master's thesis, Kean College, Union, New Jersey. (ED 329947).

Raygor, A. L. (1977). "The Raygor Readability Estimate: A Quick and Easy Way to Determine Difficulty." In P. D. Pearson, ed., *Reading: Theory, Research, and Practice* (pp. 259–263). Clemson, SC: Twenty-Sixth Yearbook of the National Reading Conference.

Robinson, F. P. (1970). *Effective Study,* 4th ed. New York: Harper & Row.

Robinson, H. A. (1978). *Teaching Reading and Study Strategies,* 2nd ed. Boston: Allyn & Bacon.

Roehler, L. R., and G. G. Duffy. (1989). "The Content Area Teacher's Instructional Role: A Cognitive Mediational View." In D. Lapp, J. Flood, and N. Farnan, eds., *Content Area Reading and Learning: Instructional Strategies* (pp. 115–151). Englewood Cliffs, NJ: Prentice-Hall.

Rothkopf, E. Z. (1976). "Writing to Teach and Reading to Learn: A Perspective on the Psychology of Written Instruction." In N. Gage, ed., *The Psychology of Teaching Methods.* Chicago: University of Chicago Press.

Schumm, J. S. (1992). "SQ3R Revisited: This Time with Learning Disabled Secondary Students." *Journal of Reading* 36:232–233.

Smith, C. R. (1991). *Learning Disabilities: The Interaction of Learner, Task, and Setting,* 2nd ed. Boston: Allyn & Bacon.

Spache, G. D. (1953). "A New Readability Formula for Primary-Grade Reading Materials." *Elementary School Journal* 53:410–413.

Thomas, E. L., and H. A. Robinson. (1972). *Improving Reading in Every Class.* Boston: Allyn & Bacon.

Vacca, R. T., and J. L. Vacca. (1986). *Content Area Reading,* 2nd ed. Boston: Little, Brown.

Wiggins, R. A. (1994). "Large Group Lesson/Small Group Follow-Up: Flexible Grouping in a Basal Reading Program." *The Reading Teacher* 47:450–460.

# *R*eading and Writing

© James L. Shaffer

# *Overview*

*I*n this chapter reading, writing, and speaking are presented as developmental communication processes that involve an interrelated relationship. For these processes to develop as fully as possible, a positive classroom environment must prevail.

This chapter discusses early writing development and continued writing development as social and trial-and-error learning. The transition experiences from oral to written communications, which can cause particular difficulty for children if they are not properly understood by the facilitative classroom teacher, are explained.

The experiential stages of writing and reading development are delineated, with attention drawn to the idea that these stages are ongoing, interrelated, and recursive; some children, because of diverse needs, will require more opportunities to experiment in these stages than others. Children's invented spellings and other approximations of written literacy are discussed. Next, suggested reading and writing goals and program attributes are explored, followed by teaching strategies, processes, and ideas for enhancing reading and writing development in the classroom. These include use of dictation, process writing, creative writing, children's literature, journal writing, and content-reading opportunities. Finally, computer technology and word processor applications that are consistent with the literature on process writing are discussed.

## *Main Ideas*

- Reading, writing, and speaking are all communication processes.
- Reading and writing are very interrelated.
- Fostering a positive writing environment is important.
- Experimentation and trial-and-error learning are fundamental to writing development.
- Writing is a social, constructive, and developmental activity.
- Understanding the transitions from oral to written language is necessary for teachers.
- Writing involves use of different semantic, syntactic, and discourse structures.
- Experiential stages in the developmental writing process are ongoing, interrelated, and recursive.
- Children from diverse backgrounds and with diverse needs will require more time and opportunities to experiment in various stages of writing.
- Numerous strategies, processes, and ideas can be used by lower-, middle-, and upper-grade elementary teachers to enhance their students' reading and writing development.

Reading and writing are communication processes that are part of the larger language-learning process. Both reading and writing involve the construction of meaning. Readers construct meaning from written language. Writers construct meaning with written language. Teaching reading and writing together makes sense because they share many of the same or similar processes and knowledge (Tierney and Shanahan 1991); they seem to naturally develop together (Sulzby and Teale 1991); and by teaching them together we help children recognize and understand the connections between the two processes (Cooper 1993), and we foster the development of thinking, which is a critical part of the construction of meaning inherent in reading and writing activities (Tierney and Shanahan 1991). Because of this, it should be clear that a reading classroom without inclusion of writing activities cannot be an effective reading classroom; writing is critical to any successful reading program.

The reading and writing activities that students engage in are literacy activities that usually involve some content to be learned, reviewed, or enjoyed. As Langer and Applebee (1986) stated: "One does not simply learn to read and write: one learns to read and write about particular things in particular ways. This is a process that begins with the cereal boxes and stop signs familiar to the preschool child, and continues in the specialized content domains of academic discourse that students encounter throughout their schooling" (p. 173).

## Reading and Writing Relationship

The reading and writing processes are without a content of their own. Instead, they are social and constructive processes to be applied to all the written-communication activities and content areas your students come in contact with both in and out of school. Reading and writing are learning and literacy tools that are not mutually exclusive or separate entities; they have a very close interrelated relationship and should be integrated into the total elementary curricula (Flippo 1980). Hennings (1994) has pointed out that since children use the various elements of language together, these elements should be taught together in a single curriculum involving students thinking and communicating. Students will develop an understanding of the relationship between reading and writing and the other communication and thought processes when they are given many opportunities to read, write, and discuss things in meaningful contexts. They can learn very early in their school experience that when their thoughts are written down, others are able to read them. Figure 8.1 depicts this relationship.

Additionally, students learn that writing is constructing meaning with thoughts written down, and that reading is constructing meaning by reading someone's thoughts that have already been written down. Although this relationship and these definitions seem to be very simplistic, such an understanding is fundamental to literacy and the written-language processes as projected in Figure 8.1.

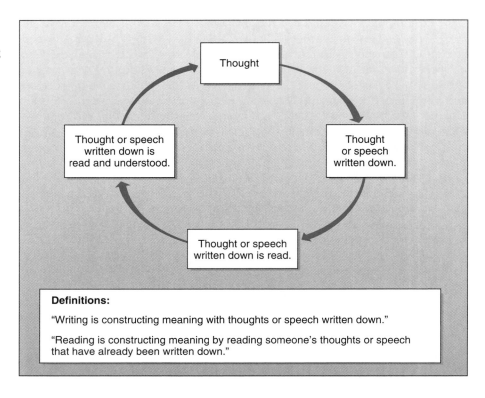

***Figure 8.1***
The interrelated relationship of reading and writing.

A review of the literature clearly indicates the close and important relationships between the teaching of reading and writing. For instance, Fitzgerald (1989) viewed revision in writing and critical reading as related language activities, both involving thought and comprehension. Wray (1994) indicated that "authorship, in the sense of creation and re-creation of meaning, should be a central focus in any model of literacy instruction" (p. 52). Tierney and Shanahan (1991) suggested that reading and writing should be viewed together, learned together, and used together. This chapter describes several recommended processes, activities, and classroom contexts for promoting an integrated teaching of reading and writing.

## *Creating an Environment for Writing*

You are responsible for creating a learning environment that is positive for both reading and writing development. Students learn to write by writing, just as they learn to speak by speaking, to read by reading, and to think and reason by thinking and reasoning. A classroom environment should be provided that will foster and encourage students to think, speak, write, and read. Each of these should be encouraged, and each will stimulate the other in a facilitative environment.

## Reflection Activity 8.1

*H*ow would you develop the necessary positive and nurturing writing environment? In your journal under the heading Reflection Activity 8.1, list as many ways as you can think of for a teacher to create an environment that will foster writing activity and development in the elementary classroom without isolating writing from thinking, speaking, and reading activities.

When you have completed this reflection activity, please compare your list with ours in Figure 8.2. This listing of suggestions for fostering positive writing experiences in the classroom was compiled by reviewing and analyzing the published literature, research, and professional opinions on writing and literacy development (Atwell 1987; Cambourne 1988; Clay 1991; Cooper 1993; Cullinan 1993; Deford 1986; Flood, Jensen, Lapp, and Squire 1991; Graves 1994; Graves and Hansen 1983; Hansen 1986, 1987; Harste, Burke, and Woodward 1984; Hennings 1994; Irwin and Doyle 1992; Morrow, Smith, and Wilkinson 1994; Routman 1988, 1994; Sulzby and Teale 1991; Templeton 1995; Tierney, Leys, and Rogers 1986; Tierney and Shanahan 1991; Tompkins and Hoskisson 1995; and Weaver 1994). As you design your reading-writing plans, remember to use suggestions that are consistent with your philosophy and classroom setting. Additionally, we want to remind you once again how strongly your beliefs about writing and literacy will affect your students' beliefs. Research confirms that students' perceptions of writing and their self-perceptions are influenced by teachers' beliefs and behaviors (i.e., Fear, Anderson, Englert, and Raphael 1987).

## *Early Writing Development*

Keep in mind that writing is a communication process, and like speaking and reading, students are socialized into writing at an early age. Toddlers and youngsters have observed members of their family and community using writing. They likely have observed (a) someone writing a letter to a friend or relative in another city; (b) another family member writing a note to put on the front door indicating that the doorbell is out of order; (c) someone doing homework or writing a shopping list; and (d) someone signing a birthday card or making a name tag for a gift. These early observations socialized children to the notion that writing is another way of communicating with other people.

Just as babies and toddlers learn to talk by trial and error, their first attempts at writing are experimental. In the beginning, they make random markings on paper just to try out the pencil and its effect on the paper. Eventually they begin to make marks that look a little more deliberate in order to replicate the writing activities they have observed. The marks become still more deliberate as the youngster gets better at imitating the writing activity of others. Often the marks look more like pictures, but children are typically able to explain these marks and pictures in a logical manner.

1. Provide an atmosphere conducive to writing with an authentic literacy environment for all students.
2. Demonstrate the usefulness of print by displaying messages, signs, charts, lists, songs, stories, and poems that children frequently use and read throughout the day.
3. Accept and allow for trial-and-error learning and approximations of written language in your classroom.
4. Provide materials and many opportunities for free exploration of reading and writing.
5. Encourage all students to read and share their own writings with you and each other in the classroom.
6. Encourage all students to dictate experiences, ideas, and stories often.
7. Model the use of writing by allowing your students to see you write. Share your writing with them, asking for their advice or input when appropriate.
8. Read aloud to students and encourage their discussion, questions, and comments.
9. Allow opportunities and time for repeated writing, sharing, and revising of writing so all students have multiple time periods and days to complete a writing piece.
10. Provide guidance and show a strong interest, but allow students to initiate their own topics and explore their own styles, voice, and forms of writing.
11. Provide texts, literature, and expectations that model rich language, literature, and writing, as opposed to simplified material and structured and stilted workbook type exercises in reading and writing.
12. Respect all students' writing.
13. Allow the students to assist, advise, and collaborate with each other on their writings.
14. Encourage a sense of community and sharing of talents, interests, and knowledge.
15. Allow much student talk and student decision-making instead of much teacher talk and teacher decision-making.

*Figure 8.2*
Suggestions for creating an environment to foster student writing.

As young children's writing abilities develop, they begin to make their markings in a linear fashion from the left side of the page to the right side (i.e., if children live in a culture that uses such a system), and their marks begin to look more and more like "scribble writing." Additionally, children know that this written language has something to do with communicating. The young child has observed how others use writing "to say something to someone." Furthermore, they are able to communicate with themselves because like family members, friends, or others they have observed, they too can read their own writing. As they make their marks or scribble writing, they are thinking about what they want to communicate and develop some marks or figures to match their thoughts.

When children enter school they need additional opportunities for their trial-and-error development. For students to continue their development as writers and readers, the trial-and-error period must continue throughout the school years. In preschool and kindergarten, opportunities for much scribble writing, reading of scribble writing, and discussion of scribble writing should be encouraged as a daily activity. Even though children's attempts may be random as they begin to write letters, or strings of letters, they should have opportunities for writing, reading, and discussing their writing attempts, and their attempts must be nurtured and valued. Later (usually by kindergarten and first grade), as children begin to use invented spelling to communicate their ideas, their writing must continue to be valued, discussed, read, and shared. As children gradually mature, their writing and reading activities will also mature, but the basic premise of trial and error must continue. With opportunity and encouragement, the children's scribble writing will develop into symbol writing and then eventually more-legible composition, and reading and discussion of these compositions will lead to more mature thinking, writing, reading, and discussion.

## Reflection Activity 8.2

*T*hink back to your early childhood. How did your family and teachers expose you to writing? Under Reflection Activity 8.2 in your reflection journal, describe these early writing experiences.

There can be no question that the writing and reading process is ongoing, with teachers guiding and helping students as needed and students helping each other while they are in the process of writing (e.g., see Atwell 1987, Cooper 1993, Deford 1986, Dunkin 1983, Hansen 1986, Routman 1994, and the many others previously cited in this chapter). The emphasis in the facilitative classroom is on meaning and clarifying meaning, rather than on correction. This is very different from the emphasis that exists in some classrooms where writing and reading activities are viewed as products to be corrected and graded by the teacher when completed. Students must be encouraged to take risks to improve their reading and writing attempts (Au and Kawakami 1986); however, when writing assignments are evaluated punitively, risk taking may result in a multitude of red marks and poor grades, which in turn may discourage students' future risk taking with writing (Flippo 1983). Cooper (1993) has indicated that the teacher should not become the "fixer" of students' writing; instead the teacher's role should be one of discussant—discussing ideas with students and noting places that need work but allowing the writers to make their own changes (p. 425). Smith (1988) noted that writers learn by learning about writing, not by getting letters, numbers, or other grades put on their efforts and abilities (p. 30).

## *Understanding the Transition from Oral to Written Language*

Although children are exposed to written language at an early age, the contexts or situations of their experiences are informal and situational, as opposed to the more formal and often context-dependent writing situations usually expected or contrived in school. These transitions from oral to written language, with both reading and writing, present some unfamiliar and sometimes confusing differences to children. Smith (1994) has explained that much of the oral and written language children learn prior to entering school is situation-dependent; the meaning is derived or conveyed by the situation in which it occurs. However, much of the language of texts is context-dependent, with language and grammatical complexities necessary to take the place of the situation (pp. 36–39). Writers use complex grammar and other conventions to help the reader understand what is going on. Transitions from the informal and situational to the formal and context-dependent can present problems for the student. Nevertheless, if you understand the complexities involved, you can make a difference and facilitate the transitions positively.

First, remember that your students' understanding of written language has been informally developed and is understood only in light of previous, but ongoing, familiar reading-writing experiences (a note on the door, a birthday card, etc.).

Second, help students to understand that their thoughts and speech written down is writing, but this is only the beginning of what is involved. Even when your students understand that, they encounter the next stage, which involves the transition from communicating with informal speech to communicating with writing and its many conventions.

Third, the transition from communicating orally to communicating in written language (reading and writing) involves semantic, syntactic, and discourse-related differences (Leu 1984; Leu and Kinzer 1995). These differences are discussed in the sections that follow.

The early familiarity with writing, as with all other knowledge including reading, comes about informally and situationally in the home and sociocultural community, and in other comfortable, familiar settings. If students are placed in a highly formal and structured situation for the teaching of writing and reading, they will have a more difficult time with this transition. Although you will want to structure and teach some skills and strategies through direct demonstration and scaffolded instruction, many of your students may benefit from a casual, relaxed, and facilitative environment where the learning of written-language skills, structures, and conventions (reading and writing) are acquired as naturally and as informally as possible.

### *Communicating with Writing Is Different from Communicating with Speech*

In speech, communication often involves setting, situation, gestures, intonation, and other inferences associated and related to "being there." Often, just a short sentence is enough to convey the necessary information when the speaker and the listener are both "there." However, in writing, as opposed to talking, it is often necessary to supply additional information to make up for the intended readers' "not being there." For instance, the writer may need to add words like "he said" or "I said" to indicate who is speaking. To convey the message or thoughts, the writer must insert missing information in a manner similar to that of playwrights. The dialogue is often not enough to convey to the reader what is meant or what is going on; that is, without the being there inferences of speech, the writer must add stage directions, descriptions, and background information. However, since your students' oral-language development is an outgrowth of being there experiences, they may have difficulty in conveying being there experiences in writing while remembering to use all the necessary stage directions and background for others to understand their work.

The facilitative teacher will understand this and allow students to experiment by trial and error over extended periods of time so that students will realize that they may need to supply more information and to fill in those stage directions and descriptions. If your students are guided and allowed to practice writing down their thoughts and speech, as well as allowed to share this writing frequently with peers and with you, they will eventually learn to revise and reconstruct their writing to include the necessary stage directions, descriptions, and background for others to read and fully understand their writing.

## *Reading Someone Else's Writing Involves Different Semantic, Syntactic, and Discourse Structure*

Just as the being there inferences are not necessarily present in students' writing, they are also missing from some of the books and other materials students will eventually be expected to read. Students who are accustomed to all the rich and visible information provided by speech may find most reading material difficult, because not only are some of the being there cues missing but also different books have different styles, voices, structures, forms, and organizational patterns.

In addition to the necessity of understanding what is being read while also trying to identify vocabulary, students have to be aware of unusual forms as well as a lack of being there cues. Leu (1984) has provided a list of the differences with which students must learn to cope. Some of these differences include the following:

1. Students will have to make use of semantic differences. Often, *pronouns* (e.g., *I, me, he, she, you, we,* and *us*), *locatives* (such as *here, there, up,* and *down*), and *temporal adverbs* (such as *today, yesterday,* and *tomorrow,* among other temporal concepts) are implied in speech. But when reading, the reader sometimes has to either infer these words from text or do without the information.

   Look at the following paragraph. Words that illustrate some of the semantic differences from spoken to written communication have been italicized.

   > *It* had been storming very hard but Tara and *her* brother, Todd, wanted to go out anyway. *"We* really will be okay out *there.* Please let *us* go *now," she* said. But *I* knew better. "No," *I* said, *"You* can't *go. It* is too dangerous. *It* will have to wait until *later."*

   To get an idea of the complexity of this simple paragraph, after reading it, try to answer the following questions.

   What does "*it*" refer to in the first sentence?

   What does "*her*" refer to?

   Who is "*we*"?

2. Students will have to cope with syntactic or word-order differences. The students' own speech, clause, and phrase patterns are predictable and

familiar, but in reading, students must often deal with different phrases, clauses, and speech patterns.

3. Students will have to analyze and interpret discourse differences. Students are most familiar with the most common two-person type of conversations. When reading, your students are often expected to read many varieties of discourse found in different narrative genre, expository patterns, and the unique structures of specialty books (like dictionaries and other reference materials).

4. Students will have to deal with symbol differences. In speech, even though the symbols are invisible, they are "just there"; but in reading, the symbols are often "not there" or are harder to find, even though they are sometimes evident in the punctuation. Young readers must learn to decipher these symbols when they are present. However, no matter how good the youngsters are at understanding punctuation symbols, the stress and intonation in reading materials must usually be predicted by the reader prior to actually seeing the punctuation, "before" the beginning of the linguistic unit (Goodman, Watson, and Burke 1987, p. 64). For example, although a question mark does not appear till the end of the sentence, a child must predict that the sentence will end with a question mark before he or she begins reading it, in order to use appropriate intonation.

This difficulty with written language symbols, combined with the "just there" stress and intonation children are accustomed to in oral language, can be problematic. Additionally, sometimes children do not notice, or they misinterpret, the punctuation clues, or false intonation clues are used by the reader because of line breaks and other confusion over sentence boundaries (Flippo 1985a, 1985b); or there is a complete omission of periods and other punctuation marks, or periods are added at the end of each line (Edelsky 1983). Milz's (1983) study showed that full and consistent use of the punctuation system takes longer to develop than other aspects of writing, and that first-grade children use space and distribution on the page as alternate ways of marking off phrases and sentences without punctuation. Wilde (1992) has provided a good summary of these symbol and sentence boundary problems and emphasized that learning to cope with these problems and differences between oral and written language is developmental and children will learn to use the symbols over time.

Errors in the implied intonation and stress can result in loss of meaning or in different meanings. Read this simple sentence: " 'Are you interested in doing this today?' the teacher asked." As you vary the invisible but numerous possible intonations of this sentence, you can detect different meanings for it. Look at the following list of possible stress and intonations, each providing a different meaning.

*"Are* you interested in doing this today?" (Stress on *are.* Meaning: "Are you or aren't you interested in doing this?")

"Are *you* interested in doing this today?" (Stress on *you*. Meaning:"Are you, not the boy next to you, interested in doing this?")

"Are you interested in doing *this* today?" (Stress on *this*. Meaning:"Are you interested in doing this or are you interested in doing something else?")

"Are you interested in doing this *today?*" (Stress on *today.* Meaning:"Are you interested in doing this today, or are you interested in doing this tomorrow or another time?")

Sensitivity to these differences between familiar speech and unfamiliar text, and strategic planning of opportunities for students to experiment with many different genre of books and other reading materials will enable students to eventually become more familiar with the very different registers, genre, and symbols of written communications. Additionally, through experimentation with reading and writing, they will also try out some of these different registers, styles, patterns, symbols, and genre and discuss how they are different and what strategies they need to use as readers and writers when they read or write the different registers, genre, and so on. These ideas are discussed later in this chapter in the teaching strategies section on using children's literature to model and stimulate writing, based on the extensive work of Cambourne (1988) and Brown and Cambourne (1987). In the next section we present information on invented spelling and other approximations of written literacy to help you understand that they are part of children's literacy development and should be encouraged and nurtured.

## *Understanding Invented Spelling and Other Approximations of Written Literacy*

Children begin to write and read long before they enter school. (Readers are referred back to the emergent literacy research fully discussed in an earlier chapter for this background.) Children spend much of their time modeling what they see adults do. If they see adults read and write, they begin to "pretend" read and write. This pretending leads to approximations of what more traditional reading and writing look like. Children's attempted modeling and resulting approximations of written literacy are "developmental writing and reading."

Chomsky (1971) and Read (1971) first began using the term *invented spelling*. Other, less common names for invented spelling include *creative spelling* and *developmental spelling* (Wilde 1992). Wilde pointed out that children's invented spellings should not be thought of as spelling errors because invented spelling is a developmental approximation, and children are not in error as they develop; they are re-creating written language through experimentation. This experimentation and inventing is an active process and results in the child's learning about written language (Chomsky 1979).

The research and literature on early writing and invented spelling does indicate that children's reading can develop through writing as soon as children take an interest in writing (Coate and Castle 1989). Invented spelling helps children learn sounds as they need them. They write letters to try to represent the sounds that they hear in words (Hansen 1987). They invent spellings as they experiment with writing and are able to try out their own developing phonics rules (Goodman 1993). Inventive spellers are especially prepared for the use of phonetic knowledge that beginning word reading requires, even though spelling has not been taught (Richgels 1995). Richgels's (1995) study with kindergarten children confirmed other studies that have indicated the strong relationship between invented spelling and reading achievement (e.g., Ehri and Wilce 1987; and Clarke 1988). Wilde's work (1992) has explained and confirmed that invented spelling eventually leads toward traditional spelling as children continue to develop their written language proficiency. For example, young inventive spellers may use one, two, or three letters to stand for a longer word (e.g., using the letter *M* for mother, or *BR* for brother). As the child matures, he or she learns more letter symbols for sounds and continues to try to approximate; eventually *M* becomes *MTR* and then *MOTR,* and finally, *MOTHER.*

Another approximation of written language that children try to model is punctuation. Wilde (1992) used the term *developmental punctuation* rather than invented punctuation. Wilde indicated that punctuation marks are rarely invented in the same way that spellings are; however, young children use punctuation differently than adults do. Wilde asserted that children's punctuations can be seen as representing their gradually more sophisticated hypotheses about how language works (1992, p. 5). For example, in the previously cited Milz (1983) study, first-grade children left spaces to indicate the ending of ideas when they wrote; this understanding that some separation was necessary, even though the children did not know how to use punctuation yet, showed great development.

Use of capitalization is another approximation of written literacy that children model and develop. Although capitalization does not involve use of punctuation, capitalization is considered an aspect of punctuation. Wilde (1992) reviewed the research on capitalization and concluded that various types of punctuation and capitalization gradually emerge in children's writing ". . . reflecting a developing knowledge of syntactic and other linguistic structures" (p. 33). For example, young children tend to begin writing with uppercase letters and gradually move to lowercase. By the time they are in third or fourth grade they can capitalize words correctly about 86 percent of the time, and about 89 percent of the capital letters they use are appropriate. Finally, Wilde (1987) found that *I* was the most likely word to be capitalized correctly, and proper names and headings were least likely.

The learning of word boundaries, or becoming aware that spaces separate one word from another, is one of the first types of punctuation that children learn (Wilde 1992, p. 119). Later children learn sentence boundaries. Sentence boundaries are eventually made with a period, question mark, or exclamation point that ends one sentence, and a capital letter that starts the next one. The learning of more-sophisticated internal punctuation usually takes longer to develop. However, learning how to use word boundaries, sentence boundaries, punctuation, capitalization, and spelling is best done by

MI IAGOL IS
FAhY

Kenneth

**Figure 8.3**
Sample of kindergartner, Kenneth's, writing
and invented spelling.
*Translation:* "My uncle is
funny."
Used with permission of Peggy Marrano,
Wildwood School, Wilmington, Massachusetts.

NNTHS IS A

KAR aD a RBO

**Figure 8.4**
Sample of kindergartner, Mark's, writing and invented spelling.
*Translation:* "This is a
car and a rainbow."
Used with permission of Peggy Marrano, Wildwood School, Wilmington, Massachusetts.

extensive opportunities for reading and writing, not by learning them as isolated skills (e.g., Calkins [1980] found that third graders in a writing classroom knew much more about punctuation than children who were taught punctuation skills but did little writing).

Finally, it is very clear from all of the research and literature we have reviewed that the teaching of reading and writing must go together from the earliest grades. Reading can be taught through writing. Writing is enhanced through reading. Reading and writing are developmental, meaning they are approximated by the child in the earliest stages, are developed by immersion in literate environments where they can be continually tried out by trial and error and are enhanced by teachers who recognize the importance of facilitating written language development. (See Figures 8.3 through 8.8 for samples of kindergarten and first-grade children's invented spellings and other approximations of written language. The translations were done by their teachers, Peggy Marrano, at Wildwood School in Wilmington, MA, and Marcia Haimila, at McKay Campus School in Fitchburg, MA.) In the sections that follow, instructional suggestions will be made to facilitate this written-language development.

**Figure 8.5**
Sample of kindergartner, Kimberly's, writing and invented spelling.
*Translation:* "Spring is a nice day."

Used with permission of Peggy Marrano, Wildwood School, Wilmington, Massachusetts.

**Figure 8.6**
Sample of first-grader, Sabrina's, writing and invented spelling.
*Translation:* "When I get home from school I play with my dolls and my sister Alyssa."

Used with permission of Marcia Haimila, McKay Campus School, Fitchburg, Massachusetts.

I YAM T
MYCOUSINS
H

**Figure 8.7**
Sample of first-grader, Sarah's, writing and invented spelling.
*Translation:* "I am at my cousin's house."

Used with permission of Marcia Haimila, McKay Campus School, Fitchburg, Massachusetts.

my TREE
isen my Bak
IYRD

I LIKE to KII
my +REE

1

2

**Figure 8.8**
Sample of first-grader, Jaclyn's, writing and invented spelling.
*Translation:*
(1) "My tree is in my back yard."
(2) "I like to climb my tree."

Used with permission of Marcia Haimila, McKay Campus School, Fitchburg, Massachusetts.

What can you observe about the children's written-language approximations and development from the writing and invented spelling samples provided in Figures 8.3 to 8.8? In your reflection journal, under the heading Reflection Activity 8.3, note your observations about the various samples and be prepared to share and explain them with peers in your class.

## Implementing an Instructional Model for Reading and Writing in the Classroom

As we have previously seen, children come to school with emerging literacy in writing and reading. Because of the differences in family, sociocultural, and community experiences and expectations, language and cognitive experiences, and socialization and affective experiences with oral and written language, the children will differ in their individual development when they start formal schooling. Some children will have a more defined understanding of oral-language, writing, and reading relationships than others.

It is extremely important for teachers to understand the needs and development of all the learners with whom they work. An understanding of children's diversities should help teachers plan for and assist each child with his or her learning and continued development (Grossman 1995). As educators learn more about all students' needs, we are in a better position to adjust our goals, curriculum, instructional plans, and materials accordingly. Many resources are available for assistance in understanding the issues surrounding at-risk learners (e.g., Barr and Parrett 1995), second language learners (e.g., Diaz-Rico and Weed 1995), learning disabled learners (e.g., Rhodes and Dudley-Marling 1988), and other diverse learners (e.g., Grossman 1995). Additionally, many resources are available to help teachers provide a culturally rich environment to enhance the learning of learners from all cultures (e.g., Block and Zinke 1995).

In Figure 8.9 the experiential stages of writing and reading have been outlined for you. The listing of stages is not intended in any way to impose a scope-and-sequence type of relationship on these language functions. Instead, we hope it will provide you with an understanding of the experiential stages involved, as we see it, in the development of the free-writing and reading usage of school-aged students. It is important to reiterate that this development will be different for each child in your class. These experiential stages are interrelated and recursive, indicating that students need unlimited and continuous opportunities for free explorations and experimentation with oral language; writing and reading; authoring and sharing; literary and discourse

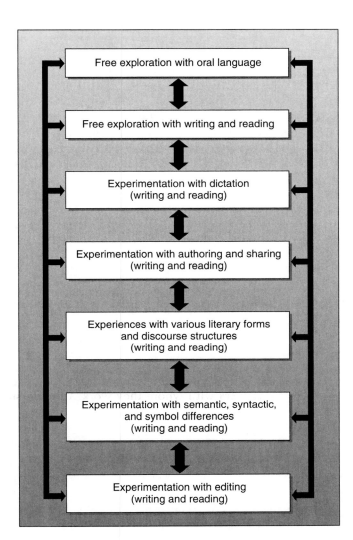

*Figure 8.9*
Experiential stages of writing and reading: interrelated and recursive.

Free exploration with oral language

Free exploration with writing and reading

Experimentation with dictation
(writing and reading)

Experimentation with authoring and sharing
(writing and reading)

Experiences with various literary forms
and discourse structures
(writing and reading)

Experimentation with semantic, syntactic,
and symbol differences
(writing and reading)

Experimentation with editing
(writing and reading)

forms; thinking and editing; and semantic, syntactic, and symbol differences throughout their school-age years. Once again, because of the diversity and the individual needs of children you will teach, some children will need more time and opportunities to experiment and explore in some stages. These children should be given all the time and opportunities they require in any and all of the experimental stages, no matter what their particular grade levels.

In the sections that follow, goals are described and program attributes are suggested and outlined for implementation of an instructional model for reading and writing in the primary grades (kindergarten through second grade) and in the middle- to upper-elementary grades (third through sixth grade).

## Kindergarten, First-, and Second-Grade Reading-Writing Programs

Most children in these school years come to their classrooms with excitement, enthusiasm, and motivation. They tend to be highly motivated and interested in engaging in the written-communication skills of writing and reading. Their image of being "grown-up" and attending school includes involvement in writing and reading activities. Most of these young children have probably been told that they would learn to read and write when they go to school. Early-grade teachers must encourage this belief and provide children with immediate opportunities to participate in real writing and reading activities.

The following is a list of suggested reading and writing goals that we believe are appropriate and nurturing for kindergarten, first-, and second-grade children. After these goals, program attributes that you could consider adopting and implementing to reach these goals are outlined.

### Primary Grades (K–2) Reading and Writing Goals

There are a myriad of writing goals that you could use to direct your early reading-writing activities. Ten possible goals that you could select are as follows:

1. Development of oral-language fluency
2. Development of an awareness that constructing meaning with thoughts and speech written down is writing
3. Development of an awareness that constructing meaning by reading someone's thoughts or speech that have been written down is reading
4. Development of a friendly, comfortable, and enthusiastic feeling toward writing
5. Development of a friendly, comfortable, and enthusiastic feeling toward reading
6. Development of an awareness and appreciation of self as an author (writer)
7. Development of an awareness and appreciation of self as a collaborator or coauthor in the writing process
8. Development of an awareness and appreciation of self as a reader
9. Development of an interest in personal writing and experimentation with a widening variety of writing
10. Development of an interest in personal reading and experimentation with a widening variety of reading

### Primary Grades (K–2) Reading and Writing Program Attributes

Five reading-writing attributes for developing your program are suggested and recommended. These suggested attributes include the following:

I. Create an environment that encourages talking and discussion.
   A. Organize chairs, desks, or tables in the room in cluster-type arrangements, rather than in rows or other arrangements, to encourage group discussion and talk.

B. Allow and plan for extensive student oral interactions and decision making, instead of a teacher-centered environment.

II. Create an environment that is conducive to writing.

    A. Prepare and make available an abundance of writing materials. This could include supplies of newsprint, recycled computer and other paper, pencils, and marking pens.

        1. These materials should be left at a writing-center-type corner with table room for your students to work there (or they can take materials back to their desks).

        2. Allow and plan daily time for students to engage in free-writing opportunities.

        3. Encourage your students to participate additionally in free writing whenever they finish other work.

    B. Encourage as well as plan daily activities for students to engage in meaningful writing activities.

        1. Students can write stories of their own choosing.

        2. Students can keep journals of their thoughts and experiences.

        3. Students can write reports concerning classroom content (science, social studies, etc.) or their own interests.

        4. Students can write on themes, stories, or ideas purposefully introduced by the teacher.

    C. Encourage as well as plan daily activities for your students to share their writing with others.

        1. Students can read their writing to others in their cluster or writing community group, or share their original stories with the whole class using the "author's chair."

        2. Students can share their writing with you.

        3. Students can collaborate or even coauthor writing with their peers.

    D. Encourage as well as plan daily activities for your students to reconsider, rewrite, or add to their writings.

        1. Students can revise their work based on input from others in their cluster or writing community group.

        2. Students can add to their writing based on further consideration of it.

        3. Students can work with their peers or you to improve their writing.

    E. Allow frequent opportunities for your students to see you write (as an author).

    F. Encourage the idea that writing is a meaning-based activity that involves writers using their own thinking-reasoning abilities to convey ideas so that readers will comprehend the written ideas.

III. Create an environment where reading is important.

    A. Prepare and make available an abundance of reading materials by adding new materials regularly and often (e.g., storybooks, magazines, comics, special-interest books, biographies, fiction, nonfiction, and all types of genre that would be of interest to your students).

1. These materials should be left in a reading center or other designated area for browsing and selection. Your students can elect to read them there or take them back to their desks.
2. Allow and plan daily activities for students to engage in free-reading opportunities.
3. Allow students to participate in free reading whenever they finish other work.
4. Design and plan their "other work" experiences and curriculum to include use of various literature and reading/writing activities.

B. Encourage as well as plan daily activities for your students to engage in meaningful reading experiences.
1. Students can read materials of their own choosing and review and do other critical work with the materials.
2. Students can read materials of their own choosing, but within a theme, cluster, topic, context or literary type.

C. Encourage as well as plan daily activities for students to share their reading with others.
1. Students can read a favorite book, story, paragraph, or idea to others in their cluster or reading community group.
2. Students can read a favorite book, story, paragraph, or idea to the teacher.
3. Students can collaborate and read something special together and of their own choosing like a favorite story or a play.
4. Students can read the same book or story and discuss it in their cluster or reading community group.

D. Encourage as well as plan frequent time for your students to read one another's writings.
1. Students can make their own books, bind them, and put them on the author table to be read.
2. Students may be willing to let special friends read their journals.

E. Allow frequent opportunities for your students to see you read (as an interested reader).

F. Encourage the idea that reading is a meaning-based activity that involves readers using their own thinking-reasoning abilities to comprehend the writers' (authors') ideas.

IV. Stimulate frequent dictation or language-experience sessions.
A. Plan opportunities for students to individually dictate to you.
1. Dictation can be based on their personal artwork.
2. Dictation can be based on their interests or ideas.
3. Dictation can be planned by you to involve any contents, topics, vocabulary, or ideas you purposefully select.

B. Plan frequent opportunities for students to dictate in small groups.
1. Dictation can be based on mutual interests or ideas.
2. Dictation can be planned by you to involve any contents, topics, vocabulary, or ideas you purposefully select.

C. Plan some opportunities for students to dictate within a large-group or whole-class setting.
  1. Dictation can be based on mutual interests or ideas.
  2. Dictation can be planned by you to involve any contents, topics, vocabulary, ideas, or field-trip experiences you purposefully select.
V. Create an environment where literature is appreciated.
  A. Read aloud daily to your students, using student-selected materials that should include
    1. Favorite books and stories.
    2. Favorite student-authored books.
  B. Plan daily times for reading aloud to your students, using teacher-selected materials that should include
    1. A variety of literary forms and genre.
    2. A selection of books to encourage their desire for further reading.
  C. Plan opportunities for students to share favorite books, stories, and special literature with the class and with you.

## Implementing the Primary Grades (K–2) Reading and Writing Program

The exact implementation of reading-writing program procedures and details in kindergarten, first, or second grade will depend on your beliefs. Look back at Reflection Activity 8.1 where you noted ways of creating a positive environment for writing. Do you want to add or delete elements from your list? Can you integrate that list with the goals and program attributes suggested for the early-grade (K–2) reading and writing program? It is important that you be able to apply the information detailed in this chapter, together with selected program goals and attributes, to implement a program that is effective for your classroom and is consistent with your own beliefs. Remember to review the experiential stages (Figure 8.9), the suggestions for fostering positive writing activity and development (Reflection Activity 8.1 and Figure 8.2), and the significance of the transitions from oral to written communication, as you plan the details of your own program.

## Third-, Fourth-, Fifth-, and Sixth-Grade Reading and Writing Programs

Students in the middle- or upper-elementary grades often come to school discouraged or disenchanted because of their earlier reading and writing school experiences. Unfortunately, some who were once highly motivated have lost their enthusiasm. If you are a middle- or upper-elementary teacher, it will be up to you to reclaim these students and develop their reading and writing interests and motivations.

If you will again examine Figure 8.9, you will note that the experiential stages have no age boundaries. As previously indicated, we see these stages as interrelated and recursive. Also, we want to remind you that the suggestions for fostering positive writing activity and development (Reflection Activity 8.1 and Figure 8.2) also have no age boundaries and should provide you with specific suggestions and guidelines for all your students. They were based on the research and literature reviewed in this chapter.

In the following section, important reading and writing goals that we believe are appropriate for students in grades three through six are suggested and listed. Note that the first ten are identical to the ten on the primary-grade list of goals, because we believe that those goals are also relevant for older children. However, our initial list of goals has been expanded to include several others. The first ten goals provide for extensive experimentation with the first four or five experiential stages in Figure 8.9, whereas the additional goals for the middle- and upper-elementary grades provide for increasing experimentation with the last three experiential stages in Figure 8.9.

Although the first ten goals provide for heaviest experimentation with the first four experiential stages, some of these goals are flexible enough to apply to all of the seven stages. In other words, we believe that kindergarten through second-grade teachers can include all the experiential stages in their classroom for some children. However, the majority of the class activity at this level will be spent experimenting in the first four or five stages.

### *Middle- and Upper-Elementary Grades (3–6) Reading and Writing Goals*

We have listed the following thirteen goals to guide you in implementing your middle- or upper-elementary grade reading-writing program:

1. Development of oral-language fluency
2. Development of an awareness that constructing meaning with thoughts and speech written down is writing
3. Development of an awareness that constructing meaning by reading someone's thoughts or speech that have been written down is reading
4. Development of a friendly, comfortable, and enthusiastic feeling toward writing
5. Development of a friendly, comfortable, and enthusiastic feeling toward reading
6. Development of an awareness and appreciation of self as an author (writer)
7. Development of an awareness and appreciation of self as a collaborator or coauthor in the writing process
8. Development of an awareness and appreciation of self as a reader
9. Development of an interest in personal writing and experimentation with a widening variety of writing
10. Development of an interest in personal reading and experimentation with a widening variety of reading
11. Development of an awareness of comprehension and thinking strategies for decoding (as a reader) and encoding "stage directions" (as a writer)
12. Development of an awareness of and experience with a variety of genre, styles, patterns, symbols, and discourse structures (e.g., narrative, expository, and reference materials) as a reader and as a writer

13. Development of an awareness and appreciation for editing written materials for spelling, punctuation, syntax, and semantic considerations

## Middle- and Upper-Elementary Grades (3–6) Reading and Writing Program Attributes

Just as the suggested goals for reading and writing in the middle- and upper-elementary grades are an extension of the goals suggested for the primary grades, the suggested reading-writing program attributes for grades three through six are also an extension of the suggested program attributes for the primary grades. In other words, we believe that creating an environment where oral language, writing, reading, thinking, language experience, and literature are encouraged and nurtured are just as important in the middle- and upper-grade reading-writing program as they are in the primary grades. However, there are additional program attributes that we would suggest you consider for the third through sixth grades. Therefore, the following outline is an extension of the primary-grade listing, but it begins with program Attribute VI (see Attributes I–V in the primary section). Once again, although there will be emphasis in grades three through six on the first four experiential stages (Figure 8.9), as noted in the suggested program goals and attributes, an additional emphasis is added for opportunities for increasing experimentation with the last three stages and the last three goals (see previously stated goals 11–13).

VI. Create an atmosphere where development of comprehension and thinking strategies for reading and writing in a wide variety of genre and discourse structures is encouraged.
  A. Plan daily opportunities for free reading and free writing and discussion.
    1. Discuss materials read and written.
    2. Discuss strategies used.
    3. Discuss metacognitive activities.
    4. Discuss semantic, syntactic, discourse, and symbol differences.
  B. Plan daily opportunities for reading and writing in a variety of literary forms and discourse structures.
    1. Discuss materials read and written.
    2. Discuss strategies used.
    3. Discuss metacognitive activities.
    4. Discuss semantic, syntactic, discourse, and symbol differences.
VII. Create an atmosphere where editing is a natural extension of writing.
  A. Develop opportunities for editing.
    1. Encourage students to use one another as editorial boards.
    2. Encourage students to use you as a reviewer.
    3. Encourage students to use other sources such as teachers, parents, siblings, other family members, and friends as reviewers.
    4. Encourage students to edit their own work according to feedback they receive and their self-reflections and judgments.

B. Publish students' edited work when they feel it is ready.
  1. Display work.
  2. Encourage work.
  3. Discuss work.
C. Refrain from using negative reinforcers such as red markings on your students' papers.
  1. Evaluate work based on ideas.
  2. Evaluate work based on content.
  3. Evaluate work based on creativity.
  4. Evaluate work based on experimentation with different structures, forms, symbols, and other text attributes.
D. Teach necessary handwriting, grammar, spelling, and punctuation skills (mechanics) as opportunities arrive within the framework of the students' natural editing.
  1. Explain these skills as a secondary priority.
  2. Explain these skills as refining or additional editing skills necessary for a wider breadth of publication and dissemination purposes.

### Implementing the Middle- and Upper-Elementary Grades (3–6) Reading and Writing Program

The exact implementation procedures and details of the middle- and upper-elementary grades reading and writing program will depend on your beliefs. To implement this type of program in theses grades, refer once again to Figures 8.2 and 8.9. Also, you will want to reexamine the suggested goals and program attributes outlined in the preceding section and in the Primary Grades (K–2) section. Finally, take advantage of the creative-writing opportunities in your middle- and upper-elementary grade program, not only to promote the development of your students' reading-writing and thinking-reasoning abilities but also to showcase their work.

## Teaching Strategies, Processes, and Ideas to Enhance Reading and Writing Development

This section provides several classroom strategies, processes, and ideas for enhancing and developing reading and writing. Additionally, several applications for the teaching of reading and writing are suggested. Some of these ideas and strategies were mentioned earlier in the chapter as part of the suggested goals and attributes for programs. These descriptions and teaching processes for encouraging reading and writing in school should enhance your developing knowledge and ideas concerning the reading-writing process and learning opportunities for your students.

### Dictation and Language Experience

Using dictation and language-experience opportunities, you can write down your students' ideas so that they can have the satisfaction of seeing their words (and thoughts) recorded. Furthermore, use of these procedures helps students see the interrelatedness of writing and reading: that writing is constructing meaning with talk and thoughts written down, and that reading is constructing meaning by reading someone's thoughts and talk that have been written down (Durkin 1993; Flippo 1983; and Sulzby 1994). Tompkins and Hoskisson (1995) have indicated that "reading and writing are connected as students are actively involved in reading what they have written" (p. 259). Finally, these teaching procedures provide for feedback to students and demonstrate that the students' ideas, thoughts, and words are important.

The language-experience approach (LEA) is based on children's language and their experiences (Ashton-Warner 1965; Lee and Allen 1963; and Stauffer 1970). It involves children telling their ideas and experiences as the teacher writes what the children verbalize or dictate. In using dictation as an instructional tool, certain guidelines are helpful. These include the following:

1. Work with individuals, small groups, large groups, or the entire class.
2. Encourage children to discuss an experience, feeling, idea, concept, topic, picture, and so on.
3. Write down the exact words that the children verbalize.
4. Match your writing speed to children's verbalizations as much as possible.
5. Give children as much time as they need to compose their ideas or to change what they want to say.
6. Do not attempt to correct errors for sentence fragments, run-on sentences, or grammar.
7. Read the dictations back to the child or children, pointing to the words as you read them.
8. Ask children to read the dictated information again with you as often as they want to.
9. Ask children to read the dictated information aloud by themselves when they are ready.
10. Save the dictation for future reading, or encourage children to keep the dictation for future reading.

Karnowski (1989) indicated that although use of the language-experience approach is not a new idea, it can be compatible with the newer emphasis on process writing. In fact, Karnowski and others (e.g., Coate and Castle 1989) have shown how use of children's language experiences, invented spellings, and process writing in the classroom can be powerful writing-development opportunities for the classroom teacher.

## Process Writing

Writing is a cognitively demanding and complex activity. Writers have to deal with multifaceted problems such as assessing topical knowledge, organizing that knowledge, taking audience and purpose into account, paying attention to rhetorical requirements and the linguistic features of written text, and managing the motor skills necessary to put their words on paper (Farnan, Lapp, and Flood 1992). Flower and Hayes (1980) described these demands as a "juggling act." Lapp and Flood (1993) explained that traditional approaches to writing instruction attempted to teach students by breaking various components of writing into single instructional disconnected units; that is, students were asked to carry out the juggling act without ever being able to examine how the actual task was done. Process approaches to writing, however, have attempted to teach students the juggling act by having them examine the process while involved in it as writers (p. 254). In fact, a study of children's perceptions of how writing should be taught (Zaragoza and Vaughn 1995) revealed that second-grade children, from various ethnic and socioeconomic backgrounds, who had been immersed in a process-writing classroom, were extremely knowledgeable about what works for them and what does not facilitate their writing. Process writing seems to foster the development of independent, empowered writers who see themselves as authors and who indeed think about and talk about their writing as authors do.

Graves (1983) explained the process of writing as a set of stages that writers use as they develop their finished pieces of writing. These stages include the following:

1. *Prewriting,* which involves thinking about the topic, discussing ideas with others, and rehearsing and thinking about how ideas could be written.
2. *Writing,* which involves putting ideas down without worrying about spelling, grammar, punctuation, and other mechanics.
3. *Rewriting,* which involves refining ideas to make them more meaningful and clear.
4. *Editing,* which involves checking the writing for spelling, grammar, punctuation, and other conventions and errors.
5. *Postwriting,* which involves publishing the writing, considering your readers' responses, and reflecting on the work.

Lapp and Flood (1993) emphasized that this set of writing stages is not discrete. According to them, writers often move between and among the stages while composing and may be in more than one stage at a time. These researchers and others (e.g., Palmer, Hafner, and Sharp 1994) have referred to the recursive nature of writing, meaning that the starting and ending points of writing are not fixed; writing is a recursive, ongoing, and interrelated process. Writers "determine their own paths and eventually will develop an approach to writing that is uniquely their own" (Lapp and Flood, 1993, p. 255). Mulcahy-Ernt and Stewart (1994) showed how all the stages of writing and reading processes are integrated and intertwined throughout the school curriculum.

Teachers who want to facilitate a process approach to writing should keep the following ideas in mind:

1. Process writing is writer centered, not teacher centered.
2. Children should be free to select their own writing topics.
3. Children should be free to decide which writing pieces they want to work on.
4. Children need to be free to allow as much or as little time as they need to work on various tasks and stages of their writing, going back and forth between stages as they see fit.

5. Attention to spelling, grammar, punctuation, and other mechanics is done in the editing stage, just before publishing the writing, and the children authors have the final say-so regarding changes to their work.
6. Sharing of writing is very important and should be encouraged during all stages of the writing process.
7. Writing communities should be established by the teacher and students to provide opportunities for more intimate peer-group discussions, reflections, editing, and sharing of work during all stages of the writing process.

Finally, Graves (1983) has used the term *writing workshop* to emphasize the importance of establishing an atmosphere that lends support to the craft of writing. This support must come from the children (peers) in the writing community, and also from the teacher as a member of the classroom community. Teachers need to become writers themselves to be part of this community. Let the children see you write your own pieces and share your own writing using the process approach (Graves 1990).

## Creative-Writing and Brainstorming Suggestions

Students sometimes need stimulation for their writing. Although it is best when writing develops from the students' own thoughts and ideas, it is acceptable for you or other students to provide stimuli at times.

### Creative Writing

There are an infinite number of creative-writing scenarios and topics you could visualize. In fact, you could think of many good ones that probably have not been used by others. Additionally, many published professional journals, teacher's magazines, and idea books contain creative-writing ideas. Because of that, a long listing of ideas, scenarios, and topics will not be discussed here. However, the following ideas are provided to stimulate your interest and provide a few examples:

1. Pretend you are a bird flying over your neighborhood. What do you see?
2. Pretend you are a stuffed animal. You've been on the shelf for two months and no one has paid any attention to you. Now someone is picking you up and holding you. How do you feel?
3. Pretend you are an animal. What kind of animal are you? What does it feel like to be that animal? What other animals are your friends? Why?
4. Pretend you are a computer and you meet a typewriter. What questions would the typewriter ask you? How would you answer those questions?
5. Your spring has just sprung. You were such a beautiful chair but after a child jumped on you your springs sprung. How do you feel?

You also could ask students to explain various phenomena like:

- The first winter's snowfall. Why is it so exciting? Can you explain it?
- Peanut butter. Where does it come from? Why does it always seem to stick to the roof of your mouth and to the sides of your teeth?

Or they could do some persuasive writing like:

- Why we need some extra recess time.
- Why a "popcorn party" on Friday is a good idea.

Or, finally, they could write some "how to" descriptions like:

- How to make my favorite dessert.
- How to give the dog a bath in the bathtub, and keep him in the tub while you are doing it.

## Reflection Activity 8.4

*R*eading the preceding suggestions should stimulate some ideas for creative writing that you could develop. In your reflection journal under Reflection Activity 8.4, list your own creative-writing scenarios or ideas that you believe will stimulate your students.

### Brainstorming

As you can see, brainstorming is another productive way to stimulate written expression. Because it can be both fun and stimulating, your students will enjoy doing it, too. Perhaps you will ask your students to brainstorm or to share and discuss some good creative-writing ideas in their writing-community groups or with the whole class. When students brainstorm and are allowed to select their own writing topics from all the interesting suggestions, they should be very stimulated indeed.

### Using Children's Literature to Model and Stimulate Writing

Children's literature provides an excellent model and stimulus for writing. Through reading children's literature, children are exposed to a variety of text structures, writing styles, genres, and writing conventions. The work of Brown and Cambourne (1987) has provided many examples of how, by immersing children in literature, teachers promote opportunities for children to think like authors and model the writing of various literary registers and genre. Routman (1994) suggested that a large number of books in various genre is important in a classroom library, and that discussion of this literature has many beneficial outcomes, including development of critical readers, writers, and thinkers. Additionally, Atwell (1987) emphasized that writing in response to literature gives children time to consider their thinking and that their thoughts help them capture new insights.

## *Trade Books: Models for Author's Chair*

Trade books are books that can be purchased by the general public in book stores, through mail-order houses, or at book fairs. This differentiates them from books that are sold by educational publishing companies to be used for instructional purposes, such as basal readers and other school-related textbooks. The literature in the field of reading education has been endorsing the use of trade books in the classroom (e.g., Allen, Freeman, Lehman, and Scharer 1995; IRA and CBC 1995; and Meek 1982). Generally, the consensus is that authentic children's literature increases children's desire to read and their interest in books.

We also know from the work of Brown and Cambourne (1987) and others that using a variety of children's literature gives children different genre and registers with which they can become very familiar. These can be used as models for children's own writing of stories and books. As readers of these literatures, children observe how writers fashion their wordings, stories, and authors' craft. Then, as writers of these various literatures (genre), children model the authors' craft that they are familiar with. For example, children who have become very familiar with the genre mysteries can write their own mysteries imitating or modeling the techniques that their mystery authors had used. Here is another example: Students familiar with the literary techniques of playwrights can write their own plays by imitating the techniques that their playwright authors had used.

Graves and Hansen (1983) suggested that in primary-grade classrooms, a special chair should be indicated as the "author's chair." Children, or the teacher, sit in the special chair to share books they have written, as well as other special books that they have read. This is the only time anyone is allowed to use that chair. Sitting in the author's chair involves reading a book or special written piece (student-authored books should be encouraged), telling the name of the author, and telling something about the author. The idea is that authorship should be revered, and that sitting in the special author's chair helps children realize that authors write books, and that they themselves are or can be authors.

## *Trade Books: Models for Bookwriting and Bookmaking*

As suggested in this chapter, students should have an opportunity to author and share their own books. You can encourage revising and editing of children's writing by suggesting and encouraging that they publish the final copy of their story or book. Bookmaking allows students an opportunity to

1. take further pride in their writing accomplishments,
2. develop an author library to share their works,
3. experiment with writing in the various genre and registers they wish to model,
4. apply their writing skills to specific themes and purposes, and
5. see writing as a meaningful, worthy, and purposeful pursuit.

You can easily gather bookmaking materials for use in your classroom. Often students are delighted to help gather needed materials by bringing supplies such as the following from home:

| | | |
|---|---|---|
| cardboard | construction paper | magic markers |
| scissors | laminating materials | fasteners |
| paste or glue | old manila folders | staplers |
| contact paper | crayons | |

Once students have made books, be sure to find a special place or author's table to display them. Make this author's table a place where other students can borrow books. Let authors read their own books and tell the others about writing them. Use a special author's chair for that purpose (Graves and Hansen 1983).

## Reflection Activity 8.5

*C*learly, children's literature can provide models and stimuli for writing. This chapter has provided a few ideas for using children's literature in this way. Can you think of others? In your reflection journal, under the heading Reflection Activity 8.5, share any additional ideas you have.

## *Journal Writing*

Journal writing is an excellent way to encourage and develop writing in your classroom. It provides opportunities for students to practice informal and reflective writing, using writing in a functional and meaningful manner. Many literacy educators have discussed the benefits of using journals for reading and writing and reflection on learning (e.g., Anson and Beach 1995; Atwell 1984, 1987; Calkins 1991; Hall and Robinson 1994; Morrow et al. 1994; Parsons 1994; and Short and Harste, with Burke 1996). Journals can be kept for many different purposes. Using these journals extends, reinforces, and supports students' fluency and confidence in their writing skills and abilities. In the brief sections that follow, four different types of journals that you could use with your students are described, and suggestions for using journals are given. For those seeking more information and suggestions for using journals in their classrooms, the authors cited in this section and in the sections that follow are excellent resources and springboards for additional ideas and resources.

## *Diaries*

Diaries can be kept in a blank-page book, pad, or notebook. Students who write their private thoughts, observations, or expressions of feelings in their diaries should be allowed to decide for themselves whether or not they want to share the contents with the class. Even if a student chooses not to share her/his diary, keeping a diary is still a valuable writing experience.

## Response Journals

Response journals are sometimes referred to as "literature logs" or "reading journals." These journals are used to keep students' reflections or reactions to books they read or on pieces they have written. They can include such things as students' predictions made before or during a reading, thoughts and ideas recorded during or after a reading, and feelings and reactions recorded after a reading or writing. Teachers can read these journals to find out about students' responses to literature and to their own writings. Students can keep these journals as a record of their readings and ideas about their readings and writings. The writings of Fuhler (1994), Fulps and Young (1991), Hancock (1993), and Parsons (1994) contain especially helpful ideas for using response journals in your classroom.

## Dialogue Journals

Dialogue journals provide an opportunity for students and the teacher to communicate about a reading or writing piece. Students, their peers, the teacher, and even parents/family members can write back and forth, discussing the reading or writing selection. These dialogues can help students think more about the selection and continually reflect on meaning. An article by Wells (1992/93) provided an in-depth look at how she used dialogue journals with her students, and an article by Grant, Lazarus, and Peyton (1992) is recommended for your use when working with your special needs students.

## Learning Logs

Learning logs are students' records of what they have learned. These logs can be used with all subject areas, and they can be used like response journals (with no teacher or peer or parent responses) or like dialogue journals (with opportunities for shared communications). For instance, students can keep a learning log for science, recording their observations and ideas regarding their science experiments. Or students can keep a learning log for social studies, recording their observations and thoughts regarding their social studies readings and assignments. Calkins (1991) is especially recommended for ideas for using learning logs with students.

## Suggestions for Using Journals

Using journals in your classroom is a personal decision and can be implemented in many different ways in all grade levels. However, the following suggestions are given to help guide this implementation:

1. Make your own journal and put some entries in it, to illustrate to students what it and the format might look like.
2. Explain the purpose for the journal writing that you plan to use.
3. Discuss with students what the journal entries might look like or include, and give them an opportunity to practice making some entries in a cooperative group or in their writing community. Emphasize that there

are many appropriate ways of making an entry, so that they do not feel restricted to a one-way approach.

4. Discuss with students how often you expect them to write in their journals.
5. Discuss with students how you plan to evaluate their journals.

## *Content-Reading and -Writing Opportunities*

Reading and writing applications can be applied to all content areas, subjects, and topics. Therefore, the reading and writing processes should not be treated as separate subject areas to be taught in isolation from content.

Because writing and reading are essential in every content area that you teach, why not purposefully plan activities and instruction in social studies, sciences, and other areas to include writing and reading? Many reading and writing practitioners and researchers have seen this potential. A review of the literature indicated that numerous educators (e.g., Heimlich and Pittelman 1986; Kucer 1986; Moore, Moore, Cunningham, and Cunningham 1994; Short et al. 1996; Tierney, Readence, and Dishner 1995; and others) have described many examples of reading and writing applications in content areas. For example, Santa, Ostrem, and Scalf (1986) have discussed ideas for using writing to help students attain a deeper understanding of history. Kucer (1986) explained how writing helps students to more fully understand course content in all subject areas. And Heimlich and Pittelman (1986) have described how you can relate content and writing through the use of semantic-mapping activities.

The practice and use of writing and reading in the content areas is a natural application of these literacy tools within a school's instructional framework, but this application should not be left just to chance. You should plan for the practical use and development of writing and reading throughout your curricula. Although discussion concerning reading in content areas was the topic of the previous chapter, we also suggest the following as planning ideas that you may want to use in your program:

1. Consider which type of reading is required for the content or topic to be studied.
2. Provide your students with opportunities to read a variety of authentic materials (e.g., library research, journal and book passages, newspaper articles).
3. Consider which types of writing are required for the content or topic to be studied.
4. Provide your students with opportunities to utilize a variety of authentic writing purposes (e.g., note taking, letter writing for inquiries, report making, journal keeping for observations).
5. Consider which type of sharing is required for the content or topic to be discussed.
6. Provide students with opportunities for authentic sharing of their readings and writings (e.g., sharing of readings, journals, research, communications, and information).

*P*lease indicate under Reflection Activity 8.6 in your journal your candid thoughts regarding the enhancement and development of reading and writing opportunities for students. Also, discuss how these thoughts fit in with your overall beliefs about reading and writing development in the schools.

We believe that strategies, ideas, and opportunities for enhancing and developing reading and writing across the curriculum are limited only by your imagination and the length of the school day. What do you believe?

## Computer Hardware and Software Considerations

Children and teachers can make use of the word processors and computer technology frequently available in today's elementary classrooms for writing and reading. The word processor can be used in several ways:

1. As another, and novel means of taking children's dictation
2. As a means of children preparing their final copy for their books and other revised writings
3. As a tool and stimulus for composing
4. As a way of helping children deal with the confusion sometimes experienced over line breaks (breaks as the end of the line of print)

The use of the word processor and computer as a tool for composing in the classroom has been getting more attention. For instance, Graves (1994) has noted that computers are helpful for spell checks and publishing students' work, allowing for easy rewrites and editing. According to Routman (1994), who has said that computers have added a new dimension to children's desire to write, word processing is a viable way to publish children's work and facilitate editing. For example, as Routman has pointed out, when drafts are printed out, double- or triple-spaced, it is easier for children to see what needs to be edited. Additionally, some children who have learning disabilities and problems with handwriting can read their own writing better when it has been printed on a word processor. However, Routman (1994) cautioned, and we concur, that use of a word processor is not a panacea for writing quality. Unless the writing process is clearly established by the teacher in the classroom, children will not necessarily value writing and editing, whether it is done on a computer or by hand.

Farris (1997) indicated that writing with a word processor involves the same steps as writing by hand with a pencil. These include prewriting, writing, rewriting, and publishing. However, the word processor can free some children from problems like illegible handwriting and frequent revisions. Others (e.g., DeGroff 1990; Genishi 1988; and Tompkins and Hoskisson 1995) have reiterated that the most valuable application of computers for the language arts is as a tool for writing; for example, to create stories, poems, and other kinds of writing in the classroom.

Finally, Flippo (1986) suggested that inexperienced readers often pause at the end of the line (line break) assuming a pause that isn't really there. Because the line seems to end, unsophisticated readers often treat the end of a line as a period. This pause causes a change in the intended intonation of the author, throwing the meaning of the passage off for the reader. Flippo (1986) further indicated that the wraparound effect of the word processor would illustrate to inexperienced readers that the line break does not warrant a pause. Young readers experimenting with dictation or other writing on the computer would quickly notice that the line break is just a coincidence of spacing and with wider or narrower margins the break would occur elsewhere. Through experimentation and trial and error using the word processor, the unsophisticated reader could develop an understanding of the line-break phenomenon.

Children can benefit most from trial-and-error opportunities afforded them with word processing usage. Rather than drill-and-practice activity (really a sophisticated workbook-type of approach), we see composing, revising, and editing with the word processor as the most appropriate usage of computers in the classroom, as they relate to reading and writing activities. The advantages for using the word processor for writing are summarized and listed for your review:

1. It is an easy way to collect one's ideas and thoughts, rearranging them as often as desired.
2. It integrates the activities of written communication: thinking, writing, and reading (and speaking too, when dictation is taken).
3. It can promote collaborative writing (coauthoring opportunities) over extended periods of time.
4. It promotes the revision and editing processes.
5. It promotes the concept of authorship, publishing, and sharing (writing and reading).

The software programs available for computer applications have been growing at a tremendous rate. Tompkins and Hoskisson (1995) have suggested that because of quality and cost considerations, and the number of new programs constantly becoming available, teachers should carefully preview software before purchasing. They also noted that children can help preview the various software programs and offer their own opinions and recommendations. Various literacy educators have recommended specific software programs and publishers. For instance, Bank Street Writer has been suggested by Farris (1997) and Tompkins and Hoskisson (1995). Quill has been recommended by Farris (1997); Strickland, Feeley, and Wepner (1987); and Tompkins and Hoskisson (1995). First Writer, Magic Slate, and Writing Workshop were also suggested by Tompkins and Hoskisson (1995) as being developed especially for elementary students and easy to use. Routman (1994) indicated that teachers and children she has worked with have especially liked the easy workability and large print of

Once upon a time there was a monster. Who was green. He had slime all over him. He lived in a small town called Woodville. One day he saw a little girl running down the road. she was yelling. The monster listened. she was saying there is a monster nearby be careful. the monster wasen't listening. He was thinking of how tasty she looked. he tried to think of a plan to eat her without letting her get away. But he couldn't.that little girl was annoying. She kept right on yelling. the monster was so mad. he started stomping and crushing down trees.then right then and there the monster had thout of a plan. he would start stomping.and he would stomp the little girl. the monster was so happy he started jumping up and down.The whole town started to run.The monster started stomping. And he ate all the people. that is the end of my tale.

**Figure 8.10**

Kelly's, age 7, original story written on a computer.

Used with permission of Robin Coughlan, Spaulding Memorial School, Townsend, Massachusetts.

Once upon a time there was a monster. Who was 🖊. He had slime all 🌴 him. He lived 🏠 a small town called Woodville. One day he saw a 👨‍👩‍👧 running 🍷 the road. she was yelling. The monster listened. she was saying there is a monster nearby be careful. the monster wasen't listening. He was thinking of how tasty she looked. he tried to think of a plan to 😈 her without letting her get away. But he couldn't.that 👨‍👩‍👧 was annoying. She kept 👉 📻 yelling. the monster was so 😠. he started stomping and crushing 🍷 trees.then 👉 then and there the monster had thout of a plan. he would start stomping.and he would stomp the 👨‍👩‍👧. the monster was so 🙂 he started jumping 🍷 and 🍷.The whole town started to 🐕.The monster started stomping. And he ate all the people. that is the end of my tale.

**Figure 8.11**

Kelly's, age 7, original story written on a computer with picture icons added.

Used with permission of Robin Coughlan, Spaulding Memorial School, Townsend, Massachusetts.

The Children's Writing and Publishing Center by Learning Company in Menlo, California; she also has suggested Sunburst in Pleasantville, New York, and Scholastic Inc., in New York City, for reputable word processing programs.

One innovative program was particularly recommended by a special needs teacher with whom we have worked. Robin Coughlan, a teacher at Spaulding Memorial School in Townsend, Massachusetts, has suggested that Kid Works 2, developed for Macintosh and Windows, available from Davidson and Associates, provides opportunities for young learners to illustrate as they write, add picture icons to their writing, and also allows children to listen to their own original stories. This program combines a word processor, a paint program, advanced text-to-speech technology, sound effects, and boxes full of picture icons. Figure 8.10 shows the original story created on this program by 7-year-old Kelly, a second grader who didn't like to write because writing by hand is especially difficult and frustrating for her and because her penmanship is poor. Kelly has been writing prolifically since introduced to Kid Works 2.

This program allows for the automatic substitution of certain words with picture icons, if a student wishes to do so. In Figure 8.11, Kelly has added picture icons to her story. Additionally, Kelly created some of her own original icons to represent special words in her story.

*W*hat possibilities do you see for using word processors in your current or future classroom's reading and writing program? If you have a student like Kelly who writes very little because of handwriting difficulties or other special situations, do you see the potential advantages of using word processors? What do you observe about Kelly's writing development from these computer-generated samples? Under the heading Reflection Activity 8.7 in your reflection journal, jot down your ideas regarding these questions.

## Summary

In this chapter we have considered the interrelated and recursive relationship between reading and writing and the importance of creating a nurturing environment for the writing development of all students. This environment includes developing reading and writing together as a natural and authentic extension of the school curriculum. This extension is exemplified in usage with all content areas and topics.

Teachers of both young and older elementary students should be aware of the importance of trial-and-error development and experimentation as vehicles for the development and enhancement of written-language processes. Students with diverse backgrounds and needs may need more time and more opportunities to experiment and develop their written-language abilities. This development should not be stifled or interrupted by punitive measures that impede students' experimentation with writing and reading.

Reading and writing discussions in this chapter have included early writing development; implementing an instructional model for reading and writing in the classroom; and teaching strategies, processes, and ideas to enhance the development of reading and writing. Finally, the possibilities for using the computer and word processor in the classroom were explored.

## Closing Activities

1. Observe kindergarten or first-grade children as they work on art or free-drawing activities. Circulate among them and note their verbalizations as they draw. In some instances you might want to stop and ask individual children to "tell" you about their pictures. Take notes and later summarize and share your findings with your peers.
2. Work with one child using dictation as described in this chapter. Summarize what transpired, and share this and the dictation with your peers.
3. Work with a small group of children taking dictation. Summarize what transpired, and share this and the dictation with your peers.
4. Meet with a small group of youngsters, and read to them some of the creative-writing ideas you suggested in Reflection Activity 8.4 for a sample of fun writing topics. Encourage them to brainstorm their own topics, and then (a) encourage them to select one topic and try writing on that topic and (b) share the brainstorming list and one or two of the students' writings with your peers.
5. Work with two or three students to write, illustrate, publish, and then bind their authored books. Using the "author's chair" or your own technique for sharing, encourage the students to share their books. Summarize and share the experience, and if possible, share these books with your peers.

6. Review some elementary-school reading materials looking for the "stage directions." Take notes and be prepared to share your findings with your peers. How could a lack of stage directions affect students' understanding? How could different styles, text structures, and organization patterns also affect students' understandings? What about students with diverse languages, or from diverse cultures? What problems might they incur?

7. Review some elementary-school reading materials and look for paragraphs to illustrate symbol differences or possible symbol misunderstandings. Particularly note sentences and paragraphs where the stress and intonations could be predicted and interpreted in several ways, each of which could change the meaning of the paragraph. Bring these paragraphs to your class and share them and their various interpretations with your peers.

8. Observe the invented spellings and other approximations of written language of two or three children in the early grades. Summarize your observations, and, if possible, bring in writing samples to share with your peers.

9. Work with a small group of students, over time, using the five stages of process writing as delineated in this chapter. Observe and take notes as children work in each stage, and as they move from stage to stage. Summarize and share your observations.

10. Experiment using one or more of the types of journals described in this chapter with a group of students. Summarize your experiences with these journals and share these experiences with your peers.

*References*

Allen, V. G., E. B. Freeman, B. A. Lehman, and P. L. Scharer. (1995). "Amos and Boris: A Window on Teachers' Thinking about the Use of Literature in Their Classrooms." *The Reading Teacher* 48(5): 384–390.

Anson, C. M., and R. Beach. (1995). *Journals in the Classroom: Writing to Learn.* Norwood, MA: Christopher-Gordon Publishers.

Ashton-Warner, S. (1965). *Teacher.* New York: Simon & Schuster.

Atwell, N. (1984). "Writing and Reading Literature from the Inside Out." *Language Arts* 61: 240–253.

———. (1987). *In the Middle: Writing, Reading, and Learning with Adolescents.* Portsmouth, NH: Heinemann.

Au, K. H., and A. J. Kawakami. (1986). "Influence of the Social Organization of Instruction on Students' Text Comprehension Ability: A Vygotskian Perspective." In T. E. Raphael, ed., *The Contexts of School-Based Literacy* (pp. 63–77). New York: Random House.

Barr, R. D., and W. H. Parrett. (1995). *Hope at last for At-Risk Youth.* Boston: Allyn & Bacon.

Block, C. C., and J. A. Zinke. (1995). *Creating a Culturally Enriched Curriculum for Grades K-6.* Boston: Allyn & Bacon.

Brown, H., and B. Cambourne. (1987). *Read and Retell.* Portsmouth, NH: Heinemann.

Calkins, L. M. (1980). "When Children Want to Punctuate: Basic Skills Belong in Context." *Language Arts* 57: 567–573.

———. (1991). *Living Between the Lines.* Portsmouth, NH: Heinemann.

Cambourne, B. (1988). *The Whole Story: Natural Learning and the Acquisition of Literacy in the Classroom.* Auckland, NZ: Ashton Scholastic.

Chomsky, C. (1971). "Invented Spelling in the Open Classroom." *Word* 27: 499–518.

———. (1979). "Approaching Reading through Invented Spelling." In L. B. Resnick and P. A. Weaver, eds., *Theory and Practice of Reading,* Vol. 2 (pp. 43–65). Hillsdale, NJ: Erlbaum.

Clarke, L. K. (1988). "Invented versus Traditional Spelling in First Graders' Writings: Effects on Learning to Spell and Read." *Research in the Teaching of English* 22: 281–309.

Clay, M. M. (1991). *Becoming Literate: The Construction of Inner Control.* Portsmouth, NH: Heinemann.

Coate, S., and M. Castle. (1989). "Integrating LEA and Invented Spelling in Kindergarten." *The Reading Teacher* 42(7): 516–519.

Cooper, J. D. (1993). *Literacy: Helping Children Construct Meaning,* 2nd ed. Boston: Houghton Mifflin.

Cullinan, B. E., ed. (1993). *Pen in Hand: Children Become Writers.* Newark, DE: International Reading Association.

Deford, D. E. (1986). "Classroom Contexts for Literacy Learning." In T. E. Raphael, ed., *The Contexts of School-Based Literacy* (pp. 163–180). New York: Random House.

DeGroff, L. (1990). "Is There a Place for Computers in Whole Language Classrooms?" *The Reading Teacher* 43: 568–572.

Díaz-Rico, L. T., and K. Z. Weed. (1995). *The Crosscultural, Language, and Academic Development Handbook.* Boston: Allyn & Bacon.

Dunkin, P. H. (1983). "The Development of Voice Range and Sense of Audience in Young Writers: Integrating Reading and Writing Experiences." In G. McNinch, ed., *Reading Research to Reading Practice* (pp. 38–41). Athens, GA: American Reading Forum.

Durkin, D. (1993). *Teaching Them to Read,* 6th ed. Boston: Allyn & Bacon.

Edelsky, C. (1983). "Segmentation and Punctuation: Developmental Data from Young Writers in a Bilingual Program." *Research in the Teaching of English* 17: 135–156.

Ehri, L. C., and L. S. Wilce. (1987). "Does Learning to Spell Help Beginners Learn to Read Words?" *Reading Research Quarterly* 22: 47–65.

Farnan, N., D. Lapp, and J. Flood. (1992). "Changing Perspectives in Writing Instruction." *The Reading Teacher* 35: 550–556.

Farris, P. J. (1997). *Language Arts: Process, Product, and Assessment,* 2nd ed. Madison, WI: Brown & Benchmark Publishers.

Fear, K. L., L. M. Anderson, C. S. Englert, and T. E. Raphael. (1987). "The Relationship between Teachers' Beliefs and Instruction and Students' Conceptions about the Writing Process." In J. E. Readence and R. S. Baldwin, eds., *Research in Literacy: Merging Perspectives* (pp. 255–263). Rochester, NY: National Reading Conference.

Fitzgerald, J. (1989). "Enhancing Two Related Thought Processes: Revision in Writing and Critical Reading." *The Reading Teacher* 43(1): 42–48.

Flippo, R. F. (1980). "The Relationship between Reading and Writing." *Carolina English Teacher* 3(1): 37–39.

———. (1983). "Reaction: The Development of Voice Range and Sense of Audience in Young Writers—Integrating Reading and Writing." In G. McNinch, ed. *Reading Research to Reading Practice* (p. 41). Athens, GA: American Reading Forum.

———. (1985a). "Evidence of the Cognitive and Metacognitive Effects of Punctuation and Intonation: Can the New Technologies Help?" In J. Ewing, ed., *Reading and the New Technologies* (pp. 92–95). London: Heinemann Educational Books.

———. (1985b). "Punctuation and Intonation: The Effects on Young Readers' Comprehension and Perception of Text." In G. McNinch, ed., *Reading Research in 1984: Comprehension, Computers, Communication* (pp. 133–137). Athens, GA: American Reading Forum.

———. (1986). "Using the Word Processor to Clarify Textual Phrasing." *Reading Horizons* 27(1): 65–68.

Flood, J., J. M. Jensen, D. Lapp, and J. R. Squire, eds. (1991). *Handbook of Research on Teaching the English Language Arts.* New York: Macmillan.

Flower, L. S., and J. R. Hayes. (1980). "The Dynamics of Composing: Making Plans and Juggling Constraints." In L. W. Gregg and E. R. Steinber, eds., *Cognitive Processes in Writing* (pp. 31–50). Hillsdale, NJ: Erlbaum.

Fuhler, C. J. (1994). "Response Journals: Just One More Time With Feeling." *Journal of Reading* 37(5): 400–405.

Fulps, J. S., and T. A. Young. (1991). "The What, Why, When and How of Reading Response Journals." *Reading Horizons* 32(2): 109–116.

Genishi, C. (1988). "Kindergartners and Computers: A Case Study of Six Children." *The Elementary School Journal* 89: 185–201.

Goodman, K. S. (1993). *Phonics Phacts.* Portsmouth, NH: Heinemann.

Goodman, Y. M., D. J. Watson, and C. L. Burke. (1987). *Reading Miscue Inventory: Alternative Procedures.* Katonah, NY: Richard C. Owen.

Grant, J. O., B. B. Lazarus, and H. Peyton. (1992). "The Use of Dialogue Journals with Students with Exceptionalities." *Teaching Exceptional Children* 24(4): 22–29.

Graves, D. (1983). *Writing: Teachers and Children at Work.* Portsmouth, NH: Heinemann.

———. (1990). *Discover Your Own Literacy.* Portsmouth, NH: Heinemann.

———. (1994). *A Fresh Look at Writing.* Portsmouth, NH: Heinemann.

Graves, D., and J. Hansen. (1983). "The Author's Chair." *Language Arts* 60(2): 176–183.

Grossman, H. (1995). *Teaching in a Diverse Society.* Boston: Allyn & Bacon.

Hall, N., and A. Robinson, ed. (1994). *Keeping in Touch: Using Interactive Writing with Young Children.* Portsmouth, NH: Heinemann.

Hancock, M. R. "Exploring and Extending Personal Response through Literature Journals." *The Reading Teacher* 46(6): 466–474.

Hansen, J. (1986). "Learners Work Together." In T. E. Raphael, ed., *The Contexts of School-Based Literacy* (pp. 181–190). New York: Random House.

———. (1987). *When Writers Read.* Portsmouth, NH: Heinemann.

Harste, J. C., C. Burke, and V. A. Woodward. (1984). *Language Stories and Literacy Lessons.* Portsmouth, NH: Heinemann.

Heimlich, J. E., and S. D. Pittelman. (1986). *Semantic Mapping: Classroom Applications.* Newark, DE: International Reading Association.

Hennings, D. G. (1994). *Communication in Action: Teaching the Language Arts,* 5th ed. Boston: Houghton Mifflin.

International Reading Association, and the Children's Book Council. (1995). *More Kids' Favorite Books.* Newark, DE: International Reading Association.

Irwin, J. W., and M. A. Doyle, eds. (1992). *Reading/Writing Connections: Learning from Research.* Newark, DE: International Reading Association.

Karnowski, L. (1989). "Using LEA with Process Writing." *The Reading Teacher* 42(7): 462–465.

Kucer, S. B. (1986). "Helping Writers Get the 'Big Picture'." *Journal of Reading* 30(1): 18–25.

Langer, J. A., and A. N. Applebee. (1986). "Reading and Writing Instruction: Toward a Theory of Teaching and Learning." In E. Z. Rothkopf, ed., *Review of Research in Education* (pp. 171–194). Washington, DC: American Educational Research Association.

Lapp, D., and J. Flood. (1993). "Are There 'Real' Writers Living in Your Classroom? Implementing a Writer-Centered Classroom." *The Reading Teacher* 48(3): 254–258.

Lee, D. M., and R. V. Allen. (1963). *Learning to Read through Experience,* 2nd ed. New York: Meredith.

Leu, D. J. (1984, November 30). *Toward a Theory of Reading Acquisition: Examining the Transition from Oral to Written Language.* Paper presented at the thirty-fourth annual session of the National Reading Conference, St. Petersburg, Florida.

Leu, D. J., and C. K. Kinzer. (1995). *Effective Reading Instruction,* 3rd ed. Englewood Cliffs, NJ: Merrill/Prentice-Hall.

Meek, M. (1982). "What Counts as Evidence in Theories of Children's Literature?" *Theory into Practice* 21: 285–292.

Milz, V. E. (1983). "A Psycholinguistic Description of the Development of Writing in Selected First Grade Students." Doctoral dissertation, University of Arizona. *Dissertation Abstracts International* 44: 3279A.

Moore, D. W., S. A. Moore, P. M. Cunningham, and J. W. Cunningham. (1994). *Developing Readers and Writers in the Content Areas, K–12,* 2nd ed. New York: Longman.

Morrow, L. M., J. K. Smith, and L. C. Wilkinson, eds. (1994). *Integrated Language Arts: Controversy to Consensus.* Boston: Allyn & Bacon.

Mulcahy-Ernt, P. I., and J. P. Stewart. (1994). "Writing and Reading in the Integrated Language Arts." In L. M. Morrow, J. K. Smith, and L. C. Wilkinson, eds., *Integrated Language Arts: Controversy to Consensus.* (pp. 105–132). Boston: Allyn & Bacon.

Palmer, B. C., M. L. Hafner, and M. F. Sharp. (1994). *Developing Cultural Literacy through the Writing Process.* Boston: Allyn & Bacon.

Parsons, L. (1994). *Expanding Response Journals in all Subject Areas.* Portsmouth, NH: Heinemann.

Read, C. (1971). "Pre-school Children's Knowledge of English Phonology." *Harvard Educational Review* 41: 1–34.

Rhodes, L. K., and C. Dudley-Marling. (1988). *Readers and Writers with a Difference: A Holistic Approach to Teaching Learning Disabled and Remedial Students.* Portsmouth, NH: Heinemann.

Richgels, D. J. (1995). "Invented Spelling Ability and Printed Word Learning in Kindergarten." *Reading Research Quarterly* 30(1): 96–109.

Routman, R. (1988). *Transitions: From Literature to Literacy.* Portsmouth, NH: Heinemann.

———. (1994). *Invitations: Changing as Teachers and Learners K–12.* Portsmouth, NH: Heinemann.

Santa, C., V. Ostrem, and J. Scalf. (1986). "Writing to Learn in Social Studies." *Wisconsin State Reading Association Journal* 30(3): 61–66.

Short, K. G., and J. C. Harste, with C. Burke. (1996). *Creating Classrooms for Authors and Inquirers,* 2nd ed. Portsmouth, NH: Heinemann.

Smith, F. (1988). *Joining the Literacy Club.* Portsmouth, NH: Heinemann.

———. (1994). *Understanding Reading: A Psycholinguistic Analysis of Reading and Learning to Read,* 5th ed. Hillsdale, NJ: Erlbaum.

Stauffer, R. G. (1970). *The Language Experience Approach to the Teaching of Reading.* New York: Harper & Row.

Strickland, D., J. T. Feeley, and S. B. Wepner. (1987). *Using Computers in the Teaching of Reading.* New York: Teachers College Press.

Sulzby, E. (1994). "I Can Write! Encouraging Emergent Writers." In K. M. Paciorek and J. H. Munro, eds., *Early Childhood Education 94/95* (pp. 204–207). Guilford, CT: Dushkin Publishing Group.

Sulzby, E., and W. Teale. (1991). "Emergent Literacy." In R. Barr, M. L. Kamil, P. Mosenthal, and P. D. Pearson, eds., *Handbook of Reading Research, Volume II* (pp. 727–757). New York: Longman.

Templeton, S. (1995). *Children's Literacy: Contexts for Meaningful Learning.* Boston: Houghton Mifflin.

Tierney, R. J., M. Leys, and T. Rogers. (1986). "Comprehension, Composition, and Collaboration: Analyses of Communication Inferences in Two Classrooms." In T. E. Raphael, ed., *The Contexts of School Based Literacy* (pp. 191–216). New York: Random House.

Tierney, R. J., J. E. Readence, and E. K. Dishner. (1995). *Reading Strategies and Practices: A Compendium,* 4th ed. Boston: Allyn & Bacon.

Tierney, R. J., and T. Shanahan. (1991). "Research on the Reading-Writing Relationship: Interactions, Transactions, and Outcomes." In R. Barr, M. L. Kamil, P. Mosenthal, and P. D. Pearson, eds., *Handbook of Reading Research, Volume II* (pp. 246–280). New York: Longman.

Tompkins, G. E., and K. Hoskisson. (1995). *Language Arts: Content and Teaching Strategies,* 3rd ed. Englewood Cliffs, NJ: Prentice-Hall.

Weaver, C. (1994). *Reading Process and Practice: From Socio-Psycholinguistics to Whole Language,* 2nd ed. Portsmouth, NH: Heinemann.

Wells, M. C. (1992/93). "At the Junction of Reading and Writing: How Dialogue Journals Contribute to Students' Reading Development." *Journal of Reading* 36(4): 294–302.

Wilde, S. (1987). "An Analysis of the Development of Spelling and Punctuation in Selected Third and Fourth Grade Children." Doctoral dissertation, University of Arizona. *Dissertation Abstracts International* 47: 2452A.

———. (1992). *You Kan Red This!* Portsmouth, NH: Heinemann.

Wray, D. (1994). "Text and Authorship." *The Reading Teacher* 48(1): 52–57.

Zaragoza, N., and S. Vaughn. (1995). "Children Teach Us to Teach Writing." *The Reading Teacher* 49(1): 42–47.

# Section III

## Meeting the Diverse Interests and Needs of All Learners

*S*ection III, "Meeting the Diverse Interests and Needs of all Learners," includes two distinct chapters. Chapter 9 looks at all of the reasons that students have to pursue individual reading, including their pursuits of new and developing interests, recreational purposes, academically oriented purposes, and reading for pleasure. Fundamental to these pursuits is the students' self-selection, self-motivation, and satisfaction of personal needs and desires. Discussion regarding the teacher's role in these pursuits; and the impact and involvement of culture, community, and family is the major focus of the chapter. Developing personal reading is given special treatment in this chapter because of its importance to meeting the diverse interests and needs of all learners. This chapter also explores ideas for working with parents and families to help promote maximum opportunities for children to engage in personal reading outside of school, in their homes and greater communities. Additionally, this chapter provides extensive listings of children's literature, and professional sources for reviewing and finding appropriate literature for all your students' interests and needs.

Chapter 10 focuses on helping teachers provide an inclusive classroom setting, one that includes culturally and language diverse learners; learners that some would call "at risk" but that we and others prefer to think of as "at promise"; and learners with special needs, challenges, and gifts/talents; as well as all other learners in the classroom. This chapter includes extensive discussion of cultural diversity, macroculture, microcultures, and multicultural education efforts. Bilingual and ESL programs are described, and scenarios involving two culturally and language diverse children, Kim and Tomas, are provided.

Additionally, this chapter includes extensive information on mainstreaming and the full inclusion model, along with information regarding learners with specific needs, challenges, and gifts, including students with Attention Deficit Disorder (ADD) and/or Attention Deficit/Hyperactivity Disorder (ADHD). Instructional ideas, procedures and strategies for teaching students in the inclusive classroom are provided.

As in other sections of this text, the chapters in Section III encourage your reflections and journal notations. Also, Chapter 10 provides a "Computer Hardware and Software Considerations" section to provide important ideas for using technology with some language diverse students and with some students with special learning needs, challenges, and gifts.

# *Developing Personal Reading: Meeting Diverse Interests and Motivations*

© David M. Grossman/Photo Researchers, Inc.

# Overview

*O* ne of the more important goals of developing children's reading is to develop their pursuit of and interest in reading independently and with pleasure. This chapter discusses the importance of developing the personal reading of each child in your classroom. A special feature of this chapter is the focus on how to meet the individual needs and interests of each student, and how to help each of them develop aspects of their personal reading. Six aspects, or purposes, of personal reading are discussed and include reading for (1) current interests, (2) new and developing interests, (3) recreation, (4) academic interests, (5) practical purposes, and (6) pleasure.

Ideas for developing each aspect of personal reading are provided at appropriate places throughout the chapter. These include use of attitude/feelings and perception questions, interest inventories and questions, reflection questions to help teachers "work in" students' interests into the classroom curriculum, sustained silent reading (SSR) procedures, reading aloud to your students and sharing good literature with them, questions to help guide your selection of reading materials, using academic interests, genre immersion, and the sharing of personal reading.

Parents and family/community life play a major role in children's attitudes about personal reading and in children's opportunities for personal reading. Parents and family are discussed and suggestions are made to include them in efforts to promote and continue children's personal reading at home and in the child's larger community life. Likewise, culture and sociocultural influences affect children's personal reading development, choices, and interests. Suggestions are made about how to use these choices and interests to promote the development of all students' personal reading.

This chapter also includes listings of professional references and resources for teachers that should facilitate their efforts to find children's literature especially for their students. This literature can include "good taste" and "good literature" choices that children find particularly interesting or relevant for their individual interests, needs, and desires.

## Main Ideas

- Personal reading is more than recreational reading.
- Current individual interests can be pursued and developed through personal reading.
- New and developing interests can be enhanced through personal reading.
- Personal reading can be for recreational purposes.

- Personal reading can be used to develop academic interests.
- Reading to enhance literary appreciation can be accomplished through personal reading.
- Personal reading can occur for practical purposes.
- Reading for pleasure is an important aspect of personal reading.
- Personal reading involves self-motivation and self-selection.
- Students' culture, community, and family all have an impact on students' personal reading.
- The aesthetic stance and individual desires are important to readers' personal reading enjoyment and involvement.
- The efferent stance is the stance readers take when they focus on the information to be learned from the text and then hopefully find information they can use and relate to in the reading selection.
- Personal reading must never be pushed or forced on students by anyone.
- Personal reading development can be promoted by the classroom teacher's understandings and the many opportunities provided for students to read inside and outside the classroom.

## *Personal Reading: A Definition*

What is personal reading? Many would define it as *recreational reading* or *the reading we do for our own pleasure.* We agree with this definition, but we believe that personal reading includes much more. Our definition of personal reading also includes *individual pursuits of interests (current, developing, and academic)*, and *individual pursuits for practical purposes. It is using reading for one's own pleasure, interests, motivations, purposes, and needs.* Figure 9.1 displays our concept of what personal reading involves. Keep in mind that all of these aspects are influenced tremendously by each individual's culture, community, family, and personal needs and desires.

 **Reflection Activity 9.1**

$W$hat do you believe personal reading is? Where does your idea of "personal reading" fit into your thoughts about the reading process, a facilitative teacher's role, and development of learners' literacy? In your journal, under the heading Reflection Activity 9.1, write your ideas about personal reading and your answers to these questions.

**Figure 9.1**
Personal reading:
aspects and influences
display.

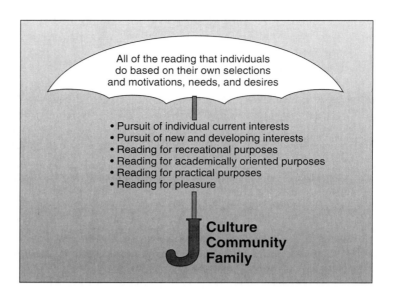

# *Enhancing Reading Opportunities*

By now you are very aware of the importance of the teacher's role in reading development. You also are aware of the characteristics and responsibilities of a facilitative teacher. An important part of the facilitative teacher's role is to help develop the personal reading of his or her students. Facilitative teachers do this by enhancing reading opportunities.

What does this mean? Simply put, it means that the facilitative teacher will use every opportunity to foster the development of personal reading, for all children. The teacher will plan instruction and learning opportunities that allow for the continued development of personal reading interests, habits, motivation, and selection. As illustrated in the personal reading umbrella in Figure 9.1, self-motivation and self-selection are fundamental. *Self-motivation refers to the kind of motivation that comes from within. Self-selection refers to one's own personal choosing.* The research and literature support the importance of self-motivation in all aspects of reading (e.g., Cramer and Castle 1994; and Guthrie 1994).

Additionally, the facilitative classroom teacher must understand the importance of each individual's experiences, background, culture, and family/community influences. Because students are diverse and unique individuals, each student may develop different meanings, insights, and understandings from any piece of literature. It is critical for teachers to understand and respect these unique and often diverse individual meanings. The "transactional" theory of reading and writing (Rosenblatt 1978, 1989) supports the idea that the meaning a reader brings to text and the meaning that the writer intended is often reconstructed into a new, developed meaning as the reader creates and makes meaning as he or she reads. Reading is a very personal experience during which readers connect the story they are reading to their own lives and to their own personal experiences with literature. They don't search for the author's "correct message," but instead they create personal meanings for themselves (Rosenblatt 1978).

## Aesthetic Stance

Rosenblatt (1978, 1991) referred to the "aesthetic" stance and response of reading as reading for deriving pleasure from what we read. This often involves "living through" the experience of the story and the evoking of feelings and associations. This aesthetic response to literature is crucial to developing an ongoing desire to read. Without the expectation of pleasure, and without the satisfaction of a pleasurable feeling from reading, people would not desire to read.

As teachers, we need to understand each child and see to it that we give all children many and continuous opportunities to anticipate reading their own choices of literature, with pleasure. Likewise, we need to ensure that we provide a classroom atmosphere and climate conducive to the pleasurable enjoyment of their selected literature. We must also always remember that what is pleasurable to one child may not be pleasurable to another child. By knowing and working with our students, we can anticipate some of their needs, desires, and motivations; however, only the individual students themselves can really know what is pleasurable to them.

## Efferent Stance

Rosenblatt (1978, 1991) also referred to "efferent" reading. *Efferent* means to carry away information from reading and hopefully relate it to what the reader already knows. When readers seek out or take information from reading materials, they are responding to the reading in relation to what they previously knew. Diverse learners, and in fact, all learners, may carry away different information from a particular reading. This must be understood and respected by the classroom teacher.

Additionally, Rosenblatt (1985) pointed out that almost every reading experience calls for a balance between aesthetic and efferent stances. As readers read, they move back and forth between aesthetic and efferent stances or purposes. However, she and others (e.g., Many, Wiseman, and Altieri 1996 and others they reviewed and cited) indicate that literature should be read and responded to by readers for primarily aesthetic stances—in other words, for pleasurable reasons. We agree, but we also believe that readers can read for efferent purposes (i.e., to seek information) and still derive satisfaction from the reading. However, for this to happen, readers must be truly motivated to seek and read the information. Figure 9.2 illustrates our conception of the aesthetic and efferent stances and shows how they can each relate to and enhance personal reading choices.

**Figure 9.2**
"Aesthetic" and
"efferent" stances, and
the relationship to
personal reading
choices.

## Reflection Activity 9.2

*F*or what aesthetic purposes or desires do you read? For what efferent purposes might you be interested in reading? In your journal, under the heading Reflection Activity 9.2, list the most compelling aesthetic and efferent purposes you can think of, for you. What can you do as a teacher to help children develop a desire to read and anticipate it with pleasure? Jot your ideas down in your journal.

## *Personal Feelings and Beliefs*

One important area that should not be overlooked is children's personal feelings about themselves as readers, and their beliefs and understandings concerning reading. Because of the research and literature in affective factors (e.g., Alvermann and Guthrie 1993; Cramer and Castle 1994), we know that children who have made positive associations with reading tend to read more often, read for longer periods of time, and read with greater interest. Children's self-perceptions of themselves as readers can influence their overall orientations and associations to reading (Henk and Melnick 1995). Therefore, it is very important that the classroom teacher is aware of each child's attitudes (McKenna and Kear 1990) and feelings about himself or herself as a reader, as well as each child's beliefs and understandings about reading.

Two assessment instruments are recommended for classroom teachers' use. One is a rating scale developed by Henk and Melnick (1995), "The Reader Self-Perception Scale," which contains thirty-three questions to which students are asked to indicate their agreement or disagreement, using five possible choices. The questions are designed to measure how each student feels about himself or herself as a reader. A second suggested assessment instrument, for determining your students' beliefs and understandings about reading, is "The Reading Interview" (Goodman, Watson, and Burke 1987, pp. 219–220). This assessment uses ten open-ended questions to probe into students' ideas and concepts.

Classroom teachers should use these or similar assessments (e.g., McKenna and Kear 1990, and others found in various reading assessment texts) or their own probing questions, to discover how their students feel about themselves as readers, and how each of their students views the reading process. Using a combination of ideas from the works of Henk and Melnick (1995) and Goodman, Watson, and Burke (1987), as well as Flippo (1997), we have developed some probing questions to help get you started. Additionally, you could develop more of your own.

## Open-Ended Questions to Find Out about Students' Feelings and Beliefs As They Relate to Reading

1. If you were asked to describe yourself as a reader, what would you say?
2. What do you think your last year's teacher thought about you as a reader? Why?
3. How do you feel when you read? Do you feel good? Do you feel bad? Why?
4. What do you think your parents and family think about your reading? Do they think you are a good reader? Do they think you are a bad reader? Who thinks these things? Why?
5. Who is a good reader that you know? What makes him or her a good reader?

Clearly, students' feelings and perceptions about reading will affect the personal choices they make about reading. Classroom teachers will need to balance their understandings regarding these feelings, as well as their understandings regarding the importance of the aesthetic stance of reading, and the personalization of meaning each reader gets from a reading, to facilitate development of students' personal reading. This is a tall order, but in the sections that follow, each of the six aspects of personal reading will be discussed, with these understandings serving as a foundation to the discussions. *We want to be clear that we do not see personal reading as a separate or discrete part of the elementary school day. Rather, we see development of personal reading as an important goal of the elementary school teacher; and the application of personal reading as a weaving into the curriculum of meaningful, interesting, motivating, and self-selected reading materials for all students, with full consideration for their diverse feelings, desires, and needs.*

# Pursuit of Individual Current Interests

To facilitate the pursuit of individual students' interests, the facilitative teacher first helps students identify their interests, which can be done in several ways. What follows is a brief discussion of them for your consideration.

## Interest Inventories and Questions

Numerous interest inventories have been developed and published in reading education texts. Most of these contain a list of questions to ask children about their reading interests, sports interests, television interests, and their hobbies. Additionally, there are often questions concerning favorite pets, animals, movies, games, and music. The intent of these interest inventories is to inquire into the individual students' interests and preferences.

Interest inventories typically use open-ended questions, where students write, list, or tell their interests, or checklist or circle responses, where students check or circle their choices. Most authors have suggested that teachers of young students, and students who may need support, read the questions to the children individually and assist them by taking dictation and writing responses to the open-ended questions for these children. Teachers of older or more independent students are usually directed to give the questions to the students, who can then record their own responses. Although we do not disagree with these methods, we favor the more personal approach of one-to-one teacher-student discussion of interests. This will demonstrate to your students that their individual interests are really important to you, and you will be ensured that each student's response is accurate, rather than a result of misunderstanding the question or directions. We also favor open-ended questions that provide more opportunities for students to express their true interests and thoughts.

In Appendix A of this book, we have provided an interest inventory (or set of questions) that you might want to use. Or you may prefer to develop your own interest inventory. It is likely that your own interest inventory will be more appropriate for your students because you will be aware of any special community, regional, ethnic, cultural, and sociocultural conditions that would add to the types of interests and desires of your students. We encourage you to consider using ours (see Appendix A) as a base, and then to add your own special questions and interest areas to anticipate and fit your students' diverse interests and needs.

## Meeting Individual Interests

Once you have assessed your students' interests, the real challenge begins. Now you must ask and answer the question, How can I meet these varied interests and diverse needs? The answer is (a) to provide many opportunities for students to go to and use the library, (b) to provide many opportunities for students to peruse and have time to read the reading materials (e.g., various genres of books, magazines, etc.) you bring into the classroom for them, and (c) to find other resources for special problem and need areas. You may also need to guide the more reluctant readers toward their indicated interests and gently suggest that they self-select and explore those materials. However, because self-selection and self-motivation are very important to personal reading, take care to only suggest and offer choices and options. Remember the aesthetic stance! You want children to "read because they desire to."

A wide variety of literature is available on almost any topic or interest area, and for many problem areas, too. Your school or public librarian can help you find the most current indexes of children's literature, which contain lists and abstracts of books and other reading materials classified by genres, topics, subjects, and authors. Additionally, many excellent professional books are available that suggest literature by topic and interest area, genre or types of literature, age level, and ethnicity. For example, see Cullinan and Galda (1994) for extensive discussions of and suggestions of children's literature; see Beaty (1994) for suggested picture books in a variety of areas and topics; see Stroll (1994) for a wide variety of magazines classified by age/grade and subject; and see Harris (1993) for children's literature suggestions for a variety of cultures. Also, Rudman (1995) provides literature suggestions to help deal with special problems, situations, and issues (i.e., divorce, death, abuse, aging, gender roles, and heritage). At the end of this chapter, a more complete list of sources will be provided.

Remember, children's interests and needs are not standard in any way. Do not limit or deter your students from reading in areas of their interests or needs to only the area you define as recreational reading. As shown earlier in this text, children may genuinely have an interest in academic areas and more practical areas (e.g., see Figure 9.2) in addition to fiction or more recreational types of reading. Meeting the individual current interests of all your students must include all types of areas, purposes, and literature.

## *Pursuit of Students' New and Developing Interests*

Once again, the use of an interest inventory, with questions you design or add for your particular students, will be a good indicator of their new and developing interests and needs. Additionally, your own observations while teaching your students will be another important guide to emerging interests and possible problems or projects they might want to pursue through reading.

### *Students' New and Developing Interests*

Children may need the most guidance with their new and developing interests. Often they are not familiar enough with a topic or interest area to know how or where to find appropriate literature. Your role should be that of a facilitator, offering suggestions, possible choices, and other options. You will need to use some of the available and most current professional books, as suggested, as well as indexes in the school and public libraries, and other sources to locate appropriate reading materials.

Some of your students will benefit the most from the individual help of a librarian, who could suggest available and interesting books and other literature relevant to their particular developing interests and needs. The school librarian is one of the classroom teacher's best resources and should be consulted for professional help whenever possible.

Additionally, you could ask students probing questions to help them verbalize their desires and needs regarding their search for particular literature on particular topics. For example, you could ask:

1. Do you wish you could get some help finding a book you really like?
2. What kind of help do you think you need?
3. Who would you like to help you?
4. When would you like this help?
5. Is there more assistance or more information you need, and where and how do you think you could get this assistance?

## Promoting Students' New and Developing Interests

When you have observed or noted an emerging or developing interest in a student, you will need to nurture it carefully. The student may not even realize he is really interested yet. Additionally, a more reluctant reader may balk at the idea that she is really interested in reading anything at all!

How do you hone and nurture these emerging or developing interests? In a low-key way—by making subtle suggestions and by making assignments conducive to the pursuit of those developing interests. Here facilitative teachers can really show their know-how and professionalism: You can design assignments related to the school's curriculum (e.g., reading, writing) and your content subjects (e.g., science, social studies) that will enhance those developing interests. (For instance, do you remember how Mrs. Argueta, in another chapter, designed her rainforest assignment to allow students to read and research areas related to their personal interests?) When students are truly interested in something, they will usually read about it, as long as you approach them with sensitivity to their feelings, needs, and desires. Remember that self-motivation and self-selection are the overall indicators of personal reading. Frankly, we see the real purpose of reading instruction as the development of individuals who will engage in personal reading for pursuit of their interests, needs, recreation, practical and academic purposes, and for just pure pleasure.

Some reflection questions that classroom teachers can ask themselves, to review the curriculum and other potential opportunities to promote students' new and developing interests, include:

1. Are there curriculum areas that we will be working on that provide opportunities to explore some specific interests of my students?
2. Are there ways of "working in" some of the other interests?
3. Can I create reading and writing assignments that are open-ended enough to accommodate for students' specific interests?

4. What other arrangements can I make to be sure that my students really have opportunities to read in their desired interests?
5. What other resources do I need to help me accommodate for every student's reading desires and needs?
6. How can I include the student's family in these efforts?

## Reflection Activity 9.3

*C*an you think of other questions that a classroom teacher should consider or review to help make sure he or she is doing everything possible to facilitate students' pursuit of their reading interests and needs? In your journal, under the heading Reflection Activity 9.3, note any questions you would add.

## *Reading for Recreational Purposes*

Recreational reading is a very important aspect of personal reading. As a teacher, one of your most important roles is to encourage and model recreational reading inside and outside of your classroom. You will want your students to be aware that reading can be pursued as a recreational activity that refreshes, relaxes, and restores; and certainly, it can be a very enjoyable pursuit.

One way to build recreational reading into your classroom schedule is to provide some specific time for it each day. During this time, all members of the classroom, including you, the teacher, will set aside their other work and activities to read their books or materials of choice—just for recreational purposes. Other ways to promote recreational reading include: allowing for ample unscheduled or unstructured free-reading time in the classroom every day; encouraging and modeling that children (and you) read books at home for recreational purposes—just to relax and enjoy; and reading enjoyable good books and other "good taste" literature to your students each day. These ideas for encouraging and modeling recreational reading will be discussed in the sections that follow.

### *Sustained Silent Reading (SSR)*

The specific, structured quiet time set aside for recreational reading, as just described, is often referred to as Sustained Silent Reading (SSR). It was introduced in 1968 by Fader and McNeil in their book *Hooked on Books: Programs and Proof.* Fader and McNeil called it USSR, the *U* standing for *uninterrupted* to emphasize the idea that for a particular time period, everyone reads, and no interruptions of any kind are permitted. Most reading educators still encourage the use and ideas of SSR today, even though some use other names like "Drop

Everything and Read" time (DEAR time). Whatever you call it, the objectives seem to be the same, that is, to (a) provide students with a specific quiet time for their silent reading, (b) allow students to observe models of appropriate silent reading behavior, (c) provide opportunities for students to sustain their silent reading for longer and longer periods of time, (d) convey to students that reading is important, (e) indicate to students that everyone can read, and (f) develop a sense of trust between the teacher and students that students are individually pursuing reading.

SSR is appropriate for most students of all age groups. It can be implemented in the elementary classroom by you or in a middle or secondary school setting by a content area teacher. There have been SSR programs implemented in entire schools, where all students, teachers, administrators, and other school staff (custodial, cafeteria, office) participate. The key benefit of schoolwide SSR programs is the modeling of reading aspect and the accompanying message that reading is important and everyone can do it.

How can you implement SSR in your classroom? It is important to set aside a specific time for recreational reading each day, encourage students to keep their recreational reading available at their desks, and keep your recreational reading available and visible on your desk. You should also do the following: (a) Have in your classroom many additional materials that are interesting and enjoyable so that students who forget or finish their books can select from these; (b) have a timer or alarm clock available to time the SSR experiences; and (c) select an appropriate length of time for SSR based on the age and maturity of your students. Typically, with younger students, you may want to begin with only five minutes, and for older students you could begin with ten minutes. Once the routine is established, the time can be gradually increased. There are no specific time regulations, but it might be realistic to eventually have the SSR last fifteen to twenty minutes in the primary grades, and twenty to thirty minutes for the upper-elementary grades. The use of an alarm clock or timer will allow you and your students to relax and read without watching the clock.

Finally, elementary teachers can do a number of things to enhance the SSR experiences for their students. These include but are not limited to (a) developing a classroom library with diverse and interesting books and other printed materials for teacher and student SSR selection (Allington 1994); (b) encouraging less-abled students to read series books with predictable characters, settings, and plots (McGill-Franzen 1993); (c) permitting students with special needs to use "talking books" and technology such as Sony's Electronic Book Player DD-8 and CD-ROM discs during SSR sessions; and (d) scheduling cooperative-learning activities after SSR sessions to promote authentic and integrated listening, speaking, reading, and writing experiences (Leal 1993; Morrow and Sharkey 1993). Working with parents and other family members to strengthen the home-literacy environment and to establish an SSR program with families would also be advantageous (France and Hager 1993).

## *Unstructured Free-Reading Time*

Unstructured free-reading time is another option for the classroom teacher. Unlike SSR, unstructured free-reading has no specific time of day and no specific duration of time. In addition, unstructured recreational reading can be done individually; that is, not all of the students in the classroom need to participate at the same time.

The unstructured approach offers flexibility to the teacher and students alike. You can offer students the option of unstructured reading time after the early completion of assignments or during other free time. Other teachers may find that it is more appropriate to set up designated times for free-reading options. Or students can choose their own times for recreational reading.

The structured (SSR) and unstructured approaches to recreational reading can, of course, be used concurrently. Or you may choose to use one and not the other. Based on discussions with several classroom teachers, advantages and disadvantages of each approach are listed. Some of these pros and cons include the following:

**STRUCTURED**

**Advantages:**

1. The students know that a particular time will be reserved every day for SSR.
2. All of the students will be doing the same thing at the same time.

**Disadvantages:**

1. Some of the students may not wish to participate in reading every day at the same time.
2. If the entire school participates in the SSR, the time chosen for schoolwide participation may not be convenient for the individual schedule of a given teacher.

**UNSTRUCTURED**

**Advantages:**

1. The reading time is flexible and can take place at the teacher's or student's convenience.
2. The atmosphere is more relaxed, without the occasional anxiety that builds up as the SSR time approaches.

**Disadvantages:**

1. Supervision of the students who are reading is much more difficult, since the teacher will probably be working with other students on other tasks.
2. The lack of structure or routine may not be in the best interest of inexperienced readers, and they may be less inclined to participate.

## Reading to Your Students

Sharing literature of all kinds with your students is a wonderful way to encourage recreational reading and help students realize that reading is a refreshing, relaxing pursuit. When you read aloud to your students, you not only are sharing literature with them, you also are "demonstrating reading." In addition, you are creating a pleasant, memorable experience for your students to remember. These experiences can be particularly important for diverse learners and for students who have shown negative or unhappy feelings and attitudes about reading.

Anderson, Hiebert, Scott, and Wilkinson (1985) indicated in *Becoming a Nation of Readers: The Report of the Commission on Reading* that the single most important thing that teachers can do for students to help ensure future success in reading is to read aloud to them. Many teachers believe that reading selected books aloud to their classes is their most enjoyable activity associated with teaching. Although the benefits and gains to be made by reading aloud to children are immeasurable (Daisey 1993; Trelease 1995), some researchers have suggested that reading aloud to children also promotes cognitive and emotional challenges without frustrations (Gersten and Jiménez 1994); literacy development (Galda and West 1992; Scott 1994); whole-class unity (Swindal 1993); individual and cultural identity (Gillespie, Powell, Clements, and Swearingen 1994); and appropriate gender, ethnic, and other perceptions (Fox 1993). However, for maximum reading-aloud benefits to occur, some have also suggested (e.g., Hoffman, Roser, and Battle 1993) that teachers have a logical and planned read-aloud program so that children know it is important and that it actually happens in the classroom. What follows is a brief listing of questions and answers you could consider when including reading aloud to children as part of your classroom experiences. These ideas were developed by reviewing various language arts and teaching with literature texts (e.g., Hennings 1994; Tompkins and Hoskisson 1995; and Tompkins and McGee 1993).

### Reading-Aloud Questions and Answers

1. What kind of reading-aloud experiences do I want for my students? What are my options?
   *Answer:* Many options exist. Some teachers prefer doing all the reading aloud themselves. Other teachers invite other fluent readers to read aloud to students, such as fluent readers in the class, the school librarian, older students, parents, or other community members. There are no limits to who can read aloud. The important criteria is that the readers are "fluent" and present an enjoyable experience for your students.

2. Is Readers' Theater an option? What would it involve?
   *Answer:* Yes, Readers' Theater is a viable option. Using Readers' Theater, a group of students in your classroom, or from an upper-grade classroom, present their story or script, by reading it like a play, to other students. Once again, when using Readers' Theater as a read-aloud option, be sure the readers are all fluent and well rehearsed so that the audience has a pleasurable listening experience.

3. Should I consider reading aloud to my students as a "treat" or an "extra" when we have time, or when they've been particularly good?
   *Answer:* No, reading aloud should not be used as a reward for good behavior, nor should it be viewed as an extra that can be squeezed in when there is time. Reading aloud should be considered a valuable way of sharing literature with your students and should be done at least once each day, more if possible.
4. I teach an upper-elementary grade. Should I be reading aloud to my students?
   *Answer:* Yes, reading aloud has no age barriers. It can be used with students at all age and grade levels, from the youngest preschool child through students in the middle- and even high-school years.
5. I think that reading aloud to students is a good idea, but we have so many curriculum requirements in my school, how can I justify the time it will take out of my class schedule each day? What do I tell the principal when she asks?
   *Answer:* You could say, "Reading aloud to the students introduces them to a wide variety of literature, nurtures their love of literature, models for them what good readers do, introduces them to a variety of authors and genres, gives me a chance to share books with children that they may not be able to read themselves, and gives me an opportunity to turn them on to reading."

In the following list, we suggest some tips for reading aloud to your students. These tips should help your reading-aloud performance, but if you are not comfortable with one or more of them, you don't have to include it. The idea is that a certain amount of showmanship, or showwomanship, is sometimes entertaining and enjoyable to your audience. Additionally, you do need to consider where you and the children sit during read-alouds; all children must be able to easily hear you read as well as see any illustrations you display. Obviously, if students can hear, see, and enjoy the read-aloud, they will have more opportunity to get maximum benefits from the experience.

## Read-Aloud Tips

1. *Be expressive.* No one likes to listen to an unenthusiastic reader who appears disinterested. Expression should not be confined to the voice, since the face can also be used to exhibit an appropriate appearance for the action of the story.
2. *Vary the loudness of the voice.* This should be tailored to fit the action of the story. For tense moments of anticipation, when everyone expects a sudden dramatic event, you can switch to a very soft voice, with slow and deliberate phrases. When the dramatic event does occur, your voice would become much louder.
3. *Show physical movement.* During the course of the reading, you can move around the room, as long as everyone can still hear you and see the illustrations. Physical movement could also entail physical expression with head, arms, and maybe even legs.

4. *Allow discussion during the reading.* Frequently students will become particularly excited about something that has taken place in the story. When this occurs, spontaneous comments and discussions can be expected. This does not demonstrate impolite behavior on the part of the students but, rather, shows that they are involved in the plot. Stop for a few seconds to let the students share their ideas.

5. *Select appropriate stopping points.* This is an important maneuver in reading aloud. There are specific rules for the selection of good stopping points, and you will learn them as you develop your techniques. Typically, the best stopping points occur when the story reaches its apex of suspense, where everyone who is listening is convinced that the next sentence will answer the question What's going to happen?

Finally, postreading discussions, rereading of favorite parts of the story, and extension activities often heighten children's enjoyment and awareness of the literature that has been read. Lively postreading discussions should focus on getting students to make connections between the literature read and their personal experiences. These connections promote appreciation and critical thinking. Rereading memorable or favorite parts of the story will provide students with a deeper understanding of the author's intent and the story line. This understanding in turn increases the quality and quantity of students' responses to the literature. Postreading extensions should encourage reflection and rethinking. Independent or cooperative-learning extensions you could use to promote students' insights and personal reactions are creative writing activities, literature journals, art and drama projects, and Readers' Theater, using the story just read as the script (Hancock 1993; Young and Vardell 1993). Another postreading activity could be to have your students critique the story read and recommend literature for future readings (Saccardi 1993/1994) or to add to the classroom library selection (Prill 1994/1995). The selection of related literature (e.g., writing by the same author or within a thematic unit) permits students to explore interrelationships, to discover patterns, and to think more deeply (Hoffman et al. 1993).

Although the next section discusses selection of reading materials, and at the end of the chapter we provide a listing of resources, we do want to point out one particular book, which is a favorite of ours, and is especially devoted to reading aloud, *The New Read-Aloud Handbook* by Jim Trelease (1995). This book contains many helpful suggestions for both teachers and parents. Additionally, it includes an annotated list of many children's books very suited to reading aloud. You could obtain the Trelease book from your library and use it as an additional source for read-aloud literature for your students.

## Selection of Reading Materials

For recreational reading, most reading material should be considered appropriate. Unless your school or school system has a censorship regulation, children should be allowed to read whatever they like, within of course the framework of "good taste." Good taste does not imply "good literature." Instead, good taste

Time for pursuit of personal reading gives children opportunities to find and to read books they want to read, books that meet their purposes, and books that they will savor, reading over and over again.
© Michael Siluk

means literature that is acceptable to your school community and to the various sociocultural groups to which you teach. In other words, good taste materials could include comic books; magazines that feature sports, music, cars/hot rods, and movie/TV stars; and popular books like series books and novels; as well as other materials that are considered by the school community and the greater sociocultural community to be acceptable and nonoffensive. Cullinan and Galda (1994) have emphasized that teachers must be sensitive to the standards of the communities in which they teach but at the same time must protect children's rights to read material that stimulates, informs, and delights them (p. 223). Furthermore, Cullinan and Galda (1994, p. 413) remind us that the International Reading Association, National Council of Teachers of English, and American Library Association all condemn attempts of censorship that try to restrict students' access to quality reading materials. You might also want to consult Simmons (1994) on the issue of censorship. However, again we remind you to be sensitive to your community and use that sensitivity to make appropriate professional decisions for your own classroom. Remember, the purpose of recreational reading is for refreshment, relaxation, and restoration, not necessarily for reading good literature.

Having made that clear, we do not want to imply in any way that we do not value good literature. Contrarily, we believe that good literature is to be valued, appreciated, and savored. We hope that having been allowed the opportunities that "rich" personal reading development encompasses, students will be exposed to good literature through the teacher and librarian reading to them and through self-discovery in the library and classroom. Also, the teacher and librarian should display an assortment of "good" children's literature for children to browse through. When many Newbery and Caldecott award books (e.g., see Roginski 1992), other classic children's trade books and stories, and quality materials from various genres are read and shared with children, and are readily available for their self-selection, some of it will be selected and read and reread.

Many lists of this good literature are available to teachers. The school and public librarians usually have published lists, anthologies, and indexes of them. Additionally, we have listed some sources, at the end of this chapter, of "good" literature suggestions and other resources for your reference and use. But before reviewing these listings, let's consider this question, What is a good book?

## Reflection Activity 9.4

*A*s previously explained, a "good book" could be "good taste literature" or "good literature," depending on the reader's orientation. However, in your journal, under the heading Reflection Activity 9.4, try answering the question, What is a good book?, from your own personal orientation and perspective. Be prepared to share your answer with your peers in class.

Obviously, descriptions of a good book will vary greatly and will probably be as diverse as any population who answers this question. Because of this, no one person's answer can really be considered right or wrong for anyone else. However, we would like to share one answer we received from a colleague who had been a fifth-grade teacher for many years. Her answer seems to grasp the spirit of recreational reading. She said, "Pick a book that makes them laugh and makes them cry, that makes them happy and makes them sad, that makes them gasp and makes them sigh, that makes them cheer and makes them mad."

The professional literature also contains many varied descriptions of what good books and good literature contain or do, and how to evaluate a book. For example, Hoffman et al. (1993) have suggested that good books have enduring stories with meaty plots that promote interest, literacy development, independence, and personal connections. Crawford, Crowell, Kauffman, Peterson, Phillips, Schroeder, Giorgis, and Short (1994) have indicated that good literature will assist students to find themselves as learners and people and will help them to learn how to negotiate interpersonal relationships. Tompkins and

McGee (1993) stated: "The best way to evaluate a picture book or a chapter book is to share it with a child and observe his or her reaction and the depth of that response" (p. 63). We agree; the most important elements are the child's joy, satisfaction, and involvement with the reading material. Once again, remember the importance of the reader's aesthetic stance (Rosenblatt 1978, 1991) discussed near the beginning of this chapter.

We have developed a listing for you of questions to help guide your selection of the reading materials you will choose to read and share with your students. This listing includes the ideas and suggestions we have found in the professional literature, especially in the works of literacy and children's literature professionals (namely, Harris 1993, and Tompkins and McGee 1993; and also in Cullinan and Galda 1994; Farris 1997; and Hennings 1994).

## Questions to Help Guide Your Selection of Reading Materials for Reading and Sharing

1. Will this book or story hold your students' attention?
2. Does the plot make sense?
3. Are the characters interesting and believable?
4. Do the characters develop as the book or story develops?
5. Are the characters stereotyped, or does the author's presentation seem biased in any way toward or against any particular group?
6. Does the style and language of the book or story seem appropriate to the particular literature?
7. Will your students be comfortable with and understand the style and the language of the material?
8. Does the book or story have a worthwhile overall theme and is it applicable to students' diverse understandings and backgrounds?
9. Is this a book or story that all your students will love and ask you to read over and over again?
10. Does this book or story exemplify the most fundamental characteristics of its genre, so that students will be likely to correctly generalize it as one example of the genre?
11. When you look at the pictures or illustrations in the book, do they seem to be accurate, authentic, and nonstereotyped representations of women (and girls), men (and boys), people of color, and people of various diverse ethnic and racial groups?
12. If this is a nonfiction book, what are the author's credentials for writing about this topic? If this is a fiction book, did an "insider" or "outsider" perspective inform the book and to what extent does the book succeed in fulfilling its apparent purpose?
13. Is there anything in this book that would embarrass or offend any child in your classroom? Is this a book that you are completely comfortable sharing with a group of mixed-race children, with a group of all-black children, and with a group of all-white children? (If not, don't choose this book.)

Finally, do not be dismayed if your students choose to read good taste literature instead of the good literature suggested from these questions and the lists at the end of the chapter. Personal reading involves personal selection and motivation. Be happy and know that you are reaching your intended goals when your students self-select and read for recreation either good taste or good literature. They are reading and learning to use reading as a means of recreation—this is the most important thing!

Therefore, the implication is that you will need to

1. Have a large variety of good taste literature available for the children's perusal and reading, according to the information you collected from the interest questions and other observations.
2. Allow children to bring in their own good taste literature, if they choose to.
3. Have a large variety of good literature available for the children's perusal and reading, according to the information you collected from the interest questions and other observations, and from the good literature sources and lists you've found in the professional suggestions near the end of this chapter. (Some of the good literature might very well fit in with the students' interests.)
4. Have a large variety of good literature available from the good literature lists for children and from librarians' suggestions.
5. Read good literature aloud each day to your students. Children enjoy being read to and as we have seen, there is much evidence to suggest that reading to children is an important aspect of literacy.
6. Frequently, every week or two, bring in new good taste and good literature to the classroom for students' perusal and self-selection, and remove most of the literature that has "been around" for more than two or three weeks. (Note, feel free to keep "favorite books" for an extended time. Many of your younger or less-developed readers will benefit from repeated readings of their favorite stories and books.)

## Reading for Academically Oriented Purposes

As already pointed out, children's personal reading can include reading for academically oriented purposes if they self-select and are self-motivated to choose these materials. If children display real interest in academic areas in their responses to your interest questions, or as determined by other observations, then they may choose to personally read in those interest areas. Using the professional books, indexes, and anthologies as suggested will help you locate reading materials for these very special academic interest areas. Remember, the goal of personal reading development is to promote individuals who are motivated to self-select reading materials for their own personal purposes and interests. As an elementary teacher, *it is important that you give students an opportunity to learn how to find materials that they want to read and then provide opportunities for them to read these materials.*

## *Using Interests to Enhance Content Assignments*

As we hope you can see, the facilitative teacher can really capitalize on these academically oriented interests. For instance, if he is teaching a unit on transportation as part of the social studies curriculum in third grade, and he has one student who has a strong current or developing interest in model railroads, the teacher can use that student as a resource or "peer teacher" when discussing railroads. The peer teacher in this case may be able to bring into the classroom model railroad cars from various historical time periods, railroad cars for different purposes, and so on. Additionally, if this student is a real model railroad buff, she may know a great deal about the historical development of the railroad in the United States. If she doesn't already know enough about railroad development, the student might be more than willing to read to learn more about it (if the teacher can assist by providing appropriate sources, and/or assist by showing the student how to locate sources) and share and explain to the rest of the class.

In an example in another chapter, Mrs. Argueta, a fourth-grade teacher, developed a research assignment that allowed students to explore various aspects of rainforests. Carmen, one of her students, was encouraged to use her current knowledge and interests in snakes and reptiles and extend it into her rainforest research. Carmen could become a peer teacher in Mrs. Argueta's class, sharing examples of snake skins, photos of reptiles and snakes, and newly found books and developing knowledge of snakes and reptiles in rainforests.

Here's one more example. Obi, an African student in Mr. Friedman's sixth-grade class, is particularly interested in the history as well as the current events of Nigeria. Knowing this, Mr. Friedman encourages Obi to share his knowledge and research with the rest of the class during their Study of Africa unit. Because of Obi's interest, he is very happy to read as much as possible about Nigeria and has a wealth of information to share with his peers.

Obviously, many more examples could be suggested. However, the important message would be the same. Your students are capable human beings who have a broad variety of current and developing interests. These interests should be tapped and enhanced for students' development. The students can read for their own interests, helping themselves and enjoying their pursuits. Additionally, they can share their learnings with other students, helping these other students as well. This show of respect for all students' academic abilities and learnings is important if we are to model to children respect and caring for all people (e.g., Tiedt and Tiedt 1995, and many others). It is also important that children are given encouragement and an outlet for displaying their academic interests and related readings.

## Reflection Activity 9.5

*C*an you think of other examples of how students' interests can be used to enhance content assignments? If so, in your journal, under the heading Reflection Activity 9.5, make note of some of these examples. (This is different, of course, than the inverse, or trying to use students' interests to get them to read content material.) Here, once again, we are more concerned with self-selection and self-motivation. We hope facilitative teachers will use their students with special interests and knowledge as resources in appropriate content instruction or study.

## *Using Personal Reading to Enhance Author Awareness and Literary Appreciation*

The more often your students are given an opportunity to read based on their personal selection, motivation, and interests, the greater likelihood that they will be exposed to a variety of literature. This exposure to a variety of literature and this immersion in a literate environment—your classroom—will help them to develop an appreciation for a variety of literary devices, a variety of authors, and a variety of ideas and concepts.

Your students will also be learning about the benefits of a literate environment by being *in* a literate environment. As students read a variety of literary materials, they will begin to develop an appreciation for many of the aspects of good literature, such as good illustrations, good bookbinding, good paper and print qualities, good plots, interesting characters, and memorable stories. Although they may not express it, you may find that your students are drawn back to some of these excellent pieces of literature to reread them, to look at the illustrations once more, or simply to enjoy and savor the good book.

Students will also begin to develop a better sense of their own preferences. If they have not been in a truly literate environment before, they may for the first time have an opportunity to experiment with their tastes. Students who have come from more literate environments will have opportunities to continue to develop and refine their tastes.

An appreciation for authors and their works is certainly a very desirable and likely outcome. For example, students who are interested in horses may find that a certain author has written several books on horses. Once students discover that author and have read and enjoyed one of her books, it is likely that they will want to read the other books about horses written by the same author. Once all the books about horses have been read, it is also likely that students may be willing to read another book on a different topic or subject by the same author. Your students will "discover" authors and develop a sense of appreciation for many of them.

Often after reading a number of books by the same author, students will also observe similarities regarding situations, plots, characters, and writing style, as well as inconsistencies. This can lead them to much more awareness and critical personal reading—a most desirable outcome. For example, one of our children, Tara, when she was an elementary student, was an avid Nancy Drew book series reader. But Tara observed that the main character of each of the books, Nancy Drew, seemed to remain a perennial teenager, approximately 18 years old, and that Nancy Drew had solved over 60 mysteries within a relatively very brief span of time. Tara's awareness of the age and time discrepancies, developed as Tara read more and more books in the series, resulted in criticism of the Nancy Drew series' author for apparently failing to realize that some readers would be aware of the age and time inconsistencies in these books. Thus, Tara was acquiring the ability to become a critical and discerning reader.

Undoubtedly, one of your curriculum goals as a classroom teacher will be to expose your students to a wide variety of literature in the many different genres. Although we again remind you to be sensitive to the importance of students' self-selection and self-motivation, you can very naturally use students' personal reading interests to enhance their genre awareness and appreciation. Here is one example: Natasha loves to read fairy tales. She's indicated this in her responses to the interest questions you posed. Why not allow Natasha to read all the fairy tales she wants for an extended period of time? Using Brown and Cambourne's (1987) literary immersion model (as previously suggested in other chapters), Natasha will immerse herself in fairy tales, and after several weeks of this immersion she will know quite a lot about fairy tales. For instance, if you asked Natasha to tell you what the characteristics of fairy tales are (or perhaps you'd say, "What are fairy tales like, Natasha?"), she would be able to generate her own list of the literary characteristics of fairy tales. (For example, she might say, "They often start with the words 'Once upon a time.'" "They often have kings, queens, princesses, princes, witches, or goblins as main characters." "They often end with the words 'They lived happily ever after,'" etc.) Using Natasha's natural desire to read fairy tales, you've given her a unique opportunity to learn a great deal about the genre, fairy tales. You could also give Natasha opportunities to write her own fairy tales, if she wishes, following her immersion, based on the list of characteristics she personally generated. When she writes, Natasha will emulate some of the author craft that a writer of fairy tales must use.

Here's another example: Maxie is very interested in reading as many mystery books as possible. He is enthralled with Sherlock Holmes and many of the other classics. You let him follow his natural desire to read mysteries. After several weeks of this immersion with mystery books, Maxie can tell you many characteristics of mysteries. (For example, he might say: "They are full of suspense." "The author tries to keep the 'who-done-it' part till the end." "But the mystery is always solved." "Very often, 'who-done-it' is a complete surprise to the reader," etc.) Again, Maxie has had an opportunity to be immersed in literature he loves, learning a great deal about that literature. When given an opportunity, Maxie can write his own mystery using many of the characteristics of a mystery that he himself generated as a result of his literary immersion. Maxie can also emulate some of the author craft involved with writing a mystery, especially the suspense, plot, and character development inherent in this type of narrative. (Also see Brown and Cambourne 1987; and Flippo 1997 for more examples and step-by-step details of how to do literary immersion with your students.)

Finally, as your students read they cannot help but be exposed to a variety of ideas and concepts. They will often be exposed to different and diverse cultures, lifestyles, and problems. The sharing of their literary experiences with one another, by discussing good and bad books, by discussing various genres, by discussing interesting ideas and problems noted in the books, as well as the use of their readings within the framework of the rest of the curriculum (in content areas and in writing) will encourage and lead to a richer vocabulary and richer experiential base for each of them. In conclusion, as Rosenblatt (1978) has explained, when students are given opportunities to write and reflect about their readings, this helps them to unravel their thinking, elaborate their ideas, and clarify their responses.

# *Reading for Practical Purposes*

Students often want to read something of a practical nature to help solve a problem, or to help do something new or different. They are motivated because they do recognize the problem, or they are really interested in learning to do something new. This type of reading is as much a part of personal reading as all the other aspects already depicted. We encourage you to include "reading for practical purposes," as needed, or as indicated by student interest, in your personal reading development efforts with students. Once again, the results of your interest questions, as well as observations you make about students' interests, problems, and needs, will be very helpful. Additionally, information you learn from talking with students' parents and families will provide you with more assistance in meeting each student's needs. (Discussion regarding working with parents and families for students' personal reading development will be explored later in this chapter.)

## *Reading for Problem Solving*

Just as we as adults have problems, children often have problems, too. Although some of the problems may be relatively small ones, to the children involved they feel big and significant. Unfortunately, many problems facing youngsters in schools today are quite serious. However, resources are available to help, and teachers need to know how to locate them (Ouzts 1994).

Previously mentioned, Rudman's book (1995) contains listings with annotations of books on many sensitive areas, such as divorce, death, adoption, foster care, family configurations, siblings, aging, abuse, sexuality, and special needs. Rasinski and Gillespie (1992) deal with some similar issues and also with drug and substance abuse issues, as well as dealing with the issue of "moving." Rudman, Gagne, and Bernstein (1994) focused entirely on books that have been selected to help children deal with "separation" and "loss." Finally, Friedberg, Mullins, and Sukiennik (1992) and Robertson (1992) focused on nonfiction and fiction books that help children understand and promote their acceptance of a wide variety of physical, emotional, and medical disabilities.

Using readings in sensitive areas to help people understand and cope with special problems is known as *bibliotherapy.* Rudman (1995) has indicated that use of books to help children grapple with their personal problems has become accepted as an important part of teaching (p. 2). She further stated that using books to help children address these concerns is not putting teachers in the role of psychologists. Instead, she argued, because many children walk into today's classrooms grappling with many problems and because teachers, next to parents, spend the most time with these children, teachers need to be competent to handle children's questions and concerns (pp. 2–3). However, Rudman has warned that to be helpful, these book suggestions must not be prescribed or forced. Instead she suggests displaying books on a given theme and allowing children to discover them, recommending titles by posting them in an accessible area, and having conferences where children and teachers feel comfortable sharing concerns and book ideas or suggestions.

Finally, Rudman has indicated that the teacher must always be sensitive to children's reactions. Ideally the reader should be able to identify with the character and action in the book. When teachers search for a variety of books to help children deal responsibly with the issue or problem, teachers should observe how the issue is treated; that is, books that provide "lessons to be learned" should be analyzed for their accuracy. The aesthetic quality of a book is still one of the most important factors to consider. Good children's literature can contain many issues and provide opportunities for students to deal with them. For example, Rudman explained that the death of Charlotte in E. B. White's *Charlotte's Web* (1952) helps readers to understand and handle the concept of death while also providing a wonderful literary opportunity (p. 3).

At the end of this chapter, selected children's books will be listed, dealing with some of the more common problems and areas of concern. These selections will be presented just to give you an idea of the availability of books in sensitive areas. Teachers wanting more information, more books, and descriptions of each book should see Rudman (1995) or one of the other bibliographies available. Additionally, when appropriate, and with the utmost sensitivity, teachers may be able to suggest some of these books to parents/families. However, care must be taken to not put the children in an embarrassing, awkward, or dangerous situation; and if it is deemed appropriate to share these book suggestions with parents/families, it is important that parents understand that the reading of the book must not be forced on their children.

 **Reflection Activity 9.6**

*H*ow do you feel about using children's literature to assist children with their concerns, problems, and needs? When do you feel it might be particularly appropriate? Write your reactions to these questions in your journal, under the heading Reflection Activity 9.6.

### Reading to "Do"

Have you ever read a "how-to-do-it" book? How to dress for success? How to refinish furniture? How to make and can preserves? How to travel cheaply? Many of us have read such material because we have a genuine desire to dress right, or to "do it ourselves," or to savor the fruits we picked this summer all year long, or to travel as much as we can afford. In other words, we were genuinely motivated.

If you have students who express an interest in a "learning-how-to" type of book, or some other practical type of reading, encourage it. Reading for practical purposes is part of life. It is a tool we all need to succeed in life. Many adult basic education programs (programs for adults who need to further develop their basic literacy and other skills) stress this type of life-skill reading because of its essentiality in helping people to function in everyday life. For example, eventually almost everyone has to read a driver's manual to take their driving tests; people also need to read job applications, menus, cookbooks, and directions "to do" or to assemble specific things. These are "basic" to our literacy needs in the larger culture in which we live. Other literacy and how-to-do-it needs and motivations may also be basic to the diverse cultures and desires of your students and their families and immediate communities (Wlodkowski and Ginsberg [1995], emphasize that motivation is inseparable from culture). Give students the opportunities to read desired materials, and provide the help they may need locating desired materials. Often public librarians and various community agencies and businesses can be extremely helpful here.

As we have cautioned you previously, mandating certain types and kinds of reading should not be a part of developing personal reading. Therefore, wait until your students express a real desire to read some specific how-to or other practical material, before suggesting it. If it is appropriate, you and the student may also decide to involve the parent/family in this reading effort. Discussion regarding parent/family involvement will be addressed later in this chapter.

## Reading for Pleasure

What does so much of personal reading really seem to be all about? You've guessed it: It is very often reading for pleasure or self-satisfaction. In most cases, if you really choose to read something, and you are really motivated to read it, you will usually derive some sense of pleasure, accomplishment, or satisfaction from doing it. We know that all reading is not necessarily pleasurable, nor should it all be. We are not suggesting that. But we are suggesting that one of the primary aspects of personal reading should be the gaining of pleasure or satisfaction from one's reading. Again, remember the importance of the aesthetic stance (Rosenblatt 1978, 1991). We want children to really feel and get the message: "Reading is a pleasure!"

How do you give them that message? Well, we hope for one thing that you will try implementing extensive personal reading development in your classroom, as described throughout this chapter. Second, we hope that you will create a comfortable, open, and unstressful environment in your classroom so that your efforts to develop personal reading will be successful. Third, we hope that you will provide the literate environment described throughout this chapter, filling your room with a great variety of children's literature of good and good taste quality in many indicated interest areas, and that you will frequently bring in new materials, replacing most books and magazines that have been "around" for more than two or three weeks. Fourth, we hope that you will model that "reading is a pleasure" by allowing your children to see you really read and enjoy your own book every day. (Let them also see you taking it home to read and enjoy when not at school.) Fifth, we hope you will make personal reading a nonpunitive activity. In other words, students will not be graded down or corrected for doing something wrong. Instead, "free" reading will be encouraged, honed, and nurtured. Reading for the sake of enjoyment, recreation, exploring interests, solving problems, or learning something new will be savored and honored. Sixth, we hope you will read aloud to your students each and every day, selecting from their favorite books, or their suggested books, or some good literature you want to introduce. Finally, we hope children will be given ample opportunity to share their own personal reading experiences with others, to suggest books to each other, and to write, when they wish, about their personal reading experiences.

## *Sharing Personal Reading: Its Importance*

Children are often very excited and proud of their personal reading choices and accomplishments. Some children relish what they have learned about, others relish "how many" books they have read, and others relish a particular story, character, or plot they came across in their personal reading. Sharing this excitement and these savored reading experiences is an extremely healthy way to achieve the goals of personal reading development. By sharing personal reading, children, (1) catch each other's enthusiasm about reading, (2) become interested in someone else's books, topics, and/or authors, and, (3) learn that reading can truly be a pleasure.

Of course, secondary benefits, which may really be primary benefits to other areas of your curriculum, are involved. During this sharing, students are often also enhancing their oral language skills, vocabulary skills, summarizing skills, analytic skills, critical skills, reporting skills, listening skills, writing skills, and, of course, their schemata in a wide variety of topics and areas.

## *Sharing Personal Reading: How To*

Personal reading can be shared in a variety of ways. Although we will suggest several, we hope that as you begin to read this section, you will already have thought of many of your own ideas. Nevertheless, here are some possibilities; we know you will be able to expand and embellish each of these to fit your own style, perspective, philosophy, classroom, and students.

1. *Sharing through discussion.* Students can form small literature circles or discussion and sharing groups to discuss one or more books each week or as often as possible for them. You will need to allow the group to pace itself based on the students' selections and available times. The Roser and Martinez (1995) book is especially recommended to help you with "book talk" ideas and to facilitate "book talk" discussions.

2. *Sharing through writing.* Students can keep response journals or literature logs of their personal readings. As suggested in another chapter, many literacy educators suggest these types of journals or logs as a means of creating opportunities for students to reflect on and react to books they have read (see Hancock 1993.)

   Students can also be encouraged to respond to "suggested" questions like the following: What did you like best about this book?, How does this book fulfill your expectations about it?, and Are there any particular ideas you'd like to discuss that relate to this book? Teachers can ask students to share their responses to these questions, or any other reflections students would like to share about a book, with the teacher and with other students through "dialogue journals." Nash (1995) has pointed out the benefits of this type of personal reflection, sharing, and ongoing dialogue through writing.

   Whatever type of journal writing you suggest for your students' use, keep in mind that the purpose of this writing is to allow students to think and feel about what they have read and give them opportunities to share these thoughts and feelings in a meaningful way for each of them (Handloff and Golden 1995).

3. *Sharing through drama, art, music, and dance.* Galda and West (1995) have suggested sharing all kinds of books through use of dramatizations. Fennessey (1995) has proposed the sharing of historical readings and enhancing understandings of these readings through use of drama, music, and dance. Zarrillo (1994) has suggested many ideas for sharing literature through various performing arts projects and through visual arts projects as well. Zarrillo's ideas include using drama, song, and dance. He also has suggested use of puppets, Readers' Theater, bulletin board displays, dioramas (three-dimensional displays), and collages (combinations of various materials, cut and pasted) to represent children's feelings about their readings. Zarrillo has noted that these sharing activities (including others, like journal writing) are excellent for including and working with learners from all diverse cultural backgrounds. Cullinan and Galda (1994) also have recommended that children make character puppets and put on their own puppet shows as a creative and fun way to share their special books with other children (p. 65).

   Following are other art, drama, and music/dance ideas we have used and particularly like. Children can create whole wall murals displaying the most interesting and exciting characters and parts of their favorite books. Students can pantomime representations of their favorite books and play "book charades," where children get to act out book titles and plots and other students must guess which book they are representing. Children can develop a musical background for their special books, creating a tape of mood or action music to go with the reading of a book, or with special parts. Finally, children can create dances to show the relationship of characters in their favorite books or to show the passage of time or special events. Obviously, different kinds of sharing and different drama, art, and music/dance options are more appropriate to some books than to others. Some children also prefer using certain mediums over others. Children should always be free to share in ways they feel are most appropriate to their particular books and their particular preferences. Also, if children do not want to share, they have the right to not do so. Again these should all be personal choices for personal reading.

4. *Sharing through recommendations.* Students may want to make recommendations about books they have read and share these with others in their class. These recommendations can be done orally or in writing. For instance, we have seen classrooms where students do "bookselling" fairs, displaying and "selling" the reading of their favorite books to one another. Or some teachers suggest that students write their recommendations about a book and put it on a card in the book jacket or pocket so that other students will have opportunities to review their peers' recommendations before selecting a book.

5. *Sharing through annotations.* Students can develop their own, or group, or whole-class annotated bibliographies. Students could develop lists providing the full citations of a book followed by a short summary. These lists can be done topically to create a continuous source of available readings categorized by interest area or topics for the use of other students, the teacher, and the teacher's future classes. If you have a computer available for your classroom, the students could use a database program (e.g., MicroSoft Works or AppleWorks) to compile, store, and manipulate their annotations by author, topic, and interest among other variables. Both you and interested students could then be given a hard copy of the book annotations available and stored on the database on particular interest areas and topics.

## Reflection Activity 9.7

*H*ow would you give children the message that "reading is a pleasure"? How would you encourage children to share their special books to give them the message that "what you think counts and is important," while also stimulating other children to want to read these special books? Please share your thoughts and ideas to these questions in your journal under the heading Reflection Activity 9.7.

The next section discusses the foundations of personal reading (or the "umbrella handle" as depicted in our Figure 9.1): culture, family, and community. This foundation is the greatest influence on children's personal reading motivations and pursuits. Because of this, it is extremely important for teachers to understand these influences and work with parents/families and the community to connect the personal reading development we are attempting to do in school with children's real lives and cultures outside of school.

# Culture, Family, and Community Connections

To a great extent, teachers control the activities and "climate" of personal reading endeavors in school. The teacher's encouragement, praise, and presence is often a catalyst for some children who may not otherwise participate. However, the personal reading that students engage in outside of school is a different matter. To ensure that personal reading development efforts are maximized for each child in your classroom, the teacher must take certain steps to make very necessary and important culture, family, and community connections both in and out of the classroom. In this part of the chapter, each of these connections is discussed.

## Cultural Connections

The professional literature abounds with books, research, and discussions emphasizing the importance of children's culture and diverse backgrounds and how these must be used to plan instruction and learning activities for children (e.g., Block and Zinke 1995; Cárdenas 1995; Díaz-Rico and Weed 1995; Grossman 1995; Lewis 1996; Tiedt and Tiedt 1995; Wlodkowski and Ginsberg 1995; and Zarrillo 1994). Of course, development of students' personal reading is a part of all of this.

Throughout this text, and this chapter, we have emphasized the importance of meeting the needs, motivations, interests, and language diversities of all learners. Here we want to reemphasize this and ask you to consider the following culturally responsive teaching conditions, as developed and depicted by Wlodkowski and Ginsberg (1995) and as further developed and then summarized by us.

1. *Teachers must find ways of including all students in the learning activity.* (This means facilitative teachers must emphasize the human purpose of what is being learned and relate it to students' personal experience. They can do this by engaging students in cooperative and collaborative learning; treating all students equally and with respect; and using approaches that facilitate the learning of diverse students, including writing groups, peer teaching, cooperative learning, and ways of sharing that can include art, drama, music/dance, and other personal-choice ways of demonstrating learning.)

2. *Teachers must find ways of developing the positive attitudes of all students.* (This means facilitative teachers must relate teaching to students' experiences, motivations, interests, and previous knowledge. Students must be encouraged to make choices in content and the methods of evaluating their work that fit their experiences, values, needs, and strengths. Teachers must be flexible in teaching styles, allow for individualization of learning, and accept students' developing understandings and skills. Approaches that can facilitate these positive attitudes include learning contracts, experiential learning, informal authentic assessments, and teaching to the interests and motivations of all learners.)

Facilitative teachers plan learning and reading opportunities to meet the needs, motivations, interests, and the language and cultural diversities of all learners—making cultural, family, and community connections whenever possible.
© Elizabeth Crews/The Image Works

3. *Teachers must find ways of enhancing meaning for all students.* (This means facilitative teachers must provide appropriate learning experiences that will challenge students to use higher-order thinking and critical inquiry. Teachers must address the real issues and real concerns of the world in which we live and relate those to the smaller but important world of each student. Reflections and discussions, classroom dialogue, and sharing of ideas are to be encouraged. Teachers must provide students with meaningful books, texts, and materials for reading, written in meaningful language, and with relevant and meaningful assignments. Approaches that can facilitate the enhancement of meaning include critical questioning, metacognitive probing, students' decision making, experimental inquiry, students' research, and project-type of learning.)

4. *Teachers must find ways of encouraging the competence of all students.* (This means facilitative teachers must use appropriate, multiple, and authentic assessments to find out about students' strategies and skills. Teachers must then build on those existing strategies and skills to help students develop other strategies that are necessary for success in school and society. Assessments and instruction must be connected with students' desires to succeed and accomplish. Teachers must accept and appreciate differences, and appreciate growth when it takes place. And students must be given opportunities to reflect on and self-assess their

own work and progress. Approaches that can facilitate the encouraging of competence include portfolio assessment, authentic assessment, self-assessment, individual conferences and feedback, narrative evaluations as opposed to "grades," and individualized instruction.)

It is obvious that to be a culturally responsive teacher you will need to understand students' cultures and backgrounds. For this understanding to take place, you will need to meet with, work with, and learn from the students' parents and families. They, and the students themselves, are your greatest resource for assessing and successfully working with each child. The next section explores some parent/family connection ideas that we hope will help you facilitate the development of every child's personal reading.

### Parent/Family Connections

The importance of working with students' parents and families is well recognized. Many reading professionals have published books and other ideas emphasizing these important connections (e.g., Morrow 1995; Rasinski 1995; Shockley 1994; and Shockley, Michalove, and Allen 1995). Working with parents/families now involves much more than just having parent conferences, or sending letters home. Today when we talk about making parent/family connections and working with parents/families, we are usually talking about collaborating with parents/families, learning about their child from them, and involving parents/families in children's assessment and instruction decisions. For instance, Flippo (1997) has devised questions and ideas for gathering information from parents about their child's literacy development and strategies and their family literacy practices. She has also suggested ways of involving parents/families in three-way reciprocal conferences (parent, child, and teacher), with each member having equal say-so and power, to assess progress and plan future outcomes. Additionally, Flippo has expanded and discussed ideas for sharing report card evaluations and home-school communications. This kind of parent/family involvement in assessment and instruction and continuous collaboration can foster the development of students' personal reading.

Parents and other family members must know that they play an essential role in their child's literacy and personal reading development. You need the connection with them, because parents' attitudes about reading can affect children's attitudes toward reading (Shockley 1994). Parents need to know what is going on in the school curricula and how they can be involved and help their child to learn (Flippo and Smith 1990). Parents also can be encouraged to help their child find literature that meets their child's interests, desires, and needs. They can take part in their child's personal reading development by sharing literature with their child, and encouraging special times each evening for family reading opportunities. Parents also can be encouraged to read aloud to their children of all ages. Flippo (1982) has recommended the following step-by-step approach for parents/family members on how to read a book to their child. You might consider sharing this information with parents, and if possible, demonstrating it for them in your classroom.

## How to Read a Book to Your Child

Reading a book to your child should be a pleasant experience for both of you, a time you and your child can relish together. Use the following list of steps only as a guide to help you and your child develop your own unique way of sharing books.

1. Carefully select a book for your child from a selection of good children's books.
   Or select several books and let the child choose one from the group.
   Or allow your child to independently select a book.
   (It is probably best to alternate your methods of selecting a book to be read from the three ways above.)
2. Talk about the book before you begin to read it so that your youngster knows the title, is familiar with the cover, and has been told the author's name. This will allow the child to anticipate the book. This will also help the child realize that someone wrote the book and that a book is someone else's thoughts, ideas, and talk written down.
3. Read the book to your child, stopping often to point at or talk about different things in the pictures, according to the child's interests.
4. As you read the book, ask questions that your child can answer by looking for clues in the pictures or making inferences from what has already been read. Allow your child time to answer, and praise your child's comments whenever possible. If you disagree with the answer, ask your youngster about it. If the answer is not at all applicable, talk about other possible answers to the same question. Be careful not to say "That's wrong," "You didn't understand," or "No, that's not right."
5. After you have read the book, talk about things in the book with which your child is familiar, or things in which the child is interested. Encourage your youngster to talk about the book.
6. Occasionally, allow your child an opportunity to illustrate a favorite part of the book after you have finished reading it. Sometimes let the child verbalize the theme of the book to you as you write down the child's exact words; then display them with the picture.
7. Very often your child will want to read a favorite book to you. Allow this whenever possible. Do not correct errors. The child is not reading words but is retelling the story from memory. This gives you a chance to observe the progress of your child's oral language and memory development. This practice and opportunity will be very good, providing that you are supportive and don't turn this into a *reading lesson*. (From *How to Help Grow a Reader* by Rona F. Flippo, 1982.)

Teachers planning to involve parents and families in their children's personal reading development might want to consider the following relevant ideas. Goodman and Haussler (1986) suggested beliefs that still serve as a facilitative point of reference from which to proceed:

1. All families offer children knowledge of reading and writing—just the forms are different.
2. Having all kinds of reading and writing matter easily accessible to children is an important aspect of literacy development.
3. Attitudes expressed by family members in the home toward reading and writing have an impact on children's learning.
4. Children learn language that is meaningful and functional to them.
5. Children should not be penalized by the school for coming from a home where more practical, less literary forms of reading and writing are valued and used.
6. Children's oral language and the extension of what they already know about literacy should be the foundation on which school reading and writing programs are built.

### *Community Connections*

Transitions from home connections to community connections involve only subtle differences. Children and their families and homes are part of the larger sociocultural community in which they live. Children and their families cannot be understood if treated apart from this community.

For example, Danling, a Laotian child, and her family live in a housing complex that is composed of families representing various diverse cultures. However, a large percentage of these families do come from several Asian Pacific cultures. Danling's family is involved in activities of their church, and when time permits, they take part in neighborhood meetings, activities, and celebrations. Unfortunately, every day after school, Danling has to go home to an empty apartment. Both of her parents work two jobs and do not get home until late in the evening. However, Danling's immediate community provides for her safety and well-being in her parents' absence. In fact, Danling often eats dinner at her friend's apartment and does her homework over there. She also spends a great deal of time at another friend's house down the street. The influence and connections between Danling and her immediate community (her family, her friend Kim's family, her friend Chiang's family, her church family, and her neighborhood) are complex, but important. These connections and influences must be part of the teacher's efforts to work with Danling. Because Danling's parents are only part of her community, her teacher, Miss Jackson, works at including and involving the other community members in Danling's personal reading development whenever possible. After all, Danling spends much of her awake hours with these other community members. Their beliefs, their attitudes, and their ideas will have an influence on Danling.

Additionally, it is also helpful to view the child as a member of his or her immediate community. As a member of this community, a child often must be involved in community life, concerns, and affairs. For example, if a child's community is in a volatile area that has been feeling unsafe to the child's family and neighbors, it is likely that issues involving safety are currently very important in that community. These issues may need to also be dealt with in school if the child is to see school as part of his or her real life. These issues may become part of the child's personal reading concerns and interests and should be honored if they are.

Community connections also include community agencies, businesses, intergenerational programs, and services that can help you with your personal reading development efforts with students. For example, many community agencies are available to help with specific problems and needs. Many community businesses are delighted to get involved and help out by coming to your classroom to share ideas and materials, by donating books and materials, and by serving as a resource in various areas of expertise. Intergenerational programs can be developed between your school, or your classroom, and older community members, or perhaps even retirement homes in your community. Arrangements can be made for these senior citizens to read aloud to children in your class. Perhaps your students could also go to a nursing home and read aloud to seniors who may no longer be able to read. Community services like those provided by the public library can often supplement what your school library does not have. Take advantage of these connections and use them all you can. Also be respectful of these connections; perhaps you and your students can think of ways to help these agencies, businesses, senior citizens, and services in some way to reciprocate for the help they provide to you.

Professional books, research, and writings have been looking at these and other community connections (e.g., Flippo, Hetzel, Gribouski, and Armstrong, in press; Morrow 1995; Morrow, Tracey, and Maxwell 1995; and Rowe and Probst 1995 will provide you with a small sampling). We suggest you think about your students' communities; connections you can make with them; the resources they can bring into your classroom; and ways you can consider and weave the students' immediate community needs, values, and issues into your classroom curricula and life.

## Reflection Activity 9.8

*R*eview the sections on culture, family, and community connections. How important do you feel these are to your students' personal reading development? Why? In your reflection journal, under the heading Reflection Activity 9.8, write your ideas.

# Professional References and Resources for Locating Children's Literature

Many resources are available to teachers for help in locating children's literature and for getting professional information concerning the use of children's literature. Some of these have already been cited in this chapter and throughout this text. However, this section of the chapter pulls it all together for your future use and for ease of reference.

## Professional Organizations

Several professional organizations are actively involved in researching, promoting, listing, and providing information about children's literature. Four of these we particularly recommend for their wealth and quality of available information. The addresses of these organizations follow: American Library Association (ALA), 50 East Huron Street, Chicago, IL 60611; Children's Book Council (CBC), 568 Broadway, New York, NY 10012; International Reading Association (IRA), 800 Barksdale Road, P.O. Box 8139, Newark, DE 19714-8139; and National Council of Teachers of English (NCTE), 1111 W. Kenyon Road, Urbana, IL 61801-1096.

## Published Lists of Children's Literature

Many professional journals, other periodicals, and organizations regularly publish lists and recommendations of children's literature, including the previously cited ALA, CBC, IRA, and NCTE. In this section we provide specific information about these lists and their sources. Many of these may be available for your reference in your school or public library.

*Booklist* is published by the American Library Association (ALA) once or twice each month. It contains listings of books recommended for library purchase for both adults and children. Books that have been judged to be outstanding are noted with a star. Bibliographies on selected topics are also included.

*Book Links* is also published by ALA. This magazine provides annotated bibliographies on many topics and themes for teachers, librarians, bookstores, and others interested in children's literature, from preschool through eighth grade. Contact *Booklist* or *Book Links,* 434 W. Downer Place, Aurora, IL 60506-9936.

*The Horn Book Magazine* is published twice a month and reviews current children's books, classified by age level and subject. It also provides articles on Caldecott and Newbery award winners, reviews books in Spanish, reviews books that have recently been republished in paperback, and provides a list of "outstanding books" each year. Contact *The Horn Book,* 14 Beacon Street, Boston, MA 02108-9765.

*Journal of Children's Literature* is published twice a year by the Children's Literature Assembly, an affiliate of NCTE. Each fall issue contains that year's list of notable children's trade books. Contact the NCTE.

*The Language Arts,* a journal published by NCTE, publishes a list of notable children's books, yearly, in its October issue. Contact the NCTE.

*Multicultural Review* reviews books for children and young adults and also reviews other multicultural materials in each of its quarterly issues. Contact *Multicultural Review,* Greenwood Publishing Group, 88 Post Road West, Box 5007, Westport, CT 06881–5007.

*The New Advocate* is published four times a year, contains articles pertinent to the use of children's literature in the classroom, and also reviews new children's books and professional resources. Contact *The New Advocate,* Christopher-Gordon Publishers, 480 Washington Street, Norwood, MA 02062.

*The New York Times Book Review* devotes a fall and a spring "Book Reviews" section to children's books. Also, in November and December, it publishes selected lists of outstanding children's books. Contact *The New York Times Book Review,* 229 West 43rd Street, New York, NY 10036.

*The Reading Teacher,* a journal published by IRA, publishes "Children's Choices" each year in its October issue. This annual bibliography is a list of books (compiled by the IRA and the Children's Book Council, CBC) chosen by children as their very favorites.

Each November, *The Reading Teacher* also publishes the "Teachers' Choices" list. "Teachers' Choices" is a list of books chosen by teachers as outstanding for curriculum use. Contact the IRA for the "Children's Choices" and the "Teachers' Choices" lists.

*The School Library Journal* is published monthly, reviewing new books for children and young adults. The reviews are categorized by four age levels and under fiction and nonfiction designations. Outstanding books are rated with a star and are included in the "Best Book" list published in each December's issue. Children's books in Spanish are also reviewed. Contact *School Library Journal,* P.O. Box 1978, Marion, OH 43306–2078.

## Professional Books

Many professional books are available to the classroom teacher looking for information about and ideas for good children's literature. Next we have cited some of these sources and organized them into categories that describe their use.

## Books for Overviews of Children's Literature

These books generally provide discussions of children's literature and suggestions for children's literature in a wide variety of genres. Many of these books also include samples of children's literature, lists of award-winning books, suggested magazines for children, addresses of publishers of children's books, and other valuable resources relating to children's literature. The full citations for each of these books can be found in the references at the end of this chapter. Many of these books may be available in your college or public libraries.

Cullinan and Galda (1994) *Literature and the Child*

Huck, Hepler, Hickman, and Kiefer (1997) *Children's Literature in the Elementary School*

Lukens (1995) *A Critical Handbook of Children's Literature*

Norton (1991) *Through the Eyes of a Child: An Introduction to Children's Literature*

Rothlein and Meinbach (1996) *Legacies: Using Children's Literature in the Classroom*

Sutherland and Arbuthnot (1991) *Children and Books*

## Books for Helping Teachers Support Classroom Reading

All of the books and resources listed in this section provide help and support for developing personal reading. However, the following four books seem particularly appropriate for ideas and suggestions that would facilitate reading, discussion of reading, and a literate environment in the early childhood and elementary classroom.

Cullinan (1992) *Invitation to Read: More Children's Literature in the Reading Program*

Cullinan (1993a) *Children's Voices: Talk in the Classroom*

Roser and Martinez (1995) *Book Talk and Beyond: Children and Teachers Respond to Literature*

Slaughter (1993) *Beyond Storybooks: Young Children and the Shared Book Experience*

## Books for Nonfiction Trade Book Suggestions

These books contain many suggested ideas for using more nonfiction trade books in your classroom curriculum.

Cullinan (1993b) *Fact and Fiction: Literature Across the Curriculum*

Freeman and Person (1992) *Using Nonfiction Trade Books in the Elementary Classroom: From Ants to Zeppelins*

## Multicultural Literature Suggestions

These books contain many good ideas for using multicultural literature in your classroom, as well as suggestions for specific children's literature for a variety of diverse cultures.

Harris (1993) *Teaching Multicultural Literature*

Hayden (1992) *Venture into Cultures: A Resource Book of Multicultural Materials and Programs*

Miller-Lachmann (1992) *Our Family, Our Friends, Our World: An Annotated Guide to Significant Multicultural Books for Children and Teenagers*

Zarrillo (1994) *Multicultural Literature, Multicultural Teaching*

Additionally, several of the books listed under "Books for Overviews of Children's Literature" also include multicultural literature suggestions. Cullinan and Galda's (1994) *Literature and the Child* is particularly recommended for its extensive section on multicultural children's literature.

## Books That Provide Literature to Help Children Deal with Special Issues, Problems, and Situations

These books provide literature suggestions for children in a wide variety of special areas of concern, including divorce, death, adoption, foster care, family configurations, siblings, aging, abuse, sexuality, special needs, separation and loss, drug and substance abuse, moving, and various disabilities. Not all of these issues are dealt with in any one of these books; however, their titles will give you a fairly good idea of their coverage.

Friedberg, Mullins, and Sukiennik (1992) *Portraying Persons with Disabilities: An Annotated Bibliography of Nonfiction for Children and Teenagers*

Rasinski and Gillespie (1992) *Sensitive Issues: An Annotated Guide to Children's Literature*

Robertson (1992) *Portraying Persons with Disabilities: An Annotated Bibliography of Fiction for Children and Teenagers*

Rudman (1995) *Children's Literature: An Issues Approach*

Rudman, Gagne, and Bernstein (1994) *Books to Help Children Cope with Separation and Loss*

## Books That Suggest Books to Read Aloud

These books provide ideas for and anthologies of good books and stories to read aloud to children.

Trelease (1992) *Hey! Listen to This: Stories to Read Aloud*

Trelease (1995) *The New Read-Aloud Handbook*

## Books That Suggest Picture Books and Predictable Books for Young Children

These books suggest ideas and literature that are particularly relevant to the needs of the teacher of young children. They suggest picture books and predictable books, use of them in the classroom, and many teaching ideas.

Beaty (1994) *Picture Book Storytelling: Literature Activities for Young Children*

Cianciolo (1990) *Picture Books for Children*

Slaughter (1993) *Beyond Storybooks: Young Children and the Shared Book Experience*

Additionally, several of the books listed under "Books for Overviews of Children's Literature" also include picture books and predictable books. Cullinan and Galda's (1994) *Literature and the Child* is particularly recommended for its extensive section on picture books.

### *Magazine Suggestions for Children*

These provide a resource of information regarding available magazines and other periodicals for children.

Stroll (1994) *Magazines for Kids and Teens*

Additionally, several of the books listed under other categories often make suggestions regarding children's magazines and newspapers.

### *Favorite Book Ideas*

These books provide listings of children's favorite books to read, and teachers' favorite books to use in the curriculum.

IRA (1994) *Teachers' Favorite Books for Kids*

IRA and CBC (1992) *Kids' Favorite Books*

IRA and CBC (1995) *More Kids' Favorite Books*

### *Research and More Professional Resources*

Many of the books already suggested in other categories provide research sources for teachers, and all of the books listed in all categories are excellent professional resources. However, the following book has been particularly prepared to provide a listing of almost all the professional resources related to children's literature that anyone might need. It provides an excellent starting place for the teacher or other educators who need information and want to see a range of what is available.

Short (1995) *Research & Professional Resources in Children's Literature: Piecing a Patchwork Quilt*

## *Children's Literature Suggestions and Examples*

This section contains a sampling of suggestions for specific children's literature titles in a wide variety of special areas, and also for various age groups of children. Of course, these are but a very small sample of the available children's literature. The professional organizations, periodicals, and books listed in the preceding sections can provide you with a more complete idea of the wealth of available literature for specific areas, genres, and ages of readers. Most of the titles cited in this section were taken from the suggestions made by authors and publishers of the professional sources we have recommended (we use them, too), and from the recommendations of librarians we know. In this first listing, we pull from the recommendations of Rudman (1995) and others, to provide a few examples of books in a variety of sensitive and/or problem areas. Following that, we list other book titles that have been designated by various age groups of children as their favorites, using a number of the annual "Children's Choices" (IRA and CBC) lists for our information.

# Sensitive Issues and Children's Problems Books

## Adoption

Lifton, B. J. (1993). *Tell Me a Real Adoption Story.* New York: Alfred A. Knopf.

Rivera, G. (1976). *A Special Kind of Courage: Profiles of Young Americans.* New York: Simon & Schuster.

Wasson, V. (1977). *The Chosen Baby,* 3rd rev. ed. Philadelphia: J. B. Lippincott.

## Aging

Ackerman, K. (1990). *Just Like Max.* New York: Alfred A. Knopf.

Hickman, M. W. (1985). *When James Allen Whitaker's Grandfather Came to Stay.* Nashville, TN: Abingdon.

Leiner, K. (1987). *Between Old Friends.* New York: Franklin Watts.

Moore, E. (1988). *Grandma's Promise.* New York: Lothrop, Lee, & Shepard.

## Child Abuse

Anderson, M. Q. (1978). *Step on a Crack.* New York: Atheneum.

Hunt, I. (1976). *The Lottery Rose.* New York: Charles Scribner's Sons.

Lowery, L. (1994). *Laurie Tells.* Minneapolis, MN: Carolrhoda Books.

Roberts, W. D. (1978). *Don't Hurt Laurie!* New York: Atheneum.

## Death

Anders, R. (1978). *A Look at Death.* Minneapolis, MN: Larner.

Burch, R. (1970). *Simon and the Game of Chance.* New York: Viking.

DePaola, T. (1973). *Nana Upstairs & Nana Downstairs.* New York: G. P. Putnam's Sons.

Mellonie, B. (1983). *Lifetimes: The Beautiful Way to Explain Children.* New York: Bantam Books.

## Disabilities

Baldwin, A. M. (1978). *A Little Time.* New York: Viking.

O'Shaughnessy, E. (1992). *Somebody Called Me Retarded Today . . . And My Heart Felt Sad.* New York: Walker and Company.

Peusner, S. (1977). *Keep Stompin' Till the Music Stops.* New York: Seabury Press.

Wolf, B. (1974). *Don't Feel Sorry for Paul.* Philadelphia: J. B. Lippincott.

### Divorce

Blume, J. (1972). *It's Not the End of the World.* New York: Bantam Press.

Krementz, J. (1988). *How It Feels When Parents Divorce.* New York: Alfred A. Knopf.

Mann, P. (1978). *My Father Lives in a Downtown Hotel.* New York: Doubleday.

### Families: Single-Parent

Gilbert, S. (1982). *How to Live with a Single Parent.* New York: Lothrop, Lee, & Shepard.

Gould, D. (1988). *Brendan's Best-Timed Birthday.* New York: Bradbury.

Johnson, D. (1990). *What Will Mommy Do When I'm at School.* New York: Macmillan.

### Families: Stepparents and Stepfamilies

Boyd, L. (1987). *The Not-So-Wicked Stepmother.* New York: Viking.

MacLachlan, P. (1985). *Sarah, Plain and Tall.* New York: Harper.

Nixon, J. L. (1985). *Maggie Too.* San Diego: Harcourt Brace Jovanovich.

Park, B. (1989). *My Mother Got Married (and Other Disasters).* New York: Alfred A. Knopf.

Sobol, H. L. (1979). *My Other-Mother, My Other-Father.* New York: Macmillan.

### Families: Extended

MacLachlan, P. (1991). *Journey.* New York: Delacorte.

Shasha, M. (1992). *Night of the Moonjellies.* New York: Simon & Schuster.

Snyder, Z. K. (1990). *Libby on Wednesday.* New York: Delacorte.

Whelan, G. (1992). *Bringing the Farmhouse Home.* New York: Simon & Schuster.

Williams, V. B. (1982). *A Chair for My Mother.* New York: Greenwillow.

### Fear

Berkey, B., and V. Berkey. (1978). *Robbers, Bones, and Mean Dogs.* Reading, MA: Addison-Wesley.

Clyne, P. E. (1977). *Tunnels of Terror.* Boston: Atlantic Monthly Press.

Mayer, M. (1991). *You're the Scaredy-Cat.* Roxbury, CT: Rainbird Press.

McCloskey, R. (1952). *One Morning in Maine.* New York: Viking.

## Gender Roles

Gauch, P. L. (1971). *Christina Katerina & the Box.* New York: Coward-McCann.

Hilton, N. (1990). *The Long Red Scarf.* Minneapolis, MN: Carolrhoda.

Isadora, R. (1980). *My Ballet Class.* New York: Greenwillow.

MacLachlan, P. (1979). *The Sick Day.* New York: Pantheon.

McPherson, S. S. (1992). *I Speak for the Women: A Story About Lucy Stone.* Minneapolis, MN: Carolrhoda.

## Heritage

Allison, D. W. (1992). *This Is the Key to the Kingdom.* Boston: Little, Brown.

Ancona, G. (1993). *Powwow.* San Diego: Harcourt Brace Jovanovich.

Bang, M. (1985). *The Paper Crane.* New York: Greenwillow.

Bryan, A. (1989). *Turtle Knows Your Name.* New York: Atheneum.

Hurwitz, J. (1980). *Once I Was a Plum Tree.* New York: Morrow.

Lawrence J. (1993). *The Great Migration.* New York: Harper.

## Hospitalization

Howe, J. (1994). *The Hospital Book.* New York: Morrow.

Rey, M., and H. A. Rey. (1966). *Curious George Goes to the Hospital.* Boston: Houghton Mifflin.

Sobol, H. L. (1975). *Jeff's Hospital Book.* New York: Henry Z. Walck.

## Love

Graham, J. (1976). *I Love You, Mouse.* San Diego, CA: Harcourt Brace Jovanovich.

Sonneborn, R. (1970). *Friday Night Is Papa Night.* New York: Viking.

Viscardi, H. (1975). *The Phoenix Child: A Story of Love.* Middlebury, VT: Paul S. Eriksson.

## Self-Awareness

Ardizzone, E. (1970). *The Wrong Side of the Bed.* New York: Doubleday.

Carlson, N. (1988). *I Like Me.* New York: Viking.

Hooks, W. H. (1977). *Doug Meets the Nutcracker.* New York: Frederick Warne.

Lee, H. A. (1978). *Seven Feet Four and Growing.* Philadelphia: Westminster.

### Sibling Rivalry

Alexander, M. G. (1975). *I'll Be the Horse if You'll Play with Me*. New York: Dial.

Dragonwagon, C. (1983). *I Hate My Brother Harry*. New York: Harper.

Hazen, B. S. (1979). *If It Weren't for Benjamin*. New York: Human Science Press.

Lexau, J. M. (1972). *Emily and the Klunky Baby and the Next Door Dog*. New York: Dial.

Zolotow, C. (1966). *If It Weren't for You*. New York: Harper & Row.

### Twins

Aliki. (1986). *Jack and Jake*. New York: Greenwillow.

Cleary, B. (1967). *Mitch and Amy*. New York: Morrow.

Fair, S. (1982). *The Bedspread*. New York: Morrow.

## *Children's Favorite Books*

Children like books for various valid reasons. In one study, conducted by Wilson and Abrahamson (1988), fifth-grade students were asked about their favorite classic books. They rated and ranked the following classics as their favorites: *Charlotte's Web; Little House in the Big Woods; The Secret Garden; The Hobbit; The Lion, the Witch, and the Wardrobe; Heidi; The Borrowers;* and *The Moffats*. When asked why *Charlotte's Web* was their highest ranked book, they indicated because (1) it was a fantasy but it was made to seem very real; (2) it was personal and it evoked an emotional response from them; (3) they loved the animal characters; and (4) they liked the author's style.

In the listings that follow, we provide you with some book titles for various age groups that children in those age groups have selected as their favorites. These titles were taken from several years of "Children's Choices" compiled and published by IRA and CBC. For full listings of each year's favorite children's books, consult the October issues of *The Reading Teacher*.

### For All Ages of Readers

*Amanda's Perfect Hair* (1993) by L. Milstein. New York: Philomel.

*Belly's Deli* (1993) by R. L. Shafner and E. J. Weisberg. Minneapolis, MN: Lerner.

*The Best School Year Ever* (1994) by B. Robinson. New York: HarperCollins.

*Chicken Sunday* (1992) by P. Polacco. New York: Philomel.

*Christmas in July* (1991) retold by W. Wegman with C. Kismaric and M. Heiferman. New York: Hyperion.

*The Grizzly Bear Family Book* (1994) by M. Hoshino. New York: North-South Books.

*It Was a Dark and Stormy Night* (1991) by K. Moseley. New York: Dial.

*Martha Speaks* (1992) by S. Meddaugh. Boston: Houghton Mifflin.

*Mistakes That Worked* (1991) by C. F. Jones. New York: Doubleday.

*Monster Mama* (1993) by L. Rosenberg. New York: Philomel.

*Not the Piano, Mrs. Medley!* (1991) by E. Levine. New York: Orchard.

*Somebody Catch My Homework* (1993) by D. L. Harrison. Honesdale, PA: Boyd's Mills Press.

*Somebody Loves You, Mr. Hatch* (1991) by E. Spinelli. New York: Bradbury.

*When I Was Your Age* (1991) by K. Adams. Hauppauge, NY: Barron's.

*The Willow Pattern Story* (1992) by A. Drummond. New York: North-South Books.

## For Beginning Independent Readers

*Big Pumpkin* (1992) by E. Silvermann. New York: Macmillan.

*Clifford the Firehouse Dog* (1994) by N. Bridwell. New York: Scholastic.

*Draw Me a Star* (1992) by E. Carle. New York: Philomel.

*Easy to See Why* (1993) by F. Gwynne. New York: Simon & Schuster.

*Five Little Monkeys Sitting in a Tree* (1991) by E. Christelow. New York: Clarion.

*The Giant Zucchini* (1993) by C. Siracusa. New York: Hyperion.

*The Great Snake Escape* (1994) by M. Coxe. New York: HarperCollins.

*How Do You Say It Today, Jesse Bear?* (1992) by N. W. Carlstrom. New York: Macmillan.

*King Kenrick's Splinter* (1994) by S. Derby. New York: Walker & Co.

*Matthew's Dream* (1991) by L. Lionni. New York: Alfred A. Knopf.

*Monkey Soup* (1992) by L. Sachar. New York: Alfred A. Knopf.

*Sheep in a Shop* (1991) by N. Shaw. Boston: Houghton Mifflin.

*Trade-in Mother* (1993) by M. Russo. New York: Greenwillow.

*When I Was Little: A Four-Year-Old's Memoir of Her Youth* (1993) by J. L. Curtis. New York: HarperCollins.

*The Winter Duckling* (1990) by K. Polette. St. Louis, MO: Milliken Publishing.

## For Younger Readers (ages 5–8)

*An Alligator Named . . . Alligator* (1991) by L. G. Grambling. Hauppauge, NY: Barron's.

*Andrew's Amazing Monsters* (1993) by K. H. Berlan. New York: Atheneum.

*Arthur's Family Vacation* (1993) by M. Brown. Boston: Little, Brown.

*Benjamin Bigfoot* (1993) by M. Serfozo. New York: McElderry Books.

*Captain Abolul's Pirate School* (1994) by C. McNaughton. Cambridge, MA: Candlewick Press.

*Courtney* (1994) by J. Burningham. New York: Crown.

*Dogs Don't Wear Sneakers* (1993) by L. Numeroff. New York: Simon & Schuster.

*Don't Wake Up Mama! Another Five Little Monkeys Story* (1992) by E. Christelow. New York: Clarion Books.

*Dragon's Fat Cat* (1992) by D. Pilkey. New York: Orchard.

*Earthquake in the Third Grade* (1993) by L. Myers. New York: Clarion.

*Miss Spider's Tea Party* (1994) by D. Kirk. New York: Scholastic.

*Mona the Vampire* (1991) by S. Holleyman. New York: Delacorte.

*Mrs. Katz and Tush* (1992) by P. Polacco. New York: Dell.

*Mucky Moose* (1991) by J. Allen. New York: Macmillan.

*The Night I Followed the Dog* (1994) by N. Laden. San Francisco: Chronicle Books.

### For Middle-Grade Elementary Readers (ages 8–10)

*Alice in April* (1993) by P. R. Naylor. New York: Atheneum.

*Best Enemies Again* (1991) by K. Leverich. New York: Greenwillow.

*Best Friends* (1993) by E. Reuter. Cedarhurst, NY: Yellow Brick Road/ Pitspopany Press.

*Doesn't Fall Off His Horse* (1994) by V. A. Stroud. New York: Dial.

*Fourth Grade Rats* (1991) by J. Spinelli. New York: Scholastic.

*The Ghost of Popcorn Hill* (1993) by B. R. Wright. New York: Holiday House.

*The High Rise Glorious Skittle Skat Roarious Sky Pie Angel Food Cake* (1990) by N. Willard. San Diego: Harcourt Brace.

*Jesse Owens: Olympic Star* (1992) by P. McKissack and F. McKissack. Hillside, NJ: Enslow Publishers.

*The Last Princess: The Story of Princess Ka'iulani of Hawai'i* (1991) by F. Stanley. New York: Four Winds.

*The Librarian Who Measured the Earth* (1994) by K. Lasky. Boston: Little, Brown.

*Meet Addy* (1993) by C. Porter. Middleton, WI: Pleasant Company.

*Muggie Maggie* (1991) by B. Cleary. New York: William Morrow.

*The River* (1991) by G. Paulsen. New York: Delacorte.

*Storm* (1993) by J. Wood. New York: Thomson Learning.

*The Wretched Stone* (1991) by C. Van Allsburg. Boston: Houghton Mifflin.

**For Upper-Grade Readers (ages 10–13)**

*Alone in the House* (1991) by E. Plante. New York: Avon.

*Crosstown* (1993) by K. Makris. New York: Avon.

*Dogs Don't Tell Jokes* (1991) by L. Sachar. New York: Alfred A. Knopf.

*The Face on the Milk Carton* (1990) by C. B. Cooney. New York: Bantam Books.

*Finding Buck McHenry* (1991) by A. Slote. New York: HarperCollins.

*Flip-Flop Girl* (1994) by K. Paterson. New York: Lodestar Books.

*Ghost Brother* (1990) by C. S. Adler. New York: Clarion Books.

*Ghost Stories* (1993) Compiled by R. Westall. Las Vegas, NV: Kingfisher Books.

*The Giver* (1993) by L. Lowry. Boston: Houghton Mifflin.

*L. Frank Baum: Royal Historian of Oz* (1992) by A. S. Carpenter and J. Shirley. Minneapolis, MN: Lerner Publications.

*Letting Swift River Go* (1992) by J. Yolen. Boston: Little, Brown.

*Mama, Let's Dance* (1991) by P. Hermes. Boston: Little, Brown.

*Nightjohn* (1993) by G. Paulsen. New York: Delacorte/Bantam Doubleday Dell.

*Rosa Parks: My Story* (1990) by R. Parks with J. Haskins. New York: Dial.

*What Daddy Did* (1991) by N. Shusterman. Boston: Little, Brown.

Finally, we want to point out that approximately 125 different awards are given each year for children's books (Cullinan and Galda 1994). These awards include the Newbery Medal, Caldecott Medal, Boston Globe-Horn Book Awards, IRA Children's Book Award, and many others. Each one of these awards uses its own selection process with some selected by children, some by adults, and some by international and/or local or regional groups. Cullinan and Galda indicate that a comprehensive listing of the various award winners is provided in *Children's Books: Awards and Prizes,* updated and published periodically by the Children's Book Council (e.g., see the 1992 publication cited in the References of this chapter). The latest publication of this material should be available in your school or public library for your use and reference.

## *Summary*

This chapter has provided you with our definition of personal reading, which involves students' self-motivated behavior to select and read from materials in areas that can include their current interests, new and developing interests, recreational readings, academic interests, practical purposes, and pursuits of pleasure. To promote the personal reading development of each student, we have provided you with ideas concerning use of interest and other relevant questions, as well as discussions about ways that teachers can use students' interests and purposes within their curriculum and overall classroom planning.

We have emphasized that each aspect of personal reading is important and that the reading of all "good taste" as well as "good literature" is to be valued. The development of each student's personal reading can be enhanced when the child's culture, family, and community are all considered and respected.

Finally, we have provided you with a listing of professional references and resources to assist you in your search for good taste literature and good literature that meets your students' interests, needs, and purposes. We have also provided a sampling of children's literature suggestions taken from a few of these professional resources, just to give you some idea of what is available.

We hope you have seen that students' personal reading pursuits can often be applied to the elementary curriculum and classroom in interesting and motivating ways. However, we also hope you will remember that personal reading must always involve students' self-motivation and self-selection and should not ever be forced. Remember, the aesthetic stance involves students' desire to read, pleasure with the particular reading, and anticipation of additional pleasure with additional readings.

## *Closing Activities*

1. In a small group, share your ideas about personal reading with others taking this course. Refer to your responses to the reflection activities in this chapter.
2. Interview two or three teachers and ask them how they define "personal reading," and what aspects they feel personal reading includes.
3. Ask one or two elementary students all or some selected questions from the interest inventory found in Appendix A of this book. Question students orally and individually, recording their responses. Share and discuss your findings with others taking this course.
4. How important are students' feelings, perceptions, and beliefs regarding reading? Why? In a small group, share your views with others taking this course.
5. As part of your field experience for this course, try using SSR with a classroom of children for several weeks. Share your observations and reactions with peers taking this course.
6. As part of your field experience for this course, select a narrative children's book appropriate for the class you are working with and appropriate to the cultural diversity and interests of the students. Read the selected book to a small or large group. Encourage "book talk" and other related discussion. Write a summary describing the results of this activity and share it with your peers.
7. In a small group, discuss how teachers could most successfully weave personal reading into their total curriculum and classroom activities.
8. How do you feel teachers can best foster, cultivate, and use children's cultural, family, and community connections as part of their personal reading development? In a small group, share your ideas with others taking this course.

### *References*

Allington, R. L. (1994). "The Schools We Have. The Schools We Need." *The Reading Teacher* 48:14–29.

Alvermann, D. E., and J. T. Guthrie. (1993). "Themes and Directions of the National Reading Research Center." *Perspectives in Reading Research* 1:1–11.

Anderson, R. C., E. H. Hiebert, J. A. Scott, and I. A. G. Wilkinson. (1985). *Becoming a Nation of Readers: The Report of the Commission on Reading.* Washington, DC: The National Institute of Education.

Beaty, J. J. (1994). *Picture Book Storytelling.* Fort Worth, TX: Harcourt Brace College Publishers.

Block, C. C., and J. A. Zinke. (1995). *Creating a Culturally Enriched Curriculum for Grades K-6.* Boston: Allyn & Bacon.

Brown, H., and B. Cambourne. (1987). *Read and Retell.* Portsmouth, NH: Heinemann.

Cárdenas, J. A. (1995). *Multicultural Education: A Generation of Advocacy.* Needham Heights, MA: Simon & Schuster.

*Children's Books: Awards and Prizes.* (1992). New York: The Children's Book Council.

Cianciolo, P. J. (1990). *Picture Books for Children,* 3rd ed. Chicago: American Library Association.

Cramer, E. H., and M. Castle, eds. (1994). *Fostering the Love of Reading: The Affective Domain in Reading Education.* Newark, DE: International Reading Association.

Crawford, K., G. Crowell, G. Kauffman, B. Peterson, L. Phillips, J. Schroeder, C. Giorgis, and K. G. Short. (1994). "Finding Ourselves as People and as Learners." *The Reading Teacher* 48:64-74.

Cullinan, B. E., ed. (1992). *Invitation to Read: More Children's Literature in the Reading Program.* Newark, DE: International Reading Association.

———. (1993a). *Children's Voices: Talk in the Classroom.* Newark, DE: International Reading Association.

———. (1993b). *Fact and Fiction: Literature Across the Curriculum.* Newark, DE: International Reading Association.

Cullinan, B. E., and L. Galda. (1994). *Literature and the Child,* 3rd ed. Fort Worth, TX: Harcourt Brace College Publishers.

Daisey, P. (1993). "Three Ways to Promote the Values and Uses of Literacy at Any Age." *Journal of Reading* 36:436-440.

Díaz-Rico, L. T., and K. Z. Weed. (1995). *The Crosscultural, Language, and Academic Development Handbook.* Boston: Allyn & Bacon.

Fader, D. N., and E. B. McNeil. (1968). *Hooked on Books: Programs and Proof.* New York: G. P. Putnam's Sons.

Farris, P. J. (1997). *Language Arts: Process, Product, and Assessment,* 2nd ed. Madison, WI: Brown & Benchmark Publishers.

Fennessey, S. (1995). "Living History through Drama and Literature." *The Reading Teacher* 49 (1): 16-19.

Flippo, R. F. (1982). *How to Help Grow a Reader.* Atlanta, GA: Metro Atlanta/Georgia State University Chapter Phi Delta Kappa. Reprinted by Fitchburg State College, Fitchburg, MA.

———. (1997). *Reading Assessment and Instruction: A Qualitative Approach to Diagnosis.* Fort Worth, TX: Harcourt Brace College Publishers.

Flippo, R. F., C. W. Hetzel, D. Gribouski, and L. A. Armstrong. (in press). "Literacy, Multicultural, and Socio-Cultural Considerations: Student Literacy Corps and the Community." *Phi Delta Kappan.*

Flippo, R. F., and J. A. Smith. (1990). "Encouraging Parent Involvement through Home Letters." *The Reading Teacher* 44 (4): 359.

Fox, M. (1993). "Politics and Literature: Chasing the 'Isms' from Children's Books." *The Reading Teacher* 46:654-658.

France, M. G., and J. M. Hager. (1993). "Recruit, Respect, Respond: A Model for Working with Low-Income Families and their Preschoolers." *The Reading Teacher* 46:568-572.

Freeman, E. B., and D. G. Person, eds. (1992). *Using Nonfiction Trade Books in the Elementary Classroom: From Ants to Zeppelins.* Urbana, IL: National Council of Teachers of English.

Friedberg, J. G., J. B. Mullins, and A. W. Sukiennik. (1992). *Portraying Persons with Disabilities: An Annotated Bibliography of Nonfiction for Children and Teenagers.* New Providence, NJ: R. R. Bowker.

Galda, L., and J. West. (1992). "Enriching Our Lives: The Humanities in Children's Literature." *The Reading Teacher* 45:536-545.

———. (1995). "Exploring Literature through Drama." In N. L. Roser and M. G. Martinez, eds., *Book Talk and Beyond: Children and Teachers Respond to Literature* (pp. 183-190). Newark, DE: International Reading Association.

Gersten, R., and R. T. Jiménez. (1994). "A Delicate Balance: Enhancing Literature Instruction for Students of English as a Second Language." *The Reading Teacher* 47:438–449.

Gillespie, C. S., J. L. Powell, N. E. Clements, and R. A. Swearingen. (1994). "A Look at the Newbery Medal Books from a Multicultural Perspective." *The Reading Teacher* 48(1): 40–50.

Goodman, Y. M., and M. M. Haussler. (1986). "Literacy Environment in the Home and Community." In D. R. Tovey and J. E. Kerber, eds., *Roles in Literacy Learning* (pp. 26–32). Newark, DE: International Reading Association.

Goodman, Y. M., D. J. Watson, and C. L. Burke. (1987). *Reading Miscue Inventory: Alternative Procedures.* Katonah, NY: Richard C. Owen Publishers.

Grossman, H. (1995). *Teaching in a Diverse Society.* Boston: Allyn & Bacon.

Guthrie, J. T. (1994). "Creating Interest in Reading." *Reading Today* 12 (1): 24.

Hancock, M. R. (1993). "Exploring and Extending Personal Response through Literature Journals." *The Reading Teacher* 46(6): 466–474.

Handloff, E., and J. M. Golden. (1995). "Writing as a Way of 'Getting to' What You Think and Feel About a Story." In N. L. Roser and M. G. Martinez, eds., *Book Talk and Beyond: Children and Teachers Respond to Literature* (pp. 201–207). Newark, DE: International Reading Association.

Harris, V. J., ed. (1993). *Teaching Multicultural Literature in Grades K–8.* Norwood, MA: Christopher-Gordon Publishers.

Hayden, C. D., ed. (1992). *Venture into Cultures: A Resource Book of Multicultural Materials and Programs.* Chicago: American Library Association.

Henk, W. A., and S. A. Melnick. (1995). "The Reader Self-Perception Scale (RSPS): A New Tool for Measuring How Children Feel about Themselves as Readers." *The Reading Teacher* 48 (6): 470–482.

Hennings, D. G. (1994). *Communication in Action: Teaching the Language Arts,* 5th ed. Boston: Houghton Mifflin.

Hoffman, J. V., N. L. Roser, and J. Battle. (1993). "Reading Aloud in the Classroom: From the Modal to a 'Model.'" *The Reading Teacher* 46:496–503.

Huck, C. S., S. Hepler, J. Hickman, and B. Kiefer. (1997). *Children's Literature in the Elementary School,* 6th ed. Madison, WI: Brown & Benchmark Publishers.

International Reading Association. (1994). *Teachers' Favorite Books for Kids.* Newark, DE: International Reading Association.

International Reading Association and Children's Book Council. (1992). *Kids' Favorite Books: Children's Choices 1989–1991.* Newark, DE: International Reading Association.

———. (1995). *More Kids' Favorite Books.* Newark, DE: International Reading Association.

Leal, D. J. (1993). "The Power of Literacy Peer Group Discussions: How Children Collaboratively Negotiate Meaning." *The Reading Teacher* 47:114–120.

Lewis, M. (1996). *Using Student-Centered Methods with Teacher-Centered ESL Students.* Portsmouth, NH: Heinemann.

Lukens, R. J. (1995). *A Critical Handbook of Children's Literature,* 5th ed. New York: HarperCollins College Publishers.

Many, J. E., D. L. Wiseman, and J. L. Altieri. (1996). "Exploring the Influences of Literature Approaches on Children's Stance When Responding and Their Response Complexity." *Reading Psychology* 17(1): 1–41.

McGill-Franzen, A. (1993). "'I Could Read the Words!': Selecting Good Books for Inexperienced Readers." *The Reading Teacher* 46:424–426.

McKenna, M. C., and D. J. Kear. (1990). "Measuring Attitude Toward Reading: A New Tool for Teachers." *The Reading Teacher* 43 (9): 626–639.

Miller-Lachmann, L. (1992). *Our Family Our Friends Our World: An Annotated Guide to Significant Multicultural Books for Children and Teenagers.* New Providence, NJ: R. R. Bowker.

Morrow, L. M., ed. (1995). *Family Literacy: Connections in Schools and Communities.* Newark, DE: International Reading Association.

Morrow, L. M., and E. A. Sharkey. (1993). "Motivating Independent Reading and Writing in the Primary Grades through Social Cooperative Literary Experiences." *The Reading Teacher* 47:162–165.

Morrow, L. M., D. H. Tracey, and C. M. Maxwell, eds. (1995). *A Survey of Family Literacy in the United States.* Newark, DE: International Reading Association.

Nash, M. F. (1995). " 'Leading from Behind': Dialogue Response Journals." In N. L. Roser and M. G. Martinez, eds., *Book Talk and Beyond: Children and Teachers Respond to Literature* (pp. 217–225). Newark, DE: International Reading Association.

Norton, D. E. (1991). *Through the Eyes of a Child: An Introduction to Children's Literature,* 3rd ed. New York: Macmillan.

Ouzts, D. T. (1994). "Bibliotherapeutic Literature: A Key Facet of Whole Language Instruction for the At-Risk Student." *Reading Horizons* 35 (2): 161–175.

Prill, P. (1994/1995). "Helping Children Use the Classroom Library." *The Reading Teacher* 48:365.

Rasinski, T. V., ed. (1995). *Parents and Teachers: Helping Children Learn to Read and Write.* Fort Worth, TX: Harcourt Brace College Publishers.

Rasinski, T. V., and C. S. Gillespie. (1992). *Sensitive Issues: An Annotated Guide to Children's Literature K–6.* Phoenix, AZ: Oryx Press.

Robertson, D. (1992). *Portraying Persons with Disabilities: An Annotated Bibliography of Fiction for Children and Teenagers,* 3rd ed. New Providence, NJ: R. R. Bowker.

Roginski, J., ed. (1992). *Newbery and Caldecott Medalists and Honor Book Winners.* New York: Neal-Schuman.

Rosenblatt, L. (1978). *The Reader, the Text, the Poem: The Transactional Theory of the Literary Work.* Carbondale, IL: Southern Illinois University Press.

———. (1985). "The Transactional Theory of the Literary Work." In C. R. Cooper, ed., *Researching Response to Literature and the Teaching of Literature* (pp. 33–53). Norwood, NJ: Ablex.

———. (1989). "Writing and Reading: The Transactional Theory." In J. M. Mason, ed., *Reading and Writing Connections* (pp. 153–176). Boston: Allyn & Bacon.

———. (1991). "Literature—S.O.S.!" *Language Arts* 68:444–448.

Roser, N. L., and M. G. Martinez, eds. (1995). *Book Talk and Beyond: Children and Teachers Respond to Literature.* Newark, DE: International Reading Association.

Rothlein, L., and A. M. Meinbach. (1996). *Legacies: Using Children's Literature in the Classroom.* New York: HarperCollins.

Rowe, R., and C. Probst. (1995). "Connecting with Local Culture." *Educational Leadership* 53 (1): 62–64.

Rudman, M. K. (1995). *Children's Literature: An Issues Approach,* 3rd ed. White Plains, NY: Longman.

Rudman, M. K., K. D. Gagne, and J. E. Bernstein. (1994). *Books to Help Children Cope with Separation and Loss,* 4th ed. New Providence, NJ: R. R. Bowker.

Saccardi, M. (1993/1994). "Children Speak: Our Students' Reactions to Books Can Tell Us What to Teach." *The Reading Teacher* 47:318–324.

Scott, J. E. (1994). "Teaching Nonfiction with the Shared Book Experience." *The Reading Teacher* 47:676–678.

Shockley, B. (1994). "Extending the Literature Community: Home-to-School and School-to-Home." *The Reading Teacher* 47:500–502.

Shockley, B., B. Michalove, and J. Allen. (1995). *Engaging Families: Connecting Home and School Literacy Communities.* Portsmouth, NH: Heinemann.

Short, K. G., ed. (1995). *Research & Professional Resources in Children's Literature: Piecing a Patchwork Quilt.* Newark, DE: International Reading Association.

Simmons, J. S., ed. (1994). *Censorship: A Threat to Reading, Learning, Thinking.* Newark, DE: International Reading Association.

Slaughter, J. P. (1993). *Beyond Storybooks: Young Children and the Shared Book Experience.* Newark, DE: International Reading Association.

Stroll, D. R. ed. (1994). *Magazines for Kids and Teens.* Newark, DE: International Reading Association.

Sutherland, Z., and M. H. Arbuthnot. (1991). *Children and Books,* 8th ed. New York: HarperCollins.

Swindal, D. N. (1993). "The Big Advantage: Using Big Books for Shared Reading Experiences in the Classroom." *The Reading Teacher* 46:716–717.

Tiedt, P. L., and I. M. Tiedt. (1995). *Multicultural Teaching: A Handbook of Activities, Information, and Resources,* 4th ed. Boston: Allyn & Bacon.

Tompkins, G. E., and K. Hoskisson. (1995). *Language Arts: Content and Teaching Strategies.* Englewood Cliffs, NJ: Prentice-Hall.

Tompkins, G. E., and L. M. McGee. (1993). *Teaching Reading with Literature: Case Studies to Action Plans.* New York: Macmillan.

Trelease, J. (1992). *Hey! Listen to This: Stories to Read Aloud.* New York: Penguin.

———. (1995). *The New Read-Aloud Handbook,* 3rd rev. ed. New York: Penguin.

Wilson, P. J., and R. F. Abrahamson. (1988). "What Children's Literature Classics Do Children Really Enjoy?" *The Reading Teacher* 41:406–411.

Wlodkowski, R. J., and M. B. Ginsberg. (1995). "A Framework for Culturally Responsive Teaching." *Educational Leadership* 53 (1): 17–21.

Young, T. A., and S. Vardell. (1993). "Weaving Readers Theatre and Nonfiction into the Curriculum." *The Reading Teacher* 46:396–406.

Zarrillo, J. (1994). *Multicultural Literature, Multicultural Teaching: Units for the Elementary Grades.* Fort Worth, TX: Harcourt Brace College Publishers.

# *L*iteracy Learning in an Inclusive Setting

© James L. Shaffer

# Overview

*T*his chapter provides elementary teachers with the knowledge they need to better understand and teach students in an inclusive classroom setting—including culturally diverse learners and learners who are considered to be "at risk," as well as those with other special learning needs and/or gifts/talents. The idea of students "at risk" (or "at promise") is discussed. Cultural diversity in one classroom is sampled, and discussion of the cultural difference model, and macroculture and microcultures is shared. Multicultural education is defined and its dimensions, principles, and contexts are presented. Bilingual and ESL (English as a Second Language) programs are discussed. Students with special learning needs, with ADHD (Attention Deficit Hyperactivity Disorder), and with gifts/talents are defined; some of their characteristics are described; and special instructional procedures for these learners are discussed. Finally, facilitative and functional teaching ideas and strategies that could be implemented by elementary teachers to meet the literacy learning needs of various students in an inclusive setting are suggested. These ideas, procedures, and strategies include language-based and interactive guidelines, multisensory procedures, the analytical-tutorial approach, and other teaching strategies. The chapter ends with a brief discussion of computer hardware and software considerations.

## Main Ideas

- The demographics of the elementary classroom have changed—classrooms are now inclusive settings where the needs of each student must be identified and appropriate instruction provided.
- "At risk" and "at promise" are contemporary labels that some educators use to identify a heterogeneous student population that may have learning, behavioral, or other special needs that should be addressed for students to experience success in school.
- Elementary teachers should be aware and accepting of their classroom's cultural diversity—its macroculture and microcultures—and meet the literacy needs of all students.
- Multicultural education promotes the appreciation of cultural differences and similarities, incorporates the strengths of cultural diversities in instructional practices, and advances democracy and equality for all.
- Bilingual and ESL programs can facilitate students' development of a second language without students having to abandon their home language or pride in their language and cultural diversities.

- Many teaching procedures and strategies that are appropriate for students with special learning needs are also appropriate for language and culturally diverse learners and all learners who might need systematic instruction and extra support.
- Mainstreaming and inclusion are service delivery models used in elementary schools to educate students with special learning needs, challenges, and/or gifts and talents.
- Elementary teachers should implement appropriate teaching ideas and procedures to meet the behavioral and other special needs and challenges of their students.
- Elementary teachers should implement specific teaching ideas and procedures (e.g., language-based and interactive, multisensory, etc.) to meet the specific needs of all their students in an inclusive setting.

If you were to ask seasoned elementary teachers, what are the most significant changes they have witnessed in the classroom, they would probably give a variety of responses. However, the vast majority of these professionals undoubtedly would use the words "at risk," "cultural diversity," and "mainstreaming or inclusion." Most of them would tell you that they are teaching more students who are at risk due to learning, behavior, or other special needs. They would also tell you that elementary students today come from more culturally diverse backgrounds, and for many, English is their second language. Finally, these teachers would tell you that the mainstreaming or inclusion of students with special learning needs has resulted in significant changes. This chapter introduces you to these students and their needs and provides you with information and ideas that should help you implement a balanced literacy program for them in an inclusive elementary classroom.

## *Students "at Risk" or "at Promise"*

The literature reports that the term *at risk* has become the primary label used by educators to identify a heterogeneous student population with learning and behavioral problems (see Brozo and Simpson 1995) and that local educational agencies have reported increased percentages of such students in the classroom (see Frazer and Nichols 1991). In this section, we present two definitions of at risk that are representative of those being used to define and label certain student populations. After doing so, however, we will discuss why this educational label, like all student labels, is problematic and is being questioned by many. Collins and Cheek (1993) indicated:

> The term is often used to describe a particular segment of the population of the United States that is thought of as underfed, undereducated . . . underprivileged . . . culturally disadvantaged, and educationally disadvantaged. These students usually experience great difficulty with reading and communicating orally in the school setting. Part of the problem can be ascribed to environmental factors; however, most of the difficulty is with language acquisition. The language of the at-risk student is typically nonstandard American English. (p. 384)

In essence, this definition indicates that students are at risk because of environment or experiences that place them at an educational disadvantage. Many of these students also have difficulty using or understanding standard English, which may negatively influence their ability to learn to read and to express themselves orally if they are not given an opportunity to learn in a bilingual environment.

Lerner (1993) provided a description of at-risk children from her perspective as a special educator:

> Children who are at risk may not be eligible under the law for services, but they are high risk for becoming children with disabilities and for having substantial developmental delays if early intervention services are not provided. . . . Three categories of [at risk] are recognized. . . . The established risk category includes children with an established diagnosis that invariably results in disability or developmental delay [(e.g., Down syndrome). The biological risk category includes] . . . children whose early medical and health history reveals significant biological conditions that do not lead invariably to developmental delay or disorder but that have a greater probability of delay and disability than is found in the general population [e.g., premature and low birth weight infants] . . . [Finally, the environmental risk category] includes children who are biologically sound but whose early life experiences have been so limiting that they impart a high probability of delayed development. Such experiences include parental substance abuse; significant family social disorganization; extreme poverty; parental intellectual impairment; disturbed parent-child interactions; low parental education; family isolation and lack of support; and a history of inadequate prenatal care, child abuse, or neglect. Children [at environmental risk] frequently lack cognitive stimulation for normal development. (pp. 254–255)

In essence, Lerner's definition suggests that at-risk students can be divided into three populations based on the factors that she believes cause their risk designation and that these students may or may not be disabled and eligible for special educational services.

As professionals, we continually find ourselves in academic quagmires that may or may not be of our own choosing (e.g., due to federal, state, or local laws and policies, and politics). Furthermore, these quagmires seriously limit our efforts or may actually prevent us from achieving the goal of educating students. According to Hammill and Bartel 1995, our use of labels has become an academic problem in that labels seem to be logical and necessary, but in actuality, most labels are educationally irrelevant and pejorative, if not stereotyping, and presuppose that the problem is within the student. The use of labels also lowers our expectations for those students labeled, as well as lowers students' expectations of their abilities.

Brozo and Simpson (1995) stated that labeling students at risk does ". . . little more than blame the victims and perpetuate conditions of failure both at home and in the school" (p. 333). Sleeter and Grant (1994) react against the at-risk label and the problems caused by stereotyping:

[W]hen teachers hear they are receiving a new student who is "at risk," certain images and personal characteristics of students often rush forward. Research on stereotyping also finds people to be more accepting of individuals who fit a stereotype than individuals who do not. Stereotypes seem to give us a map of reality that suggests how to interpret and act toward people, and individuals who do not fit that map make us uncomfortable. Rather than questioning the stereotype, however, we often avoid or put down the persons who do not fit. (p. 92)

We agree with Brozo and Simpson (1995) and Sleeter and Grant (1994), and we would also add that the use of the at-risk label has no educational relevance. When teachers are told or determine that they have a student at risk, they receive no insight into instructional strategies they can use to educate this student. Unfortunately, because of the more common view of at risk, focus could be placed on the student's ethnicity, language facility, gender, disability status, or socioeconomic status. One "enabling" term we would like to see used more often, to replace "at risk"—or what Brozo and Simpson (1995) referred to as "transposing our deficit-ridden language to a language of hope for and expectation of success" (p. 333)—is the term "at promise." Heath and Mangiola (1991) wrote about "children of promise"; and Banks (1994) described the "cultural difference" perspective or model to be one that rejects the idea that ethnic minority students, and other students unfortunately labeled as "at risk," have cultural deficits. Banks maintained that if we treat students as culturally deprived or at risk in some way, we will approach their instruction very differently than if we see their cultural differences as strengths that can enrich our and their lives.

## *Cultural Diversity*

What is meant by cultural diversity? What is involved? And how does cultural diversity impact schools? These are important questions that we will help you reflect on in this section.

Let's take a look at one scenario of a culturally diverse classroom in a Massachusetts community to see some examples of cultural diversity. We will call the school Neighborhood School, and we will call the community Center Towne. Ms. Lee is the teacher, and she herself is second-generation Chinese American. She has been fortunate to get this combination first- and second-grade teaching position because jobs have been especially hard to find in this part of Massachusetts for the past few years; however, her own cultural heritage and her ability to speak fluent English, as well as fluently speak two different dialects of Chinese, were particularly helpful in attaining the position. Ms. Lee's fluency in Chinese will be especially useful because she has four children of Chinese ethnicity in her classroom who are in various stages of learning English and who speak different dialects of Chinese. Her other students include: three Laotian Americans, two Cambodian Americans, five African Americans, two Vietnamese Americans, four European Americans, and three Latinos (two newly from El Salvador and one from Guatemala, who has been in the United States since he was a toddler.) Needless to say, their ethnicity, cultures, languages, community identifications, and religions are quite diverse!

Classroom teachers will need to meet the needs of students from many culturally and language diverse backgrounds.
©James L. Shaffer

Ms. Lee wants to provide quality education for all of her students. She has many who are in the process of acquiring English as a second language. She also knows that these children, even though of similar ages, have various differences regarding their literacy development, linguistic and cognitive strategies, cognitive abilities, special needs, and interests and motivations. She plans to facilitate their learning by getting to know each of her students' strengths and needs and using various materials, instructional strategies, and motivations to help them develop as readers, writers, and learners in her classroom. Because of the cultural diversity of her classroom, school, and community (Center Towne), Ms. Lee plans to use the community (parents, families, and other community members) as much as possible to reach her goals for these students.

To help her get started, Ms. Lee gathers professional literature that she will use as resources to help inform her instruction. For instance, she uses a book by Samway, Whang, and Pippitt (1995) to help her develop ideas for a cross-age tutoring program between her classroom and another classroom in Neighborhood School. She uses Harris's book (1993) (and many other sources cited in this text) to locate children's literature from a variety of cultures representative of children in her classroom. She also reads books and articles on multicultural education, multicultural literacy, and culturally responsive teaching that include Banks (1994), Cárdenas (1995), Diamond and Moore (1995), Gersten and Jiménez (1994), Schumm, Vaughn, and Leavell (1994), and Wlodkowski and Ginsberg (1995).

## The Cultural Difference Model

So, what ideas and model will Ms. Lee use to accomplish her goals when there is so much diversity in her classroom? Well, one idea that especially appeals to her is the cultural difference model (Banks 1994). Because she herself had first-hand experience as a child in school of negative expectations (or a cultural deficit model), Ms. Lee believes that a model that respects each child's differences and uses those differences as positive materials to enrich the classroom would be just right for her very diverse classroom and students. We have depicted the ideas of this model to show you specifically what Ms. Lee believes: (1) the school and the teacher, not the cultures of the students, are responsible for low academic achievement; (2) the school and the teacher must change in ways that will result in respect for all students and teaching strategies that are consistent with students' cultural characteristics; (3) teaching strategies will be culturally sensitive and enriched to enable students to achieve; (4) the school and teacher will not ignore or try to alienate students from their cultures but instead use their cultures in positive ways; and (5) the school and teacher will view other languages spoken by their students as strengths, rather than as problems to overcome (Banks 1994).

## Reflection Activity 10.1

*C*ultural diversity is part of all of our lives and is part of school experience. In your reflection journal, under the heading Reflection Activity 10.1, reflect on what cultural diversity means to you and how you can use it in positive ways in your classroom. Will you use a "cultural difference model"? Why?

In the next sections we discuss the sociological terms *macroculture* and *microculture* to provide you with some additional background pertinent to a discussion of cultural diversity and acceptance of cultural values.

## Macroculture

Most people could say they have a lot in common with their immediate and distant relatives, and they could give a number of reasons that this is true (e.g., "We're family"). But Chinn (1994, p. 565) posed the question, "Have you noticed how your classmates, roommates, and friends from different ethnic groups seem to have quite a lot in common with you?" Have you? Do you know why this is so? According to Chinn:

> This is true, in part, because we all belong to the macroculture, the core, or universal, culture of this country. Our macroculture evolved from Western European traditions. No longer limited to white Anglo-Saxon Protestants, the macroculture is composed of many different ethnic groups, particularly middle class. Traits such as individualism, industriousness, ambition, competitiveness,

self-reliance, and independence are highly valued by the macroculture. . . . Most educators, regardless of their ethnic background, belong to the middle class and subscribe to the values of the macroculture. (p. 565).

Our *macroculture*, the national culture of the United States or the "American identity," began with the founding of our country and has continued to evolve since the 1880s. Gollnick and Chinn (1994) reported that its genesis was rooted in white Anglo-Saxon Protestant and agrarian traditions, and because so many middle-class members adopted these institutions, this provided the framework for traits and values that came to be regarded as "American." In addition to ethnic, socioeconomic, religious, and agrarian traditions, our macroculture was also strongly influenced by the earlier population's dominant gender (male), age (middle age), geographic region (Northeast), and exceptionality status (nondisabled) among other factors.

Today, many of our institutions continue to exhibit the heritage of our "Founding Fathers," but the influences of some of the earlier dominant cultural factors have lessened. As a country, we have moved, through "sea-to-sea" geographic expansion and the industrial revolution, from an agrarian to a metropolitan or small town society. We are in the midst of changes in the way we view people and are in an information age revolution. The American identity is also being strongly influenced by changing population demographics (the increasing cultural diversity of our people), political debates (liberal vs. conservative), and the thoughts and actions of various diverse groups reacting to contradictions within the core culture (e.g., reacting against sexism, racism, discrimination, and other exclusions).

Because culturally diverse and other diverse groups define, value, accept, and identify differently with the macroculture, the national culture is changing to mirror their differences. Individualism, freedom, and the other values listed by Chinn (1994) continue to be core macroculture traits, but we have also become concerned with equality and opportunity for all persons and the acceptance and appreciation of human differences. Finally, the macroculture of our pluralistic society is also being defined and influenced by our membership in various microcultures. We are a part of the dynamics of the American macroculture, and as educators, we will affect our school's macroculture and significantly influence the core culture traits and values.

## *Microcultures*

Gollnick and Chinn (1994) defined *microcultures* as subsocieties within the United States that have distinctive cultural elements and institutions not common to the American macroculture but that also share some cultural patterns with the national culture. Microculture identity results from traits and values associated with ethnic or national origin, language, gender, sexual preference, age, religion, geographic region, place of residence, and disability status. Gollnick and Chinn (1994) noted that people may share membership in one microculture but may not share membership in other microcultures. For example, all women and girls are members of the female microculture, but they do not all belong to the same ethnic, religious, cultural, or sexual preference groups. Furthermore, as Chinn (1994) also indicated, different individuals identify with their microcultures to a greater or lesser extent than others. For example, one individual may be a Latino who functions as a nonethnic (or, in other words, does not take an active part in the cultural community and Puerto Rican, Central American, or Mexican heritage of his family/culture). Another individual may be a Latino who closely identifies with his heritage and takes an active role in Mexican American affairs, culture, and activities.

Finally, Gollnick and Chinn (1994) stated that our cultural identity will be based on our membership in different microcultural groups and the interactions of these groups with the macroculture. For example, membership in one microculture will have a profound effect on traits and values in other microcultures. To this end males and females in particular ethnic and religious groups are expected to assume specific gender roles as children, youths, and adults and thus tend to assume these roles. Additionally, the relationship and interaction of our microculture(s) with the national cultural also affect our cultural identity. For example, if we are members of microcultures compatible with the dominant culture, we develop certain traits and values. We then accept, promote, and "school" our children and charges in the macroculture. However, if our membership is in groups that are at variance with the dominant culture, we learn other characteristics and appreciations. We may then view ourselves as beholden, discriminated against, or oppressed and "school" our children and charges in these characteristics or values. Thus, as the macroculture changes and we change membership in microcultures, our traits and values change.

## Reflection Activity 10.2

*T*hink back on a particular year/grade of your elementary school experiences (e.g., third grade) and try to recall the macroculture and microcultures in your classroom. Under Reflection Activity 10.2 in your reflection journal, describe the macroculture. Then, list the different microcultures in this classroom and describe the microcultures with the most and fewest student members. With respect to the macroculture, discuss your own ethnicity and microcultures and to what extent you "fit" the macroculture of the classroom. Finally, describe which aspects of the macroculture may have promoted or negatively affected your literacy development.

## *Multicultural Education and Literacy Learning*

We have introduced you to the concepts of macroculture and microculture and cultural identity and diversity. Clegg, Miller, and Vanderhoof's (1995) review of the literature suggested that these concepts are becoming more important as we move into the twenty-first century, because by the year 2000 one in three U.S.

residents "will be a person of color" and by the year 2020 ". . . nearly half of the school-age population will belong to ethnic and cultural groups other than European American" (p. 3). And, if you are teaching in a large school district today, Fitzgerald (1993) reported that you should not be surprised to find that one-third of your class would be English as a second language students (remember Ms. Lee's classroom as an example). To meet the needs of the increasing number of students in culturally diverse groups, local school districts are engaging in the educational reform that is called "multicultural education."

## *Definitions*

Although the definition of multicultural education is evolving and professionals disagree on the types of diversity it addresses (Sleeter and Grant, 1994), a number of definitions have been proposed and used to restructure programs and curricula to meet the needs of all students from all cultures. We present here three definitions by noted authorities that school districts may use to guide multicultural education efforts. First:

> Multicultural education is an idea, an educational reform movement, and a process whose major goal is to change the structure of education institutions so that male and female students, exceptional students, and students who are members of diverse racial, ethnic, and cultural groups will have an equal chance to achieve academically in school. It is necessary to conceptualize the school as a social system to implement multicultural education successfully. Each major variable in the school, such as its culture, power relationships, the curriculum and materials, and the attitudes and beliefs of the staff, must be changed in ways that will allow the school to promote education equality for students from diverse groups. (Banks and Banks 1993, p. 1)

Second:

> Education that is multicultural provides an environment that values cultural diversity and portrays it positively. Students' educational and vocational options are not limited by gender, age, ethnicity, native language, religion, class, or disability. Educators have the responsibility to help students contribute to and benefit from our democratic society. Diversity is used to develop effective instructional strategies for students in the classroom. In addition, multicultural education should help students and teachers think critically about institutionalized racism, classism, and sexism. Ideally, educators will begin to develop individual and group strategies for overcoming the debilitating effects of these societal scourges. (Gollnick and Chinn 1994, p. v)

And third:

> [Multicultural education refers] . . . to educational practices directed toward race, culture, language, social class, gender, and disability, although in selecting the term we do not imply that race is the primary form of social inequality that needs to be addressed. We see racism, classism, and sexism as equally important. [Also, it is a term] . . . that educators increasingly use to describe education policies and practices that recognize, accept, and affirm human differences and similarities. . . . (Sleeter and Grant 1994, pp. 33; 167)

## Reflection Activity 10.3

*W*hat do you think? How would you define multicultural education? Which diverse groups do you believe multicultural education should address? In your reflection journal, under the heading Reflection Activity 10.3, please answer these questions, and then see how we responded in the next paragraph.

We support Banks and Banks's position that multicultural education is an idea or movement, that schools should be viewed as a social system for implementing multicultural education, and that all school variables must be changed to promote educational equality for diverse groups. We are also in agreement with Gollnick and Chinn's statements that multicultural education provides an environment that values diversity and portrays it positively and that it promotes the use of diversity to develop effective instructional practices. And we believe, like Sleeter and Grant, that race should not be the main or only focus of multicultural education—racism, classism, and sexism are all problems, and multicultural education should seek to recognize, accept, and affirm all human differences and similarities. As to which diverse groups should be addressed by multicultural education, we would agree with those identified by all of these authors. All peoples, of all colors, races, languages, cultures, religions, sexes, ethnicities, sexual preferences, and abilities or disabilities deserve understanding and respect. Because your classroom will represent many microcultures, it will be important to know and understand some of the important issues, dimensions, principles, contexts, and programs that are part of multicultural education and efforts.

### *Multicultural Education Assessment and Programmatic Issues*

Banks (1993, p. 4) asserted that multicultural education is an ongoing process and not "something we 'do'" to achieve the objectives of multicultural educational reform. You do not "do" multicultural education this year and implement another program or reform next year to meet the needs of your students. Sleeter and Grant (1994) stated that the long-term school goals of multicultural education are to "[p]repare citizens to work actively toward social structural equality; promote cultural pluralism and alternative lifestyles; [and] promote equal opportunity in the school" (p. 211). Facilitative teachers will foster cultural diversity and equal opportunity and prepare students to address social equality issues. It has also been stated (see Gollnick and Chinn, 1994) that it will be you, the classroom teacher, who will be the key as to whether or not culturally diverse students achieve academically and are able to assimilate in the broader society.

Facilitative teachers will be concerned with multicultural education throughout their professional careers and will be working to ensure that students become full members of our society. If teachers are to achieve multicultural educational objectives, it is critical that students are evaluated with unbiased assessments and that you design their learning programs around appropriate dimensions, principles, and contexts.

A review of the literature (see Bender, 1995; Chinn, 1994) reveals that the problems of biased assessment and its negative consequences have been ongoing concerns of professionals. For example, you will read that biased assessment practices confound all educational endeavors and that three primary variables contribute to biased assessments—the characteristics of the examiner, the attributes of the tests, and the characteristics of the examinee. Thus, facilitative teachers are encouraged to take every step possible to engage in unbiased assessment procedures. Because unbiased assessment data are essential to plan and evaluate multicultural education, assessment activities must be structured to produce these unbiased results. We have listed the following guidelines that you may want to adopt to promote unbiased assessments:

1. Select assessment procedures that are compatible with the characteristics of your culturally diverse students' microcultures.
2. Use informal and qualitative techniques in lieu of formal assessments.
3. Administer formal tests that have been appropriately standardized (e.g., your culturally diverse student groups were accurately represented in the norming population).
4. Use two or more assessment procedures to secure needed data. At least one of these assessments should be individualized or administered in a one-to-one format.
5. Ensure the content validity of your assessment items by manipulating examples to correspond with the students' backgrounds and experiences.
6. Conduct assessments in the students' native language.

Finally, it is recommended that the examiner and examinee have congruent microcultures. This is paramount when assessment results are to be used to make decisions that may have a lifelong effect. If you find yourself in a critical assessment situation where you and a student have different microcultures, what would you do? One strategy we would suggest is that you ask a colleague or a parent or community member who is of the same microculture as the student to help you conduct the assessment.

## Multicultural Education Dimensions, Principles, and Contexts

Banks (1993) stated that multicultural education programs should be developed around four dimensions. These dimensions and general goals include the following.

### Content Integration

Content integration involves the use of examples and content from a variety of microcultures in teaching. In addition to your and your students' microcultures, use examples and content from other microcultures that your students will encounter outside the classroom.

## Knowledge Construction

Students must be helped to understand, investigate, and determine how the implicit cultural assumptions, frames of references, perspectives, and biases with a discipline influence the ways that knowledge is constructed. We encourage you to engage in this knowledge construction through collaborative consultation (to be discussed in the next section) and across the curriculum.

## An Equity Pedagogy

An equity pedagogy exists when teaching is modified to facilitate the academic achievement of students from diverse racial, cultural, gender, and social-economic groups. As a facilitative teacher, you should determine your culturally diverse students' strengths and needs (e.g., linguistic, cognitive, and affective) and design appropriate instructional practices.

## An Empowering School Culture

You should examine grouping and labeling practices, sports participation, disproportionality in achievement, and the interaction of the staff and the students across microcultures. This will permit you to support the development of a school climate that empowers all students from all culturally diverse groups. Adopting certain principles within your multicultural program will ensure that you teach "multiculturally" and that your classroom models democracy and equity. Seven principles recommended by Gollnick and Chinn (1994, p. 297) that you could adopt are:

1. Place the student at the center of the teaching and learning process.
2. Promote human rights and respect for cultural differences.
3. Believe that all students can learn.
4. Acknowledge and build on the life histories and experiences of students' microculture membership.
5. Critically analyze oppression and power relationships to understand racism, sexism, classism, and discrimination against microcultures.
6. Critique society in the interest of social justice and equality.
7. Participate in collective social actions to ensure a democratic society.

We believe you will maximize your students' literacy learning success by developing your multicultural education program around the four dimensions described, by adopting the seven principles identified, and by believing that you can make a difference.

There are many contexts that can be structured and designed to meet the literacy needs of students in your multicultural classroom. These contexts have been discussed by numerous professionals (e.g., Banks 1994; Banks and Banks 1993; Gollnick and Chinn 1994; Sleeter and Grant, 1994; and the many others cited in this chapter) and include but are not limited to the following.

### School and Classroom Environment

Promote a diverse and multicultural school climate. Hall bulletin boards and exhibits, children's literature in the school library, curriculum materials used throughout the school, and school activities and celebrations should be balanced culturally. School administrators and teachers should have diverse cultural backgrounds. You should work closely with your principal and peers to integrate the community and family into the reading and learning program. Welcome opportunities to share new and different cultural experiences.

### Teacher Attitudes and Beliefs

Be enthusiastic about and dedicated to "multicultural awareness," because your attitude, beliefs, and behavior will be a model for your students. Your classroom actions have a definite impact on all of your students. Be positive and accepting. Do not transmit biased messages and treat all students equally and respectfully. Engage in teaching activities that stimulate and motivate your students' desires to learn and that "fit" your students' learning needs. Finally, use your students' unique cultures and experiences to enrich the classroom curriculum.

### Instructional Context

Instructional context includes all the other contexts described (school and classroom environment, materials and literature, and teacher attitudes and beliefs) as well as the instruction, expectations, amount of teacher control, and the amount of student control in the classroom. The context for your instruction with culturally and language diverse students must fit their needs, strengths, interests, motivations, and also fit your needs for autonomy and control. Each teacher must develop an instructional context that is appropriate for the child and for himself or herself (see Flippo 1997, and Lipson and Wixson 1991, for help regarding determining an appropriate context of instruction for you and your students).

## Reflection Activity 10.4

*I*n your reflection journal under the heading Reflection Activity 10.4, further develop your definition of multicultural education to include the development of reading, writing, and other language skills and strategies. How would you promote these in your multicultural classroom?

In the next sections we discuss special language and learning programs that many schools are using to enhance the language and cognitive learnings of their culturally and language diverse students. See how these fit with the ideas you generated in Reflection Activity 10.4.

# Bilingual and ESL Programs

More and more schools and school districts are recognizing the language and cognitive needs of culturally/language diverse students. As we saw in Ms. Lee's classroom, many students enter school with diverse languages and often they are just beginning to learn English. In recognition of the importance of students' own home languages, "bilingual programs" are often available to encourage learning in children's own languages while gradually helping students learn English (to help students become more active participants in the macroculture). The objective is fluency and literacy in both languages (Díaz-Rico and Weed 1995). Of course, to enable this to happen, teachers must be found who are fluent in the students' home languages and who have an understanding and knowledge of the culture, history, literature, and issues of the students' and families' countries of cultural heritage. In other words, ideally a teacher will have completed a bilingual teacher preparation program for the particular language/culture she or he wishes to teach and will be able to provide a context that supports and extends students' home language and culture.

Schools and school districts also offer programs known as English as a Second Language (ESL) programs for learners who have their own home language but are in need of learning English to assimilate into the macroculture. The emphasis of these programs is on learning English. Most of the instruction is in English. Less attention is given to helping students retain their own home languages and cultures. ESL teachers usually do not have as much preparation as bilingual teachers do in the culture, history, literature, and issues of the students' and their families' countries of cultural heritage. Additionally, because ESL teachers teach in English, they do not have to have the same fluency in the home languages of their students as bilingual teachers must have. ESL teachers may have children from many cultural/language backgrounds in the same classroom (as Ms. Lee did) and will teach them all in English. Many excellent sources are available for teachers with ESL students (e.g., Ashworth and Wakefield 1994; Durkin 1995; and Spangenberg-Urbschat and Pritchard 1994). And we particularly recommend Díaz-Rico and Weed (1995) for more insight and details regarding bilingual learning programs. Also, the Samway, Whang, and Pippitt (1995) book should be helpful to all teachers with language/culturally diverse learners, whether or not the teachers are ESL, bilingual, or just general education classroom teachers.

In the next sections we will visit Ms. Lee's classroom again at the Neighborhood School in Center Towne to see how she handles the instruction of two children in her classroom, Kim and Tomas.

## Kim's Story

Kim is a Chinese American child who speaks fluently in the Mandarin dialect her family uses at home. Although she is in first grade this year, she speaks almost no English. However, she is fortunate because her teacher, Ms. Lee, is also fluent in the Mandarin dialect, and she can teach Kim reading, writing, and all the content subjects in Kim's home language. Kim's family seems anxious for Kim to finally learn English, but Ms. Lee will first do all her instruction in Mandarin for Kim and very gradually give her opportunities to develop English. In this way, Ms. Lee can build on Kim's existing linguistic background and will also use concepts, ideas, and images familiar to Kim to enhance her cognitive learnings. Ms. Lee will be able to provide bilingual instruction for Kim because she knows the culture and language of Kim's home. When Kim is interested in learning the English words to represent her ideas, Ms. Lee will teach her. Additionally, Kim will also learn English by being immersed in this predominantly English language classroom, since Ms. Lee will need to communicate with most of the other students in English, as she doesn't share any other common language with them. It will also be helpful to Kim to have the other Chinese American children to communicate with—two of them are already fairly fluent in English but can also speak Mandarin. Ms. Lee believes that eventually Kim will be bilingual in Mandarin and English and will retain her strong Chinese identity, culture, and pride in her ethnicity.

### Tomas's Story

Tomas is a second-grade Latino boy who has recently immigrated from El Salvador with his family. He speaks no English, and neither do his mother, brothers, and sisters. However, his father speaks some English, and so does one of the other Latino children in the class—Edwardo, who is from Guatemala. Ms. Lee plans to use Tomas's father and Edwardo as much as possible to help her teach Tomas. Because Ms. Lee does not speak any Spanish, she must teach Tomas as an ESL student. However, because she believes strongly in the cultural difference model, she will do her best to help Tomas retain his own language and culture and will encourage his pride in his own ethnicity. Ms. Lee is confident that eventually Tomas will learn English, and she will do her best to help him learn how to read and write in English. She will, however, try to find children's literature depicting Latino (hopefully some from El Salvador) children and family life for Tomas's and the other Latino children's reading instruction, and she will use the assistance of the school librarian and the sources cited in this text to find this appropriate literature.

## Reflection Activity 10.5

*D*o you see some of the challenges inherent in providing bilingual instruction and ESL instruction in the classroom? Do you have ideas that you feel would enhance Ms. Lee's chances of success with Kim and with Tomas? In your reflection journal, under the heading Reflection Activity 10.5, jot down your ideas.

Gersten and Jiménez (1994) have indicated that many instructional practices that teachers use when working with students with special needs and with those students considered at risk also seem to be effective for teaching ESL students to read. Others (e.g., Graves, Graves, and Braaten 1996) have shown how several of these instructional practices work in inclusive classrooms with all learners who require extra support. Some of these suggested teaching strategies include: (1) vocabulary development, frequent checks on students' understanding of new vocabulary, and meaningful application of new vocabulary; (2) questioning students regarding their reading, encouraging them to elaborate on their responses, and paraphrasing students' comments and answers; (3) use of consistent language with students with minimum use of synonyms and idioms; (4) use of scaffolded instruction, teacher coaching, and teacher modeling; and (5) using approaches that involve high levels of student involvement and interaction.

In the remaining sections of this chapter, we focus on other students with special learning needs, challenges, and gifts and talents. Because the literature indicates that many of the same teaching strategies and procedures have been found effective with language and culturally diverse students, students considered at risk/at promise, and students with other special learning needs, we believe that many of the strategies suggested in the second half of this chapter will be applicable for many students in the inclusive and in the culturally diverse classroom. Additionally, many of the teaching strategies suggested throughout this text are also appropriate and should be considered. Of course, we believe that the facilitative teacher will carefully review procedures and only select those that meet his or her individual students' needs, strategies, motivations, interests, and cultures, designing the most appropriate literacy and learning program possible.

## *Students with Special Learning Needs and Challenges*

To meet the needs and help children with specific handicaps (today the term is "disabilities"), federal legislation was enacted in 1975. As a result of that legislation, schools and school districts have endeavored to develop models or procedures to facilitate special education delivery. In this section of the chapter we provide information concerning this legislation, as well as provide descriptions of the two models: mainstreaming and full inclusion.

First, the legislation: Many elementary students with special learning needs and challenges are identified and defined in the 1975 federal legislation Public Law (PL) 94-142 (the Education for All Handicapped Children Act) and its 1990 reauthorization PL 101-476 (the Individuals with Disabilities Education Act—IDEA). These students are eligible for a free and appropriate education in the least restrictive environment, must have an individualized education program (IEP), are entitled to needed technology and assistive devices, and have due process, nondiscriminatory evaluation, confidentiality, and other rights. PL 101-476, IDEA, uses "people-first" language to identify and define disabled populations. Later in this chapter we discuss these populations.

Two instructional delivery systems to meet the academic and nonacademic needs of students with special needs and challenges have been used by schools and school systems. These systems are mainstreaming and inclusion.

## The Mainstreaming Model

Wood (1989) has defined mainstreaming as:

> a joint venture of both regular and special education personnel. The focus of mainstreaming is to provide instructional options for the special student within the regular classroom and to provide special education only when this is the best educational practice. In the mainstream, educators share their skills and time to develop an education climate designed for success. (p. 4)

According to Wood (1989), students with disabilities are placed in general education settings and only receive special education services when necessary. General and special educators would then work together in the "mainstream" to plan appropriate educational experiences for these students. We would add that mainstreaming is the collaborative effort of general and special educators to meet the academic and social needs of special needs students in general education classrooms with their own age-group peers.

The following two general arguments have been used to promote mainstreaming:

1. Some, who have written on the topic from the perspective of advocates, have emphasized ethical issues: Mainstreaming is the *right* thing to do because, unlike special class and resource class programming, it does not require segregating . . . [students with disabilities] from their peers.
2. Some, in general agreement with the arguments concerning [an] overemphasis on physical setting[s] . . . [are] look[ing] . . . [for] ways of facilitating the principal of mainstreaming. They have investigated different ways of structuring what goes on in the classroom, as well as different ways in which educational personnel can be used to enhance the chances of successful mainstreaming. (Hallahan and Kauffman 1991, pp. 57–58)

It has also been suggested (see Wood 1989) that the mainstreaming model should be used because it benefits both students and professionals. All students concerned acquire a more heterogeneous view of society, learn and accept differences, participate in "normal" school functions, and have equal opportunities for academic achievement and development of their self-concepts. And, general and special education professionals, through collaboration, improve their knowledge base, communication skills, interpersonal abilities, and problem-solving skills.

## Collaborative Consultation

A primary key to successful mainstreaming involves collaborative consultation with special educators. Idol, Nevin, and Paolucci-Whitcomb (1994) defined collaborative consultation as

> an interactive process that enables groups of people with diverse expertise to generate creative solutions to mutually defined problems. . . . Collaborative consultation can be characterized by the following . . .: (a) Group members agree to view all members . . . as possessing unique and needed expertise; (b) they engage in frequent face-to-face interactions; (c) they distribute leadership responsibility and hold each other accountable for agreed-on commitments; (d) they understand the importance of reciprocity and emphasize task or relationship actions based on such variables as the extent to which other members support or have the skill to promote the group goal; and (e), they agree to consciously practice and increase their social interaction and/or task achievement skills through the process of consensus building. (p. 1)

Idol et al. (1994) also suggested that three factors will significantly affect the effectiveness of your collaborative consultation processes—knowledge base; interpersonal communicative, interactive problem-solving skills; and intrapersonal attitudes. Your knowledge base is elementary education curricula, assessment, instructional interventions and materials, and classroom and student management. You will be the "elementary education expert" and must assume this leadership role in all interpersonal communications and interactive problem solving (i.e., discussion and decision-making sessions). Your intrapersonal attitudes are the beliefs, values, and experiences you bring to the collaborative consultation process.

## *The Full Inclusion Model*

Full inclusion involves the elimination of pull-out and separate programs by "integrating" general, remedial, and special education. Initially, requests for inclusion, or a unitary school system, were centered in special education (Stainback and Stainback 1992), but reading educators have also questioned the efficacy of separating children for educational purposes (Allington 1994a). The inclusive movement has its roots in the mainstreaming efforts of the late 1970s and the 1980s (Lindsey, Ghose, and Ramasamy, in press). Inclusive education discussions resulted from debates on the need to restructure teacher education and general education by promoting an effective-reflective teacher corps (LaBoskey 1994) and by improving the quality of instruction for all students (Spring 1994). What is full inclusion and why are local education agencies across the United States implementing unitary systems?

We provide here five brief definitions of full inclusion that are representative of advocates of integration. Full inclusion is . . .

> "the education of all students in neighborhood classrooms and schools" (Stainback, Stainback, and Jackson 1992, p. 3).
>
> "a term used to describe the placement of children with disabilities in a regular education classroom with children who do not have disabilities" (Haas 1993, p. 4).

"the provision of appropriate educational services to all students in regular classes attended by non-disabled students of the same chronological age in their neighborhood school, including students with severe disabilities" (Giangreco and Putnum 1991, p. 245)

"the belief that instructional practices and technological supports are presently available to accommodate all students in the schools and classrooms they would otherwise attend if not disabled. Proponents of full inclusion tend to encourage that special education services generally be delivered in the form of training and technical assistance to 'regular' classroom teachers." (Rogers 1993, p. 2).

"to place and instruct all children—regardless of the type of disability or the level of severity—in their neighborhood school, in the regular classroom. In this setting, multidisciplinary teams of professionals mutually adjust their collective skills and knowledge to invent unique, personal programs for each student. All staff members are involved in making decisions, teaching, and evaluating the students' needs and progress. An underlying aim of the full-inclusion model is the complete elimination of special education, which is viewed as an unnecessary 'second system' " (Lerner 1993, p. 152)

According to Stainback et al. (1992), Haas (1993), and Giangreco and Putnal (1991), full inclusion involves all students attending neighborhood schools in general classrooms with children of similar chronological ages; and according to Rogers (1993) and Lerner (1993), full inclusion can occur today because (a) general education classes have the instructional practices and supports needed to meet the needs of all students and (b) "regular" education teachers will receive the assistance they need to understand and work with the included students. And general and special educators will form multidisciplinary teams to design, implement, and evaluate each student's educational program.

A number of other points are pertinent to defining full inclusion. First, and as stated by Wisniewski and Alper (1994), full inclusion is more than the placement of students with and without disabilities in the same classrooms (physical proximity). Students are educated together for the purpose of active and mutual academic and social interactions. Second, and as noted by York (cited in Luster and Ouder 1994), "Inclusion is not a place. It cannot be defined in terms of minutes in a day, and what it means to specific individuals will vary" (p. 3). Third, as proposed by Stainback, Stainback, East, and Sapon-Shevin (1994), full inclusion creates a "community" of professionals and learners. Professionals collaborate to plan and implement appropriate instruction to achieve teaching-learning outcomes while learners work and learn together to develop mutual support systems.

Although a number of different rationales are being used to foster the movement toward full inclusion, advocates seem to provide several justifications for a unitary school system. One of the prevailing arguments mirrors the findings of the 1954 historic Supreme Court case *Brown v. Board of Education*—"separate is inherently unequal" and segregation denies students with disabilities equal access to education (Chinn 1994). When students are segregated, they are not only viewed as "second-class" citizens but also receive "second-class" education. Also, full inclusive advocates contend that integration provides direct training, experiences, and appropriate role models (Hunt and Marshall 1994). For students, this direct training and these interactions promote independence, academic achievement, and social-emotional development. And inclusive advocates argue that segregated programs divide the attention and efforts of educators, and pull-out programs disrupt both teaching and learning (Allington 1994a). When professionals collaborate, the quality of education is improved for all students, and educating students in one setting permits blocks of time without interruption for coherent instruction. A fourth argument (see Pearman, Barnhart, Huang, and Mellblom 1992) suggests that it is illogical to assume, and the data do not support the position, that students can be removed from their natural settings to be "fixed" and then "returned."

## Multidisciplinary Teams

Full inclusion will result in the education of all students in general classrooms and the delivery of needed services in these settings. And it will not only significantly increase the heterogeneity of the student population but also necessitate that professionals from varied disciplines work together to achieve teaching-learning outcomes. To this end you will find yourself collaborating with other professionals within your school or district in multidisciplinary teams to meet the individual needs of your students. By definition, a multidisciplinary team is two or more professionals from different disciplines working together in collaborative consultation to achieve a common objective. With respect to multidisciplinary team activities, you will be a "full and equal" partner with other professionals in all collaborative efforts involving your students. You will be the "elementary education expert"; thus you must bring this expertise to bear in all decision making. Furthermore, it will be your and other team members' knowledge, intrapersonal attitudes, interpersonal communication abilities, and interactive problem-solving skills that determine the success or failure of the multidisciplinary endeavors on behalf of your students.

You will find multidisciplinary activities both rewarding and challenging, and these activities can result in your professional development and your students' academic and nonacademic growth. Depending on the services needed by specific students, you will be teaming with general and special education professionals, paraprofessionals, and related service personnel to determine, carry out, and evaluate your students' educational programs.

## Student Empowerment Strategies

If full inclusion is to be successful, professionals will need to develop their inclusive knowledge base and be committed to integration. Also, they will need to realize and execute their leadership roles but at the same time function effectively within the multidisciplinary team concept. However, there is a third factor that will determine the success or failure of inclusive education. This factor is student empowerment, specifically students developing mutually supporting systems.

It is important that you collaborate with multidisciplinary team members to empower your students. Strategies we have discussed throughout this text that you can use to help all students (with and without special learning needs and challenges) develop mutual support systems are cooperative learning groups, peer and cross-age tutoring efforts, and buddy or other partner work. In addition to promoting literacy learning, these strategies facilitate reciprocal understanding, trust, and responsibility.

## Reflection Activity 10.6

*S*tudents with mild, moderate, and severe disabilities/challenges may be included in your elementary classroom. In your reflection journal under Reflection Activity 10.6, answer the following questions: In general, do you support inclusive education—why or why not? Do you believe inclusion and multidisciplinary-team concepts will facilitate literacy learning for students *with* and *without* special needs/challenges? Do you believe students with more severe needs/challenges should be included in elementary classrooms—why or why not?

The following sections provide overviews of the various populations that were traditionally and typically included in the "special education" designation. As you have read, many of these learners are now instead included in the general elementary classroom. You will see, as we cite some of the literature, that some of the old labels and designations are still being used by some; however, whenever possible, we use terminology that is more indicative of the purposes and hope of inclusion. Labels can be damaging. For instance, Slavin (1996) would like to see terms like *mainstreaming* and other labels that brand students by perceived deficiencies disappear. (Frankly, we would, too.) Slavin has indicated the solution would be "neverstreaming" or completely wiping out labels, and in reality possibly preventing many learning and behavioral problems from ever developing. We suggest you read Slavin (1996) and others (e.g., Allington 1994b, 1995) for arguments against labeling children in special education programs and special reading programs.

As you read the information provided on each population of special learners, please keep in mind that all learners must be treated with dignity and respect, and their special needs and gifts should be viewed as challenges for both you and for them. These challenges should not label or separate them in any way from others in your classroom. Instead, we hope that you will facilitate the development of all who are put in your charge and find ways to do so that will enhance their self-concepts, self-respect, and interests and motivations in learning.

## Students with Mild Disabilities/Challenges

According to Lerner (1993), the designation *mild disabilities* is a relatively new term used to group different populations of students with special needs/challenges for general and special education purposes. Smith, Price, and Marsh (1986, p. 50) indicated that the designation mild disabilities includes students who were previously labeled as "educable mentally retarded," "learning disabled," and "emotionally disturbed/behaviorally disordered," as well as referring to the "borderline student." Hannaford (1993) reported that some students designated as having mild disabilities have difficulties perceiving, thinking, learning, socializing, and handling their emotions. Even though this population consists of students with various special needs/challenges, their actual outer behaviors are really more homogeneous than heterogeneous, which tends to validate a single classification system. However, with respect to reading abilities, this student population is as heterogeneous as the rest of the elementary-age students (e.g., with little reading to advanced reading skills and strategies).

## Students with Special Communication Challenges

Students with special speech or language needs usually have problems communicating. They may have difficulty understanding or using oral language—or both. These students, of course, can vary greatly in their speech/language, academic, and classroom behaviors. Many of your students with speech/language needs will receive special services from a speech pathologist or clinician.

## Special Speech Challenges

Students who have special needs/challenges regarding their speech usually are experiencing one of three difficulties: articulation, voice, or disfluency. Each is described in the sections that follow.

*Articulation.* Articulation is the production of speech sounds or phonemes, and elementary students can manifest three types of articulation difficulties: Omissions involve leaving out one or more phonemes. For example, instead of saying *baby* the student says *_a_e*, omitting the /b/ sound; or, omitting /s/, "I want to *i*ng my *o*ng by my *e*lf" for "I want to sing my song by myself." Additions occur when the student adds one or more phonemes. For example, the student says *belue* for *blue* or *sumber* for *summer.* Substitutions involve the substituting of sounds. The classic example is the substitution of /w/ for /r/—*wabbit* for *rabbit.*

Articulation difficulties in and of themselves will not directly affect your students' acquisition of literacy skills. The etiology of the articulation problem is what must be considered. If the students misarticulate because they have an auditory-discrimination problem, these same students may also have difficulty developing phonic abilities.

*Voice.* Voice disorders are associated with vocal deviation in pitch (e.g., using too high a pitch for age and sex), degree of loudness (e.g., speaking too softly), and quality (e.g., speaking harshly). Problems in voice are due to laryngeal disorders or growths or to vocal abuse. Students you suspect have a voice disorder should be immediately referred to a physician.

Like articulation difficulties, voice disorders will not affect your students' reading development. Hoarseness is the number-one form of voice difficulty, and this condition, as well as pitch or loudness deviations, could affect your students' oral-reading proficiency. Therefore, students with this difficulty should be asked to volunteer to read aloud.

*Dysfluency.* Dysfluency, or stuttering, involves acute disruptions in the rhythm of speech. Stuttering can be characterized by prolongation of sounds, excessive hesitations, long pauses, or excessive interjections. Dysfluency is believed to have both physiological and psychological bases. If one of your students stutters, this student should not be asked to read aloud or forced into contributing to discussions, if he or she doesn't indicate a desire to do so.

## Special Language Needs

Silliman and Stack (1994) stated that "[l]anguage is the system by which human beings communicate" (p. 291). Kirk, Gallagher, and Anastasiow (1993) defined language as ". . . an organized system of symbols used to express and receive meaning" (p. 265). A number of definitions of special language needs have been published by language specialists. These definitions primarily focus on an inability to acquire, understand, or express language.

The special language needs of elementary students could include the following.

***Poverty of Expression.*** This condition is related to a student still using telegraphic speech. For example, you may hear a student say, "Go home have fun" for "I want to go home and have fun." Poverty of expression is also associated with making grammatical and syntactical errors. For "This is my pencil," the student says, "This are my pencil."

***Linguistic Problems.*** Students with linguistic problems may have difficulty understanding how language is structured or organized. These students manifest a number of specific characters, but their single most common attribute is that their verbal-language competence is well below that of their peers. Some of your students with linguistic problems may have been three or even four years old when they actually began talking.

***Symbolization Problems.*** Students with language problems can have difficulty understanding and using the symbols of their language. This directly manifests itself in these students' having problems learning to read, to write, to spell, and to do mathematics.

***Additional Characteristics.*** Other behaviors manifested by students with language problems may include poor speech, limited vocabulary, using "baby talk," not following verbal directions, having short attention spans and being easily distracted, and mixing the meanings of simple words, among the other language behaviors already described. With respect to reading ability, your students with special speech and language needs exhibit heterogeneous behaviors. These students may read very little or may excel in reading.

## Students with Sensory Challenges

This designation includes students with a vision or hearing loss. Specifics regarding each of these sensory challenges are provided.

## Students with Visual Challenges

Obviously, depending on the severity of the visual impairment, students would experience more or fewer challenges in school settings. Because the most severe of impairments is blindness, it is important that you know the legal definition of it as well as have some ideas about methods and materials for use with different degrees of visually impaired learners. First, the legal definition follows:

> Visual impairment or visual disability can be used to describe a visual limitation of 20/70 or worse. The "20/70" refers to the diagnosis made by using the Snellen chart; it means that the person could see no more at a distance of 20 feet than someone with adequate vision can see at a distance of 70 feet. Those persons whose visual acuity falls between 20/70 and 20/200 are considered partially sighted. . . . The clients in a rehabilitation setting whose visual acuity falls between 20/200 and 20/500 are described as having partial vision, low vision, or useful vision. Clients with 20/500 or worse . . . are termed totally blind or having no useful vision. (Vander Kolk 1981, p. 2)

Teachers should know that students who are legally blind can learn in the classroom and "learn best through tactile and auditory senses" while individuals with partial sight or low vision can use their intact visual abilities with magnifying devices or other aids to learn (Holbrook and Healy 1994, p. 389) Of course, students with visual challenges, low vision or blind, are heterogeneous with respect to the characteristics they exhibit in the elementary classroom. Many of these students have residual vision but use telescopic or magnifying devices (e.g., hand-held, closed-circuit television, etc.) and special materials (e.g., talking books, braille, etc.) for learning purposes. Their academic abilities are comparable to other children of their age, but some of these students, usually depending on their age when they became visually impaired, may need specific instruction to develop associations (e.g., names and objects), to understand some concepts (e.g., clouds), and to learn to move about the classroom, building, and school grounds (e.g., orientation and mobility training). For students with visual challenges, it is also important that, when possible, you promote the use of vision, help them develop auditory and haptic modality skills, encourage use of nonoptical and optical devices as needed, and reduce blindisms (i.e., repetitive motions such as rocking back and forth).

### Students with Hearing Challenges

Hearing, like visual challenges, can be defined from a quantitative or educational perspective (Hunt and Marshall 1994). Quantitative or legal definitions state the degree of hearing loss as assessed audiometrically in decibels (dB). Telford and Sawrey (1981, p. 381) have summarized the quantitative or dB loss definition:

> *Class 1. Mild losses (20 to 30 dB).* People with hearing losses in this range learn to speak by hearing . . . and are borderline . . . hard-of-hearing and . . . normal.
> *Class 2. Marginal losses (30 to 40 dB).* People with such losses usually have difficulty in hearing speech at a distance of more than a few feet . . .
> *Class 3. Moderate losses (40 to 60 dB).* With amplification of sound and the assistance of vision, people in this range can learn speech aurally.
> *Class 4. Severe losses (60 to 75 dB).* People with hearing losses in this range will not acquire speech without the use of specialized techniques. Most such people are considered "educationally deaf." They are borderline . . . hard-of-hearing and deaf.
> *Class 5. Profound losses (greater than 75 dB).* People with this range seldom learn language by ear alone, even with maximum application of sound.

PL 94-142 has defined hearing impairments from an educational or functional perspective. According to this definition:

> Deaf is the term used to describe a hearing impairment which is so severe that the child is impaired in processing linguistic information through hearing with or without amplification, which adversely affects educational performance.
> Hard of hearing is the term used to describe a hearing impairment whether permanent or fluctuating, which adversely affects a child's educational performance but which is not under the definition of deaf. (Larson and Miller 1982, p. 449).

In essence, students with a hearing challenge will have a diagnosed hearing loss (that can be measured in decibels lost) that may affect their educational growth and development.

Students with various hearing challenges can exhibit a host of characteristics alone or in combination. The three most important factors that affect these characteristics are age of onset (e.g., hearing loss occurred before or after the speech-language developmental period), type of hearing loss (e.g., conductive, sensorineural, or mixed/both), and degree of impairment (e.g., mild to profound). Most of these learners will have usable residual hearing, those with a conductive hearing loss may use amplification or hearing aids, and there is no research to suggest that the intellectual skills of these students are different from their hearing peers. However, these students' language facility and academic achievement is significantly affected by age of onset and degree of loss, so students who have a severe or profound hearing loss at birth may have more severe language and academic learning problems. Because a hearing loss can impede the development of oral language, and oral language can be the basis for social interactions, students with a hearing disability may have difficulty interacting with you and their peers and, consequently, may have difficulty developing and maintaining friendships. A lack of social interactions and friendships can negatively affect social-emotional development as well as academic achievement.

If students with hearing challenges are to succeed in the classroom and reach their literacy potential, facilitative teachers must use multidisciplinary, collaborative, and home-school procedures to plan and conduct their instructional program. In addition, we encourage you, whenever possible, to promote these students' uses of residual hearing and hearing aids, assist them in developing visual and haptic modality skills, encourage their use of lipreading, and facilitate their oral language development.

## *Students with Physical Challenges*

These students have mild to severe motor or movement limitations and may or may not be confined to wheelchairs. The most common cause of a physical disability is a central-nervous-system injury.

According to Esposito and Campbell (1993): "Individuals who are physically challenged have significant disabilities in posture and movement. These disabilities may be acquired through accident or disease, such as individuals with paralysis. . . . Some individuals are born with a movement disability. Disabilities can range from mild to severe. The most prominent dimension among individuals with physical disability is the degree of impairment to the motor system that is present. Individuals may be totally unable to move the arms, legs, or body but may be able to move the head or their eyes. Some individuals have upper extremity movement but movement patterns may be limited or uncoordinated" (p. 160).

Students with physical disabilities/challenges will be quite heterogeneous but may have various difficulties that may affect their learning in an inclusive classroom setting. For example, they may have mild to severe problems in the area of motor skills (e.g., balance, gross, fine, etc.) and oral language (e.g., some will be nonverbal and use assistive-augmentative devices to communicate). Or they may require assistance from peers or paraprofessionals to fully participate in classroom activities. A multidisciplinary team approach, particularly collaborating with related services personnel (e.g., physical and occupational therapists, speech pathologist, etc.), and home-school programming are two ways to provide classroom access and opportunities for a comfortable learning environment for students who are physically challenged.

### Students with Attention Deficit Disorder (ADD) and Attention Deficit/Hyperactivity Disorder (ADHD)

The number of children, youths, and adults being identified with ADD and ADHD has increased significantly, and there has been considerable attention in local and national media regarding these designations. This section is intended to broaden your understanding of ADD and ADHD and to suggest collaborations and strategies to use to meet the needs of these students. Students with ADD and ADHD may or may not be considered as having a disability and eligible for special education services (e.g., a student with LD who is also ADD or ADHD receives special education services because of the learning disability) but do have legal rights for educational accommodation and are protected under Section 504 of the 1973 Rehabilitation Act (Henley, Ramsey, and Algozzine 1996). Who are these students and what can you do to accommodate their literacy learning?

Shaywitz and Shaywitz (1992a) stated that "[at]tention deficit disorder (ADD) currently represents one of the most frequently diagnosed neurobehavioral disorders in childhood, affecting perhaps as much as 20 percent of the school-aged population" (p. vii). The 20 percent figure is probably high, but unquestionably, millions of children, youths, and adults have been identified as ADD and represent one of three subtypes or groups: ADD without hyperactivity, ADD with hyperactivity, and ADD with aggression (Shaywitz and Shaywitz 1992b). However, in the American Psychiatric Association's (1994) *Diagnostic and Statistical Manual of Mental Disorders* (*DSM-IV*), attention deficit/hyperactivity disorder (ADHD) is the diagnostic classification they use and define as ". . . a persistent pattern of inattention and/or hyperactivity that is more frequent and severe than is typically observed in individuals at a comparable level of development" (p. 78). According to criteria in *DSM-IV*, children with ADHD represent 3 to 5 percent of the school-age population (data for youths and adults are limited) and can be classified as one of three subtypes: ADHD predominantly inattentive, ADHD predominantly hyperactive-impulsive, and ADHD combined inattentive and hyperactive-impulsive. "In its severe form, the disorder is very impairing, affecting social, familial, and scholastic achievement" (American Psychiatric Association 1994, p. 81). Although professionals debate the diagnostic disability classification of ADHD (see Reid, Maag, and Vasa 1994), you are likely to have students identified as ADHD in your classroom.

## Characteristics

Students with ADHD manifest varied characteristics and behaviors of inattention, hyperactivity, and/or impulsivity. These students tend to exhibit normal sensory acuity, and intellectual, perceptual, and social-emotional abilities ranging from below average to above average. These students' reading, spelling, and arithmetic achievement can be significantly below their peers without ADHD, and approximately 50 percent may be designated as having a reading disability. These observations are supported by the research of Dykman and Ackerman (1992), among others. Furthermore, students with ADHD may exhibit varying behaviors due to their gender and present grade-placement differences (Shaywitz, Holahan, Marchione, Sadler, and Shaywitz 1992).

The specific behaviors of inattention, hyperactivity, and/or impulsivity are identified by the American Psychiatric Association (1994, pp. 83–85).

## General Teaching Strategies

The efforts teachers put forth to meet the needs of students with ADHD will take one of two approaches. If the student has also been identified as having a disability within IDEA guidelines and is already receiving special education or related services, the teacher will collaborate with the student's parents and professionals in the school to develop and implement an individualized education program (IEP). If the student has not been identified as having a disability within IDEA guidelines, the teacher will collaborate with the student's parents and school and community professionals (e.g., a clinical psychologist who made the ADHD diagnosis) to provide the student with classroom modifications under the mandates of Section 504 of the Rehabilitation Act of 1973. This collaboration could involve monitoring the students' taking a psychostimulant medication and observing the effects of the medication. Lerner (1993) reported that the three most frequently prescribed stimulant medications are Ritalin (methylphenidate), Cylert (pemoline), and Dexedrine (dextroamphetamine). You should know that

> [a]lthough stimulant medications have been found to significantly enhance behavioral and academic functioning among groups of children with ADHD, their effects on the behaviors of individual children are idiosyncratic and dependent upon several factors, including (a) the specific task or activity under investigation and (b) the dosage  . . . Thus, treatment evaluation must involve the multiple measures collected across several doses of medication. (Anastopoulos, DuPaul, and Barkley 1992, p. 278)

Carefully monitoring students' classroom activities and providing parents with feedback will both maximize the effectiveness of the medications and minimize negative side effects such as lethargy, insomnia, appetite loss, withdrawal, and isolation (Smith 1991).

Collaborating to meet the needs of students with ADHD will also result in the use of specific behavior management strategies and instructional principles. Lindsey, Cheek, and Kritsonis (1989, pp. 324–325) have reviewed the literature to identify strategies that can be used to increase students' attention. They recommend:

1. Use well-organized and structured reading activities.
2. Use reading materials and tests that are simple, straightforward, and have few graphic distractions.
3. Give short assignments.
4. Schedule one activity at a time.
5. Remove visually distracting elements from the classroom.
6. Plan activities that require the students to engage in verbal and motor responses (e.g., role playing) and vary them to hold students' interests.
7. Encourage students to use page markers, line markers, or index cards with slots cut the width and length of a line of text to keep their place.
8. Use lots of positive reinforcement when the student is "attending" during reading instruction.
9. Use educational technology and audiovisual aids to reinforce concepts being taught.
10. Use learning goals, questions, outlines, and other adjunctive aids to focus attention and increase comprehension.

Finally, a number of other strategies can be used to manage hyperactivity. These strategies include but are not limited to (a) establishing realistic behavioral expectations; (b) designing and implementing well-organized and structured academic activities; (c) scheduling extended or brief literacy assignments based on activity levels; (d) incorporating motor or movement activities within literacy assignments (e.g., students move from seated to standing activities); (e) providing the students with a zone-of-movement area (e.g., a 5-foot-by-5-foot marked zone around desks); and (f) collaborating with professionals to implement student-centered biofeedback and relaxation programs (Bender 1995; Mercer and Mercer 1993).

## *Other Students with Special Gifts and Talents*

This population of students is just as heterogeneous as the other populations we have discussed, and these students will provide you with unique experiences that will help you to further develop your teaching abilities. Can you imagine having a 9-year-old who plays violin on weekends for your city's symphony in your classroom? Or students whose artistic, language, or reading abilities are so advanced that they stand out as truly special? Who are these students?

A number of definitions have been given to define students with gifts and talents. The definitions have usually focused on intellectual ability, creativity, and different types of intelligences (e.g., linguistic, logical-mathematical, musical, etc.). However, one definition that is accepted in many circles, has been adopted by the U.S. Congress, and is included in the Gifted and Talented Children's Educational Act, stands out because of its broad acceptance, that is,

"gifted and talented children" means children, and whenever applicable, youth, who are identified at the preschool, elementary, or secondary level as possessing demonstrated or potential abilities that give evidence of high performance capabilities in areas such as intellectual, creative, specific academic, or leadership ability, or in the performing and visual arts, and who by reason thereof, require services or activities not ordinarily provided by the school. (Silverman 1982, p. 172)

Stated simply, students with gifts and talents can or have the potential to achieve far beyond their peers in various areas. They will be or can become superior thinkers, academic achievers, artists, dancers, or class leaders.

Maker, Nielson, and Rogers's (1995) work reflects some of the more recent thinking regarding giftedness, special talents, diversity, and problem-solving abilities. Building on Gardner's (1983) theory of multiple intelligences, Maker et al. have presented a continuum of problem-solving types and have shown how these are related to giftedness and to identifying problem-solving abilities. Also, like Gardner (1983), these researchers have emphasized that culture, language, and environment do not determine whether or not an individual will be gifted but that these do influence the specific ways that a student's giftedness may be expressed. For example, they explain that oral storytelling may be a common form of linguistic giftedness in some cultures, whereas writing (e.g., poems or short stories) may be more common in others. Also, they indicate that the particular form of language may influence the expression of giftedness and provide the example that Navajo has many rich, descriptive words but few nouns and word categories. This difference (in this one example) might influence the expression of linguistic giftedness. Finally, they show how family values and environment can influence motivation and opportunities for developing some forms of giftedness. One example they provide is that students whose parents are musicians will have more opportunities and motivation to develop musical giftedness than children whose parents have little interest in music.

The intelligences, problem-solving types (or types of giftedness) presented by Gardner (1983) and further developed by Maker, Nielson and Rogers's work (1995) include: linguistic, logical-mathematical, spatial, bodily kinesthetic, musical, interpersonal, and intrapersonal.

In summary with respect to classroom behaviors, students with gifts and talents exhibit heterogeneous attributes. Many of their gifts and talents have been developed based on their cultures, languages, and environments and the opportunities and motivations these have presented. They, of course, tend to have "normal" general characteristics (e.g., height, weight, etc.); but they can demonstrate superior achievement in academic areas (e.g., they could be your best reader, mathematician, geographer, etc.) and/or can show persistence, order and structure, excellent memory, acute powers of observation, high levels of energy, and superior powers of abstraction and critical-thinking abilities. Students with talents may also have average intellectual and academic abilities and exhibit exceptional creativity (e.g., ability to generate original ideas) and may excel in the visual and performing arts, personal skills, and body-kinesthetic skills. As would be expected, the reading abilities of your students with gifts and talents can be as diverse as any other population in your classroom.

Meeting the literacy needs of students with special learning considerations, challenges, and gifts/talents in the classroom is a rewarding experience for both the teacher and the students.
© James L. Shaffer

We recommend the use of multidisciplinary, collaborative, and home-school programming to meet some of the needs of these exceptional learners. We also suggest that you use any opportunities you can to motivate all of your learners to increase their chances of discovering and developing their giftedness and talents. Sternberg (1995/1996) shared many ideas for developing creativity among your learners—which we believe could lead to discovering hidden gifts and talents. In addition, we suggest that you use appropriate ideas, methods, and materials recommended throughout this text to design literacy instruction for your students. If you are asked to participate in your school district's utilization of other models to educate students with gifts and talents (e.g., early admission, telescoping grades, etc.), we recommend that you consider doing so.

We have presented many populations of learners with specific needs, challenges, and gifts. It is important to continue to keep in mind that even though we have designated them into certain populations to better describe their needs, challenges, and/or gifts, each learner is unique, and each learner has the potential for some degree of success in school. It is all up to you!

## Reflection Activity 10.7

*H*ow will you see to it that each learner in your class is treated with respect and is treated as special for his or her positive attributes? How will you help each learner discover his or her own potential gifts and talents? How will you work with students with special needs, challenges, and gifts, without labeling them or making them self-conscious of challenges they may face? In your reflection journal, under the heading Reflection Activity 10.7, answer these questions.

# Instructional Ideas, Procedures, and Strategies

We believe that facilitative teachers promote the literacy learning of students with cultural and language diversities, and with specific needs, challenges, and gifts by designing and implementing instructional programs based on effective ideas, procedures, and strategies. In this section we provide an array of teaching ideas and strategies that should help you plan your instructional program. We suggest that you select from these, as well as others presented throughout this text to develop appropriate instruction for all your special learners that both meets their needs and fits in with your own beliefs and definition of reading.

## Language-Based and Interactive Ideas

Later in this text, we present several language-based and interactive teaching approaches. The use of one or more of these approaches, and specifically tailoring its (their) procedures to meet the needs of students in an inclusive setting, should be strongly considered. These approaches, as noted, stress the importance of developing students' prior knowledge and language abilities. Some students with special learning needs have limited prior knowledge and less-developed language abilities. These approaches also stress the utilization and integration of speaking, listening, reading, and writing activities within authentic contexts. The literacy needs of students in an inclusive setting are promoted when they engage in receptive and expressive language activities in realistic and functional circumstances. Finally, to ensure that the approach(es) you use permit(s) you to select objectives and outcomes, to determine students' degrees of learning, and to account for student differences we also suggest that you use a planning-learning pyramid (Schumm et al. 1994) to design and conduct literacy activities (see a later chapter for application details).

Many professionals (e.g., Hammill and Bartel 1995; Henley et al. 1996; Mercer and Mercer 1993) have suggested ideas that can be used to structure effective literacy learning events and promote your students' language development. Also, Mercer and Mercer (1993, pp. 381–382) have recommended ideas and guidelines to promote students' language comprehension. We feel that most of these ideas are both language based and interactive, in that most of them involve the natural and frequent use of the learner's language and the learner's opportunity to interact in meaningful ways:

> The components (e.g., morphemes) of the formal language system should not be taught separately . . .

> Language should be taught in various natural settings (e.g. classroom, cafeteria) and not . . . in isolated groups . . .

> Language skills should be taught in connection with other curriculum content . . .

> The content of . . . [the student's] message should be reacted to first, since it is most important in the communication process. . . .

Generalizations of language [can] be [modeled], so that [the student] . . . will learn how to apply [them] to novel situations . . .

[E]stablish eye contact and maintain attention before presenting information. Cue . . . [the student] to listen through the use of silent pauses or instructions to listen to or look at the teacher. This helps to establish a mental set for listening.

Present new concepts in as many modalities as possible (e.g., auditory, visual, and kinesthetic), and use gestures to augment verbal presentations . . .

Explain to . . . [the student] that listening is an active process that requires . . . [him/her] to behave in certain ways, and teach . . . [him/her] to identify good behaviors associated with good listening (e.g., look, think about what is said, and repeat to yourself) . . .

Be sensitive to . . . [the student's linguistic complexity] and adjust the rate and complexity of instructional language accordingly. . . . [Where possible] use structurally simple and short sentences . . . and limit the number of new and unfamiliar words presented in a single lesson to five or less . . .

[Teach the student] to use semantic organizers when reading that display key concepts as clusters of related ideas and, thus, provide a verbal (semantic) and a graphic-structure (organizer) component.

### *Multisensory Procedures*

The multisensory concept for developing students' literacy abilities is based on two premises: First, we learn through our senses and assimilate our world by seeing, hearing, smelling, tasting, and touching. Second, the more senses tapped during the teaching-learning process, the greater the chances are that learning takes place. Having students use more than one sense at a time in a lesson (e.g., having them see, hear, and touch a bird) is believed to be more effective than having them use one or both of the traditional senses used in school (e.g., only seeing and hearing a bird). There is one drawback, however, to the multisensory teaching strategies: When you stimulate multiple senses, you sometimes confuse or overwhelm some students. For example, and this is not an exact analogy, have you ever had three or more people trying to show and tell you the same thing at the same time? You probably could not process anything that was going on or you only understood in bits and pieces. Nevertheless, you will have students who do profit from multisensory experiences.

We would recommend that you consider using one of the following multisensory strategies within your reading program for your students who need this type of instructional support.

### *Gillingham and Stillman's (1970) VAK Strategy*

Gillingham and Stillman advocated the Visual-Auditory-Kinesthetic (VAK) multisensory strategy. Using the VAK procedure, students associate and learn eight VAK links. For example, you want to teach students the letter *r* and its sound /r/. The students would be shown the letter *r* and write *r* for the V-K link. They would then hear the /r/ sound and write *r* for the A-K link. Finally, the students would write the letter *r* and pair it with another *r* for the K-V link. And, the student would write the letter *r* and produce the /r/ sound for the K-A link. The VAK strategy and corresponding links could be used to teach some students how to read words, phrases, and sentences.

### Fernald's (1943) VAKT Strategy

The most powerful multisensory strategy you can use with students is the Fernald Visual-Auditory-Kinesthetic-Tactile (VAKT) strategy. This strategy has four stages, but the basic premise of the technique involves the students seeing, hearing, tracing, and writing what they are to learn. For example, you want to teach your students how to read the word "was." You give them flashcards with the word *was* on it. The students see *was* (V), you say /was/ (A), the students write *was* (K), and the students trace *was* (T). Fernald's VAKT strategy can be used to develop synthetic- and analytic-phonic abilities, sight vocabulary, and phrase-reading abilities.

### Dwyer and Flippo's (1983) Multisensory Spelling and Sight-Word Strategy

Dwyer and Flippo (1983, pp. 171–172) have also developed a multisensory procedure, based on Fernald's VAKT strategy, which can be used in both reading and spelling activities. The procedure promotes visual memory through sensory reinforcement and uses the following steps:

1. Look at the word carefully.
2. Talk about the word to determine its meaning and pronunciation.
3. Close your eyes, visualize the word, and write it in the air.
4. Write the word on paper without looking at it.
5. Check its spelling, and write it again from memory.
6. Write the word in a sentence.

Because some students need still more reinforcement, you can try the following additional steps:

1. Take an 8½-by-11-inch (roughly 20-by-30-centimeter) sheet of clear acetate, the kind frequently used with overhead projectors.
2. Perforate the acetate all over by running it through a sewing machine with an unthreaded needle, making rows approximately ¼ inch (1 centimeter) apart. This is to make the surface rough.
3. Attach the acetate along one side of a piece of cardboard so that the acetate can be easily lifted.
4. A word to be learned is printed in large letters on paper and placed under the acetate.
5. The word can now be viewed through the acetate, and the student can trace each letter with the index finger while saying the word. The perforations feel rough and help the reader be conscious of tracing the letter shapes.
6. The whole word is pronounced.

The student sees the word, "feels" it, and hears it. Although time-consuming, the multisensory procedure helps strengthen visual memory. With most students, the number of tracings needed to learn to spell new words become fewer and fewer until tracing becomes unnecessary.

Review is essential for long-term retention of difficult words, so establishing a word bank for each student is advisable.

### Analytical-Tutorial Word Identification Strategy

Descriptions of a variety of procedures for developing students' reading abilities are included in the professional literature. Lindsey, Beck, and Bursor (1981) have proposed a strategy for developing and reinforcing some of your students' vocabulary and sight-word learning. You begin the process by using a modified language-experience approach (LEA):

1. The student dictates a story to you, and you write it down.
2. The student reads the story and then types it (with or without assistance).
3. The student rereads the story and works with you to identify high-frequency sight words to be learned.
4. The Fernald VAKT strategy is used to have the student learn the words "on sight."
5. You and the student develop a vocabulary-and-story file.
6. The student reviews the filed vocabulary and stories.

After the student has shown he/she can read the story and knows the high-frequency vocabulary, Lindsey, Beck, and Bursor suggested that you would then work with a teacher of a lower grade level to develop a cross-age tutorial program. Your students are taught how to conduct a one-to-one tutoring lesson and then are paired with younger students. The older students tutor the younger students, teaching them how to read the dictated story and emphasizing the designated vocabulary and sight words.

### Cooperative Learning

Cooperative learning, or learning through doing and solving a group assignment, is a learning strategy that holds promise for meeting the literacy needs of students in an inclusive setting. This grouping format involves assigning students to work together to accomplish an objective or to solve a problem. Such activities require students to interact in a positive and task-oriented way if they are to succeed in their efforts. You will find that cooperative-learning procedures can be fun to implement and will prove to be quite useful. The basic steps you should consider to organize a cooperative group activity include:

1. Identifying the group's purpose—literacy objectives.
2. Determining the size of the group.
3. Providing students with guidelines to ensure that they understand the group's purpose and how to work together cooperatively.
4. Monitoring the group's endeavors.
5. Evaluating the group's activities and outcomes.

Mercer and Mercer (1993) have described two unique variations of cooperative learning or grouping that you may want to use with your students with special learning and behavior needs: Student Teams-Achievement Divisions (STAD) and Teams-Games-Tournaments (TGT) (see Mercer and Mercer 1993). With STAD, you teach a lesson to a small or large group. Immediately following the lesson, the group or team of students works together to ensure that all students have developed the required knowledge or abilities. The students are then assessed individually without peer support. TGT also begins with you teaching a lesson, followed by the students working together to learn concepts or skills. A tournament, however, replaces the individual quizzes and students compete as teams to earn points.

## Pretend Play and Story Making

Liam and Watson (1993) noted that students' literacy development is facilitated when classroom strategies are shifted from teacher-directed instruction to student-initiated activities involving the functional use of language in natural settings. Pretend-play situations can be an excellent medium for promoting your students' functional language usage. To encourage pretend play, you will need to provide opportunity, space, and many reading and writing props. Roskos (1988) suggested that you (a) create and frequently use play centers that facilitate sustained pretend play and prompt experimentation with reading (e.g., an office area, a travel agency, a store, a bank, or a play school); (b) ask students to share their pretend stories and record them on chart paper for extended language-experience activities; and (c) observe more closely the literacy at work in the pretend play of students.

## Use of Music, Songs, and Lyrics

Music, songs, and lyrics can be used to not only manage students' classroom behaviors (see West et al. 1995) but also develop their cognitive and academic abilities. Flippo (1988) did an extensive review of the research and found that the possibilities for using music, songs, and lyrics as material for reading and writing development are limitless. The activities should be very motivating for your students, and the students can select their own favorite songs (e.g., ethnic, popular, ballads, etc.). Additionally, sheet music, recordings, cassette players/recorders, radios, and musical instruments can be brought to class for a never-ending supply of materials for the students to choose from. You will want to have a lot of writing material available to record the students' words for later use.

## Behavior Management Strategies

Finally, one of the challenges you will face in an inclusive literacy setting is developing or managing the behaviors of some of your students with special learning or behavioral needs who do not respond to your classroom management procedures or are unable to control their behaviors with self-monitoring and self-management methods you have taught them to use. For these students it may be necessary to design and implement a specific approach to developing or increasing appropriate general classroom and literacy behaviors (e.g., see Hammill and Bartel 1995; Henley et al. 1996; Mercer and Mercer 1993). This section describes five behavior management strategies you may want to apply, either alone or in combination, to promote appropriate behaviors or to deal with crisis situations.

### Counseling

The use of counseling techniques is a very standard procedure for trying to manage students' behaviors. You could counsel learners with special needs in large groups, small groups, or one-to-one. You could take the directive-counseling approach, that is, structuring the counseling session and showing these students how to solve their problems. You can also use the nondirective approach, which is structuring the counseling environment but having the students identify and solve their own problems.

### Modeling

This technique is another traditional approach used in the schools to manage students' behaviors. You should consider using three steps to implement a modeling program: First, identify the behavior you want students to model (or exhibit) and identify a student in the class who already exhibits this behavior. Second, when the selected student exhibits the desired behavior, point out this behavior manifestation to the class and reward the student for exhibiting it. Third, when the students model or exhibit the desired behavior, you should reinforce them and verbally praise them in front of their classmates.

### Reality Therapy

Reality therapy can be a very effective behavior-management procedure, because it helps students to take responsibility for their own behaviors. Students who become responsible for their actions (i.e., they take charge of their lives and do not blame others for their problems) have a sense of involvement in the educational process and develop feelings of self-worth. Five steps you could use to implement a reality-therapy program in your elementary classroom are as follows: (1) interact with a student when he or she is exhibiting a desired behavior; this interaction develops rapport and confidence; (2) during one of these positive interactions, ask the student if what he or she is doing is of value. If the student says "Yes, I like what I am doing," go to the next step; (3) work with the student and formulate realistic plans that would get the student to continue exhibiting the positive or valued behavior. Write a contract based on the plan and both you and the student sign it; (4) help the student to follow the contract. If the student follows the contract, he or she will exhibit positive changes in behavior. A new plan and contract is then designed and signed for bringing about other behavioral changes; and (5) if the contract is not met, you and the student tear up the old contract, and no questions are asked or excuses given. A new plan and contract for smaller behavioral changes are developed and signed (i.e., the old contract may have been based on too great a behavioral change).

## Behavior Modification

This behavior-management technique has as its objective the strengthening, weakening, or maintenance of your students' exhibited behaviors. You would identify a behavior that you want to change and manipulate the environment to bring about that change. For example, if you wanted students to sit at their desks during reading instruction, you would reward these students with a primary (e.g., manipulative object) or secondary (e.g., verbal praise) reinforcer when they are sitting in their chairs. Conversely, if you wanted to stop students from speaking out without first raising their hands, you would ignore them when they speak out but reward them when they raise their hands.

## Life-Space Interviewing

Life-space interviewing (LSI) is the most effective technique you can use to manage and reduce crisis situations. It is an interview procedure that can be used daily and with nearly all crises (e.g., arguments, fights, etc.). Its purpose is to help students to understand crises and to make decisions to avoid these disruptive activities. Six steps you would use to implement LSI are (1) provide students in crisis the opportunity to give their impressions of what happened and why; (2) question the students to be sure all facts and details are presented; (3) get the students to tell you what they can do to prevent such a crisis from occurring in the future; (4) where students cannot give a remedy to the situation, you describe the crisis situation and possible consequences; (5) after describing the crisis and consequences, you outline steps the students can take to prevent such future crises; and (6) you and the students work together to develop strategies that can be taken to prevent future crises.

In addition to the preceding five strategies, you may want to use role playing and play therapy (structured and unstructured) to develop your students' appropriate classroom and literacy behaviors. You may not want to role-play highly emotional situations with certain students or to permit selected students to engage in play therapy without fully understanding the rules for playing.

## Reflection Activity 10.8

*M*any teaching ideas, procedures, and strategies have been described that could be used with some culturally and language diverse learners, and with some learners with specific needs, challenges, and gifts. Which did you like best? Why? How would you use those selected to enhance the learning, and reading and other literacy skills of special learners? Are there others you would also include from other chapters? If so, which ones and why? In your reflection journal, under the heading Reflection Activity 10.8, note your ideas.

# Computer Hardware and Software Considerations

Your school district's technology specialist will assist you in securing state-of-the-art hardware (e.g., a multimedia system) and software (e.g., authoring programs such as Apple's HyperCard) that will be conducive to promoting literacy in an inclusive setting. As discussed previously this person can also assist you in accessing local area networks (e.g., library LANs) and telecommunication avenues (e.g., the Internet).

You should also consult ESL professionals who can provide guidance for using English-development software (e.g., Intechnica International's *I Speak English* [1993] series and Merit's ESL Demons). Although we would highly recommend that you use such multimedia software to develop your students' English receptive and expressive language abilities, there is one traditional approach that we would also suggest you consider for this purpose. Your limited-English-speaking and English as a Second Language (ESL) students can benefit from the comprehensible input plus language-experience approach (CI + LEA) as described by Moustafa (1987). This approach has you using concrete object such as large pictures or models that can be pointed to again and again in conjunction with oral language to help students acquire more oral English before the LEA portion of the lesson. Once the students are thoroughly familiar with the concrete objects or pictures, you use the objects to pose questions like "Where are they?" "Who's that?" and "What's he doing?" When the students answer the questions, you reaffirm the answer in a complete sentence such as "Yes, they are at the playground." Using this procedure, sight words are emphasized and reinforced, and students use their acquired vocabulary and sentences relating to the concrete object or picture to develop dictated language-experience stories. Moustafa reported success with varied ESL students including Spanish, Vietnamese, Cambodian, Korean, Tagalog, and Hmong first-language speakers.

Special educators will work with you to obtain and use adaptive input devices (e.g., adaptive keyboards or touch screens) and adaptive output devices (e.g., speech synthesizers or large print and braille processors). The ultimate goal of your technology program for students in an inclusive setting is the matching of literacy objectives with student characteristics and hardware and software attributes. Multidisciplinary, collaborative, and home-school activities will help you ensure this match and should help promote your students' literacy learning.

## Summary

This chapter introduced the idea of teaching literacy in an inclusive setting. Students from all cultural and language groups were included in this setting. Instructional models and procedures that could be applied when working with students in inclusive settings were provided. Extensive discussion was also provided on areas and issues that included "at risk"/"at promise" students, cultural diversity, multicultural education, and bilingual and ESL programs. The issues of diversity, mainstreaming, and inclusion in the elementary classroom were discussed. Students with various special needs, challenges, and gifts were described, and specific considerations to provide age-appropriate instruction were depicted. The chapter concluded with ideas for and descriptions of teaching strategies that can be used in the elementary classroom to meet the literacy needs of all students, including culturally and language diverse learners, and learners with special needs, challenges, and gifts/talents.

# Closing Activities

1. In a small group, discuss the following concepts presented in this chapter: (a)*At-Risk*—should this term be used to label students in the elementary classroom? Why or why not? (b) *At Promise*—should this term be used to identify students who might need extra support? Why or why not? (c) *Multicultural Education*—should a course on multicultural education be included in the preservice elementary education degree program? Why or why not? (d) *Full Inclusion*—should all elementary students be educated in general education classrooms in neighborhood schools and not removed (or segregated) for special education or other educational services? Why or why not? Be prepared to summarize your discussions at the next class meeting.

2. Using the library resources at your institution, secure two articles that address cultural diversity and multicultural concepts in the elementary classroom. Compare and contrast the general positions presented in both articles. Also, infer and discuss each of the authors' probable attitudes toward reading development and other literacy learnings.

3. Using the library resources at your institution, read two articles on bilingual programs and two more on ESL programs. Based on what you have read, what are the similarities and differences between the programs? How might each type of program serve the special needs of students, teachers, and schools?

4. Using the library resources at your institution, examine the recommendations various educators have suggested for meeting the literacy needs of elementary students with special needs and challenges. In outline format, describe how their recommendations compared or contrasted with those we suggested in this chapter.

5. As part of the field activities in this course, visit an elementary school in your area that has an exemplary multicultural education program, a full inclusion program, a bilingual or ESL program or all of these. Interview administrators and teachers to determine their multicultural education and full inclusion (1) definitions, (2) goals and objectives, and (3) professional collaborations and parental-family-community activities. Additionally, observe literacy lessons and record what instructional ideas and strategies the teachers used to meet the needs of students from culturally diverse backgrounds and those students with special needs. Ask the teachers how they use students' language and cultural diversities as strengths in the classroom. Take notes on your findings and be prepared to share them in class.

## References

Allington, R. L. (1994a). "The Schools We Have. The Schools We Need." *The Reading Teacher* 48:14-29.

Allington, R. L. (1994b). "What's Special about Special Programs for Children Who Find Learning to Read Difficult?" *Journal of Reading Behavior* 26 (1):95-115.

Allington, R. L. (1995). "Literacy Lessons in the Elementary Schools: Yesterday, Today, and Tomorrow." In R. L. Allington and S. A. Walmsley, eds., *No Quick Fix: Rethinking Literacy Programs in America's Elementary Schools* (pp.1-15). New York: Teachers College Press.

American Psychiatric Association. (1994). *Diagnostic and Statistical Manual of Mental Disorders,* 4th ed. Washington, DC: American Psychiatric Association.

Anastopoulos, A. R., G. J. DuPaul, and R. A. Barkley. (1992). "Stimulant Medication and Parent Training Therapies for Attention Deficit-Hyperactivity Disorder." In S. E. Shaywitz and B. A. Shaywitz, eds., *Attention Deficit Disorder Comes of Age: Toward the Twenty-First Century* (pp. 273-292). Austin, TX: PROED.

Ashworth, M., and H. P. Wakefield. (1994). *Teaching the World's Children: ESL for Ages Three to Seven.* Markham, Ontario: Pippin Publishing Limited.

Banks, J. A. (1993). "Multicultural Education: Characteristics and Goals." In J. A. Banks and C. A. Banks, eds., *Multicultural Education: Issues and Perspectives,* 2nd ed. (pp. 3-28). Boston: Allyn & Bacon.

————. (1994). *An Introduction to Multicultural Education.* Boston: Allyn & Bacon.

Banks, J. A., and C. A. Banks, eds. (1993). *Multicultural Education: Issues and Perspectives,* 2nd ed. Boston: Allyn & Bacon.

Bender, W. N. (1995). *Learning Disabilities: Characteristics, Identification, and Teaching Strategies,* 2nd ed. Boston: Allyn & Bacon.

Brozo, W. G., and M. L. Simpson. (1995). *Readers, Teaching, Learners: Expanding Literacy in Secondary Schools,* 2nd ed. Englewood Cliffs, NJ: Merrill/Prentice-Hall.

Cárdenas, J. A. (1995). *Multicultural Education: A Generation of Advocacy.* Needham Heights, MA: Simon & Schuster.

Chinn, P. (1994). "Exceptional Children from Diverse Cultural Backgrounds." In N. Hunt and K. Marshall, eds., *Exceptional Children and Youth* (pp. 562–602). Boston: Houghton Mifflin.

Clegg, L. B., E. Miller, and W. Vanderhoof. (1995, Spring). "A Case for Multicultural Education." *Education Today: News for Early Childhood, Special and Elementary Educators,* 1–4.

Collins, M. D., and E. H. Cheek, Jr. (1993). *Diagnostic-Prescriptive Reading Instruction: A Guide for Classroom Teachers,* 4th ed. Madison, WI: Brown & Benchmark Publishers.

Diamond, B. J., and M. A. Moore. (1995). *Multicultural Literacy: Mirroring the Reality of the Classroom.* New York: Longman.

Díaz-Rico, L. T., and K. Z. Weed. (1995). *The Crosscultural, Language, and Academic Development Handbook.* Boston: Allyn & Bacon.

Durkin, D. (1995). *Language Issues: Readings for Teachers.* New York: Longman.

Dwyer, E. J., and R. F. Flippo. (1983). "Multisensory Approaches to Teaching Spelling." *Journal of Reading* 27:171–172.

Dykman, R. A., and P. T. Ackerman. (1992). "Attention Deficit Disorder and Specific Reading Disability: Separate but Often Overlapping Disorders." In S. E. Shaywitz and B. A. Shaywitz, eds., *Attention Deficit Disorder Comes of Age: Toward the Twenty-First Century* (pp. 165–183). Austin, TX: PROED.

Esposito, L., and P. H. Campbell. (1993). "Computers and Individuals with Severe and Physical Disabilities." In J. D. Lindsey, ed., *Computers and Exceptional Individuals* (pp. 159–177). Austin: TX: PROED.

Fernald, G. (1943). *Remedial Techniques in High School.* New York: McGraw-Hill.

Fitzgerald, J. (1993). "Literacy and Students Who Are Learning English as a Second Language." *The Reading Teacher* 46:638–647.

Flippo, R. F. (1988). "The Use of Music, Songs, and Lyrics in Reading Instruction." In C. Anderson, ed., *Reading: The ABC and Beyond* (pp. 55–61). London, England: Macmillan Education.

————. (1997). *Reading Assessment and Instruction: A Qualitative Approach to Diagnosis.* Ft. Worth, TX: Harcourt Brace College Publishers.

Frazer, L., and T. Nichols. (1991). *At-Risk Report: 1990–91: Executive Summary.* Austin, TX: Austin Independent School District, Office of Research and Evaluation.

Gardner, H. (1983). *Frames of Mind: The Theory of Multiple Intelligences.* New York: Basic Books.

Gersten, R., and R. T. Jiménez. (1994). "A Delicate Balance: Enhancing Literature Instruction for Students of English as a Second Language." *The Reading Teacher* 47 (6):438–449.

Giangreco, M. F., and J. W. Putnum. (1991). "Supporting the Education of Students with Severe Disabilities in Regular Education Environments." In L. H. Meyer, C. A. Peck, and L. Brown, eds., *Critical Issues in the Lives of People with Severe Disabilities* (pp. 245–270). Baltimore: Paul H. Brookes.

Gillingham, A., and B. Stillman. (1970). *Remedial Training for Children with Specific Disability in Reading, Spelling, and Penmanship.* Cambridge, MA: Educators Publishing Service.

Gollnick, D. M., and P. C. Chinn. (1994). *Multicultural Education in a Pluralistic Society,* 4th ed. New York: Merrill/Macmillan.

Graves, M. F., B. B. Graves, and S. Braaten. (1996). "Scaffolded Reading Experiences for Inclusive Classes." *Educational Leadership* 53 (5):14–16.

Haas, D. (1993). "Inclusion Is Happening in the Classroom." *Children Today* 22:34–35.

Hallahan, D. P., and J. M. Kauffman. (1991). *Exceptional Children: Introduction to Special Education,* 5th ed. Englewood Cliffs, NJ: Prentice Hall.

Hammill, D. D., and N. R. Bartel. (1995). *Teaching Children with Learning and Behavior Problems,* 6th ed. Austin, TX: PROED.

Hannaford, A. E. (1993). "Computers and Exceptional Individuals." In J. D. Lindsey, ed., *Computers and Exceptional Individuals* (pp. 3–26). Austin, TX: PROED.

Harris, V. J., ed. (1993). *Teaching Multicultural Literature in Grades K–8.* Norwood, MA: Christopher-Gordon Publishers.

Heath, S. B., and L. Mangiola. (1991). *Children of Promise: Literate Activity in Linguistically and Culturally Diverse Classrooms.* Washington, DC: National Education Association, Center for the Study of Writing and Literacy, and American Educational Research Association.

Henley, M., R. S. Ramsey, and R. F. Algozzine. (1996). *Teaching Students with Mild Disabilities,* 2nd ed. Boston: Allyn & Bacon.

Holbrook, C., and M. S. Healy. (1994). "Children Who Are Blind or Have Low Vision." In N. Hunt and K. Marshall, eds., *Exceptional Children and Youth* (pp. 386–425). Boston: Houghton Mifflin.

Hunt, N., and K. Marshall. (1994). *Exceptional Children and Youth.* Boston: Houghton Mifflin.

*I Speak English: Program Overview.* (1993). Midwest City, OK: Intechnica International.

Idol, L., A. Nevin, and P. Paolucci-Whitcomb. (1994). *Collaborative Consultation,* 2nd ed. Austin, TX: PROED.

Kirk, S. A., J. J. Gallagher, and N. J. Anastasiow. (1993). *Educating Exceptional Children,* 7th ed. Boston: Houghton Mifflin.

LaBoskey, V. K. (1994). *Development of Reflective Practice: A Study of Preservice Teachers.* New York: Teachers College Press.

Larson, A. D., and J. D. Miller. (1982). "The Hearing Impaired." In E. L. Meyen, ed., *Exceptional Children and Youth: An Introduction* (pp. 444–480). Denver: Love Publishing Company.

Lerner, J. W. (1993). *Learning Disabilities: Theories, Diagnosis, and Teaching Strategies,* 6th ed. Boston: Houghton Mifflin.

Liam, H. J. L., and D. J. Watson. (1993). "Whole Language Content Classes for Second-Language Learners." *The Reading Teacher* 46:384–393.

Lindsey, J. D., F. W. Beck, and D. E. Bursor. (1981). "An Analytical-Tutorial Method for Developing Adolescents' Sight Vocabulary." *Journal of Reading* 24:591–594.

Lindsey, J. D., E. H. Cheek, and D. G. Kritsonis (1989). "Maintaining Reading-Disabled Students' Attention During Reading Instruction." *Child Language Teaching and Therapy* 5:321–326.

Lindsey, J. D., C. Ghose, and R. Ramasamy. (in press). "The Full-Inclusive Perceptions of Graduate Students in General and Special Education." *Educational Research Quarterly.*

Lipson, M. Y., and K. K. Wixson. (1991). *Assessment and Instruction of Reading Disability: An Interactive Approach.* New York: HarperCollins.

Luster, J. N., and C. Ouder. (1994, November 10). *Special Educators' Language: Do We Understand Each Other?* Paper presented at the Mid-South Educational Research Association, Nashville, Tennessee.

Maker, C. J., A. B. Nielson, and J. A. Rogers. (1995). "Giftedness, Diversity, and Problem-Solving: Multiple Intelligences and Diversity in Educational Settings." In K. M. Paciorek and J. H. Munro, eds., *Early Childhood Education 95/96,* 16th ed. Guilford, CT: Dushkin Publishing Group/Brown & Benchmark Publishers.

Mercer, C. D., and A. R. Mercer. (1993). *Teaching Students with Learning Problems,* 4th ed. New York: Merrill/Macmillan.

Moustafa, M. (1987). "Comprehensible Input PLUS the Language Experience Approach: A Long-Term Perspective." *The Reading Teacher* 41:276–286.

Pearman, E. L., M. W. Barnhart, A. M. Huang, and C. Mellblom. (1992). "Educating All Students in School: Attitudes and Beliefs About Inclusion." *Education and Training in Mental Retardation* 27:176–182.

Reid, R., J. W. Maag, and S. F. Vasa. (1994). "Attention Deficit Hyperactivity Disorder as a Disability Category: A Critique." *Exceptional Children* 60:198–214.

Rogers, J. (1993, May). "The Inclusion Revolution." *Research Bulletin* (Number 11). Bloomington, IN: Center for Evaluation, Development, and Research.

Roskos, K. (1988). "Literacy at Work in Play." *The Reading Teacher* 41:562–566.

Samway, K. D., G. Whang, and M. Pippitt. (1995). *Buddy Reading: Cross-Age Tutoring in a Multicultural School.* Portsmouth, NH: Heinemann.

Schumm, J. S., S. Vaughn, and A. G. Leavell. (1994). "Planning Pyramid: A Framework for Planning for Diverse Student Needs During Content Area Instruction." *The Reading Teacher,* 47 (8): 608–615.

Shaywitz, S. E., and B. A. Shaywitz, eds. (1992a). *Attention Deficit Disorder Comes of Age: Toward the Twenty-First Century.* Austin, TX: PROED.

———. (1992b). "Introduction." In S. E. Shaywitz and B. A. Shaywitz, eds., *Attention Deficit Disorder Comes of Age: Toward the Twenty-First Century* (pp. 1–9). Austin, TX: PROED.

Shaywitz, S. E., J. M. Holahan, K. E. Marchione, A. E. Sadler, and B. A. Shaywitz. (1992). "The Yale Children's Inventory: Normative Data and Their Implications for the Diagnosis of Attention Deficit Disorder in Children." In S. E. Shaywitz and B. A. Shaywitz, eds., *Attention Deficit Disorder Comes of Age: Toward the Twenty-First Century* (pp. 1–9). Austin, TX: PROED.

Silliman, E., and J. Stack. (1994). "Children with Communications Disorders." In N. Hunt and K. Marshall, eds., *Exceptional Children and Youth* (pp. 288–335). Boston: Houghton Mifflin.

Silverman, L. K. (1982). "The Gifted and Talented." In E. L. Meyen, ed., *Exceptional Children and Youth: An Introduction* (pp. 168–195). Denver: Love Publishing Company.

Slavin, R. E. (1996). "Neverstreaming: Preventing Learning Disabilities." *Educational Leadership* 53 (5):4–7.

Sleeter, C. E., and C. A. Grant. (1994). *Making Choices for Multicultural Education,* 2nd ed. New York: Merrill/Macmillan.

Smith, C. R. (1991). *Learning Disabilities: The Interaction of Learner, Task, and Setting,* 2nd ed. Boston: Allyn & Bacon.

Smith, T. E. C., B. J. Price, and G. E. Marsh. (1986). *Mildly Handicapped Children and Adults.* St. Paul, MN: West.

Spangenberg-Urbschat, K., and R. Pritchard, eds. (1994). *Kids Come in all Languages: Reading Instruction for ESL Students.* Newark, DE: International Reading Association.

Spring, J. (1994). *American Education,* 6th ed. New York: McGraw-Hill.

Stainback, S., and W. Stainback, eds. (1992). *Curriculum Considerations in Inclusive Classrooms: Facilitating Learning of All Students.* Baltimore: Paul H. Brookes.

Stainback, S., W. Stainback, K. East, and M. Sapon-Shevin. (1994). "A Commentary on Inclusion and the Development of a Positive Self-Identity by People with Disabilities." *Exceptional Children* 60:486–490.

Stainback, S., W. Stainback, and H. J. Jackson. (1992). "Toward Inclusive Classrooms." In S. Stainback and W. Stainback, eds., *Curriculum Considerations in Inclusive Classrooms: Facilitating Learning of All Students* (pp. 3–17). Baltimore: Paul H. Brookes.

Sternberg, R. J. (1995/1996). "Investing in Creativity: Many Happy Returns." *Educational Leadership* 53 (4):80–84.

Telford, C. W., and J. M. Sawrey. (1981). *The Exceptional Individual,* 4th ed. Englewood Cliffs, NJ: Prentice-Hall.

Vander Kolk, C. J. (1981). *Assessment and Planning with the Visually Impaired.* Baltimore: University Park Press.

West, R. P., K. R. Young, K. Callahan, S. Fister, K. Kemp, J. Freston, and T. C. Lovitt. (1995). "The Musical Clocklight: Encouraging Positive Classroom Behavior." *Teaching Exceptional Children* 27:46–51.

Wisniewski, L., and S. Alper. (1994). "Including Students with Severe Disabilities in General Education Settings: Guidelines for Change." *Remedial and Special Education* 15:4–13.

Wlodkowski, R. J., and M. B. Ginsberg. (1995). "A Framework for Culturally Responsive Teaching." *Educational Leadership* 53 (1):17–21.

Wood, J. W. (1989). *Mainstreaming: A Practical Approach for Teachers.* New York: Merrill/Macmillan.

# Section IV

## Assessment and Organizing for Instruction

S ection IV, "Assessment and Organizing for Instruction," consists of three chapters that explore topics related to assessment, approaches to teaching reading, and organizing and managing reading instruction in the classroom. Included are the use of portfolios for assessment, authentic assessment, and other informal assessment procedures, as well as formal tests to measure reading achievement and skills. Assessment decisions are explained as determined by the teacher's purposes, and assessment is viewed as an ongoing classroom activity.

The whole language, the interactive, and the skills-based perspective are recapped. Additionally, the facilitative teacher perspective—one that balances the use of approaches with students' needs, skills, strategies, motivations, and cultures—is reviewed; and five approaches for teaching and/or developing reading are presented. These approaches are the language-experience approach, individualized-reading approach, literature-based approach, basal reader approach, and eclectic approach. All of these approaches are discussed as viable options for the classroom teacher. No one approach is endorsed, as each has its place in the classroom. Instead, the idea that teachers will use many, several, or any one of these approaches to meet the current needs, skills, strategies, motivations, and cultures of their individual students is promoted. Also included is a description of an integrated curriculum.

An overview of classroom organization and management considerations and procedures is presented. Ms. Walker, a third-grade teacher, must make decisions to manage her classroom in ways that will facilitate effective instruction. Various types of groupings are explored, as well as use of a planning-learning scheme; use of materials; development of learning centers; organizing, managing, and evaluating technology in the classroom; and organizing for and encouraging parent and family participation. Finally, professional development is discussed as a way of continuing reflection and learning beyond the scope of this text, course, and certification requirements.

Many opportunities for reflections are interspersed throughout this section, and journal notations are encouraged. A culminating reflection journal activity is provided at the end of the last chapter to provide readers with an opportunity to apply many of the various ideas presented throughout this text.

# *A*ssessment in the Elementary Classroom

© Will & Deni McIntyre/Photo Researchers, Inc.

*Overview*

$T$ his chapter identifies procedures that may be helpful in providing appropriate reading instruction to students. Topics explored in this section relate to the definition and purpose of assessment, the types of assessment procedures that are available for use in your elementary classroom, and how you can most effectively use this assessment information. Specific types of assessment procedures are authentic, informal, and formal. Although authentic assessment is typically regarded as informal and classroom-based, we will treat it separately from the category of informal assessment in order to focus more on the use of portfolios. Other informal procedures discussed are observation measures, attitude and interest inventories, various types of reading inventories and other qualitative-assessment strategies, and additional sources of assessment information. Formal procedures discussed include achievement tests and group and individually administered reading tests.

## Main Ideas

- Some type of assessment is essential to facilitating reading instruction.
- Many types of assessment procedures and materials are available to you; however, for the purposes of our discussion, they fall into the categories of authentic, informal, and formal.
- Decisions to use one procedure or one type of assessment technique over another are determined by your purposes.
- Whatever your purpose or whatever procedures you use, care should be taken when analyzing and using the results.

Assessment is the process of gathering information relevant to a particular purpose. In the classroom, it usually refers to the process of determining the abilities of students to understand information that is most important to a particular content or learning situation. One can attempt to assess a student's abilities in most school-related areas, but one of the most frequently assessed areas is reading. In this chapter, we will focus on the assessment of reading strategies and other reading-process-related areas.

## The Assessment Component

Assessing reading skills and strategies involves many variables that make assessment complex. Student variables that influence assessment results include experiental backgrounds, prior knowledge/schemata, motivations, interests, and varying cultural perspectives. Types of reading instructional materials used, among many other factors, also affect results.

Test factors can also interact to create stumbling blocks in accurately assessing students. Two major test attributes you should be concerned with are validity and reliability. Other variables, such as teacher time, attitude toward assessment, numbers of students being taught, and physical constraints of the classroom, combine with the factors previously mentioned to produce additional problems for assessing students' strategies. Indeed, although many factors interact with the reading environment to impede assessing each student's reading skills and strategies, you should try to learn as much as possible about the assessment process and your students' learning strategies, interests, schemata, backgrounds, motivations, abilities, and cultures because assessment is an essential component of any successful learning program.

Your decisions regarding assessment procedures and areas you are interested in assessing will be greatly influenced by your own beliefs. We believe that the preferences teachers show for certain types of assessment procedures, and the skills, strategies, or areas they choose to assess, are good indicators of their overall beliefs concerning the reading process and literacy instruction. In other words, if you believe it is important to test phonic skills, then you are more likely to believe that phonic skills are crucial and that they should be dealt with as an essential part of the total assessment and instructional reading program.

## Reflection Activity 11.1

*I*n your reflection journal under the heading Reflection Activity 11.1, list all of the areas, skills, or strategies and other reading-related aspects you believe are important to assess, and note your reasons for believing that they are important.

## Purposes of Assessment

The information gathered about students will greatly influence teachers' perceptions of students' abilities, needs, and interests. This information often influences decisions about what type of instruction a student should have. Since the primary purpose of assessment is to gain as much useful information as possible in a brief period of time, it is very important that the facilitative teacher first analyze objectives or purposes before beginning the assessment process.

In analyzing purposes for assessment, you should first remember that assessment data are essential to plan instruction to develop students' reading abilities and interests, and that valuable information about students can be obtained through the use of appropriately selected and analyzed assessment procedures. However, other purposes for assessing your students in reading and reading-related areas could include:

1. Determining a student's overall reading ability.
2. Examining a student's ability to use graphophonic, syntactic, and semantic cues in reading.

3. Analyzing a student's grasp of the process of comprehending the printed page and the interactive processes of getting meaning from what he or she reads.
4. Determining a student's cognitive concepts and experiential background in various content areas.
5. Determining a student's strengths and needs, to give you the insight to help that student become a more proficient reader inside and outside of the classroom.

## Types of Assessment

Now that we have established a definition of assessment and its various reading-related purposes, we will examine the various types of assessment procedures available to classroom teachers to help determine students' reading strengths and needs. In general, assessment techniques are typically divided into two categories: *informal* (or nonstandardized) and *formal* (or standardized). However, to include the most recent developments in assessing reading instruction, we have elected to add a third category, *authentic* assessment. Although authentic assessment is an informal assessment gathering procedure, we believe that a thorough and separate treatment of this assessment type is important to the facilitative teacher's understanding of the overall assessment process. Both authentic assessment and informal assessment procedures are flexible and useful to the teacher in classroom situations. We believe procedures should form the basis for day-to-day assessment of children's progress in becoming better readers.

Formal assessment procedures, however, are often more strictly controlled, in that guidelines relative to test setting, directions, and time lines are explicitly stated and must be followed. Most of the widely used formal tests are standardized by the use of norm groups (i.e., your students' performances will be compared with how students of similar characteristics performed on that particular test), and technical test information is usually included, which discusses reliability (the test will yield the same results consistently) and validity (to what extent the test actually does measure what it purports to measure), among other psychometric concepts. Tables of norms are also included and indicate the size of the sample (number of students tested in the norm or comparison groups), so that some comparisons among students and between school districts can be made.

## Authentic Assessment

Relatively recent trends in reading instruction suggest that the more traditional ways of assessing students' reading abilities—the use of formal (standardized) assessment procedures and basal reader unit tests to measure reading growth and/or reading skills—may not be the best or most effective means of evaluating students' progress. We believe that many school districts have relied too heavily on these assessment tools while overlooking other assessment procedures that more closely mirror the actual daily and weekly instructional activities that are inherent in the reading instruction provided in the classroom. Facilitative teachers need to know how well their students are doing every day, so that they can provide the appropriate instruction to meet their needs. Thus, the most effective means of gathering daily information about students' progress in reading may be through the use of authentic assessment procedures.

What is authentic assessment and where did it originate? In recent years, there has been a significant and very influential philosophical shift in the way reading is thought about and taught to elementary school children. As you may recall, we discussed the different perspectives that have influenced reading definitions and instruction and the differences between those evolving perspectives; these perspectives and definitions have also influenced the area of assessment, particularly the gathering and analysis of data that sample children's strategies and skills in reading. Due to the influences of the whole language and interactive perspectives of teaching reading, it became clear that assessment procedures needed to be focused on the changing thinking and instructional needs of teachers in language-based and interactive classrooms. Thus, to assess children's strategies and skills in reading, real children's literature and real content assignments and materials would need to be used rather than the more contrived assignments and materials often found in workbooks or basal reading series tests.

Authentic assessment, then, is the use of appropriate procedures to gather information about students' reading skills and strategies in a fair and unbiased manner that represents the actual reading assignments and materials necessary to do their classroom work. It can be integrated with meaningful writing activities emphasizing various genres, authentic children's literature and authentic content assignments, enabling teachers to utilize such authentic assessment procedures as responses to literature, critical writing activities, using journals, mapping content information, reading guides, story frames, and Readers' Theater.

One of the most effective ways of gathering authentic assessment data is through the use of portfolios. The use of portfolios in the elementary classroom is quickly becoming a popular and highly effective way of empowering children with greater responsibility in the learning and assessment process, as well as empowering teachers with more accurate and specific assessment data gathered through numerous authentic avenues.

## *Portfolios*

What is a portfolio and how does it work? The dictionary defines a portfolio as a flat, portable case for collecting loose sheets of paper, manuscripts, and drawings. Artists, financial planners, journalists, and now educators are utilizing portfolios to develop an authentic representation of their activities. Valencia (1990) has drawn on an artist's perception of a portfolio and asserted that artists use the portfolio to demonstrate their skills and achievements. Artists' portfolios usually include samples of their work that exemplify their expertise. Artists may include works in various media, works on one subject to show their

refined skills, and works collected over time to reveal their growth. Portfolios give the teacher and the student a similar opportunity to portray the work of each student in a class. Portfolio contents can be used to assess students' understandings and strategies. In many different ways, the portfolio offers us the opportunity to capture each student's growth over time.

Valencia (1990) has defined a portfolio as a purposeful collection of student work, records of progress, and evidence of achievement collected over a period of time. As you construct and refine your personal definition of assessment, it will be helpful to keep in mind the following four principles of portfolio assessment in reading that have been developed by Valencia:

1. Sound assessment is anchored in authenticity—authenticity of tasks, texts, and contexts. . . .
2. Assessment must be a continuous, ongoing process. . . .
3. Because reading is a complex and multifaceted process, valid reading assessment must be multidimensional—committed to sampling a wide range of cognitive processes, affective responses, and literacy activities. . . .
4. Assessment must provide for active, collaborative reflection by both teacher and student . . . (p. 338).

Thus, portfolios are a collection of student work over an extended time and provide teachers, students, parents, family members, and administrators with a continuous profile of student growth and accomplishments. In this respect, portfolios have a real role in assessment, but they are more than a means of evaluation. Portfolios can be used to diagnose student strengths and weakness; portfolios provide teachers with a basis for appropriate student instruction.

> They [portfolios] are tied to our definition of literacy. When we read and write constantly, when we reflect on who we are and who we want to be, we cannot help but grow. Over time, portfolios help us identify and organize the specifics of our reading and writing. They catalogue our accomplishments and goals from successes to instructive failures. (Graves and Sunstein 1992, p. xii)

By this time, you may be asking yourselves, what exactly do portfolios look like? Well, it is difficult to say exactly. They can take the form of file folders, large envelopes, expandable file folders, boxes, as well as any other suitable container. We prefer expandable file folders because they can hold quite a bit of the students' work and are easily accessible. We like Valencia's (1990) discussion in which she describes a portfolio as larger and more elaborate than a report card, but smaller and more focused than a steamer trunk. She has suggested that a portfolio is similar to a large expandable file folder that holds a variety of samples of each student's work, the teacher's observational notes, the student's own periodic self-evaluations, and progress notes contributed by both the student and teacher collaboratively.

## Content of Reading Portfolios

As we discuss the implementation of reading portfolios, we should consider the many options for the contents of portfolios. Once that decision is reached, you should also decide how to collect and organize the contents so that it will be useful for your students, their parents, families, and yourself. Typically, the student will assemble a collection of materials during the school year with some tasks being assigned and others selected by the student (Calfee and Perfumo 1993). You should select appropriate data based on observations of student reading behaviors and accomplishments, while some of the materials assembled will represent a collaborative effort between you and your students.

## Student Responses

In the category of student responses, portfolio contents may include: (a) favorite poems, letters, or comments; (b) written responses to literacy components (plot, setting, character development, criticism, and theme); (c) writings that illustrate critical thinking about reading; (d) interesting thoughts to remember from books that have been read; (e) story retellings; (f) reading response journals; (g) literature/reading logs; (h) reflections about inclusion of portfolio contents; and (I) peer comments.

## Student Products

Students will also have products to include in their portfolios. These may include: (a) projects, surveys, and reports from reading; (b) literature extensions (scripts, visual arts, webs, charts, story frames, time lines); (c) self-portraits that are simply drawings of "self"; and (d) thematic projects.

## Teacher Observations

Students should be observed both formally and informally throughout the school year, with records of these observations included in each student's portfolio. Observational data may include: (a) analyzed audiotapes of student readings; (b) anecdotal records of reading behaviors; (c) checklists of reading behaviors; (d) analyzed oral think-alouds about readings; (e) rubrics, which are guides for assessment; (f) results of informal reading inventories, word lists, and word analysis skills; (g) running records with miscue analyses; (h) progress reports or report cards; and (i) records of teacher/student conferences and interviews (Farr and Tone 1994; Glazer and Brown 1993; Hill and Ruptic 1994). For example, as you discuss a reading log entry with a student you should make notes of strengths, areas for further growth, strategies used by the student, connections made with other books or authors read, and/or personal experiences. These observational data guide you toward future instructional decisions.

Other important portfolio contents are not easily categorized. For example, you may ask parents/family members to make comments or complete a check sheet after reviewing the contents of their child's reading portfolio. These parent responses can be a significant component of the portfolio because they will provide valuable insight into the growth of the student. A table of contents, either prepared by you, designed by the student, or completed collaboratively between the student and you, should be included to aid in understanding and organizing the portfolio. A table of contents is essential to organizing the portfolio contents, but since the portfolio is always changing, so must the table of contents (Farr and Tone 1994; Valencia, Heibert, and Afflerbach 1994). Photographs of student projects too large for the portfolio or collaborative projects with other students also can be included. The use of photographs can be a meaningful, though expensive, addition to a student portfolio.

Whatever you and your students decide to include in a reading portfolio, the contents must be organized in a usable and meaningful way. Contents can be organized in many ways, but ideally, the organization is a collaborative effort between the student and yourself (Farr 1992).

## Types of Reading Portfolios

Three different types of reading portfolios can be used to help organize the ever-growing contents and provide authentic information for assigning grades. These include: (a) a teaching (working) portfolio, (b) a showcase portfolio, and (c) a teacher's observational portfolio.

### Teaching (Working) Portfolio

According to Farr and Tone (1994), the teaching (working) portfolio is the central focus for reading assessment. They have compared the working portfolio to the portfolio of a photographer. The photographer has a collection of photographs taken that are good, but not quite as good, as photographs chosen for display. Similarly, students select items for their working portfolios that show thought, reflection, and effort, but these items are not what the students consider to be their finest work. It is the working and thinking about the contents in this type of portfolio that will help students mature into critical readers and develop realistic views of personal performance. Students would select finished products considered to be their "best work" from the teaching (working) portfolio to become a part of the showcase portfolio.

## Showcase Portfolio

A showcase portfolio contains items that are selected by the students and considered by them to be their best works (Tierney, Carter, and Desai 1991). As with the photographer, these items are intended for display and for sharing with many audiences. You should provide some guidance in the selection process, but with a showcase portfolio, it is important that the student is the decision-maker.

## Teacher's Observational Portfolio

The facilitative teacher's observational portfolio is similar to folders that teachers have kept for years. It includes: (a) checklists, (b) teacher notes about students' reading behaviors, (c) parent/family progress reports, (d) notes received from parents/family about their student's reading progress or problems, and (e) any other pertinent information related to the student's reading. By using the observational portfolio, you will be able to organize this data in one easily accessible location. Contents of this portfolio can be especially helpful in parent/teacher/administrator conferences.

## Evaluating Students' Portfolio Work

At this point, you may be wondering how classroom teachers can evaluate the products and contents of students' portfolios. Certainly, if students' portfolios collections are to be used as an assessment of their reading and other literacy abilities, growth, skills, and strategies, you must have some means to make evaluation decisions about the quality of this work and students' progress. Use of rubrics and anchor papers can facilitate these evaluation needs.

## Rubrics and Anchor Papers

The move from traditional standards of assessment to new ways of looking at student performance is an essential component of portfolio assessment. The rubric, a description of performance for certain task or activity, is one standard for looking at student work. Rubrics contain words and phrases to assist in explaining a work sample to students, parents/family members, other teachers, and administrators. In other words, a rubric is a set of criteria for scoring students' work that will go into their portfolios. The teacher determines, preferably in collaboration with the other teachers in the school, or at least, within the grade level, the criteria that will be used to score students' work. When you develop the performance criteria (rubrics) for your students' work, it is crucial that there is consistency within your performance levels for your classroom, and it is also essential that the same levels of consistency exist within your grade level. One key point that we have not yet mentioned is that, for portfolio assessment to be effective in a school, *everyone* must participate. The reasons

**Figure 11.1**

An example of a
reading rubric.

Developed by Heather
Gaspard, Judy Burch, and
Nora Miller, Audubon
Elementary School, Baton
Rouge, Louisiana. Used
with permission.

---

**Reading rubric**

---

Response to reading activity

**3**    The response presents a substantial amount of information from the story. The information used is accurate and relevant resulting in correctly responding to 5 or 6 parts of the task.

---

**2**    The response contains a moderate amount of information from the story. Some minor inaccuracies may appear. Some of the information may be irrelevant to the task resulting in correctly responding to 3 or 4 parts of the task.

---

**1**    The response presents a minimal amount of information from the story. It may contain frequent or serious inaccuracies. Irrelevant information from the story may outweigh relevant information resulting in correctly completing 1 or 2 parts of the task.

---

**0**    The student makes no attempt to respond to the story by completing the task.

---

Response to reading activity—Personal reaction

**1**    There is evidence that the student makes a personal response to the story.

---

**0**    There is no evidence of a personal response or the response does not make sense.

---

Scoring: Proficient 4 • Beginning 3 • Developing 1 or 2

---

for this include consistency in setting performance criteria (using rubrics), ensuring a fair and equitable grading system for each child, matching authentic instruction ("real" literature and "real" content assignments) with authentic assessment, and ensuring logical and consistent performance expectations for children as they progress from one grade in school to another. A final comment about rubrics is that they need to be constructed by you for your classroom and also in collaboration with the other teachers in your school to ensure that each student is evaluated in an unbiased and equitable manner.

An integral component of developing performance criteria (rubrics) for students is the use of anchor papers. Anchor papers serve as model criteria for scoring reading and writing activities that will be included in the students' portfolios. These anchor papers are actual samples of the student's work and represent the various performance levels that would be represented in the rubrics. They are important because they allow for consistency in scoring. You must select the papers that you believe most closely represent the performance level suggested by your rubric. In the early stages of this process, you may feel somewhat insecure about developing rubrics and in selecting anchor papers that match the various performance levels, but you will become more comfortable with this process as you gain experience in using this type of assessment (see Figures 11.1, 11.2, and 11.3 for examples of reading and writing rubrics and an anchor paper).

**Figure 11.2**

An example of a writing rubric.

Developed by Heather Gaspard, Judy Burch, and Nora Miller, Audubon Elementary School, Baton Rouge, Louisiana. Used with permission.

**Writing rubric**
Writing a story

Name _____ Date _____

Content:

Picture:
0  No picture, picture does not pertain to story.
1  Picture pertains, but has few details.
2  Detailed picture that pertains to story.

Story:
0  Disorganized, no attempt.
1  Some attempt at organization, moderate use of story elements.
2  Ordered logically, includes elements of the story.

Sentences:
0  No evidence of sentences making sense.
1  Sentences sometimes make sense.
2  Majority of sentences make sense.

Mechanics:

Spelling:
0  No high frequency words spelled correctly, approximations not close.
1  Some high frequency words spelled correctly, some good approximations.
2  Spells many high frequency words, good approximations.

Punctuation:
0  Uses no punctuation or capitals appropriately.
1  Beginning to use appropriate punctuation and capitalization.
2  Uses capitalization and punctuation appropriately.

Appearance:

Format:
0  No spacing.
1  Some spacing.
2  Appropriate spacing.

Handwriting and Neatness:
0  Handwriting not legible.
1  Beginning to use correct letter formation.
2  Generally uses correct letter formation, is legible.

Developing 0–6 • Beginning 7–11 • Proficient 12–14

In concluding this section on portfolios, we believe that this type of assessment can enhance student learning and can provide you with a realistic understanding of the student's needs, skills, and strategies. It also more fully empowers the students and you to make sound decisions about the learning process based on information obtained that is realistic and indicative of classroom instructional environment.

**Figure 11.3**
An example of an anchor paper: A first-grade student's response to a reading activity.

*Translation:* I had wrote about Superman.
He blowed up a house because
they had a bad guy.

Used with permission of Heather Gaspard, Audubon Elementary School, Baton Rouge, Louisiana.

## Informal Assessment Procedures

Because of the flexibility and usefulness of informal assessment procedures, you may find yourself on a day-to-day basis using these techniques and relying on the information they provide. Perhaps the most important benefit to be derived from informal assessment procedures is that they enable you to immediately adjust instruction for your entire class and to enhance your individualization of reading instruction for specific students. Other specific purposes of informal assessment have been identified by Collins and Cheek (1993) and those purposes that we believe may be of interest to you include:

1. Studying, evaluating, or assessing a student's reading behavior.
2. Tracing a student's growth in reading over a period of time.

3. Supplementing information obtained from formal assessment procedures.
4. Acquiring information not readily available from other sources.
5. Facilitating the establishment of groups for reading instruction.
6. Selecting materials and teaching techniques appropriate to a student's needs and interests.
7. Providing specific information to parents during conferences.

In an effort to give you as much information as possible regarding informal assessment, we discuss several procedures that facilitative teachers can use to evaluate students' reading skills/strategies. These informal procedures include observing reading behaviors, administering attitude and interest inventories, and using a variety of reading inventories.

## Observation of Behaviors

Observation is an important assessment tool, particularly when it is used in conjunction with other assessment strategies. Through observation, teachers can gain valuable information about students' skills, strategies, interactions, behaviors, and needs. From observation, you may first get indications that a problem is developing. Reading progress can also be determined by using observations.

Structured observations can take either of two forms: anecdotal or checklist. Anecdotal records are detailed notes taken on individual students, with dates recorded for each observation. Although it is very time-consuming, this type of observation and record-keeping procedure can reveal important information. For example, consistent patterns of behavior are often revealed through the analysis of anecdotal records. Also, these records are very helpful in observing students with varied reading needs because they permit greater insight into these students' specific reading behaviors (i.e., you can focus your time and attention on specific skills, strategies, or perceived needs).

Checklists can also be used to structure observations. They are more time efficient than anecdotal records in that they can be used with individual students or with large groups. A checklist can be one page (see Figure 11.4) or several pages and tailored to record general reading skills/strategies or specific behaviors. The checklist is not as in depth as the anecdotal record in recording reading behaviors but can be quite useful in appropriate situations. Items on a checklist should include specific behaviors that can be observed and are important or closely related to reading instructional objectives. Space should also be provided for the teacher to make "additional comments." The number of items on the checklist should be kept to a minimum to keep it from becoming overwhelming. Some of the items that may be included on a reading checklist are as follows:

1. Comprehension of reading material.
2. Motivation and interest in required reading material.
3. Interest in recreational or other personal reading.
4. Vocabulary usage and recognition of unfamiliar words.
5. Ability to use higher-level cognitive skills.

**Figure 11.4**
Partial checklist for
observation purposes.

Name _____ Grade _____ Age _____

Teacher _____ Date _____

_____ 1. Reads effectively and functionally during content reading activities and assignments.

_____ 2. Enjoys reading independently to pursue individual interests and purposes.

_____ 3. Uses effective oral reading techniques such as phrasing, holding book correctly, and fluency.

_____ 4. Uses effective silent reading techniques, such as concentrating, holding book correctly, rereading or going back to clarify or better understand, and reading at a consistent pace.

_____ 5. Activates prior knowledge and experiences when reading orally and/or silently.

_____ 6. Participates in class discussions based on readings and related assignments.

_____ 7. Recognizes words in context and, when appropriate, out of context.

_____ 8. Uses various vocabulary strategies effectively.

_____ 9. Comprehends information effectively and provides evidence of metacognitive awareness.

_____ 10. Uses study strategies effectively, such as summarizing, outlining, and interpreting charts, tables, maps, and diagrams.

Additional comments:

Although observation can take place during specific reading times, or even when the students are reading for leisure, you may choose to observe students informally for several days. Some specific steps Collins and Cheek (1993) have recommended for using an observation checklist are as follows:

1. Select or design a checklist that meets the needs of your particular classroom situation.
2. Have a checklist for each student you are to observe.
3. Know the checklist well to expedite its use in the observation process.
4. Set aside specific periods of time for observations.
5. Note any problems that the students exhibit during the observation periods. (You should give specific attention to areas designated on your checklist.)

Observations are beneficial in assessing the strengths and needs of students, but the data collected should always be done over a period of time and used in conjunction with findings from other types of assessment strategies.

# Attitude and Interest Inventories

Two important components of the reading process revolve around the attitudes and interests of your students. Facilitative teachers know that students' interests and attitudes about reading and the materials to be read are essential to their students becoming effective readers.

Attitude inventories are often divided into one of two categories: retrospective or introspective. Retrospective inventories are designed with items that enable students to examine why they succeed or fail in reading. This instrument involves more of an objective analysis between the student and the teacher. Introspective inventories, however, require a more subjective analysis on the student's part. Students attempt to recall what occurred in their minds during the reading process by examining their own thought processes. Because of the similarities of retrospective and introspective inventories, it is often difficult to separate these instruments into clearly defined categories. Since most attitude inventories do assess both areas, our suggestions for analyzing student attitudes will encompass both areas.

Another widely used procedure for assessing students' attitudes is the autobiography. This informal strategy can be an oral or written account of the student's reading history, but you should seriously consider using the oral autobiography for those students who may be reluctant to write, or who have more-limited writing skills. Whichever method you choose, it is important to involve each student in this process. For many students, the reading autobiography will be their only opportunity to express their feelings about reading, and you should not be surprised or offended if some of your students express hostility or frustration toward the reading program. Many children have developed poor attitudes about reading from the reading programs implemented in their schools, and it will be one of your primary responsibilities to turn these attitudes around by being more sensitive to, and utilizing, your students' attitudes and interests. In some instances, you may wish to use a checklist form of autobiography, but you should always keep in mind that a checklist will limit the quantitative and qualitative responses of your students. However, an option available to you to increase the validity and content of your students' responses involves using open-ended questions such as

Do you enjoy reading? Why or why not?

What kind of reading do you like best? Why?

What kind of reading do you like least? Why?

What kind of reading material do you have in your home?

What do other members of your family like to read?

Another useful procedure for analyzing attitudes in the classroom is the use of class discussions. Through this interaction between you and your students, you can determine which topics or reading materials they like or dislike, or what topics or materials they have been actively reading.

Likewise, another effective procedure you could use to analyze your students' attitudes is the interview. This informal procedure involves a one-to-one interaction between you and the student and is structured to give students an opportunity to express their feelings about reading and about themselves as readers.

The following suggestions are intended to assist you in gaining specific data and insight into your students' interests.

One very simple method of determining your students' interests is through observation—observing which books they choose to read, their degree of concentration and enjoyment as they read, their eagerness to share what they read with others, and their desire to read more books. Another important signal is the degree of attention you observe among students when a story is read to the class. All of these clues will help in determining student interest and help you provide suitable book selections for students.

You can obtain more detailed information about your students' interests and the kinds of materials they like to read by having them give brief "book" reviews. Rather than focusing on book reports, these brief oral or written reviews can give you an indication of interest without boring some students and frustrating others. This informal procedure gives you the opportunity to determine the types of stories that interest your students and to encourage students to read by having them share their favorite stories with others in the class. The information that you gather in this manner allows you to direct assignments toward each student's particular interest.

Another way of determining your students' interests is to allow them to examine and rate a series of book titles. In this particular activity, you would list on a handout, chalkboard, or transparency a number of book titles for your students to rate. Their preferences for certain titles would enable you to provide the more appropriate ones for each student in your classroom.

Perhaps the most common way of determining students' interest is through the use of an interest inventory. The primary purpose of an interest inventory is to give you a structured and specific instrument to explore the interests of the students. It is easy to construct and to use because you determine the types of questions to be asked, put them into a questionnaire format, and then administer the inventory individually or in groups. After you have administered the inventory and interpreted the results, you can use the information to provide materials appropriate to each student's interests and motivations. In interpreting interest inventories, it is important to note that the interests of students can frequently and quickly change. These changes occur because of age, other interests, other needs, other motivations, peer-group pressure, and teacher influence. Thus, it is important that you update the information gathered from your interest inventory continuously.

### Reading Inventories

You will find that some of the more practical informal assessment procedures available to teachers involve the administration and interpretation of one or more of the various types of reading inventories. Most of these instruments can be constructed and given relatively easily, and the others can be purchased from commercial publishers. The descriptions of three types of informal reading inventories and suggestions for using them effectively follow.

## Simplified Reading Inventory (SRI)

The Simplified Reading Inventory (SRI) is a broad screening tool used to determine whether reading materials are appropriate for students' abilities. The SRI is a simple procedure and is not intended to give specific assessment information. It merely assists teachers in choosing materials with specific characteristics (e.g., subject or topic) that enhance students' motivation and learning. Results from this inventory can also indicate a need for additional testing.

The SRI is very easy to develop and administer. First, you select a passage from a basal reader, content text, or other appropriate instructional materials. The passage should be directly related to your reading objectives and approximately one hundred words in length. Second, you give the passage to your students and ask them to read several sentences aloud. We recommend that you use a one-to-one setting to administer an SRI (since many students feel awkward or uncomfortable when required to read before a group). Having students read the passage can indicate whether the material may be too difficult for instructional purposes.

A number of factors should be considered if you employ SRI procedures. Since the SRI is primarily a screening tool and is not intended to give specific assessment information, it should be used at the beginning of reading instruction to determine whether the materials are beyond the reading abilities of students. If students do not have a schemata for the particular material or concept in reading, they may not be able to read it, no matter how strong their reading abilities. Also, because the SRI is simplistic in its construction and application, it is not refined to pinpoint specific reading needs; it should be used in combination with other assessment procedures. The use of other assessment strategies is particularly important if you determine that a student is unable to read the passage adequately.

## Informal Reading Inventory (IRI)

The Informal Reading Inventory (IRI) is one of the most widely used individually administered informal assessment tools used in the classroom to determine students' reading ability levels (Klesius and Homan 1985), and many believe it provides the most complete and useful information about readers (e.g., Shearer and Homan 1994). Teachers can purchase a number of commercial IRIs; they can also engage in the time-consuming but often beneficial task of creating their own. An IRI is composed of graded passages designated grade 1, grade 2, etc., with accompanying comprehension questions for each passage. Because it is an individually administered oral and silent-reading assessment, an IRI affords teachers the opportunity to examine individual students' strengths and needs in vocabulary, word identification/word recognition, and comprehension skills and strategies. Figure 11.5 provides a sample of an IRI graded passage with comprehension questions for the teacher to ask.

*Figure 11.5*

IRI graded reading passage and comprehension questions.

**Grade 5: Teacher's copy**

Introduction: This story tells about a king of long ago. Try reading it to discover some interesting things about the king and how he ruled his kingdom.

Many legends of the Middle Ages tell stories of a great king. His name was Arthur. He was the ruler of the people of England. Arthur was a popular leader. He made his kingdom a peaceful place to live. He selected knights to join him in the great meeting hall. There they discussed problems.

These heroic men were shrewd leaders. Their ideas became law. The men held discussions at a table called the Round Table. Legend says the Round Table was created by Merlin, the magician. The marble table could be magically folded up and then it could be carried in a coat pocket.

The shape of the table was very important. A round table has no head chair. Every seat is equal. So every knight felt equal in power. It was a great idea for helping find solutions to problems.

141 words

Comprehension questions and possible answers:

1. What would be a good title for this story?
   (answers may vary)

2. Where did this story take place?
   (in England)

3. Who did Arthur select to sit with him around the Round Table?
   (the knights)

4. What is meant by the word "heroic"?
   (men that were brave like the knights)

5. What did the knights do after they discussed the problems of the kingdom?
   (passed resolutions, made laws and rules)

6. Why was the shape of the table important?
   (it had no head chair, every seat was equal)

7. What makes you think that King Arthur was a good ruler?
   (he let others help him rule, he let others share in the power of the kingdom)

8. Why is it important for lawmakers to feel equal in power?
   (each wants his opinion valued, each wants to feel he has a valuable contribution to make, no one wants to feel that another has all the power)

### Scoring guide

| Word recognition: | | Comprehension: | |
|---|---|---|---|
| ___ IND | 0–2 errors (miscues) | ___ IND | 0–1 incorrect |
| ___ INST | 3–7 errors (miscues) | ___ INST | 2 incorrect |
| ___ FRUST | 14+ errors (miscues) | ___ FRUST | 4 or more incorrect |

Although it takes approximately twenty to thirty minutes to administer this instrument to each student, the information gathered is well worth the time and effort. The IRI should be given at the beginning of the school year so that you can use the information to help make instructional decisions concerning students' skills and strategy needs. It should also be given to those students who did not do well on the SRI in order to obtain more specific reading data. Since IRIs are such valuable assessment tools and are used by so many educators, many have been developed and are available through commercial sources. However, you may prefer to construct your own IRI, suited to your needs, your students, classroom situation, and classroom materials. You should be aware, however, that many reading experts (see Cooter 1990 and others cited in his work) have criticized IRIs around issues of reliability, passage content, question selection, and various technical procedures. Teacher-made IRIs are subject to even more of this criticism.

Nevertheless, to construct your own IRI you should follow these steps:

1. Secure a graded-word recognition test such as the *Slosson Oral Reading Test,* or you may wish to develop your own word list by randomly selecting about twenty words from an appropriate source. You could select words from the lowest appropriate-level basal (probably preprimer) to the highest level available (probably eighth grade). The purpose of this step is to develop informal word list tests based on reading vocabulary to determine your students' sight-word familiarity. Keep in mind, however, that these tests or word lists are not used to measure the primary function of reading—comprehension. You administer the graded word tests to determine an approximate starting point to begin the administration of the IRI.

2. Select a series of graded passages (from a hundred to two hundred words) from your instructional materials (preprimer through middle school). The readability levels of each of the graded passages should be carefully checked using a valid readability-analysis procedure such as the Fry Readability Graph. The passages can come from your basal program, content texts, or supplementary materials; or you can write them using selected vocabulary words. However, because of some of the criticisms previously cited, you should be aware that writing your own passages may further make your inventory subject to additional reliability, content, and technical problems. The content of the passages should be interesting to help motivate the readers. Two passages should be selected at each level (one for oral and the other for silent reading).

   (If you choose to write your own passages, remember to consider interest level, readability level, syntax, and concepts. Writing original passages for your IRI is commendable, and in some situations, may even be preferable, but be careful to communicate your ideas effectively. It may be prudent to have a few of your students read and react to the passages to assist you in determining their usability.)

3. Develop a set of comprehension questions for each passage (from five to ten questions). Word-meaning, literal-, inferential-, and critical-comprehension questions should be generated. The questions should emphasize reading skills such as finding the main idea, sequencing events, cause-and-effect relationships, comparison and contrast, moods, and author opinions. The greater the number of questions, the more precise the comprehension-assessment outcome. Also, it is important to evenly distribute the categories of questions that you ask.

4. Prepare the passages and the questions. The reading levels of the passages and the comprehension questions need to be identified on the teacher's copy, but not on the student's copy. Appropriate type size and spacing should be used. For instance, if you are assessing primary-age students, you should use larger type and wider spaces between the lines. (See Figure 11.5 for an example of what a teacher's copy of an IRI passage, with comprehension questions and a scoring guide, might look like.)

The procedures you would use to administer a commercial IRI or one that you developed would include the following:

1. Establish rapport with the student and give a brief explanation of what is to be done.

2. Administer the word-list tests to determine where to start the assessment of the student's oral reading.

3. Select a passage that is a little below the student's indicated level as determined by the word-list test. Introduce the passage, suggesting a purpose for reading it.

4. Have the student orally read the passage. Record oral-reading errors (miscues) (e.g., insertions, omissions, and so on) by marking them on the teacher's copy of the passage. Figure 11.6 presents a marking procedure you can use to code and mark errors (miscues) as you have students orally read selected passages. Because of differences in philosophies, some teachers may not want to use all of these markings; however, we include all the markings that are traditionally used. (For instance, some teachers and/or reading experts would not mark "mispronunciations," believing that students of diverse languages/cultures might pronounce a word "differently" and still know the word. Some would not mark "teacher pronounced words" because they wouldn't assist students with unknown words, believing that this would interfere with observing students' own strategies for dealing with unknown words in text.)

5. Ask the first set of comprehension questions and record the responses.

6. Have the student silently read the second passage. You may want to give the student permission to ask for help with words, recording the words that were asked.

**Figure 11.6**
IRI marking
procedure.

```
                        Sample IRI marking procedure

Mispronunciation ..... place MP over the word mispronounced and write the word as
                       mispronounced

Substitution ............. draw a line through the word with the new word written above

Teacher ................... place TP over the word
pronounced words

Insertion ................. put a caret (^) with the word written in

Omission ................ circle the words or punctuation omitted

Repetition ............... place R over the word(s) repeated

Hesitation ............... put dashes (-------) between words with hesitations of more than
                          five seconds duration

Self-correction ......... place SC over the word the student self-corrected
```

7. Ask the record set of comprehension questions and record correct and incorrect responses.
8. Administer other oral- and silent-reading passages until the independent, instructional, and frustration reading levels are determined for each.

The specific definitions for each of the IRI reading levels you can obtain are

*Independent Level.* The level at which students are able to read fluently and fluidly, without assistance. It is an area of maximum comprehension.

*Instructional Level.* The level at which students are taught in reading. At this level students experience some difficulty in word recognition and comprehension but still fall within the parameters of the specified criteria for instructional purposes.

*Frustration Level.* The level at which students experience difficulty in recognizing words and comprehending the information read. Students would often find reading at this level to be frustrating.

There has been discussion over the years concerning which set of criteria is better for determining the preceding three reading levels. Since the criteria developed by Betts in 1957 continue to be the most widely used today, we have included them for your consideration. However, you may wish to modify these or use criteria found in commercial reading inventories.

| Level | Word recognition (percent correct) | Comprehension (percent correct) |
|---|---|---|
| Independent | 99 percent and above | 90 percent and above |
| Instructional | 95–98 percent | 75–89 percent |
| Frustration | 90 percent and below | 50 percent and below |

When the IRI data have been analyzed, you will be able to identify your students' independent, instructional, and frustration levels. And, an analysis of their word recognition errors (miscues) and comprehension will help you plan appropriate reading instruction. This analysis can provide insight concerning students' graphophonic, syntactic, and semantic strengths and needs if the teacher applies qualitative reading miscue analysis procedures (see next section).

A number of situational factors should be considered when an IRI is administered to obtain reading information for instructional purposes. These factors include:

1. Even though the IRI looks complicated and is an individually administered instrument, it can be fairly easily and quickly administered.
2. Since the IRI is administered individually, you are able to examine specific word recognition/identification and comprehension strategies and difficulties during both the oral- and silent-reading procedures. You can also use the IRI as a listening comprehension inventory to assess your students' listening comprehension abilities. This procedure requires you to orally read the passages to the students and then to ask the accompanying comprehension questions. An 80 percent correct response criterion is recommended to determine students' instructional-listening levels. Once the student falls below the 80 percent correct response level, the testing should be discontinued. The last passage at which the student responded correctly to 80 percent of the questions is considered to be the student's instructional listening comprehension level.
3. IRIs should be administered at the beginning of the school year to assess specific strategies and/or difficulties and to help formulate instructional plans; but they can also be administered throughout the year to provide continuous reading assessment data to inform instruction.
4. Commercial inventories are available and can be utilized if you do not have time or do not wish to develop your own IRI. However, because there are many commercially available IRIs, you should take the time to review several and select one that best meets your philosophy and needs.

### Miscue Analysis Inventory

Although the reading inventories that we have discussed so far are helpful tools, they are designed primarily for a quantitative analysis of your student's reading abilities. After administering these inventories you may want to take a second look at your findings and qualitatively analyze them. Such an effort would help you to gain more insight into the importance of your students' deviations from text or miscues and to qualitatively as well as quantitatively examine all reading data. Miscue analysis is a qualitative assessment procedure that can be used with students' reading data.

Miscues are text deviations that students make while reading. Researchers have found that some miscues enhance comprehension for readers, since these "positive miscues" are meaningful substitutions, insertions, omissions, and self-corrections made while reading (Beebe 1979/1980, D'Angelo 1982). Because such miscues can actually improve readers' comprehension, you should consider this when making quantitative decisions about your students' oral reading skills/strategies.

However, all miscues are not positive. Students can also exhibit the use of "negative miscues" (D'Angelo 1983, Goodman 1969). These are miscues that are meaningless substitutions, insertions, or omissions and do not indicate enhanced understanding on the part of the reader. Additionally, less-abled readers demonstrate little self-correcting strategies. It is also important to analyze the types of miscues made to determine whether students' comprehension was positively or negatively affected. In other words, qualitatively analyzing students' reading deviations avoids penalizing them for miscues that enhance their reading comprehension. Additionally, miscues will provide you with useful information about your students' reading strategies.

An example of an instrument specifically designed for the qualitative assessment of reading errors is the *Reading Miscue Inventory* (RMI) (Goodman, Watson, and Burke 1987). The RMI is predicated on the principle that oral reading errors (miscues) can be analyzed to better understand how the reader derives meaning from language. The four basic assumptions that provide the foundation for the development of the RMI are (a) all readers bring an oral-language system to the reading process; (b) all readers bring the sum total of their past experiences to the reading process; (c) reading materials represent the language patterns of past experiences of the author; and (d) reading is an active language process, which involves constant interaction between the reader and the text (Goodman and Burke 1972).

Five steps are typically used to administer the *Reading Miscue Inventory.* Although we are unable in this section to give you a comprehensive description of these important steps, we would like to give you some basic knowledge about what occurs in each. The five steps and their general objective(s) include the following:

1. Ask the student to read for fifteen to twenty minutes an unfamiliar passage that is above the student's independent reading level.
2. Record the oral reading on tape.
3. After the reading, ask your student to retell the story. If portions of the text are omitted, you should ask probing questions about them. The level of comprehension attained by the student in retelling the story indicates a satisfactory or unsatisfactory performance.
4. After the student has finished reading and retelling the passage, you should analyze the miscues and code them onto a coding sheet provided in the RMI. Miscues are coded according to graphic similarity (words that look alike, such as *point* and *pint*), sound-alike similarity (*bat* and *pat*), dialect variation, intonation changes, and syntactic and semantic changes.
5. After analyzing the miscues for their effect on comprehension, plan appropriate strategy instruction as necessary.

Again, the primary purpose of the RMI is to carefully analyze each miscue that a student makes and to observe its effect on the meaning intended by the material. It differs from other oral reading inventories in that the quantity of errors made is secondary to their quality or effect on readers' comprehension. Although the RMI is an excellent instrument for examining the language strategies of a student, you may find it somewhat complex and time-consuming to use in its entirety. However, the principle underlying the miscue analysis inventory can and should be applied whenever possible when you analyze your students' oral-reading skills/strategies. This principle can be applied to the analysis of oral-reading miscues on the Informal Reading Inventory (IRI) or any other oral-reading procedure, including use of authentic materials. Teachers can use shortcuts and do modified miscue analysis on students' oral readings. Rather than using lengthy coding sheets, teachers can use simplified analysis forms or notebook paper to record and review miscues (see Flippo [1997] for her description of modified miscue analysis procedures). Remember that miscues can be positive or negative, and you can determine the nature of your students' miscues and use this analysis to improve their reading strategies' instruction.

### A Closing Comment

The preceding discussion of informal assessment procedures should provide you with basic information essential to securing and using informal data to plan a successful instructional-reading program. It is clear that to develop a successful reading program, you should utilize those informal procedures that are best suited to your particular situation. Attempting to provide reading instruction without such information may result in choosing inappropriate materials for students to read, selecting the wrong reading strategy or skills to meet a particular student's needs, and negating the effective utilization of supplementary reading materials. This can be especially harmful for students experiencing difficulty with reading, students with special needs, and students from diverse sociocultural backgrounds. On the other hand, the use of sound, informal, assessment data in planning and implementing your reading program will result in better motivated, less frustrated, and more successful readers.

## Formal Assessment Procedures

As mentioned earlier in this chapter, the other major category of assessment procedures involves the use of formal standardized tests. Formal instruments and procedures follow specific administration procedures, utilize norming standards, and consider test reliability and validity factors among other subjects. Because of the features inherent in formal assessment procedures, you will probably not use these instruments as frequently as you would informal procedures. However, you should be familiar with these types of formal tests that you may be required to administer and possibly score and analyze as well. These tests measure academic achievement, including reading, mathematics, spelling, and other abilities.

# Achievement-Test Batteries

Achievement-test batteries are used by many school districts as a means of securing varied academic information about their students and as indexes on how well the students in the district are achieving. They provide such data as a review of students' knowledge in various areas of the curriculum, the extent to which students have acquired specific information, and the extent to which they have learned various skills. This information is also sometimes used to compare a particular school district with other school districts. More to the point, the primary function of administering achievement-test batteries is to examine the overall effectiveness of instruction in the various curriculum areas.

As you use achievement tests to evaluate instruction in the varied curriculum areas, it is important for you to remember that the information obtained from these batteries relates to achievement and is not diagnostic in nature (i.e., the data are general rather than specific). The tests tend to be group-administered, are rigidly standardized using norms from large samples of the school-age population, and yield information that can help the school district to examine students' relative position in comparison to other students throughout the country. However, extreme care should be taken to ensure that the norm groups used are appropriate for students for these comparison purposes. Scores from achievement-test batteries are reported in numerous ways, including percentile ranks, stanines, or grade equivalents. Care should be taken when interpreting these derived scores.

Percentile ranks are derived scores ranging from 0 to 100 (actually 1 to 99) that rank a student according to the score of others in a group who are above or below that student's score. On the normal curve, the 50th percentile rank is at the mean while the 16th percentile rank is one standard deviation below the mean, and the 84th percentile rank is one standard deviation above the mean. For example, a student with reading achievement at the 55th percentile rank has attained a higher reading score on the test than 55 percent of those taking the test. Percentile rank scores can be reported in quartiles (e.g., the first quartile is the 0 to 25th percentile) and deciles (e.g., the first decile is the 0 to 10th percentile), but they cannot be averaged, added together, subtracted, or treated arithmetically in any manner.

Stanines are represented on a normal curve by a nine-point scale (i.e., dividing the range of scores into nine parts) with a mean of five and a standard deviation of approximately two. Test scores at the first three stanines (1,2,3) are considered below average, at the middle three stanines (4,5,6) average, and at the last three stanines (7,8,9) above average. Teachers usually find these types of scores more usable for assessment, because they represent a wider range of achievement and are better suited to fluctuations that may occur in students' scores.

Grade equivalents (e.g., 1.6, 2.5, and so on) represent a derived score converted from comparing a student's raw score on a standardized test with the norming table(s) of the test. These scores are usually expressed as a grade level divided into tenths. For example, the grade equivalents for the third grade range from 3.0 to 3.9, with 3.0 representative of the lowest point in the third grade and 3.9 the highest point. The addition of a tenth of a point in each grade level represents one month. In other words, the grade equivalent 3.5 represents the third grade, fifth month of school. Although the use of grade equivalents in reporting test scores has continued to be used, teachers should be very cautious when interpreting and using these scores to begin instructional procedures, since they are derived and extrapolated and are not an accurate representation of students' skills, strategies, schemata, interests, or other reading attributes; and they can be very damaging (e.g., the International Reading Association [1981], admonished use of them). Therefore, teachers must use extreme care in using them to report, discuss, or evaluate a student's reading ability. Here's an example: The grade equivalent score of 3.5 only means that a student scored the same raw score as the average of raw scores of students in the norming group who happened to be in the fifth month of third grade (most of the students in the norming group would have scored a higher or lower raw score—the reported raw score for any grade is only an average of all the raw scores in that grade). An older student who received a 3.5 grade equivalent score could be unfairly placed in reading materials for which he or she was far too mature to enjoy, if a teacher or parent believed that the student read at this grade level. Conversely, a very young child who was believed to be reading at 3.5 grade level could be placed in far too sophisticated reading materials for the child to enjoy and for which he or she didn't have interest in or schema for.

Numerous achievement-test batteries have been published that your school could adopt or you could administer if you are given permission to do so. Four tests that are widely used are the *California Achievement Tests* (CTB McGraw-Hill, Monterey, CA), the *Comprehensive Test of Basic Skills* (CTB McGraw-Hill, Monterey, CA), the *Metropolitan Achievement Test* (The Psychological Corporation, San Antonio, TX), and the *Stanford Achievement Test* (The Psychological Corporation, San Antonio, TX). Specific strengths that have been associated with achievement-test batteries include the following:

1. Information about various curriculum areas is provided to school districts.
2. Achievement batteries are easily administered by classroom teachers.
3. Strict norming procedures are followed in developing these instruments.
4. Data obtained can help in reviewing students' achievement over time.
5. Criterion-referenced data on specific reading skills are provided by some of the tests.

The weaknesses that have been identified with achievement tests are as follows:

1. To ascertain any in-depth diagnostic data, teachers need to conduct an item analysis.
2. The scores obtained tend to represent the students' frustration level.
3. The effectiveness of the instruments can be negated by a faulty testing environment, such as placing large numbers of students together to take the tests.

4. Because silent-reading skills are required to take these tests, the tests may reflect reading ability rather than content knowledge.
5. Local norms are not always available for school districts to use.

Achievement tests are perhaps most useful in providing your school district with information about the total school population and how it compares with others, as well as reviewing total curriculum in terms of whether instruction and coverage are adequate. However, information concerning individual students' strengths and weaknesses is not an appropriate use of these tests and, if provided, should be used with utmost caution.

## Reading Tests

Although a variety of reading tests are available to the teacher, these formal instruments can be grouped into three categories: survey reading tests, group diagnostic reading tests, and individual diagnostic reading tests. In the following section, we provide a brief description of these categories and examples of each. You may find yourself in a situation where some prior knowledge as to the purpose of these tests will be helpful in interpreting assessment data derived from these instruments.

### Survey Tests

Survey reading tests are group tests that have been constructed to give as much information as possible with a relatively brief expenditure of time. They are easily administered by classroom teachers and yield useful group and individual-student reading data. Some factors that have led to the popularity of survey reading tests are that the instructions are clearly presented, they do not take a lot of time to administer, and typically they are well constructed and normed. The only major disadvantage associated with survey reading tests is that they are typically designed for general screening and not diagnostic purposes.

Scores yielded by survey reading tests are presented in percentiles, stanines, and grade equivalents. Reading competencies that these tests tend to assess are comprehension, vocabulary, and depending on the instrument, rate of reading. The scores obtained from survey tests are on students' frustration reading level, not instructional or independent levels, as is the case with the results from achievement-test batteries. The primary advantage of giving a survey reading test is that the information secured provides teachers with a place to start in the assessment process. These tests are screening devices, and their scores should only be used as a global overview of students' reading ability and not for any instructional decision making.

One of the most widely used survey reading tests is the *Gates-MacGinitie Reading Tests* (Riverside Publishing, Chicago, IL).

### Group Diagnostic Reading Tests

Many school districts use group diagnostic reading tests. Two of the reasons for their popularity are (1) their ease in administration and interpretation and

(2) the diagnostic information they provide on students' reading strengths and needs. Since more information can be obtained from these instruments as compared with survey tests, some school districts prefer the group diagnostic tests, even though they are usually more costly and time-consuming to administer. Another primary advantage of the group diagnostic reading tests is that they have subtest scores in areas other than just vocabulary and comprehension. The *Stanford Diagnostic Reading Test,* or *SDRT,* is one of the more popular group diagnostic reading tests (The Psychological Corporation, San Antonio, TX).

### Individual Diagnostic Reading Tests

Individually administered diagnostic reading tests are generally not given by classroom teachers. They have been designed to be given by reading specialists to analyze traditional facets of reading and to provide a more thorough assessment of various reading problems. The tests are typically administered only to students who exhibit the need for more or for additional reading diagnostic assessments. Since the tests are complex in nature and must be administered in one-to-one testing situations, they are more time-consuming and require more expertise to give, score, and interpret. Although these diagnostic tests are especially valuable in analyzing selected students' strengths and needs, you may prefer using the informal or the other types of formal procedures discussed earlier in this chapter. Two individual diagnostic reading tests that have been widely used in school districts are the *Diagnostic Reading Scales* (CTB McGraw-Hill, Monterey, CA), and the *Durrell Analysis of Reading Difficulty* (The Psychological Corporation, San Antonio, TX).

### A Closing Comment

As we have discussed, there are numerous advantages and disadvantages to using these formal assessment instruments in the classroom. The information yielded by these formal tests can be useful, but you must be cautious when using the results and you should understand the various strengths and weaknesses of each type of test you use. Obviously, the instruments that provide the more in-depth diagnostic information about students require more time and experience. Thus, you must decide which instrument is better suited to your situation at any one particular time.

## Other Assessment Procedures

We have discussed authentic assessment procedures, as well as other informal and formal quantitative and qualitative assessment procedures that you can use in your elementary classroom. These procedures have been suggested as a means of determining the needs of students, and then providing the appropriate instruction. Some of these procedures require different experiences and levels of expertise, but they all provide ways of learning more about students. The following discussion involves the use of other sources from which assessment information can be obtained to further facilitate your ability to understand and meet the reading needs of your students. Additional information can be gathered from such sources as parents/family members, students' self-assessments, peers, other teachers, and cumulative records.

## Parents/Family Members

A valuable resource in obtaining reading-assessment information about your students is parents and/or other family members. Although the parents' perspective about their children may not be altogether objective, you should try to use this avenue for securing information to its fullest potential. Parents are ready sources of information about their children's interests, motivations, behaviors at home, home reading habits, time spent watching television, and interactions with peers. Parents/family members can also give you information about their children's attitude toward school and how parents perceive their role in helping their children learn to read.

Information from parents can be gathered through informal and formal conferences and questionnaires. In our opinion, the more effective method of gaining information from parents about students would be through conferences. The conference format and questions should be structured so that parents are comfortable and their right to privacy is not violated. If teachers experience difficulty in scheduling conferences with parents, they can construct questionnaires and send them home for parents to fill out. This is a more indirect approach, which may not elicit in-depth information but as least would secure some parent/family data. No matter which method you select, it is important to involve parents in the assessment process because their cooperation and support is vital to the success of your reading program.

## Students' Self-Assessments and Peers

Another source of assessment information that you may want to consider is that of students' self-assessments and assessment by interaction with peers. Observing students as they interact with classmates can give a teacher insight into students' feelings of self-worth, attitudes toward other students, roles in the school environment, differences in interaction at playtime versus instructional time, peer pressure and its effect on overall performance in the classroom, and interaction with peers as it affects students' rapport with the teacher. Students' self-assessments can provide information concerning students' views of themselves as readers, self-concepts as readers, and perceived use of reading strategies. Peer-assessment and self-assessment information can be gathered conducting informal and formal observations, using retrospective and introspective reports, and scheduling conferences with students and their peers. Carefully analyze self and peer data to learn as much as possible about individual students' strategies, motivations, self-concepts, and other reading-related information. These data should be viewed and used as one more component of the assessment process.

## Other Teachers

Information obtained from other teachers can be very helpful and should be gathered in the assessment process. Yet, this is a resource that is often not used as fully or as cautiously as it should be. For example, many teachers have been in situations where they have asked several other teachers about a particular student's performance in reading and were given several contrasting perceptions. This is certainly frustrating from an assessment perspective but happens because student-teacher relationships depend on numerous variables, which affect every teachers' perception of each student. Additionally, because different teachers have different philosophies regarding what is important in the reading process, it is possible that what one teacher perceives as a strength might not be viewed as such by another teacher. Because of this, you should ask the requested questions, and then carefully analyze responses for the particular information you are seeking.

In securing information from other teachers, try to focus on specifics, such as your students' strengths and needs in various skill and strategy areas, previous placement in a basal reading program, previous instruction provided, and types of reading materials used. One question that you could ask is, "Which approaches were the most effective with which individual students?" Teachers frequently make the mistake of asking colleagues general questions about students when they really should have asked specific questions to get data that will assist them in developing appropriate instructional programs. If possible, avoid asking questions that require subjective judgments because they will elicit answers that are opinions in nature and not necessarily provide you with needed information.

## Cumulative Records

A final source of information that you may choose to consult for assessment data is the cumulative records that follow students throughout their school careers. These records tend to have personal and family demographic data, health histories, scores from standardized tests that students have taken, information about school conduct and disciplinary actions, and other information that might affect a students' performance in your class. Because students' cumulative records can contain a great deal of information, do not assume that they provide more valid or accurate information than your other assessment data. Cumulative records are just one additional piece of assessment information and should not be relied on any more or less than other assessment data.

*S*everal informal and formal procedures have been described. Did you note some that would be appropriate to assess the areas, skills, strategies, and other reading-related aspects you listed at the beginning of the chapter? Please review that list and the reasons you gave (or your purposes) for wanting to assess them. Then under Reflection Activity 11.2 in your reflection journal, indicate which assessment procedures you would select to measure those areas and why. Be as specific as you can.

## Summary

This chapter discussed several topics in the reading-assessment process. The primary focus was on determining the needs of students through the use of authentic, informal, and formal-assessment procedures. In the authentic assessment section, the primary emphasis was on using assessment procedures that are more closely related to instruction in the classroom and on using authentic materials in teaching reading, such as "real" literature and "real" content materials that more closely reflect real life uses and purposes for reading. The use of portfolios as a way of gathering authentic assessment information was discussed. The three types of portfolios presented were teaching (working), showcase, and teacher observational portfolios. The use of rubrics and anchor papers as an integral component of portfolios was also discussed.

In the informal category we described the use of observation measures, attitude and interest inventories, and various types of reading inventories, such as the Simplified Reading Inventory, the Informal Reading Inventory, and miscue analysis. Formal testing procedures discussed included achievement tests, and group and individually administered reading tests. Other assessment sources discussed involved parents/families, self and peers, other teachers, and cumulative records.

## Closing Activities

1. In a small group, share your list of areas (Reflection Activity 11.1) that you would want to assess. Then, discuss the assessment procedures you indicated you could or would use to assess these areas (Reflection Activity 11.2).
2. Interview a classroom teacher and an elementary principal and find out their beliefs about (a) what assessment involves and (b) how students' reading skills, strategies, and abilities should be assessed. Summarize your findings and be prepared to share them in class.
3. Select one of the informal procedures discussed in this chapter and develop an assessment tool to be used with first- or second-grade students to measure any reading or reading-related area or skill. If at all possible, try it out with one student or a small group of students during your field component and summarize the results.
4. Respond to the following statement: "The areas a teacher chooses to assess and the procedures selected to make those assessments are good indicators of the teacher's overall beliefs about reading and reading development." Write a short response paper.
5. In a small group, discuss the extent to which assessment is important in providing appropriate reading instruction to students in an elementary classroom.
6. Using the library resources at your institution, analyze the research regarding assessment in the area of reading education in the previous ten years. Determine the extent to which the current focus on reading assessment has shifted from formal to more informal procedures. Summarize your conclusions in a brief report.

Beebe, M. J. (1979/1980). "The Effect of Different Types of Substitution Miscues on Reading." *Reading Research Quarterly* 15:324–336.

Calfee, R. C., and P. Perfumo. (1993). "Student Portfolios: Opportunities for a Revolution in Assessment." *Journal of Reading.* 36:532–537.

Collins, M. D., and E. H. Cheek. (1993). *Diagnostic-Prescriptive Reading Instruction: A Guide for Classroom Teachers,* 4th ed. Madison, WI: Brown & Benchmark Publishers.

Cooter, R. B. Jr. (1990). *The Teacher's Guide to Reading Tests.* Scottsdale, AZ: Gorsuch Scarisbrick Publishers.

D'Angelo, K. (1982). "Correction Behavior: Implications for Reading Instruction." *The Reading Teacher* 35:395–398.

———. (1983). "Insertion and Omission Miscue of Good and Poor Readers." *The Reading Teacher* 36:778–782.

Farr, R. (1992). "Putting It All Together: Solving the Reading Assessment Puzzle." *The Reading Teacher* 46:26–37.

Farr, R., and B. Tone. (1994). *Portfolio and Performance Assessment (Helping Students Evaluate Their Progress as Readers and Writers).* Fort Worth, TX: Harcourt Brace College Publishers.

Flippo, R. F. (1997). *Reading Assessment and Instruction: A Qualitative Approach to Diagnosis.* Ft. Worth, TX: Harcourt Brace College Publishers.

Glazer, S. M., and C. S. Brown. (1993). *Portfolios and Beyond: Collaborative Assessment in Reading and Writing.* Norwood, MA: Christopher-Gordon Publishers.

Goodman, K. S. (1969). "Analysis of Oral Reading Miscues: Applied Psycholinguistics." *Reading Research Quarterly* 5:9–30.

Goodman, Y. M., and C. L. Burke. (1972). *Reading Miscue Inventory.* New York: Macmillan.

Goodman, Y. M., D. J. Watson, and C. L. Burke. (1987). *Reading Miscue Inventory: Alternative Procedures.* New York: Richard C. Owen Publishers.

Graves, D., and B. S. Sunstein, eds. (1992). *Portfolio Portraits.* Portsmouth, NH: Heinemann.

Hill, B. C., and C. Ruptic. (1994). *Practical Aspects of Portfolio Assessment: Putting the Pieces Together.* Norwood, MA: Christopher-Gordon Publishers.

International Reading Association. (1981). "International Reading Association Position on the Misuse of Grade Equivalent Scores." Newark, DE: International Reading Association.

Klesius, J. P., and S. P. Homan. (1985). "A Validity and Reliability Update on the Informal Reading Inventory with Suggestions for Improvement." *Journal of Learning Disabilities* 18 (2): 71–76.

Shearer, A. P., and S. P. Homan. (1994). *Linking Reading Assessment to Instruction: An Application Worktext for Elementary Classroom Teachers.* New York: St. Martin's Press.

Tierney, R. J., M. A. Carter, and L. E. Desai. (1991). *Portfolio Assessment in the Reading-Writing Classroom.* Norwood, MA: Christopher-Gordon Publishers.

Valencia, S. W. (1990). "A Portfolio Approach to Classroom Reading Assessment: The Whys, Whats, and Hows." *The Reading Teacher* 43:338–340.

Valencia, S. W., E. H. Hiebert, and P. P. Afflerbach, eds. (1994). *Authentic Reading Assessment: Practices and Possibilities.* Newark, DE: International Reading Association.

# *A*pproaches for Instruction

© Rita Nannini/Photo Researchers, Inc.

# *Overview*

*T*his chapter discusses the selection of approach(es) to meet the reading instructional and developmental needs of every student in the elementary classroom. We believe that these needs can be met most effectively through the implementation of the facilitative teacher perspective, employing an interactive language-based and integrated classroom learning environment that balances use of a variety of approaches and materials. The primary purpose of using a variety of approaches and materials to meet each student's needs is to help all students be the best readers that they can be. In reviewing our perspective of reading, we reiterate that we believe that no matter which approaches and materials are used, it is appropriate to use direct, skills, and strategy instruction as needed.

In this chapter, we recap the major perspectives of reading; our facilitative teacher perspective is reviewed and then five approaches are presented. These include the language-experience approach, the individualized-reading approach, the literature-based approach, the basal reader approach, and the eclectic approach. Additionally, the integrated curriculum is discussed as another opportunity to balance instruction, using the eclectic idea of pulling from what is most appropriate from various approaches and ideas.

## *Main Ideas*

- Facilitative teachers review approaches for instruction and then select those that best fit their own beliefs about reading and the needs, strategies, motivations, and cultures of their students.
- A number of approaches are used in the schools for reading instruction. Approaches vary from holistic to skills-based and in between.
- Classroom teachers should be aware of ideas and research that can affect what we know about teaching and learning.

Learning to read is one of the most important tasks that students undertake. In most instances, there is a direct correlation between learning to read well and success in elementary, secondary, and postsecondary classroom instruction. The actual process involved as educators teach reading and students learn to read is one of the most widely debated issues in the field of general and special education. The debate has many facets but revolves primarily around the issue of which approaches are the most effective in developing students' reading abilities. According to Smith (1965), we have at various times in our history emphasized an alphabet-spelling system (the 1600s and 1700s), a whole-word method (1800s), a synthetic phonics method (the late 1800s and early 1900s), a new look-say method (the early 1900s), and the basal method (approximately 1930 to the present). Even within the current discussions about the basal approach, there have been major debates and instructional changes relative to whole-word, phonics, language-experience, and linguistic factors. These changes have been further complicated by arguments concerning the merits and demerits of skills-based approaches and meaning-emphasis approaches. Some reading educators recommend the adoption of a skills-based approach and stress the importance of teaching word-identification skills. Yet other reading educators suggest the adoption of a meaning-emphasis approach and stress the teaching of comprehension. What is the best reading approach for you to use in your elementary classroom?

## Reflection Activity 12.1

*B*ased on all you have read thus far in this text, what do you think? Is there one best approach to use? Why or why not? In your reflection journal under the heading Reflection Activity 12.1, try answering these questions. Then continue to read this chapter for information about several approaches you might have cited.

## *Selecting the Most Appropriate Reading Approaches*

According to the National Assessment of Educational Progress (1993), 85 percent of the teachers in the United States use a basal reading program; however, it also reported that 46 percent of the teachers used both basals and trade books.

Although the basal reading system is still the most widely used approach in teaching reading in the United States, you should consider certain basic factors before selecting the basal or any other approach to teaching or developing reading. These factors include (a) your philosophy and definition of reading and reading instruction; (b) the characteristics of your students (e.g., motivations and interests; language, cognitive, and cultural experiences; cognitive and linguistic strategies; prior knowledge and schemata; and sociocultural background); and (c) your school and classroom context and environmental conditions (e.g., class size, equipment and materials, etc.). Even if your school district is committed to the use of a basal reading system, you could supplement your basals with authentic literature and materials and use other approaches as well. The selection of these other approaches should primarily depend on the needs of your students, but you must also consider your beliefs and reading perspective as well as the other factors cited.

In selecting a reading approach to use with students, facilitative teachers should be aware of each student's strategies, strengths, motivations, and needs and then match the appropriate approach or approaches accordingly. In the following sections, we recap the three major perspectives or philosophies of reading, review our facilitative reading perspective, and then present five approaches to teaching reading in the elementary classroom to help you understand the instructional attributes, advantages, and limitations of each and the influence of the major perspectives. These approaches are widely used in the United States with varying degrees of success, depending on effective and adequate instruction and the needs and characteristics of the reader. As these approaches are reviewed, ask yourself which fit with your current philosophy and theory of reading instruction.

 **Reflection Activity 12.2**

*O*nce again, we'd like you to stop and reflect. Please go back to the reflections you wrote in Chapter 1 (Reflection Activity 1.1, Parts A, B, and C) and examine the perspective and definition of reading that you wrote. Have they changed? If so, how? Feel free to amend them now and indicate in you reflection journal, under the heading Reflection Activity 12.2, any changes you noted.

## *The Whole Language Perspective: A Recap*

The whole language perspective encompasses the view that an integrated reading and writing curriculum that uses authentic literature to empower students and teachers to learn together in a democratic learning community leads to successful reading experiences for students. The influence of this perspective has been widespread and has affected the way many teachers view and think about reading. These holistic views have persuaded many school districts and publishing companies to reexamine their approaches and materials for teaching reading. For example, basal reading publishers are making more efforts to include authentic literature in their programs. Additionally, many teachers are supplementing these programs with trade books and other real literature. This interest in authenticity of materials, instruction, and approaches is an outgrowth of whole language ideas.

## *The Interactive Perspective: A Recap*

The interactive perspective encompasses the view that reading involves interaction with text, and that readers develop meaning by combining information from text with their own prior knowledge, purposes, motivations, and situations. The influence of this perspective has also been widespread and has affected the way many teachers, school systems, and publishing companies view and think about reading. Interaction with text, self-awareness, strategies, and motivations for reading are being attended to more than ever in classrooms, schools, and published materials. For example, basal programs are making more efforts to make their materials interactive. Interest in interaction between the reader and text, metacognitive strategies, and other cognitive processes are an outgrowth of interactive perspective views.

### The Skills Perspective: A Recap

The skills perspective encompasses the view that reading involves the learning of many skills, including phonics and other word identification and analysis skills, and that teachers must provide this instruction in direct and systematic ways. The influence of this perspective has also been widespread and has affected the way many teachers, school systems, and publishing companies view and think about reading. Direct instruction, skills instruction, as well as phonics and other word recognition instruction, continue to be attended to in classrooms, schools, and published materials. For example, basal programs present reading skills and introduce vocabulary in a systematic way. Interest in ensuring that students have basic reading skills, sight vocabulary, phonics, and other word recognition skills, and presentation of this instruction using direct approaches are an outgrowth of the skills perspective.

## The Facilitative Teacher Perspective

In the beginning of this text, we shared our ideas and beliefs with you and suggested that they represent a "balance" from what we value most from the evolving skill-based, whole language, and interactive perspectives of reading. We further indicated that we have embodied these ideas and beliefs in "the facilitative teacher perspective"—this is the teaching perspective that "balances" the use of methods, procedures, materials, and instruction to utilize what is most appropriate for specific individual students' learning (see Figure 12.1).

Figure 12.2 highlights the facilitative teacher perspective and indicates where each belief has evolved from. As you will see, because these beliefs represent a balance between the three major perspectives of reading, no particular approach or method of reading instruction can be advocated for all students or all situations.

Our following discussion of each of the approaches to teaching or developing reading is intended to demonstrate that each of these approaches can have a place in the elementary classroom program. They can stand alone or be used in conjunction with each other to provide reading instruction and continued development. We see each as having promise for the facilitative teacher's purposes: that is, to provide effective, language-based, interactive, and integrated instruction for all students while meeting their individual needs, motivations, and interests. No matter what your perspective and beliefs about reading, we believe that you will find that you can use one or several of these approaches to meet the needs of all your students.

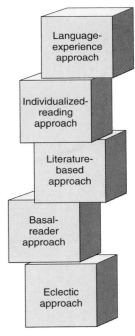

**Figure 12.1**
The facilitative teacher perspective: Balancing use of approaches with students' needs, skills, strategies, motivations, and cultures.

- Reading development is based on students' emerging experiences with language.
- The reader's comprehension is of paramount importance.
- The reader's prior knowledge and experiences affect his/her understanding of what he/she reads.

- Reading is an interactive process and involves the cognitive processing of information in the text and the use of many skills, strategies, and resources to gain meaning.
- Readers interact with text to develop meaning, meaning that will be shaped by a combination of text, experience, prior knowledge, purpose, and situation.
- Students should receive direct instruction, as needed, in various strategies to help them develop their proficiency as readers.

- It is necessary at times for teachers to provide direct instruction in skills (including phonics) to students needing this instruction.

- The decoding of print is part of reading.

*Figure 12.2*
The facilitative teacher perspective and beliefs: Using and balancing ideas from the evolving skills-based, whole language, and interactive perspectives.

# The Language-Experience Approach

The continued development of language as an effective communication skill is one of the most important responsibilities of the elementary teacher. One important goal is that students develop an understanding of the relationship between language and writing. A reading approach that integrates language-, writing-, and reading-instructional activities can increase the likelihood of many students becoming successful readers.

Jagger (1985) contended that several important themes suggest that using students' language and having them learn through their language is the most appropriate reading-instructional procedure. The logical themes that led to Jagger's conclusion included the following:

1. *Language learning is a self-generated, creative process.* Children learn language without direct instruction. They learn it in a variety of ways (e.g., through experience or by listening to others) and experiment with and practice their language in situations where language is purposeful.
2. *Language learning is holistic.* The language components of function, form, and meaning are learned simultaneously. Children acquire new and more complex forms and functions for language when they have a need for new and more complex meanings. Through this process they learn that the forms used to express meaning and intention can vary according to purpose and content.
3. *Language learning is social and collaborative.* Language is acquired by children in meaningful interactions with others who provide models. These individuals also support children's language learning by responding to what children are trying to say and do, rather than to form.
4. *Language learning is functional and integrative.* Children do not first learn language and then learn how to use it. Language acquisition and the ability to communicate by means of language are simultaneous functions. The process also stimulates children's ability to use language to think and learn.
5. *Language learning is variable.* Because language learning is inherently variable, the meanings, forms, and functions of children's language depend on children's personal, social, and cultural experiences.

The writings and research of those supporting an emergent literacy view of reading and writing development (e.g., see Strickland and Morrow 1989; Sulzby and Barnhart 1992; Teale and Sulzby 1986; and others) tend to agree with these conclusions.

The language-experience approach is designed to capitalize on the preceding five language themes. This approach also motivates students to want to read and effectively demonstrate the connection between oral and written language. The language-experience approach places great emphasis on the use of your students' own language and experiential backgrounds.

Allen (1973, p. 158) portrayed the ideas of the language-experience approach in his scenario of a student's reflections:

> What I can think about, I can talk about.
> What I can say, I can write, or someone can write for me.
> What I write, I can read.
> I can read what I can write and what other people can write for me to read.

Hall (1978) defined the language-experience approach as "a method in which instruction is built on the use of reading materials created by writing down children's spoken language" (p. 1).

These ideas and definition provide the foundation of the language-experience approach: using children's own language as the basis for their reading instruction in the elementary classroom. With this emphasis, the language-experience approach utilizes the integration of language, reading, and writing as integral components of the reading process. Usova and Usova (1993) found that an integrated art and language arts program for at-risk first-grade children using language experience, whole language, and basals improved reading, writing, and language ability.

In implementing the language-experience approach, it is important to be logical and systematic in designing and conducting reading activities. If you use this reading approach, consider the following specific steps suggested by Collins and Cheek (1993):

1. Use the approach with individual students, small groups, or large groups depending on the purpose of the lesson.
2. Discuss an experience that is common to the group or that seems important to the individual student. To facilitate this discussion, you could use a stimulus such as a field trip, an actual object, or a picture of an event or object.
3. Prepare the students to tell their own story about the above discussion by having them summarize ideas from the discussion and by giving a title to the ideas discussed. Have students contribute by sharing their specific ideas about the experience.
4. Write each contributed idea in a sentence on the board or on a chart. The sentences could be written in story or paragraph form. The students' stated title should be written above the writing.
5. Read each idea after it is written, sweeping your hand under each line to emphasize left-to-right sequencing. Then, with your students, read the sentences as a story.
6. Discuss written-language elements and principles within the story by pointing out capital letters, proper names, contractions, and abbreviations, among other written elements.
7. Have the student(s) copy and file the story. During the following days, reread the story and teach the vocabulary and concepts. Some skill instruction can also occur, if desired.

In addition to these suggestions, you can also encourage your students to relate their own experiences in class and write their own stories/ideas independently. These more self-directed written stories can be shared with the entire class or with just the teacher. Students with limited English could be encouraged to tape their stories, so that you can later use this to write their stories with them. Such activities will help students to develop their understandings regarding the connection between oral and written language.

The computer can also be used to implement the language-experience approach in the classroom. Grabe and Grabe (1985) suggested that computers could be used for word-processor-generated stories, sequence stories, and interactive literature. Flippo (1986) indicated that the use of language-experience techniques using a word processor could make children more aware of sentence structure, word groupings, phrase boundaries, and terminal punctuation. Additionally, Flippo stated that the processes of inserting, deleting, and rearranging are all part of the general process that students go through as they develop control over language. Heller (1993) also has suggested that the use of the word processor with first graders to explore oral and written language is an especially effective way to implement the language-experience approach. Moxley and Barry (1985) found that teaching spelling with a computer within the context of a language-experience approach proved to be successful.

The language-experience approach does provide a positive and viable means of developing students' reading; however, this approach does have both limitations as well as strengths. As already suggested, some strengths are (a) students' language is used as the basis for reading instruction; (b) students are motivated because of high interest; (c) students' self-esteem is enhanced; (d) students' use of left-to-right sequencing, capitalization and punctuation, and word boundaries are developed naturally; (e) students' oral-language skills are promoted; and (f) students develop more awareness of the language, reading, and writing connection. Some limitations of the language-experience approach include (a) it is an instructional approach with no sequential development of skills; (b) teacher-made and student-made materials are emphasized, since there are very few commercial materials available; (c) some students may suffer from the lack of repetition of vocabulary-development activities because there is no controlled vocabulary like that found in basal programs; (d) overuse of this approach may become boring to the student; and (e) a great deal of teacher time is required for successful implementation of the approach.

The language-experience approach does facilitate the development of oral and written language for younger students who are just beginning to read, as well as for all students who are language diverse and learning to write and read in a second language. Because of this, it can be a valuable instructional procedure in the elementary classroom. It need not be your only approach for teaching reading, but it could be a primary approach for use with some students and an excellent supplementary approach for use with others. (Also see Sampson, Sampson, and Allen 1995; and our reading and writing chapter; for additional applications regarding use and extensions of the language-experience approach.)

# The Individualized-Reading Approach

The individualized-reading approach involves a planned program for individual students. Although the term *individualized* may imply one-to-one instruction, much of the instruction can take place in groups. What is individualized are decisions as to what instruction, materials, and assignments each student will take part in. Back in 1949, Olson indicated that students' performance can be enhanced when instruction permits seeking, self-selection, and student-directed pacing. An individualized approach can be used with large or small groups of students or with individual students. It can also be used alone or as a supplement to other reading approaches.

Bagford (1985) suggested a number of guidelines that could be used to implement an individualized-reading approach. The guidelines we especially recommend include:

1. Use this approach in conjunction with programs that include some direct instruction (a basal program would qualify).
2. Students at every grade level should have a regularly scheduled time when they can select their own reading material.
3. Spend time with your students discussing the importance of ideas expressed in their specific individualized readings.
4. Students learn to read by reading, so it is important to devote instructional time to allowing students to actually read.

Also, when using an individualized-reading approach, Collins and Cheek (1993) recommend steps to be included. Those that we believe are particularly important and would fit most philosophies are as follows:

1. Be aware of each student's interests, motivations, strategies, and cultures. Obtain a sufficient number of library books or other materials appropriate for all involved students.
2. Organize the books according to topics and interests to assist students in locating appropriate materials. Have students select the book that they want to read. If you assist your students in the selection process, remember to consider factors other than readability level (e.g., interest and motivation). If you are concerned that a book may be too difficult for a student you can ask the student to read several pages of the selected book to you to help determine whether the book is appropriate. However, remember that if a student really wants to read a book, no matter its difficulty, you should let the child do so.
3. Have the students read their selected books and then sign up, when they are ready, for an individual conference with you to discuss the ideas, topics, or story. The conference could last from five to twenty minutes and provide you with an opportunity to ask questions, to listen to the student read a short selection to assess word-identification and oral-reading skills and strategies, and to assist the student with skill and strategy development.

4. When students are reading their individual books, provide assistance if needed and suggest that students list words that they do not recognize or understand.

Many variations of the preceding implementation guidelines and steps can be undertaken by a facilitative teacher. These variations should be based on your students' interests, motivations, needs, cultures, cognitive and linguistic experiences, and other factors, and by your own developed philosophy and theory regarding reading, teaching, and learning.

Some strengths of the individualized-reading approach are (a) it requires student-centered, personal, and individualized interactions between teachers and their students; (b) it increases grouping flexibility and individualized instruction; (c) it reduces possibilities of negative comparisons between students because everyone is reading a different book; (d) students read books of personal interest to them at their own rates; and (e) it enables students to experience success, which enhances their self-esteem. Some limitations of the individualized reading approach include (a) it is time-consuming for teachers to obtain books and materials necessary for implementing this approach; (b) it is time-consuming for teachers because of the organizational processes involved in planning and record keeping; (c) the students' reading vocabulary is not controlled; (d) there is a lack of sequential skill development; and (e) students needing more direction may have difficulty staying on task.

The individualized-reading approach can be very effective if used appropriately. Remember to consider its strengths, limitations, and potential when deciding whether its use is appropriate for students in your classroom. The approach is more effective when used with students who can work well independently. However, one of your responsibilities as a facilitative teacher will be to provide more of these opportunities for your students to become independent learners. As you encourage independence, you may find that more students will be able to succeed in an individualized reading approach environment. As they become more self-directed, managing individualized instruction will also become easier for you. Individualized reading can be used as a primary approach for some students and as a supplementary approach, combined with direct instruction, for other students.

## *The Literature-Based Approach*

Although the literature-based approach and the individualized-reading approach have similarities, they have different origins. The individualized-reading approach is grounded in child development theory, whereas the literature-based approach has been very strongly influenced by the whole language movement. The primary similarity between the two approaches is the extensive use of authentic children's literature to teach reading.

The primary focus of the literature-based approach to teaching children to read is to use authentic or "real" children's books and literature. Many of the basic tenets inherent in whole language are found in literature-based reading instructional programs. These include, in addition to authentic literature and

authentic assessment, the use of thematic units, integrating reading and writing, and collaborative learning. Within our perception of what constitutes literature-based instruction, we perceive some differences between the literature-based approach and what is advocated by the whole language perspective. These differences are primarily in the areas of direct instruction and skills instruction. We believe that both direct instruction and strategy and skills instruction are permissible and appropriate when children require this element in their reading program. Literature-based instruction can include these when the instruction is provided in context and as part of the literature reading, review, and discussion.

In examining the foundation upon which the literature-based approach is laid, we invite you to examine the eight characteristics provided by Savage (1994):

1. Trade books, which are the centerpiece of the literature-based curriculum, are used intensively. Other types of literature, stories and poems, and material from other content areas are part of the daily reading activities. A primary focus is for students to interact and share information in a positive and less stressful environment.
2. Another integral element is reader response. Students interact with each other through discussion, drama, art, and writing. This constant interaction allows students to gain a deeper understanding of what they are reading.
3. "Read-alouds" are another vital element of literature-based instruction. Teachers read aloud to students throughout the day, initiating situations where students and the teacher can share common reactions and experiences.

4. An important feature of literature-based reading instruction is sustained silent reading. This is an activity that is done daily, where specific times are set aside for both teachers and students to read books that they choose.

5. Perhaps one of the more important characteristics of the literature-based approach is the extensive use of thematic units. Trade books, content textbooks, fiction, and any other appropriate sources are used to investigate specific topics. It is a way of teaching across the curriculum, so that students can be aware of the more holistic nature of learning. For example, a third-grade teacher might choose to implement a thematic unit on "frogs." Students could then research frogs in trade books, their science textbook, library resource material, and any other appropriate sources.

6. Classroom libraries are an essential ingredient in a literature-based program, but in situations where you are a new teacher, or a beginning teacher, or have limited funds, use your school and/or public library to supplement your resources.

7. Another element in literature-based programs is author study, where students study about those authors who wrote their stories and poems. Studying authors that they enjoy will encourage students to become more involved in the classroom activities by becoming authors themselves and writing original stories and poems.

8. Teachers are the key to any successful literature-based program. It is essential for children to witness your enthusiasm and zest for literature. Remember that positive modeling is a "must" in teaching children to read.

In examining the characteristics of a literature-based program, it is important to remember that an appreciation of literature as well as an understanding of its content is desirable. One of the primary goals of a literature-based program is to instill in children the belief that reading is not only for learning school-related information but also for enjoyment. This idea of instilling in children the belief that reading is useful and relevant to their everyday lives is one of the primary concerns of educators who believe that the use of prescribed stories and regimented workbook pages inherent in the way many teachers have used basal programs could turn children off to reading. The National Council of Teachers of English (1983) has stated that children should (1) realize the importance of literature as a mirror of human experience, (2) develop greater insights from reading literature, (3) develop an appreciation of writers from diverse backgrounds and experiences, (4) learn how to share and write about various forms of literature, (5) appreciate the beauty and rhythms of the language in literature, and (6) develop lifelong reading habits.

We believe that the literature-based reading approach is creative and exciting, with a number of outstanding features that we find appealing. It is an approach that can be very effective when used by a facilitative, creative, and experienced teacher; however, we do have some reservations about the abilities of first-year teachers to use this approach effectively. This approach requires considerable knowledge of children's books, well-developed classroom management skills, and an extensive classroom and/or school library. However, we do believe that the current trend toward the use of authentic literature in elementary classrooms as the primary instructional delivery system is both appropriate and in the best interests of children.

In summary then, some advantages of the literature-based approach are as follows: (a) it is flexible, allowing freedom in grouping and the ability to adjust instruction to meet the needs of the student; (b) it uses rich and varied language from the different sources of literature; (c) skills and strategies are taught within the parameters of the literature that the students are reading, not as isolated activities; (d) students enjoy a heightened sense of involvement with authentic literature and tend to develop more positive attitudes toward reading material in which they are interested; and (e) children are exposed to a greater variety of authentic literature. Disadvantages of a literature-based approach are that (a) it requires a great deal of planning and organization, (b) knowledge of authentic literature, (c) experience in implementing this type of instructional program, (d) an extensive classroom and/or school library, and (e) a supportive school environment (Collins and Cheek 1993; Savage 1994).

## The Basal Reader Approach

As mentioned at the beginning of this chapter, basal readers have been in use in this country for approximately seventy years. The use of basal readers as the primary approach for teaching reading is well known and extensively discussed in the literature. However, the degree of reliance on basals by classroom teachers has been and continues to be a source of debate among reading educators. Basal programs use graded books (and stories) and teacher's guides to present reading skills as a hierarchy, commonly referred to as a scope and sequence of skills.

The hierarchy of skills found in basal reading programs is designed to indicate to teachers at which grade levels certain reading skills are introduced and should be taught. Thus, the reading skills taught in the first grade form a basis for those skills encountered in the second and later grades. Technically, for the basal's hierarchy to be effective, students should master skills as they are taught, so that they can use these skills to help learn those skills introduced later in the scope and sequence. The problem with this philosophy, however, is that students do not learn the introduced skills at the same rate, nor do they bring the same perspectives to the reading process. Such factors as the characteristics of the reader (e.g., experiential background, interests, motivations, prior knowledge, and linguistic and sociocultural differences) that alone or in combination affect reading-skill development.

Criticisms of basal reading programs abound. Durkin (1981) found that basal reader teacher's manuals can negatively influence reading instruction by giving more attention to assessment, application, and practice exercises than to direct, explicit instruction. Durkin (1984) has also stated that teachers must share some of the responsibility for the ineffectiveness of basal readers, since there is a tendency among teachers to ignore many of the instructions given in manuals. Green-Wilder and Kingston (1986) found that basals could serve as a better model for students if the value of reading would be depicted in stories as an integral part of daily life. Templeton (1986) has suggested that some basal readiness activities should be avoided or postponed, while there should be more emphasis on direct experience with books and shared reading at this level. Finally, Shannon and Goodman (1994) published an entire edited book of criticism covering every major aspect and component of basal readers; and in 1988, Goodman, Shannon, Freeman, and Murphy published a critical review of basals for the NCTE Commission on Reading. Yet, despite these and other criticisms of basal reading programs, the widespread use of this approach in teaching reading mandates that you should be as familiar as possible with it. You may be expected to use basal readers as the basis of at least part of your reading program.

The primary purpose of a basal reading program is to develop proficient readers through the use of a series of books that introduces new skills, new vocabulary, and that progresses in reading difficulty. There are typically one or more of these books at each level beginning at the preprimer stage and continuing through the eighth grade. Each of the books is a prerequisite to the next level. Thus, a book at the preprimer level might be referred to as Level 1 or Level A, depending on the series being used, and the numbering or lettering would continue through the numbers of levels present in a particular series.

In addition to the various books or "readers" at each level, basal reading programs contain numerous other materials that are designed for both teachers and students. Materials that can be included for the teacher's use are (a) teacher's manuals, (b) pictures of characters found in the basal readers and vocabulary cards, (c) audiovisuals, (d) management systems that include assessment procedures and record-keeping strategies, and (e) other supplementary word-identification and comprehension materials. Materials normally included for students are (a) a reader or readers for each level, (b) workbooks for each level, (c) supplementary games and activities, and (d) paperbacks designed for high-interest, low-vocabulary recreation use.

Baumann (1992) discussed the problems inherent in basal readers and concluded the following: no adaptations or rewrites of excerpts from children's literature should be used; literature should be authentic; instruction should be provided only for authentic reading skills and strategies; basal assessment techniques should employ more authentic measures to improve teacher decision making about appropriate instruction for students; teachers' guides should suggest, not direct, instruction; workbooks and skill sheets should ask students to respond in more open-ended and reflective ways; and basal materials should be presented as one tool that can be used to promote students' literacy and not the total program or only means that teachers can use to teach children to read.

Companies that publish basal readers have made a concerted effort to improve the quality of their products. For example, more authentic literature is being used in the readers and the quality of the supplemental materials has improved dramatically. Efforts have been made to include multicultural literature, and literature depicting various ethnic groups; and women, girls, men, and boys in nonstereotypical roles and activities. There is also somewhat less emphasis on developing isolated skills. More emphasis is being placed on language-based activities involving student collaboration, student-teacher interaction, and the development of higher-order thinking skills. In addition to these efforts, some of the paperbacks are presented in big books and predictable book formats, which many children seem to be more motivated to read.

These materials are designed to provide you and your students with the means to effective instruction and efficient reading. Detailed lesson plans that follow a Directed Reading Activity (DRA) format can also be provided to assist you in using the basals properly. To obtain the desired results from basal programs, you should employ logic and good judgment in following the teacher's manual. Use the manual appropriately, but do not follow it word for word. Integrate your ideas and other approaches into the activities suggested by the teacher's manual.

Some of the strengths of using a basal reader approach are as follows: (a) each reader in the series is graded; (b) the vocabulary in each reader is controlled, with repetition of words to help students remember the words; (c) teacher's manuals offer many valuable suggestions and may provide sample lesson plans; (d) basal reading programs include most major components of a total reading program, such as vocabulary development, word identification, oral and silent reading, recreational reading, and comprehension; and (e) basal programs have a built-in systematic and comprehensive skills program.

The basal reading approach also has the following limitations: (a) the syntactic structure found in most basal readers is often different from that of the students reading them; (b) the use of controlled vocabularies can create dull, repetitive stories of questionable literary value; (c) stories in older basals have typically emphasized middle-class situations and values rather than presenting a diverse sociocultural perspective; (d) since basal reading programs are considered to comprise a total reading program, there is a tendency for some teachers to neglect other experiences that could enhance their overall reading program; (e) some teachers may follow the teacher's manual verbatim without considering the specific needs of their individual students; and (f) many believe that the use of basal reading groups has perpetuated "ability grouping," which tends to label students and has damaged many students.

Because of the widespread use of basal reading programs throughout the United States, numerous suggestions have been proposed for improving their instructional value. A realistic evaluation of present reading philosophies and instructional practices indicates that basal readers will remain an integral part of most classroom reading instruction for some time to come. Thus, perhaps the most logical basal reader approach for you to take is to modify, vary, and supplement your basal reading program as necessary to counter some of the limitations and criticisms. Consider the following modifications:

- Use more authentic literature in the form of trade books to enhance your basal instruction.
- Encourage your students to respond to what they are reading through such venues as discussion groups, journals, cooperative groups, drama and art activities, and extensively use writing with your basal reading program.

- Use "read-alouds" as an integral part of your daily activities and encourage students to share their excitement about what they are reading.
- Make sustained silent reading an important component of your daily reading activities.
- Use thematic units to integrate reading across the curriculum.
- Use portfolios to assess your students' progress as part of your basal reader and other reading/writing activities.

Finally, in the early 1990s, the Center for the Study of Reading, partially supported by funding from the U.S. Department of Education, developed and published *A Guide to Selecting Basal Reading Programs*. The *Guide* consists of booklets focusing on major areas of reading instruction and was designed to provide both a systematic process to initially select elementary reading programs and valuable research-based guidance to improve existing programs. Teachers and school systems considering adoption of basals could refer to this resource for specifics on all major aspects of reading instruction using the basal (see Dole, Osborn, and Lehr 1990).

## *The Eclectic Approach*

Although reading professionals have their own ideas about which approaches are the most effective ways of teaching reading for specific students, it is clear to the majority of reading educators that there is no one best way to teach reading. If a single best approach for all students existed, we would have identified that approach by now and adopted it in all school districts so that all teachers would be using that one approach. The fact is, there is not one ultimate approach or ultimate material. Instead, the majority of reading educators would advocate the use of a variety of approaches and materials to cultivate the reading development of students. This use of a variety of approaches and materials has become known as "the eclectic approach." The eclectic reading approach, then, is an approach that combines and balances the desirable aspects of all current approaches to meet the needs of specific, individual students.

In using the eclectic approach, teachers match students' needs, strategies, and motivations with those features of the various approaches that would best enhance the individual students' reading development. To use the eclectic approach effectively, you need to be very familiar with your students' needs/motivations and the attributes of a variety of approaches. The primary strength of the eclectic approach is its ability to meet the needs of every student in your classroom when implemented by a knowledgeable, facilitative teacher. Its primary limitations are that it requires considerable teacher knowledge and the careful planning and coordination of a variety of reading activities, assignments, and materials.

## *An Integrated Curriculum*

Spiegel (1992) alluded to the possibility of bridging the gap between holistic and more traditional approaches to teaching reading by implementing more of an integrated curriculum. We include it here because we believe that an integrated curriculum represents a balanced or more eclectic approach to reading instruction and learning. In the facilitative teacher chapter of this text, our description of the integrated-facilitative classroom represents a similar idea.

Lapp and Flood (1994) further discussed the possibilities of an integrated curriculum and suggested some first steps in implementing this type of curriculum. They indicated that teachers should select a theme that will make instruction as relevant as possible, and they should be sure to encourage students to participate in selecting this theme. It should be broad enough to encompass the skills and information required for a specific grade level. Teachers should collect texts and other materials related to this theme. The materials can be gathered from the classroom, the school library, and any other appropriate source. After collecting materials, teachers should determine specific goals and objectives that they want to accomplish and then plan activities to meet those objectives. How each phase of the instructional plan and the corresponding activities will be carried out should then be determined. This step includes plans for whole-class activities and grouping. Teachers can identify ways that the students can expand the theme, and plan for meaningful, authentic activities to assess students' growth.

The following are advantages of an integrated curriculum:

1. Students are presented with a more holistic picture that reveals the relationship between ideas and concepts within the parameters of a specific theme.
2. The process of communication becomes more authentic.
3. Students expand their personal bases of ideas through sharing.
4. Interaction among students increases respect and cooperation.
5. Students develop a greater sense of responsibility.
6. Teachers become facilitators rather than dispensers of information.
7. A sense of community develops within the classroom.
8. Grouping patterns tend to emerge naturally.
9. Assessment is continuous and authentic.

If you use a basal program, you might consider modifying and enhancing your program by implementing some of the preceding suggestions, or you may want to develop your own innovative and creative reading program that is more eclectic and balances what you like best from several of the approaches in this chapter and the ideas represented by the integrated curriculum.

## Reflection Activity 12.3

*T*his chapter has presented a variety of approaches to teaching or developing reading. There are those in favor of and those opposed to each of these approaches, and each of the approaches has certain advantages and disadvantages. Does this confuse you? How do you stand? What additional information do you need to help you more fully understand these issues and approaches and to make instructional decisions? In your reflection journal under Reflection Activity 12.3, please note any questions you may have, additional information you would like, and sources you might want to read. Later we hope you will research these questions, concerns, and sources to help you find answers. All teachers must constantly do this to keep abreast of the large and growing fields of knowledge related to teaching reading. We hope you will also take the time to find your answers.

## Summary

In an effort to present a variety of approaches to teach and develop reading in the classroom, the three major perspectives were briefly recapped, then our facilitative teacher perspective and five approaches to reading instruction were presented. These approaches included the language-experience approach, the individualized-reading approach, the literature-based approach, the basal reader approach, and the eclectic approach. Strengths and limitations of each approach were discussed to assist in understanding the possible uses of each. The idea that many approaches can be used within a classroom to meet the needs, interests, motivations, skills, strategies, and cultures of all students was highlighted. An integrated curriculum was suggested as one way of eclectically balancing use of many approaches and ideas.

## Closing Activities

1. In a small group, share and discuss how you were taught to read in school. What approaches do you remember being used? How did they, or do they, affect your feelings about reading?
2. In a small group, discuss the extent to which basal readers have exerted a positive and/or negative influence on the teaching of reading in the elementary classroom for the past seventy years.
3. As part of your field activities in this course, implement the literature-based approach with a small group (no more than five) of primary-grade children. Place particular emphasis on the integration of writing into the lesson. Summarize your results, and if possible bring the related writings the children developed to class to share with your peers.
4. At the library, research one of the questions or areas noted in Reflection Activity 12.3. Summarize your findings in a brief report, and if possible, share the report with your peers in class.

### References

Allen, R. V. (1973). "The Language Experience Approach." In R. Karlin, ed., *Perspectives on Elementary Reading* (p. 158). New York: Harcourt Brace Jovanovich.

Bagford, J. (1985). "What Ever Happened to Individualized Reading?" *The Reading Teacher* 39 (2): 190–193.

Baumann, J. F. (1992). "Basal Reading Programs and the Deskilling of Teachers: A Critical Examination of the Argument." *Reading Research Quarterly* 27 (4): 390–398.

Collins, M. D., and E. H. Cheek. (1993). *Diagnostic-Prescriptive Reading Instruction: A Guide for Classroom Teachers,* 4th ed. Madison, WI: Brown & Benchmark Publishers.

Dole, J. A., J. Osborn, and F. Lehr, project coordinators. (1990). *A Guide to Selecting Basal Reading Programs.* Urbana-Champaign, IL: Adoption Guidelines Project, Reading Research and Education Center, Center for the Study of Reading, University of Illinois at Urbana-Champaign.

Durkin, D. (1981). "Reading Comprehension Instruction in Five Basal Reader Series." *Reading Research Quarterly* 16: 515–544.

———. 1984. "Is There a Match Between What Elementary Teachers Do and What Basal Reader Manuals Recommend?" *The Reading Teacher* 37 (8): 734–744.

Flippo, R. F. (1986). "Using the Word Processor to Clarify Textual Phrasing." *Reading Horizons* 27 (1): 65–68.

Goodman, K. S., P. Shannon, Y. S. Freeman, and S. Murphy. (1988). *Report Card on Basal Readers.* Katonah, NY: Richard C. Owen Publishers.

Grabe, M., and C. Grabe. (1985). "The Microcomputer and the Language Experience Approach." *The Reading Teacher* 38 (6): 508–511.

Green-Wilder, J. L., and A. J. Kingston. (1986). "The Depiction of Reading in Five Popular Basal Series." *The Reading Teacher* 39 (5): 399–402.

Hall, M. A. (1978). *The Language Experience Approach for Teaching Reading,* 2nd ed. Newark, DE: International Reading Association.

Heller, M. F. (1993). "Hearts and Rabbits: Computer-Assisted Language Experience Stories." *Writing Notebook: Visions for Learning* 10 (3): 15–17.

Jagger, A. (1985). "On Observing the Language Learner: Introduction and Overview." In A. Jagger and M. T. Smith-Burke, eds., *Observing the Language Learner* (pp. 1–7). Newark, DE: International Reading Association.

Lapp, D., and J. Flood. (1994). "Integrating the Curriculum: First Steps." *The Reading Teacher* 47 (5): 416–419.

Moxley, R. A., and P. A. Barry. (1985). "Spelling with LEA on the Microcomputer." *The Reading Teacher* 39 (3): 267–273.

National Assessment of Educational Progress. (1993). Executive Summary, 1992 National Assessment of Educational Progress.

National Council of Teachers of English. (1983). "Forum: Essentials of English." *Language Arts* 60: 244–248.

Olson, W. C. (1949). *Child Development.* Boston: D. C. Heath.

Sampson, M. R., M. B. Sampson, and R. V. Allen. (1995). *Pathways to Literacy: Process Transactions,* 2nd ed. Ft. Worth, TX: Harcourt Brace College Publishers.

Savage, J. F. (1994). *Teaching Reading Using Literature.* Madison, WI: Brown & Benchmark Publishers.

Shannon, P., and K. Goodman, eds. (1994). *Basal Readers: A Second Look.* New York: Richard C. Owen Publishers.

Smith, N. B. (1965). *American Reading Instruction.* Newark, DE: International Reading Association.

Spiegel, D. L. (1992). "Blending Whole Language and Systematic Direct Instruction." *The Reading Teacher* 46 (1): 38–44.

Strickland, D., and L. Morrow, eds. (1989). *Emerging Literacy: Young Children Learn to Read and Write.* Newark, DE: International Reading Association.

Sulzby, E., and J. Barnhart. (1992). "The Development of Academic Competence: All Our Children Emerge as Writers and Readers." In J. W. Irwin and M. A. Doyle, eds., *Reading/Writing Connections: Learning from Research* (pp. 120–144). Newark, DE: International Reading Association.

Teale, W., and E. Sulzby. (1986). *Emergent Literacy: Writing and Reading.* Norwood, NJ: Ablex.

Templeton, S. (1986). "Literacy, Readiness, and Basals." *The Reading Teacher* 39 (5): 403–409.

Usova, C. J., and G. M. Usova. (1993). "Integrating Art and Language Arts for First Grade At-Risk Children." *Reading Improvement* 30 (2): 117–21.

# *O*rganizing and Managing Classroom Instruction

© James L. Shaffer

# *Overview*

*T*opics to be discussed in Chapter 13 revolve around the need to organize and manage instruction in the elementary classroom. Suggestions for implementing whole-class instruction, individualized instruction, and varied groupings are provided. In the discussion on grouping, several intraclass grouping strategies are explored. These include (a) achievement/ability groups; (b) skill and strategy groups; (c) interest/motivation groups; (d) peer, cross-age, and intergenerational groups; and (e) cooperative learning groups. Also discussed is the use/limitations of interclass groupings. Other topics include (a) a planning-learning scheme; (b) techniques for managing instruction; (c) arranging for effective instruction; (d) using materials; (e) developing learning centers; (f) organizing, managing, and evaluating technology; and (g) organizing for parents and other family members' participation. Finally, professional development is discussed as a way of continuing reflection and learning.

## *Main Ideas*

- Organizing the elementary classroom facilitates instruction.
- Whole-class learning is useful for some instructional events.
- Individualized instruction is an effective instructional procedure.
- Grouping can be done according to different purposes.
- Managing group activities is an important aspect of instruction.
- A planning-learning pyramid or scheme can be used to match instructional practices with students' needs.
- Arranging classrooms for instruction can facilitate students' literacy development.
- Materials should be evaluated before they are assigned for student use.
- Learning centers can be used to reinforce instructional practices.
- Teachers can organize, manage, and evaluate technology in their classrooms.
- Organizing for parent and family participation and involvement is important.
- Professional development and continued reflection and growth are goals that can be developed in a number of ways.

It is one thing to read about many different philosophies, teaching strategies, reading approaches, and types of learners, but it is quite another thing to actually use such information to organize and manage a classroom for instruction in the most facilitative and effective way. Consider the following scenario.

It is the first day of school, and Ms. Walker has thought about and planned how she will organize her classroom. This year she is teaching the third grade, and past experiences have shown her that many students can work alone, but others cannot without close supervision. Last year was frustrating for Ms. Walker as well as for her students. There was a lot of off-task behavior and a great deal of wasted time in the classroom because of continual disruptions, both internal and external. No matter how hard she tried, Ms. Walker did not feel that she had accomplished much with her students. The thought of another year like that caused her to decide to investigate ways of improving the instructional environment in her classroom.

## Organizing the Elementary Classroom

In considering the different ideas, Ms. Walker knew she needed to examine various techniques for organizing her classroom for instruction. She realized that in heterogeneous, or mixed-group, classes there are often a wide range of reading abilities, interests, motivations, strategies used, and needs among students. This year's class, for instance, ranged from students exhibiting little reading vocabulary and skills to students reading at the sixth-grade instructional level—as measured quantitatively with an Informal Reading Inventory (IRI). A closer analysis of the class revealed the following range:

| Instructional Levels | Number of Students |
|---|---|
| Sixth-grade level | 2 |
| Fifth-grade level | 3 |
| Fourth-grade level | 4 |
| Third-grade level | 11 |
| Second-grade level | 4 |
| First-grade level | 2 |
| Below first grade | 2 |

Additionally, Ms. Walker remembered some of the other assessment strategies that had been suggested in her elementary reading-education course and also assessed her students qualitatively. She found that they had a wide variety of personal and academic interests, that they used various reading strategies for getting meaning from text, that there were many differences among students in their use of word-identification procedures, and that they had varied cultural, experiential, linguistic, and cognitive backgrounds.

"Well," thought Ms. Walker. "Even though all of my students are in the third grade, they are heterogeneous! I will have to change my classroom organization and management practices if I am to meet my students' needs, motivations, and interests."

Ms. Walker felt that to adjust instruction to more effectively meet the various abilities, interests, motivations, cultural and linguistic diversities, strategies used, and skill and other needs in the class, she had to be better organized. Many reflections and decisions were necessary to fully implement her organizational plan.

First, she thought back to the reading education course she took to complete her teacher certification requirements. She had used the text by Cheek, Flippo, and Lindsey (1997), *Reading for Success in Elementary Schools*. As a result of her reflection during that course, she had further developed her own personal philosophy of reading and learning. Many of her ideas coincided with what Cheek et al. called the facilitative teacher perspective. Yes, Ms. Walker feels she is a facilitative teacher and she would provide the necessary environment to facilitate reading and learning this school year!

Ms. Walker's professional development activities also convinced her that she would utilize the general suggestions recommended by Wiggins (1994), Heron and Harris (1993), and Collins and Cheek (1993) to organize her classroom. This school year she would do the following:

1. Collaborate with professionals and paraprofessionals to determine instructional practices and outcomes
2. Recognize and accommodate students' individual differences
3. Assess students' strengths and needs using qualitative and quantitative procedures
4. Plan for literacy instruction on a daily basis
5. Use available resources effectively
6. Design whole-class, large-group, and small-group activities
7. Employ book buddy, peer tutoring, and other student-directed concepts
8. Implement effective instructional procedures for individual students
9. Establish school-to-home and home-to-school literacy programs
10. Evaluate continuously

Finally, Ms. Walker decided to experiment with Mercer and Mercer's (1993, pp. 104–105) recommendations for arranging special areas or centers and for seating students. She would develop a classroom setting that included

1. Learning centers for literacy, mathematics, science, and social studies.
2. Carrels for individual or dyad student activities.
3. A center for computer activities.
4. An area for recreational reading.
5. A teacher center for teacher-student conferences and for monitoring classroom activities.

The student seating arrangement plan she would use to start the school year involved the following:

1. Arranging seats/desks so that all students could easily see her presentations
2. Arranging seats/desks so that she has easy access to each student
3. Arranging seats/desks so that she can readily observe students as they work
4. Arranging desks depending on the desired teaching-learning outcome(s)
5. Seating students who are off-task or who are easily distracted in the middle of the classroom near the front

Ms. Walker was confident and looking forward to meeting the challenges of the new school year. She believed she could make the necessary organizational changes in her classroom that would be appropriate for her situation, her students, and her beliefs about reading and learning.

$W$hat suggestions would you make to help Ms. Walker organize her third-grade classroom for instruction? In your reflection journal under the heading Reflection Activity 13.1, describe organizational procedures you would use and list any information you feel would be necessary to make these decisions.

Effective classroom instruction and organization depends on the teacher providing the necessary and most appropriate organizational framework, and the students becoming actively involved in the learning process. Studies in teacher effectiveness (e.g., see Brophy 1979; Rupley and Blair 1980), other professional publications (e.g., see Zabel and Zabel 1996), and reviews of research and literature (e.g., see Reutzel and Wolfersberger 1996) have suggested that effective classroom organization and environment enhances instruction. Teachers who are good classroom managers have integrated rules and procedures into a workable pattern that students learn early (Biehler and Snowman 1990). Thus, good classroom managers are more likely to be effective classroom teachers.

In organizing your classroom, remember that your students may differ significantly in cultural, linguistic, cognitive, and experiential backgrounds; maturity; interests; motivations; needs; and prior knowledge. For example, and as noted in another chapter, you may find that a large percentage of your class are language or culturally diverse students and that English is their second language. Additionally, some of your students, particularly those with special learning challenges, may require special teaching and classroom settings that should be considered and addressed when designing instructional activities. Burns, Roe, and Ross (1996) have suggested a number of recommendations you may want to keep in mind as you design your organizational plans to include an appropriate arrangement and context for all students' learning:

1. No simple classroom pattern or structure is better than another. The local situation, the strengths of individual teachers, and the abilities of the students involved will help to dictate the best system for a particular school.
2. Many criteria should be considered in deciding on a particular organizational plan. Results of informal or formal tests, students' interests, and specific goals of instruction are but a few you should use.
3. Organizational patterns should be flexible and should be altered as better ways are discovered.
4. There is no absolute criterion that specifies proper group size within a class. Working with special learning needs usually requires small groups. However, where students can assume responsibility for independent work, the number in a group may be greater.

5. Structure and orderly organization are desirable but so are positive and supportive environments.
6. Individualized learning experiences can benefit all students.
7. Whole-class instruction can meet academic objectives and provide students with a sense of class oneness and should be included.

The facilitative teacher also must give careful attention to organizing literacy activities to meet the needs of all diverse learners. Kameenui (1993, pp. 381–382) has proposed six principles to consider when designing and implementing reading instruction for these learners:

1. Instructional time is a precious commodity; do not lose it (i.e., use the most efficient methods).
2. Intervene and remediate early, strategically, and frequently (e.g., provide more frequent reading opportunities).
3. Teach fewer strategies more thoroughly (e.g., focus on the most important literacy outcomes).
4. Communicate reading strategies in a clear and explicit manner, especially during initial phases of instruction.
5. Guide student learning through a strategic sequence of teacher-directed and student-directed activities (e.g., move from teacher-directed to student-directed activities).
6. Examine the effectiveness of instruction and educational tools by formatively evaluating student progress (e.g., measure student performance continuously to make appropriate educational decisions).

Additional literacy teaching-learning suggestions recommended by Holdaway (1984); Reutzel and Wolfersberger (1996); Smith, Finn, and Dowdy (1993); and other professionals that can be used to meet the needs of all students include the following:

1. Establish a favorable environment in which the conditions for learning are maximized—one in which literacy is of high value, purposeful, inviting, and satisfying.
2. Design activities that take students through the various stages of learning—acquisition, proficiency, maintenance, generalization, and adaption.
3. Be humanistic but have high expectations for teaching-learning outcomes.
4. Use appropriate reward systems to reinforce students for good work and completing tasks.
5. Establish language in action by allowing students to learn through doing in authentic tasks, texts, and contexts.
6. Provide daily instruction that includes modeling or inducing reading and writing strategies—participating in problem solving from print, encouraging predictions, and rewarding risk-taking and self-correction behaviors.

7. Secure materials appropriate to students' interest and abilities and use technology and other media for instructional and supplementary purposes.
8. Involve students in literacy decision-making processes and maximize student-directed learning and interactions through heterogeneous cooperative grouping patterns.
9. Use buddy systems and other peer support groups to promote the literacy development of all students.
10. Work with caregivers and family members to encourage school-to-home and home-to-school literacy activities.

If you find that organizational and management changes are needed in your classroom, perhaps the suggestions being considered by Ms. Walker and those just listed, along with your own philosophy of reading and learning, will be helpful. Making organizational decisions or changes in a classroom can involve whole-class instruction, grouping strategies, management techniques, and arranging the classroom to facilitate these procedures.

## Whole-Class Instruction

Whole-class instruction is a frequently used organizational structure for implementing reading and other instruction in the elementary classroom; however, it should not be the only grouping you use since it often does not meet the needs of individual students. There are, however, times where the use of whole-class instruction is both appropriate and practical. For example, when introducing a new unit, you could meet with the entire class to discuss the information that your students need to complete their specific and varied assignments, to set a purpose for their varied activities and assignments, and to introduce vocabulary and concepts relative to the unit. Additionally, whole-class instruction can often be used effectively for other activities that include the teacher reading stories to the class, dramatizations, students sharing experiences with one another, role playing, and introducing various reading activities. When common material has been studied or read, you can discuss and share the literature within the whole group. Whole-class instruction certainly has its place in the classroom for academic and class unity objectives (Burns et al. 1996).

You can maximize the benefits of whole-class instruction by collaborating with professionals and paraprofessionals (Zucker 1993), conducting brief mini-lessons (White and Lawrence 1992), moving quickly to individual or small group follow-up activities (Sanacore 1993; Wiggins 1994), and employing buddy systems (Lake 1992) and other peer work groups.

## Individualized Instruction

There have been different understandings of individualized instruction over the years. Some educators have believed that it involves a strictly one-to-one instructional relationship, with each student working on a different task. Others felt that individual instruction could occur in other organizational frameworks. Currently, individualized instruction is viewed as instruction designed to accommodate each student's needs, strategies, skills, interests, and purposes in reading and learning. Every student does not need to be on a different task, but each must receive instruction appropriate to his or her needs and motivations. This perception of individualized instruction has led to the belief that it can often be effectively used in grouping formats, since there will likely be other students in the class who need similar instruction in specific areas and strategies, or who share similar interests and motivations. To determine appropriate placement of students in these varied learning groups, you must rely on effective assessment, which you can achieve through a combination of formal, informal, and authentic assessment procedures as was described in another chapter. Individualized instruction is facilitated by clustering students according to similar skill and strategy needs and preferences, and according to their interests and motivations as determined by assessment information. Individualized reading instruction can be used with all learners. It is not just for learners experiencing difficulty or requiring additional instruction. For example, Dooley (1993) has noted, "[a]ppropriate, differentiated reading programs are essential for the academic growth of highly capable readers and for the preservation of their desire to learn" (p. 547). Permitting students to select instructional materials and activities during individualized practices will also promote achievement of literacy objectives (Palmer and Codling 1994).

## Reflection Activity 13.2

*H*ow would you define individualized instruction? Additionally, how individualized does individualized instruction have to be? As just described, some educators have believed that it must be one-to-one in nature, whereas others will tell you that it can involve group instruction and activities—if students are assessed and grouped according to their needs, interests, and so on. In your reflection journal under Reflection Activity 13.2, describe and draw a continuum of individualized instruction that ranges from one-to-one instruction to small-group and large-group activities. After developing this continuum, indicate and mark where you stand on it. Next, write your definition of individualized instruction and justify your position on your continuum.

Independent-reading activities are another way of providing individualized instruction to students. These activities do not have to be done alone or apart from the rest of the class, and they provide students with a choice in the types of materials they would like to read. Again, an informal assessment procedure such as the interest inventory and self-selection of materials could ascertain this information. There could be flexibility in the independent-reading activities, and the students could be allowed to express themselves through various activities that are developed to be applied to their independent readings. For instance, students could express themselves through writing poems, short stories, or research reports; role playing with other students; presenting a

**Figure 13.1**
Example of a reading contract.

---

**Reading contract**

Date _Sept. 10_

I, _Matt Burke_, agree to undertake and complete the following reading assignments:

1. _Study 10 Dolch words each day this week._
2. _Show that I know these words._

If I complete the above assignment(s) of this contract, I will earn _a grade of A if I show that I know all the words, B if I know most of them, and C if I know at least half of them._

Student Signature _Matt Burke_

Teacher Signature _Ms. Walker_

---

play; or creating a docudrama using equipment from the media center. Such activities stimulate independence and decision-making strategies and also foster a receptive, innovative, and interesting learning environment, which further stimulates learning. Independent-reading activities should be teacher- and student-directed (Lewin 1992) and offer school-to-home and home-to-school literacy opportunities (Shockley 1994).

Contracts can be used to delineate individualized assignments. The primary focal point of contracts is the joint decision making between teacher and student concerning the assignment (see Figure 13.1.) A series of goals and specific objectives are agreed to by the teacher and student. Other topics, such as the period of time needed to complete a task and what each task includes, should also be decided. The teacher and student can actually sign the contract to make it more formal. You can also allow students to negotiate for the grade they want based on the quality and quantity of work completed.

Finally, individualized instruction can be greatly enhanced by the use of paraprofessionals, parents, and volunteers. Using these helpers in the classroom requires maximum teacher organization. Students could work with these support persons individually or in small groups implementing the teacher's instructional plans. When paraprofessionals, parents, or volunteers are available, teachers can give extra assistance to individual students and can manage all aspects of instruction in the classroom more effectively. These assistants also enable teachers to spend less time on such tasks as discipline and more time on instruction.

In summary, individualized instruction can enhance the learning of all students. Use of individualized instruction techniques, combined with other instructional groupings, based on students' needs, motivations, and strategies, are recommended to develop a balance that, on the one hand, provides appropriate instruction for each student and, on the other, emphasizes the need for interaction among students through the use of various grouping strategies.

## Varied Grouping

Grouping is probably used more often in the elementary schools than any other type of organizational structure. According to Collins and Cheek (1993), the use of varied groups for teaching-learning purposes has several advantages:

1. It allows the classroom teacher more flexibility in instruction.
2. It permits teachers to devote more time to individual students than would be possible in a whole-class type format.
3. It facilitates more appropriate adaptation of materials and resources to meet the needs of individual students.

Also, the use of varied grouping arrangements can result in significant improvement in students' reading strategies and attitudes toward reading (Swift 1993). There appears to be no "magic" student number for groups (Flood, Lapp, and Nagel 1992). Two students would form a dyad, small groups could consist of three, four, five, or six students, and large groups could consist of seven to ten students or half the class.

Many different types of grouping strategies are found in the elementary classroom. These vary from school to school and from classroom to classroom, and some teachers may have discovered that a particular grouping strategy works better for them than another. Whatever grouping arrangements are selected, the teacher and students should feel comfortable with them. Furthermore, it is important all students feel "included" and not "excluded." As Knight (1994) stated: "[The teacher's] role, ultimately, is to make certain that all students in . . . [his or her] care see themselves as integral parts of a community of learners. When we belong, we learn" (p. 499).

Two grouping structures used by elementary teachers are homogeneous and heterogeneous. In homogeneous grouping, students are grouped according to perceived similar achievements, abilities, or needs. This is sometimes referred to as "tracking" in the upper grade levels. Unfortunately, one of the false beliefs about homogeneous grouping is that it eliminates the need for further grouping within the classroom. Actually, the use of homogenous grouping in a classroom or school does not negate the need for additional grouping or for more individualized instruction. It is very unlikely that any students in a classroom would be reading at exactly the same level, would have exactly the same needs, would have the same metacognitive awareness and other strategies of reading, would require exactly the same skill and strategy instruction, or would have exactly the same interests, motivations, and cultures. Instead, heterogeneous grouping implies "mixed" grouping.

## Intraclass Grouping Options

Students in a classroom may also be grouped intraclass and interclass. Intraclass groupings allow for the use of several grouping strategies for instruction within the same classroom. Five basic intraclass grouping strategies are achievement/ability groups; skill and strategy groups; interest/motivation groups; peer, cross-age, and intergenerational groups; and cooperative groups (see Figure 13.2). A discussion of each of these grouping strategies follows.

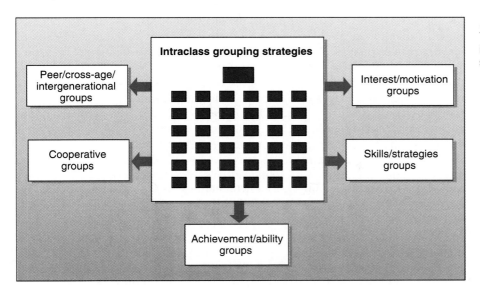

**Figure 13.2**
The five basic intraclass grouping strategies.

Intraclass grouping strategies

Peer/cross-age/ intergenerational groups

Cooperative groups

Interest/motivation groups

Skills/strategies groups

Achievement/ability groups

## Achievement/Ability Groups

Achievement/ability grouping is still the most widely used of all the grouping strategies. It is a type of homogeneous grouping (as previously described). The idea is that students are assigned to groups based on their perceived or assessed reading achievement. Allington and Cunningham (1996) pointed out that this achievement assessment, even if accurate, has nothing to do with students' "abilities." In fact, many students are unfairly placed in ability groups and treated as if they were of lesser ability, with instruction slowed down for them, when what they really need is more accelerated and intensive experiences with print, stories, and books. Evidence also indicates that factors other than actual reading achievement may enter into this placement process. Haller and Waterman (1985) reported that factors such as overall achievement, work habits, classroom behavior, personalities, and occasionally home environment are considered by teachers when placing students in achievement (or ability) reading groups. Jongsma's (1985) review of the literature found that the distribution of achievement within a given class or school and organizational constraints (e.g., teacher time, resources, materials, etc.) also play a more important role in group formation than an individual student's ability. Assuming that reading achievement is the primary criterion in forming groups, those students performing at the highest level are grouped together and those performing at the lowest level are grouped together. Those students perceived as reading at levels between the high and low groups are usually placed in one or more middle groups.

If using achievement groups, it is important to exercise caution. Students who are placed in the lower reading groups should be continually evaluated to monitor their appropriate placement. Also, avoid situations in which students are labeled as poor readers and not given the opportunity to improve their position in the classroom. The presumed purpose of using achievement groups is to provide effective instruction to all students, and thus flexibility in grouping strategies is important. Students should be moved from one group to another as their needs dictate, not locked into a group placement for an entire school year, or for the rest of their school years! Unfortunately, achievement/ability groups tend to be relatively permanent entities without upward mobility (Hiebert 1983).

Facilitative teachers must also strive to stay abreast of the ever-emerging research and literature on achievement/ability/homogeneous groupings. Although some support exists for using homogeneous grouping for some selected curricula (e.g., Hereford 1993), for some selected students (see Mills and Tangherlini 1992), and for some students with gifts and talents (see Fiedler, Lange, and Winebrenner 1994), numerous educators and professional organizations are against these grouping practices (e.g., see Allington and Cunningham 1996; Flood et al. 1992; and Stanovich 1986 and others reported in this chapter and other places in this text). Flood et al. (1992) reported that "growing evidence has shown that the exclusive use of ability groups for language arts instruction can be deleterious on student learning, particularly for those children assigned to the lowest groups" (p. 613).

In addition to the negative impact on students' social status and emotional development (Burns et al. 1996), it has also been reported that homogeneous ability grouping results in unequal instruction and treatment (Young 1990), and in no differences in academic gains when compared with other grouping patterns (Slavin 1993), even for gifted students (Slavin 1991). The National Council for the Social Studies adopted a position statement, based on research and the goal of "citizenship education," against ability/achievement grouping in social studies ("Ability Grouping in Social Studies" 1992). Again, if you decide to use achievement grouping in your classroom, it is important that you do so with extreme caution and flexibility. This care and sensitivity should be exercised with all populations of students, even those considered gifted and talented. Finally, better ways of grouping exist and are suggested in this chapter. Also, teachers could consider the use of accelerated instruction and experiences (as suggested by Allington and Cunningham 1996) and some of the learnings from the Accelerated Schools model (see Knight and Stallings 1995) to provide rich literacy experiences for their students with lower achievement, rather than putting them in a low group.

Cooperative grouping promotes the development of elementary students' literacy learning, interactions, and sociocultural appreciation.

© James L. Shaffer

## Reflection Activity 13.3

*H*ave you ever stopped to wonder, "How must it feel to be in the low reading group?" Did you or someone close to you ever have that experience? Under the heading Reflection Activity 13.3 in your reflection journal, address some issues related to the student in the low group. How must he or she feel? Can reading time be thought of as positive? How does the student feel about being labeled a "low reader?" What are your feelings about this type of grouping?

Heterogeneous grouping is a more positive alternative. Heterogeneous grouping includes students of various abilities and needs in the same classroom. A school with heterogeneous grouping implies that the classrooms have been mixed, with students randomly assigned regardless of their perceived ability levels, needs, or other assumed similarities. Heterogeneous grouping permits students of varying abilities, strategies, skills, and cultures to interact and to learn together.

If you are planning to use achievement/ability groups in your classroom, as you review assessment data, consider these ideas derived from Collins and Cheek (1993):

1. If achievement tests are used for grouping purposes, combine these results with your findings from informal procedures such as teacher observation and other informal-reading assessments.
2. Do not rely on any one assessment, test, or judgment alone for reading-group placement; it is important to use multiple data to view the students' skills, strategies, and needs from several perspectives.

If you use achievement/ability groups, it is essential that you be concerned with individual student needs. Meeting these needs within such a grouping format is just one of several grouping patterns available to teachers.

## *Skill and Strategy Groups*

Skill and strategy grouping arrangements can be an integral part of all reading programs when students need assistance in developing specific literacy skills and strategies. Additionally, this type of grouping can be implemented in a reading program that uses various materials and approaches, including literature-based, basal, eclectic, and individualized programs. Skill and strategy grouping is considered to be short-term grouping and is not designed for continuation over a prolonged period of time. Since the primary purpose is to strengthen a specific skill or strategy area, the student leaves the group when the skill or strategy is learned. Furthermore, a student may be in many different skill or strategy groups (e.g., metacognitive awareness, sight vocabulary, inferential comprehension, etc.) during any particular time.

Wiggins (1994), Unsworth (1984), and Flood et al. (1992) have made suggestions for grouping students by skill or strategy needs:

1. There are no permanent groups.
2. Groups are periodically created, modified, or disbanded to meet new needs as they arise.
3. Groups vary in size depending on the group's purpose.
4. Group membership is not fixed; it varies according to needs and purposes.

You can use skill and strategy groups as a means of individualizing instruction in the classroom. After assessing all your students' reading skills and strategies and other needs, utilizing procedures described in the assessment chapter, you can use this information to assign students to skill and strategy groups. For instance, you may assess your students in numerous skill and strategy areas (e.g., main idea, cause-and-effect relationships, metacognitive awareness, or graphophonic awareness), and you may have noted that certain students needed instruction in one or more of these areas and formed a skill or strategy group for each area. Students needing this type of instruction are called together periodically to work in that specific skill or strategy group. Some students are only in a few skill or strategy groups, others are in many. There is no "level" stigma with these groups, as each group has little to do with achievement or ability levels. You provide materials, instruction, and practice with the skill or strategy to all students in that group. Some groups have only three or four students in them, others have nine or ten. Material can be from students' content textbooks, library books, newspapers, student- or teacher-developed material, or other materials.

Figures 13.3a and 13.3b are examples of some of the skill and strategy assessment results from groups in Ms. Walker's class. Note how she developed particular skill and strategy groups for that class. As you can see, the skill and strategy groups are numerous, with as many as thirteen students in one group (pronoun referents) and as few as three in another (phonics). Some students

**Figure 13.3a**
Skill and strategy assessment results from Ms. Walker's class.

| Student's names | Main idea | Cause and effect | Metacognition | Sequencing | Structural analysis | Context clues | Phonics | Sight words | Pronoun referents |
|---|---|---|---|---|---|---|---|---|---|
| Matt | X | ✓ | X | X | X | X | ✓ | X | X |
| Kristi | X | ✓ | ✓ | ✓ | ✓ | ✓ | ✓ | ✓ | X |
| Sam | X | X | X | X | ✓ | X | ✓ | ✓ | X |
| Shauna | ✓ | ✓ | ✓ | ✓ | ✓ | X | ✓ | ✓ | X |
| Tyrone | ✓ | ✓ | ✓ | ✓ | ✓ | ✓ | ✓ | ✓ | ✓ |
| Maxie | X | X | X | X | ✓ | ✓ | ✓ | X | X |
| Jesse | X | ✓ | ✓ | ✓ | ✓ | X | ✓ | X | X |
| Kate | ✓ | X | ✓ | ✓ | ✓ | ✓ | ✓ | ✓ | X |
| Hannah | ✓ | ✓ | ✓ | ✓ | ✓ | ✓ | ✓ | ✓ | ✓ |
| Jill | X | ✓ | ✓ | ✓ | X | ✓ | ✓ | ✓ | X |
| Tyler | ✓ | ✓ | X | ✓ | X | ✓ | ✓ | ✓ | ✓ |
| Stephen | ✓ | ✓ | X | ✓ | ✓ | X | ✓ | ✓ | X |
| Ajay | X | ✓ | ✓ | ✓ | ✓ | ✓ | ✓ | ✓ | X |
| Sarah | ✓ | ✓ | ✓ | ✓ | ✓ | ✓ | ✓ | ✓ | ✓ |
| Rachel | ✓ | ✓ | ✓ | ✓ | X | X | X | ✓ | ✓ |
| Elizabeth | ✓ | X | ✓ | ✓ | ✓ | ✓ | ✓ | ✓ | ✓ |
| Ai-Ling | ✓ | ✓ | X | ✓ | ✓ | ✓ | ✓ | ✓ | ✓ |
| Jacob | ✓ | ✓ | ✓ | ✓ | ✓ | ✓ | ✓ | ✓ | X |
| Maria | X | X | X | X | X | X | ✓ | ✓ | X |
| Michael | ✓ | ✓ | ✓ | ✓ | X | ✓ | ✓ | ✓ | ✓ |
| Chin | ✓ | X | ✓ | ✓ | ✓ | ✓ | ✓ | ✓ | ✓ |
| Felita | X | X | X | ✓ | ✓ | X | X | X | X |
| Sean | X | X | X | ✓ | X | X | X | X | X |

OK ✓    Needs Instruction X

are in many groups (Maria and Sean are in seven or eight different groups), other students are in only one (Elizabeth and Jacob and Chin) or two (Kristi, Shauna, Kate, Tyler, and Ajay) groups, and a few are not in any groups (Tyrone, Hannah, and Sarah). Because skill and strategy groups are flexible, based on individual needs, and diagnostically strategic, they provide an excellent alternative to or can be used in conjunction with achievement/ability groups.

## Interest/Motivation Groups

Another useful grouping that has been used successfully is by interest or motivations. Students with similar interests work together to examine, read, and reflect on literature represented by their interests and purposes. A positive

**Figure 13.3b**
Skill and strategy
groups in Ms. Walker's
class.

| **Main idea group** | Matt Kristi Sam | Maxie Jesse Jill | Ajay Maria Felita | Sean |
| --- | --- | --- | --- | --- |
| **Cause and effect group** | Sam Maxie Kate | Elizabeth Maria Chin | Felita Sean | |
| **Metacognitive awareness strategy group** | Matt Sam Maxie | Tyler Stephen Ai-Ling | Maria Felita Sean | |
| **Sequencing group** | Matt Sam Maxie | Maria | | |
| **Structural analysis group** | Matt Jill Tyler | Rachel Maria Michael | Sean | |
| **Context clues group** | Matt Sam Shauna | Jesse Stephen Rachel | Maria Felita Sean | |
| **Phonics group** | Rachel Felita Sean | | | |
| **Sight words group** | Matt Maxie Jesse | Felita Sean | | |
| **Pronoun referents group** | Matt Kristi Sam | Shauna Maxie Kate | Jill Stephen Ajay | Jacob Maria Felita | Sean |

aspect of interest grouping, as with skill and strategy grouping, is that students of all abilities are grouped together, which allows for meaningful interactions without stigma. Additionally, interest groups are very purposeful groups for students because they meet to read about and explore their mutual interests. This highly motivational grouping format can be used interchangeably with skills and strategy grouping.

Interest/motivation and skill and strategy groups provide the opportunity for students to interact with all their peers, thus enhancing motivation and the desire to want to read more. Additionally, interest/motivation groups are positively focused as opposed to negatively focused on needs or ability levels. Such groups make reading more enjoyable and less of a frustrating task. Since interest grouping is a motivational format, unenthusiastic students tend to develop more of a desire to read. It is especially helpful for including language and culturally diverse students and other diverse learners. Students are able to learn from the experiences of others in the classroom, which broadens their language base and improves their opportunities for reading development. Interest/motivation groups in the elementary classroom can be a valuable part of your organizational plans for reading, writing, and learning. This type of grouping strategy not only encourages students to interact but also provides a positive adjunct to achievement/ability groups and/or skill and strategy groups. It also provides the opportunity for the development of social skills and more active participation of students in their own learning process.

## *Peer, Cross-Age, and Intergenerational Groups*

A grouping strategy that has proved useful in elementary classrooms is peer tutoring, that is, one student tutoring another student. A variation, in which older students work with younger students across grade levels, is referred to as cross-age grouping or tutoring (see LeLand and Fitzpatrick 1993/1994; Marden, Richard, and Flippo 1991; and Samway, Whang, and Pippitt 1995); the primary purpose is for older students to improve the reading or other skills of younger students. Interestingly enough, research (e.g., Rekrut 1994) has indicated that the reading skills of not only the younger students but also the older students are improved. Thus, both the tutored student and the student doing the tutoring are being helped. In many instances, students who would usually not read certain types of books will read them to better assist their tutees. As a result of this, both the tutee and the tutor learn.

Our experiences with peer and cross-age grouping have been positive. It is an effective way to motivate all students. There are also other positive effects. For instance, student tutors and tutees develop a more positive image of their reading abilities and a more positive self-concept: the tutees because of the additional attention they are getting, and the tutors because they are helping someone else (acquiring regard and respect) while reviewing important academic concepts.

In utilizing peer or cross-age grouping, only those students who want to assist or tutor should be selected. It is important that the prospective tutor exhibits patience and tolerance in working with other students. Also, if using peer tutoring, make sure that students want such assistance, because some prospective tutees could be embarrassed or offended by this grouping strategy; however, when developing cross-age tutoring relationships, younger students are typically not uncomfortable with the idea of someone older offering help. Finally, it is important to appropriately match tutors and tutees in terms of ability to work well together.

An extension of cross-age tutoring/grouping is intergenerational tutoring. This can involve use of older persons (i.e., older family members, senior citizens, and other community members) volunteering their assistance in the classroom and/or students volunteering their services to elderly seniors, older family members, or others needing reading assistance in the community. For example, this could involve seniors reading to children or helping children with their work in the classroom (Coolidge and Wurster 1985). Or it could involve students going to a nursing home to read to elderly seniors who are no longer able to read on their own. However, the most recent intergenerational efforts have focused on home/school literacy connections, fostering the literacy skills of both the students and their families (see Morrow, Tracey, and Maxwell 1995; Paratore 1995; and Rockwell 1996 for examples of such home/school and community literacy connections).

## Cooperative Learning Groups

Cooperative learning uses the dynamics of group working relationships. Cooperative learning involves students working in small groups to accomplish a common goal or common work, or solve a common problem. The literature to date (Johnson and Johnson 1994; Opitz 1992; Stevens, Slavin, and Farnish 1991; Swengel 1990) has supported cooperative learning in the elementary classroom. Cooperative learning facilitates the interactions of students with varied cultural backgrounds to promote multicultural knowledge and awareness.

In cooperative learning activities, students of varied abilities, skills, and strategies are grouped to solve or resolve a problem, research information, or achieve another specific goal. The entire group is given responsibility for accomplishing the task. Students must organize, plan, and guide each other, and everyone has a role in completing the task.

Johnson and Johnson (1994) indicated that cooperation pervades human nature and human life, and they provided details regarding many approaches to cooperative learning and grouping. Overall, cooperative learning and grouping involves the following: positive interdependence of students, the individual accountability of students, use of social skills, and group processing activities. The teacher's role in more formal cooperative grouping involves planning for the types of groups and groupings, deciding instructional objectives, making preinstructional decisions, explaining the task and the necessary cooperation, monitoring and intervening as necessary, and evaluating and processing students' learnings. However, there are many occasions for using more informal cooperative groups, which would involve less structure; and Johnson and Johnson also suggested that long-term base groups could be used to provide for support/assistance and peer help with academic work. (This would be very similar to some peer group relationships previously described.)

Johnson and Johnson (1994) reported many positive results and dynamics of cooperative learning and grouping. However, even though the results do seem very positive, McCaslin and Good (1996) pointed out that their reviews of research on cooperative learning indicated that some possible, not so positive outcomes could include: students' misconceptions, students' shift of dependency from the teacher to a peer, students valuing the product more than the process, students valuing the process more than the academic product, students' receipt of differential attention and status, students' belief they are not able to contribute, students learning they do not need to contribute, and problems with group accountability. We believe that many of these possible problems are more likely to occur when the teacher has not planned, monitored, intervened, and evaluated students' learning. As with all other groupings, students need a facilitative teacher who knows what he/she is trying to accomplish and why, and who organizes, plans, and orchestrates learning.

## Interclass Settings

A second major grouping procedure is interclass or cross-class. The primary purpose of this grouping procedure is to permit teachers to try to develop a homogeneous setting to facilitate their reading instruction. Interclass grouping is accomplished by integrating students from several classrooms into reading groups according to their reading levels. Students are then taught reading in these supposedly homogeneous groups, with each teacher working with a specific group (e.g., all the students in third-grade classes would be divided into groups based on reading-ability levels).

Although interclass grouping was created to reduce the range of reading levels within a classroom setting, this goal is based on the assumption that once ability grouped, students would all have similar needs, strategies, and skills. Unfortunately, this leads to the inaccurate belief that such a grouping procedure eliminates the need for smaller-group instruction and individualized instruction. However, as discussed earlier, this is not true.

Another problem of interclass grouping is that teachers may know very little about particular students, since contact is limited to one daily reading period. Some difficulty may also develop in coordinating instruction among teachers, and reading may become isolated from the rest of the curriculum. Because the integration of reading, writing, and other pursuits into the total curriculum is essential to effective instruction, all of these problems/disadvantages should be carefully considered before interclass grouping is selected.

# Managing Instruction

Managing instruction involves planning, organizing, and balancing many aspects of classroom management. These include establishing a planning-learning framework, having a basic design for implementing instruction, arranging the classroom, using materials, developing learning centers, organizing and managing technology, and organizing for parents' and other family members' participation.

## A Planning-Learning Pyramid

After assessing students' prior knowledge, interest, and literacy skills and strategies, the facilitative teacher evaluates the data collected to determine literacy and other learning objectives, group arrangements, and instructional materials and methodologies. Selection and implementation of appropriate procedures will contribute significantly to achieving program goals and meeting the needs of individual students. To best meet the needs of all students, no matter how diverse, a flexible planning-learning framework to help teachers plan and structure learning outcomes is recommended. Such a framework, a planning-learning pyramid, adapted from the work of Schumm, Vaughn, and Leavell's (1994) planning pyramid, is presented in Figure 13.4.

Schumm et al. (1994) proposed the following rationale for utilizing a planning-learning framework or pyramid:

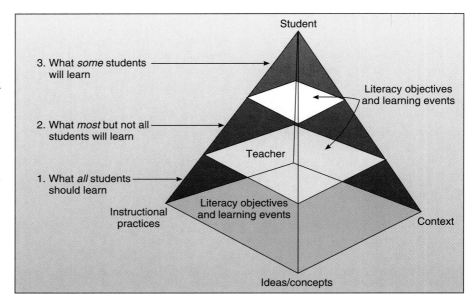

**Figure 13.4**

Basic components of the planning pyramid, including three degrees of learning and five points of entry.

Adapted with permission from Schumm, Vaughn, and Leavell, "Planning Pyramid: A Framework for Planning Diverse Student Needs During Content Area Instruction," *The Reading Teacher* 47:608–615. Copyright © 1994 International Reading Association, Newark, DE.

Labels in figure:

3. What *some* students will learn

2. What *most* but not all students will learn

1. What *all* students should learn

Student

Teacher

Literacy objectives and learning events

Literacy objectives and learning events

Instructional practices

Context

Ideas/concepts

> [It is] a way of thinking about planning instruction for all student learners . . . [but] not a rigid formula for instructional planning . . . [It is] a flexible tool strongly influenced by individual teacher thinking. Teachers' beliefs, theories of learning, teaching experiences, interest and prior knowledge of the . . . [curricular area], and willingness to adhere to state and district . . . guidelines can and should influence how teachers use the . . . Planning Pyramid. Use and interpretation of it will not be the same for all teachers. (pp. 610–611)

In actuality the planning-learning pyramid is a "mental template" based on two major components, degrees of learning and points of entry. However, due to the interactive and dynamic nature of your literacy objectives and learning events, and individual students' needs, you cannot separate these components.

## Degrees of Learning

The body of the pyramid represents all of the classroom teacher's literacy objectives and learning events, and it is subdivided into three degrees of learning.

The literacy objectives and learning events in the bottom third of the pyramid are for *all* students—the teacher would ask him/herself, "What do I want all of my students to learn?" "What teacher- or student-directed activities can I use to achieve these objectives?" Teachers then review their literacy objectives and determine which are paramount for all students' present and future growth. Then, they select the most appropriate instructional practice(s) to ensure that all students have an opportunity to achieve these objectives. For example, you might be implementing a thematic unit on bees. One literacy objective for this unit would be for all students to know what a bee is (schemata). Appropriate instructional practices to achieve this objective would be visiting a local apiary, watching a movie about bees, and observing bees through the classroom windows.

The literacy objectives and learning events in the middle area of the pyramid are for *most* students—the teacher would ask him/herself, "What do I want most of my students to learn?" "What teacher- or student-led instructional practices can I use to achieve these objectives?" According to Schumm et al. (1994), these literacy objectives ". . . can include additional facts, extensions of base concepts, related concepts, or more complex concepts" (p. 611). Teachers then review their literacy objectives and determine which are important for most students' present and future growth. Then, they select the most appropriate instructional practice(s) to ensure that most students achieve these objectives. Again, using the thematic unit on bees, you might want most of your students to be able to develop a written report on the different types of bees—workers, drones, and queens. Appropriate instructional practices to achieve this objective would be a whole-class language-experience activity on the types of bees and following that up with a workshop to assist students in writing their reports.

The literacy objectives and learning events near the top of the pyramid are for *some* students—the teacher would ask him/herself, "What do I want some of my students to learn?" "What teacher- or student-directed activities can I use to achieve these objectives?" The literacy objectives at this level are more complex, detailed, or incidental in nature and will be learned or understood by some students. This learning or understanding occurs in and out of the classroom through formal and informal processes. Teachers then review their literacy objectives and determine which are important for some students' present and future growth. Then, they select the most appropriate instructional practice(s) to ensure that some students achieve these objectives. For example, and again using the thematic unit on bees, one literacy objective at the top of your planning-learning pyramid for this unit might be for some students to know specifics about the "symbiotic relationship" between bees and plants. Appropriate instructional practices to achieve this objective would be discussing in a small or large group, or encouraging student research on the "symbiotic relationship" between bees and plants, to learn how bees pollinate flowers while foraging.

## Points of Entry

A point of entry for planning literacy events is represented by each pyramid axis. Teachers consider these points before implementing any instructional practice. With respect to the teacher's point of entry, teachers would reflect on their literacy beliefs and philosophy, state and district curricular mandates, interest and experiences with the literacy objectives and possible learning events, and available resources. Teachers then use the result of these reflections to select their instructional practices. With respect to ideas/concepts, the teacher would determine what learning events would help students learn the ideas and concepts relevant to the literacy and learning objectives. Where possible, language experiences should be maximized through integrated processes (e.g., reading and writing). With respect to context, teachers would determine classroom organizational and environmental factors that affect literacy learning. Classroom organizational factors could include grouping arrangements, available resources, and instructional time (e.g., three weeks are needed but there is an extended school holiday in two weeks). With respect to instructional practices, teachers reflect on the literacy and other learning events they want to implement within and across the different degrees of learning (e.g., assessment and instructional). For some students, the instructional practices needed for literacy learning could remain the same. However, for some students, particularly those with special learning needs, an instructional practice could be effective at one degree of learning but ineffective at the next level (e.g., cooperative grouping). Or, it may not be effective at any degree of learning (e.g., whole-class grouping).

The final axis is the student, located at the top of the pyramid, which may be the most important entry point for planning purposes. As Schumm et al. (1994) noted, it may not be possible for teachers to consider each and every student individually when developing unit and lesson plans. However, if teachers are to succeed in meeting their literacy objectives through the use of appropriate literacy events, determining and planning for student differences is imperative. As you have read throughout this text, facilitative teachers consider their students' interests, motivations, prior knowledge, experiential backgrounds, languages, and cultures, among other variables, when designing literacy instruction. You have also read that collaborating with professionals, paraprofessionals, and parents/caregivers and other family members will also assist you in determining students' needs and appropriate learning events. It goes without saying that determining and planning for student differences will promote student-centered instructional practices.

Using a flexible planning-learning pyramid, such as the one presented here, should help teachers structure their own inductive and deductive reasoning as they attempt to match instructional practices with students' differences and literacy objectives. Using degrees of learning and points of entry will promote student-centered literacy and other learning.

### A Basic Design for Implementing Instruction

Mercer and Mercer (1993) stated that:

> To succeed in school, students . . . need a systematic instructional program that is planned according to their individual needs. This individualized approach does not imply that each student must be taught in a one-to-one or small-group instructional format. It *does* mean, though, that the student receives daily instruction tailored to his [or her] educational need. (p. 5)

Use of a planning-learning pyramid would provide a way to plan a student-centered program that accounts for student differences and literacy objectives. So, how do you deliver this tailored instruction in a systematic manner? We suggest the Directed Reading Activity (DRA) for implementing many literacy-learning objectives. The DRA is especially appropriate for many objectives that require the systematic sequencing of events or that involve review or introduction, direct instruction, guiding reading and writing, and specific follow-up instruction.

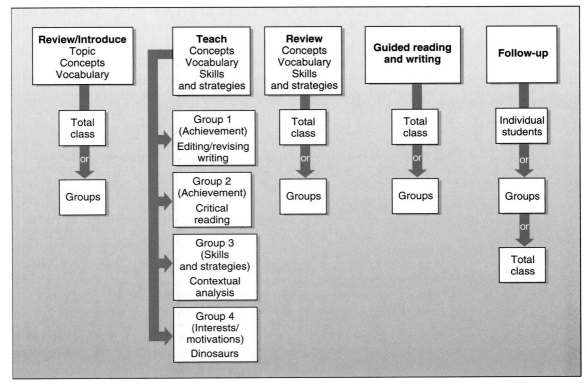

*Figure 13.5*
Basic design for implementing reading instruction.

In Figure 13.5 a basic design for implementing reading instruction in the elementary classroom is presented. Two achievement groups, one skill and strategy group, and one interest/motivation group, utilizing a DRA format were used in the design. This design can be expanded and used with more or other groups. The time periods and suggested activities are for demonstration purposes only. Facilitative teachers will want to adjust times for reading instruction based on their own and on their students' needs and the requirements of their schools—ideally integrating reading and writing into all subjects and areas of curriculum.

Managing groups and individualized instruction in an elementary classroom is a task that requires experiences, discipline, and good organizational skills (Flood et al. 1992; Wiggins 1994). Since most literacy instruction moves from the whole-class format to group and individualized arrangements and then back to a whole-class activity, you may want to consider the following suggestions by Collins and Cheek (1993) to structure your group procedures: (1) time the activities for each group so that one group does not finish well ahead of the others; (2) provide alternatives for those students who finish their assignments early; and (3) provide a variety of interesting activities appropriate to students' needs, interests, and motivations.

Leal (1993), Holdaway (1980), and Baker (1994) have also made suggestions that have applicability for managing instruction and structuring groupings:

1. Plan brief individual conferences with each student, at varying intervals of five to ten days. This provides opportunities for the student to share a personal reading experience with you. You will, at such times, be in a position to monitor the students' reading experiences, to assess the student, to offer guidance, and to make a practice assignment where necessary.
2. Students can keep a log of personal reading activities, and you can check and discuss the content of the logs as needed.
3. Students can engage in independent-reading activities between conferences, and they can use a range of options to report their readings.
4. Students may use designated learning centers as well as engage in cooperative learning activities.
5. Flexible groups can be used to accommodate for interests/motivations, skill and strategy needs, and other purposes.
6. Implement reading and writing minilessons or workshops to address specific literacy concepts and skills. These minilessons/workshops would be daily and last no longer than ten to fifteen minutes.
7. Students can assume leadership roles in determining group purposes. They can also select group activities and lead group discussions.

Flood and Lapp (1994) recommend a procedure that provides guidance for direct instruction, utilizing children's literature and writing, and is adaptable for most skill and strategy development:

1. *Select a book/story for reading purposes.* Collaborate with students to select books that offer quality literature.
2. *Encourage connections.* As the book/story is being read, you should have the students connect text concepts with their prior knowledge.
3. *Schedule time to read the book/story aloud.* Where possible, use different tones of voice and appropriate phrasing to convey the author's message. Also, show students pictures and illustrations that accompany text.
4. *Have the students write a response to the book/story to promote reflection and thinking.* For younger students the response may be a drawing, single word, or one sentence. Older students should respond in their reading journals.
5. *Have a whole-class, large group, or small group discussion about the book/story and the students' reflections.* Where possible, relate text concepts to student experiences. Also, discuss characters, settings, events, and plots.
6. *Revisit the book/story for specific purposes.* These visits could address reading, writing, or strategy development.
7. *Extend the activity to other books/stories written by the same author or on the same topic or theme.* This extension could occur through independent reading, book buddy, reading workshops, and other teacher-directed and student-led activities.

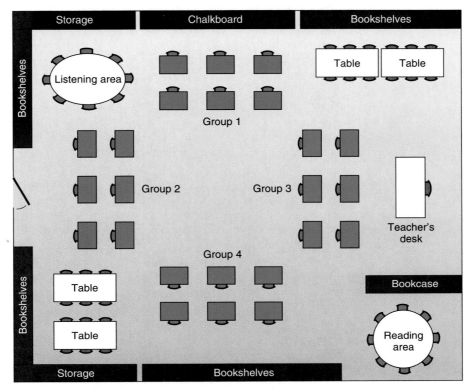

*Figure 13.6*

A sample class arrangement for group and individualized reading instruction (groups can be achievement, skill and strategy, interest/motivation, peer/cross-age/intergenerational, or cooperative learning groups).

## Arranging the Classroom

An integral component of organizing and managing instruction involves the physical arrangement of the classroom, because classroom arrangement can be either a benefit or a limitation to certain types of organizational procedures. Obviously, teachers are limited by certain physical constraints that are beyond their control, such as time, space, economic considerations, and the goals and objectives of individual schools and districts. An immediate problem that you may face is the type of equipment found in the classroom. For example, you may have to deal with a room full of desks, which does not particularly facilitate grouping and individualized instruction in the classroom. Nevertheless, these desks can be arranged in a way that still meets the needs of students. Figure 13.6 is a diagram representing a room arrangement that features grouping and individualized instruction. This is, of course, not the only way of organizing a classroom, but it is presented simply as a means of illustrating one possible arrangement.

In arranging the classroom, you might want to obtain tables in addition to the students' desks. With your principal's approval, you may want to eliminate some desks and replace them with tables, because grouping is usually more easily implemented with tables in the classroom. Other suggestions to facilitate classroom arrangement include (a) using free-standing bookcases arranged perpendicular to the wall for developing work areas and using the backs as added display space for students' work; (b) developing many areas for small-group or individual work, including a reading area, listening area, drama and art area, sharing area, and flexible learning-center area; (c) using pillows, carpet pieces and carpets, or an old couch to make areas comfortable; (d) developing storage areas and systems for the students to store and to retrieve their work; and (e) using every possible wall space for displaying students' work. Additionally, having available plenty of writing materials (e.g., newsprint, lined paper, pencils, etc.) and reading materials (e.g., library books, magazines, etc.) is important. Students should have easy access to such materials.

Another important consideration in the physical arrangement of the classroom is attractiveness (Reutzel and Wolfersberger 1996). Classrooms should be clean, neat, practical, and interesting, because attractive rooms may enhance learning by promoting student motivation and enthusiasm. Student-developed or -involved bulletin boards, pictures, and other displays encourage students to be productive and take part in learning. Students can have responsibility in developing bulletin boards and other displays during the year.

## Using Materials

After you have organized the groupings for instruction and learning and arranged the physical facilities to suit you and your students' needs, your next task is to provide appropriate instructional and supplementary materials. Materials should be matched to the students' instructional needs, cognitive experiences, cultural and linguistic backgrounds, and interests/motivations; and a wide variety of materials should be available for use in and out of your classroom. Such materials could be supplementary to your basal reading series, teacher-made, student-made, or from the library or elsewhere. Students with opportunities to choose from a wide variety of appropriate and interesting materials tend to be more interested and more motivated to read, write, and learn.

The following suggestions have been recommended by Wray (1994), Mercer and Mercer (1993), Miletta (1992), McGill-Franzen (1993) and other professionals to help teachers provide appropriate instructional and personal reading materials, fiction and nonfiction:

1. Secure materials that have field-test or research data to support their effectiveness.
2. Evaluate materials presented before purchasing them (e.g., Figure 13.7 presents evaluation guidelines you may want to use).
3. Obtain materials that reflect your literacy objectives and the interests and needs of your students (e.g., topics and complexity).
4. Provide materials that facilitate students' critical thinking and literacy abilities (e.g., series books with predictable characters, settings, and plots).

**Figure 13.7**
Evaluation guidelines
for instructional
materials.

Title of materials: _____

Author(s): _____

Publisher: _____

Copyright date: _____

| | Yes | No |
|---|---|---|
| **Content** | | |
| 1. Meets needs, interests, and motivations of students. | ___ | ___ |
| 2. Appropriate for and addresses different culturally diverse groups. | ___ | ___ |
| 3. Uses current material. | ___ | ___ |
| 4. Written in an understandable style and language for intended students. | ___ | ___ |
| **Scope** | | |
| 1. Complements other materials being used. | ___ | ___ |
| 2. Objectives match those of teacher and/or school system. | ___ | ___ |
| 3. Can be easily adapted to various teaching styles. | ___ | ___ |
| 4. Can be easily integrated into current curriculum. | ___ | ___ |
| **Readability** | | |
| 1. Vocabulary load appropriate for intended students. | ___ | ___ |
| 2. Concept load appropriate for intended students. | ___ | ___ |
| 3. Language structure appropriate for intended students. | ___ | ___ |
| 4. Other aspects of qualitative readibility appropriate for intended students. | ___ | ___ |
| **Format** | | |
| 1. Size and spacing of type appropriate for intended students. | ___ | ___ |
| 2. Has durable binding. | ___ | ___ |
| 3. Margins are adequate. | ___ | ___ |
| 4. Illustrations are adequate and appropriate for intended students. | ___ | ___ |
| **Teacher's guide** | | |
| 1. Lesson plans are adequate. | ___ | ___ |
| 2. Identifies concepts, vocabulary, and skills and strategies to be taught. | ___ | ___ |
| 3. Provides suggestions for using supplementary materials. | ___ | ___ |
| 4. Gives adequate directions to the teacher. | ___ | ___ |
| **Evaluation** | | |
| 1. Provides individual and group assessment procedures. | ___ | ___ |
| 2. Suggests follow-up activities. | ___ | ___ |

**General rating**

_____ Recommended without reservation.
_____ Recommended with reservation.
_____ Not recommended.

5. Provide materials that promote the integration of receptive and expressive language processes (e.g., related-writing activities for authorship).
6. Acquire materials that can be used in teacher-directed and student-led literacy activities (e.g., easy and difficult books).
7. Provide materials in different print formats (e.g., big books).
8. Secure materials that can be used to develop thematic units (e.g., selected holidays).

A primary consideration in evaluating reading materials is their readability. Some of this information is usually provided by publishers; however, it may only represent an average (the quantitative) readability level for an entire set of materials, and at best is only partial (quantitative) information. In some instance, such information is not provided at all. Thus, you may have to use a readability formula to ascertain this quantitative aspect, as well as to later examine the material qualitatively. Several limitations should be considered if you use a quantative-assessment technique:

1. They provide only an estimate of the level of a given selection.
2. Concepts in the text under analysis cannot be measured.
3. Formulas are calculated in different ways, thus providing different levels for the same material.
4. The degree of difficulty of vocabulary causes fluctuations in readability levels.
5. The syntax and semantic style of certain materials may affect readability levels.
6. The students' reading performance is affected by their experiential, linguistic, cognitive, and language/cultural backgrounds, and their interests, purposes, motivations, and prior knowledge relating to the materials to be read.

Although many problems are associated with readability formulas, they can be useful in some situations. When you use them, remember that they provide only a quantitative estimate and should be used in conjunction with qualitative considerations and teaching judgment in selecting appropriate materials. There are many readability formulas available. One that is flexible and easy to use is the Fry Readability Graph presented in Figure 13.8.

As previously mentioned, readability formulas are quantitative assessments of reading materials, and as such they do have limitations. That is why it is essential for you to know and understand the importance of making qualitative judgments about materials. Publishers cannot furnish you with a qualitative assessment of their materials' appropriateness for your students. Only you can do this. The following is a list of some qualitative considerations or questions to use in conjunction with the quantitative readability-estimate information to evaluate the appropriateness of instructional materials:

1. How difficult are the concepts discussed or mentioned in the material?
2. How much prior experience would students need to understand the concepts?
3. What are the presupposed schemata for understanding the concepts presented?
4. Is the material presented in natural and uncomplicated syntax?
5. Would students have the linguistic experience to deal with the syntax, semantic, and graphophonic cues inherent in this material?
6. In what type of discourse or expository structure is this material written?
7. Are students familiar with this structure? How difficult would this structure be for them?

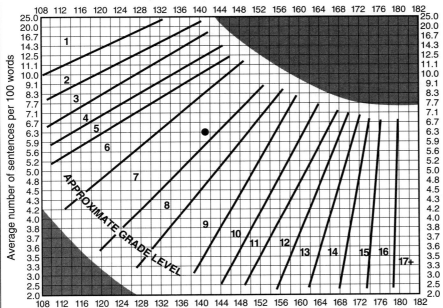

**GRAPH FOR ESTIMATING READABILITY — EXTENDED**
by Edward Fry, Rutgers University Reading Center, New Brunswick, N.J. 08904

Average number of syllables per 100 words

*Figure 13.8*
Fry Readability
Graph—extended.

From E. B. Fry (1977).
"Fry's Readability Graph:
Clarification, Validity, and
Extension to Level 17."
*Journal of Reading* 21:
242–252. Reproduction
permitted—no copyright.

Directions: Randomly select 3 one hundred word passages from a book or an article. Plot average number of syllables and average number of sentences per 100 words on graph to determine the grade level of the material. Choose more passages per book if great variability is observed and conclude that the book has uneven readability. Few books will fall in gray area but when they do grade level scores are invalid.

Count proper nouns, numerals and initializations as words. Count a syllable for each symbol. For example: "1945" is 1 word and 4 syllables and "IRA" is 1 word and 3 syllables.

| Example | Syllables | Sentences |
|---|---|---|
| 1st Hundred Words | 124 | 6.6 |
| 2nd Hundred Words | 141 | 5.5 |
| 3rd Hundred Words | 158 | 6.8 |
| Average | 141 | 6.3 |

Readability 7th grade (see dot plotted on graph)

8. Is the material organized in an easy-to-use and easy-to-read format?
9. Are easy-to-use reading aids available in this material (index, table of contents, glossary, chapter introductions, chapter summaries, outlines, illustrations, and so on)? Can students use these aids effectively?
10. Does the material look appealing, is it of interest to students, and is it presented in a way that stimulates their interest and would motivate reading?

It is important to emphasize the positive aspects of the instructional process by arranging materials in your room in a way that best facilitates instruction. You will need to change the materials in your classroom periodically, so that materials can be kept current and stimulate your students' interests. Materials can be displayed in several places including shelves, bookcases made from cement blocks, a library area or corner, learning centers, or a reading area or corner. Your students' work can be illustrated and bound for display purposes, and bulletin boards can also contain colorful and interesting activities for students to engage in.

You may wish to establish a listening center with tapes, discs, and headphones. Be sure to include paper, pencils, and crayons for follow-up activities. You could develop a computer center with appropriate hardware and software, which we have discussed throughout this text. It is important for students to assume some responsibility for keeping the classroom and centers neat, and to return materials to their appropriate place. This can best be accomplished by familiarizing your students with instructional materials through modeling and the use of small-group activities.

## *Learning Centers*

Learning centers are very useful for providing practice with specific skills and strategies in reading, writing, and other learning areas, for individuals or for small groups. Learning centers can also be used as open areas containing high-interest reading materials, or for specific practice in content areas such as math and science, as well as reading. Mercer and Mercer (1993, pp. 156–157) have provided twelve suggestions for developing effective learning centers:

1. Make them neat and attractive.
2. Make them a pleasant and comfortable place to work.
3. Appeal to student interest and curiosities.
4. Give simple and clear directions.
5. Make the evaluation activity important (e.g., follow up student work as much as possible).
6. Organize the center at first according to specific directions and gradually add materials and activities as resources and time permit.
7. Include activities that involve more than one student.
8. Explain and demonstrate how to use the center, particularly when a new material or activity is added to the center.
9. Coordinate movement to and from the center with other activities (usually through scheduling).
10. Do not limit the use of center activities to the physical area designed as the learning center. In many instances, students can be directed to other areas in or outside of the classroom for completion of activities.
11. Make changes to maintain enthusiasm for a given center. Some centers will change every day, others will change once a week, and still others can remain constant for a longer period.

12. When several centers are in use in one classroom, give careful attention to the balance of design in the centers. Some provide for active involvement, and others are for more quiet activity. Some require only short attention; others demand time for long-term development. Some offer experiences in reading and writing; others require extensive motor activity. Some are designed for individual work; others require the cooperative efforts of pairs or small groups. Some are open-ended and experimental in nature; others are more structured in presentation of content. Some are completely student-structured; others are prepared by the teacher.

Centers are especially helpful to teachers in organizing and managing the classroom, because they provide alternative activities for students. They can provide reinforcement activities and give students an opportunity to work independently. The primary value of learning centers is that they can provide your students with instructional activities that are worthwhile and useful. They can also provide you with an effective delivery system for the reinforcement of classroom instruction.

## *Organizing, Managing, and Evaluating Technology*

When used appropriately in literacy settings, technology empowers both teachers and students. However, for this empowerment to occur, you must have a realistic understanding of technology and structure its use. First understand that technology is neither a panacea nor will it "cure" learning problems or overcome ineffective teaching practices (Lewis 1993). Second, accept technology as one of the many media or contexts to be used to "mediate learning, production, and communication" (Daiute and Morse 1994, p. 229). Third, take the stance that technology does not supplant or compete with traditional teacher- or student-directed formats and that it is effective in individual, cooperative group, and whole-class formats (Hofmeister and Thorkildsen 1993). Fourth, use learning and instructional theories and principles to design technology-related activities (Gardner and Edyburn 1993). Fifth, take into account students' differences when planning specific technology events and expect different outcomes (Cavalier, Ferretti, and Okolo 1994). Finally, collaborate with other professionals and engage in professional development to determine effective procedures for integrating literacy curricular demands with technology.

A myriad of excellent suggestions are recommended by educational technologists for organizing, managing, and evaluating technology programs; these include:

1. Developing your technology literacy through collaborative and individual activities.
2. Evaluating hardware and software before purchasing.
3. Securing state-of-the-art technology (e.g., multimedia computers).
4. Obtaining different types of software (e.g., application, simulation, etc.).
5. Using technology for personal productivity purposes (e.g., record keeping).

6. Using technology for instructional productivity (e.g., teaching-learning outcomes).
7. Matching technology with curricular objectives and students' needs (e.g., Scholastic's WiggleWorks trade books and related software).
8. Designing technology activities across grouping formats (e.g., individual, cooperative, etc.).
9. Teaching students how to use application programs (e.g., word processing, database, etc.).
10. Establishing systems to manage students' access to and use of technology.

The following strategies are from those recommended by Gardner and Edyburn (1993, pp. 301–302) to help facilitate and observe students' use of technology:

1. Be physically available and prepared to interact with or assist students working at the technology station.
2. Take a minute or two to observe students' technological activities and the auditory or visual feedback they receive.
3. Listen to statements made by students regarding their technology performance. (For example, if you hear a student complaining "Why can't I save this story?" you could move to the technology station and assist this student in saving his or her story.)
4. Use anecdotal procedures to record students' technology performance. (An analysis of your notes could help pinpoint strengths and needs and help you structure the format and content of minilessons.)

Finally, the technology component must be evaluated to determine which activities you will maintain, modify, or eliminate. According to Gardner and Edyburn (1993, pp. 303–304), you can increase the validity and reliability of this evaluation if you do the following:

1. Create a classroom atmosphere that reinforces the importance and routine of collecting specific information about students' computer performance.
2. Use software programs that store useful performance information and develop a routine that provides sufficient time to access and interpret this information.
3. Record performance data from summary screens.
4. Establish consistent procedures for the collection and recording of performance data.
5. Have students assume the responsibility for recording their own performance.
6. Create and adhere to a schedule to formally and informally collect progress data.
7. Design a means to measure students on skills and information learned at the computer.
8. Elicit students' self-reports. After observing a situation where a student appears to have problems, ask the student to describe what he or she found hard or why he or she was having difficulty. Another self-report

method that can be used is the "think-aloud" procedure to assess students' application of cognitive strategies or thinking skills. An example of a think-aloud application would be to ask students to work at the computer and orally describe how they are thinking and problem-solving to complete the task.

## Organizing for Parent and Family Participation

The involvement of parents, caregivers, and other family members in literacy learning is important. Because of this, many states and school districts have developed parent/family advocacy and volunteer programs ("Family Resource Centers" 1994) and support the U.S. Department of Education's efforts, under the Goals 2000 legislation, to establish parental resource centers in each state ("Parent Initiative Set" 1994). Parents, family members, and other caregivers who are interested in working with their children and with you are important sources of assistance and information. Efforts to secure their support will strengthen your literacy program.

In this section, we suggest some steps that can be taken by classroom teachers to maximize family/parent involvement and participation, as gleaned from reviewing related literature (e.g., Rasinski 1995; Rockwell 1996; Shockley 1994; and others mentioned in this chapter and throughout this book).

1. Decide how you would like to involve parent/family members. For instance, do you view them as possible volunteers to help you during instructional or other program activities? Do you want them involved in other ways as well? How? List your ideas regarding the specific participation and involvement you want to cultivate.

2. Organize a meeting or other means of communicating your ideas and hopes for this desired involvement. It is important, too, that parents are given an opportunity to know and understand your perspective and beliefs about reading/learning. Use these communication efforts to share/explain your views. During such a meeting you can share your ideas with parents/family members, see how they would like to be involved, and plan with them accordingly. Figure 13.9 presents an outline for such a meeting that you may want to consider early in the school year. Frequent family conferences should be scheduled throughout the school year to review participation and involvement activities and outcomes and to modify plans accordingly. Whenever possible, involving children in the planning and review process is very beneficial.

3. Use the information from your parent/family meeting or other communication efforts to plan and schedule parents' involvement and participation. You can most easily accomplish this by reviewing your overall plans for the remainder of the school year and pinpointing anticipated dates for curriculum themes, special projects, field trips, and so on, and by reviewing your weekly class schedule. Decide where

**Figure 13.9**
Sample outline for a parent/family meeting.

I. Introduce yourself and your perspective/philosophy regarding reading, learning, and parent/family participation and involvement.

II. Present and explain your list of needs for parent participation, involvement, and help. For example:
  A. Review the list and pass around sign-up sheets with days of the week available and times available for areas such as reading to children, working with skill groups on practice activities, sharing information and personal interests and skills, field trip assistance, small project assistance inside and outside of the classroom, etc.
  B. Ask parents to suggest other areas they can help in, or other ways they can be involved. Provide a sign-up sheet for those. (Be sure to get parents' names, their child's name, phone number, and work number, on all sign-up sheets to make future use of these lists easier.)

III. Use this opportunity to explain your use of homework and to explain your method of grading, etc. (Explain anything unusual about your program.)

IV. Allow parents an opportunity for questions and concerns regarding your philosophy, approaches, and program.

V. Determine if subsequent meetings are desired, and if so, determine the best day and time for those parents attending.

specific parents'/family members' interests and contributions can best fit, and schedule them in. If you need assistance that parents/family members from your classroom cannot provide, seek it and schedule it from the broader community (e.g., from the fire or police department if you want a featured guest speaker who provides community service and if none of the parents from your classroom have these types of positions).

4. Is any special training or orientation necessary for some of the scheduled parents/family members to more effectively participate? Are any special materials required? Plan for and make arrangements to meet these needs/requirements on a timely basis. If you need outside assistance to provide this training or materials (e.g., librarian support or community assistance), request it. One especially helpful source is the International Reading Association's newsletter, *Reading Today,* that features a special section, "Parents and Reading." It contains ideas that you can photocopy and provide to participating parents, as well as other parents/family members to generate their interest/involvement.

5. Evaluate the effectiveness of these efforts on an ongoing basis. Frequently solicit feedback, recommendations, and other suggestions from participating (and nonparticipating) parents, family, and community members. Use these suggestions to continually reflect on and modify, as necessary, parent/family/community opportunities and involvement in your classroom.

## Reflection Activity 13.4

*I*n your reflection journal under the heading Reflection Activity 13.4, answer the following questions: (a) How will you utilize parents, other family members, and other caregivers, as well as interested community members to enhance learning in your classroom? (b) What responsibilities do you feel toward students' parents and family members? (c) Will you want to provide additional information to help them nurture their preschool and other school-aged children? (d) Do you believe it is your role to facilitate reading and literacy development beyond your classroom doors? If so, where (in what places?) would you concentrate your efforts?

## *Continued Professional Development*

You are about to finish reading this book and complete the parallel reading education course. We hope both have provided you with the reading and facilitative-teaching insight and knowledge that you need. It is the goal of certification and teacher preparation programs to help teachers develop their understandings, reflections, and their own perspectives to become the most effective teachers that they can be (Flippo and Radley 1995); if we have done this we are very pleased. However, facilitative and professional teachers continue their reflections, learning, and development throughout their careers.

Because it is often easy to think that growth stops with a teaching certificate, facilitative teachers ensure their continued development through reflection, self-assessment, and ongoing professional efforts. There are many ways to continue growing and developing professionally. There are a number of activities/opportunities that you can use for professional growth after the teaching certificate (Flippo 1996). These activities/opportunities include

1. Attending professional conferences that focus on reading and literacy-related areas.
2. Joining professional organizations that focus on literacy.
3. Reading professional journals and newsletters such as those published by the International Reading Association.
4. Making presentations at local, state, and national conferences.
5. Planning classroom research activities involving your own students and classroom setting.
6. Trying out innovative approaches and monitoring their progress.
7. Involving parents, family, and community members in your school reading program.
8. Creating a facilitative environment in your classroom that enhances reading and learning.

How will you know when you are an effective facilitative teacher? How will you know when you can consider yourself a true professional? We think you will be able to answer these questions easily, and we wish you success as you grow and develop professionally.

## Reflection Activity 13.5

*W*e began this book by asking you in Chapter 1 to describe or to diagram what you thought reading was. We also asked you to define reading. Now, we ask you to turn back to that original description/diagram and your original definition and look over what you wrote/drew. Then review your reflection journal for additional ideas you noted concerning your developing philosophy and definition of reading as you read through this text (e.g., see Reflection Activity 12.2). Next, under the heading Reflection Activity 13.5 in your reflection journal, state or restate your "most current" philosophy and definition of reading, and cite any differences you have noticed about your perspective as you reflected throughout this text. Finally, describe activities you are interested in engaging in to continue your professional reflection, growth, and development.

## *Summary*

This chapter has provided ideas and suggestions for organizing and managing an elementary classroom for effective reading instruction. It has included discussions on various grouping procedures, as well as provided a scheme for planning instruction to meet teaching objectives, using a DRA model to plan various group instruction; and other techniques and procedures to effectively manage space, materials, technology, and parent/family/community involvement. Additionally, this chapter has endeavored to help readers pull together the ideas from this text and use them to consider their current philosophies and beliefs regarding reading and to suggest that professional growth can be enhanced by continued reflection and other development efforts.

## *Closing Activities*

1. As part of your field activities in this course, observe the organizational and management practices used in several elementary classrooms. Take notes during your observations (focusing on practices you agree and disagree with and why), and share your notes with your peers.
2. Using the library resources in your institution, examine research information relating to the impact of effective organizational and management procedures on reading instruction in the elementary classroom. Summarize your research findings and share them with your peers.
3. Go back to Reflection Activity 13.2 and reexamine your position regarding the degree of individualization you believe in. Ink in your position on the continuum. Then, in a small group in class, share and discuss your individualized instruction continuums and beliefs.
4. In a small group in class, share and discuss your answers to the questions in Reflection Activity 13.4 concerning parent and family involvement efforts, and education, including how you see your responsibilities and opportunities in these areas. Your group will develop an organizational plan for parent/family involvement and develop ideas for parent education, sharing these with the rest of the class.

# Culminating Activity for Text: Reflection Activity 13.6

*Y*ou are preparing for the new school year at your elementary school. Describe how you would integrate the following elements into your instructional program:

1. Literacy-related assessment in the classroom
2. Use of various approaches to teaching reading
3. Organization and management of the classroom
4. Integration of reading and writing
5. Effective utilization of children's literature
6. Provision of equitable and appropriate instruction for students with diverse languages, cultures, and special learning challenges
7. Assessment and planning for continued professional reflection, growth, and development

Use your reflection journal, under the heading Reflection Activity 13.6, to develop an outline of how you would integrate the above elements.

*References*

"Ability Grouping in Social Studies." (1992, September). *Social Education* 56:268–70.

Allington, R. L., and P. M. Cunningham. (1996). *Schools That Work: Where All Children Read and Write.* New York: HarperCollins.

Baker, E. E. (1994). "Writing and Reading in a First-Grade Writer's Workshop: A Parent's Perspective." *The Reading Teacher* 47:372–377.

Biehler, R. F., and J. Snowman. (1990). *Psychology Applied to Teaching,* 6th ed. Boston: Houghton Mifflin.

Brophy, J. E. (1979). "Teacher Behavior and Its Effects." *Journal of Educational Psychology* 71:733–750.

Burns, P. C., B. D. Roe, and E. P. Ross. (1996). *Teaching Reading in Today's Elementary Schools,* 6th ed. Boston: Houghton Mifflin.

Cavalier, A. R., R. P. Ferretti, and C. M. Okolo. (1994). "Technology and Individual Differences." *Journal of Special Education Technology* 12:175–181.

Collins, M. D., and E. H. Cheek Jr. (1993). *Diagnostic-Prescriptive Reading Instruction: A Guide for Classroom Teachers,* 4th ed. Madison, WI: Brown & Benchmark Publishers.

Coolidge, N. J., and S. R. Wurster. (1985). "Intergenerational Tutoring and Student Achievement." *The Reading Teacher* 39:343–346.

Daiute, C., and F. Morse. (1994). "Access to Knowledge and Expression: Mulitmedia Writing Tools for Students with Diverse Needs and Strategies." *Journal of Special Education Technology* 12:221–256.

Dooley, C. (1993). "The Challenge: Meeting the Needs of Gifted Readers." *The Reading Teacher* 46:546–551.

"Family Resource Centers Get Parents Involved." (1994). *Reading Today* 12:12.

Fiedler, E. E., R. E. Lange, and S. Winebrenner (1994). "Ability Grouping: Geared for the Gifted." *Education Digest* 59:52–55.

Flippo, R. F. (1996). "After the Teaching Certificate, What Next: Opportunities for Professional Development and Growth." *New Teacher Advocate* 4 (1).

Flippo, R. F., and K. Radley. (1995). "Reflections of a Student Teacher and a Student Teacher Supervisor: 'Morning News' A Strategy That Works!" *The Reading Professor* 18 (1): 43–54.

Flood, J., and D. Lapp. (1994). "Developing Literacy Appreciation and Literacy Skills: A Blueprint for Success." *The Reading Teacher* 48:76-79.

Flood, J., D. Lapp, and G. Nagel. (1992). "Am I Allowed to Group? Using Flexible Patterns for Effective Instruction." *The Reading Teacher* 45:608-616.

Gardner, J. E., and D. L. Edyburn. (1993). "Teaching Applications with Exceptional Individuals." In J. D. Lindsey, ed., *Computers and Exceptional Individuals,* 2nd ed. (pp. 273-310). Austin, TX: PROED.

Haller, E. J., and M. Waterman. (1985). "The Criteria of Reading Group Assignments." *The Reading Teacher* 38 (8): 772-781.

Hereford, N. J. (1993). "Making Sense of Ability Grouping." *Instructor* 102:50-52.

Heron, T. E., and K. C. Harris. (1993). *The Educational Consultant: Helping Professionals, Parents, and Mainstreamed Students.* Austin, TX: PROED.

Hiebert, E. H. (1983). "An Examination of Ability Grouping for Reading Instruction." *Reading Research Quarterly* 18:231-255.

Hofmeister, A., and R. Thorkildsen. (1993). "Interactive Videodisc and Exceptional Individuals." In J. D. Lindsey, ed., *Computers and Exceptional Individuals,* 2nd ed. (pp. 65-107). Austin, TX: PROED.

Holdaway, D. (1980). *Independence in Reading: A Handbook on Individualized Procedures,* 2nd ed. Portsmouth, NH: Heinemann.

Holdaway, D. (1984). *Stability and Change in Literacy Learning.* Exeter, NH: Heinemann.

Johnson, D. W., and R. T. Johnson. (1994). *Learning Together and Alone: Cooperative, Competitive, and Individualistic Learning,* 4th ed. Boston: Allyn & Bacon.

Jongsma, E. (1985). "Grouping for Instruction." *The Reading Teacher* 38:918-920.

Kameenui, E. J. (1993). "Diverse Learners and the Tyranny of Time: Don't Fix Blame; Fix the Leaky Roof." *The Reading Teacher* 46:376-383.

Knight, J. (1994). "Learning in the Community." *The Reading Teacher* 47:498-499.

Knight, S. L., and J. A. Stallings. (1995). "Implementing the Accelerated School Model in an Urban Elementary School." In R. L. Allington and S. A. Walmsley, eds., *No Quick Fix: Rethinking Literacy Programs in America's Elementary Schools* (pp. 236-251). New York: Teachers College Press.

Lake, V. A. (1992). "Valentine Book Buddies." *Learning* 20:80-83.

Leal, D. J. (1993). "The Power of Literacy Peer Group Discussions: How Children Collaboratively Negotiate Meaning." *The Reading Teacher* 47:114-120.

LeLand, C., and R. Fitzpatrick. (1993/1994). "Cross-Age Interactions Builds Enthusiasm for Reading and Writing." *The Reading Teacher* 47:292-301.

Lewin, L. (1992). "Integrating Reading and Writing Strategies Using an Alternating Teacher-Led/Student-Selected Instructional Pattern." *The Reading Teacher* 45:586-591.

Lewis, R. B. (1993). *Special Education Technology: Classroom Applications.* Pacific Grove, CA: Brooks/Cole.

Marden, M. R., M. Richard, and R. F. Flippo. (1991). "Fifth Grade/Kindergarten Mentor Program: Beginnings." *New England Reading Association Journal* 27 (2): 2-4.

McCaslin, M., and T. L. Good. (1996). *Listening in Classrooms.* New York: HarperCollins.

McGill-Franzen, A. (1993). " 'I Could Read the Words!': Selecting Good Books for Inexperienced Readers." *The Reading Teacher* 46:424-426.

Mercer, C. D., and A. R. Mercer. (1993). *Teaching Students with Learning Problems,* 4th ed. New York: Merrill/Macmillan.

Milleta, M. M. (1992). "Picture Books for Older Children: Reading and Writing Connections." *The Reading Teacher* 45:555-556.

Mills, C. J., and A. E. Tangherlini. (1992). "Finding the Optimal Match: Another Look at Ability Grouping and Cooperative Learning." *Equity & Excellence* 25:205-208.

Morrow, L. M., D. H. Tracey, and C. M. Maxwell, eds. (1995). *A Survey of Family Literacy in the United States.* Newark, DE: International Reading Association.

Opitz, M. F. (1992). "The Cooperative Reading Activity: An Alternative to Ability Grouping in the Classroom." *The Reading Teacher* 45:736-738.

Palmer, B. M., and R. M. Codling. (1994). "In Their Own Words: What Elementary Students Have to Say about Motivation to Read." *The Reading Teacher* 48:176-178.

Paratore, J. R. (1995). "Implementing an Intergenerational Literacy Project: Lessons Learned." In L. M. Morrow, ed., *Family Literacy: Connections in Schools and Communities.* Newark, DE: International Reading Association.

"Parent Initiative Set in the United States." (1994). *Reading Today* 12:9.

Rasinski, T. V. (1995). *Parents and Teachers: Helping Children Learn to Read and Write.* Ft. Worth, TX: Harcourt Brace College Publishers.

Rekrut, M. D. (1994). "Peer and Cross-Age Tutoring: The Lessons of Research." *Journal of Reading* 37:356–362.

Reutzel, D. R., and M. Wolfersberger. (1996). "An Environmental Impact Statement: Designing Supportive Literacy Classrooms for Young Children." *Reading Horizons* 36(3): 266–282.

Rockwell, R. E. (1996). *Parents and Teachers as Partners: Issues and Challenges.* Ft. Worth, TX: Harcourt Brace College Publishers.

Rupley, W. H., and T. R. Blair. (1980). "Teacher Effectiveness Research in Reading Instruction: Early Efforts to Present Focus." *Reading Psychology* 2:49–56.

Samway, K. D., G. Whang, and M. Pippitt. (1995). *Buddy Reading: Cross-Age Tutoring in a Multicultural School.* Portsmouth, NH: Heinemann.

Sanacore, J. (1993). "Whole-Language Grouping That Works!" *Education Digest* 58:67–71.

Schumm, J. S., S. Vaughn, and A. G. Leavell. (1994). "Planning Pyramid: A Framework for Planning Diverse Student Needs during Content Area Instruction." *The Reading Teacher* 47:608–615.

Shockley, B. (1994). "Extending the Literature Community: Home-to-School and School-to-Home." *The Reading Teacher* 47:500–502.

Slavin, R. E. (1991). "Are Cooperative Learning and 'Untracking' Harmful to the Gifted?" *Educational Leadership* 48(6): 68–71.

———. (1993). "Ability Grouping in the Middle Grades: Achievement Effects and Alternatives." *The Elementary School Journal* 93:535–552.

Smith, T. E. C., D. M. Finn, and C. R. Dowdy. (1993). *Teaching Students with Mild Disabilities.* Ft. Worth, TX: Holt, Rinehart & Winston.

Stanovich, K. E. (1986). "Mathew Effects in Reading: Some Consequences of Individual Differences in the Acquisition of Literacy." *Reading Research Quarterly* 21:360–407.

Stevens, R. J., R. E. Slavin, and A. M. Farnish. (1991). "The Effects of Cooperative Learning and Direct Instruction Reading Comprehension Strategies on Main Idea Identification." *Journal of Educational Psychology* 83:8–16.

Swengel, E. M. (1990, April 23–26). *Restructuring the School System to Involve All Students in Peer Helping.* Paper presented at the annual conference of the National Peer Helpers Association, Flagstaff, Arizona.

Swift, K. (1993). "Trying Reading Workshop in Your Classroom." *The Reading Teacher* 46:366–371.

Unsworth, L. (1984). "Meeting Individual Needs through Flexible Within-Class Grouping of Pupils." *The Reading Teacher* 38:298–305.

White, M. C., and S. M. Lawrence. (1992). "Integrating Reading and Writing Through Literature Study." *The Reading Teacher* 45:740–743.

Wiggins, R. A. (1994). "Large Group Lesson/Small Group Follow-Up: Flexible Grouping in a Basal Reading Program." *The Reading Teacher* 47:450–460.

Wray, D. (1994). "Text and Authorship." *The Reading Teacher* 48:52–57.

Young, T. A. (1990). "Alternatives to Ability Grouping in Reading." *Reading Horizons* 30:169–183.

Zabel, R. H., and M. K. Zabel. (1996). *Classroom Management in Context: Orchestrating Positive Learning Environments.* Boston: Houghton Mifflin.

Zucker, C. (1993). "Using Whole Language with Students Who Have Language and Learning Disabilities." *The Reading Teacher* 46:660–670.

# *Appendix*

## *The Flippo Interest Inventory*

Directions: This inventory can be given orally to both younger and older students, or you can have your older students complete it independently. To obtain accurate and complete information, it is recommended that you record students' oral responses exactly as they give them to you. If older students ask for assistance with their written responses, feel free to help them.

1. What are the things (topics) you like most to read about? Why?
2. What are the things you like most to do? Why?
3. Are there some new things (topics) that you are interested in learning about? Why?
4. What would you like to do when you grow up? Why? List or tell everything you can think of that you would *really* like to do.
5. What kinds of things do you like to read about, or watch TV or movies about, just for fun or excitement? Why?
6. Have you heard or read about anything new or unusual (in school or at home) that you would like to learn more about? Why?
7. Do you like to do things by following directions such as cooking, building or assembling, sewing, or writing away for things? Which do you like? Why?
8. What is your favorite kind of music?
9. Do you have any special hobbies? What are they? Why are they especially interesting?
10. Do you have any favorite sports? What are they?
11. Do you have any pets? What kinds?
12. Are you interested in any role-playing games? If so, which ones? (*Note:* You may want to reword these questions for use with younger students.)
13. Do you have some special concerns or problems that you would like to explore, work on, or change? If so, would you like some help finding resources or information? (*Indicate to students:* They do not have to answer these questions, but if they do, their answers will be confidential. *Also Note:* You will need to reword these questions for use with younger students.)
14. If you could do anything in the world and money was no object, what would you like to do? Why?
15. If you could go anywhere in the world and money and time were not problems, where would you like to go? Why?
16. What are the names (titles) of your favorite books? Who are your favorite authors?
17. Of all the books and authors listed in item 16, which/who is absolutely your favorite book and author? Why?
18. If you wanted to tell people about this book (and/or author), and convince them to read it (read books by him/her), what would you say?
19. If some people wanted to give you a number of books, magazines, or other types of printed materials to read, what kind should they give you? Why? Can you name some particular titles?
20. If a writer told you she/he would write a book, just for you, about *anything,* but she/he needed to know what you would want in the book, what would you say?

**A**

# *Appendix*

## *Professional Organizations and Journals*

## *Organizations*

American Educational Research Association (AERA)
1230 17th Street, NW
Washington, DC 20036-3078
    AERA is an association of researchers who are involved with all aspects and fields of educational research. Because of its wide diversity, there are various divisions and special interest groups within AERA. National meetings are held annually.

American Reading Forum (ARF)
College of Education
Concordia University
7400 Augusta Street
River Forest, IL 60305
    ARF is an organization of professional educators associated with all aspects of research in reading. A national conference is held each year.

Association for Childhood Education International (ACEI)
11501 Georgia Ave., Suite 315
Wheaton, MD 20902
    ACEI is an association whose primary interest is the education of children from infancy through early adolescence. It has local, state, and regional branches, and holds an annual national meeting.

Association for Supervision and Curriculum Development (ASCD)
1250 North Pitt Street
Alexandria, VA 22314-1453
    ASCD is an association whose primary focus concerns those issues directly related to instruction and learning in the schools, as well as professional development, supervision of instruction, and curriculum development.

College Reading Association (CRA)
83 Sharon Street
James Madison University
Harrisonburg, VA 22801-2715
    CRA is an organization of professional educators concerned with teacher education, clinical practices in reading, adult reading, and college reading instruction. A national meeting is held annually.

Council for Exceptional Children (CEC)
1920 Association Dr.
Reston, VA 22091
    CEC is an association of special educators, interested in the special needs of students. National meetings are held annually.

International Reading Association (IRA)
800 Bardsdale Rd.
P.O. Box 8139
Newark, DE 19714-8139

The IRA is the largest association focusing on reading, other literacy instruction, and related issues of concern to reading teachers. The association sponsors numerous special-interest groups on a variety of topics. International, regional, state, and local meetings are held annually. Many countries hold additional affiliate meetings. The IRA also sponsors a World Congress meeting every two years.

National Association for the Education of Young Children (NAEYC)
1509 16th St., NW
Washington, DC 20036–1426

NAEYC provides educational resources for improving the quality and availability of services for children from birth through age eight. It has local, state, and regional affiliates, and holds an annual national meeting.

National Council of Teachers of English (NCTE)
1111 West Kenyon Rd.
Urbana, IL 61801-1096

NCTE is an association of teachers and others interested in all areas of the language arts, including writing and reading and related areas of literacy. National and regional meetings are held annually. Most states have chapters that are affiliated with the national group.

National Reading Conference (NRC)
200 North Michigan, Suite 300
Chicago, IL 60611

NRC is an organization of professional educators concerned with all aspects of research related to reading and other literacy processes.

# *Journals*

*American Educational Research Journal*

Published quarterly by the American Educational Research Association, 1230 17th St. NW, Washington, DC 20036-3078. Presents reports of original research on all aspects of education.

*English Journal*

Published monthly from September to April by the National Council of Teachers of English, 1111 West Kenyon Rd., Urbana, IL 61801. Presents discussions on a variety of topics related to the teaching of English and related disciplines. Emphasis is on practical applications and suggestions for teachers.

*Exceptional Children*

This is the journal of the Council for Exceptional Children, 1920 Association Drive, Reston, VA 22091. It publishes articles about the concerns of special educators and the treatment of exceptional students.

*Journal of Adolescent & Adult Literacy*

Published eight times a year by the International Reading Association, 800 Barksdale Rd., Newark, DE 19714-8139. Includes articles and discussions of research and practical suggestions for those interested in the teaching of reading to adolescents and adults.

*Journal of Educational Psychology*
 Published by the American Psychological Association, 750 First Street, NE, Washington, DC 20002–4242. Contains articles on learning, focusing on issues of instruction, development, and adjustment at every educational level.

*Journal of Educational Research*
 Published by Heldref Publications, Helen Dwight Read Educational Foundation, 1319 18th St., NW, Washington, DC 20036–1802. Presents articles, book reviews, and discussions on all aspects of education and educational research.

*Journal of Literacy Research*
 Published quarterly by the National Reading Conference, 200 North Michigan, Suite 300, Chicago, IL 60611. Presents articles related to all aspects of reading and other literacy research.

*Language Arts*
 Published monthly by the National Council of Teachers of English, 1111 W. Kenyon Rd., Urbana, IL 61801. Presents articles on the teaching of language arts with practical application for classroom teachers.

*Lectura y Vida*
 Published four times a year by the International Reading Association. Includes articles in the Spanish language for those teaching early childhood through adult-aged students.

*Reading Horizons*
 Published quarterly by the College of Education, Western Michigan University, Kalamazoo, MI 49008–5197. Emphasizes discussion of the teaching of reading at all levels.

*Reading Improvement*
 Published four times each year by Project Innovation of Mobile, P.O. Box 8508, Spring Hill Station, Mobile, AL 36608. Includes articles that concern various aspects of reading instruction.

*Reading Psychology*
 Published quarterly by Taylor & Francis Ltd., 4 John Street, London WC1N 2ET UK. The Editorial Office is: Department of Educational Curriculum, Texas A & M University, College Station, TX 77843. Publishes research and other articles in the fields of literacy, reading, and related psychology disciplines.

*Reading Research and Instruction*
 Published quarterly by the College Reading Association, Editorial Office, 215 MCKB, Brigham Young University, Provo, UT 84602. Includes reports of research and practice in reading education and related instructional areas.

*Reading Research Quarterly*
 Published quarterly by the International Reading Association. Reports findings of research in reading and other literacy areas.

*The Elementary School Journal*
 Published five times a year by the Center for Research in Social Behavior, University of Missouri–Columbia, 1507 East Broadway, Columbia, MO 65211. Presents articles concerning research in elementary schools and topics related to elementary education.

*The Reading Teacher*
 Published eight times per year by the International Reading Association. Includes articles containing practical suggestions for teachers of all learners up through age 12.

*Teaching Exceptional Children*
 Published four times a year by the Council for Exceptional Children, 1920 Association Drive, Reston, VA 22091. It includes articles describing practical materials and methods to use with exceptional students in regular and special-education settings.

# Index